The Art of Being Human

W9-BKO-338

The Art of Being Human

The Humanities as a Technique for Living

ELEVENTH EDITION

Richard Paul Janaro
New World School of the Arts

Thelma C. Altshuler
Professor Emerita, Miami-Dade College

PEARSON

Boston   Columbus   Indianapolis   New York City   San Francisco   Amsterdam
Cape Town   Dubai   London   Madrid   Milan   Munich   Paris   Montréal   Toronto   Delhi
Mexico City   São Paulo   Sydney   Hong Kong   Seoul   Singapore   Taipei   Tokyo

Editor in Chief: Sarah Touborg
Senior Publisher: Roth Wilkofsky
Editorial Assistant: Devon Bacso
Executive Marketing Manager: Wendy Albert
Senior Product Marketer: Jeremy Intal
Marketing Assistant: Frank Alcaron
Managing Editor: Melissa Feimer
Program Manager: Barbara Cappuccio
Project Manager: Joe Scordato
Operations Specialist: Mary Ann Gloriande

Senior Digital Project Manager: Rich Barnes
Pearson Imaging Center: Corin Skidds
Full-Service Project Management: Lumina Datamatics, Inc.
Composition: Lumina Datamatics, Inc.
Printer/Binder: LSC Communications/Kendallville
Cover Printer: Lehigh Phoenix
Cover Design: Pentagram
Cover Art Director: Kathryn Foot
Cover Art: Franco Fortunato, "Il Cielo"

Copyright © 2017, 2012, 2009 by Pearson Education, Inc. or its affiliates. All rights reserved.
Printed in the United States of America. This publication is protected by copyright, and permission should be obtained from the publisher prior to any prohibited reproduction, storage in a retrieval system, or transmission in any form or by any means, electronic, mechanical, photocopying, recording, or otherwise. For information regarding permissions, request forms and the appropriate contacts within the Pearson Rights & Permissions Department, please visit www.pearsoned.com/permissions/.

Acknowledgments of third party content appear on the appropriate page within text or on the credit pages in the back of this book.

PEARSON and ALWAYS LEARNING are exclusive trademarks owned by Pearson Education, Inc. or its affiliates in the United States and/or other countries.

Unless otherwise indicated herein, any third-party trademarks that may appear in this work are the property of their respective owners and any references to third-party trademarks, logos or other trade dress are for demonstrative or descriptive purposes only. Such references are not intended to imply any sponsorship, endorsement, authorization, or promotion of Pearson's products by the owners of such marks, or any relationship between the owner and Pearson Education, Inc. or its affiliates, authors, licensees or distributors.

Library of Congress Cataloging-in-Publication Data
Janaro, Richard Paul, author.
   The art of being human : the humanities as a technique for living / Richard Janaro, New World School of the Arts; Thelma Altshuler, Professor Emerita, Miami-Dade College. —Eleventh edition.
      pages cm
   ISBN 978-0-13-423873-9 (alk. paper)
  1. Conduct of life—Textbooks.   2. Humanities—Textbooks.   I. Altshuler, Thelma C., author.   II. Title.
   BJ1581.2.J36 2016
   001.3—dc23

                                                                                          2015037055

2   16

Student Edition
ISBN 10:   0-13-423873-7
ISBN 13: 978-0-13-423873-9

Instructor's Resource Copy
ISBN 10:   0-13-423896-6
ISBN 13: 978-0-13-423896-8

Books à la carte
ISBN 10:   0-13-424046-4
ISBN 13: 978-0-13-424046-6

This book is dedicated to Dr. Milton E. Ford, in memoriam, 1941–2014

Contents

Preface

The eleventh edition of *The Art of Being Human*, like its predecessors, introduces students to the joys of the humanities—those disciplines that reflect the best efforts of human culture through the ages and around the globe. As always, our aim is to communicate our enthusiasm for the humanities both as the source of experience for the mind and the emotions, and as a path to self-knowledge. By becoming acquainted with the creative arts and learning to think critically about them, students will inevitably better understand themselves and the world they live in.

The Art of Being Human tells the story of outstanding achievements in the humanities throughout history and across the world's many cultures. We acknowledge the contributions of the past because people very much like us lived there, and those people created remarkable works that continue to move us today. What they said and did can shed light on the present. And we explore the works of modern and contemporary artists, knowing only that some of these will become, like their predecessors, classics and even masterpieces. Whenever we revisit this text, we find new reasons to rejoice and new stimuli for the senses in work from both past and present, and from cultures and peoples around the world.

How This Book Is Organized

The Art of Being Human is unique among introductory texts in the humanities because of our focus both on the humanistic arts—literature, music, art, performance—and on persistent philosophical themes including religion, morality, happiness, and freedom. Unlike the typical chronologically organized text, *The Art of Being Human* allows us to explore themes and disciplines individually and also to draw significant connections among them.

Chapters 1 to 3 offer a basic foundation for the study of the humanities. We define what we mean by "the humanities" in Chapter 1; in Chapter 2, we emphasize the importance of critical thinking in understanding the disciplines and themes that are presented and discussed in the text; and in Chapter 3, we describe the role of myth as it underlies our study of the humanities.

Chapters 4 to 9 provide accessible, comprehensive explorations of the basic disciplines of the humanities: literature, art, music, theater, musical theater and dance, and film and television.

Chapters 10 to 16, which set this text apart from other introductory humanities texts, offer wide-ranging discussions of themes that have proved central to cultures around the world. These themes—including religion, morality, happiness, love, freedom, the role of nature, and the challenge of death and life-affirmation—introduce the philosophical questions that have confronted humankind throughout its existence, and the ways in which they have impacted and been reflected in the arts.

What's New in This Edition

For this new edition, we've created an extraordinary new learning architecture: REVEL. Every feature that students formerly may have accessed through MyHumanitiesKit or MyArtsLab is now embedded in this new cross-platform environment—music, architectural panoramas, Closer Looks, studio technique videos, self-tests, and so on. You can zoom in on a piece of art, switch on the chapter audio, and listen to the text being read to you while you look at the image. You can begin your day at home, working with a chapter on your laptop, get on the bus, continue working on your smart phone, arrive at school, and open the chapter on your tablet. REVEL is as fully mobile as you are, and you can use it on any device, anywhere and anytime.

We firmly believe that this new learning architecture will help your students engage even more meaningfully in the critical thinking process, helping them to understand how cultures influence one another, how ideas are exchanged and evolve over time, and how this process has led us to where we are today. Perhaps most important, the connections drawn in this text (and emphasized in the REVEL architecture) allow students to better understand themselves.

The Art of Being Human has remained popular through ten editions because the humanities are alive and will be alive forever—and as a part of our daily lives, they constantly grow and change. Thus, the present text includes a number of important revisions necessary to keep our special approach to the humanities vital. Indeed, there is very little throughout the eleventh edition that has not been reexamined, revised, or rewritten. In particular, we have focused on bringing the book clearly into the twenty-first century with new material in virtually every chapter about contemporary works and contemporary thought. In addition to the new REVEL platform, you will find the following changes:

- **Major additions to every chapter on the disciplines of the humanities** are designed to introduce students to contemporary figures and works. These additions include:
  - New sections on **poetry in our time** and **the post-modern novel** (Ch. 4)

- New sections on **abstract expressionism, performance and installation art,** and **digital art** (Ch. 5)
- Expanded discussions of **rock, hip-hop,** and **rap** (Ch. 6)
- New discussions of contemporary playwrights including **David Mamet, August Wilson,** and **Tony Kushner** (Ch. 7)
- New sections on **rock and jukebox musicals,** and **the Broadway "spectacular"** (Ch. 8)
- New sections on **science fiction, animated film,** and **the "comic book" blockbuster** (Ch. 9)
- A completely new section on **television,** focusing on **the "new golden age" of television drama** (Ch. 9)

- **An expanded emphasis on critical thinking** is reflected in:
  - **New image captions** that invite students to form their own opinions about what they are seeing
  - **A Critical Focus,** a feature at the end of each discipline chapter (Chs. 4–9), that offers a lens through which students may look closely at a single work, or compare two or more works within a genre, and invites them to use their critical skills to respond to questions about these works—to analyze and compare, for example, poems about dying young by Walt Whitman, Wilfred Owen, and A.E. Housman, or to discuss the appeal of "bad" characters like Tony Soprano and Omar Little of *The Wire*

- **Revisions and updates to the thematic chapters** (Chs. 10–16) reflect both contemporary thought and a more wide-ranging focus on global cultures.
- **Learning Objectives** aligned with major heads throughout each chapter, and **Looking Back** sections at the end of each chapter, guide students to focus on the important overall concepts introduced in each chapter.
- **Musical selections** that are being made available for listening via the REVEL are indicated by an 🔊 icon in the printed text.

Enduring Strengths in *The Art of Being Human*

No book enters an eleventh edition unless it is built on a sound foundation. The eleventh edition of *The Art of Being Human* continues to reflect our belief that a non-chronological structure can lead to a deeper understanding of the humanities disciplines. We retain here our focus on the individual artistic disciplines and on philosophical themes that have been central to the study of the humanities through the years. This new edition builds on the many strengths that have made this text highly respected and easy to use. These strengths include:

- *Full coverage of the humanities. The Art of Being Human* discusses all the important disciplines and examines

connections to issues that remain of vital importance. Students are encouraged to explore how the arts and social themes relate to their own lives.

- *Individual treatment of disciplines and themes.* The book's topical organization allows students to explore one artistic mode or theme at a time, rather than having to cover multiple disciplines and themes in each chapter, often the case in chronologically organized texts.
- *Flexible organization.* Each chapter stands on its own, so the book can be taught in any sequence and can be easily customized to meet the goals of any number of introductory courses on the humanities in two- and four-year colleges.
- *Diverse range of traditional and contemporary examples of all the arts. The Art of Being Human* strives to familiarize students with the reach of the humanities by including many examples of literature and art from cultures around the globe. We address issues that remain of vital importance for an increasingly global society.
- *Accessible writing style.* We strive to explore the world of the humanities in a contemporary idiom that students can easily understand.
- *An impressive visual program.* The more than 250 color images provide students with a rich visual appreciation of the arts. All of the images and their captions are tied directly to discussions within the text.

Our hope is that students who read this book will discover much about themselves, in addition to gaining an understanding of human culture that will prove rewarding in their ongoing development. If, as Katherine Mansfield once said, a great poet must first be a great poem, what shall we say of the fully realized human being? Won't such an individual be not only a poem but also a song, dance, painting, play, movie, or new idea? These are distant stars at which to aim, but a journey too easily accomplished may not be worth the effort.

Pearson Choices and Resources

Pearson humanities titles are available in the following formats to give your students more choices—and more ways to save.

Explore REVEL—dynamic content matched to the way today's students read, think, and learn.

Ideal for the unique approach to the humanities reflected in *The Art of Being Human,* REVEL includes:

- Spoken audio
- Pan/zoom and scale markers for nearly every image
- Writing prompts of several varieties to foster critical thinking

- 360-degree architectural panoramas and simulations of major monuments
- Media interactives and videos, including "students on site" videos shot and narrated by proficient student learners
- Quizzing that allows students to check their understanding at regular intervals

Fully mobile, REVEL enables students to interact with course material on the devices they use, anywhere and anytime.

REVEL's assignability and tracking tools help educators:

- Ensure that students are completing their reading and understanding core concepts
- Establish a clear, detailed schedule that helps students stay on task
- Monitor both class assignment completion and individual student achievement

Build your own Pearson custom course material.

For enrollments of at least 25, the Pearson Custom Library allows you to create your own textbook by:

- Combining chapters from best-selling Pearson textbooks in the sequence you want
- Adding your own content, such as a guide to a local art museum, a map of monuments in your area, your syllabus, or a study guide you have created

A Pearson Custom Library book is priced according to the number of chapters and may even save your students money. *To begin building your custom text, visit* www.pearsoncustomlibrary.com *or contact your Pearson representative.*

Explore additional cost-saving options.

- The **Books à la Carte edition** offers a convenient, three-hole-punched, loose-leaf version of the traditional text at a discounted price—allowing students to take only what they need to class. *Students save 35% over the list price of the traditional book.*

Instructor Resources

- **PowerPoints**

Instructors who adopt the text may gain access to a robust collection of PowerPoints illustrated with images from the text, additional media, and class discussion prompts.

- **Instructor's Manual and Test Item File**

This is an invaluable professional resource and reference for new and experienced faculty that includes time lines, checklists of major concepts, and teaching strategies. The test bank includes multiple-choice, short-answer, and essay questions. Available for download from www.pearsonhighereducation.com

- **MyTest**

This flexible online test-generating software includes all questions found in the Test Item File. Instructors can quickly and easily create customized tests with MyTest at www.pearsonmytest.com

Acknowledgments

The "we" of this preface includes not only the authors but also others who have worked long and hard helping to improve the book. Our independent development editor Ginny Blanford was instrumental in creating the content new to this edition, in expanding our focus on the contemporary, and in selecting new images. The oversight of our editor, Roth Wilkofsky, and the work of freelance development editor Margaret Manos were invaluable. Our production team—Joseph Scordato and Barbara Cappuccio of Pearson, Cynthia Cox of Ohlinger Publishing Services, and Haylee Schwenk of Lumina Datamatics—kept us on track and on schedule. Our text and art permissions editor, Peggy Davis at Pearson, and researchers, Jennifer Simmons and Tom Wilcox of Lumina Datamatics, handled complicated tasks adroitly, with skill and patience. All became part of a team, and through their efforts we discovered the true meaning of *synergy*.

Our magnificent cover image is the work of Italian artist Franco Fortunato, and we are grateful to him for granting permission for its use, as well as to John Bryant of Hofstra University for facilitating our communications with Signore Fortunato.

We would also like to acknowledge the letters from students and teachers who support what we are doing and who have made valuable comments about how we could do it even better, and the thorough, caring reviews of the previous edition provided by Pamela Painter DeCius, Saint Leo University; Laura Jones, Atlanta Technical College; Debra Justice, Ashland Community and Technical College; Connie LaMarca-Frankel, Pasco-Hernando State College; Abigail Lewsader, Texas State Technical College; Nancy Smith, St. Petersburg College; Lindsey Smitherman-Brown, Tallahassee Community College; Patricia Swenson, California State University/Northridge; and Nancy Taylor, California State University/Northridge. And we are tremendously grateful for the detailed discipline-specific reviews provided by Robert Arnett, Old Dominion University; Ryan Ebright, The University of North Carolina/Chapel Hill; Gary Poe, Palm Beach Atlantic University; Jennifer Rosti, Roanoke College; and Derek Williams, Florida Agricultural and Mechanical University.

To write a humanities text is perhaps the best way to discover the humane characteristics of others and the secret of all meaningful endeavor, which is that *no one can work alone.*

Richard Paul Janaro
Thelma C. Altshuler

The Art
of Being Human

PART I

Exploring the Humanities

Chapter 1
The Humanities: A Shining Beacon

Learning Objectives

1.1 Define "the humanities."

1.2 Summarize the gifts of the humanities.

1.3 Explain why Leonardo da Vinci is considered the perfect model of the "infinite" person.

Figure 1.1 Leonardo da Vinci, *Mona Lisa*, c. 1503–1507.
Why has this tiny work become the most famous painting in the world? What magic does it have?
GL Archive/Alamy

Defining the humanities is no longer as simple as it once was. At one time, the word "**humanities**," which grew out of the term " **humanism**," simply meant the study of what the best minds of classical Greece and Rome—the great artists, writers, and philosophers—had accomplished. During the Renaissance, the huge artistic and political revolution that swept over Western Europe beginning in the fourteenth century, interest revived in the cultures of ancient Greece and Rome—cultures that had been left largely unexamined during the thousand-year span following the fall of Rome. The intelligentsia of the Renaissance believed that only through a study of classical art, literature, and philosophy could a person become *fully* human.

These **disciplines** became known as *the humanities*. In time, the term grew beyond the study of Greek and Roman cultures to include those of major Western European countries: first Italy, then France and Spain, then Britain and, finally, Germany. As cultures multiplied, so did the disciplines people needed to study in pursuit of humanness. Music, theater, and dance began to flourish during the Renaissance, and scholars discovered that these disciplines were also part of the ancient world's legacy.

More recently, this ethnocentric view of the humanities—the study of Western cultures—has expanded again to acknowledge the vast contributions of cultures beyond Europe. The art, music, theater, and literature of China, Japan, and other Asian nations, as well as those of Africa and the Americas, have become important additions to the study of the humanities.

Being Fully Human

1.1   *What are the humanities?*

In this book, we define the term *humanities* as broadly as possible. Yes, we still need to pay attention to extraordinary artistic and intellectual achievements that have been singled out for special praise and that now represent what is sometimes called the "humanistic tradition." All of us belong to the human race and should want to know as much as possible about the distinguished contributions of those who have gone before. We may also find in our study of the humanities our response to the traditional mandate: Know thyself. By exploring the contributions of others, we begin to see how we ourselves might contribute—not, perhaps, as great artists or writers or musicians, but as more thoughtful and critical human beings.

We do need to recognize that the "humanistic tradition" was for many centuries limited more or less to the contributions made by *men* of the classical and then the Western European worlds. Plato and Michelangelo and Shakespeare continue to deserve our admiration and reward our study. But our study should and does include those persons, both male and female, past and present, from around the globe, who may be little known or not known at all, who nevertheless left behind or who now offer a myriad of wonderful songs, poems, and provocative thoughts waiting to be appreciated.

The humanities are also the creative and intellectual expressions of each of us in moments of inspiration, whether they happen in the shower or just walking down the street on a balmy day when our spirits are lifted by the sheer joy of being alive. In these times of global fears and a future of uncertainty, in these times of dizzying technological advances that can be both marvelous and bewildering, when it can be hard to pinpoint our identity in time and space, the humanities offer a safe haven, a quiet harbor where we can moor our vessels and, at least for a time, confirm who we are.

Each of us is more than a gender, an age, an address, an occupation. Each of us embodies thoughts, expressed or not, the capacity to be moved, the need to laugh or cry, longings for things just beyond our reach. The humanities give us stories to inspire our imagination, ideas to stimulate our intellect, musical sounds to excite our passions, and the knowledge that we can respond to the creativity and thoughts of others.

Studying the humanities allows us to look inward to see what *we* think and what creative impulses lie dormant and cry out to be released. A greater knowledge of the humanities helps us confront our true identity. A major aim of this book is to show how a study of the humanities can be the starting point for the journey into self-knowledge.

Studying the Humanities: The Importance of Critical Thinking

The humanities comprise not only the inspiring achievements themselves, but also the *study* of those achievements, as well as the critical process by which scholars and critics analyze and interpret them and then communicate their findings to others so that the works they study will never be forgotten. And the humanities are the critical process by which we ourselves look squarely at and come to appreciate what is there for us to read, see, or hear. This process, often called *critical thinking*, is essential to being effectively human, especially as the world's tempo increases. In fact, so crucial is critical thought, and so important are the humanities in developing it, that the following chapter is devoted solely to the subject.

The humanities offer a technique for living accessible to every human being who wants to do more with life. They offer a way of life filled with moments of critical thought and aesthetic pleasure, and they are urgently needed in our world.

The humanities are addictive. Once you let song and story, music and dance, and words and ideas into your life, you can never live without them. And you should never *have* to. The humanities may best be appreciated in our quiet moments, and quiet can also be addictive in a noisy world. *If only everyone on earth would insist on these quiet moments, wouldn't the world be a happier (and a safer) place?*

In a world that has become a global village, in a world with all its hovering threats of terror attacks and dirty bombs, with so many who are more than willing to sacrifice their own lives to kill others, in a world of environmental woes, a world in which cynics wonder about the value of living—in such a world there are always the humanities to lift our spirits. Art and music and literature, stories and songs, all the marvels of the human mind, the architectural and engineering achievements, or just noticing the first spring flower keep reminding us of what it means to be truly human.

Humankind will not necessarily prevail just because we are living longer. Genetic scientists envision replacing the gene responsible for aging; eventually, they promise life expectancies that were once found only in literary fables. (Perhaps some of us may live to celebrate our "eleventy-first birthday," like Bilbo Baggins of *The Hobbit*.) Existing on and on without coming to terms with who we are and without knowing how to reach a safe haven inside when the world gets maddeningly chaotic about us might not be the best technique for living. The humanities help make longer life spans abundantly richer.

Redefining the Humanities in a Wider World

The key to the richer life is to be as open-minded as possible. One of the dangers of living longer is becoming too firmly enclosed by the values many of us have held since our earliest days. The humanities cannot fail to inspire open-mindedness. Exploring the literature, music, art, and patterns of thought of other cultures is indispensable to our own development. Why? The answer is simple: The world has grown too small for us not to care what is happening all around us; and the world *is* just that—all around us. So we need to balance a sharper awareness of who we are with a broader understanding of who *they* are; for they are part of us, and we of them.

The cultural history of Western civilization, as traditionally presented, simply will no longer suffice. During the time of the ancient Greeks, for example, were there not many women who thought great thoughts and secretly wrote great poems?

While the much heralded early civilizations, like those of Egypt, China, Japan, Rome, and Greece, have received abundant attention and been the subject of countless critical and historical studies, they do not tell the whole story of human genius. Rich cultures flourished in Africa; in South and Central America; in the North America that was inhabited long before Columbus "discovered" it; in the lands that produced Islamic art, science, and philosophy, lands once thought too mysterious for the Western mind to understand; in lands of the unknown people who built Stonehenge in England and the 30-foot statues that stand at eternal attention on Easter Island. While owners were sipping juleps on plantation verandas, slaves in their humble shanties were weaving elaborate tales and singing complex songs to keep their heritage alive.

The primary mission of this book is, therefore, to show you that a wonderful, a magical world of human devising has existed for as long as humanity has existed and that it is still there, waiting each day to be discovered anew. It is the world of the humanities. The humanities are here. They are just outside your door, waiting. They are even inside *you* if you know where to look. All you have to do is open that door or get in touch with your creative self and extend a welcoming hand. If you do, your life will be changed very much for the better. And you will want to run out into the street and share the wonder with everyone you meet!

Gifts of the Humanities

1.2   *What are the gifts of the humanities?*

Economics tells us that the wants of people are insatiable, but resources are limited. Because almost everything is scarcer than we would like, treasured possessions, as well as basics such as food and shelter, come with a price tag. Even water is becoming scarce; it may not be long before we have to pay premium prices just to slake our thirst, let alone water our lawns. Do we have enough money to buy everything we want? The answer is usually NO!

With the humanities the problem is reversed. *The resources of the humanities are unlimited*, but all too often our wants are meager. In the economic world, we can't always be rich by choice, but in the world of the humanities, we can be "poor" by choice.

Several decades ago, during a severe recession, banks attracted savings deposits by offering gifts to those who would forego spending and open CD accounts instead. People walked out with new toasters, blenders, steam irons, and luggage; and, of course, bank reserves swelled. Such incentives are cyclical in nature, but the humanities always have gifts that are there for us regardless of what the economy is doing. Here are some of them.

Beauty

Ever since philosophy began, ever since thoughtful people started asking what makes life good, the answer often involved something called **beauty**. Its close connection with pleasure has always seemed apparent. It is pleasant and desirable to see beautiful things and beautiful people. People prefer to live amid beauty than amid ugliness.

Though people may debate whether a particular person or piece of music is beautiful, there is widespread agreement that something deserves to be called beautiful if the arrangement of the parts is pleasing, if it seems *right*. The rightness of the arrangement determines the pleasure that it gives us. When there is something in an arrangement that seems *not* right, we are less attracted, possibly even repelled. What are the criteria for something seeming *right*? That is, admittedly, the tricky part.

Is judging an arrangement—of a painting, a person's face, a story, a dramatic moment—as right or not right entirely subjective? Yes and no. Culture can play a role—some cultures perceive symmetry as right, some prefer asymmetry; some find delicacy important, others prefer strength. To some extent, we must rely for our standards on those works that have, over centuries, retained the capability to move us.

Leonardo da Vinci's *Mona Lisa* (Figure 1.1) is probably the world's most famous painting. Each week thousands flock to the Louvre Museum in Paris to see the portrait of the lady with the enigmatic smile. Since its creation in the years between 1503 and 1507 innumerable art historians and critics have given their opinions of what makes this a great work. They may differ in the specific elements they praise; some appreciate the haunting face or the ambiguity of the gaze, others the mysteriousness of the landscape behind the face. Not everyone will agree that the subject herself is a beautiful woman—that judgment may be colored by cultural standards—but they tend to agree that *Mona Lisa* is a beautiful work of art.

AESTHETIC PLEASURE   The pleasure that beauty inspires in us is called **aesthetic**. Yet what kind of pleasure is it? One answer is that the beautiful inspires within us *a feeling of well-being that is its own justification*. True, the attraction of a shiny new car may have less to do with its pure beauty than with the pride we feel in owning it, or if it belongs to someone else, by the envy we feel. When a beautiful face passes by, we might long for closer contact with it, but we would not have such a desire if we did not first make an aesthetic judgment. The critics who have written volumes about the "secret" of the *Mona Lisa* have already made an aesthetic judgment and are now trying to find the words to describe why the arrangement of the parts is right. A universal definition of beauty that fits every example may be impossible to find, but suffice it to say that few of us would deny that the beautiful does indeed exist.

The humanities are, in part, a catalog of works that have tallied a host of positive votes from people who have spent their lives in pursuit of the beautiful and who hold up road signs for us in our own quest. Be advised, however, that the pursuit is endless, and the catalog needs almost daily updating. The road signs often vary from one culture to another. If we are to expand our capacity for aesthetic pleasure, we need to experience many versions of the beautiful and try to see them from other points of view.

In the Asian wing of New York's Metropolitan Museum of Art, tucked away in a corner that the visitor can easily miss, is a sculpture called *Water Stone* (Figure 1.2) by the Japanese artist Isamu Noguchi (1904–1988). It is a gray stone fountain of uneven shape with a perpetual flow of water that, at first glance, appears to be a sheet of clear glass sitting motionless on top but, in reality, trickles slowly down the side so that the escaping water is always equal to the new supply being pumped up from below. The trickle creates a soft sound that soothes and mesmerizes the visitor who takes the time to sit on the bench provided. One woman reported that she sat there entranced for nearly an hour.

The arrangement of parts in *Water Stone* includes the shape and texture of the stone, the varying shades created by the falling water, and, most important, the sound. But you don't have to be in a museum to experience the beauty of similar arrangements. A woodland stream, flowing over rocks of different shapes, will create varied shadings, and if you shut your eyes and really listen to the water, you will discover that it has a variety of sounds, depending on wind and the different rocks over which it flows. In truth, all you need to

Figure 1.2 Isamu Noguchi, *Water Stone*, c. 1987.
Would your experience be different if you found a similar group of stones in a natural setting? What differentiates the beauty of art from the beauty of nature?
The Metropolitan Museum of Art. Image source: Art Resource, NY

do to experience in full how the humanities can take you to that quiet oasis we mentioned is find a stream in the woods, or study closely the different colors in rainwater gushing alongside a curb. When you search for the beautiful, you will be astonished to realize how close it is.

Of course, the arts can do more for us than provide an aesthetic moment. Sometimes they may convey a message the artist believes is important. In fact, some take the position that meaning is what we primarily look for in any work. Yet it does a disservice both to the artist and to the viewers if we always insist upon looking for a message. (After all, what is the message in water slowly trickling down the side of a stone sculpture?) Many artists, as well as poets and novelists, object to those critics who analyze their work, evaluating it solely in terms of the important—or unimportant—meanings they find.

The humanities can be enjoyed for both their aesthetic and communicative functions. Learning to distinguish one from the other is an important part of *critical thinking*, the subject of the chapter that follows.

Beautiful Movement

The perfection of movement cannot fail to inspire a sense of awe and admiration. Movement is as much a part of being human as breathing. Few of us move in perfect synchrony, but almost all of us experience joy when we see it done right. Even though our own movements may lack the coordination of, say, the skilled dancer, there is also aesthetic pleasure for us not just in watching others, but in getting up and swaying, gliding, or shaking to a rhythm. We have patterned our lives to meeting deadlines and reaching destinations. Perhaps that's why people like, for a change, to be on the dance floor and simply move in rhythm. Are they trying to get somewhere in particular? No. The pleasure of the movement is its own reason for existing.

The French artist Edgar Degas (1834–1917) loved to paint dancers (see Figure 1.3). Degas's many paintings of ballerinas depict the beauty of women and the elegance of their movements. Portraying beauty and elegance may not have been his only intent; other paintings depict working women in other circumstances, and he may have been intrigued by the role of women in the working world. But clearly ballerinas gave him aesthetic pleasure. His paintings give that same pleasure to us.

Figure 1.3 Edgar Degas, *The Dance Class*, c. 1874.
Can a painting provide us with the same experience we have watching actual dancers? How might these experiences differ?
Scala / Art Resource, NY

So do the serene gliding, graceful leaps of a figure skater, the seemingly impossible spins of a snow boarder or X Games athlete, the angular pops of hip hop dancers, and the fluid grace of champion runners. The arrangement of the parts in a given movement seems right, even if we don't see their function. Many of us are not as coordinated or as strong and well-trained as a great dancer, skater, or runner. If we were, then their art might seem less beautiful.

Language

Words in varied combinations are the means by which we communicate to ourselves and with each other. Through language, we make ourselves understood to others, and we are able to understand what we read and what others are saying. The need for language becomes apparent at an early age; we develop a love of language if we are fortunate enough to be around adults who talk to us (but not in baby talk), who enjoy reading, and who read to us.

Children develop through recognizable and documented stages. Most children between the ages of 2 and 3 become word-conscious. The need to attach a name to everything in sight appears to be an inborn instinct. Parents as well as older siblings can be annoyed at hearing the persistent "What's that?" throughout the day, even as they are happy that the insatiable demand for words is proceeding as it should. At this stage, children like to repeat sentences and phrases they hear in their surroundings, unconcerned that they have no idea what these words mean. Children like the sound and the "taste" of words. Unfortunately, the insatiable need to add to and replenish our vocabulary does not always stay with us.

ACQUIRING MODELS How or when some of us lose the need for more words is a complex mystery. Unraveling it is perhaps less important than the awareness that *it does not have to happen*. That's where the humanities come in. Through reading, through listening to great language on the stage or screen—or, better yet, through reading poetry aloud—we acquire models of how to say things in ways that make others sit up and take notice. People experienced in using the humanities as a technique for living sometimes make a point by directly quoting well-known lines, assured that their friends will catch the reference.

One of the most famous lines in all of drama is the beginning of Hamlet's third soliloquy: *To be or not to be: that is the question.* When people on similar wavelengths are discussing whether, for example, to stay home and watch television or go downtown for a costly evening of eating out and seeing a movie, the comment "Ah, that is the question" communicates instantly that the speaker is not leaning one way or the other but is wide open to suggestions. Directly quoting or providing variations on famous lines that you know others will recognize is not only fun but cuts down on the need for details and circular discussions.

The most popular work of the medieval English poet Geoffrey Chaucer (c.1343–1400), *The Canterbury Tales*, contains a collection of unforgettable stories as well as famous descriptions of the people who tell them. Chaucer was a master at capturing the essence of his characters with swift strokes of his pen, and many of his descriptions are part of the reservoir of language in the minds of people who read. One of the characters is a lawyer who is always in a hurry and apparently so busy that he could easily have been the envy of lazy people. After describing the man and his behavior in detail, Chaucer adds: "Yet he seemed busier than he was." Who knows how many thousands of readers over the last 600 years have used some version of this line in referring to people who display the same kind of feverish but essentially meaningless activity? A high school student, asked why he is not doing his homework, responds: "I'm very busy with other things." We roll our eyes and say, "He seems busier than he is."

The sixth-century BCE Greek philosopher Heraclitus is famous for having said: "You cannot step twice into the same river." By this he meant that life is constant change, that the only thing stable in all the universe is the fact of change itself. A number of more recent writers have amended his aphorism to say that we can't even step *once* into the same river, because water flows without cease—or, more ironically from environmentalists, because the water has disappeared altogether, as is true for some parts of the Colorado River. Clearly, the versatile language derived from the humanities even increases the chance that an urgent cause may win more supporters.

APPRECIATING VARIETY   The humanities help us to appreciate a variety of ingenious phrasings and offer us models of how language can be expertly manipulated. One of the greatest comedies ever written, Oscar Wilde's 1895 *The Importance of Being Earnest*, is a storehouse of witty lines illustrating that one way of saying something is not necessarily as good as another. In one scene, the hero, Jack Worthing, is being interviewed by his fiancée's mother, a social lioness with biting wit, who investigates his credentials as a suitor (see Figure 1.4). She asks the nervous young man whether he smokes. Sheepishly he admits that, well yes, he does smoke. Her unexpected reply: "I'm glad to hear it. A man should always have an occupation of some sort." Not only is the lady staying one step ahead of him with her wit, but she is making an indirect statement about the indolence and lack of purpose of the upper classes.

Another master of language was the thirteenth-century Persian poet known as Rumi, who left us a treasure trove of clever and moving sentiments. One memorable line, often rendered as "The wound is the place the Light enters you," may have influenced the twentieth-century Canadian poet and songwriter Leonard Cohen, whose "Anthem" includes the line, "There is a crack in everything, that's how the light gets in."[1]

Playing with language has evolved into a high art. Like the beautiful, good language needs no further justification. A person characterized by others as someone with "a way with words" or "a flair for language" generally earns respect (unless, of course, it turns out that the person never has anything else to offer *except* words).

Yet just as a novel or play or movie can be spoiled when authors use words and idioms that have become so commonplace they are no longer effective, so too is the everyday language of most people littered with terminology employed over and over. Yet such hackneyed language keeps slipping from our tongues without our even noticing. We insert "like" into our speech so frequently that we hardly notice it's there.

EVERYDAY SPEECH   In addition to the omnipresence of the word "like," ordinary speech is now sprinkled frequently with "y'know" or "know what I'm sayin'," and we often use "go" instead of "said": "I go . . . and then he goes . . .". In addition, we are encouraged to use abbreviations (BTW for "by the way," LOL for "laugh out loud," and so on), or to replace language altogether with emoticons, as we communicate more and more often by text message rather than in face-to-face dialog. Language is always changing, and perhaps now it is changing faster than ever before. Consider these sentences: "I need a new iPhone because the apps I have just aren't working," or "We stayed up all night binge-watching *Orange Is the New Black*." Apps? Binge-watching? Ten years ago, words and phrases like these didn't exist.

But do we pay attention to the words that we hear? Do they startle us with their cleverness? Do we remember a memorable turn of phrase? Does language help us grow? Listen carefully to the speech patterns of

Figure 1.4   Brian Bedford as Lady Bracknell in a 2009 production of *The Importance of Being Earnest* at the Roundabout Theater in New York.

Oscar Wilde's plays are famous for their use of wit and wordplay. Has the emergence of social media changed the way we use language? How?

Joan Marcus Photography

people with whom you are conversing. If their language tends to be fresh and interesting, chances are they spend a lot of time reading. Perhaps your own language reflects the same habit. We hope so.

Here is an excerpt from a poem by Taylor Mali, who has had a varied kind of life, having taught for nine years, studied acting with the Royal Shakespeare Company, and then become a poet and advocate of teaching literacy in the classroom. The poem is titled "Totally like whatever, you know?"

> *In case you hadn't noticed,*
> *it has somehow become uncool*
> *to sound like you know what you're talking about?*
> *Or believe strongly in what you're saying?*
> *Invisible question marks and parentheses (you know?)'s*
> *have been attaching themselves to the ends of our sentences?*
>
> *Even when those sentences aren't, like, questions? You know?*[2]

Ideas

Language is not only the vehicle through which we can display our savvy in everyday dealings with others; it is also the means by which we formulate ideas. Still, all of us have flashes of ideas that we can't quite catch hold of because the words aren't there. A statement attributed to Albert Einstein (perhaps incorrectly) suggests that "If you can't explain it simply, you don't understand it well enough." When someone explains a complicated idea such as the theory of relativity and we nod to signify understanding, we are more or less guaranteeing that we would be able to deliver the identical explanation in our own words. Very often we cannot.

Words are the means by which we think. If we have no words, we cannot have ideas. We *can* have intuitions without words, but they are not the same as ideas. Intuitions are, of course, vital human resources. We don't need words to find a piece of music exciting. Intuitions are necessary for a full appreciation of much that the humanities have to offer. But through our philosophers, novelists, and poets, we derive a love for exciting ideas. After reading a stimulating passage that makes an explosive point, one often says to oneself, "Oh! I wish I'd thought of that!" (And don't we all glow with pride when we advance an idea that meets with approval, even admiration, an idea others wish *they* had thought of?)

Thinking helps us keep our sanity—even in our world of rapidly accelerating change and technological marvels that are said to think *for* us. Fortunately, the brain can still be what makes us want to do more than just survive. Thinking keeps us in touch with ourselves and the world around us. Thinking comes in a variety of forms. Rigorous studies such as mathematics, physics, and economics provide powerful exercise for the brain, but not all of us are adept at these disciplines.

Yet happily, we have the humanities, which widen both our emotional range and our understanding of many things: the past, the present, human behavior, the workings of the creative mind, and the many unanswered questions that philosophers, scientists, and theologians have asked for centuries.

TEACHING BY ASKING: THE SOCRATIC METHOD The Society for Philosophical Inquiry movement is the brainchild of Christopher Phillips, author of *Socrates Café* (2001), which describes various venues, all with that name, in which society members gather to discuss and share ideas. The format for the meetings is inspired by the teaching methods of Socrates (469–399 BCE), mentor of Plato (427–347 BCE).

Socrates and his young students would gather in an Athenian grove and discuss specific questions, such as "What is justice?" As recorded by Plato—since the master himself, as far as we know, wrote nothing down—the discussions took this form:

The question is posed by Socrates.

ONE STUDENT SAYS:	*"Justice is whatever is in the best interest of the ruling party."*
SOCRATES ANSWERS:	*"Can the ruling party ever pass a law that is for some reason not in its best interest?"*
STUDENT:	*"I suppose it could happen."*
SOCRATES:	*"If it did happen, would the people be justified in breaking that law?"*
STUDENT:	*"I don't think so. A law is a law."*
SOCRATES:	*"In other words, it would be wrong to break a law just because somebody thought it was not in the best interest of the ruling party."*
STUDENT:	*"Well . . . maybe it could be broken."*
SOCRATES:	*"If you thought the law could be broken and I said it couldn't, which of us is right?"*
STUDENT:	*"I guess in that case we're both right."*
SOCRATES:	*"Is this your idea of a just society—one in which anyone can decide whether to obey a law or not? Would you want to live in such a society?"*
STUDENT:	*"I . . . suppose I wouldn't."*
SOCRATES:	*"Then justice really has to be defined as something that is absolute and not only in the best interest of the ruling party or the individual who decides not to obey a certain law."*

Socrates here demonstrates the Socratic method—that is, teaching by asking questions that stimulate critical thinking, rather than lecturing. The point of a discussion at a Socrates Café is not to solve all the problems of the world. It is to apply the technique of the ancient philosopher and the techniques of other thinkers to puzzling questions of the past and present. Clearly "justice" is one such issue. It has never been defined to everyone's satisfaction. Whether one agrees or not that justice is absolute and unchanging or that there is no applicable principle other than "might makes right," the discussion and defense of ideas are ways of strengthening our mental faculties. Like dancing, thinking needs no further justification.

A Deeper Sense of the Past

The humanities allow us to see more than our personal past. Through the humanities we may immerse ourselves in the firsthand experiences of those who actually lived and often struggled in the past—lived and struggled with many of the problems that face us today. These experiences help each of us to better understand what living is all about. *The realized human being is an accumulation of what has gone before and how that affects the present.*

Through the humanities, we can live more than once: here and now, and yesterday as well. Those who refuse to browse among the cumulative treasures of human expression have only themselves to blame if they find themselves trapped in one solitary existence.

Like all of us, the past has its right to be heard. It did not, we know, allow for the *full* representation of its genius, for the contributions of both men and women from a variety of cultures. Still, the past has its own glory, even as it stands. The statue of Venus de Milo has been around for many hundreds of years. It no longer has arms, but, gazing at it, we cannot help seeing the idealism, the adoration of the female form that must have motivated the unknown classical artist. Becoming familiar with treasures of the past brings us closer to those who came before us, inspires in us the pride of belonging to the continuity of our species. The love of beauty is timeless and universal, and the past, as reflected in the humanities, has more than its share of beauty, not to mention ideas and great language.

Some treasures from the past embody issues that still face us. *The Oresteia*, an epic tragedy consisting of three plays by the Greek dramatist Aeschylus (525–456 BCE), is based on a very ancient myth about the murder of a mother and her lover by a son seeking revenge for his father's death at their hands. In the final play, *The Eumenides*, Aeschylus creates the world's first courtroom drama, in which the hero is acquitted on the grounds that his mother's crime had been greater than his. She had killed a man who was also a great warrior and leader of his people. The son, Orestes, has killed an adulterous woman and her lover.

The decision to acquit the hero was made nearly 2,500 years ago and delivered from the stage at the Theater of Dionysus; the verdict is still discussed today. Theater history teachers often point out that while the acquittal does not sit well with everyone, especially feminists (who argue that it discriminates against the gender of the victim and ignores the fact that the murdered husband had a mistress), the work is nonetheless a milestone in the early history of democracy. There was, after all, a trial. Reading or watching performances of *The Oresteia* can generate discussion about whether the law, even in a democracy, judges all persons equally.

Even more modern works can give us all a deeper sense of history, of how those who lived before us thought and felt. Consider, for example, the novel *To Kill a Mockingbird*, which almost every American schoolchild reads at some point. Doesn't this story help many of us better understand not only the persistent issues of racism and injustice in this country, but also the emotions and sensibilities of childhood itself? Don't countless readers recognize something of themselves in the young protagonist Scout? And certainly a painting like Picasso's *Guernica* (see Figure 5.33) can help us know the chaos and calamity of war.

Developing a profound respect for the classical works of Socrates, Aeschylus, or the sculptor of the Venus de Milo, or for the works of more recent artists such as Harper Lee and Picasso, does not mean choosing to ignore the achievements of everyone else. At the same time, having profound respect for today and a wider vision of tomorrow does not mean that we ought to ignore what can be justly celebrated from yesterday.

Becoming an "Infinite" Person

1.3 *Why is Leonardo da Vinci considered the perfect model of the "infinite" person?*

By sharpening our awareness of the present—the issues, the important themes and varied ways of presenting them—and by linking us to the past, the humanities provide a wider view of life. As this book unfolds, you will be learning much more about the humanities and what the various disciplines are and how they can deeply affect your life. Your view of the humanities and the world will continue to expand, and you will be on your way to becoming an infinite person.

Let us consider the very model of humanism, the very essence of the infinite person, Leonardo da Vinci (1452–1519). So broad was the range of his curiosity and creative genius that history has accorded him that rarest of titles: *uomo universale*, universal man. He is also called a **Renaissance man**, meaning a man of the broadest possible learning and a widely diverse range of interests and achievements. Since Leonardo's time, that label has been given to many people, both the famous and the not-so-famous, who refused to be limited to just one field of endeavor, though it is doubtful that many will ever match what Leonardo accomplished: planning early versions of the airplane and the submarine; speculating about the human circulatory system long before William Harvey "officially" discovered the circulation of the blood; building the first hydrometer to measure the displacement of water; inventing the science of meteorology long before the proper instruments to make accurate predictions were available. His *Vitruvian Man*, a drawing based on the work of the architect Vitruvius, suggests a perfect blend of art and science: an attempt to portray a realistic figure representing ideal proportions (Figure 1.5). And on top of all the scientific and technological contributions, there are his works of art, including the *Mona Lisa* (Figure 1.1).

The example of Leonardo da Vinci suggests that, while few may hope to approach his genius, all of us can do more with our lives than we are doing at this very moment. There are so many books to read, so much music to hear, so many plays to see, so many great films to view. We may not become Renaissance persons, but infinite choices await us. The more we absorb from the humanities, the more we expand our knowledge, our capacity for understanding both ourselves and others. In a sense we become infinite, intertwining with innumerable lives in myriad combinations.

Here are just three advantages of becoming an infinite person.

- First, the infinite person commits no crimes against humanity. He or she is no longer narrowly preoccupied with self and its immediate needs, its sense of having been unfairly used, its desire to avenge wrongs against itself.
- Second, the infinite person is free of rigid prejudices and never works consciously to restrict others from exercising their right to assemble, speak their minds openly, practice their own religion, and follow their own preferences, as long as, in being free, they do not themselves limit the freedom of others.
- Third, the infinite person does not jump to quick conclusions but looks at all sides of an issue before making a judgment, recognizes that no judgment is final, and is always willing to reconsider in the light of new data. This person is therefore not constrained by family and social traditions and willingly seeks out the source of imposed or inherited beliefs so as to reevaluate them. "That's how we've always done it around here" is not the mark of the infinite person.

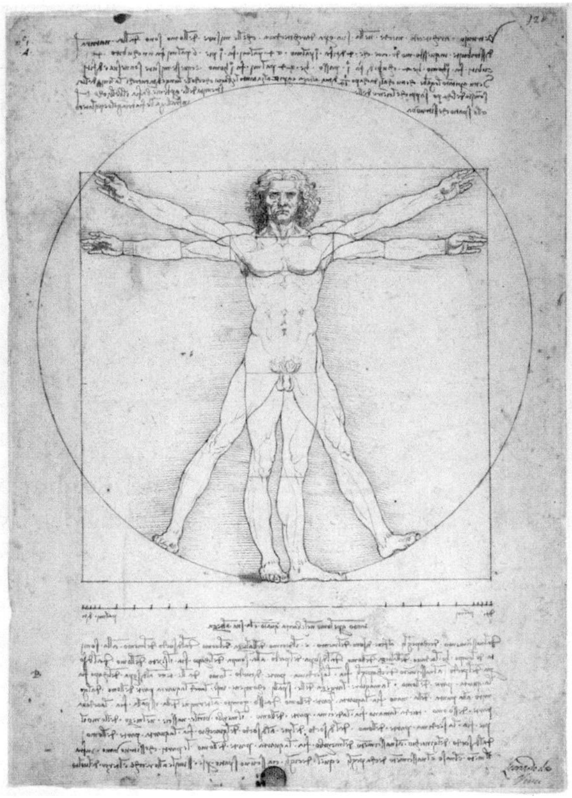

The book you are about to read is thus not only a visit to the treasure house of the humanities, the stupendous creative and intellectual achievements of human beings. It has the underlying purpose of convincing you that you cannot fail to want to expand your life, to fill every moment with art and thought, once you realize that all it takes is the willingness to do it.

Figure 1.5 Leonardo da Vinci, *Vitruvian Man*, c. 1490.
Why do you think this drawing has remained famous for over 500 years?
© Cameraphoto Arte

Looking Back

In this chapter,

- we discussed what we mean by the humanities and how the definition of the humanities has changed and broadened in recent centuries,
- we looked at the various gifts that we receive when we include the humanities in our lives, and
- we discussed the concept of the "infinite" person, and how Leonardo da Vinci represents this concept.

Key Terms

aesthetic An experience in the arts or in life, such as watching a sunset, that we value for no reason beyond itself.

beauty A pleasing arrangement of parts that affects us aesthetically.

discipline In the humanities, a given art form—literature, visual art, music, drama, dance, and cinema—as well as a field of academic study (such as "literary theory" or "history of dance").

humanism A movement begun in the early Renaissance that extolled and studied the creative and intellectual legacies of classical Greece and Rome, leading to the conviction that only through such study could one become fully human; a term that is now expanded to include the study of contributions from all cultures.

humanities Once limited to "the best products of the best minds," narrowly defined as classical Greek or Roman, but later expanded to include Western European achievements and, more recently, the creative expressions of men and women around the world.

Renaissance man A label often applied to Leonardo da Vinci, indicating his display of genius in many areas from art to science; now used as high praise for anyone who has earned a reputation for high achievement in several fields (e.g. Albert Einstein).

Chapter 2
The Humanities and Critical Thinking

Learning Objectives

2.1 Discuss the importance of critical thinking in understanding the value of the humanities.

2.2 Distinguish between Apollonian and Dionysian responses to the humanities.

2.3 Identify three ways to exercise the mind and become a critical thinker.

2.4 Differentiate between the role of a professional critic and that of the individual responding to a creative work.

2.5 Identify the characteristics of "literalist" and "figuratist" critical responses.

These two representations of the same historical figure represent the Apollonian and Dionysian sides of human personality. How do they differ from one another? Do you react differently to each?

Figure 2.1 Michelangelo, *David*, c. 1501–1504.
© Studio Fotografico Quattrone

Figure 2.2 Donatello, *David*, c. 1430–1440.
Leemage/Corbis

In the introductory chapter, we said that the study of the humanities includes understanding the critical process—that is, the process by which we observe, analyze, and evaluate works of art. In this chapter, we will explore the processes used by those who do that kind of work for a living—professional critics and scholars. But we will also explore the ways in which most of us who are not professional critics can enrich our lives by using some of the same techniques: becoming objective in how we evaluate what we see, read, or hear; integrating pure emotional responses with analysis; and delaying a final judgment until we have all the data.

The Importance of Critical Thinking

2.1 *What is the importance of critical thinking in understanding the humanities?*

The critical thinking skill has a strong carryover into everyday life. We should not make snap judgments about other people or blindly accept opinions expressed in the media if we happen to be fond of the anchor or commentator, and—of vital importance to the conduct of our own lives—we should listen carefully to what others tell us before we make up our minds. All too often we are guilty of quickly deciding this is true or that is poppycock, or he is not to be trusted, or she always knows what she is talking about. Worse, we often place people in the wax museum of our mind, attaching labels that never change: bossy, lazy, dull, naive, and so on and on. From great literature and drama, we learn that people are far more complex than the stereotype labels we often attach to them.

Critical thinking sharpens the mind. If we start early enough in life and continue to exercise our critical faculties throughout our lives, chances are good that our mind will not desert us late in life. Toward the end of William Wharton's 1981 novel *Dad*, the main character, en route to his father's funeral, has a sudden glimpse of his own aging.

> *I'll become a bore to others, a drag in conversation, repeat myself, be slow at comprehension, quick at misunderstanding, have lapses in conceptual sequences. All this will probably be invisible to me. I won't even be aware of my own decline.*[1]

The older we get, the more precious does the mind become. Many, early on, seek what they term "altered states," achieved through substance or alcohol abuse. A reason often given is that life is too complex: we have too many responsibilities—school, parental problems, money problems, relationship problems—so escape is not only pleasant but absolutely necessary. Even if we use these escape mechanisms in relative moderation and there are no lasting effects, we are missing the opportunity to effectively use that most wonderful commodity, the mind.

Those who miss the chance to develop critical thought may be too concerned with the specific details of everyday life to go beyond what seems most personally important at the moment. None of us can engage in thought to the exclusion of making practical decisions. There are times when "What shall I wear to the party?" becomes the most important question we face. But the individual who is *solely* concerned with practicalities of the moment *all* the time is a *noncritical thinker*. We all think noncritically from time to time. But our efforts to use our critical faculties—and to focus on events and concepts beyond ourselves and our small circle of day-to-day friends and activities—will be well rewarded.

Instructors of English comp classes often assign personal narratives because students are much more skilled at writing about themselves than about larger questions. When well done, the personal narrative can result in a book like Frank McCourt's *Angela's Ashes* (1996), about growing up poor in Ireland, or Marjane Satrapi's compelling graphic novel about her childhood in Iran, *Persepolis* (2000). Memoirs can also be self-indulgent and uninteresting. At their worst, memoirs can be, as Daniel Mendelsohn points out in an essay called "But Enough about Me,"

[U]nseemly self-exposures, unpalatable betrayals, unavoidable mendacity . . . memoir, for much of its modern history, has been the black sheep of the literary family . . . motivated, it would seem, by an overpowering need to be the center of attention.[2]

Ideally, thinking about ourselves leads us to self-knowledge, and self-knowledge leads us to a more profound understanding of the world and of humankind. Let's not get distracted by taking selfies!

Apollonian and Dionysian Responses to the Humanities

2.2   *What distinguishes an Apollonian response to the humanities from a Dionysian response?*

The German philosopher Friedrich Nietzsche (1844–1900) wrote a book in 1872 titled *The Birth of Tragedy from the Spirit of Music* in which he revisits the great age of drama in fifth-century (BCE) Athens. He points out that the art form had begun a century earlier as choral music and dance, without spoken dialog. As it evolved, certain soloists became distinct from the chorus, and through their dialog, they told stories based on ancient myths. *The Oresteia* by Aeschylus is one such story. Most popular were the tragic myths, stories of powerful and rich men (often rulers) who, because of a fatal flaw of character, fell from the heights of strength into the depths of despair and ruination. Not all of the tragedies, including *The Oresteia* itself, fit this description exactly, but they are all filled with horror, suffering, and the extremes of human pain. They have scenes that are among the most shattering ever devised.

What bothered Nietzsche was that, in lecturing or writing about tragedy, teachers and critics sometimes forgot that the roots of the art form were in dance and music. He believed the proper response to viewing a tragedy was to allow oneself to respond emotionally, the way we respond to music. He found that viewers and critics alike were focusing on the central characters' moral failings, on the consequences of breaking a moral law. As a result, Greek tragedies were evaluated and discussed in terms of the *lessons* they taught, not the strength of their emotional impact. Nietzsche believed it was wrong to encourage people to view tragedy through reason rather than emotion, wrong to insist on the moral philosophy behind a play at the expense of appreciating the force and the fury that drive it.

He then made a famous distinction between two ways of responding not only to drama but to events in real life. He identified as **Apollonian** that side of the human personality dominated by reason and disciplined analytical, rational, and coherent thought: in short, the side that responds to Greek tragedy by seeking its meaning. He dubbed as **Dionysian** that side of the human personality dominated by feelings, intuition, and freedom from limits: the side that responds emotionally to music as well as to the force and fury of tragedy.

Nietzsche derived these opposing terms from Greek mythology. Apollo was the god of the sun (hence of light and truth) and Dionysus was the god of the vibrant energy of the earth (hence of emotion, spontaneity, and intuition). (See Figures 2.1 and 2.2 for Renaissance representations reflecting these two descriptions.) Nietzsche believed the goal of life was to achieve a balance between reason and emotion—to be able to think clearly; to be steady, reliable, and responsible for one's actions; AND to be able to feel, to enjoy the fruits of the vine (so to speak), to express both love and hate (when necessary) unguided by a concern for rules.

We shall have occasion to refer many times throughout this book to Apollonian and Dionysian elements in the humanities. If critical thinking is a major goal of studying the humanities, the distinction between the two sides of our personality should be our starting point. It is impossible to study the humanities without seeing how one or the other, or often both together, inform a given work. The symphonies of Beethoven, for example, trigger a Dionysian, or emotional, response, but our critical, Apollonian side also appreciates their monumental structures.

The Apollonian response also means looking at a work objectively before evaluating it. Critical thinking begins on the Apollonian side; writing a critical analysis is always Apollonian, even though a strong emotional response may have inspired the analysis. One can be enraptured by a musical performance *without* wanting to analyze it further. If this is the case, however, the comment "It was great; I was carried away by it" must not be confused with a full critical statement. It has to be recognized for what it is: a statement of a personal experience. "I liked it" is personal and Dionysian. "I liked it because it had . . ." may be introducing an Apollonian evaluation. Both are valid; but they should not be mistaken for each other.

The Popcorn Syndrome

A word of caution: It is all too easy to give the critical mind a vacation, to surrender to the Dionysian excitement of the moment and decide that further considerations are not important. Doing so will not stretch our mental capacities and should be avoided unless a given work clearly does not warrant time and mental energy.

More seductive is the popcorn experience, often felt at the movies. When we label something a "popcorn movie," we are generally suggesting that we can simply sit back, munch on popcorn, and be entertained without having to think. A huge number of films and television shows belong to this category, as indeed do many popular novels called "good reads" or "beach books."

The novels by Suzanne Collins that comprise the *Hunger Games* trilogy (*The Hunger Games*, 2008; *Catching Fire*, 2009; and *Mockingjay*, 2010) are hugely popular, and not just with the young adults for whom they were intended. The novels tell the story of a dystopian society that controls its populace by pitting teenagers, selected by lottery, in battle-to-the-death "games" and the emergence of a genuine heroine who eventually inspires a successful revolution. It is told in such fast-moving, cinematic prose that the reader cannot wait to turn the page. Exciting? Yes. Suspenseful? Indeed. Great literature? Here one must pause and reflect. Is the story totally believable? Is there serious depth to the main characters? Do the novels leave the reader with what we may call "residual thoughts"? Or are they, like many others, just popcorn fun?

The truth about these books (and the films made from them) is that they are probably not great literature, but they do raise profound and compelling questions about tyranny, exploitation, and revolution. If we read (or watch, popcorn in hand) and never contemplate those questions, it is our loss.

Of course, we may also decide that *any* novel or film that is *so* entertaining—from the speed and violence of Mad Max's adventures to the silliness of Adam Sandler's comedies—is worthwhile. Popular music, films, novels, cartoons in newspapers and magazines—all that entertains and amuses us for even a short time—can be called, at the very least, the "temporary humanities." Like all emotional responses, fun is a legitimate way to spend some time. Some of us stop there.

There is a deeper, more satisfying definition of "entertainment," however. Having enjoyed the *Hunger Games* trilogy as a series of "good reads," we might let the characters of Katniss and President Snow resonate a bit in our minds. We might think about a society that forces children to fight one another and consider whether such outrageous things could (or do) happen in our world today. We might analyze how America (for an America of the future is the setting for these books) could have become the society depicted in them: What would have needed to happen to turn America into such a place? We might find that our understanding of this series was deeper and more profound than we could have imagined.

The critical mind, perceiving that a response to a piece of music like Duke Ellington's "Take the 'A' Train" or Taylor Swift's "Shake It Off" has been largely Dionysian, might later consider those elements that caused the response: The syncopations and rhythms? A unique timbre in the singer's voice? The universality of the lyrics, or the unexpected shifts in tempo? No two analyses will be exactly the same; nor need they be.

Critical thinking is valid as a process, not as the absolute determination of good or bad. The important thing is that the unexamined Dionysian response—perhaps limited to "Man, that was terrific!"—is a suitable response as far as it goes, but it will not, alone, move us forward; it will not contribute much toward balancing the two forces in our lives. While acknowledging our very human emotional responses, we should always seek to find the *why*—the reasons that a work of art or literature or performance has moved us in that way.

Empathy and Alienation

Sometimes the artists who create paintings, or dance, or theater work hard to engage our emotional responses—and sometimes they push against that impulse. The characters or works they create may encourage our empathy, or they may encourage a very different response: alienation.

EMPATHY   **Empathy**, the process by which we identify with a character or a performer so that for a short time we believe we are that person, is a Dionysian trick of our nature. Empathy is crucial to the entertainment process. If you, for example, should arrive late for a circus performance and sit down just as the tightrope walker's act has begun, what you would see is not only the death-defying performer higher up than you might ever care to be but also hundreds of seated patrons swaying back and forth. They would be projecting themselves into the precarious journey, gasping each time the walker (as part of the act) appears about to fall.

In similar fashion, you and your fellow audience members in a movie theater are in the passenger seat of a car careening wildly out of control, dodging the elevated pillars along Canal Street in New York, or feeling the sad abandonment of a lover. Television and movie directors know about Dionysian empathy and readily design opportunities for indulging in it. If the heroine, trapped in a mountain ravine with flood waters inching upward, attempts to scale the rock wall, she has to be successful at first and then *must* slip when she is halfway up and appear to be doomed. You give free reign to your empathetic imagination because deep down you know all will be well in the end, but you will feel cheated if all is well from the start.

Just why empathizing with near-death experiences should qualify as entertainment has been debated for centuries. It may be traceable to the eighteenth-century shift away from the on-stage blood and gore of popular tragedies, including many of Shakespeare's, that featured hands being chopped off, tongues and eyes being ripped out, horrors that could rival the bloodiest slasher movie of today. The eighteenth century on both sides of the Atlantic introduced a more genteel way of life for the upper classes and those who imitated them. Shakespeare and his contemporaries went into a period of decline, or else their works were revised with all the horrors eliminated. But little by little, as society became more respectable, at least on the surface, stage entertainment began reintroducing melodramatic elements for audiences that enjoyed escape from their morally upright lives. In the nineteenth century, the circus was born, with its empathy-inducing trapeze and high-wire acts and its wild animal encounters. All of this led inevitably to our present-day Dionysian orgies on film and television.

Sometimes we can be lulled into empathizing with a less than noble character. Walter White, the chemistry-teacher-turned-meth-manufacturer in the hit television series *Breaking Bad*, at first appears tremendously sympathetic—just given a diagnosis

Figure 2.3 Bryan Cranston as Walter White in TV's *Breaking Bad* (2008–2013).
What makes us feel empathetic toward a character in film or television? How can a director manipulate that tendency toward empathy?
Ursula Coyote/AMC/Everett Collection

of terminal cancer, with little money set aside to care for his family and a sense that he has failed in life—but gradually emerges as monstrous. And yet because the series is so skillfully structured, the audience remains empathetic with Walt long past the time when he has begun to violate the moral and ethical principles that most of us hold dear. Indeed, the series creator, Vince Gilligan, has said that he set up the challenge deliberately: to see how long he could keep the audience empathizing with Walt.

<u>ALIENATION</u>   The flip side of the Dionysian coin when it comes to such entertainment can be called Apollonian alienation. The term **alienation effect** was coined by Bertolt Brecht (1898–1956), an important German playwright of the early twentieth century. Brecht wanted to make sure audiences did not become so emotionally involved in plot and character that they failed to heed his messages. He often injected vaudeville slapstick, songs, and dances into very serious material, hoping to prevent empathetic responses.

The critical thinker need not be restricted by the intentions of the author or performer. Attending a play or film with strong emotional undercurrents or reading a powerful novel filled with moving, tragic moments, we may both acknowledge and appreciate the feelings evoked, but we may, at the same time, look analytically at the work. We might ask: *Why is the hero's downfall so terrifying when he is not a very good person? How does the author make us care about what is happening to him?* When we begin to identify the ways in which the artist or author has nudged us toward certain feelings—the artistic strategies being used—then the viewing or reading experience becomes that much richer. We can seize the opportunity to expand our minds.

When we think critically, when we push ourselves beyond emotion, we tend to retain stronger memories of our experiences and find enjoyment in discussing works with others who may have differing views, or who may have identified other creative strategies embedded in the work we are discussing. Mutual agreement doesn't matter. The process of building "brain muscle" does.

The Importance of Knowing When a Purely Emotional Response Is Appropriate

We are not insisting that it is always better to analyze in Apollonian fashion. This is not an *either-or* activity. To enter the Sistine Chapel in the Vatican and gaze up at the magnificent ceiling created by Michelangelo (Figure 2.4) is, for many people, to be quite literally bereft of words. No language is needed to explain that these artistic arrangements are right, magnificently right. For these viewers, looking at the ceiling is to experience what Plato would have called "pure beauty." Time stops; practical concerns disappear.

For others, this same experience comes from listening to an Indian sitar master play a *raga*, or from watching an exquisite Japanese *kabuki* drama, or from discovering a pre-Columbian carving in a small room at a museum. It is the quiet joy of being conscious at the highest level. When you get to a summit like this, you *know* it!

Great works like Picasso's *Guernica* or Michelangelo's *David*, the symphonies of Beethoven, the tragedies of Shakespeare, the ceramics of the Chinese Ming

Figure 2.4 Michelangelo, *Creation of Adam*. c. 1512.
When is it appropriate to have a purely emotional response to a work of art? Do you think your first response to the Sistine Chapel ceiling would be emotional or analytical?
The Gallery Collection/Fine Art Premium/Corbis

dynasty—all these have powerful emotional effects on many viewers and listeners long before any intellectual judgment is attempted.

Beethoven: Symphony No. 9 in D Minor, IV

What emotions are evoked for you when you listen to Beethoven's Ninth Symphony?

Even trained professional critics, who analyze the creative work of humankind for a living, are no doubt equally affected before they take a deep breath, stand back, and begin a rational analysis of a work. If a work does not move us emotionally, there is little point to the rational analysis. Unfortunately, that emotional appeal is often left out in formal lectures on the humanities.

The Importance of Responding Critically

Critical thinking carefully defines, describes, and analyzes something: an election, an important decision, a question that has puzzled or intrigued philosophers for centuries, a new electronic invention, a movie, a novel, Number 1 on the Top 40, or a decision about whether to move into your own apartment. Critical responses, as we have said, build our mental strength. They usually involve the following steps:

1. Defining what we want to determine (*What made this film special?*)
2. Acknowledging our instinctive, emotional responses (*How did it make me feel?*)
3. Collecting information and considering all pertinent factors (*What can I find out about the artist's intentions and the craft that was at work here?*)
4. Evaluating the work or the topic in its proper context (*What can I find out about the historical and artistic context in which this work was produced?*)
5. Accepting characters unlike yourself (*Can I like these people—or at least understand them—even though I have nothing in common with them?*)
6. Forming an opinion with evidence to back it up (*Using all the information I have gathered, along with my initial emotional response, what can I say about this work?*)

Developing the skill of analysis and objective evaluation helps us to deepen our appreciation of the humanities and also allows us to have a better sense of what finally is truly worth our time.

Exercising the Mind

2.3 *In what ways might we exercise our critical minds?*

Most of us get up and go when we feel the need to exercise our bodies, especially when something has prevented our moving about (such as being cramped for hours in an airplane seat). Those who have suffered illnesses from a lack of exercise may be encouraged to alter the way they live and be urged to run, walk, take stairs instead of elevators, and participate in those activities to avoid that sluggish feeling well known to nonexercisers. Yet far too many of us have no trouble, and experience no guilt, when we allow their minds to be sluggish. The critical responses we have discussed in the previous section come much more easily to minds that are trim and fit. And getting there doesn't even involve a diet!

Critical thinking is enhanced as we engage in three important activities: defining and solving problems, challenging assumptions, and recognizing contexts.

Defining and Solving Problems

Critical thinkers are always identifying and solving problems, even hypothetical ones. Try this one.

> *Three salesmen traveling together in a blinding rainstorm spot a hotel and decide to get a room. The night clerk tells them the price for a triple room is $90. Accordingly, each man gives the clerk $30. After they go upstairs, the clerk double-checks the rate and realizes the room costs only $85 dollars. He gives the bellhop five singles and instructs him to give this money to the three salesmen. On his way upstairs, the bellhop stops and thinks, "They will be checking out early in the morning when the night clerk is no longer there. How would they ever know the true cost of the room?" He then decides to give the salesmen a $3 refund, and he pockets $2 for himself. The problem: After their "refund," each man has paid $29 for the room, bringing their total to $87 ($29 \times 3 = 87$). Adding the $2 pocketed by the bellhop, the total is $89. What happened to the missing dollar?*

The error occurs in the way the problem is presented. The room actually cost $85, not $87. The men received $3 back, and the bellhop pocketed two. So now we are back to the original $90. A problem such as this one helps us to be careful about how we report an event and to listen carefully for inconsistencies and contradictions in the way others report.

Having developed the habit of critical analysis, we are prepared to confront a real problem in our own life. The family member who needs help is a problem thousands face each day. Suppose you have a brother who constantly overspends, is heavily in debt, and cannot curb his extravagance. One reason is that he always counts on being rescued by responsible relatives—for example, *you*.

The first step in solving such a problem is to define it—to determine whether a problem actually exists. Whether or not to pay off your brother's debts may not be a problem if you decide not to assume ownership of it. Whose problem is it? It's yours if you wish to avoid the pain of guilt you think you'll experience if you turn your back. But the problem belongs to your brother or to other family members if you decide to withdraw with a clear conscience. If the rest of the family also declines with a clear conscience, then only your brother has a problem.

Family bonds are likely to be pretty strong, but you have to weigh all the factors. Does your brother overspend very often? Is your brother capable of earning enough money to pay the debts? If not, will he listen to a rational argument in favor of spending within his limits? Merely paying off the debts to "avoid the hassle" may send the wrong signal.

This problem may not always be solvable, but it is definable. We have just engaged in the act of reasoning. Sometimes easy solutions evade us and we must settle on one, hoping for the best. Yet we are less likely to find a successful answer if we have not fully analyzed the problem—if we have not been critical thinkers.

Challenging Assumptions

Assumptions are a fact of everyday communication. They are the beliefs on which opinions are based and conclusions drawn. Often these are *buried*; that is, they lie beneath what people are saying without being acknowledged as assumptions, and often they are the real message that is being communicated. When we think critically, we listen carefully, always seeking what is actually being said.

Suppose a newspaper reader turns to you and says that a convicted murderer has been released after being confined to a mental hospital for ten years. In the opinion of the staff, that person is no longer a menace to society. The reader then observes, "There ought to be a law against letting people escape the death penalty by pleading insanity and then releasing them so they can kill again."

The above statement makes no pretense to be factual. It is understood that the speaker is expressing an opinion. The assumptions buried beneath the opinion, however, may not be recognized. Here are some possibilities:

1. The question of insanity should have no bearing on a court case.
2. The defendant was not really insane anyway.
3. The state or federal legislature should control how defendants plead.
4. Once a murderer always a murderer.
5. Those in charge of mental hospitals are not qualified to make accurate judgments about when to release a patient.

The easy response is to nod in agreement with the reader's observation, because careful debate in this instance involves careful analysis of the buried assumptions, and many of us don't want to invest the time needed for making this analysis.

Now suppose that the newspaper reader and the listener in the above example both work to exercise their mental faculties as often as possible, attempting to balance their inner Apollo and Dionysus. The reader might communicate a different version of the newspaper story: "Abel Parsons has been released from the mental hospital where he has spent the last ten years. If you remember, he pleaded guilty by reason of insanity."

The listener might respond: "Does the article cite any reasons for his release?"

"One. The psychiatrist who has observed him for the whole time called in three consultants, and they all agreed that Parsons appears to be totally rehabilitated."

"Have they provided any sort of monitoring system to keep tabs on what he does at least for a while?"

"It doesn't say."

"I would think they'd *have* to set something up. Don't you agree?"

The two people have not solved a thorny legal problem. What they *have* done in this hypothetical conversation is made an attempt to get at the objective facts of the newspaper story rather than make assumptions about it—that is, they have tried to think critically about the problem.

Recognizing Contexts

Everyone and everything exists in a **context**, a framework of circumstances and relationships. Knowing that nothing exists independent of one or more contexts, those who try to think critically avoid making large-scale generalizations and absolute evaluations. We are all, of course, tempted at times to simplify, to distill contexts down to something manageable. We are all capable of obscuring the truth, not only of the past but of what happened just yesterday when the full context of an event is unpleasant or embarrassing to relate. Using the well-practiced skill of rationalizing, we tell others (as well as ourselves) a convenient and palatable version of an event—say, a bitter argument with a sibling, in which the absent family member is usually the culprit and we are the victim. By the time we have finished telling the story, the context within which the argument took place has become fixed in our mind exactly as we have described it. And chances are that that doesn't come close to what *really* happened.

While dedicated critical thinkers are not immune to reinventing contexts or selecting those that can be comfortably dealt with, they are less likely, upon reflection, to feel good about substituting imagination for reality.

HISTORICAL CONTEXT   One of the gifts of the humanities we described earlier is a sense of the past, which provides us with *historical context*. A casual browser in a secondhand store filled with attic discards might grow impatient. Those with a sense of the past, however, might be intrigued, interested in examining toys, dolls, or clothing that reveal much about bygone periods.

The more we know about the past, the more we understand the importance of historical and cultural context. And the more we learn to recognize context, the less likely we are to evaluate everything in terms of today. In reading books or watching movies from the past, critical thinkers know better than to judge them only in contemporary terms. *Gone With the Wind* (1939) is recognized by professional film critics as a milestone in movie-making, although contemporary viewers will find much of it sentimental and dated. Certainly many of us have a viscerally negative response to the inherent racism in the film, as did some viewers—and particularly, of course, African-Americans—when it was released in 1939. But we can nevertheless recognize that the film was ground-breaking in its use of color cinematography, its sweeping symphonic score, and the remarkable performances of both Vivien Leigh as Scarlett O'Hara and Hattie McDaniel, the first African-American Academy Award winner, as Mammy. No art can exist apart from how it is viewed in a contemporary context. Whether a given work belongs to the past or the present, we can appreciate its positive achievements without endorsing all of its ideas or techniques.

Knowledge of historical context makes us more tolerant of outmoded styles—for example, of black-and-white film or nineteenth-century opera. The novice viewer might easily lose patience with a three-hour performance in which arias seem to suspend the flow of the story, and the performers have been chosen for the power of their voices rather than their physical appearance or acting ability. More experienced opera-goers, and those who think critically about the value of opera, know that superb voices singing thrilling music can more than compensate for outmoded conventions.

ACCEPTING ADAPTATIONS   Sometimes a work from earlier times is restaged or even rewritten for modern audiences. Often purists prefer the original, but adaptations may draw new audiences into an appreciation for old stories. Those who think critically are typically willing to accommodate either version—as long as both are examples of well-made art. One such modernized update of a familiar and much loved work is the 1989 musical *Miss Saigon*, based on *Madame Butterfly* (1904), an opera by Giacomo Puccini (1858–1924). (See Figures 2.5 and 2.6.) By modern standards, sentimentality, racism, and sexism abound in the original story of a Japanese geisha who falls in love with, marries, and has a child by an American naval officer, who abandons her shortly after their wedding. The latter, we discover, later takes an American wife, and in 1904 audiences would have understood why his Japanese "marriage" is out of the question and a return to America is morally and socially necessary. They would have wept as Cio-Cio San, the abandoned wife, prepares to commit suicide in the presence of her son, but applauded when she tells him to remember that he is an American and places a flag in his little hands just before she dies a tragic, but morally respectable, death.

Figure 2.5 Scene from Puccini's *Madame Butterfly*, **Opera Bastille, Paris, 2006.**
SuperStock

Figure 2.6 Scene from Claude-Michel Schönberg's *Miss Saigon*, **Dancap Productions, 2010.**
When a work is adapted to another artistic medium, how might context change its meaning?
Robbie Jack/Corbis Entertainment/Corbis

The context of *Miss Saigon* is the unpopular and divisive mid-twentieth-century war in Vietnam. Many U.S. soldiers, finding themselves far from home, entered relationships with Vietnamese women—a situation the French creators of *Miss Saigon*, Claude-Michel Schönberg and Alain Boublil, found strikingly parallel to the events in *Madame Butterfly*. This time the heroine, Kim, is a young Vietnamese bar-girl, forced into prostitution. She sleeps with an American soldier who, after learning she is only 17 and an orphan, takes her under his wing. When the chaotic evacuation of Saigon takes place in 1975, the soldier, Chris, is forced to leave Kim behind—never knowing that she is pregnant with his son. Back in the United States, Chris marries, but eventually returns to Southeast Asia with his new wife to look for Kim. Kim is first overjoyed and then, when she realizes that Chris is married and that his wife will not consider taking her son back to safety in the United States, despondent. As in Puccini's opera, the heroine commits suicide; she sacrifices herself to gain a better life for her son, whom, she assumes, Chris and his wife will now be forced to adopt.

The historical context of the two stories is dramatically different. Early audiences of the Puccini opera may have sympathized with the American officer, but contemporary audiences find his behavior reprehensible. Audiences for *Miss Saigon* empathize with both Chris and Kim, understanding the tragedy and inhumanity of a particular war, and of war in general.

Viewers who know both versions of this story may well find deeper resonances than those who are familiar with only one or the other, and critical viewers will enjoy discussing not only the differences and similarities, but also the ways in which historical context impact our perceptions of these two works of art.

A Guide to Critical Viewing, Professional and Personal

2.4 *How are the roles of a professional critic and of an individual responding personally to a creative work different?*

Professional critics—those who write for a living about film, art, dance, literature, and other creative undertakings—often begin, like the rest of us, as untrained, unanalytical viewers, listeners, and readers. Some study the arts they review in academic courses, but many do not. They have simply read and observed and listened, training themselves to recognize the techniques employed by the artists whose work they evaluate. They internalize—or sometimes create—the standards by which these works are judged. Reading professional criticism and seeing the kind of things that professional critics notice, as well as their reasons for suggesting whether an experience is worth our time, is one excellent way to develop the skills of critical analysis.

The Role of the Professional Critic

Criticism on the professional level is a career. The best critics earn high salaries for giving their widely respected opinions. Their work can be found on the pages of leading newspapers such as *The New York Times* or the *San Francisco Chronicle*, magazines such as *The New Yorker*, *Rolling Stone*, *Film Comment*, or *Opera News*, as well as Internet sites such as *Wired* and *Slate*. Most professional critics are not "trained" *per se* as critics—they do not get degrees in "how to write criticism." Rather, they are first and foremost lovers of the art forms that they evaluate, and because of that passion, they have learned about the art form and taught themselves how to communicate their own knowledge and opinions to others. Often, professional critics take rambling paths to their final destination—but some, like the late film critic Roger Ebert (1942–2013), know almost from birth what they want to do. Ebert started writing movie reviews as a student at the University of Chicago (which happened to be home to the oldest college film society in the country) and just never stopped.

What professional critics have to say about something can help us decide among the many choices open to us. In the world of the humanities, with so much that is Dionysian to stir the emotions and, sometimes, to cloud our judgment, the voice of the professional critic can serve as a model for our own growing critical skills.

Sometimes the analytical voice may be simply *too* analytical to suit us. A famous example involves the 1965 Academy Award-winning musical *The Sound of Music*, which has retained its popularity as a fixture on cable television. Most critics writing for prestigious magazines and newspapers disliked the film for a variety of reasons: its one-dimensional characters; its sentimentality (as when the austere, military-minded father tearfully tells his children's governess, "You have brought music back into my house"); its predictability (we never doubt that the family will escape the pursuing Nazis).

Pauline Kael (1919–2001), the film critic for *McCall's*, a women's magazine, wrote a review of *The Sound of Music* that was particularly scathing. Quotes echoed throughout the country. Kael called the movie (among many other things), "a sugarcoated lie that people seem to want to eat"—a comment that not only denigrated this movie that most viewers loved, but also implicitly denigrated the viewers themselves. Kael was fired, which prompted responses from other film critics, among them Larry Devine of the *Miami Herald*, who recommended that the magazine "go back to the recipes and footcare"—in itself, of course, a snobbish put-down of women's magazines. The kind of review Kael wrote, and the kind of put-down that followed from Devine, have given many professional critics a reputation for being arrogant snobs.

We must hasten to say, however, that Kael went on to enjoy a long career as the film critic for *The New Yorker*, and her thoughtful, if sometimes challenging, reviews set the standard for film criticism in the 1970s and 1980s.

THE CHARACTERISTICS OF A GOOD CRITIC We suggest that there are two categories of professional critics: those who are basically reviewers, who provide brief plot synopses or descriptions of artworks (and who may be more likely to offer praise for works that have potential mass appeal); and those who establish and hold to consistent critical principles, looking for—and writing about—the elements that constitute a work of art. The attitude of serious critics is: Because we have such a limited stay on this earth, we want to be emotionally moved, to be intellectually challenged, and, above all, to be in the company of writers, artists, composers, directors, actors—creative people of all kinds—who respect the intelligence of their audiences.

Alex Ross, the music reviewer for *The New Yorker*, has tastes that range from Bach to be-bop to film scores. He is always looking for serious art, even in works denounced by other critics as beneath their consideration. He reviews chamber music at Lincoln Center, as well as rock; his interest in the 1960s band Velvet Underground helped establish that group as a forerunner of the punk and alternative rock movements. In urging his readers to keep an open mind about the dissonant atonal chords of contemporary concert music, Ross uses other musical forms to make his point: Such chords, he writes, "crop up in jazz; avant-garde sounds appear in Hollywood film scores; minimalism has marked rock, pop, and dance music from the Velvet Underground onward. Sometimes the music resembles noise because it *is* noise, or near to it, by design."[3] The word "design" alerts the reader who is still entertaining doubts that music that on first hearing sounds like nothing but noise may be worth a closer listen.

In perhaps their most useful role, professional critics serve as teachers to those of us without substantial backgrounds in a particular art form. They get down to specifics about the work they are reviewing, and almost always their philosophy of what constitutes art in the form is evident. Take, for example, this review written by Alastair Macaulay of the Joffrey Ballet Company's performance in the choreographer Sir Frederick Ashton's *Cinderella*. The performance, Macaulay writes, moves the audience

> *into a new realm of form, where Ashton's wealth of vocabulary and luxurious style expands the whole stage world immensely . . . And the greatest and most chilling of Ashton's many inventions are the strikes of doom that arrive at the midnight hour. . . . [The supporting dancers] all fuse into an impersonal machine, the workings of a giant clock in which Cinderella finds herself trapped. She is barred by one wall after another. . . . In few other ballets is the poetic drama of ballet so potent.*[4]

In these few sentences, the critic has informed us that a great ballet performance is one that "expands the whole stage world immensely" by providing unexpected "inventions" like the brilliant use of scenic technology to tell us what midnight means to the heroine. It is not that we don't know this; it's just that the way it tells us the old story is new and thrilling. If Macaulay had said merely that the ballet is "fresh and really good," our knowledge of ballet would not have increased.

The Personal Critical Response

We don't need the training (or salary) of a professional critic to engage in the process of evaluation after a careful and fair viewing, listening, or reading. Let's use a poem to understand what's meant by personal critical response. Here is "The World Is Too Much with Us," by William Wordsworth (1770–1850), who lived in England's Lake District at a time when the Industrial Revolution was beginning to have an impact and many people were moving from the country to the cities seeking a more lucrative lifestyle. The poem remains an iconic expression of the limitations of living for economic gain.

> *The world is too much with us; late and soon,*
> *Getting and spending, we lay waste our powers:*
> *Little we see in Nature that is ours;*
> *We have given our hearts away, a sordid boon!*
> *This Sea that bares her bosom to the moon;*
> *The winds that will be howling at all hours,*
> *And are up-gathered now like sleeping flowers;*
> *For this, for everything, we are out of tune,*
> *It moves us not.—Great God! I'd rather be*
> *A Pagan suckled in a creed outworn;*

So might I, standing on this pleasant lea,
Have glimpses that would make me less forlorn;
Have sight of Proteus rising from the sea;
Or hear old Triton blow his wreathéd horn.[5]

What can we do to help ourselves become critical thinkers? Let's look at five actions we can all take to be more analytical about Wordsworth's poem—and all creative human endeavors.

Don't jump to conclusions. The first step in becoming an informed personal critic is *not to jump to a hasty conclusion*. "I don't like it" or "I love this poem" is an irrelevant remark at this early stage in the process.

Ask: What have I seen, or read, or heard? The next step is to determine what it is you have just read. Describe the poem as clearly and objectively as possible. A possibility: The poem contains (or appears to contain, which might be a more conservative, more cautious approach, at least in the beginning) a regretful realization that, in a concern for material welfare, we no longer live on close terms with nature; and from a current perspective, we are less and less likely to enjoy nature given what so many are doing to ensure their own profits. But more than two centuries after its creation, the poem continues to remind us that the wondrous beauty of the natural world is its own justification. Noticing how the seasons affect the landscape, how plants and flowers will grow and bloom wherever they are given space, costs nothing and yields treasures that money cannot buy.

Explore context and speculate about ideas. Wordsworth could not have known about environmentalism as such, but he is already aware that the commerce of everyday life, the "getting and spending," is creating a danger that the natural world would be ignored, uncared for. And so he thinks of an ancient time when mythology turned nature into a wondrous force to be dazzled by and always respected.

If you are adventurous and enjoy probing a little deeper, you can obtain information about the poet's life from the Internet. You would learn that, as Wordsworth grew older, he feared he was losing the inspiration he used to feel when he was out in nature. You would also learn that this poem was written in 1804, perhaps during a transition phase in the poet's development—that is, at a time when, in reaching full maturity, he might have begun to fear that, though he was profiting from writing, he was doing so at the cost of his inspiration. If you wanted to advance this idea, you would do well to tread softly, however. Though many literary scholars take the plunge and read autobiography into every work by an author, the poet in this case might have been making a general statement applicable to all people.

In any case, speculation about ideas in a work sharpens our critical faculties, even if it doesn't say the last word about what we are reading. The important thing is to separate probability from possibility. It is virtually certain that Wordsworth was upset about the pursuit of material gain, and it is possible that, at the age of 34, he feared he might be losing the passion that fired his youth.

Consider craft and technique. The next stage in the critical process is to look at the poet's *craft*—that is, the handling of language, **imagery** (the pictures in your mind that the poem communicates), and the way the requirements of the medium do not interfere with the poet's expressive needs. What makes poetry different from prose is that poets are able to compress a great deal into fewer words than prose requires.

"Getting and spending" in three words describes our whole economic system. That is compression of thought in a memorable sequence, one that has been used over and over, even by economists themselves. Wordsworth makes us see an ocean in the image of the sea baring its bosom to the moon. Just saying "the sea" would have served his purpose, but not equally well. The aptness of the phrasing in creating the picture in our minds extends our pleasure in reading the poem because the image allows for intricacies that even great paintings of the sea cannot provide. The reason?

The image makes us find the intricacies for ourselves. A painting is what it is. We do not see beyond it.

Consider form. Finally, the poem is a **sonnet**, a demanding literary form in which the poet is restricted to 14 lines. In the past, poets challenged themselves by using rhyming lines and writing in a definite rhythm. Often rhythm and rhyme are forced, as in "Backward, turn backward, oh time in your flight, / And make me a child again, just for tonight." One suspects that anyone who would write such a line wouldn't mind being a child again for a longer period, but "just for tonight" allows for the rhyme. The rhythm of the lines makes it impossible for us not to see that the requirements of the form have totally taken over the poet's individuality. Rhythm and rhyme, not the poet, are the stars.

If you read Wordsworth's poem aloud to find the rhythmic pattern, you discover that the pattern is quite rigid: Unaccented syllables are almost always followed by accented ones; very rarely do two accented or unaccented syllables appear side by side. At the same time, when you read it without stressing the rhythm, the words flow naturally and manage to keep the rhythm unnoticed. The rhyming pattern is also quite regular. (The first and fourth lines rhyme, as do the second and third, the fifth and eighth, the sixth and seventh, and, finally, the ninth, eleventh, and thirteenth, and the tenth, twelfth, and fourteenth.) Yet in reading the poem aloud, following the natural progression of it, you don't find the rhymes jumping out of their context.

But, you may ask, so what if the rhythm and the rhyme are not obtrusive? One answer may be that when the poet works within rigid guidelines without having them dictate his content we admire his craft, his poetry-making skill. Being aware that the poet has carefully concealed the artistry behind the poem happens to be one of the pleasures of responding critically. When the pianist performs a complicated jazz solo or a sonata by Mozart, we should not have to think about the musician's years of practicing eight hours a day. When the ice skater glides across the arena in perfect sync with Debussy's "Clair de Lune," we should believe that we can strap on a pair of skates and do the same thing.

Debussy: "Clair de Lune"

Art is the illusion that there is no art. Only when the skater attempts a triple axel and falls do we then watch future leaps with apprehension, painfully aware of the difficulty involved. Of course, we don't forget that the art *is* there; but when we keep being reminded of it, strangely enough, the art isn't there anymore. You don't want the actor to let you know how great he or she is. Critical thinkers can discover that for themselves.

The same guidelines that we used to analyze Wordsworth's poem can be applied to critical analysis of almost any work of art—a painting, a piece of music, a play or dance.

- Don't jump to hasty conclusions. Don't make your first response "I love this" or "I hate this."
- Decide what you have just seen or heard. Describe it as objectively as possible, with as much detail as you can offer.
- Think about context. When was this work created? What might have influenced its creation—in the creator's life, in the world at large?
- Speculate about ideas. What might have been the creator's intent? Does the work have meaning beyond its simple beauty?
- Think about craft and technique. How well does the creator use the available tools—imagery and language in literature, color and shape in paintings, and so on?
- Think about form. Does this creation fit into a formal category? If so, how well does it reflect the "rules" of that form—or does it intentionally break them, surprising the viewer or reader or listener?

Literalists and Figuratists

2.5 *What are the main characteristics of "literalist" and "figuratist" critical responses?*

If you meet someone in a theater lobby and casual chitchat leads to comments about the movie just seen, you can usually tell whether the person you're talking with is striving to think critically *by that person's use of language.* Those who are simply not interested in going beyond their own experiences will relate everything back to themselves: "The movie was too gory for me. I prefer a nice love story." (Or it could go the other way: "*I hate gooey love stories; give me good old-fashioned horror any time."*) Those who are looking for more from their experiences with art may refer to larger concepts or general principles. This expanded curiosity is often born from involvement in the humanities: listening, viewing, or reading a great deal and thinking about the experience.

As with critical and noncritical thinking, literalist and figuratist speakers do not comprise two opposing, non-overlapping groups. Rather, speech, like thinking, tends to fall on a continuum, and we all, at one time or another, move back and forth on it. In general, however, those who tend to think noncritically may be called **literalists**, a term derived from their habit of *not* seeing general principles. They are tuned into what is happening at the moment, and their opinions are often shaped by popular views expressed by friends who are just like them or by what Fox News or MSNBC has been saying about issues such as global warming, big government, and the state of the economy. They tend to prefer ideas that are prepackaged, as if in supermarket plastic, that never need to be taken apart and analyzed.

Those who tend to spend their time at the critical thinking end of the continuum may be called **figuratists**, a term derived from the fact that their language uses imagery (that is, figures of speech) and suggests wide experiences in many fields, including the humanities. Even if they are talking about the present moment, they are likely to see it in broader terms. Rather than "I know what I like," the figuratist might comment on cliché-ridden dialog, hackneyed camera-work, or the relevance—or irrelevance—of the film's themes to the larger world. The figuratist might say, "Here's what this film [or novel, or painting] taught me about human nature, about the human condition."

Literalist Speech

Literalists are limited to what we may call the "everyday concrete." They are also likely to listen haphazardly to what a figuratist is *generally* saying, latching on to the very last thing that was mentioned.

> **F:** *So many of the so-called professionals I run into don't seem to be what I would call experts. I'd love to meet one who could give me sound answers to important questions: where to live, whether to change jobs, where my children could get the best education.*
>
> **L:** *I didn't know you had children.*
>
> **F:** *I don't.*
> *(Blank stare)*

The figuratist is really saying that there is no certainty, not even when you are dealing with people who are expected to be experts. He or she is citing specific, hypothetical examples to arrive at general principles. Friends of "F" may have children, but not necessarily. Being broadly interested in what is happening in the world, "F" probably knows a good deal about educational systems, has read widely on the subject, has viewed panel discussions, and so on. Their conversation continues.

> **F:** *I think my students don't know the difference between the classroom and their bedroom.*
>
> **L:** *My neighbor says her son likes to sleep in class.*
>
> **F:** *The least their parents could do is send them to school with pillows.*
>
> **L:** *I don't think that would be wise.*

No further comment.

Figuratist Speech

Figuratists, especially those who devote considerable time to reading great literature, often use figurative speech or metaphoric language—that is, language that means something other than what is being directly said—even in every-day conversation. Their wide range of reading and experience may give them a quick wit; effective ways of communicating occur more naturally to them than to people who have spent less time with books. For example, at a recent opening of a bad play, a figuratist, talking to friends afterward in the lobby, commented: "Sitting through this was like giving CPR to a statue." Somehow, "The play was boring" just doesn't have the same zing.

Figuratists are adept at twisting words, which in their original context were just mildly clever, and making them shine with brilliance. There is a story, probably apocryphal, about an arrogant British playwright (in some versions Noël Coward, in others George Bernard Shaw) who sent an invitation to the opening night of one of his productions to the admired statesman Winston Churchill, known for his low tolerance for fools (or, in some accounts, to Churchill's son, Randolph). The note purportedly read: "Sir, here are two tickets for the opening of my play. Bring a friend—if you have one." Churchill allegedly responded: "Can't make the opening. Will come second night—if there is one."

Shakespeare probably penned more frequently quoted lines than any other writer in the English-speaking world—so many, in fact, that when we watch a play like *Hamlet*, we sometimes have to shake off our shocked feeling that the great dramatist used so many clichés! "This above all, to thine own self be true," "There is nothing either good or bad but thinking makes it so," "To be or not to be…," "Though this be madness, yet there is method in it," "Sweets to the sweet: farewell"—all from *Hamlet*. And we haven't even started on the 36 other plays or the 154 sonnets. Often, we play with these famous lines, tweaking them into personal comments: From a chocolate lover, for example: "Sweets to the sweet: farewell, teeth!"

The most often repeated of the great lines are those that contain wisdom behind wit, so that the critical thinker knows there is no way to improve upon them. The legendary baseball player and manager Yogi Berra (1925–2015) is credited with many familiar, if not always grammatical, remarks. His most famous remark—"It ain't over till it's over"—referred to his beloved baseball (there's always one more at bat—until there isn't) but has entered our everyday language as a way of implying that there is always hope, no matter how dire the situation may seem.

Although most of his best-remembered remarks have the feel of folk wisdom from an untutored philosopher, Berra was an educated man, and one suspects that, as he grew older and realized how famous his comments were becoming, he may have worked at giving them more depth and an entirely original style. Take, for example, "In theory there is no difference between theory and practice. In practice there is." This sly bit of wisdom sneaks up on us. It could be rephrased like this: "People who spend their lives talking theories really need to see what's out there." But how much more charming (and memorable) it is as Yogi phrased it.

Critical thinking is indispensable to the art of being human. There will always be times when we will insist, "I'd rather not think about this. I'd rather just enjoy myself." But the fact is, it is possible to both think and enjoy. *Thinking just might be the ultimate way to enjoy living.* Thinking (and speaking) well mark the lover of the humanities, which provide a perennial reservoir of inspiration to sharpen our critical faculties.

Looking Back

In this chapter,

- we explored the importance of thinking critically about the humanities,
- we identified and differentiated between an Apollonian and a Dionysian response to the humanities,
- we talked about the importance of exercising the mind, just as we exercise our bodies,

- we offered a guide to critical viewing, reading, and listening, and identified the role that professional critics play, and
- we differentiated between "literalist" and "figuratist" language in responding to creative works.

Key Terms

alienation effect The use of theatrical techniques designed to distance the audience from an emotional response and to encourage instead a social-critical one, sometimes called "making the familiar strange."

Apollonian Term derived from Nietzsche's symbolic reference to the Greek god of light and truth; used to describe something or someone that is orderly and rational.

context As used in this chapter, the environment, background, or special circumstances in terms of which a given work is best understood. Historical context is the influence that the ideas, values, and styles of a particular time have on a society, work of art, or philosophy.

critical thinking The faculty of rational and logical analysis; looking at subjects objectively, gathering all information, and then drawing conclusions about the subject based on evidence; the opposite of jumping to hasty conclusions based upon a purely emotional response.

Dionysian Term derived from Nietzsche's symbolic reference to the Greek god of wine and vegetation; used to

describe spontaneity as well as a lack of order and structure, signifying the passionate and creative (often impulsive) aspects of art, society, or an individual.

empathy Identifying with another actual person or a character in a book, film, or play; becoming, in a sense, that person and being totally involved in his or her problems.

figuratist A critical thinker whose use of language is characteristically colorful, often playful, filled with metaphors that suggest a greater interest in the general than in just the particular.

imagery Found especially in poetry, the pictures the poet creates in your mind that communicate in a few words what ordinary prose cannot, or at least not as economically.

literalist The noncritical person whose language reflects a concern for the immediate moment, especially as what is happening or being viewed relates to the self.

sonnet A 14-line poem that imposed on poets tight rules of length, rhythm, and rhyming pattern.

Chapter 3
Myth and the Origin of the Humanities

3.1 Define "myth" and "mythology."

3.2 Recognize and differentiate among various mythological archetypes.

3.3 Discuss how myths provide explanations for otherwise unexplainable phenomena.

3.4 Characterize the myths of childhood.

3.5 Understand the role of popular mythology and common sayings.

3.6 Analyze how myths influence the humanities.

Figure 3.1 A statue of Hercules, Minerva, and Mercury in the façade of Grand Central Station in New York City, c. 1913. Thousands of people see this sculpture every day. Can you think of other instances where mythology plays a role in our everyday lives?
Tetra Images/Alamy

Long before people could read about the arts in print and before arts such as music and dance were formalized, the humanities could be found in **mythology**. Music and dance probably began as rhythmic accompaniments to stylized movements in which people honored and appeased the gods and observed certain stages of life, such as the transition from youth to adulthood. Early forms of the drama occurred when people pretended to be brave hunters stalking wild animals needed for their survival or heroic warriors battling evil spirits. In Paleolithic cave drawings, such as those found in Lascaux, France, our ancestors depicted both the animals on which their survival depended and themselves in the act of hunting those animals. In reimagining the hunt, they endowed their deeds unwittingly with mythic significance.

Early people in societies that were of necessity closely knit preserved their history by weaving stories of their past—stories about where they may have originated and their relationship to the gods; stories about great hunters, warriors, and leaders; and eventually, stories designed to illustrate the difference between right and wrong.

Though not a separate discipline of the humanities, mythology underlies much of the work created in *all* disciplines. Literature, visual art, music, drama, cinema—all may have roots in **myths** that are sometimes unique to a given culture, but in many instances are universal, found in one version or another in most cultures. For this reason, mythology is an appropriate starting place for our study of the humanities.

What Is Myth?

3.1   *What is myth? What is mythology?*

A myth is a traditional story, typically without a known author, that is ostensibly based in historical events but often serves to explain something beyond normal understanding: the phenomenon of nature, the origin of humanity, the creation of the world, or some cataclysmic event. The term *mythology* typically refers to the study of myths, or to collections of myths that form the customs, belief system, religious rites, and so on of a specific people. Thus we can speak about the mythology of a Native American nation, or the mythology of a specific hero such as King Arthur. Religions are essentially collections of myth; we tend, however, to label our own stories and beliefs as religious truths, and the stories and beliefs of other cultures as mythology.

The Role of Myth in the Humanities

In this chapter, we discuss the role mythology played in shaping the humanities, including the mythic elements in some famous literary works. We also discuss the fact that all of us have our own personal mythology, which began in early childhood when we objectified our fears and our secret longings, divided the world into good and evil, and found heroes with whom we identified. Our myths stay with us for life and grow up with us, fulfilling psychological needs at every stage of our development.

In examining the mythic roots of many works in the formal disciplines of the humanities, we can see that Shakespeare's portrait of King Henry V is one of a nearly perfect hero, the champion and defender of a people, the one who seems indestructible. But so is Frodo, the tiny hobbit of *The Lord of the Rings*, who sacrifices home and security to save Middle Earth from the terrible Sauron. Such heroes are often portrayed in epic poems—the Arabian poet and adventurer Antar (525–608) in his own *Mu'allaqat*, the Mesopotamian epic of *Gilgamesh* (c. 2100 BCE), or the epic of *Sundiata* (c. fourteenth century), a hero and founder of the African empire of Mali. The hero is one of innumerable mythic *archetypes*, or models that become part of our subconscious and help us organize our thinking about how we understand the world, the nature and purpose of human life, and the events of our own lives.

WHAT MYTH IS *NOT* We need, at the outset, to demolish some common misconceptions about myth. It has become a deceptively simple four-letter word used in a variety of ways not necessarily related to the humanities, though closely tied to our personal needs. In popular usage, myth is *something erroneous yet widely believed*—something to be refuted by rational adults, such as "the Myth of Climate Change," or MYTH OF CALORIES EXPOSED; EAT ALL YOU WANT AND GET THIN! Another misuse of the word is patronizing, in the sense of "old stories once believed by naive people in a prescientific age that didn't know better."

If myths could be easily dismissed as just false and outmoded beliefs, they would not be the subject of this chapter. But mythology belongs to and affects large numbers of people. Knowledge of myth is basic to cultural literacy. Myths are not necessarily untrue. They are stories containing beliefs and character types that remain with us for life and drive many of our ideas, our hopes, and our dreams (see Figure 3.1).

WHAT MYTH CAN DO If nothing else, myths can be interesting stories, unrestricted to literal facts, truthful psychologically and emotionally. They help us to understand how a given culture characterizes itself and other cultures with which it engages. They help us to understand how individuals think and to be aware of their underlying needs. Above all, knowledge of mythology renders us less likely to make snap judgments about right and wrong, because we realize that the sharp distinction between right and wrong is itself a mythic archetype. But we must also realize that the belief in right versus wrong is not necessarily false. All we are saying is that certain beliefs, certain ways of organizing our thoughts, are deeply ingrained and *true* in a certain sense of the word. Right from the start, we must learn that "true" has more than a scientific laboratory definition.

Myths are almost as necessary for survival as breathing and eating. In addition to influencing both the humanities and, as we shall see, psychology, myth affects the behavior of people all over the world. Myths help explain the great mysteries of creation, birth, death, the afterlife, love, and power; they may center on magic numbers, on circles, on the arduous journey, or on the unspoiled garden. Some of these myths date back to very early people, but all recur in many forms. They are symbols in our culture and in our unconscious minds that help us shape the way we view ourselves and our world. They are vital to the study of the humanities.

Archetypes in Mythology

3.2 *What defines a mythological archetype?*

Even if myths were only a collection of stories about recognizable families, feuds, passion, and revenge, they would be enjoyable as literature. Reading them, we are struck by similarities in stories and characters. We might ask ourselves why certain of these are found again and again and often influence the way we ourselves think and react to what others do. Scholars look even further. They seek in myth a common thread, a chance to learn whether the stories tell us something important about the human condition. For this they turn to a theory of psychologist-philosopher Carl Jung (1875–1961), who maintained that all persons are born with an instinctive knowledge of certain **archetypes**, the models that allow people to comprehend experience and cope with the enormous and often baffling task of being human. Jung believed these models—characters such as heroes, villains, and clowns; events such as quests or journeys; symbols such as the cross or the sun—appear in cultures all over the world, though they may take different forms. Archetypes—which together comprise a shared body of buried assumptions—are transmitted from one generation to another through what Jung labeled the **collective unconscious**.

From the unconscious emanate determining influences which, independently of tradition, guarantee in every single individual a similarity and even a sameness of experience, and also of the way it is represented imaginatively. One of the main proofs of this is the almost universal parallelism between mythological motifs.[1]

Jung's theory is not accepted by all psychologists or scholars of myth, but without it or another comprehensive theory to replace it, we have a difficult time accounting for the continued appearance of certain myths and mythic elements: tales of a terrible flood and the salvation of one good man; the stories about dangerous journeys into the land of death and darkness; and, above all, tales about the major stages in the life of a singular human being—sometimes partly divine—known as the *hero*. There are, however, some alternative explanations.

One is the *external* theory, the most scientific of the possibilities. According to this theory, stories were spread along migratory routes. Myths originated in specific places and then were transported as people warred, traded, and intermarried with each other. In general, we do find myth similarities among certain cultures whose migrations can be traced.

An example of the migratory spread of old stories is the way the religious beliefs and practices of the Yoruba tribe, whose home is the present-day Nigeria, were transported to Cuba, where they were modified and adopted by a whole new body of listeners. Once in the New World, the enslaved Yoruba needed to mask their own beliefs, and gradually Catholic monotheism was grafted onto the original religion as a way of hiding the continuing existence of African pantheistic beliefs. From this emerged *Santería*, which continues to be practiced in Cuba, and its pantheon of heavenly protectors that includes both African gods and Christian saints.

Yet another explanation for the universality of myth is the predictable one that human beings share common needs, regardless of geography and level of cultural sophistication, and thus certain elements found in all myths must play their part in helping people cope with the conditions in which they find themselves. Similar needs do not necessarily imply contacts between cultures or a mandatory belief in a collective unconscious. If human needs are very much the same everywhere, why shouldn't myths be as well?

The Hero as World Myth

The hero is an archetype found in almost every culture; hence the label *world myth*. Because their appeal is so strong, heroes re-emerge again and again: Look, for example, at the recent success of the *Thor* films (*Thor*, 2011; *Thor: The Dark World*, 2013; and a third expected in 2017). The original Thor, the Norse god of thunder, appears prominently in Germanic myth, wielding his hammer and serving eventually as a pagan symbol in opposition to the Christianization of Scandinavia; in today's films, he reappears in New Mexico (land of alien invasions) to vanquish humankind's enemies. Loki, who is a simple mischief-maker—another archetype—in Norse mythology, is reconstituted as the chief villain in the contemporary Thor films.

The Irish novelist James Joyce coined the term **monomyth** to convey his belief that the concept of the hero is pretty much the same everywhere. The concept of the hero's journey as monomyth was later developed by the American mythologist Joseph Campbell (1904–1987), whose work, particularly his landmark study *The Hero with a Thousand Faces* (1949), argues that all myth comprises variations on a single basic story: that of the hero on a quest. Regardless of how each culture views existence and its particular survival needs, stories of heroes seem to be essential. As early as 1909, Otto Rank, a disciple of Sigmund Freud, indicated the characteristics of the hero in Western mythology.

The hero is the son of parents of the highest station. His conception takes place under difficulty. There is a portent in a dream or oracle connected with the child's birth.

The child is then sent away, or exposed to extreme danger. He is rescued by people of humble station, or by humble animals, and reared by them. When grown, he discovers his noble parentage after many adventures, and, overcoming all obstacles in his path, becomes at last recognized as the hero and attains fame and greatness.[2]

Freud, a pioneer in the psychological interpretation of mythology, maintained that the two families in the monomyth—the noble and the common—represent the parents as they appear at different stages of the child's development. Jung argued that the components, or motifs, of this pervasive myth were primordial images, or archetypes. For Jung, they were a profound part of universal expectations of life. *Everyone* is prone to believe in and await the coming of a hero.

THE BIRTH OF THE HERO   The hero's birth typically occurs under wondrous circumstances: bowing trees; a shower of gold penetrating the ceiling of a room in which a young girl has been confined; the visit of a god in the guise of some other creature, animal or human; and mysterious prophecies. Often the hero has been sired by a supernatural being.

From the beginning of human awareness, the phenomenon of birth has preoccupied and baffled people. Eventually they came to know the causal sequence that led to reproduction. But they must have marveled over the sequence that made such a miracle possible! Even for "ordinary" mortals, the birth of a child is a glorious event; announcements are mailed, friends offer congratulations, and a birthday remains a special day throughout life. In a real-life version of the prophecy that attends the birth of a hero or heroine, the parents are offered best wishes, a way of urging providence to take note of the infant, to destine the child for love and success. Those whose glorious future does not materialize may even believe themselves to have been cursed by fate.

EARLY RECOGNITION OF THE HERO   The hero destined for greatness must be recognized early in life, often after accomplishing a spectacular physical deed—such as the young Arthur's removal of the sword Excalibur from the stone that had held it until the rightful owner should come along, or Theseus' superhuman ability to lift a heavy stone that covered a golden sword and sandals, evidencing he was a king's lost son. (One version of the myth, however, credits him not so much with strength as with ingenuity in lifting the stone by devising a lever!) Sometimes recognition comes through fulfillment of a prophecy, as when Jason (of Argonaut fame) arrives in the kingdom of Iolcus wearing only one sandal, as was foretold.

The theory behind the monomyth is that the theme of early recognition identifies a universal need for acceptance. In the painful stages of early adolescence, the child asks "Who am I?" and fears that the answer will be "You're nobody." Children are so small compared to the adults around them that it's no wonder they lack a sense of worth.

Many of us later admit that in childhood we harbored fantasies of secretly being children of a prominent, even royal, family, stolen from the cradle by thieves or given away by our true parents. This unknown identity allows the extraordinary child to live with such average people and to perform dreary domestic tasks unsuited for noble beings. One day, the child-turned-adolescent feels, the recognition of special status will surely arrive. One only has to look at the popularity of the Harry Potter books for proof of the widespread appeal of such myths.

THE HERO'S GREAT DEED   Every hero performs a great deed. It typically occurs in young adulthood, at a time when the hero has left home and is separated from the parents. It is a mythical version of the universal rite of passage, the attainment of adult status at puberty. (Think of Luke Skywalker using the Force to lift his ship from Yoda's swamp in *The Empire Strikes Back*, if you've seen it.) All mythologies recognize the importance of the transition to adulthood.

Almost every early culture required the accomplishment of an arduous task to signify the end of childhood: enduring bitter cold, surviving the wilderness, recovering a magic item from a ferocious guardian, conquering a predatory beast. Theseus destroyed the Minotaur of Crete, a creature with the head of a bull and the body of a man, which had demanded the regular sacrifice of the finest Athenian young men and maidens (Figure 3.2). In order to kill the Minotaur—an extraordinary feat in itself—Theseus had first to find the dreaded creature by making his way through a labyrinth, a series of deceptive passages, which Freud-oriented myth commentators have viewed as the journey through the maze of childhood sexual stages. According to Freudian interpretation, the ultimate discovery and killing of the Minotaur thus becomes the young adult's arrival into sexual maturity.

Many of the great deeds in mythology are physical, but others are purely mental. Oedipus, the protagonist of the great Sophoclean tragedy, achieved greatness by solving the riddle of the Sphinx—half monstrous bird, half woman—who devoured and would continue to devour those who could not give the correct answer to this question: *What creature goes on four feet in the morning, two feet at midday, and three feet at twilight, and goes slowest when on the most feet?* When Oedipus arrived, Thebes was in a chaotic state of panic, for no one could solve the riddle. But Oedipus did. The answer is *man, who crawls on all fours as a child and therefore goes slowest, walks upright as an adult, and uses a cane near the end of his life.* The furious Sphinx killed herself, and Oedipus was made king, only to suffer disastrous consequences.

74. *Minotaurum Theseus vincit.*

Figure 3.2 *Theseus and the Minotaur*, from an early Italian edition of Ovid's *Metamorphoses* (1606).
How do you define a "hero"? Must a hero's great deeds be physical ones, like Theseus' slaying of the minotaur, or are there other kinds of heroism?
Los Angeles County Museum of Art.

The need to celebrate a hero's successful and wondrous feat stays with us through life. We love to watch and empathize with milestone achievements: the inauguration of the new president; the Academy Award ceremonies; the placing of a ribboned gold medal around the neck of an Olympic champion. We mark the milestones in our personal lives: birthdays; graduation; the first date; the first kiss; a letter of acceptance; getting the desired job; marrying; becoming a parent. All too often, however, we prefer to identify with the publicized deeds of celebrities and downplay the importance of our own achievements, especially if we have deep-rooted feelings of unworthiness.

THE HERO'S LOSS OF POWER   Myths of the West seldom end when the heroes are happy and successful. Fairy tales do. (When the prince marries Cinderella, we never hear a word about the heroine's relationship with her family, in-laws, or children.) In adult mythology, however, the hero, like Oedipus, usually falls from greatness. King Arthur must live on to see Camelot destroyed, his noble kingdom shattered. In the West, the story of the hero tends to be tragic.

If heroes lose their power, a possible compensation is that their death is usually glorious and their former greatness acknowledged. When Oedipus, who blinded himself so that he might never again look upon his misbegotten children, says, "I am the unclean one who has defiled this land" and makes his way to exile in the desert, the chorus asks the fearful question: Why does this happen? Why is Oedipus guilty of patricide and incest when he was doomed by a prophecy to perform these deeds? Why not blame the gods for his unkind fate? Yet in accepting full responsibility for his deeds, he retains his noble status. In Sophocles' play, the doomed hero walks *unbowed* from the city. The grieving citizens make a respectful path for him. A vast presence is departing, and he will be mourned for many years to come. In a sequel to the play called *Oedipus at Colonus*, the hero, nearing the end of his life, is suddenly visited by a brilliant light that he somehow is able to see, though still blind, and within which the mystery of human suffering is made clear to him, if not to us.

Great heroes fail, but their failures only testify to the bigness of their lives. It's almost as though mythology is saying "You can't have it both ways. You are either uncelebrated but perhaps content, or you take the risk of greatness, knowing that it doesn't last."

The hero's nobility is seldom recognized during his lifetime. In fact, there is sometimes outright hostility toward him. Before he undergoes a violent death, Theseus is blamed by his once-loyal subjects for the Spartan invasion of Athens at a time when he was gone from the kingdom. They even drive him out of the city, forcing him to seek the hospitality of the rival king who eventually kills him. But later the citizens realize the mistake they have made and erect an enormous tomb to honor his memory.

The history of Western civilization has recorded many instances of actual heroes, rejected or highly controversial during their lifetimes but revered after death: Joan of Arc and Galileo, to name two. The Irish playwright George Bernard Shaw ends his play *Saint Joan* on a note of irony as church officials regret having burned Joan at the stake. To their surprise she suddenly appears, telling them that since she is now a spirit, she is free to come and go as she wishes. If they *truly* want her to come back, she has the power to do so. Whereupon, they turn away and leave the stage. Alone, Joan looks upward and speaks the final lines of the play: "O Lord who madest this beautiful earth, when will it be ready to receive thy saints? How long, O Lord, how long?" Perhaps the appeal of this myth is that, though we may have secret feelings of unworthiness, the fallen hero (or disgraced politician or celebrity) is no better off.

THE HERO BEYOND THE WEST   Asian and Middle Eastern mythology have their hero stories, but they seldom concern the exploits of a singular mortal who is to be revered and celebrated to the exclusion of ordinary human beings. The Buddha himself (by birth a prince named Siddhartha) achieved great humility, never sought power, and discouraged his followers from looking upon him as a deity of some sort.

Joseph Campbell has pointed out that whereas

> *the typical Occidental hero is a personality, and . . . necessarily tragic . . . the Oriental hero is the monad [a simple indivisible unit]: in essence without character . . . untouched by . . . the delusory involvements of the mortal sphere. And just as in the West the orientation to personality is reflected in the concept and experience even of God as a personality, so in the Orient, in perfect contrast, the overpowering sense of an . . . impersonal law . . . harmonizing all things reduces to a mere blot the accident of an individual life.*[3]

Judaic and Islamic traditions contain many stories of Moses and Mohammed respectively and their feats of leadership, but both prophets are regarded as spiritual forces, not as mighty conquerors. Before his death, Moses asked that his burial site be concealed so that no elaborate memorial could be built in his memory. The Islamic laws taught by Mohammed assume "the brotherhood of man . . . [the] equality of all believers . . . and absolute submission to the will of God [Allah]."[4]

In Chinese mythology, great dynastic rulers are cited for their virtue and their social achievements. Huang Ti, for example, the so-called Yellow Emperor, made agriculture possible and encouraged the development of a musical scale. He is celebrated for having driven out the barbarians, but his success came not from his unique superhuman valor but from the help of the gods, who looked with favor on his virtuous character. Confucius occupied himself not with metaphysical beliefs about the spirit behind the universe but with practical advice for those who would rule: Walk the straight and narrow and live for the good of society. In Western mythology, King Arthur comes close to the Confucian ideal, but he was also a brave warrior of consummate fighting skill and would have been less revered if he had not been. He certainly meets the Western "requirement" that the hero be a singular individual capable of astonishing physical feats.

THAT SPECIAL SOMEONE The archetype of the hero is still very much with us. Celebrities, today's demigods and demigoddesses, may not be the literal progeny of deities and mortals, but they are as vivid in the public mind as their bygone counterparts. Their exploits are followed in magazines, gossip columns, and television interviews, and they set the trend in clothes, hairdos, and language.

There are still those who perform Herculean tasks and win admiration, the Stephen Hawkings of our world. We may admire the new home-run king, the world's fastest runner, the first astronauts in space, the first woman to walk the length of Tibet on foot, the first blind climber to reach the top of Everest, actors who receive Oscars for their first screen roles, and Nobel-prize winners, often unknown before their achievements catapult them to celebrity status. We keep looking for that special someone who solves all problems. The archetype of the mysterious stranger has been particularly important in American mythology, perhaps because of the early dangers encountered in settling so vast a land and the democratic structure of a frontier society in which leaders were not born into their roles but had to prove themselves.

A classic example of the "special someone" myth can be found in George Stevens's 1953 film version of Jack Schaefer's *Shane*, a popular novel set in the American West. The film (still available on DVD and television—and well worth your time) features a retired gunfighter who rides out of the Wyoming mountains on a white horse, rescues a group of peaceful farmers from the lawless cattlemen intent on driving them off their land, shoots the leader of the bad guys, and then rides back into the misty land of his origin.

Today, we continue to wait for the special person, such as the politician with no ties to lobbyists who will stand up for the right and the just regardless of what they might mean for a political future; who will finally be able to make all the industrial nations of the world understand that they cannot keep sending carbon atoms into the air; and who will "fix" ailing economies by convincing special interest groups that there is more to life than making as much money as they possibly can.

Archetypal special people have traditionally been males (with a few brilliant exceptions such as Joan of Arc), perhaps because the humanities have a long history dominated by mythmakers who were not women. Females abound in myth history, but they have often been portrayed (by men) as the troublemakers of this world. As mythology continues to be created, however, its heroes have been appearing in both genders.

Movies and TV shows are, of course, rich sources of myth. Weapon-brandishing women exist on equal terms with men and kill monsters with the best of them: think Jennifer Lawrence in the *Hunger Games* films (Figure 3.3) and Shailene Woodley

Figure 3.3 Jennifer Lawrence as Katniss Everdeen in *The Hunger Games, Mockingjay: Part 1*, 2014.
Can women be heroes? Is your response to a female hero different from your response to a male hero?
Murray Close/Lionsgate/courtesy Everett Collection

in *Divergent*, not to mention the various female characters in the *X-Men* series. The Chinese film *Crouching Tiger, Hidden Dragon* (2000) featured a beautiful heroine who was almost supernaturally adept at the martial arts and could even fly. Shu Lien became a worthy successor to the popular but once exclusively male traditions of kung fu and karate. Even Disney recently offered a female-centric film, *Brave* (2012), in which the princess held her own and lived happily ever after *without* a prince.

The Power of Numbers

Humanity long ago discovered that numerical units were basic to the design of both the earthly and the heavenly universe. In *The Divine Comedy*, Dante makes abundant use of the number "3" representing the Trinity. The poem is divided into three parts—*Inferno, Purgatory,* and *Paradise.* The last two parts contain 33 cantos, or chapters, corresponding to the age at which Jesus died; the first part has one extra canto to bring the total to what was considered the perfect number, 100.

Hebrew tradition also has mystic numbers. The letters of the Hebrew alphabet have number equivalents, and certain combinations of numbers are believed by some to hold the secrets of the universe. A school of Hebrew mysticism called Kabbalah studies the numerical complexities of Hebrew scripture. For example, some scholars have determined that there are 620, not just 10, commandments: 613 that were present in the five books attributed to Moses and seven that were added later by rabbis. Not by coincidence, these scholars observe, is the fact that the Ten Commandments contain 620 Hebrew letters.

People still have mystic feelings about numbers and sequences, believing, for example, that deaths come in threes, and awaiting the news of two more whenever a prominent person dies. At the Golden Gate Bridge in San Francisco, which has allegedly been the site of more suicides than any other place in the world, the city used to keep an official count of "jumpers," even designating which pillar each had jumped from. However, when the total reached 1000 in 1995, they called a halt to the record-keeping, certain that it only served to encourage unstable individuals to try for a particular number. There was even a story at the time that the city had announced a thousandth suicide before it actually happened, providing a fictitious name and occupation, along with an announcement that funeral services would be private—knowing all too well that the idea of being the thousandth might encourage a suicide that would not otherwise happen.

The Circle

The circle is an archetype that affects our lives profoundly. Because the circle is an unbroken line without beginning or end that encloses a uniform space, people have used it to symbolize oneness, completeness, and eternity. In myth, it appears as a shield, a ring, a pendant, the sun, and the moon, as well as in markings on cave walls or on stones. Countless circular structures, some dating back many millennia, are found throughout the world: temples, stone circles, and, of course, that most intriguing of all ancient monuments, Stonehenge (Figure 3.4), a large circle of heavy stones on Salisbury Plain in southwest England, the origin and purpose of which have been the subject of many changing theories over the years. Perhaps a religious structure, perhaps a burial ground, perhaps a giant calendar—no one really knows. For mythologists, however, Stonehenge—whatever its original purpose—reinforces the myth that the universe is a finite circle.

Asian and Western minds apparently came to similar conclusions about the universe. Both decided on the circular, geometrically perfect shape, which made the universe seem somehow *manageable*—that is, within the scope of human imagination, if not control. Contemporary science continues to debate the nature and extent of the universe and indeed whether "circle" does or does not really apply. Is it a random collection of planets and suns formed in the aftermath of an original explosion? Does it extend infinitely? Yet, at the same time, physicists continue to seek uniformity in physical laws. Einstein's general theory of relativity maintains that space is both infinite and *curved* and that gravity so warps space that no object can travel in a straight line forever.

For Asian cultures, the circle has traditionally symbolized the order behind *nature*. The *yin* and *yang* of Taoist philosophy, which represent the attraction of opposite forces that keep the universe in balance, are artistically depicted as overlapping halves of a black and white circle. East and West tend to see the human mind differently, however. To oversimplify, most Western cultures view the human mind as a self-contained circle. Asian cultures tend to view consciousness as a flowing river; thoughts and feelings come and go. The idea of the personal ego as a walled city, independent and closed, is a strange concept to the traditional Asian mind.

At the same time, for many Asian cultures, the circle is a symbol of the oneness of nature and the living beings who inhabit it, while the vocabulary of circles in the West is often narrowly related to self. Western "holistic" medicine treats the "whole person." When we feel unsure of where we want to go with our lives, we speak of trying to "get it together," and if we feel that we are losing control, friends might offer to help us "pick up the pieces."

Except for different images of the mind, both Asian and Western traditions seem to have always embraced the idea that everything makes sense, and the circle supports that. The circle provides an organizing principle, a coherent whole; it does not suggest chaos. Universal humanity does not want to

Figure 3.4 Stonehenge, England, built c. 2500 BCE.
Visitors have found Stonehenge mysterious and breathtaking for centuries. Why do you think this might be?
Bartlomiej K. Kwieciszewski/Shutterstock

think of itself as adrift and abandoned, an existence that cannot be comprehended. In fact, circle dances, favored in many cultures from Africa to the American south, underline the unbroken community of humankind; everyone is connected, and no one is abandoned.

The circle also represents immortality. The Hindu and Buddhist concepts of reincarnation and the cycles of existence, shared by many Westerners, are obvious examples. What is the belief found the world over in some form of an afterlife, and especially the belief in reincarnation, but the concept that existence has no end—like a circle?

The Journey

One of the major archetypes in Western mythology offers a noncircular view of the meaning of existence. The difficult journey, or quest, is another way of depicting the course of human life. Life-as-a-journey implies both purpose and a final destination as opposed to a random series of disconnected happenings. We think of life as moving from one stage or "phase" to another; again, this implies that we can make sense of life.

The mythic hero usually sets out on a journey fraught with danger and has a challenging task that must be performed at the conclusion. Fearful obstacles threaten the hero as he goes: dense, maze-like forests; dangerous beasts; and magical potions that induce slumber and prevent motion. But sooner or later, the journey continues.

Our expectations thus formed by the myth, we look for progress in our own lives and in those of others. We expect the obstacles. We say, "No pain, no gain." We are sure the journey will prove worth the effort. Accomplishing the big task will mean recognition and approval. When others seem not to succeed in their journey, we say, "He's never really grown up" or "She's still at the same old job!" (This notion that we must continually make progress also scares us, as is evident in so many recent movies in which the heroes are, more or less, adults who remain immersed in the concerns of childhood.)

The mythical journey is also a quest. The hero searches for his homeland, a buried treasure, the Holy Grail. Attainment of the goal gives shape and purpose to life. And here we note a conflict in the two key symbols: Whereas the circle guarantees life without end, the journey is supposed to yield important results. We don't mind applying the circle to universal order or to the shape of the mind as a self-contained whole, but we resist thinking of life as just one thing after another without purpose, without direction. We hate to think of ourselves as "going around in circles." We like to think that, regardless of life's continual changes, its ups and downs (there are always mythical mountains to cross), life *does* come to something after all.

The journey in Asian mythology is a series of happenings, not necessarily in a sequence and without a necessary final task. In the myth that surrounds the figure of Bodhidharma, the monk who brought Buddhism from India to China, the hero stops to meditate on a mountaintop for nine years, during which his legs fall off. But the story merely points out that this is what occurred; it does not call it a tragedy. For the East, life is indeed one thing after another, and each day has to be accepted for what it is. For the West, a journey without a successful destination is worthless. "She died before her time" is a Western mythic observation. So is "Here he is, 35 years old, and what has he done with his life?"

The Garden

In the West, as we have said, journeys are supposed to have successful destinations, but related myths question these destinations—myths that say we are heading down the "wrong path" and myths that look back to the past and say "Would that we had never embarked on this journey; we have lost too much."

Myths of a Golden Age, when things were better, extend far back in the Western tradition. In fact, the usual downfall of the hero implies that what was once good is now gone. With the death of King Arthur went all hope of another Camelot. Many myth scholars believe that the archetype of the Golden Age had its origins in the biblical account of the Garden, the earthly paradise Adam and Eve called home until they were cast out for eating the forbidden fruit from the Tree of Knowledge.

The Hebrew Bible also contains a countermyth with a countersymbol to the Garden. Adam and Eve are expelled from *their* Garden, but Abraham and his descendants are offered the hope for a Promised Land, Canaan, the fertile land of milk and honey. Moses leads the Children of Israel out of captivity in Egypt, but he does not live to reach his destination. His followers, however, find that Canaan is anything but a joyful paradise where they can live happily ever after. It is constantly attacked, conquered, and occupied. Yet the promise made by God to Abraham projects the Garden into the future. The Golden Age has yet to come, but come it will.

In the eighteenth century, writers in Europe and America revived the Garden myth as they mourned the shift from rural to urban living. They lamented the wretched lives of the urban poor, densely packed into crime-ridden, filthy slums. The teeming cities represented for these writers the antithesis of the Garden, and they celebrated the unspoiled countryside and the happy, unschooled innocents who lived there, uncorrupted by the greed and arrogance of cosmopolitan life. Writers and dramatists began to cast their eyes far afield, imagining the paradise of remote lands, where the sun shines warmly all year long, food is abundant, and inhabitants live in perpetual harmony.

PRIMITIVISM   This literary movement was inspired by the philosophy of *primitivism*, which held that those who lived far from cities in what was called a "state of nature" were happier, less apt to commit crime, and more willing to share the fruits of the land than their more educated and wealthier counterparts. The key spokesperson for primitivism was the French philosopher Jean-Jacques Rousseau (1712–1778). Rousseau restated the myth of the Garden, blaming government and social controls, both products of so-called civilization, for the corruption of humanity. In doing so, he created the archetype of the *noble savage* who is untutored but astute in the ways of nature, infinitely resourceful, and able to provide food and shelter for his family.

Primitivism led to the popularity on the stage and in fiction of this new mythic figure. In England, the "man Friday" of Daniel Defoe's Robinson Crusoe was far more adept at living without the comforts of civilization than the shipwrecked British gentleman who depends on him for survival. In America, Mark Twain created Huck Finn and sent him floating down the Mississippi River on his raft with his good friend Jim, and, at the end, "lighting out for the territories"—suggesting a way of life representing a perpetual escape from civilization, its moral codes, its social demands, and its unhappy inhabitants. Sir James M. Barrie gave the world Peter Pan, who eludes the aging process and lives a boy's carefree existence in Never-Never Land.

THE NEW WORLD   The "discovery" of America in 1492 gave rise to a new version of the Garden archetype—the New World—which continues to influence us today. First came the explorers, proudly planting their nations' flags on the "virgin" soil (while Native Americans watched). Next came boatloads of pilgrims seeking a new start in life and freedom to worship as they wished. Then by the thousands came immigrants seeking prosperity in streets supposedly paved with gold. As the eastern half of the United States became densely populated and the dream of prosperity gave way to the reality of long hours of work and crowded tenements, the archetype of the Garden moved out to the frontier, the wide-open West. Pioneers left their homes by the thousands, seeking a new Canaan. Some prospered. Many did not. The promise of the New World still holds out hope for millions throughout the globe.

When they come to the Promised Land, modern immigrants, like their predecessors, bring with them a strong archetype—the family—as well as the customs, traditional beliefs, and rituals that hold families together. Sometimes the newcomers are received with enthusiasm, and sometimes they are rejected. Often members of the younger generation drift away, become part of the new culture. The elders sometimes intensify the traditional rituals, hold even more tightly to their customs, close themselves in for fear of losing their identity, self-respect, and dignity. Disenchanted by the New World, they remember their old country, where things were better, people were nicer, and the streets were safer. Like Dorothy in the Land of Oz, they discover that maybe their original home wasn't so bad after all. The Garden always seems to be somewhere else. But if this archetype can cause disillusionment, it can also be the source of hope.

Gods as Human Beings

As an archetype, the Greek god is written about and depicted in statuary as a larger-than-life mortal. Like some other early cultures, the Greeks had ambivalent feelings about their deities. They feared them because of their enormous power and because they could be unpredictable (the gods could strike down anyone they chose, at any time, and for any reason), and they also resented them. The Greeks believed that nothing in the universe was as important as human beings. If there were to be gods, they must be **anthropomorphic**, made in the image of humanity, and not the other way around as in Judaism, Christianity, and Islam.

The archetypal term "Greek god," describing a very handsome man, usually refers to Apollo, who was always portrayed as the epitome of physical perfection and whose name itself has become an archetype of male beauty. "Greek goddess" (or often just "goddess"), describing a woman of surpassing beauty, usually refers to Aphrodite or the Roman Venus. Despite the fact that we don't run into an Apollo or a Venus every day, the enduring myth suggests that such physical perfection, though godlike, *is* attainable by certain mortals.

The Greek deities were thought of as residing on Mount Olympus, which is a very real place, in much the same way that our own deities live high up in the Hollywood Hills or on the slopes of Aspen or along the Grande Corniche, the topmost road on the French Riviera and home to the wealthy (*and* "beautiful") people of this world. Zeus and Hera, the king and queen of the other deities, were married celebrities who held grudges against each other and fought bitterly. Many human woes were ascribed to the fact that Zeus and Hera were often on opposite sides in a war, each plotting against the other. *In humanizing their gods, the Greeks in effect deified themselves!*

The Greeks were not alone in attributing human qualities (and particularly human failings) to their gods. If we think about it, most gods are to some extent anthropomorphic: They are vain; they get angry; they make demands; they are sometimes vengeful. Perhaps we can only comprehend gods who share some of our own traits. Or perhaps the case is simply that we were created in their image.

Myth as Explanation

3.3   *How do myths provide explanations for otherwise unexplainable phenomena?*

Mythology consists of much more than the archetypes that shape the way we interpret our world and what happens to us in it. For our ancestors, two major aspects of being alive must have been very baffling. One was the mystery of natural phenomena. The other was how to account for all the trouble that seemed to be part of life. Mythology was their way of understanding the mystery of the universe and the pain and hardships of living in it.

If science had been at the disposal of our ancestors across the globe, they might have turned away from mythmaking in favor of observation and experimentation. Lacking science, they created stories to account for what they could not otherwise explain. We should be grateful that they did, for these ancient stories, along with the music and dances that must surely have accompanied group ceremonies, became the foundation on which the humanities now rest securely. The myths they wove made the natural world and its amazing phenomena seem less remote and frightening and helped remove the fear that life was innately evil, that bad things happened without cause.

Much of what we call the humanities concerns itself with finding acceptable explanations for life's tragedies, even if these explanations are at odds with scientific evidence. For example, in 1927 the American author Thornton Wilder (1897–1975), most well known for his innovative play *Our Town*, published the novel *The Bridge of San Luis Rey*. The novel is about a footbridge built across a steep gorge in the Andes Mountains of Peru. Thousands had traveled across it for years, but on this particular day, the bridge collapses, and five unsuspecting travelers are suddenly hurled to their deaths.

The novel then presents the story of each victim and poses the question, "Why this person?" Although scientific explanations are abundant, the author prefers to leave the door open for the possibility that divine intervention was responsible. Is it more comforting to believe everything happens for a reason instead of believing that life is a series of random, senseless occurrences? Our ancestors must have thought so and may have left explanatory myths as their legacy to us.

Creation

Even the greatest scientists have wrestled with the agonizing questions: Why is there something when there might have been nothing? Is there an essential principle that requires existence to exist? Or did it spring accidentally from nothing? And if so, how and why? Why are *we* here? Why haven't we discovered intelligent life anywhere else in the universe—at least so far? Mythology supplies a number of different answers, and the quest continues.

One creation myth recounted in the *Upanishads*, the sacred books of India, says: At first he was lonely and afraid but, above all, he "lacked delight (therefore, we lack delight when alone) and desired a second. . . . This Self then split into two parts; and with that, there were a master and a mistress."[5] But this first woman was afraid to be touched and so hid from her male Self. She turned into various animals, but he pursued her and mated with each of her manifestations until the natural world, as we know it, was formed. The story does not explain where the original Self came from, but once that is accepted, everything else follows in a cause-and-effect sequence.

Most Asian belief systems have no clear-cut story of creation. The Buddhist Dharma constitutes the orderly principle that guides the universe, which had no beginning; therefore, the natural world, which is the outer garment of this order, must have always existed. Confucianism, a major Chinese philosophy, stresses the social world and one's duties within it and avoids the question of how it began, which does not matter as much as how life is lived.

In another major Chinese philosophy, Taoism (DOW-ism), we find a creation story that resembles those of non-Asian cultures, giving further credence to Jung's theory that early cultures developed similar myths without traceable communication with each other. In this story, the universe was at first a dark formless void, as it is described in the Hebrew Bible. Within this void, a single egg came into being inside of which was the fetus of what would eventually become the giant Pan-Gu. After attaining colossal size, Pan-Gu stretched his arms. The egg broke, and the lighter half floated upward to become the sky while the heavier part sank downward to become the earth. Ever since, the operation of the universe has depended on the attraction of opposites—astonishingly prophetic of the modern electromagnetic theory of nature!

In Greek mythology, precreation is depicted in a similar fashion. It is called the "formless confusion of Chaos" existing only in darkness. Chaos in some mysterious way gave birth to children: one was Gaea, or Mother Earth; others were Night and Erebus, or Death. Night placed an egg in the depths of Erebus, and from it was born Love (though we are not sure how this love was defined). Love's first act was to create Light and Day.

Greek myths tell us that the gods came after the creation, but this order is not surprising when we consider that in the Greek myths the power of Fate appears to be greater than that of the gods. For the Greeks, the power of Fate always existed, was responsible for the coming of Night and Death, and must therefore be reckoned as *the* divine force.[6]

The creation myth of the Haida people, who live primarily on islands off the coast of British Columbia in Canada, suggests (in common with many other Native-American creation myths) that first came animals, some endowed with godlike powers. In the Haida myth, a raven, alone on his island, sees a number of small human figures protruding from beneath a clam shell (Figure 3.5). With some difficulty, because they are frightened, he persuades them to emerge into this new world, and they become the first Haidas.

Many other cultures attribute the origin of the natural world to a divinity that preceded its existence. Judaism, Christianity, and Islam share a common belief that the world was brought into existence by an all-powerful and singular creator. Working within this tradition, the English poet John Milton (1608–1674) in his epic poem *Paradise Lost* assumes the preexistence of both God and a chaotic universe which was transformed into the orderly cosmos the poet knew. According to Milton's interpretation, in the beginning there was

> *the vast immeasurable Abyss,*
> *Outrageous as a Sea, dark, wasteful, wild,*
> *Up from the bottom turn'd by furious winds*
> *And surging waves, as Mountains to assault*
> *Heav'n's highth, and with the centre mix the Pole.*
> *Silence, ye troubl'd waves, and thou Deep, peace,*
> *Said then th'Omnific Word, your discord end.*[7]

Figure 3.5 Bill Reid, *The Raven and the First Men*, 1980.
Why do you think many Native-American creation myths rely on animals or insects, rather than classical gods?
Keith Douglas/All Canada Photos/Corbis

In the modern world, a debate continues between those who believe that the universe had no known beginning and those who believe it cannot have always existed. Modern science is deeply committed to the law of cause and effect, yet when it comes to the question of whether there was a *first* cause, a deep division of opinion remains. The theory that the origins of the universe can be traced to a big bang, a huge explosion of a single particle, is widely held. Once this explanation is accepted, the theory manages to explain all that followed. But where, some ask, did the single particle come from? One answer has been that it came from nothing, but that we need not assume that "nothing" is necessarily empty.

It is interesting to note that one of today's crucial unsolved questions is remarkably similar to those asked by our earliest ancestors.

The Natural World

One theory about Stonehenge, the remarkable stone circle on England's Salisbury Plain, suggests that it was erected as a means of predicting the seasons by following the position of the sun with respect to the stones at various times of the year. This may have been true; perhaps Stonehenge could help predict the seasons. Yet Stonehenge cannot explain *why* there are seasons. Why is it not always summer? Why the bitter cold, when people can freeze to death and food may be scarce? Why the reawakening of spring? Nature is surely something to inspire wonder, apprehension, and worship. Many early myths sought to explain nature, and early rituals—ceremonial dances as well as animal and human sacrifice—were often created in an effort to control it.

In Scandinavian communities, for example, the fertility deity was Freyr, who was thought to bring rich harvests to the earth. He did so by wooing a maiden, symbolizing the union of earth and sky. Rituals that honored Freyr and the abundance he gave were, Scandinavians thought, essential to survival. In almost all early cultures, help from the gods was sought if crops should fail or were insufficient. If the gods didn't cooperate by bringing rain (or stopping it), then food might be gathered from the sea—if the storm god could be appeased.

In Greek mythology, Apollo, the sun god, drove his chariot across the sky each day, thus accounting for the rising and setting of the sun, just as Apollo's sister Artemis presided over the moon at night. The king of the gods, Zeus, was responsible for hurling thunderbolts, and Poseidon controlled the sea. But these activities could be altered at the whim of the gods. Thus the sea might be made so calm that no ships could move when Poseidon wished to punish a fleet that failed to honor him. Or a sea monster might appear, sent by Poseidon in response to the prayer of a mortal as when Theseus prayed for the destruction of his son, who he believed had committed adultery with his stepmother.

Early peoples performed what was called "sympathetic magic," the acting out of ceremonies designed to affect the behavior of the gods. Thus people terrified by the darkness of the winter solstice, the longest night of the year, in countries throughout the world attempted to evoke the return of the sun through the lighting of candles, as if the sun—or the powers in charge of light—would imitate the lesser light below.

EXPLAINING THE SEASONS Most cultures created explanations for the changing of the seasons. The Greeks, for example, suggested that the seasons resulted from the love of Demeter, goddess of the earth, for her daughter Persephone. So joyful was Demeter at the very thought of her daughter, that when Persephone was near, Demeter provided people with a superabundance of all the good things the earth could yield. One day, however, Hades, lord of the underworld, glimpsed the girl, captured her, and took her to be his bride. Demeter so mourned her loss that the earth came to be covered with the ice and snow of perpetual winter.

If Zeus had not intervened, all human life would have ended. But he was so touched by Demeter's grief that he arranged for Persephone to live with her mother for all but four months out of the year; those she owed to her husband. When Persephone is in the underworld, the earth freezes over, and when she returns, her happy mother allows the earth once again to bloom.

Another explanation occurs in the myth of Dionysus, the male deity who governed the abundance of the earth. Winter came about because he died and in the underworld was torn to pieces and eaten. Mysteriously, he was somehow resurrected and became whole again, and spring returned—but only temporarily. Each year Dionysus meets his terrible fate again.

RENEWAL AND SACRIFICE The descent into the underworld of both Persephone and Dionysus can be regarded as sacrifices that ensured rebirth. This idea, that without sorrow or death there can be no springtime joy, was an early belief that has captured the minds of writers and philosophers ever since.

For the Greeks, vegetation could be connected to the involvement of gods with beautiful mortals. The blooms of the hyacinth and the narcissus celebrated the transformation of their namesakes from death to eternal life in nature. Hyacinthus was a beautiful young mortal dearly loved by Apollo, who was accidentally killed by him while they were playing a game of discus throwing. (Note that once again the Greeks attributed human failings to their gods.) Apollo then had the dead body transformed into the hyacinth.

The German-American classicist Edith Hamilton (1867–1963), whose 1942 book *Mythology* popularized the study of myth for many, interprets such transformation stories in a somewhat ominous way. They are, she speculates, vestiges of ancient human sacrifice rather than of accidental death. Ancient people sometimes selected a number of handsome young people for sacrificial rituals designed to appease the gods. According to Hamilton, when the Greeks told their myths in later years, they revised the stories to rid themselves of this violent era in their past:

> *It might happen, if the fields around a village were not fruitful, if the corn did not spring up as it should, that one of the villagers would be killed and his—or her—blood sprinkled over the barren land. . . . What could be more natural then, if a beautiful boy had thus been killed, than to think when later the ground blossomed with narcissus or hyacinths that the flowers were his very self, changed and yet living again? So they would tell each other it had happened, a lovely miracle which made the cruel death seem less cruel.*[8]

The sacrifice of animals was probably performed each year at the spring festivals honoring Dionysus to ensure the god's return and the renewal of the growing season. At the drama festivals, the tragic protagonist who fell from his high position became a kind of symbolic sacrifice so order could return to the state.

From what is now Ghana, in West Africa, comes a story of how the country flourished and was prosperous because each year a beautiful girl was given to a devouring serpent. (Serpents figure frequently in mythology around the world.) One year, however, when the girl was led to the pit where the serpent waited, her betrothed was also waiting. The brave young man stood by while the serpent twice spat venom on the girl, because he knew that only on the third try could the reptile be destroyed. At the appropriate moment, the young man beheaded the serpent—only to find that it kept growing new heads, eventually seven in all. The girl was saved, but the serpent had its revenge. As the last head was cut off, it flew away, saying, "For seven years, seven months, and seven days, Ghana will receive neither water nor rains of gold." A drought ensued, destroying the populace and a once-great empire.

Unlike the stories of Persephone and Dionysus, which appear to explain a recurring pattern of the natural world, this tale provides an explanation for what was probably a singular, and very real, catastrophe.

Human Suffering

Sometimes known as the *problem of evil*, suffering caused by natural catastrophes (such as the devastating tsunami of 2004 that took more than 200,000 lives in Southeast Asia) and by the inhumanity of regimes (such as that of the Nazis in the early twentieth century) has been and continues to be analyzed by philosophers, theologians, and writers. Our ancestors asked the same questions we hear now: Why are some people consumed with hatred, envy, and greed? Why are there famines, plagues, and wars? Like many contemporaries, they wanted to believe there were reasons for the suffering people had to endure. The idea that terrible things happened without cause was unacceptable because it suggested a universe ruled by chaos, a universe in which humankind was powerless. In creating stories that explained suffering, our ancestors were able to reassure themselves that order did indeed prevail in the universe and that if they acted in an appropriate manner, they might escape misfortune.

WOMAN AS TRANSGRESSOR   A common explanation for suffering was an early act of transgression against divine law: offending a god or disobeying a command. Often, these acts are performed by a woman. The Greek myth of Pandora, for example, explains how human misfortune came about because of a woman's curiosity. Beloved by Zeus, Pandora was given a magical box in which each of the other gods had placed something she is not to know. Frustrated by the gnawing desire to discover what treasures are concealed inside the box, she disobeys Zeus and opens the box, out of which fly death, sorrow, plagues, war, and every other calamity visited upon mortals ever since. Alarmed, Pandora slams the box shut, not knowing that trapped inside is the gift of hope.

In the Judeo-Christian tradition, God commands Adam and Eve not to eat the forbidden fruit growing on the Tree of Knowledge. (The fruit, often depicted as an apple, is not identified in Genesis, and apples are not native to the Middle East.) Tempted by the serpent, Eve eats the fruit, and Adam does the same. Genesis does not say that Eve prevailed upon Adam to follow her into sin, though later versions turned the story into a myth of woman's weakness. In Milton's *Paradise Lost*, God judges Adam more harshly than he does Eve because, even though Eve has sinned first, Adam, being a man, should have known better.

In an African myth of the Burundi tribe, a woman is again blamed for bringing about human suffering. At first, human beings are not touched by Death because divine dogs protect them. One day Death approaches a woman and promises to give her and her family special protection. When the woman opens her mouth to speak, Death jumps in. Questioned by the chief of the gods concerning the whereabouts of Death, the woman lies and says she has not seen him. The chief of the gods, being all-mighty and all-knowing, recognizes that the woman is lying and allows Death to dwell inside the woman and all of her descendants.

According to another tale found in the African oral tradition of the Buganda (in what is now Uganda), Kintu, the first man, and his wife Nambi are hurrying to leave the land of the sky in order to flee Death. They have been warned not to delay their escape, but Nambi decides to go back for grain. Death follows her as she attempts to rejoin her husband. As a result, death becomes the punishment for all future generations, a motif notably similar to that found in Genesis.

A legend found in Mexico and Central and South America is that of *La Llorona* ("The Weeping Woman"). So popular is this figure in oral storytelling that numerous versions of her persist. In one version, she is a phantom, never seen, but heard weeping at night, mourning her children, for whose deaths she is responsible. In another version, she is a spirit doomed to wander forever in search of the children she neglected during her lifetime. Still another version shows her to be blatantly evil, a woman who lures men to follow her only to suffer violent death. In this telling, the woman resembles the Sirens of Greek mythology, the sea maidens whose seductive singing lures sailors to their doom, and the Lorelei of Germanic lore, a lovely maiden who sits on a rock, combing her hair and singing so beautifully that sailors wreck their ships trying to reach her.

The La Llorona tales are often told as a warning to unmarried pregnant girls who, finding themselves abandoned, have no recourse but to give up their babies. Presumably, repeating the story of a mother mourning her lost children reminds young girls of what can happen when they indulge in practices forbidden by religion and family.[9]

CURIOSITY AND DISOBEDIENCE: THE STORIES OF ORPHEUS AND LOT The tragic results of curiosity and disobedience are also found in two other famous myths, one from the Greeks and the other from the Hebrew Bible. Both illustrate a universal belief that some things are better left unknown. In the Greek myth, an extraordinary musician named Orpheus is in love with the beautiful Eurydice, who dies and is taken to the underworld. Orpheus follows her and uses the gorgeous strains of his lyre to convince the king of the underworld that Eurydice should be returned to the land of the living. His request is granted, with one condition: Orpheus must walk straight up the path without turning around to make sure that Eurydice is following.

He almost keeps the pact, but at the last minute, unable to bear the suspense, he turns around, only to see his beloved being reclaimed by the powers of darkness, lost to him forever.

The prizewinning 1959 Brazilian film *Black Orpheus* (well worth hunting down), set during the night of Carnivale in Rio de Janeiro, tells essentially the same tale. A figure wearing the mask of death pursues the modern Eurydice through a crowded street, finally seizing her and carrying her into an empty building and down an endless spiral staircase. The modern Orpheus follows them, but instead of being given the chance to return to life with her, he dies also. The morning finds the two lovers, together, impaled on the sharp spikes of an aloe plant. In this modern retelling, death is not the result of curiosity or disobedience, but—more tragically—something that occurs without any purpose at all.

In a biblical tale, Lot and his family are allowed to escape the destruction of Sodom and Gomorrah, with one condition—that they flee the city without turning around to see what is happening. Lot's wife, however, cannot resist the temptation, and when she turns around, she is transformed into a pillar of salt.

Asian traditions do not speak of human suffering as caused by disobedience to a divine command; rather, they blame selfish acts by individuals for the world's ills. In Hindu belief, what happens to a person is the result of *karma*, a summation at death of how one's life has been conducted. If it has been less than morally satisfactory, the spirit is reborn into a new body and a less fortunate social position in which hunger and poverty dominate. If it has been mainly satisfactory but not perfect, the spirit is reborn with a chance to live a better life. Thus Hindus speak of "good karma," which means a life blessed by good deeds in a past existence, while "bad karma" is just the opposite.

Cursed by Fate

The Greeks introduced another way of accounting for human woes, and that was Fate. It was visually represented as three sisters: one wove the thread of life, another stretched it out, and the third cut it. In addition to having a person's lifespan determined by the whim of Fate, Greek mythology also developed the concept that many people were followed throughout their lives by the unkindness of Fate because of a transgression they themselves committed in the past, or one that was committed by an ancestor for which they are paying the price. Two of the greatest Greek tragedies are trilogies about noble families cursed by Fate because of past sins.

The Oresteia by Aeschylus (c. 525–456 BCE) consists of three plays about the doomed family of Atreus, who kills his brother's children and then serves them to him as food. He commits this atrocity as an act of vengeance against the brother for having forced his wife into adultery. The two sons of Atreus, who must bear the consequences of their father's sin, are Menelaus, king of Sparta, and Agamemnon, a Greek warrior. Menelaus marries the beautiful Helen, who runs off with the Trojan prince Paris, thus precipitating the Trojan War. Agamemnon fights the ten-year war on his brother's side, returning home only to be lured to his death by his wife, whose lover stabs him. The two adulterers are in turn murdered by Agamemnon's son Orestes, with the assistance of his sister Electra. The Furies, ferocious mythic women whose duty it is to haunt and terrify evil-doers, pursue Orestes, taunting him demonically day and night until he is exonerated by the goddess Athena in the world's first known theatrical trial scene.

The doomed family of Cadmus includes his son Oedipus and the four children sired by Oedipus and borne by his wife Jocasta, who is also his birth mother. Cadmus, a wealthy citizen, offends the gods by bragging that, because of his business success, he is just as powerful as those deities. The disasters visited upon his offspring are punishments for his arrogance.

The tragedy of the doomed Oedipus is told in three plays by Sophocles: *Oedipus the King*, *Oedipus at Colonus*, and *Antigone*. By the fifth century, Athenians had developed a highly sophisticated urban civilization, and, though the old myths still formed the basis for many plays of the period, they were subject to question. In particular, the Oedipus plays deal with the issue of whether the protagonist, suffering because he had long ago killed his father and then married his mother without knowing the truth of his parentage, should accept responsibility for his actions when he was doomed by Fate to commit them. Sophocles resolves the issue by having his protagonist willingly accept responsibility as a means of maintaining his dignity. "The gods willed that I should slay the man I didn't know was my father," he says, "but the hand that struck the blow was mine."

Greek mythology and the tragedies it inspired remain of enduring relevance because the question of whether any of us really has free will is still very much alive. It is at the core of many a court case involving dilemmas of responsibility. Inherited traits, family abuse, poverty, and a bad environment frequently enter into arguments for the defense.

Myths of Childhood

3.4 *What characteristics distinguish the myths of childhood?*

Our earliest encounters with literature, the stories told or read to us, probably influence our expectations of later life. Childhood tales—despite their frequent violence and terror—usually satisfy the child's (or even the parent's) need for security by bringing the action to a happy conclusion. ("And they all lived happily ever after.")

Adults like to escape from the demands of everyday life by giving in to their childhood love of magical kingdoms, witches, wizards, and perils that are inevitably overcome. Fables from distant childhood have been kept alive, particularly in the heavily sanitized versions presented in Disney films. Both the young and the not-so-young have made huge box-office successes of *Snow White, Beauty and the Beast, The Lion King, Frozen*, and many more. Similarly, audiences flocked to Tim Burton's 2010 *Alice in Wonderland* and *Maleficent* (2014), the tale of Sleeping Beauty told from the viewpoint of the queen, played by Angelina Jolie—traditionally a figure of evil, but here redeemed. This section deals with some childhood tales and their themes that are too important not to be considered as valid introductions to the humanities.

How We Get Our Values

Children who still hear about the Three Little Pigs learn that hard work and diligence, not fun and frivolity, pay off in the long run. Red Riding Hood's journey would certainly have been a lot safer if she had heeded the advice about not speaking to strangers; the tale of the child on her way to Granny's house teaches children a lesson about disobedience. Sleeping Beauty, threatened with awful consequences if she pricks her finger on a spindle, cannot resist the temptation to explore a hidden spinning wheel and so suffers the inevitable wound. Like so many childhood stories, that of Sleeping Beauty contains dire warnings about disobedience—but also suggests that things will turn out all right in the end.

Not every tale is so reassuring, especially if we read them in the original versions. In the Grimm Brother's original telling, for example, Little Red Riding Hood's Granny is torn limb from limb, not gently ingested, and in a number of their tales, the hardships children face echo a reality in the larger world. The series of contemporary children's books called *A Series of Unfortunate Events* by Daniel Handler (b. 1970) who writes under the pen name Lemony Snicket, brings back the sense that everything does *not* always end well—but that clever children can make their own way through the darkness.

Not all childhood mythology is designed to teach. Many of the stories offer comfort and security, even as they reflect the stress of modern life. Characters can face very real dangers and frightening villains. Sauron, whose domain includes Mount Doom in J.R.R. Tolkien's *Lord of the Rings* and who represents evil incarnate, is ultimately conquered, but only after a furious battle sequence. In Maurice Sendak's classic children's book, *Where the Wild Things Are*, a little boy sent to his room without supper sails out of his bedroom (without adult permission, of course) into a mysterious new land where he encounters weird, fantastic, sometimes frightening creatures, all vividly illustrated by the author. But, despite the odds, the boy manages to return safely—and to find his supper waiting for him, still hot. The myth appeals to the need for escape from humdrum, sometimes burdensome, reality, as well as the need for reassuring safety and love.

The Importance of Being Attractive and Rich

The old fairy tales, still popular, reinforce stereotypical gender roles, class distinctions, and the notion that good and evil are based on physical appearance. People named Charming, Beauty, and Snow White are not only physically attractive but morally pure. The labels Wicked Witch and Stepmother are given to unattractive characters—typically female—who are up to no good. Cinderella is both breathtakingly beautiful and hard-working. By contrast, her stepsisters are selfish, ugly, and possessed of unfortunately large feet.

Fairy tales take place in magic kingdoms dominated by a class system, for, after all, they originated in a time when it was believed that nobility was inborn. People may not have believed literally in the blue blood of one small segment of the populace, but they were reminded time and again that "class will tell." The heroine of a tale called "The Princess and the Pea" is so innately sensitive, so clearly a member of the upper class, that she spends a sleepless night because a single pea under a pile of many mattresses irritates her. The pea has been deliberately placed there as a test of her true aristocracy. The values embedded deeply in these tales may ultimately be harmful, but they also provide good stories, and who bothers to analyze them when children drift off to happy sleep?

The Importance of Names

In one folktale, a lower-class heroine, a miller's daughter, is engaged to a prince on the strength of a false promise—that she can transform flax into gold. She is locked in a room and told to fill it with the precious metal; if she can't manage it, she will be put to death for her lie. Of course she doesn't know how. Help comes from a little man who tells her he can perform the magic, provided she promises to give him her firstborn child. Since the poor girl is not yet married and is in danger of losing her life if she doesn't perform the task before morning, she agrees. The gold appears, the marriage takes place, and in due time a child is born. When reminded of her agreement, the queen begs for another chance, which she gets. The condition is that she must tell the little man his name. Her first guesses are not even close, but she eventually is victorious when she overhears him boasting "Rumpelstiltskin is my name."

The myth probably appeals to children at the age when language is becoming important. During dramatic presentations of the story, young audiences continually scream the name to the actress playing the heroine. Perhaps it helps children affirm their own identities, for they too have names, and names, as they are learning, are all-important, especially unusual names that make one unique.

The Dark Side

Though modern childhood mythology does not shy away from confronting real dangers, even the time-honored fairy tales can evoke multiple responses. Amid the magic kingdoms and beautiful characters lurk goblins, bats, and skulls. Through these and other dark elements, like the terrifying forest and the flying monkeys in *The Wizard of Oz*, children learn that life is not always sunny.

The beautiful Snow White appears to die from biting into a poisonous apple given to her by her jealous stepmother. She is even placed in a glass coffin, though in real life, children are generally shielded from close contact with death. Of course, the kiss of a prince restores her to life and leads to the usual proposal of a royal marriage.

Much emphasis is placed on the threat of being eaten. In *Hansel and Gretel*, still popular as children's theater and as opera, the wicked lady in the tempting gingerbread house warms her oven in dreadful preparation for roasting the two children. In the nick of time, they are rescued and the lady herself consigned to a painful death.

In his 1986 musical *Into the Woods* (filmed in 2014), Stephen Sondheim brings together all of the major characters from the fairy tales and puts them into small houses on the edge of a wood; they become symbols of the true dangers in the world. Mythical illusion is continually shattered in the musical. After their marriage, Cinderella discovers that Prince Charming is having many affairs. When confronted, he explains: "I was raised to be charming, not sincere." Jack's excursion up the magical beanstalk and his defeat of the giant in the first act leads to tragic—and shocking—consequences in the second, when the wife of the dead giant retaliates, laying waste to the kingdom and killing several characters, including an audience favorite, the baker's wife. Traditional myths help the makers of the humanities to communicate dark messages.

Roald Dahl's *Charlie and the Chocolate Factory*, filmed in 1971 (as *Willy Wonka & the Chocolate Factory*) and again in 2005, is not precisely the wholesome entertainment its title might appear to promise. Rather than a delightful fable about a wondrous world of unbelievable candy, it turns instead into a dark story of how greed destroys. The children who can't resist the many temptations of Willy Wonka's factory drown in a chocolate river or are crushed in mixing machines. The purity and common sense of the young hero is, however, recognized by the factory's proprietor, and he is allowed to ride a magic elevator into a never-never land free of greed and corruption.

Some parents seek to avoid frightening their children (especially at bedtime) by eliminating all threatening motifs, by making sure that hungry wolves are not allowed to eat either little pigs or old ladies. One mother was distressed, however, when her child burst into tears at the bland ending by demanding to know whether the wolf was still hungry!

Is it important for each generation of children to be taught the old fables? The filmmaker George Lucas (b. 1944) may have thought so when he conceived the idea for a nine-movie series called *Star Wars* in the early 1970s. A devotee of the mythologist Joseph Campbell, Lucas produced the three films covering the middle part of his story (*Star Wars*, 1977; *The Empire Strikes Back*, 1980; and *Return of the Jedi*, 1983) and then shelved the project for 15 years. These first films, however, cover the meat of the tale—a hero's quest if ever there was one. Relying on Campbell's archetypes, *Star Wars* tells the story of Luke Skywalker, whose noble lineage is unknown to him when he begins his journey. Luke is tested in all the traditional ways, doubts himself, but eventually learns to trust "the Force"—the inner power that will guide him to do the right thing. But the Force is challenged constantly by "the Dark Side," epitomized by the faceless warrior Darth Vader. Just in case someone reading this book does not know the *Star Wars* story, we won't reveal who Darth Vader turns out to be—but suffice it to say that it fits the mythic mold.

Popular Mythology

3.5 *What role do popular mythology and common sayings play in our culture?*

Much of what we say and how we react to certain situations has roots in mythology, both past and present. Whether we know it or not, we keep creating and perpetuating myths. The fables of the Greek writer Aesop (sixth century BCE) contain many stories and morals that stay with humanity from age to age, including the tortoise who wins the race against the swifter hare and the fox who decides that the grapes he is unable to reach are probably sour anyway. The latter story is the source of the term "sour grapes," applied to anyone claiming "I didn't want it anyway." Aesop gave practical advice, but it was often contradictory: The morals of his fables include both "Look before you leap" and "He who hesitates is lost." Still, either moral can be words of wisdom, depending on the situation.

Many popular beliefs are quoted without regard to their origins. Discovering the roots of popular mythology is not a plea for being more realistic. Its purpose is to encourage the *habit* of identifying certain patterns of thought and emotion, so they can be more readily evaluated as either still vital or no longer useful. In a sense, it is also an introduction to the critical appreciation of the humanities.

Common Sayings

All of us hear them; nearly everyone uses them. Life would be different without them. They are expressions of beliefs that may have originated in ancient stories, religious teachings, or frequently repeated slogans. Some may consider them misconceptions, but most of them are rarely challenged. Those who scoff may simply not be analyzing why the belief has found such wide acceptance. Here are a few common beliefs that constitute our everyday mythology.

"WHAT GOES AROUND, COMES AROUND"   The saying helps many of us account for bad things that happen. It is easier for us to believe that bad things are not random, like a lightning strike, but are the logical result of a misdeed. Thus, if we avoid such misdeeds in the future, all will be well.

"MOTHER NATURE"   As long as nature continues to be personified as a maternal force, many people will believe that, despite neglecting what is happening to the planet, somehow we will all be nurtured and protected by the mother of us all.

"THEY'LL THINK OF SOMETHING"   The ending of some Greek plays resolved terrible problems by having an actor dressed as a god come down to the stage, essentially out of nowhere. The plot device, known as *deus ex machina*, has become a standard critical term for plot contrivance. In popular mythology, the *deus* is sometimes medical research. Like the cavalry riding to the rescue, like the mysterious stranger who appears just in time, science will solve every problem, find a cure for every disease in the nick of time. Because "they" have helped so often before, they can be expected to help every time. If rescue is inevitable, every rule of good health can be violated for our bodies or our cities while we wait for our rescuers.

"ALL YOU NEED IS LOVE"   Whether we are told that love is "the sweetest thing" (as in a 1932 popular song), or that it "makes the world go round" (as in the 1961 musical *Carnival*), or that it's "all you need" (as in the Beatle's 1967 song of that title), many of us believe that love is as important—and as healing—as breathable air. Although more people live alone than ever before, most still seem to believe that having a companion—someone to love, someone who loves—is the one thing that will make living worthwhile. A first failure requires the search for the right choice next time, and a newly single person's claim of being happy is often met with disbelief and offers of matchmaking. There is someone, the myth tells us, for everyone. We all have our Prince Charmings or our Sleeping Beauties out there, if we can only find them.

"IT MUST BE FATE"   Fate, also called destiny, plays an important role in Greek mythology and is one of its major legacies. It is still present in the way people react to events. The sense of destiny can offer comfort, relief, and freedom from responsibility because, if something is "meant to be," no one is to blame. Fate doesn't always bring tragic consequences; it can also bring good fortune, love, and happiness. It can be the source of perpetual hope.

"JUST DESERTS"   Early on, we learn that Santa Claus rewards only good children, while naughty ones receive a piece of coal, getting what they deserve. Life without the myth of deserving is unimaginable. It underlies our whole system of justice, for example. It probably acts as a deterrent to untold numbers of people who might otherwise commit crimes, or may even provide comfort to people who are serving long sentences in prison for crimes they did commit: "After all, I *deserve* this."

"US VERSUS THEM"   The desire to be part of a group and therefore at odds with people in another group is well established. It may encourage school spirit and often promotes family unity, but it can also lead to gang rivalries, wars, mob violence, and a lifelong distrust and hatred of "the other." Coaches and sergeants urge their charges to fight more ferociously by reinforcing the "us/them" distinction, and in time of war it can help to bring about both national unity and inflexible mistrust of the enemy. Belonging to a privileged group underlies the racism implicit in those films of the early twentieth century in which ethnic minorities are treated as inferior. The belief presupposes the superiority of one group over the inferiority, or even non-humanness, of another.

"THERE'S ALWAYS ROOM AT THE TOP"   Belief that anyone can achieve unlimited success is both a spur to ambition and a cause for major disappointment in those who never get there. The very word "top" is loaded with preconceptions and expectations. At the top are corporate executives, entertainers, athletes, and political leaders. The pervasiveness of the belief is indicated by sales of how-to books and enrollment in seminars promising a quick and guaranteed path to the top. (Of course, if "the top" is to have any meaning, there must be a lot of people underneath.)

Literature abounds with tales of those who buy into the mythology of upward mobility. The Horatio Alger novels of the early twentieth century all have heroes or heroines who start off poor and become wealthy either by hard work or accident. (The popular novels by Jacqueline Suzanne from later in the century have heroines who do the same, although their success sometimes comes from calculated marriages.) There are also a plethora of films based on performers who inevitably become stars after early disappointments. The myth is so deeply ingrained in Western culture that many believe it is their *duty* to move up.

"ISN'T THAT JUST LIKE A (MAN/WOMAN)?"   **Gender roles** —models of appropriate behavior and functions for men and women—were for a long time codified and unchanging. For many cultures, these have been religiously defined, and failure to observe the rules can have serious consequences. Even among those who consider themselves enlightened, old myths that men are this and women are that often lurk in the background. Men like adventure movies; women like romances and romantic comedies. Men never ask for directions when lost. Women never pass a shoe store without walking in. In 2004, Martha Stewart, called the queen of the domestic divas, was arrested, tried, convicted, and jailed in a business scandal. Her supporters argued that she had been the victim of the masculine cultural mythology that resents a woman's success: The woman who gets ahead is "pushy," "bossy," and "unfeminine"; a successful man is "assertive" and, often, a widely admired executive.

"EVERYBODY DOES IT" The equation that goodness equals weakness accounts for the cynical acceptance of cheating, or "cutting corners," as an understandably human practice at all ages and places: on the playground, in class, in a courtroom or personnel office. Using test answers dishonestly acquired is only one example, with "everybody does it" furnishing the rationale. It is, after all, the way of the world. To the victor belong the spoils, presumably, regardless of how the spoils are obtained.

Does anybody think mythology has no relevance to ordinary living?

How Myth Influences the Humanities

3.6 *How do myths influence the humanities?*

Throughout the rest of this book, especially when we introduce you to the formal disciplines, we shall have many occasions to point out the myths, stories, and archetypes that underlie a given work. In the final section of this chapter, we want to offer some prominent uses of myth found in literature, drama, and cinema. You will see how a knowledge of mythology greatly enhances the appreciation of what is read or seen.

Myth and Poetry

"The Lotos-eaters" by the British poet Alfred, Lord Tennyson (1809-1892) is more meaningful, for example, if we are familiar with the myth that appears in Homer's *Odyssey* about a seductive land where Odysseus' ship is driven by a storm. Here the lotus plant grows in abundance, and the inhabitants urge the shipmates to eat it, as they do—but the effect, a blissful forgetfulness, is so powerful that the sailors must eventually be dragged back to their ship and chained to their oars. The trance-like state induced by the lotos plants is beautifully described in the last stanza of Tennyson's poem, where "surely, surely slumber is more sweet" than the boring toils and tragedies of the daily lives we all lead. The myth of the lotos-eaters infuses Tennyson's poem with a relevance to his own age—the beginning of the Industrial Revolution—where life must have seemed particularly despairing.

> VIII
> *The Lotos blooms below the barren peak:*
> *The Lotos blows by every winding creek:*
> *All day the wind breathes low with mellower tone:*
> *Thro' every hollow cave and alley lone*
> *Round and round the spicy downs the yellow Lotos-dust is blown.*
> *We have had enough of action, and of motion we,*
> *Roll'd to starboard, roll'd to larboard, when the surge was seething free,*
> *Where the wallowing monster spouted his foam-fountains in the sea.*
> *Let us swear an oath, and keep it with an equal mind,*
> *In the hollow Lotos-land to live and lie reclined*
> *On the hills like Gods together, careless of mankind.*
> *For they lie beside their nectar, and the bolts are hurl'd*
> *Far below them in the valleys, and the clouds are lightly curl'd*
> *Round their golden houses, girdled with the gleaming world:*
> *Where they smile in secret, looking over wasted lands,*
> *Blight and famine, plague and earthquake, roaring deeps and fiery sands,*
> *Clanging fights, and flaming towns, and sinking ships, and praying hands.*
> *But they smile, they find a music centred in a doleful song*
> *Steaming up, a lamentation and an ancient tale of wrong,*
> *Like a tale of little meaning tho' the words are strong;*
> *Chanted from an ill-used race of men that cleave the soil,*
> *Sow the seed, and reap the harvest with enduring toil,*

Storing yearly little dues of wheat, and wine and oil;
Till they perish and they suffer—some, 'tis whisper'd—down in hell
Suffer endless anguish, others in Elysian valleys dwell,
Resting weary limbs at last on beds of asphodel.
Surely, surely, slumber is more sweet than toil, the shore
Than labour in the deep mid-ocean, wind and wave and oar;
O, rest ye, brother mariners, we will not wander more.[10]

Similarly, we can read *Endymion* by the English poet John Keats (1795–1821) more easily if we know the fable about the handsome shepherd who, while sleeping on a hill, so arouses the moon goddess with love for him that she casts a spell causing him to sleep forever. He will never wake up, but he will never grow old. The myth of eternal youth is universal for obvious reasons.

Our reading of the poem *Prometheus Unbound* by the English poet Percy Bysshe Shelley (1792–1822) is enhanced by knowing the story of the mythical Titan who stole fire from the gods, giving it to mortals. Prometheus was punished for his transgression by being shackled to a gigantic rock; every day thereafter a huge vulture ate his liver, which would grow back the following day while the vulture waited to devour it once again, the cycle of torture repeated without end.

Myth, Death, and Visions of an Afterlife

Even when death comes in mythology, there is always the question of what comes afterward. Two major kinds of afterlife are described: one sometimes known as paradise, the other a dark, often dismal—and in many stories, eternally painful—place.

In Greek mythology, the souls of brave warriors were believed to reside in an eternal paradise called the Elysian Fields after having been spared the pain of death. When it came time for them to die in battle, a benevolent god lifted them up and escorted them to a place of peace. Similarly, in the Arthurian tales of the Middle Ages, King Arthur's body is placed on a magical ship that bears him to the far-off land of Avalon, where he will presumably live on forever. And in the twentieth-century mythic trilogy *The Lord of the Rings*, Frodo, the hobbit hero, embarks on a long and treacherous journey to destroy the magic ring that has caused so much pain and death. After bringing peace to Middle Earth, which is his world, he sails away to the West—perhaps to an afterlife, but certainly to a form of paradise—in the company of elves. In an ending that resembles Arthur's fate, author J.R.R. Tolkien describes Frodo's final seaward journey in unforgettable terms:

> *Then Frodo . . . went aboard; and the sails were drawn up, and the wind blew, and slowly the ship slipped away down the long grey firth; and . . . went out into the High Sea and passed on into the West, until at last on a night of rain Frodo smelled a sweet fragrance and heard the sound of singing that came over the water. And then . . . the grey rain-curtain turned all to silver glass and was rolled back, and he beheld white shores and beyond them a far green country under a swift sunrise.*[11]

In view of today's environmental concerns, the myth of a green afterlife has much appeal. The Greeks also had Hades, or the Underworld, where the souls of nonwarriors had to live after crossing the River Styx that led from the land of the living to the land of the dead. While it was dark and cheerless, it was not, however, a place of torment.

Myth as Teacher

Much of Asia's rich mythology is relayed in the form of **parables**, simple stories told to illustrate moral or spiritual lessons, as in the story of Ryokan, which suggests that we should all be generous with whatever possessions we have:

> *Once there was a monk named Ryokan living a simple life of poverty and meditation. One night a thief enters the monk's little hut and steals his food as well as the clothes off his back. Instead of being angry, Ryokan says "I only wish I could give you the moonlight on my floor."*[12]

Roman mythology is kept alive in a number of enduring tales, such as that of Baucis and Philemon. Rumors of their virtue reach the ears of Jupiter, king of the gods, who has become so disgusted with humanity's evil ways that he plans to destroy it and start over. But before doing so, he decides to see for himself whether there is any truth to the rumors. Disguised as a poorly clothed, weary, and hungry traveler, he visits the neighborhood of Baucis and Philemon, going first from house to house. Everyone turns him away until he reaches the home of the reputedly virtuous pair. Poor as they are, they welcome him, build a fire for him, and give him all the food they have.

After the god finally reveals his true identity, he bids them name their wish. So they ask to be allowed eventually to die together. Jupiter grants the wish; and when they die, he transforms them into intertwining trees.

Myth in the World Today

As we have seen, myths can become part of our everyday awareness. We can find mythology in films, television shows, literature—even comic strips. Who are Superman and Batman if not mythic characters? And for that matter, who are Dominic and Brian, the lead characters in one of the most popular film franchises of the twenty-first century, *The Fast and the Furious* (Figure 3.6), if not modern incarnations of mythic heroes? Surely we all know that no myth contains the full truth. Moreover, some mythology interferes with our judgment, and some is downright superstition. Even so, there are those dazzling mazes and those magic rings and the wonderful stranger who comes out of nowhere. We need a little mist in our gardens.

In a little known yet powerfully haunting novel, *Memoirs of a Midget* (1921) by British author and poet Walter de la Mare (1873–1956), the tiny heroine is at one point forced to earn a meager living in a carnival sideshow, watching as people either laugh or show cruel pity. After many nights of agony, during which she learns not to look at the crowd, a mysterious force suddenly compels her to raise her head:

> . . . my eyes chanced to fall on a figure, standing in the clouded light a little apart. He was dressed in a high-peaked hat and a long and seemingly brown cassock-like garment, with buttoned tunic and silver-buckled belt. Spurs were on his boots, a light whip in his hand. Aloof, his head a little bowed down, his face in profile, he stood there, framed in the opening, dusky, level-featured, deep-eyed—a Stranger. What in me rushed as if on wings into his silent company? A passionate longing beyond words burned in me. I seemed to be

Figure 3.6 Vin Diesel and the late Paul Walker as Dominic Toretto and Brian O'Connor in *The Fast and the Furious*, 2001.

What do these characters have to do with mythology? Why might we call them "mythic"?

Scott Garfield/Universal Pictures/Everett Collection

carried away into a boundless wilderness—stunted trees, salt in the air, a low, enormous stretch of night sky, space; and this man, master of soul and solitude.[13]

Nothing is made of this incident for a long time. We forget about it. The story moves forward as if it never happened, until one night the midget disappears, leaving behind only this cryptic note: *I have gone with him.* The identity of the stranger is never revealed—or even whether there had been anyone there at all. We never know where the midget has gone or what fate befell her. Yet none of that seems to matter. Have we not wished, at least once, that a dreadful problem could be solved by the sudden appearance of an outsider who knew all about us and knew exactly what to do?

Real life has its outsiders, its strangers, such as the paramedics who respond to frantic 911 calls within minutes and who always seem to know exactly what to do. Mythology is alive and well. We can be thankful; we need it.

Looking Back

In this chapter,

- we defined "myth" and "mythology,"
- we explored what we mean by "archetypes" and examined the roles played in mythology by various archetypes, including the hero, the power of numbers, the circle, the journey, the garden, and the role of gods as mortal beings,
- we discussed why humans create myths as explanations for otherwise unexplainable events,

including the creation of the world and human suffering,

- we summarized some myths of childhood, and
- we examined the role of mythology in popular culture, as well as its foundational role in the study of the humanities.

Key Terms

anthropomorphic Having human characteristics.

archetype A model (e.g. the hero, the circle, the journey) that, through mythology, becomes part of our subconscious and an addition to the way we organize our thinking about ourselves, human beings in general, and the nature of the universe.

collective unconscious Jung's phrase for the universality of many myths and archetypes among cultures, some of which could not possibly have had any contact with each other.

gender roles The way acceptable male and female behavior and functions are defined in a given culture.

monomyth Reference made by Irish novelist James Joyce to what he considered a fundamental myth of all cultures: that of the hero. Also known as the *world myth*.

The concept was developed by Joseph Campbell. In Western mythology, the hero is a special individual ordained by fate to be the doer of wondrous deeds, often as the savior of a whole group of people. In many Western myths, the hero's power does not last.

mythology (1) The collective myths of a specific culture or group of cultures; (2) the organized study of myths, either those of world cultures or of a specific culture.

myths Tales and beliefs transmitted from generation to generation, or springing up as part of the popular mind in a current generation, many containing psychological truth or fulfilling some deep-rooted need.

parable A simple story told to illustrate a moral or spiritual lesson.

PART II

Disciplines of the Humanities

Chapter 4
Literature

⌄ Learning Objectives

4.1 Define the terms "classic" and "masterpiece."

4.2 Evaluate the function that written texts can serve in establishing a cultural history.

4.3 Differentiate among forms of poetry including lyric poetry, the sonnet, haiku, religious poetry, and modern poetry.

4.4 Discuss the rise of the novel and the ways in which the form has changed in the past 100 years.

4.5 Describe how most contemporary short stories differ from earlier versions of this genre.

Figure 4.1 E. Vela, *A conversation between Don Quixote and Sancho Panza,* **19th century.** What is it about Don Quixote that has made him such a popular character for over 500 years?

Mary Evans Picture Library/Alamy

Who hasn't told a story? Who hasn't elaborated on an incident that occurred, embellished it with more excitement, more color than it had? In this sense, we are all born story-tellers.

A few become professionals at it, but anyone can become involved in what others write and thus share *their* imaginations. Alas, some of us lose interest in reading when we leave school and head off to our daily jobs. To those of you who feel this way, we issue an ardent plea: Go back and look for your imagination! You've left it somewhere. It's not lost—you can't ever *really* lose it. Pull it out of the drawer or down from the attic, wherever you've stored it. It's worth it.

How did "literature" begin? Our guess is that the literary impulse was felt long before written languages were available to preserve the earliest expressions of it. In the visual arts, cave drawings date back millennia. Using our imaginations (which we just found in that drawer), we can suppose that early (*very* early) people were already performing—dancing, chanting, and pounding away with stones and sticks. Why would we think, then, that some forms of literature didn't appear just as early in human history?

Classics and Masterpieces

4.1 *What makes a "classic"? What makes a "masterpiece"?*

Let's assume that people are natural-born poets and storytellers (and, by natural progression, readers). There is no good reason, then, to look upon literature as an esoteric art, locked away in libraries. In this chapter, we'll look carefully at a few examples of the major types, or **genres**, of literature: the epic, the poem, the novel, and the short story. We'll see how they may have evolved and what needs they may have served.

Some of the works we will study are **classics**. They have endured, and they continue to be relevant and to move us years, even centuries, after they were written. Some have earned the right to be called **masterpieces**—works that in style, execution, and resonance far exceed what other writers have created in the same genre. For example, although many poets were writing successful sonnets in Shakespeare's time, most of *his* sonnets tower above those of his contemporaries. They are more profound, more sophisticated in technique (handling of meter and rhyme), and distinguished by a more intricate use of words by a writer who may have commanded the largest vocabulary of any writer before or since. Indeed, much of our accepted wisdom springs from memorable statements in Shakespeare's poems and plays.

Some classics—but not all—also qualify as masterpieces. Time and circumstances give continuing relevance to a classic; a masterpiece can always stand on its own and will find admirers in any age—once it is discovered. Sometimes a masterpiece is not recognized as such until long after it first appears. Herman Melville's *Moby-Dick* was a commercial failure when it was published in 1851; not until scholars began writing about it in the early twentieth century did its reputation as a masterpiece begin to grow.

This chapter addresses itself to literature of the past and present that springs from the soul of human beings and through which we come to understand ourselves and others with whom we share the amazing condition of being alive. We are going to discuss a few representative works that have achieved literary distinction, some well-known, others less familiar but all with much to offer.

Literature as History

4.2 *What function do written texts—literature—serve in establishing cultural histories?*

At some point—we don't know exactly when, except that it was many thousands of years ago—groups must have felt the need to identify, to *define* themselves. They knew they had common bonds that came from their strivings. Imagine how you would feel if you suddenly developed amnesia and had no clue about your past history. Wouldn't you become obsessed with the desire to locate yourself in time and space?

The Basic Literary Impulse: Identity

Early in *The Grapes of Wrath* (1939) by the American novelist John Steinbeck (1902–1968), a simple incident illustrates how important it is to people to leave behind a record of themselves. Steinbeck saw the westward migration of dispossessed Oklahoma farmers of the 1930s as an example of how human society developed. Trying to get to California, the longed-for promised land of abundant work and prosperity, these "Okies" were despised nobodies robbed of their roots and their identity. When a family pulled into an orchard looking for work, the question was always "How many hands for picking?"—never "What is your name?"

During the arduous journey, Grampa Joad, patriarch of the novel's central family, dies. The family buries him by the side of the road in some desolate, nameless place. But leaving the body unidentified is unthinkable. His grandson Tom writes a brief note and puts it on the body. The note says, with all the simplicity of a folk poem:

> *This here is William James Joad, dyed of a stroke, old, old man. His fokes bured him becaws they got no money to pay for funerls. Nobody kilt him. Just a stroke an he dyed.*[1]

Some pharaohs of ancient Egypt spent most of their adult lives designing their own monumental tombs, many of which survive to this day. The great pyramids identify not only the rulers but the culture that bore them. Egypt established its past and present identity through art and architecture. Other cultures did it through stories, often passed on orally, and in some cases their efforts can be traced back thousands of years. The literary impulse was originally the same thing as the need to establish identity and a history.

An Early Epic: *Gilgamesh*

In the days when literature was transmitted and preserved either orally or in some kind of written form (or sometimes both), the **epic** emerged as the literary genre of many early societies. An epic is a long narrative poem recounting the actions and adventures of a hero who exemplifies strength, courage, and cunning, but not necessarily moral virtue. When survival was the predominant concern of a people, their epic heroes had to seem unconquerable, as indeed they hoped their society was.

One of the oldest epics is *Gilgamesh*, the story of a tyrannical king who lived around 4,000 years ago in a land that is now Iraq. Inscribed on 12 tablets, *Gilgamesh* was discovered in the ruins of an Assyrian library dating from the seventh century BCE. Classical scholars believe the story has its origins (as do many epics) in a cycle of songs and poems created to celebrate the deeds of a real person, a king in the city of Uruk in 2750 BCE. Over the course of a thousand years, the songs and poems became popular throughout Mesopotamia, and eventually Babylonian poets transformed them into a singular epic poem that was compiled, scholars suggest, by a Babylonian priest named Shin-eqi-unninni.

Central to the poem are the swashbuckling exploits of a superman. So formidable did Gilgamesh become, so devastating to all who stood in his way, that even the gods were intimidated. So they created a gentler, more compassionate counterpart named Enkidu. Some scholars have interpreted Enkidu as Gilgamesh's other self, the side with humane principles. Early in the epic, the two superheroes engage in a tremendous wrestling match that ends in a tie, suggesting that both aggressiveness and kindness are necessary for human existence.

Enkidu dies in the story, but Gilgamesh lives on, undefeated, and still a mortal problem for the immortal gods. Was the author saying that, even though kindness is a necessary element in the human personality, it is less likely to outlast aggressiveness?

Many early cultures created poetic epics that began to establish and support cultural identities. Among these are the *Mahabharata*, from the Indian subcontinent; *Sundiata*, or *Son-Jara*, from Africa; Britain's *Beowulf*; and the *Edda* saga from Norway.

An Early Masterpiece: Homer's *Iliad*

The *Iliad* marks a considerable change in the nature and purpose of the genre. Like *Gilgamesh*, it has a showdown between two supermen. The *Iliad* is unusual, however; it not only provides its audience with a history and an identity—the typical work of an epic—but it also extols the glory and virtue of an enemy.

The *Iliad* is not only a prime example of early literature but one of the treasures of human culture. It has been traditionally attributed to Homer, who may have lived anytime between 1200 and 850 BCE. For a long time, classical scholarship tended to believe that the poem was composed over several centuries and therefore could not be attributed to a single poet. More recent scholarship, however, suggests the poem is too unified *not* to have been the work of a single genius.

When it comes to very ancient works, assigning authorship is always a risky business, but as the traditional joke says, "If it wasn't by Homer, it may have been written by somebody else named Homer." Nothing is definitively known about Homer except that, according to legend, he may have been blind.

THE *ILIAD* AS CULTURAL HISTORY   The *Iliad* seems to have been an ambitious effort to give the nation of Greece a cultural history, a sense of continuity. The epic describes events that occur in the last few weeks of the ten-year war against Troy, known to Homer as Ilion, hence the poem's title, which means "The Song of Ilion." Why song? The answer may be that those who initially performed the poem could remember the lines better if they were sung.

The absence of written languages is a most important point to remember about much early literature. Even though *Gilgamesh* was discovered on clay tablets, it was set down in *cuneiform*, wedge-shaped characters that **symbolize** things; it was not a language as such, with words that stand for things. Certainly a work such as the *Iliad* was more likely performed orally than written and read. A bard—or rhapsodist, as he was also known—was a professional man hired and paid by powerful rulers and their court to present their "history." Naturally that history was about the exploits of ancestral rulers who were also brave warriors. Common people would not enter the literary scene in any major way for more than 2,000 years.

The *Iliad* is subtitled "The Wrath of Achilles." Achilles qualifies as a mythic hero; he shows great prowess in battle and has a reputation for being unconquerable—with only one tragic weakness. His mother, hoping to make him immortal, holds the infant Achilles by one heel and dips him into the river Styx. Thus the heel she holds remains vulnerable, and it eventually leads to his demise. We still use the term "Achilles' heel" today to describe an individual's vulnerable spot.

Homer's epic begins with the story of how Agamemnon, one of the Greek generals, reluctantly surrenders his mistress, a Trojan captive, in a prisoner exchange, but insists on taking Briseis, the mistress of Achilles, for himself. In retribution, the Greek hero Achilles refuses to fight, and his withdrawal turns the tide in favor of the Trojans.

Early listeners among the Greeks, hearing the story for the first time, would have been in suspense wondering how their ancestors managed a victory.

According to one popular legend, the Greeks offered the Trojans a huge wooden horse as a peace-making gift (Figure 4.2). Inside were Greek soldiers, who crept out in the middle of the night, slaughtering both citizens and every royal prince they could find. Historians believe that the story of the horse was totally fictitious; at any rate, it does not appear in the *Iliad*.

Much later, the story of the Trojan War was part of a great literary work, the Roman epic the *Aeneid* by Virgil (70–19 BCE), where the story does appear. The *Aeneid* attributes the founding of Rome to Aeneas, a Trojan prince who manages to escape the slaughter. A Roman writer would no doubt have been only too delighted to depict the Greeks as devious, dishonorable warriors, using gimmicks like the wooden horse to win the war. If the seeds of the Roman Empire were in Troy, and Troy had been conquered, it is in the spirit of literature-as-history to show that the conquest was an inglorious one.

That the story of the horse is not found in the *Iliad* does not, however, mean that the work is written as a chest-beating rah-rah glorification of a Greek victory. Not that the Greeks are shown as cowards. Achilles was already established as a hero of titanic proportions, and Greek sympathizers would have waited eagerly for him to re-assert himself. The plot is complicated by the fact that almost all of the gods become involved. Some side with the Greeks, others with the Trojans; and the tide of battle flows both ways until Achilles and Agamemnon are reconciled, and Achilles agrees to meet the gallant Trojan warrior Hector in single combat to determine the final outcome.

Had the victory over Troy been accomplished solely by Achilles' slaying of Hector, the *Iliad* might have been a prime example of literature meant to glorify a nation's past. We cannot know whether Homer intended it as such. But what emerged contains not only the Greek victory, but also the tragedy of the losing side.

Hector, a prince and Troy's most important defender, is treated so sympathetically that the true climax of the epic is Hector's death at the hands of Achilles, who ties the

Figure 4.2 Giovanni Tiepolo, *Procession of the Wooden Horse into Troy*, 1760.
Although the story of the Trojan horse doesn't appear in the *Iliad*, it has taken hold in popular imagination. Why do you think this story became so well-known?
World History Archive/Alamy

body of the slain warrior to his chariot and drags it ignominiously around the walls of Troy, afterwards selling it back to the Trojans. The *Iliad*, while rooted in Greek history, is essentially a tragic poem about a fallen hero—a hero who was not Greek! Virgil's *Aeneid* is a nationalistic poem. The *Iliad*, ultimately, is not.

Aeneas is portrayed as the perfect hero: strong, brave, and intelligent. Troy is shown to have fallen because the destiny of Aeneas was to found a city much greater than Troy. Yet, although the *Aeneid* is as thrilling and as wondrous as an epic should be, it is less gripping than the human drama of the *Iliad*.

THE *ILIAD* AS TRAGEDY   There exists, of course, the possibility that the *Iliad* went through several centuries of change as a memorized poem, sung generation after generation by unknown bards. It may have been gradually altered to become a tragic epic. The Greeks, after all, developed the art of theater, and their dramas were originally tragic in nature, indicating that, as a nation, they loved to be moved by stories of noble people who suffer a downfall. In the plays, the fall of the hero comes about because of a fatal flaw in an otherwise good person. The *Iliad*, as we have it today, anticipates the age of Greek tragedy.

Does Hector have a tragic flaw? In a sense, he does. He is characterized as a brave warrior who goes beyond what is expected of him because, like all warriors, he wants to be remembered for great deeds of valor. The ambition to be known for bravery is characteristic of a hero, to be sure, but it can also be a fatal weakness born of the pride that drives human greatness. Pride would become the major theme of the Greek—and indeed many later—tragedies. The *Iliad* may be said to be the first major work in the literature of the Western world, not only for its soaring poetry but for the *humanization* of its major characters, Hector in particular.

"Humanization" in this sense explains what makes certain literary characters stand apart from others. It is very close to a term that actors often use to define what they are looking for in a character they're going to play: *polarity*, or the binary extremes that exist in people's natures. In playing a role, the actor first determines major characteristics defined by the playwright—for example, *he is a jealous husband; she is a faithful wife*. Then the actor tries to locate the opposite of these characteristics—*he loves his wife very much and doesn't want to lose her; though faithful, she resents his jealousy and secretly wishes she could have a fling*. Great writers have always known that human beings are never just one thing or another. If characters are given certain unwavering traits instead of the contradictory natures we all share, the result is melodrama, rather than tragedy.

Like all tragic heroes, Hector has a blind side. Several times before his mortal combat with Achilles, his arch enemy, he has been warned that he almost certainly will die. His wife, Andromache, has pleaded with him not to leave her and their son. Her own father and seven brothers were slain by Achilles in earlier battles: There is, she tells him, no way to defeat this warrior who is surely favored by the gods. But Hector is resolute. He firmly believes that he and he alone has the strength and courage to defeat Achilles.

> *Nay, go thou to the house and busy thyself*
> *with thine own tasks, the loom and the distaff,*
> *and bid thy handmaids ply their work: but war*
> *shall be for men, for all, but most of all for me,*
> *of them that dwell in Ilios.*[2]

Most of all for me.

This is not only courage; this is also pride. Here is the polarity in Hector's character; here is Homer's humanization of him. Hector *assumes* he is the only one who can save Troy, just as so many human beings close their minds to the possibility that someone else might be able to perform a difficult task better than they can.

This supreme confidence in himself causes Hector to fight with reckless abandon against overwhelming odds—and to fail, weakening his city's defenses as well.

To create a great tragic figure like Hector is to create an ironic contradiction. The very thing that destroys Hector (and Troy) is his bravery, but bravery is also the source of human greatness. The suggestion—to be echoed over and over in many enduring literary works—is that *to be great is to be tragic*. Did Homer make this discovery so many thousands of years ago? In composing the *Iliad*, he was apparently caught up with something more imposing than victory, more glorious: the realization that human beings in their finest hour always reach beyond their abilities; that they will never achieve the goals they set for themselves but must nonetheless pursue them only to fail. If this is a truth of existence, then the question is whether it is better to have failed at something tremendous than to have stayed within limitations and won trivial successes. Great literature inspires big, unanswerable questions like this.

THE *ILIAD* AS MASTERPIECE   The *Iliad* deserves its place of honor as the first literary masterpiece of the Western world. The poet establishes a fundamental principle of much great literature: *real life is not a simple struggle between good and evil*. Hector may be the most noble character in the *Iliad*, but Achilles is not therefore the villain; indeed, by most definitions (including the ones we have provided here), he is its hero. The subtitle of the poem, "The Wrath of Achilles," suggests that the warrior's outrage against Agamemnon is indeed the force that drives the plot. Homer as historian presents, without judgment, the story of Achilles' anger as he knows it. If the author is less compassionate toward the Greek warrior than he is toward Hector, he duly recognizes the man's strength and courage, as well as his place in Greek history.

What makes the *Iliad* not only a great epic but also a great tragedy is, however, the struggle inside Hector between his desire for glory and his understanding of his wife's anguish, his sensitivity to her ardent pleas born out of his deep love for her. As a reader, you will find that the impact of many masterpieces arises from conflict *within* the characters, not *between* them.

The Russian playwright Anton Chekhov (1860–1904) observed that evil flows *through* people, not *from* them. Hector's pride leads him into a violent battle in which not only he but many others are slain. Achilles' refusal to fight costs the Greeks many lives and a more honorable victory. Both men believed their cause was righteous. Neither man could be described as evil, yet their actions had disastrous consequences. That is the way of tragedy and, as the great writers such as Homer knew, the tragic way of humanity.

If Homer had lived in the modern world, who knows how he might have responded to the Holocaust, the 9/11 terrorist attacks, or the bitter fighting in Iraq, Afghanistan, and the Middle East? Big questions, difficult answers. Great literature, whether from the past or the present, makes us feel, makes us think—and inevitably we are changed.

Poetry

4.3   *How do the forms of poetry discussed here—the lyric poem, sonnet, haiku, religious poetry, and modern poetry—differ from one another?*

Though we have talked about it here as a form of history, the epic is also narrative poetry that tells a story in rhythmic language. Narrative, as found in *Gilgamesh* and the *Iliad*, was probably the earliest genre of poetry; but as early societies grew in sophistication and produced artists who could be identified by their style, technique, and typical themes, poetry evolved into numerous forms. By the time of the Greek poet Sappho in the sixth century BCE, poets were highly trained and respected members of society. They worked in a written language expected to be elevated above everyday talk—that is to say, above *prose*.

Lyric Poetry

The Romans inherited from the Greeks the desire to cultivate the arts of civilization. These included the pleasurable pursuits of good food, wine, mineral baths and massage, and all forms of sexual expression. But civilized pleasures also included historical writings such as the epic, as well as poems expressive of personal feelings. Especially popular among the Romans was **lyric poetry**, so named because it was usually sung to the accompaniment of a *lyre*, a stringed instrument similar to but much smaller than the harp.

SAPPHO: THE FIRST LYRIC POET?   Sappho may have been the first poet on record to write about deeply personal feelings, even referring to herself by name in poetic prayers to the gods. Sappho (Figure 4.3) is known to have accompanied herself on the lyre and may have composed most of the music as well. She would have used the kind of musical notation that we know existed at the time, but so far none of the music has been discovered.

Among Sappho's favorite subjects are the joys and the sorrows of being in love. Apparently a woman of strong physical needs, she introduced into literature one of its most enduring themes: unrequited passion—a theme that, as we shall see, became wildly popular during the Renaissance and, indeed, is central to many contemporary popular songs.

In one of her most famous poems, *Ode to Aphrodite*, Sappho implores the goddess of love to have pity on her as she languishes in the agony of romantic frustration:

Figure 4.3 Roman bust of Sappho, copied from a lost Hellenic bust, 2nd century.
Do you read—or write—love poetry? What accounts for the enduring popularity of love as a literary subject?
Prisma Archivo/Alamy

ODE TO APHRODITE

> *… and thou, gracious Vision,*
> *Leaned with face that smiled in immortal beauty,*
> *Leaned to me and asked, "What misfortune threatened?*
> *Why I had called thee?"*
>
> *"What my frenzied heart craved in utter yearning,*
> *Whom its wild desire would persuade to passion?*
> *What disdainful charms, madly worshipped, slight thee?*
> *Who wrongs thee, Sappho?"*
>
> *"She that fain would fly, she shall quickly follow,*
> *She that now rejects, yet with gifts shall woo thee,*
> *She that heeds thee not, soon shall love to madness,*
> *Love thee, the loth one!"*
>
> *Come to me now thus, Goddess, and release me*
> *From distress and pain; …*[3]

Other writers may have carried this theme to greater heights, but Sappho will always be remembered as a distinguished pioneer in poetic art—as well as the founder of the first known school for women.

Lyric poetry also flourished in Rome, and again the primary subject was love, a popular Roman pastime. Much of this verse is highly artificial: high-flown words that professional poets knew would please their public. Since upper-class Roman women wielded considerable power and independence and were known to reject suitors, the theme of unrequited passion was often expressed from the male point of view. And to this theme, many Roman poets added that of betrayal and infidelity, of a sworn lover's being false.

The lyric poetry of Greece and Rome was largely forgotten during the early and late Middle Ages, when poetry, like art, became for Christians a way of expressing the mystic experiences of the devout, as they tried to escape from worldly temptations and find God. But the classical theme of love, including the pain it could inflict, were revived during the Renaissance (beginning in the fourteenth century), when women once again claimed the right to reject men's pleas for their favors. And during the early nineteenth century, in what was known as the Romantic period, some think that British poets including John Keats and Percy Bysshe Shelley brought lyric poetry to its fullest flowering.

The Sonnet

The **sonnet** is a 14-line poetic form first employed by Italian poets in the early Renaissance, during the revival of interest in classical art and literature. While the form was modern in its time, the usual subject—the pain caused by unsatisfied love—was of classical origin. The poet Francesco Petrarca (1304–1374), known to the English-speaking world as Petrarch, played a large part in the classical revival. He recognized the genius of the *Iliad*, for example, and had it translated into Latin. He is best known, however, for having developed the sonnet. The demands of the form, the discipline of having to put all his thoughts and feelings into 14 rhymed and rhythmic lines, challenged him, as it has challenged poets ever since.

Over the centuries, a number of variations on the sonnet have emerged, but the basic form is still the Petrarchan. The rhythm, called iambic pentameter, also became the fundamental rhythm of English poetry and is closely identified with the sonnets and plays of William Shakespeare, who was heavily influenced by Petrarch.

In poetry written in **iambic pentameter**, each line has five repetitions of an unstressed syllable followed by a stressed syllable. Each pair of syllables is called a *foot*, similar to a bar of music. For example, the word *decide* is an iambic foot. The line "Decide on when to go or not, my dear" is an example of iambic pentameter: It consists of five repetitions of the pattern; when we read it aloud, we hear the accents on every second syllable. Writing 14 lines following the rigid pattern of rhythm without that pattern being heavily obvious—and therefore boring—isn't easy.

In good sonnets, the lines have a sense of inevitability about them and give no suggestion that the poet was straining to keep the rhythm going or to seek rhymes. When read aloud, the poem should not sound overly rhythmic, like a waltz being played for a beginner's dance class. That the meter is there should be a happy discovery. In the following lines from a mercifully obscure poem, the rhythm (not to mention the rhyme) hits you squarely in the face.

> *He writes to us most every day, and how his letters thrill us!*
> *I can't describe the joys with which his quaint expressions fill us.*

The English language falls easily into iambic patterns; ordinary English speech frequently tends toward the iambic. Great poets in the language, like Shakespeare, know that rhythm has an emotional effect (as it does in music), but they don't want it to overwhelm the words. Compare the above lines with the opening lines from one of Shakespeare's most famous sonnets (XVIII). Note that to discover the iambic meter you have to distort the natural flow of the words.

> *Shall I compare thee to a summer's day?*
> *Thou art more lovely and more temperate.*[4]

The challenge to sonnet writers grows more rigorous still. Each line must fit not only the rhythmic pattern, but also a defined rhyme scheme. The poet must find rhyming words that somehow retain a sense of spontaneity and elegance. Rhyme may have originated as an aid to memory, but it remains an essential ingredient of much poetry; it is still employed by poets who like the musical resonance that rhyme can create, as well as the challenge of having the rhymes not seem forced. In Petrarchan and Shakespearean sonnets, rhymes are placed in certain sequences and cannot be varied. The great poets are somehow able to stay within the bounds of the rhyme scheme and still find freedom of thought.

THE PETRARCHAN OR ITALIAN SONNET The sonnet form popularized by Petrarch is characterized by an octet (eight lines) with the rhyme scheme *abbaabba*, followed by a sestet (six lines) that can be more flexible but generally follows a rhyme scheme of either *cdecde*, or *cdcdcd*. The two parts of the sonnet typically have different functions: The first eight lines introduce a problem, a desire, or a doubt, while the sestet may solve the problem, or respond to the desire or doubt—or simply comment on the earlier lines.

Here is one of the famous sonnets written by Petrarch to the love of his life, a 23-year-old married woman he called Laura. "Love's Inconsistency," translated by Sir Thomas Wyatt, captures the mixture of pain and joy well known to everyone who has fallen deeply into a love that is not returned.

LOVE'S INCONSISTENCY

> *I find no peace, and all my war is done;*
> *I fear and hope, I burn and freeze likewise*
> *I fly above the wind, yet cannot rise;*
> *And nought I have, yet all the world I seize on;*
> *That looseth, nor locketh, holdeth me in prison,*
> *And holds me not, yet can I 'scape no wise;*
> *Nor lets me live, nor die, at my devise,*
> *And yet of death it giveth none occasion.*
> *Without eyes I see, and without tongue I plain;*
> *I wish to perish, yet I ask for health;*
> *I love another, and yet I hate myself;*
> *I feed in sorrow, and laugh in all my pain;*
> *Lo, thus displeaseth me both death and life,*
> *And my delight is causer of my grief.*[5]

Many of the rhymes are not exact, but we may assume the translator had a difficult time being faithful to Petrarch's original words in Italian. "Done" and "seize on" are stretching verse conventions quite a bit, as are "prison" and "occasion" and "life" and "grief" in the concluding couplet. Scholars have noted that the rhyme scheme developed by the great poets of the Italian Renaissance, including Petrarch, is more amenable to the Italian language than to English. In Italian, many words use the same endings, and finding multiple rhymes for one sound is easier than it is in English, where endings are much less consistent.

SHAKESPEARE'S SONNETS Among the glories of literature in our language are the 154 sonnets penned by William Shakespeare (1564–1616), universally acknowledged as the master of English verse, not only for the complexity of his thought, but also for the unsurpassed manner in which he handles both rhythm and rhyme.

Shakespeare's favored rhyme scheme differed from Petrarch's; most of his sonnets use an *ababcdcdefefgg* pattern, perhaps because it is more accommodating to the English language. Perhaps because finding rhymes in English can be so challenging, much English and American poetry—most of the speeches in the *plays* of Shakespeare, for example—abandon rhyme altogether. **Blank verse** is poetic language that has rhythm but not rhyme. You probably wouldn't want to listen to a play in which the dialogue rhymed like an Italian sonnet. But one of the marvels of the Shakespearean play is that the rhythm is there underneath the dialog—like a faint drum—but is seldom obvious to the ear.

Shakespeare's plays are written for the most part in unrhymed iambic pentameter. When Shakespeare ends a scene with a **couplet**, two lines that rhyme, he is using a poetic scheme that might seem obvious and undramatic in lesser hands, but he manages to make the rhymes seem perfectly natural. Here is Hamlet's famous couplet spoken after he learns that his uncle murdered his father, whose ghost has demanded vengeance, a violent crime that the young man is afraid he may not have the will to commit:

> *The time is out of joint: O cursed spite,*
> *That ever I was born to set it right!*

Though Shakespeare takes rhyming liberties in his sonnets from time to time, one aspect of his genius certainly has to be an extraordinary vocabulary (said to have included over 30,000 words) from which he was able to draw forth words that perfectly fit rhythm, rhyme, and meaning. The sonnets are generally expressions of love, sometimes obsessive adoration, which is not always returned.

The identity of the person (or persons) to whom these poems are addressed has aroused considerable debate among Shakespearean scholars. However, poetry was popular during the Elizabethan age (sixteenth-century England) and the subject matter was generally love in both its positive and negative guises. In this respect, Elizabethan poetry was for its time similar to the popular songs of the 1930s and 1940s with **lyrics** that either extolled the beauty of the beloved or mourned the heartbreak of a broken romance. Like the songwriters of those times, Elizabethan poets did not always write from personal experience. Writing good poetry was a profitable business, and the youthful Shakespeare, who came to the big city of London from the small town of Stratford-upon-Avon without a great deal of money, realized he might be able to support himself with his skills as a writer of both plays and poems. In Sonnet XXIX, he speaks of the joy that love can bring.

SONNET XXIX

> *When, in disgrace with fortune and men's eyes,*
> *I all alone beweep my outcast state*
> *And trouble deaf heaven with my bootless cries*
> *And look upon myself and curse my fate,*
> *Wishing me like to one more rich in hope,*
> *Featured like him, like him with friends possess'd,*
> *Desiring this man's art and that man's scope,*
> *With what I most enjoy contented least;*
> *Yet in these thoughts myself almost despising,*
> *Haply I think on thee, and then my state,*
> *Like to the lark at break of day arising*
> *From sullen earth, sings hymns at heaven's gate;*
> *For thy sweet love remember'd such wealth brings*
> *That then I scorn to change my state with kings.*

The meter of the poem cheats only here and there. "And trouble," for example, is an iambic foot with an extra, unstressed syllable, but the rest of the line follows the rhythmic pattern. The rhythm of a poem is often apparent only through **scansion**— that is, by examining the meter. Shakespeare does not want his lines to sound *overly* rhythmic. The secret of Shakespearean verse is to read it as if it were prose. Meter and rhyme are often only quietly there. They function like subtle background music in a well-directed film. The genius of the poet is his ability to merge form and content into a unified whole.

The only punctuation marks in Sonnet XXIX are two semicolons and a sprinkling of commas. As a result, the thought extends beyond the rhyming word, leading us naturally into the next line, and the rhymes are glossed over because we don't pause between lines as we read. For the most part, Shakespeare's fertile mind was able to make rhythmic and rhymed lines fit together logically and inevitably. Larks *do* arise!

USING METAPHORS AND CONCEITS   Poets often employ various forms of figurative language. A **metaphor** is a form of expression in which an abstraction such as "justice" or "love" is represented by something that is visual and concrete. Although metaphor is used in all forms of literature, it is the soul of poetry. To say "There is no justice" is less effective than a poet's telling us that "Justice is the blind lady dropping her scales."

Shakespeare lived in an age when the English language was bursting with words taken over from the various cultures with which England had interacted: German, Scandinavian, and, of course, French. The linguistic resources stored in his brain and always readily available for his pen gave him the power to express and investigate complex ideas for which verbal abstractions were not adequate vehicles. So Shakespeare also experimented with metaphor, one of the most famous examples being from *Romeo and Juliet*, when Romeo, seeing Juliet emerge onto her balcony, wonders, "What light through yonder window breaks?" and then answers his own question: "It is the east, and Juliet is the sun."

A generation younger than Shakespeare, John Donne (1572–1631) is famous for special kinds of metaphors called metaphysical **conceits**, extremely elaborate and extended associations between two dissimilar things. The circumstances of Donne's life help explain his unique manner of communicating complex feelings and ideas with wide-ranging references: He went from soldiering in English expeditions against the Spanish to the Anglican priesthood, eventually becoming dean of St. Paul's Cathedral in London. The development of his poetic works reflects these contrasting modes of living. The poems of his youth express sensuality, cynicism, and a humorous approach to life, while those of his later years exhibit a fervent spirituality. The deeply religious older man, however, retained a strong undercurrent of the younger man's sexual urges, and in the following sonnet, one of his most celebrated, the two sides of his nature merge. The struggle to achieve mystic exaltation and free the self from sin is described in sexually explicit terms.

HOLY SONNET XIV

> *Batter my heart, three person'd God; for you*
> *As yet but knock, breathe, shine, and seek to mend;*
> *That I may rise, and stand, o'erthrow me, and bend*
> *Your force, to break, blow, burn, and make me new.*
> *I, like an usurpt town, to another due,*
> *Labor to admit you, but Oh, to no end,*
> *Reason your viceroy in me, me should defend,*
> *But is captiv'd, and proves weak or untrue.*
> *Yet dearly I love you, and would be loved fain*
> *But am betroth'd unto your enemy:*
> *Divorce me, untie, or break that knot again,*
> *Take me to you, imprison me, for I*
> *Except you' enthrall me, never shall be free,*
> *Nor ever chaste, except you ravish me.*[6]

Donne expands his conceit to include not only a violent sexual encounter ("except you ravish me") but also a startling plea to God to divorce him from Satan or else to "untie" him, suggesting a kind of mystical adultery. Donne seems to have been deeply in love with his wife, perhaps explaining why it may have been natural for him to associate the sexual and spiritual bonds between two individuals. But only a great poet would have had the creative audacity to make God one of those two.

John Donne has fascinated critics and scholars for centuries as a writer of great complexity with a hidden self that may never be completely understood apart from his writing. Poetry is the key that unlocks the door to the hidden self, which has no language until a poet finds a way to liberate it.

Haiku

The Japanese **haiku** is founded on oneness with the natural world. The haiku is a short poem (no more than 17 syllables, distributed over three lines—five, seven, five) in which the writer captures an incisive thought or an image derived from direct observation of nature, but in words that ordinary language cannot match. The thought or the image becomes fixed forever in the reader's memory. Its nearest counterpart is Zen painting, in which the artist captures the essence of an object in a few brushstrokes.

Much of this poetry springs from the Buddhist tradition, which discourages lengthy rational sequences in favor of sudden intuitive insights. Many poets use haiku as a vehicle for exploring their inner selves; for bringing them into closer contact with nature; and for the delight of children, many of whom learn to love poetry from the apparent simplicity of the form.

Parallels to the haiku are abundant in the world of visual art, especially among artists who like to create a scene or express a thought using as few details as possible. In the painting shown here, *Shrike* (Figure 4.4), by the Japanese artist Miyamoto Musashi (1584–1645), a samurai and Zen Buddhist also known as Niten, the focus is on just two central objects: a bird and a caterpillar crawling up the tree branch apparently unaware that the shrike perched atop the branch will soon end its life. Like many haiku, the painting says more about life than a great abundance of words could match.

Simple Forms, Profound Meaning

In the centuries that followed the tremendous literary and dramatic achievements of Shakespeare's age, many different poetic forms became popular. Poets continued to write sonnets, but they also expressed themselves in a variety of other ways. The British artist and poet William Blake (1757–1827) was fascinated by what a serious writer might do with nursery rhymes. Blake shows in some of his verse how a simple, popular form becomes, in the hands of a master, an unforgettable way of expressing a truth that is both personal and universal.

WILLIAM BLAKE, *SONGS OF INNOCENCE* AND *SONGS OF EXPERIENCE*   Unlike today when modern poets can set down their thoughts and feelings in whatever form they deem suitable, in Blake's time it was still customary for a poet to choose among available verse models and adhere closely to their requirements. In two of his most famous achievements, collections known as *Songs of Innocence* (1789) and *Songs of Experience* (1794), Blake met the challenge of simple, childlike verse, heavily rhythmic and forcefully rhymed (unlike the Shakespearean sonnet). But underneath their sing-songy music lies Blake's sorrow over the inevitable loss of childhood innocence and the adult's unavoidable confrontation with what life holds.

The most famous poem in *Songs of Innocence* is called "The Lamb," and it is paralleled in *Songs of Experience* by another, equally famous poem, "The Tiger." Taken together, the pair make a powerful statement. Both poems speak to religious themes, but their contrasts could not be greater.

Figure 4.4 Miyamoto Niten, detail from *Shrike*, early 17th century.
How does this delicate painting reflect the techniques of haiku?
Burstein Collection/Fine Art Value/Corbis

THE LAMB

> Little Lamb, who made thee?
> Does thou know who made thee?
> Gave thee life and bid thee feed,
> By the stream and o'er the mead;
> Gave thee clothing of delight,
> Softest clothing, wooly, bright;
> Gave thee such a tender voice,
> Making all the vails rejoice.
> Little Lamb, who made thee?
> Dost thou know who made thee?
> Little Lamb, I'll tell thee,
> Little Lamb, I'll tell thee.
> He is called by thy name,
> For he calls himself a Lamb.
> He is meek, and he is mild;
> He became a little child.
> I a child, and thou a lamb,
> We are called by his name.
> Little Lamb, God bless thee!
> Little Lamb, God bless thee![7]

Even though the poem suggests a nursery rhyme and is written in a childlike style, lurking behind its surface innocence is the knowledge that lambs were sacrificial animals and also that Christ, who "calls himself a Lamb," was himself a sacrifice. The poem suggests the darker world of experience that is to come.

In *Songs of Experience*, Blake uses the same childlike verse but expresses emotions that come to us as we grow and begin to experience the world's evil.

THE TIGER

> Tiger! Tiger! burning bright
> In the forests of the night:
> What immortal hand or eye,
> Could frame thy fearful symmetry?
> In what distant deeps or skies
> Burnt the fire of thine eyes?
> On what wings dare he aspire?
> What the hand dare seize the fire?
> And what shoulder, and what art,
> Could twist the sinews of thy heart?
> And when thy heart began to beat,
> What dread hand? and what dread feet?
> What the hammer? what the chain?
> In what furnace was thy brain?
> What the anvil? what dread grasp
> Dare its deadly terrors clasp?
> When the stars threw down their spears,
> And water'd heaven with their tears,
> Did he smile his work to see?
> Did he who made the Lamb make thee?
> Tiger! Tiger! burning bright
> In the forests of the night:
> What immortal hand or eye,
> Dare frame thy fearful symmetry?

The poem combines simple language, childlike patter—and huge questions. Blake was 37 when he wrote this poem. The child's narrative viewpoint of "The Lamb" is now that of a grown up, sobered by the world. "Did he who made the Lamb make thee?" is as electrifying a line as exists in the entire range of the humanities and will always speak deeply to anyone who has ever asked the awful question: "If God is good, why is there evil in the world?" Philosophers have pondered this question, and millions of words in complex prose have been written in answer to it. But it took poetic genius to ask it in eight short words that echo through time, defying an answer.

As with all great literature, explanations only scratch the surface. Just as the innocence of "The Lamb" is tempered by the dark reminder of sacrifice, so too is the fearfulness of "The Tiger" tempered by the recognition of the animal's magnificence: "burning bright." Is this a compensation? Does evil fascinate even as it terrifies? Or do the two poems, taken collectively, hint at a divine order behind the universe that is beyond our ability to understand? Great literature unsettles, disturbs, and makes us wonder, even as it thrills us with its power.

Religious Poetry

The urge to communicate with, and sing the praises of, a deity is as old as humanity itself and, like dance and music, an early component of the humanities. The key word here is "sing," for much prayer was and continues to be sung or sometimes *intoned* (defined as a prolonged monotone or chant). The precise kind of intonation varies from religion to religion as well as among the different sects within a particular faith. Buddhist monks, Roman Catholic clerics during a mass, the cantor in a synagogue, priests in a tribal ceremony, worshippers in the mosque—all chant in their own styles.

What is chanting but intoning words in rhythm and often in rhyme: in short, poetry? Protestant believers singing a hymn are putting poetry to music. Great composers such as Mozart and Beethoven adapted prayers and chants into enormous symphonic works requiring full orchestras and large choirs. Words in rhythm, the building blocks of poetry, are integral to human religious experience.

The psalms in the Hebrew Bible, attributed to King David, contain many personal expressions of joy in God's creation and faith in the transcendent power of God's love. One of the most enduring of the psalms, as translated in the 1611 King James bible, is Psalm 23, beginning "The Lord is my shepherd." The metaphor describing the relationship between a loving God (the shepherd) and humankind (his cared-for flock) has been a cornerstone of Judeo-Christian religions.

GERARD MANLEY HOPKINS   The poet Gerard Manley Hopkins (1844–1889) was an ordained Catholic priest who, after years of conflict between his urge to put poetry first in his life and his belief that giving in to poetic inspiration was self-indulgent, finally convinced himself that his inspirations came from God. He dedicated the rest of his short life to poetry that paved the way for **modernism**, while at the same time reaffirming God's glory. In the following widely admired poem, he views God and the natural world as being one, a concept that was prevalent during the latter half of the nineteenth century.

GOD'S GRANDEUR

> *The world is charged with the grandeur of God.*
> *It will flame out, like shining from shook foil;*
> *It gathers to a greatness, like the ooze of oil*
> *Crushed. Why do men then now not reck his rod?*
> *Generations have trod, have trod, have trod;*
> *And all is seared with trade; bleared, smeared with toil;*
> *And wears man's smudge and shares man's smell; the soil*
> *Is bare now, nor can foot feel, being shod.*
> *And for all this, nature is never spent;*
> *There lives the dearest freshness deep down things;*
> *And though the last lights off the black West went*

Oh, morning, at the brown brink eastward springs—
Because the Holy Ghost over the bent
World broods with warm breast and with ah! bright wings.[8]

The best way to study this poem is to read it aloud a number of times. There is no need to break it down into images, metaphors, and possible meanings. Like Hopkins's world, it is a unity that cannot be divided, only appreciated. This much-heralded revolution in poetic language stems from the poet's immersion in Welsh poetry and its influence on the development of what he called "sprung rhythm," the sudden interruption of the poetic flow. This interruption is illustrated in the famous last line, when Hopkins, after giving us the powerful image of the Holy Ghost exclaims "with ah! bright wings." The purpose of sprung rhythm is to make us trip over the words and thus see with new eyes—something poetry has always tried to do. Most poets work unceasingly to find better ways to do it.

The Birth of Modern Poetry

Poetry is generally called "modern" if it has been written within the last hundred years or so, although some nineteenth-century poets such as Walt Whitman wrote blazing blank verse that feels as modern as anything written today. To some, modern can also mean "less accessible than poetry used to be." The fear for many is that modern poetry, like modern art and music, will prove too difficult to understand. Although some poets of the modern era may seem obscure on first reading, most of them *are* approachable if we are patient—and, above all, if their work is read aloud. The difficulty that readers often face is that many modern poets, abandoning traditional forms such as the sonnet, do not use strict rhythm and rhyme and, like e .e. cummings, distort standard grammar. We need, however, to grant poets the right to create their own forms and their own way of using language.

EMILY DICKINSON   The American poet Emily Dickinson (1830–1886), an introverted, reclusive woman, found in poetry an outlet for the thoughts and feelings she kept locked away inside her. Only three of her poems were published during her lifetime, but many more were found after her death in little packets hidden away in a drawer. She is now considered one of the greatest poets of the nineteenth century, if not of all time. (See Figure 4.5.)

Dickinson had the uncanny ability to take simple, universal experiences and translate them into their final form, as in:

After great pain a formal feeling comes—
The nerves sit ceremonious like tombs;
The stiff Heart questions—was it He that bore?
And yesterday—or centuries before?

The feet mechanical go round
A wooden way
Of ground or air or ought
Regardless grown,
A quartz contentment like a stone.

This is the hour of lead
Remembered if outlived
As freezing persons recollect
The snow—
First chill, then stupor, then
The letting go.[9]

Dickinson is on the very threshold of modern poetry, except that she, unlike some of our contemporaries, anchors her feelings in traditional iambic meter with half of the lines rhyming in couplets. Her pre-modernism is suggested by the fact that the

Figure 4.5 Daguerreotype of Emily Dickinson at age 16.
Dickinson rarely left her house in Amherst, MA. How might this isolated life have influenced the poetry she wrote?
Wendy Maeda/Boston Globe/Getty Images

other half do not rhyme and there is no consistent pattern. The poem above, for example, begins with two consecutive (more or less) rhyming couplets, followed by a series of (primarily) non-rhyming lines broken only by *grown* and *stone*, and then *snow* and *go*. There is something magical about that final coupling of "snow" and "go." "Letting go" so obviously follows after chill and stupor that it seems almost by accident that "go" should be a rhyme. Try thinking of a non-rhyme that would work as the final line. As we have said before, art is the illusion that there is no art. The words of a great poem just seem to have fallen into place by their own accord. Behind a bad poem we can detect the poet's hard work.

We might call Dickinson a transition poet. She has one foot in the world of the lyric poem and the other in the coming world of modern poetry, in which rhythm and rhyme schemes, if indeed they exist at all, are not allowed to get in the way of what the poet wishes to express. Many modern poets turn increasingly to an almost proselike sentence structure, but they can suddenly do a grammatical about-face, as Dickinson does in "The feet mechanical go round/ A wooden way/ Of ground or air or ought/ Regardless grown . . ." Here the old Apollonian–Dionysian split is evident. The sentence has a standard grammatical structure of subject and verb, but note that the poet uses the adjective "mechanical" instead of the expected adverb form "mechanical*ly*"; and then we have the three nouns, "ground," "air," and "ought" (the latter a verb used as a noun). No matter how much great pain has numbed us, there are duties we have to perform whether we want to or not. The poem is both simple and complex, proselike and poetic in the highest sense of the word. The pairings are Dickinson's signature style, making much of her work instantly recognizable as hers.

To move beyond the strangeness of some of the words is to realize that the poet is crystallizing the universal experience of grief. Anyone who has felt the pain of losing a loved one or the agony of rejection or defeat knows about the numbness that follows the shock. Dickinson makes the numbness seem normal, reassuring those who share her thoughts that they are part of the human fellowship. Here we join forces with a poet who is sharing her very soul.

THE HARLEM RENAISSANCE POETS From time to time there emerge conscious artistic movements, gatherings of writers or artists drawn together by the common aim of bringing their culture, their statements, to the attention of a wider audience. One such movement was the Irish Renaissance of the early twentieth century. Another was the Harlem Renaissance, which from the mid-1920s to the mid-1930s launched the careers of dozens of African-American artists, writers, and poets.

On the night of March 21, 1924, Charles S. Johnson, editor of the literary magazine *Opportunity*, invited a number of distinguished white literary figures, including the playwright Eugene O'Neill, to attend a celebration of African-American literature. The poet Georgia Douglas Johnson (c. 1880–1966) was among those who presented work. Now considered the first major female African-American poet of the twentieth century, she adapted the traditional style of the lyric poem while communicating anything but lyrical images of the painful hardships endured by a neglected but crucial sector of America. "Black Woman" illustrates how a modern poet makes the reader see life with a different set of eyes, as Hopkins had done half a century earlier.

BLACK WOMAN

Don't knock at my door, little child,
I cannot let you in,

You know not what a world this is
Of cruelty and sin.
Wait in the still eternity
Until I come to you,
The world is cruel, cruel, child,
I cannot let you in!
Don't knock at my heart, little one,
I cannot bear the pain
Of turning deaf-ear to your call
Time and time again!
You do not know the monster men
Inhabiting the earth, Be still, be still, my precious child,
I must not give you birth![10]

Although Johnson gives her theme away early in the piece, the poem is not really complete until the shock of the final line in which she suddenly abandons the metaphor of someone knocking and confronts us with the reality of the woman's plight. Johnson's structure almost defines modern poetry, which is intended to move, startle, and give sudden insight, and it does so with ever-increasing complexity. Having to compete with other linear media and, more particularly, with visual media requiring little thought, a good many modern poets go their own ways knowing they will reach a small, understanding audience, one that is accustomed to seeing with new eyes and will work, if need be, to grasp what can be the mystery of that last line.

Johnson's poem is a direct appeal for greater understanding of the pain many women endure. She was one of many poets and writers who emerged from the Harlem Renaissance, among them Countee Cullen, Claude McKay, Zora Neale Hurston, and James Baldwin. Perhaps the most famous was Langston Hughes (1902–1967), whose poem "Harlem" from his 1951 collection, *Montage of a Dream Deferred*, not only gives us the title for the 1959 play by Lorraine Hansberry, *A Raisin in the Sun*, but also suggests the consequences of long-standing racial injustice, asking whether a dream deferred for too many years simply dries up, or festers—or explodes.

Poetry in Our Time

Although books of poetry sell very few copies, we should not despair for the well-being of the genre. Once upon a time, poetry was an oral art form, and poems were passed down from troubadour to troubadour. Then, for several centuries, poetry was less and less frequently read aloud. And now, it seems, we have entered an age where we have the best of both worlds.

Much formal poetry has indeed become a largely silent language; it exists on the printed page. For this very reason, it need not be grasped immediately; it can be read and reread, studied, thought about, returned to days later. It occupies its own space, its own corner of the world, into which the reader is invited, a space where a private dialog takes place between the poet's thoughts and the reader's mind. Such dialog creates a special kind of bond that exists nowhere else but in the humanities.

But there is another world that consists of poetry intended to be recited aloud—the world of poetry slams and rap—and there is still another, even more ubiquitous, world of the song lyric. Indeed, literature scholars have long since come to agreement that the lyrics written by Bob Dylan rank as some of the finest poetry of the last 50 years. From Gershwin to Sondheim to Springsteen, from

Snoop Dogg to Drake to Kanye West, we are witnessing a flowering of poetry that can be as rigid in format, and as compelling in sentiment, as anything that has come before.

Many date the beginning of "modern" poetry to the billowing oceans of language produced by the nineteenth-century American master Walt Whitman (1819–1892). At the same time that careful stylists such as Matthew Arnold (1822–1888) and Alfred, Lord Tennyson (1809–1892) were writing finely crafted poems of elegant beauty, Whitman was going wild, revising his masterwork *Leaves of Grass* over and over, adding to and compounding its hugely individual, shockingly unrhymed portrait of self and humanity. From Whitman came free verse and the freedom to write openly about sexuality, anger, and towering emotions.

AUDRE LORDE The poet Audre Lorde (1934–1992) was uniquely positioned, as an African-American lesbian, to comment on a variety of social and cultural issues in her widely admired poetry. Her work focused not only on the challenges of negotiating a world that was often hostile, but also on her own internal identity struggles, as is clear from this early poem, "The House of Yemanjà."

My mother had two faces and a frying pot
where she cooked up her daughters
into girls
before she fixed our dinner.
My mother had two faces
and a broken pot
where she hid out a perfect daughter
who was not me
I am the sun and moon and forever hungry
for her eyes.

I bear two women upon my back
one dark and rich and hidden
in the ivory hungers of the other
mother
pale as a witch
yet steady and familiar
brings me bread and terror
in my sleep
her breasts are huge exciting anchors
in the midnight storm.

All this has been
before
in my mother's bed
time has no sense
I have no brothers
and my sisters are cruel.

Mother I need
mother I need
mother I need your blackness now
as the august earth needs rain.
I am

the sun and moon and forever hungry
the sharpened edge
where day and night shall meet
and not be
one.[11]

Lorde lived in an era—the last half of the twentieth century—when questions of identity were paramount; we were all searching inside ourselves to discover who and what we were. She finds in herself two distinct selves, both traceable to her mother, who was of mixed race and could "pass" for white. Compare Lorde's journey through the world to the one described by Georgia Johnson, earlier in this chapter.

The Novel

4.4   *When did the novel first appear, and how has the form changed in the past 100 years?*

The emergence of the novel as a literary form was inevitable. The novel is essentially a long narrative, and the great epics discussed earlier are long narratives of adventures, battles, conquests, and complicated human relationships—all the stuff of fiction. In this respect, the *Iliad* and the *Aeneid* could be considered forerunners of the novel, and they certainly are not the only examples. Throughout the world, every culture has produced stories, either written or communicated orally. Much of the Hebrew Bible contains narratives: for example, the story of Moses leading the children of Israel out of bondage and the story of the patient Job whose faith is put to a severe test. In fact, the Colombian novelist Gabriel García Márquez suggested in his autobiography, *A Life*, that "fiction was invented the day Jonah arrived home and told his wife that he was three days late because he had been swallowed by a whale."

India, China, and Japan, all embrace literary traditions that preceded Homer, suggesting that story-telling developed along with human communication skills. Many literary historians believe that the world's first "official" novel was *The Tale of Genji* written by a Japanese aristocrat, Lady Murasaki Shikibu, over a thousand years ago (Figure 4.6). Though filled with brave deeds and heroes, it is written, unlike the great epics of the classical period, as prose, not poetry.

France in the late Middle Ages produced a number of prose tales called **romances**. These were stories of knighthood, chivalry, and love affairs between brave knights and their fair ladies (often married to other men). From England came the tales of King Arthur and the knights of the Round Table. Not only were they artful narratives, but they also created a whole mythology that continues to influence the human dream. In addition to Camelot, these tales gave prominence to the search for the Holy Grail, which has become a lasting symbol of the elusive prize that human beings continue to seek.

Our word "novel" comes from the Latin *novellus*, meaning new and unfamiliar. Early in the Italian Renaissance the author Giovanni Boccaccio (1313–1375) used the

Figure 4.6   Scene from *Tale of Genji*, color woodcut, date unknown.
Written over a thousand years ago by Lady Murasaki in Japan, this work includes heroes and brave deeds. Why is it generally considered a novel, rather than an epic?
Akg-images/Newscom

Italian word **novella** to describe the short prose narratives he wrote. It is very possible that the sense of "novelty" contained in the term was intended to distinguish fictional stories from those that supposedly had a basis in truth.

The Early Novel in the Western World

Early Western literature, especially the **picaresque** tale, flourished in Spain. These often quite long stories narrated the adventures of a soldier of fortune living the carefree life on the open road and getting involved in all sorts of intrigues and love affairs. The Spanish also had tales similar to the King Arthur legends, dealing with the adventures on the road of brave and dashing knights who were superheroes; tremendous in battle and noble and chivalrous toward their true loves.

The first known major novelist of the Western world was Miguel de Cervantes Saavedra (1547–1616), whose life span closely parallels Shakespeare's. His *Don Quixote* (written between 1612 and 1615) remains one of the most popular and beloved of all novels. The central character is an old man who has read so many stories of brave knights that he has gone mad and believes himself to be one of them. Riding a broken-down old horse named Rocinante and attended by his faithful squire Sancho Panza, he goes off in search of glorious adventure (Figure 4.1). Intended originally as a satire on the ridiculous excesses of the wandering knight story, *Don Quixote* became, in the opinion of many, a tragic tale of an idealist who sees the world not as it is but as it ought to be: a world in which people are driven by the noblest of motives, chivalry prevails, and love means forever. As an adventure story, *Don Quixote* influenced the work of many novelists who followed, setting the pattern for long, loosely structured yarns that would find a home in the magazine serials of the eighteenth and nineteenth centuries. The serial was a publishing gimmick, each episode ending with the hero or heroine in a perilous strait, and thus keeping the reader coming back to purchase more issues.

The English novel had its true beginnings in the eighteenth century. The coming of the magazine fostered a passion for fiction that had potential novelists busily scribbling. But the period was also one of a passion for science and its search for truth. Those who dictated the taste of the reading public insisted that a lengthy published work, to be worth the time spent in reading it, must at least pretend to be a true story. Consequently, much fiction was passed off as biography or autobiography, and this meant that the author's real name was often omitted. For example, *Gulliver's Travels* (1726) by Jonathan Swift and *Robinson Crusoe* (1719) by Daniel Defoe, two enduringly popular works of fiction, pretended to be nonfictional accounts of actual adventures, and *Pamela: Virtue Rewarded* (1740), by Samuel Richardson was an **epistolary novel**, consisting solely of letters "written" by its 15-year-old heroine.

American writers were slow to gain recognition and respect abroad. In the early nineteenth century, British critics were asking, "Who reads an American book or goes to see an American play?" These questions incurred the wrath of American authors, who promptly responded in a variety of ways. There was Washington Irving (1783–1859) and his satiric novel masquerading as nonfiction, *A History of New-York from the Beginning of the World to the End of the Dutch Dynasty, by Diedrich Knickerbocker* (1809), which took an irreverent swing at Thomas Jefferson's democratic ideology. Irving became the first American writer to win the long-awaited praise from abroad.

The "Golden Age" of the Novel: The Nineteenth Century

By the mid-nineteenth century, the novel had moved into a place it has yet to abandon as the most popular of literary forms. In the United States, the early efforts of Washington Irving were followed closely by those of James Fenimore Cooper (1789–1851), who romanticized the American wilderness in such novels as *The Last of the Mohicans* (1826) and *The Deerslayer* (1841), and then by the triumvirate of American authors whose work continues to move us, although in very different ways: Nathaniel Hawthorne

(1804–1864), Samuel Clemens, known as Mark Twain (1835–1910), and perhaps the greatest of all, Herman Melville (1819–1891). Hawthorne's novels *The Scarlet Letter* (1850) and *The House of the Seven Gables* (1851) won almost unanimous praise in England. Melville's *Moby-Dick* also appeared in 1851, although it sold many fewer copies than his earlier novels; Melville died a forgotten man and was not hailed as a great novelist until many years after his death, in the 1920s, when critics rediscovered his masterpiece.

Others were carving out great reputations throughout Europe: Charles Dickens (1812–1870) in Britain; Victor Hugo (1802–1885) in France; and, in Russia, Fyodor Dostoevsky (1821–1881) and Leo Tolstoy (1828–1910). Many of the novels written by these giants continue to hold a place in our cultural pantheon—not least through their adaptations in opera (*Moby-Dick*), musical theater (*Les Miserables, Oliver!*) and on film (*Anna Karenina, War and Peace*). And their enduring characters—Huck Finn, Oliver Twist and Fagin, Captain Ahab—have become simply part of our cultural vocabulary.

The Modern American Novel

By the end of the nineteenth century, American novelists Edith Wharton and Henry James were making their presence felt on both sides of the Atlantic. Mark Twain had already written *Huckleberry Finn*. Serious American writers were not playing catch-up with their European counterparts any longer. And important novels could bring wealth and fame, not to mention return a publisher's investment. That's why an eager young writer named F. Scott Fitzgerald (1896–1940) could sit down with great deliberation and resolve to write "the great American novel." We are all familiar with that phrase, which has become for many a great American myth, something to be aspired to but never quite realized. In fact, the pursuit of the great American novel became itself a theme for many American writers whose novel-writing heroes usually shed their youthful idealism, confront a harsh world, and realize that the perfect novel can never be written.

F. SCOTT FITZGERALD   Two novelists of the early twentieth century, F. Scott Fitzgerald and Ernest Hemingway, exemplify two kinds of writers, different in their style and themes, but both representatively American nonetheless. Fitzgerald wrote in rich, complex prose, evoking a still classic portrait of the 1920s: the **Jazz Age** of short-skirted flappers, bathtub gin, sleek roadsters, and endless rounds of wild parties—a carefree period that would come to a crashing end in 1929, when the stock market dropped through the floor and countless investors jumped out of windows.

Fitzgerald was an observer and critic of this careening culture. His *The Great Gatsby* (1925) is the tragic story of a man who dedicates his life to the pursuit of wealth (derived from sources outside the law), gives lavish parties that are the talk of affluent Long Island society, and seems to have realized the American dream (see Figure 4.7). But when he makes love to a woman he knows is married and allows her to drive recklessly in his Rolls Royce, causing the death of another woman, his actions lead to his own predictably violent death.

The final passage of the novel illustrates Fitzgerald's frequently imitated style and also provides a glimpse into Jay Gatsby, one of the few truly tragic figures in American literature:

> He had come a long way to this blue lawn and his dream must have seemed so close that he could hardly fail to grasp it. He did not know that it was already behind him, somewhere back in that vast obscurity beyond the city, where the dark fields of the republic rolled on under the night.[12]

ERNEST HEMINGWAY   Vastly different from Fitzgerald is Ernest Hemingway (1899–1961), who recreates the rugged individualist hero of earlier American fiction such as *The Deerslayer* and *Huckleberry Finn*, but places him in a number of different locales where he is tested for courage. In *A Farewell to Arms* (1929), he appears as

Figure 4.7 A scene from Baz Luhrman's 2013 film of *The Great Gatsby*, starring Leonardo DiCaprio and Carey Mulligan.
What happens when a book becomes a movie? Why do many critics argue that bad books make great movies, while great books make bad movies?
AF archive/Alamy

Frederic Henry, a World War I ambulance driver, who falls in love with a nurse only to see her die. Bitter and angry at the civilization that has ruined not only his life but, in his eyes, the world itself, he deserts the army, an early representative in a long line of alienated American "drop-out" heroes.

As Hemingway grew older, however, his sensibilities and values changed. Some Hemingway scholars believe that he became obsessed with maintaining his own physical conditioning as well as his magnetic appeal to women. His heroes were transformed into strong, silent, intensely masculine figures, stoically able to experience and conquer extreme dangers, always falling in love with, then losing, strong women. Biographers see the Hemingway hero as a portrait of the man he longed to be.

Perhaps the alienation of Frederic Henry in *A Farewell to Arms* weighed heavily on Hemingway's conscience. The death of Catherine as well as the futility of war motivate his running away, but to the later Hemingway, it would have been an act of cowardice. The theme of the mature Hemingway novels and stories is the attainment of a courageous stand against all of life's brutalities.

Hemingway's 1940 novel about the Spanish Civil War, *For Whom the Bell Tolls*, has what many critics have regarded as the author's most memorable portrait of the stoic, courageous hero, one who is willing to die for a cause that is not his own. The American Robert Jordan joins a band of Spanish guerillas battling a repressive government. When the superior government forces seem to have them trapped in the mountains, Jordan orders the guerillas to escape while he mans a machine gun, holding off the advancing army long enough to ensure their safe exit.

The scene includes a moving farewell to Maria, a woman with whom he would have gladly spent the rest of his life. Like much of Hemingway's fiction, this novel lacks a traditional happy ending; yet it does have the author's characteristic take on what constitutes happiness. For Hemingway, happiness is having conquered the coward who lives inside each of us. One literary historian has observed that Robert Jordan is Frederic Henry redeemed. Henry saves himself when he deserts the army; Jordan, who might have saved himself, chooses not to.

The Post-Modern Novel

The more-or-less realistic novel—a work of fiction that tracks characters who might actually live real lives—continues to thrive in the works of writers such as John

Updike, Alice Walker, and Jonathan Franzen. But early in the twentieth century, more and more often novelists began experimenting with form and content to produce works that readers often found dense, difficult, and even obscure. Some, like James Joyce's *Ulysses*, also brought down the wrath of the censors. But as the reading public grew used to experimentation, admiration for this new kind of fiction blossomed. Writers as different as Thomas Pynchon and Toni Morrison in the United States and Gabriel García Márquez in Latin America assembled extraordinary bodies of work.

THOMAS PYNCHON   Born in 1937 in Glen Cove, NY, Pynchon began writing as a student at Cornell University. His first novel, *V.* (1963), centers on the search for a mysterious character known only as V. by a former Navy sailor named Benny Profane, part of a group called The Whole Sick Crew. The novel, like Pynchon's later work, moves chaotically among a large cast of characters with very strange names who indulge in bizarre behaviors. Its timeframe and settings range from nineteenth-century Florence to contemporary New York City. The sentences are long and complex, a sea of words, reflecting the impossibility of nailing down reality with language.

V. both appealed to the generation coming of age in the chaotic 1960s and, for their elders, seemed to hold a key to understanding what was happening in a rapidly changing world. Pynchon is notoriously reclusive, granting no interviews (although he did permit himself to be portrayed on *The Simpsons!*). His 1973 novel *Gravity's Rainbow* won both a Pulitzer Prize and a National Book Award. Pynchon's style—the page-long sentences and fragmented structure—is reflected in the work of many twenty-first-century writers, perhaps most notably Michael Chabon.

TONI MORRISON   The most recent American writer to win the Nobel Prize in Literature (1993), Morrison was born in 1931 in Lorain, Ohio, and worked as an editor for many years while she published her own fiction; during those years, she was also responsible for bringing many young black writers into the mainstream of American literature. Her novels focus almost exclusively on the black experience and the consequences of slavery, but they are far from narrow. Her acknowledged masterpiece, *Beloved* (1987), tells the fragmented story of an escaped slave woman who is haunted by the ghost of her dead baby. When we reach the final, shattering conclusion, we are all complicit in the guilt of an unbearable act, and we must all share the knowledge that such acts are sometimes a symbol of humanity, not a negation of it.

GABRIEL GARCÍA MÁRQUEZ   Márquez (1927–2014) is central to the rise of **magical realism** in fiction in the latter half of the twentieth century. One of a group of Latin American novelists whose works have drawn praise over the last half-century, García Márquez was born in Colombia and lived much of his life in Mexico. His sprawling tales—*One Hundred Years of Solitude*, and *Love in the Time of Cholera*, in particular—draw on Latin American folk tales and the stories García Márquez heard from his grandfather, who raised him. Although the realistic characters and settings he creates, most notably a small Colombian village called Macondo, are often enveloped in what appear to be magical events, García Márquez always insisted that everything he wrote was based in truth—but that his reality was simply different from that of others.

The Short Story

4.5   *How do most contemporary short stories differ from earlier versions of this genre?*

A case could be made—in fact, *has* been made—for the argument that the short story is essentially an American invention, along with jazz. We have to be cautious, however, because much depends on what we mean by the short story. If we simply mean a brief tale featuring one central action, then we'd have to concede that the Bible got there long before there *was* an America. The stories of Cain and Abel, Joseph and his brothers, Ruth, Abraham's near sacrifice of Isaac, not to mention the Garden of Eden itself, must be considered literary masterpieces as well as religious writings, models of tales that waste few words; and that is precisely what great short stories do.

Magazine Fiction

The form itself gained recognition and respectability early in the nineteenth century on both sides of the Atlantic with the growing popularity of the magazine. Along with weekly or monthly installments of long novels, magazines printed pieces of short fiction that could be read in one sitting, presumably because writers could not produce lengthy fiction fast enough to meet the demand. Besides, large sums of money awaited those who could devise a fantastic story, especially one involving murder and ghosts in eerie castles and building to a shattering climax. Financial returns on a novel came much more slowly.

When we think of such stories, the name Edgar Allan Poe (1809–1849) immediately comes to mind. With his dark and brooding atmosphere, his old castles with their locked doors and cobwebs, his ghostly voices echoing down dark hallways, Poe made enough money to support his two tragic habits, drinking and gambling. Though he appears to have been rather unhappy in his brief lifetime—which may explain the fantastic world of the imagination into which he continually escaped—he left behind a treasury of short fiction, such as "The Gold-Bug" and "The Murders in the Rue Morgue," that clearly established American preeminence in this field.

Later, in France, the short story became swept up with a literary trend known as *realism*—a strong reaction against the earlier novels and stories of sheer fantasy. Character became as important as, if not more important than, plot in the novel; and the short story was expected to climax in a revelation, offering an insight into some aspect of human nature or life itself. The revelation was often an ironic one.

The Use of Epiphany in Short Stories

The sudden insight into life or human nature which short stories often give us is called an **epiphany**, a term borrowed by Irish novelist James Joyce from its biblical meaning: the visitation to the baby Jesus by the three wise men. Joyce and subsequent literary critics used the term to mean an action or a line of dialog that reveals a truth, as the arrival of the wise men revealed the truth of Jesus's holiness.

One story that has achieved international renown largely because of its shattering epiphany is "The Lottery" by Shirley Jackson (1916–1965), who often combines the chilling aspects of Poe with climactic meaningfulness. "The Lottery" moves us in a number of ways. While it rewards the discerning reader with an epiphany that widens and deepens with each reading, it also offers a suspenseful and realistic surface tale of an annual prize-drawing ceremony in a typical, peaceful small town, with the nature of the "prize" carefully withheld until the horrifying climax. As townspeople gather for the drawing, each one takes from a black box a small scrap of paper. All of the scraps are blank, we later discover, except one, which has a black mark on it. The one who draws this is declared the "winner," but the prize is death. (Shades of *The Hunger Games!*)

Early in the story, the symbolic nature of the events is hinted at. There are rumors being discussed that some towns are thinking of abandoning the lottery. Then an elderly denizen comments that this is a bad idea: "Lottery in June, corn be heavy soon." We realize that the author is showing us the survival of an ancient sacrificial ritual in which one person is slain so that the gods will provide an abundant harvest. The story is not about an agricultural ritual. It is about the survival of many primitive instincts we believe are long buried.

The Short Story Today

Many stories published in recent years have dispensed with the once required epiphany. Increasingly popular—and critically praised—are stories about believable people and complex relationships with which the reader can identify. This literary trend parallels what is happening in novels and dramas. Contemporary writers are reflecting the *zeitgeist* (or general outlook) of our age: There is no overarching theory that applies to people and their cultures the world over.

But sometimes there is a monumental occurrence that absolutely requires a response from our literary sentinels. The event that will most likely define the early part of our century took place on September 11, 2001, just before nine o'clock in the morning. So devastating was this event that we knew our lives were changed forever, and all of us would forever remember what we were doing when the planes struck the World Trade Center. Not surprisingly, writers were slow to gather their thoughts and feelings together enough to compose poems or dramas or fiction about the disaster. And also not surprisingly, one of the greatest short story writers of our age was among the first.

JOHN UPDIKE, "VARIETIES OF RELIGIOUS EXPERIENCE"   John Updike (1932–2009), prolific almost to the end of his life, published his response to 9/11 in *The Atlantic* under an intriguing title that does not give away the subject matter, "Varieties of Religious Experience," borrowed from the great work by William James. Though Updike was an ardent believer for most of his life, his use of "religious" here represents a broad spectrum of how people reacted and what interpretations, if any, they could muster. (James's book makes the point that there is no one universal religion or one way to define religious experience.)

The story shifts focus from one set of characters to another, each in entirely differing circumstances—from a Cincinnati man visiting his daughter in Brooklyn and able to see the disaster from the terrace of her penthouse, to a pair of parking garage attendants, who represent the least affected, "carrying on a joshing conversation," to a businessman in a plush office high up in one of the towers, to the pilots of the planes, getting drunk the day before on unfamiliar hard liquor and watching pole dancers in a sleazy Florida bar, to the thoughts running through the mind of a plane-fearing woman on the ill-fated flight out of Newark on which a group of passengers overpowered the hijackers and forced the plane to crash in a Pennsylvania field. The Cincinnati man on his daughter's terrace may well represent Updike's own reaction on that never-to-be-forgotten day, beginning with one of the most powerful opening lines in recent fiction: *"THERE IS NO GOD*: the revelation came to Dan Kellogg in the instant that he saw the World Trade Center South Tower fall." But then he finds himself in a vortex of conflicting attitudes that finally resolve themselves.

> *Heartland religiosity, though its fundamentalism and bombastic puritanism had often made him wince, was something Dan had been comfortable with; now it seemed barbaric.*[13]

Like most modern short story writers, Updike draws no conclusions (how could he?). At the same time, his rich imagination and humanity allow him to empathize with so many kinds of people. The story ends not exactly on a note of hope but from the perspective of innocence. As Dan and his granddaughters look at the lights later shining up from Ground Zero, the older girl refuses to go onto the terrace. She says, "Children shouldn't see what you're looking at. It's scary."

> *"Don't be scared," her younger sister told her. . . . "My teacher at school says the lights are like the rainbow. They mean it won't happen again.*[14]

We know Updike had his doubts.

This chapter has offered an introduction to a very complex subject by focusing on particular examples from major genres of literature. It makes no claim to being an exhaustive study. We have sampled a few important works by way of encouraging you to make the reading of literature an ongoing part of your life. We hope you will take it from there. Once you open the pages of literature, short or long, prose or poetry, you will discover infinite worlds and dimensions of reality that can carry you to a place only the humanities know about: your own private island of imagination.

A Critical Focus: Exploring the Poetry of Dying Young

Certain topics appear time and time again in literary texts: coming-of-age in novels (*Huckleberry Finn, Catcher in the Rye,* and *To Kill a Mockingbird,* for example); religion (the work of Flannery O'Connor, William Blake, and Gerard Manley Hopkins); utopia (the perfect world) and dystopia (the nonfunctional world) in works such as Orwell's *1984,* Sir Thomas More's *Utopia,* and Veronica Roth's *Divergent* trilogy. One of the most common topics in literature of all forms—novels, short stories, and poetry—is the tragic death of a young person.

The nineteenth-century American poet Walt Whitman (1819–1892) saw the Civil War up close; he volunteered in army hospitals, tending to the wounded, for much of the War. "Come Up from the Fields, Father" is a view of youthful death once removed, as it feels to those left behind.

Come up from the fields father, here's a letter from our Pete,
And come to the front door mother, here's a letter from thy dear son.

Lo, 'tis autumn,
Lo, where the trees, deeper green, yellower and redder,
Cool and sweeten Ohio's villages with leaves fluttering in the moderate wind,
Where apples ripe in the orchards hang and grapes on the trellis'd vines,
(Smell you the smell of the grapes on the vines?
Smell you the buckwheat where the bees were lately buzzing?)

Above all, lo, the sky so calm, so transparent after the rain, and with wondrous clouds,
Below too, all calm, all vital and beautiful, and the farm prospers well.

Down in the fields all prospers well,
But now from the fields come father, come at the daughter's call,
And come to the entry mother, to the front door come right away.

Fast as she can she hurries, something ominous, her steps trembling,
She does not tarry to smooth her hair nor adjust her cap.

Open the envelope quickly,
O this is not our son's writing, yet his name is sign'd,
O a strange hand writes for our dear son, O stricken mother's soul!
All swims before her eyes, flashes with black, she catches the main words only,
Sentences broken, gunshot wound in the breast, cavalry skirmish, taken to hospital,
At present low, but will soon be better.

Ah now the single figure to me,
Amid all teeming and wealthy Ohio with all its cities and farms,
Sickly white in the face and dull in the head, very faint,
By the jamb of a door leans.

Grieve not so, dear mother, *(the just-grown daughter speaks through her sobs,*
The little sisters huddle around speechless and dismay'd,)
See, dearest mother, the letter says Pete will soon be better.
Alas poor boy, he will never be better, (nor may-be needs to be better, that brave and simple soul,)
While they stand at home at the door he is dead already,
The only son is dead.

But the mother needs to be better,
She with thin form presently drest in black,
By day her meals untouch'd, then at night fitfully sleeping, often waking,
In the midnight waking, weeping, longing with one deep longing,
O that she might withdraw unnoticed, silent from life escape and withdraw,
To follow, to seek, to be with her dear dead son.[15]

The British poet A. E. Housman (1859–1936) wrote what is perhaps the most famous poem of all on this subject, "To an Athlete Dying Young," which first appeared in his collection *A Shropshire Lad* in 1896.

> The time you won your town the race
> We chaired you through the market-place;
> Man and boy stood cheering by,
> And home we brought you shoulder-high.
>
> Today, the road all runners come,
> Shoulder-high we bring you home,
> And set you at your threshold down,
> Townsman of a stiller town.
>
> Smart lad, to slip betimes away
> From fields where glory does not stay,
> And early though the laurel grows
> It withers quicker than the rose.
>
> Eyes the shady night has shut
> Cannot see the record cut,
> And silence sounds no worse than cheers
> After earth has stopped the ears.
>
> Now you will not swell the rout
> Of lads that wore their honours out,
> Runners whom renown outran
> And the name died before the man.
>
> So set, before its echoes fade,
> The fleet foot on the sill of shade,
> And hold to the low lintel up
> The still-defended challenge-cup.
>
> And round that early-laurelled head
> Will flock to gaze the strengthless dead,
> And find unwithered on its curls
> The garland briefer than a girl's.[16]

Another British poet, Wilfred Owen (1893–1918), is considered one of the First World War's greatest voices. His "Anthem for Doomed Youth" uncovers the anonymity of death on the battlefield, where no one sings or strews flowers. The poem anticipates Owens' own death on the front lines at only 25.

> What passing-bells for these who die as cattle?
> —Only the monstrous anger of the guns.
> Only the stuttering rifles' rapid rattle
> Can patter out their hasty orisons.
> No mockeries now for them; no prayers nor bells;
> Nor any voice of mourning save the choirs,—
> The shrill, demented choirs of wailing shells;
> And bugles calling for them from sad shires.
>
> What candles may be held to speed them all?
> Not in the hands of boys but in their eyes
> Shall shine the holy glimmers of goodbyes.
> The pallor of girls' brows shall be their pall;
> Their flowers the tenderness of patient minds,
> And each slow dusk a drawing-down of blinds.[17]

- How do these poems differ from one another? How are they similar?
- What marks the era when each one was written, if anything?
- What is the setting of each of these poems? Who is speaking? How does the setting and the perspective of the speaker influence the experience we have in reading each of them?
- Do you think one poem gives a more realistic picture of the tragedy of dying young than another? Why?

Looking Back

In this chapter,

- we discussed the differences between a "classic" and a "masterpiece,"
- we explored how literary texts serve to establish cultural histories,
- we looked closely at several poetic forms, including lyric poetry, sonnets, haiku, religious poetry, and modern verse,
- we discussed how and when the novel appeared as a distinct literary genre and traced its history, and
- we examined a short story in depth.

Key Terms

blank verse Poetry that has rhythm but not rhyme.

classic A literary work that continues to be read for years, even centuries, after its initial appearance because it remains relevant.

conceit As a literary term, an elaborate description of something in terms of something else; example given was Donne's sonnet "Batter My Heart," in which mystical exaltation is expressed in sexually charged language.

couplet Two lines of poetry that rhyme consecutively; used by Shakespeare to conclude a sonnet.

epic A genre of literature; a long narrative poem recounting the actions of a hero who exemplifies strength, courage, and cunning, but not necessarily moral virtue.

epiphany A sudden insight into life or human nature that often serves as the climax in a work of fiction, particularly a short story. The author James Joyce adapted this term from its original religious context.

epistolary novel A novel composed solely of letters written from one character to another.

genre Broadly in the humanities, any distinct category within a discipline, such as in literature the epic, the sonnet, the novel, or the short story; generally imposes certain requirements and limitations on the writer: e.g. a sonnet must have 14 lines; a haiku must have 17 syllables.

haiku Traditional Japanese poetic genre in which the poet presents one image, usually derived from an observation of nature, which may also contain an underlying thought; usually limited to three lines: 5 syllables/ 7 syllables/ 5 syllables.

iambic pentameter Classical rhythmic scheme widely used in English verse; consists of five repetitions in a poetic line of an unstressed followed by a stressed syllable, as in the line "When in disgrace with fortune and men's eyes."

Jazz Age Phrase coined by F. Scott Fitzgerald to denote the decade of the 1920s; connotes a free style of life among affluent youth preoccupied with partying, heavy drinking, fast cars, and sexual promiscuity.

lyric Literally "of a lyre," which was an ancient musical instrument, hence words sung to music.

lyric poetry Rhythmic, often rhymed, music-like poem; usually deals with the poet's feelings, especially of love.

magical realism The integration of strange, seemingly magical events into a work of literature or art that is otherwise realistic.

masterpiece Here, a literary work acknowledged to tower above others of its time because of its style, execution, memorable characters, or profound meaning; not necessarily recognized in its time.

metaphor Widely used literary device; offers writers a way to describe something highly abstract in terms of something else that is more concrete.

modernism Term frequently employed by literary critics and historians to categorize work that breaks with traditions and conventions of the past.

novella A work of fiction that is shorter than a novel but longer than a short story.

picaresque An adventure tale consisting of a series of often funny adventures (and misadventures) centered on an appealing but often roguish hero.

romance Here, a literary genre popular in the Middle Ages revolving around the exploits of a brave and handsome knight and his love for a beautiful lady, often married to someone else.

scansion Reading a poem, aloud or silently, examining its meter so as to determine whether it has a definite rhythmic pattern, such as iambic pentameter.

sonnet Genre of poetry requiring the poet to express a thought in 14 lines, controlled by a strict rhythm and rhyme scheme; invented by Renaissance Italian poets and employed in Shakespeare's poetry.

symbolism A way of communicating meaning that goes beyond the "surface meaning" of a story or novel; of expressing a thought that cannot be directly stated because of its complexity.

Chapter 5
Art

Learning Objectives

5.1 Explain why all art can be seen as imitation.

5.2 Identify key characteristics of classical, medieval, and Renaissance art.

5.3 Describe the major art movements of the eighteenth and nineteenth centuries.

5.4 Analyze why "art as alteration" is an appropriate way to characterize twentieth- and twenty-first-century art.

5.5 Discuss the impact of technology in the creation of photographic and digital art.

5.6 Explain why architecture can be considered art.

Figure 5.1 Jeff Koons, *Puppy*, Guggenheim Bilbao Museum, Spain, 2005.

© Jeff Koons, Installation at Guggenheim Museum Bilbao. (Stainless steel, soil, geotextile fabric, internal irrigation system, and live flowering plants, 486 × 486 × 256 inches. 1234.4 × 1234.4 × 650.2 cm.)

Figure 5.2 Michelangelo Buonarroti, *Moses*, c. 1515.
Compare Jeff Koons's *Puppy* (Fig. 5.1), installed at the Guggenheim Bilbao in Spain, and Michelangelo's *Moses*, commissioned for the Tomb of Pope Julius II, San Pietro in Vincoli, Rome, pictured above. Are both of these sculptures art? What criteria can we use to determine what is art?
© Vincenzo Pirozzi

In August of 1911, in the midst of the worst heat wave in Parisian memory, the year when the supposedly unsinkable *Titanic* was being built, amateur painter Luis Beroud arrived at the Louvre Museum, ready to continue copying the *Mona Lisa*, an effort he had been at for several days. At that time, amateurs with the proper credentials were allowed to make copies of famous paintings as long as the canvases they used were not the same size as the original. When Beroud finally looked up, he saw that Leonardo's masterpiece was not in its usual place, hanging between two much larger paintings. The guard on duty, who had been napping, seemed undisturbed. Someone must have taken it to be photographed, he said; that was not uncommon.

That proved not to be the case: the *Mona Lisa* had been stolen. It was eventually recovered and a confession was obtained from Vincenzo Peruggia, an impoverished Italian who said he wanted to restore the work to its rightful home in Italy. But investigators were certain that Peruggia had not acted alone, and the mystery of the audacious theft has never been completely solved. Early on, no less an august figure than Picasso was under suspicion.

The heist shook the art world. And it raised some interesting questions. What, for instance, if the painting eventually returned to the Louvre turned out to be an exquisite fake—technically worth much less than the original (or, for that matter, less than an original by another important artist, perhaps van Gogh), but quite beautiful in itself? What difference would that make in its value to viewers? Does the artist's reputation make a piece of art valuable? Or is the value intrinsic to the art?

What if artists provide us with creations—on canvas, or in marble or bronze—that do not resemble anything immediately identifiable? What is art? Who decides? Sometimes history decides, as happened with Vincent van Gogh and Caravaggio. Sometimes acclaim comes during an artist's lifetime, as it did for Michelangelo, Leonardo, and Picasso. Sometimes judgments vary during and after an artist's lifetime. The jury is still out when it comes to Jeff Koons, a contemporary sculptor who creates huge reproductions of, for example, "balloon" animals in stainless steel and flowers. Is this art or is it, as some critics contend, *kitsch*? Is it worth the millions of dollars that investors pay for it? What criteria should we use for determining what is or is not *art*?

This chapter offers a brief introduction to the visual arts: painting, sculpture, architecture, photography, and digital art. We encourage you to approach the subject without bias, without defined expectations. Be open to what may at first seem unfamiliar, even crazy. Above all, do not expect a neatly packaged definition of art that can apply to every work by every artist. As Robert Thiele, a contemporary avant-garde painter, once said, "Art is what the artist does."

The Need to Imitate

5.1 *Why can all art be seen as imitation?*

Astonishing cave paintings dating back to the days of Paleolithic cultures teach us that even the earliest humans expressed themselves through art. Although the artistic technique may appear unsophisticated to us, we can clearly recognize the subject—usually animals, such as a bison, familiar to the cave dwellers (see Figure 5.3). The exact motivation of the artists remains unknown, but one thing about the work speaks for itself: *early artists developed a technique for imitating what they saw.* Some of the paintings seem to express feelings as well—fear of the animal's power, or perhaps a sense of mastery over that power. A good bet, however, is that early artists must have enjoyed imitation because they had an instinctive knowledge of how to do it. *They liked to transfer to a two-dimensional surface what they saw in their three-dimensional world.*

All visual art, regardless of when it was produced, is imitation. Some of it—and only some of it—strives for a **likeness** of the physical world, the familiar world. Some of it imitates the world of imagination inside the artist, and often it is rejected because it is *not* familiar.

Imitation, therefore, needs to be broadly defined and understood. The term does not refer exclusively to what looks absolutely real and authentic. In the humanities, imitation means that the artist uses reality as a starting but not necessarily an ending point. Sometimes a work of art that has the external appearance of reality is actually making a comment about life. But we need to be cautious if we find we like a certain work because we know what it is "saying."

The painting *A Bar at the Folies-Bergère* by the French artist Édouard Manet (1832–1883), who was influenced by both the Realist and the Impressionist movements, does not represent photographic realism, but its likeness to reality is clear (see Figure 5.4). The expression on the barmaid's face might suggest either boredom with her necessary

Figure 5.3 Cave painting of a bison, Santander, Spain, c. 25,000-35,000 BCE.
What does this painting from many centuries ago suggest to you about the innately human need to recreate the familiar world?
Gianni Dagli Orti/Fine Art/Corbis

Figure 5.4 Édouard Manet, *A Bar at the Folies-Bergère*, 1882.
What seems most striking to you about Manet's *A Bar at the Folies-Bergère*—the beauty of the painting's shapes, colors, and figures, or the social commentary implied by the expression on the woman's face?
De Agostini Picture Library/Getty Images

job or quiet dissatisfaction with the disparity between her own circumstances and those of her affluent customers. One *could* therefore say that the painting is making a social comment—but we have no way of knowing whether that was the intent of the artist. In fact, this painting represents a very particular location and includes specific individuals, but we still don't know whether Manet intended a social message—we only know what our own perception is of that message.

We miss out on a great deal if we demand strict **realism** in every work we view. The artist may be imitating things we have never seen and never will see except on that canvas or in a bronze shape. In all its myriad forms, realistic or not, art enhances our world.

Let Me See!

An artist's need to imitate grows out of a particular way of seeing: seeing intensely, noticing details, shapes, and colors. Unfortunately, most of us tend to see selectively, except in isolated moments when a landscape or a sunset calls us sharply to attention. Children tend to see as the artist sees, and perhaps that is why Picasso urged people not to grow up, to come to the world each day as the child does.

Though we may have seen more intensely as children than as adults, most of us probably did not imitate what we looked at—at least not very accurately. Remember what you did when your elementary school teacher asked you to draw a house? Unless you were an instinctive artist, you were content to make the generic two-dimensional house (three rectangles and a triangle), just as you made stick figures to represent people. You made the *symbol* of a house, because by now you were acquiring language, and the inner world of symbolism was taking over your life.

The generic house and the stick figure got the job done for most of us. We assumed everyone knew what we meant when we drew that skeleton of a house. We were drawing the *idea* of the house. Why bother to imitate a real house? Isn't that what cameras are for?

Some artists can produce an astonishing likeness of the original. The Dutch masters of the seventeenth century were so good at faithful rendering that many artists who came later may have decided it was unwise to compete and began instead to experiment with other techniques and other goals.

What were those goals? One is the imitation of inner reality. Just think of your dreams. Every object, every location is made up of bits and pieces of other things. If you could hold onto a moment of a dream long enough to draw it, you would be, at least for a time, a modern artist. In a sense, the imitation factor is still there, except that a strange new world is being imitated. When the artist's production offers unfamiliar stimuli to us, we need to look at it nonjudgmentally, trying to absorb all that is there to behold.

The treasure of art, however, is that its reality lives on after its subjects die. The final product is an *addition* to reality, not simply a way of reproducing it. The artist always contributes something new, something that never before was put together in precisely that way. Leonardo's *Mona Lisa* is not Mona Lisa. The latter left the earth long ago; the former will never die.

Styles and Media

Now that we know all visual art is imitation, but that imitation does not always mean creating a direct likeness, we can talk about the varied styles and methods—or **media**—of imitation. Imagine a school where everyone else is content to draw rectangles and stick figures, except for one pupil who wants to be different, who wants her drawing to look like the real thing. Already we have a *style* decision.

The young artist, however, feels confined by the sheet of paper handed out for the assignment. A two-dimensional surface does not offer enough freedom or originality,

Figure 5.5 Michelangelo Buonarroti, *David***, 1501–1504.**
Is seeing this photograph of Michelangelo's *David* the same as seeing the sculpture itself? How does the medium used for a work of art change our experience of that work?
© Studio Fotografico Quattrone

so she brings a bar of soap to school and proceeds to carve a tiny three-dimensional model of a real house. Not only is this a departure from the *style* of the others, but soap is a different *medium* from paper.

The medium of imitation can be just as exciting as the act of imitating itself. Standing close to Michelangelo's statue of Moses (Figure 5.2) or David (Figure 5.5), we are astounded at how lifelike the artist was able to make the marble seem. A painting of David is not the same as the statue, even though we might recognize that both imitate the same character. The medium enters strongly into the experience of art.

If the basic urge of the artist is to imitate the appearance of people, places, and things, the basic style is therefore *Art as Likeness*—although artists differ widely in how they define and create that imitative world. A myriad of artists claim to be reproducing reality, yet we nonetheless find in their work a variety of styles, media, and approaches.

Creating Likeness in Different Styles

5.2   *What are key characteristics of classical, medieval, and Renaissance art?*

Even when the ultimate aim is to create something that looks very much like the real thing, artists can greatly differ in the kind of likeness they transfer from the external world to a medium. The marble bust sculpted in fifth-century BCE Greece may seem very different from a clay or wooden sculpture from New Guinea, in the Pacific Islands—and the intentions of the artists may differ—but to the viewer, both appear to be the heads of males (see Figures 5.6 and 5.7).

In this section we investigate *Art as Likeness* in both painting and sculpture, looking at major achievements and styles in its long history. We shall then be prepared to understand when and why artists began to consider other possibilities of artistic expression.

Figure 5.6 Roman, *Antinous,* **detail, 2nd century CE.**

G. Dagli Orti/De Agostini Picture Library/Getty Images

Figure 5.7 A traditional carving from a village in Papua New Guinea.

Compare the head of Antinous (Fig. 5.6) with the carving from New Guinea. How might cultural differences account for these different representations of a human figure?

Dozier Marc/Hemis-Fr/Alamy

Classical Art

The words *classic, classical,* and *classicism* have slightly different connotations. A *classic* is a work of art—a painting or sculpture, but also a novel or poem, a play, a film, a piece of music—that continues to be not only admired but also viewed, read, performed, seen, or played long after it was created. Critics will sometimes enthusiastically label a new work an "instant classic"; the implication is that the work will endure, will still be relevant many years from now. Of course, no one can really know how long a contemporary work will survive. The irony is that the creators of acknowledged classics seldom were aware their works would live on. On the other hand, history is also filled with artists confident they have created a "classic," only to have their work forgotten almost immediately.

In the visual arts, the term **classicism** or *classical period* is generally used to refer to the early part of a historical period when a culture's distinct artistic styles and media first flowered. Because cultures evolve on their own timelines, their classical periods date to different historical eras.

EARLY ISLAMIC, INDIAN, AND ASIAN ART Classical Islamic art generally dates from the time of the prophet Mohammed (570–632 CE) through the eleventh century. It is highly abstract and geometrical in nature, imitative not of the familiar world but of the artist's vision of the spiritual world. Islamic classical art was primarily decorative, used on tapestries, rugs, holy buildings, and the residences of high-ranking persons.

The ancient period of Indian Classical art extends from about 3500 BCE to 1200 CE. Some of it, like Islamic art, is abstract, but much Indian art is amazingly lifelike. Sculptures of nude males show painstaking effort to duplicate in stone the soft textures and muscles of the human body.

Classical Chinese art dates from around 500 BCE to the fall of the Han Empire in 220 CE. Ancient pottery displays lifelike figures of men and animals, similar to those in the cave drawings, suggesting the central importance of the successful hunt. There are also many fantastic masks meant to depict the faces of gods, who, of course, could not resemble human beings.

Ancient Japanese art has the oldest history; there is evidence of human settlements in Japan 30,000 years ago. Pottery and household utensils unearthed by archeologists cannot be precisely dated but are assumed to be older than almost any other comparable artifacts. Findings suggest that ceramic art was highly advanced, combining form and function. Jugs and plates served not only for practical household needs but for aesthetic pleasure as well. They tend to have unusual shapes and are often elaborately decorated with abstract designs indicative of a style of living that required the beautiful as well as the useful.

EARLY WESTERN ART In Western culture, classical art means the sculpture, wall carvings, **frescoes** (wall paintings), mosaics, and architecture of Greece and Rome, spanning the sixth century BCE through the fifth century CE. Because the statues and buildings of many tourist-visited ruins are white or gray, the popular image of this art is of stone shapes that lack color. In fact, classical artists were fond of color; age, weather, and other factors have taken their toll, however, and the colors have faded. Most of the gleaming white columns found on the Acropolis of Athens, for example, were originally painted in bright colors.

Stone and marble were abundant in this classical world, and artists made generous use of these media. The artists responsible for decorating the city of Athens in the fifth century BCE liked to work in marble, but they left it for the most part in an unpolished state. The Romans, who incorporated Athens into their empire in 146 BCE, were intent on rivaling or, if possible, eclipsing that city's monumental achievements in art. Roman sculptors vigorously polished their marble, establishing the process that has been followed ever since.

Figure 5.8 *Artemision Bronze*, c. 460 BCE.
© Marie Mauzy

Figure 5.9 *The Charioteer*, c. 475 BCE.
The statues shown in Figures 5.8 and 5.9 both date from the 5th century BCE. The *Artemision Bronze* is thought to represent a god; *The Charioteer* almost certainly depicts a human. What, if anything, suggests "god" or "human" to you in the two statues? Why might a god have been portrayed as a perfect human?
© Marie Mauzy

Classical Athenian buildings were designed and constructed with mathematical precision, in keeping with the Greek love of numerical and geometric harmony. The statues were mainly depictions of gods and goddesses cast in human forms. They were likenesses of noble, heroic beings, larger than life and thus not direct likenesses of particular human beings. In this sense, they represented the perfection of *humanness*, which the artists apparently considered the appropriate way to imitate the appearance of the divine. By depicting their deities as human beings, the artists were also elevating humanity to a godlike level.

A statue known as the *Artemision Bronze* (Figure 5.8), named for Cape Artemision in Greece where it was found, has been traced back to 460 BCE, early in the classical period. It is a near perfect likeness of a human being, and art historians believe its subject was either Zeus or Poseidon, the god of the sea (Neptune in Rome). It is sometimes called *The God from the Sea.*

One of the best preserved of all the great works from the fifth century BCE is *The Charioteer* (Figure 5.9). Also cast in bronze, it shows that classical Greek artists did indeed imitate real people. The likeness is that of a young man, a chariot driver, who was certainly not a god. Yet his features are without flaw. His face is noble. He could well be a god, even as the *Artemision Bronze* could well be a perfect human. *The Charioteer* is clearly the work of a sculptor who knew anatomy. The veins of the young man's right arm (the left is missing) as well as his feet are rendered with painstaking fidelity to life, and the folds of his garment are so believable that they almost beg to be touched.

Figure 5.10 The Parthenon, c. 447 BCE.
The floor of this great symbol of Athenian glory appears to exemplify the Golden Section: a ratio of 1 to 1.68 between the shorter and longer sides.
© Marie Mauzy

THE PARTHENON The classical Greek world is typified by the Parthenon (Figure 5.10), built as a temple for the goddess Athena. But it also represents the Athenians' passion for the ordered world of mathematics. The floor of the Parthenon was for a long time believed to embody a particular formula discovered and expressed mathematically by Euclid (c. 300 BCE), one of the early founders of geometry. Legend has it that Euclid was fond of handing friends a stick and asking them to indicate where they would divide it that was aesthetically satisfying to them. He found that nearly everybody divided the stick in about the same place, which was not the center. So he began to measure the ratio between the two sections and discovered that it tended to be 1 to 1.68. Expressed verbally, Euclid's law states that the most pleasing relationship between two connecting sections is such that the smaller is to the larger what the larger is to the sum of the two. Euclid called it the law of the **Golden Section**.

Fascinated by the theory, mathematicians and art historians have sought—and claim to have found—the Golden Section in a variety of places, including, in addition to the floor of the Parthenon, the foundations of many Roman ruins, the floor plan of medieval cathedrals, the pages of medieval illuminated manuscripts, and in much Renaissance art and architecture. There is some doubt that the exact Euclidean ratio exists in all the places claimed for it, but researchers say many come astoundingly close.

Beginning in the fourth century BCE, there was a movement in Greek art toward greater realism and less idealization. It is known as the period of Hellenistic Art. Whereas the chariot driver is an ordinary mortal with the appearance of a god, Hellenistic statues depict gods with the more defining features of mortals. There is less geometry and more genuine likeness, suggesting that actual models may have been used. By the third century and following, even more ambitious attempts at realism were to be found. These artists began to choose subjects that were far less serene than those of their predecessors, more dynamic, with strong appeal to the passions. They often captured moments of sensuality and the agony of death throes for a new kind of public, one that demanded excitement from art. The *Laocoön* (Figure 5.11) is a first-century sculpture depicting in graphic detail the anguish of a father and his two sons as they are being strangled by sea serpents. The figures are not idealized—unless their agony represents the "perfection" of pain. The Romans would imitate

Figure 5.11 *The Laocoön*, c. 200 BCE.
How does this portrait of a father and his sons being attacked by serpents reflect a change in Hellenistic art?
Asier Villafranca/Shutterstock

the quieter classicism of the fifth century, but they were also heavily influenced by the vivid realism of the later period.

Despite the endurance of certain Hellenistic works like the *Laocoön,* Greek and Roman art leaves the general impression of a civilization that valued balance and harmony. In fact, what we call "classical" music, which emerged in the middle to late seventeenth century, is linked to a revival of interest in that aspect of the classical world and demonstrates such order.

Medieval Art

Much Christian art from the fifth to the fifteenth centuries had one purpose: to remind the faithful of the life and death of Jesus, Mary, the saints, and the disciples. Artists who were selected by the church devoted their talents to the sacred adornment of church interiors. Like the Greeks and Romans centuries before them, medieval artists imagined spiritual beings in human terms, though their work is not very lifelike. Medieval art generally presents the *idea,* not a faithful imitation, of its subjects.

In the painting of the Madonna reproduced here (Figure 5.12) by the artist Cimabue, the mother seems more or less realistic, but the face of the baby Jesus in no way suggests that of an actual infant. It belongs to an adolescent, as it does in nearly all such paintings. Medieval artists thought of the infant Jesus as being already wise. Here we see the *idea* of the divine child, not the appearance of a real-life baby.

Nearly all of the professional art was done by men. One exception was the art of embroidery, which flourished in both France and England during the period. The Bayeux tapestry (Figure 5.13) is not really a tapestry at all but a series of panels embroidered in colored yarn on a linen background. It stretches 203 feet and tells the story of the Battle of Hastings in 1066, in which Normans under William the Conqueror defeated the Saxon army of King Harold. The tapestry is believed to have been commissioned by William's half-brother and was once attributed to Queen Matilda, William's wife. But subsequent research reveals it was more likely made years later by English embroiderers.

Classical ideas were by no means completely dormant during the Middle Ages, however. Medieval cathedrals, built during the eleventh and twelfth centuries, utilized classical principles of mathematical order. They were, of course, strongly reflective of the Christian religion, and their floor plan—a central aisle called the *nave* and a smaller chapel on each side—was shaped like the cross. They are considered the finest examples of the **Gothic** style. A sixteenth-century Italian art historian named the style after the "barbarian" Goths, the Teutonic invaders who had conquered Rome. The label was meant to connote a barbaric departure from classicism, perhaps because of the demonic-looking gargoyles—statues of ugly, evil monsters designed to frighten away malevolent spirits. But there was nothing barbaric about the plan of construction. With their soaring towers reaching up to heaven and their stone buttresses, the cathedrals were so finely engineered that no mortar was needed originally to attach the stones to each other.

Figure 5.12 Cimabue, *Maestà,* **1280–1285.**

Artists of the Middle Ages commonly portrayed the baby Jesus as a small adult, as Cimabue does here, rather than an infant. What reasons might they have had for doing this?

© Studio Fotografico Quattrone

GIOTTO The work of the Florentine artist Giotto di Bondone (1266/67–1337) introduced new techniques and prepared the way for the artistic realism of the

Figure 5.13 Scene from the Bayeux Tapestry, c. 1070s.
What might have prevented women from creating more art in the Middle Ages?
Erich Lessing/Art Resource, NY

Renaissance. Along with a number of colleagues, Giotto brought new life to the art of decorating church interiors.

Giotto was concerned not only with *what* the eye sees but *how* it sees. If you look, for example, at railroad tracks stretching ahead of you for miles, you will see that they do not appear to stay the same distance apart. The distance gradually *shrinks* until, at some point, the tracks converge. An illusion of sight, it is known in the art world as **perspective**, and Giotto was one of the first artists since antiquity to paint figures and objects larger or smaller depending on where they stand relative to the viewer.

Most art historians regard the frescoes on the wall of the Scrovegni Chapel in Padua as Giotto's masterpiece. There are 37 scenes from the lives of Christ and the Virgin. Throughout the fresco cycle, Giotto concerned himself with representing spatial depth. One of the most powerful of the scenes is the *Lamentation of Christ* (Figure 5.14). A rocky ledge behind the figures indicates that the figures are in the foreground of a landscape, and the overlapping of the figures helps define movement back into space. Moreover, two seated figures are seen from the back, facing the same direction as the viewer and thus bridging our space and that of the painted scene. In earlier medieval work, figures and objects tended to appear to be on the same plane.

Like many artists of the Renaissance to come, Giotto created frescoes, an art form that would come into its own a century after his death. Giotto used a mural painting technique called buon ("true") fresco by which water-based paint was applied on wet plaster. This technique creates durable murals because as the painted plaster dries the pigments are bonded to the surface of the wall. The artist has to work quickly, however, without making mistakes. In Giotto's day, a wall to be frescoed would be prepared with a rough undercoat of plaster called the *arricio*. When the *arricio* dried, the artist's assistants would use reddish-brown pigment or charcoal to copy the master artist's composition onto the wall, creating underdrawings called *sinopia*. A second coat of very thin plaster (the *intonaco*) was applied over the *sinopia*; once this plaster was set, but not fully dried, the artist completed the mural in segments, using pigments mixed with water.

In contrast, for his *Last Supper* in the refectory of Santa Maria del Grazie in Milan, Leonardo da Vinci employed an experimental mural painting technique by applying

Figure 5.14 Giotto di Bondone, *The Lamentation of Christ,* **1304–1306.**
How does Giotto's use of spatial depth change the experience of looking at this fresco?
© Studio Fotografico Quattrone

an oil and tempera paint directly to a wall of dried *intonaco*. The artist's radical experimentation with technique resulted in an unstable work that eventually began to flake off the wall.

Renaissance Art

The *Renaissance,* meaning "rebirth," began in Italy in the fourteenth century. Giotto is sometimes categorized as "early Renaissance." He certainly had much to do with the transition from medieval, two-dimensional art to a more full-bodied way of painting. The Renaissance would become a vast movement encompassing not only art but also drama, music, and politics.

The movement spread from Italy throughout western Europe, finally reaching the British Isles late in the sixteenth century. At first a revolution in art, bringing the world a vibrant, pulsating realism never before known, it led to a political and social revolution against the tight controls of religion. This movement sometimes deemphasized the next world as the sole concern of human beings and instead focused on leading the good life in *this* world—but religious themes remained of primary importance. The Renaissance reinstated science as a legitimate source of knowledge and held a greater respect for individual achievement. Artists such as Donatello, Fra Angelico, and Botticelli in Italy, and Van Eyck, Dürer, and Hans Holbein in the north, brought a sensuality and realism to their art that had not been seen in many years.

FILIPPO LIPPI Filippo Lippi (1406?–1469), who is better known as Fra Lippo Lippi largely because of Robert Browning's famous poem about him, typifies the Renaissance spirit. Forced into monastic orders at the age of 8, he had a hard time suppressing his desire to escape from the confines of his cell. Finally he lost the battle and began to sneak out at night, roaming the countryside, drawing people and objects that caught his eye. A forerunner of the great Italian Renaissance artists of the sixteenth century, Lippi was recognized for his genius at a very young age and was commissioned to paint biblical scenes. So astonishingly real were his figures that he was

Figure 5.15 Filippo Lippi, *The Annunciation*, c. 1435–1440.
What differences are there in the depiction of the Virgin Mary between this work and Cimabue's
Madonna and Child in Figure 5.12?
Courtesy of National Gallery of Art/Samuel H. Kress Collection

accused of using forbidden human models (see, for example, Figure 5.15). There were even rumors that he hired prostitutes to pose for his depictions of the Virgin Mary.

CLASSICAL DISCIPLINE AND INDIVIDUAL EXPRESSION   In the humanities, the term "renaissance" signified a renewed interest in the knowledge and art of the classical world—in part because that world had been ignored for so many centuries, but also because classical artists and thinkers were concerned with making sense of, and bringing beauty to the only life they knew for certain.

Renaissance artists combined classical discipline with something new: the demand for freedom of individual expression. The Renaissance constitutes the greatest single revolution in the history of Western art and thought, though centuries earlier the Arab world had kept alive the teachings of Greek philosophy, especially those of Aristotle, with his desire to analyze the human condition and his anticipation of the scientific method.

At first, the artistic revolution was a quiet one: artists experimenting with more lifelike representations of the human form. As the years went by, however, the revolutionary fires grew more intense. Artists began to react boldly against religious traditionalism and demand the right to practice their craft without constraints and fear of censorship.

Perhaps the most infamous of these was the Baroque artist Michelangelo Merisi, known as Caravaggio (1571–1610). Caravaggio's paintings are remarkable for their powerful contrasts between bright light and dark shadow (see Figure 5.22), which influenced many later artists, and for their unidealized, even gritty, depictions of Christ, Mary, and the saints as human beings who once walked the earth, even among the poorest populations. Caravaggio also produced extraordinarily sensual images of androgynous young men offering fruit and flowers, or playing music. The artist never lacked for important commissions, but he was involved in all manner of criminal activity, perhaps including murder, and he died at 39 alone on a beach south of Rome, in circumstances never fully explained. Although he was almost forgotten after his death, Caravaggio's reputation was rescued in the twentieth century, and he is now acknowledged as one of the most remarkable and influential painters in the history of art.

THE HUMAN BODY   Of particular interest to the artists of the Italian Renaissance was that in classicism the human body was depicted in the nude. True, the nude human form as displayed in ancient times had been made geometrically perfect and thus not truly lifelike, but classical art set in motion the interest of the new artists in realistic anatomy. Both Leonardo and Michelangelo performed anatomical dissections to help them understand the human body. In its pose and its idealized, heroic form, Michelangelo's *David* reveals his study of ancient sculpture, particularly of male nude athletes in the prime of life. We also know from surviving drawings that Michelangelo and his contemporaries studied the human body from live models.

The new art had two dominant characteristics. First, continuing in Giotto's tradition, it tried to make the eye of the viewer see things and people as they appeared in real life, continuing to use perspective to achieve the illusion of three dimensions. Second, it invited an emotional response from the viewer. Compare the heroic *David* of Michelangelo (Figure 5.5) to the androgynous, sexualized *David* of Donatello (Figure 2.2), also based on the study of the antique. Donatello's sensual David was made for a private patron, a member of the Medici family, while Michelangelo's heroic David was commissioned by the church, a more conservative patron. The edgy sensuality of the *David* by Donatello, who died a century before Michelangelo, elicits a different response from that of Michelangelo's heroic sculpture.

The Florentines reacted powerfully and emotionally to the classical style of Michelangelo's *David*. It is Renaissance in subject as well as in form: The subject—the boy about to take on the giant Goliath—was not only biblical but also contemporary and political. The Republican citizens of Florence saw David as a symbol of their relatively small city, challenging the recently expelled Medici and perhaps also the other mighty Italian cities such as Venice, Genoa, and Rome for supremacy in art and urban sophistication.

The obsession of Renaissance artists with imitating life as precisely as possible owes something to the general spirit of the age. The new realism, with its charged emotions, its sense of the dramatic, and its introduction of new ways of seeing and imitating life, brought together an astonishing array of great artists, most of them located in or near Florence. Many of these artists have achieved places of honor in the history of the humanities, but Leonardo, Michelangelo, and Raphael were accorded almost instant immortality.

LEONARDO DA VINCI   The oldest of the three giants of art, Leonardo (1452–1519) came to Florence from the nearby town of Vinci. He excelled in so many fields—as a painter, sculptor, architect, inventor, and at least *conceiver* of such astounding marvels as the submarine and the airplane—that he richly deserves the label bestowed upon him in his lifetime, *uomo universale*. The label has been translated as "Renaissance man."

At least two of Leonardo's works stand out as definitive examples of their respective genres: the mural *The Last Supper* (Figure 5.16) and the portrait *Mona Lisa*. Commissioned in 1494 as a sacred fresco for the refectory

Figure 5.16 Leonardo da Vinci, *The Last Supper*, 1494–1498.
Where does your gaze focus when looking at this painting? How does the artist make that happen?
© Studio Fotografico Quattrone

(dining hall) of Santa Maria del Grazie in Milan, *The Last Supper,* which shows the final gathering of Jesus and his 12 disciples before his arrest and crucifixion, took three years to complete. *The Last Supper* is celebrated for a number of reasons. First, it is a triumph of perspective. Designed to occupy the entire far wall of the dining room, the mural presents the illusion that the room actually extends into the painting, continuing on into the natural world glimpsed through the windows behind Jesus and the disciples.

Second, Leonardo employed a technique known as **chiaroscuro**, in which the strong contrasts between light and shadow provide three-dimensionality and drama. Chiaroscuro was used by earlier Renaissance artists, as well as by later artists including Caravaggio and Rembrandt, who exaggerated the contrast between light and dark even more dramatically. The use of perspective contributed to the illusion of reality, but the interplay of dark and light was necessary for a totally authentic experience of vision. Leonardo's use of a lighting system in which contours are soft and hazy like smoke (described by historians as *sfumato*) is particularly effective.

Third, the mural is a notable example of Leonardo's genius for capturing the endless complexity of human beings, reproducing not just physical but *psychological* likeness. Jesus has just said: "One of you which eateth with me shall betray me" (Mark 14:18). While he remains the calm center of the group, his pronouncement creates an emotional storm among all the others, save one. Only that one knows the betrayal has already taken place.

Does the painting show which one is Judas, the betrayer? Look carefully. From the viewer's perspective, Judas is third to the left of Jesus, his arm leaning on the table, and he appears to be holding the bag of coins he has received for pointing Jesus out to the Romans. The magic of Leonardo is nowhere better illustrated than in the fact that we do not need to see the bag to identify Judas. He leans away from Christ and is the only disciple in shadow.

Leonardo is like a stage director. By his placement of the characters and the direction of their eyes, he controls the manner in which the viewer watches the scene. And *watch* is a more appropriate word than *see*; though a painting is a static object, depicting a moment frozen in time, *The Last Supper* unfolds as a drama being witnessed on a stage.

Leonardo's complex faces, especially that of Jesus, are the parallel in visual art to what modern theater calls *subtext,* a technique whereby the playwright lets the audience know what is happening below the surface by having a character remain silent or else speak a very few words. Given the author's skill at creating the proper subtext, great performers on the stage can provoke thoughts and pique the curiosity by a slight glance or by the silences that precede or follow their words. Similarly, a great artist like Leonardo is able somehow to show what is happening inside a subject's mind. In Christ's face we can read sorrow, because he knows who the betrayer is and knows that the deed cannot be undone. There is resignation to his imminent death on the cross. And, astonishingly, we see understanding and forgiveness, too.

Through both the placement of his figures—Judas and Jesus, for example—and his ability to suggest the inner life, Leonardo greatly influenced the development of dramatic art. Max Reinhardt, one of the great theater directors of the last century, counseled his students and apprentices to study Leonardo if they wanted to learn how best to stage a scene. Konstantin Stanislavsky, who founded the modern school of truthful acting, was known to have spent many hours in his classes analyzing the dramatic elements in works such as *The Last Supper*.

LEONARDO, *MONA LISA*   Leonardo also goes far beyond surface realism in another masterpiece, the *Mona Lisa* (see Figure 1.1). The work has become the most famous single work of art in the world, attracting huge numbers of visitors each day to the Louvre Museum in Paris.

What is all the fuss about? How do we account for the extraordinary stature of a panel measuring 30 × 21 inches? One reason, of course, may be that widely discussed mysterious smile. We do not always find this kind of psychological complexity in portrait paintings, because artists customarily were and are still hired to render both a realistic likeness *and* an idealized rendering of the sitter. The expression on the face, still a source of debate and the subject of many volumes of interpretation, will probably elude definitive understanding forever.

A close look at the painting, however, reveals that the mouth is shown with only the faintest trace of a smile. Just as interesting is the fact that the sitter, the wife of a Florentine merchant, is looking at something or someone not shown in the painting—just *what* we can never know. But this adds to the mystery.

Many have suggested that, in this work, Leonardo revealed the essential ambiguity of all human faces and personalities—that, by creating a work that shows both an idiosyncratic human being and a representative noble woman, he has both particularized and generalized his subject. In its grand pyramidal composition reminiscent of images of the Virgin Mary, in the placement of the figure in a serene and confident pose that includes the arms and hands, and in the blending of human figure and untamed nature in an atmospheric, hazy light, the *Mona Lisa* presents a compelling yet mysterious representation of the sitter. She does not avert her eyes, as is usual in Renaissance portraits of elite women, but sets her gaze with self-assurance in the direction of the viewer. While Renaissance portraits of women typically emphasized the sitter's high status through jewels and elaborate clothing—interpreting her, that is, as an elite *type*—Leonardo explores instead the sitter's individuality, adding to her mystery and her modern appeal.

MICHELANGELO   What Shakespeare is to theater and Beethoven is to music, Michelangelo is to sculpture. Before he came upon the scene, sculpture was thought to be a skill at best, ordinary decoration at its least. Michelangelo Buonarroti (1475–1564) helped to change the reputation of sculpture, making it an art form of the highest order. He did it through an effort of will and physical strength that are almost unimaginable.

As a youth, Michelangelo learned from artists of the fifteenth-century Florentine style, but he soon realized that he wanted more than what they were teaching. He wanted to create figures that were totally his, that bore his unmistakable mark. In fact, he was so confident that no one would confuse his style with another artist's that he signed his name to a work only once—and that was the *Pietà* in the Vatican, created when he was just 22 and somewhat less self-assured than he would become in a short time.

As Michelangelo matured, his work began to show a tension between classicism and the expression of passion. The Vatican *Pietà* (Figure 5.17), however, viewed by the thousands who daily visit St. Peter's, shows the crucified son lying across the lap of his grieving mother. Michelangelo did not focus on physical suffering as was the case in earlier depictions of the subject. His sculpture contains more of the *idea* of pain than the *essence* of it. There is a serenity about the work that is uplifting indeed, but a little removed from an effort to capture in marble a most extreme human emotion.

In contrast is the *Pietà Rondanini* (Figure 5.18), created when the artist was in his 80s. The sculptor may have attempted to destroy the work before anyone could see it, so convinced was he that it was unworthy of his most severe critic, whom he believed to be God. Presumably it was originally intended for his own tomb, but now we are left with only fragments—or, as some scholars suggest, an intentionally unfinished work. Most clearly seen is the face of Mary, on which Michelangelo indelibly

Figure 5.17 Michelangelo Buonarroti, *Pietà*, 1498–1499.
Izzet Keribar/Getty Images

Figure 5.18 Michelangelo Buonarroti, *Pietà Rondanini*, c. 1550s–1564.

Michelangelo Buonarroti's *Pietà* (Fig. 5.17) and his *Pietà Rondanini* (above) vary significantly. To what might we attribute the striking differences between these two sculptures, both depicting the same event?

De Agostini Picture Library/Getty Images

chiseled the pain missing in the youthful work. This sculpture is intensely personal art, a statement by a genius who is not happy with what he has done, a genius who has felt the sorrow unknown to most human beings: the sorrow of having not quite ascended to the very highest level possible for a mortal. Of course, the judgment of the ages has been that Michelangelo did indeed attain this level, but he never enjoyed the knowledge of what he had achieved. A story repeated over and over in the humanities!

Michelangelo's restless, unceasing quest for perfection helps explain why he was not content to stay only with sculpture. He also aspired to be the greatest painter the world had ever known. His biggest challenge—even greater than that of the 17-foot block of marble that became the *David*—was a task given him by Pope Julius II: to paint the ceiling of the Sistine Chapel inside the Vatican. Michelangelo's imagination was immediately stirred. There was the height itself, as close to heaven as his art was ever likely to take him. There was the huge expanse of the ceiling, allowing for a series of paintings on religious themes that would at the same time present to the viewer a totally unified effect. And there was the challenge that fresco posed, for the plaster had to be applied to the ceiling and painted before it was completely dry. The artist worked for four long years, standing on a scaffold for hours at a time while plaster continually dripped down on his face. But Michelangelo was both passionate and businesslike in his work. He had assistants, and the project was carefully planned—and viewed by few until the gasp-filled unveiling. Never for a moment did the artist fear that the pontiff would be disappointed, but Michelangelo may still have harbored the fear that the work had not satisfied God.

That Michelangelo not only sought perfection but did so in such challenging media as marble and fresco tells us why he has come to symbolize the Renaissance itself. The unending quest for greatness is surely a sign of an enormous human ego, quite consistent with the period's stress on individualism and human achievement. At the same time, to offer up that ego in the service of God was to renounce worldly fame as well as the self.

Sometimes losing the struggle against ego added further to his anguish. He was adored by a huge public. Prospective patrons offered incredible sums for his services. How could he not have felt a measure of pride when he saw on all sides confirmation of his greatness? His letters reveal someone who was always at odds with himself, always fighting to suppress his ego. On the other hand, some critics have suggested that to believe God was the only audience suitable for one's work constitutes arrogance of cosmic scope.

His style—sometimes referred to by the word *terribilità,* which means "awesomeness"—reflects the need to challenge the medium in the way that the matador challenges the bull. But Michelangelo cannot be the only artist whose creative process was inspired by the difficulty of the medium. Many—perhaps most—artists overcome obstacles that might stop the rest of us in our tracks. No medium surrenders willingly; the struggle, for some, makes the conquest worthwhile. Referring to the permissiveness in modern poetry and modern theater, where great liberties are allowed in language and structure, the critic Andrew Sarris has made the telling observation that where everything is possible, nothing matters.

Yet great art often hides or disguises the effort that goes into it. If we sit in the front row at the ballet, we will hear the heavy breathing and see the drops of sweat falling to the stage. We may understand the level of effort that exists underneath it all. Sitting farther back, we see only the beauty and fluidity of movement. But we have to know the passionate striving is there, underneath it all. We've said it before, but it bears repeating: *Art is the illusion that there is no art.*

Figure 5.19 Raphael Sanzio da Urbino, *The Alba Madonna,* **1510.** Consider the difference between this Madonna and children and the one by Cimabue in Figure 5.12. What has changed in the centuries between these works?

Courtesy of National Gallery of Art/ Andrew W. Mellon Collection

RAPHAEL Raphael (1483–1520), the last born of the three great Florentine Renaissance artists, died only a year after Leonardo and nearly half a century before Michelangelo. This fact is important to remember, for when we consider how much Raphael achieved in a relatively short lifespan we can only speculate on what he might have done had he lived longer. Raphael had the advantage of observing the techniques of his two predecessors, and his work clearly shows their influence, their carrying art toward more and more intense realism, especially Leonardo's characteristic interplay of light and shadow, a technique Raphael employs in the *Alba Madonna* of 1510 (Figure 5.19). Raphael uses a brighter lighting system, different from Leonardo's hazy *sfumato* and earthy colors.

The painting also illustrates how far the technique of realistic perspective had progressed from the time of Giotto. The hills in the distance, painted near the top, are much smaller than the figures of the infants Jesus and John the Baptist. Moreover, the Virgin Mary looks like a real woman, while both children look their appropriate age. The divine nature of Mother and Child is indicated by the adoring look on the face of the Baptist, and especially by the large cross that the children hold, as well as by other symbolic elements; otherwise this could be a study of an ordinary family.

The naturalistic effect comes from the light Raphael gives to his sky and from the dark interior of the cloak from which the Virgin's arm extends, as well as from her right sleeve. The background also shows a contrast between light and shadow, and there is shade in the foreground, suggesting that the figures may be near a tree.

In 1508, Raphael, already famous, was called to Rome by Pope Julius II, who commissioned him to paint four frescoes for the Vatican Palace illustrating theology, philosophy, poetry, and justice. The most famous of these is the fresco celebrating

Figure 5.20 Raphael Sanzio da Urbino, *The School of Athens*, **1509–1511.**
What is suggested about the culture of the Renaissance by the fact that the two central figures in this painting are Plato and Aristotle?
Richard Osbourne/Alamy

philosophy, now called *The School of Athens* (Figure 5.20). In the work we see, again, a highly sophisticated use of perspective, with a multitude of ancient philosophers congregating in a vast hall built in a classical style. In this symmetrically balanced composition, the figures are painted in accurate proportion relative to the two arches in the background and the two statues of ancient gods that tower over them, and each figure is painstakingly detailed, despite the fact that, in order to recreate so large a scene, the artist had to paint with extremely minute strokes on the wet plaster.

The work of Raphael and the other great artists of the Italian Renaissance has made Florence and Rome art centers that attract many thousands of visitors yearly and millions more through the magic of virtual tours on the Internet. Eventually you may have the opportunity to see the originals up close; life offers few comparable experiences.

TWO WOMEN OF THE POST-RENAISSANCE   Sophonisba Anguissola (c. 1532–1626) and her five sisters were all trained artists, but Sophonisba was the first female to achieve an international reputation for her art. So precocious was her talent for realistic portraiture that the great Michelangelo agreed to teach her and later expressed admiration for her work. Georgio Vasari, the first major critic and art historian of the Italian Renaissance and author of the male-dominated *Lives of the Artists,* credited Sophonisba with having produced "rare and beautiful" work and placed her above all other female artists. (This suggests that she was probably one of many women who practiced the art of painting, although few achieved reputations as grand as those of their male counterparts.) Sophonisba achieved success as a portrait painter and became the official court painter to the Spanish king; she also created more intimate portraits, including one of her sisters enjoying a game of chess.

Several generations younger was Artemisia Gentileschi (1592–1652), whose reputation has eclipsed Sophonisba's. Art historians now consider Artemisia the most important female artist of the post-Renaissance, though only 34 of her works have survived. In her time, she was scorned by both critics and male colleagues as too aggressive—that is, "unfeminine"—in promoting her work.

Scorn for her spread to the public sector when she was involved in a sex scandal that became the topic of gossip in Florence. She accused a fellow artist, Agostino Tassi, of raping her and demanded that he be arrested and brought to justice. The trial lasted seven months, during which several of Tassi's male friends testified that Artemisia was generally known as promiscuous. Another witness saved the day by testifying that Tassi had, in his presence, openly boasted of the rape. Her reputation somewhat restored (though still a bit tarnished from all the negative publicity), Artemisia persevered. Feminists and art historians have debated the effect of the trial on her paintings, citing in particular their frequently violent themes. One of her most acclaimed works, *Judith Slaying Holofernes* (Figure 5.21), depicts the biblical heroine Judith, who seduced the Assyrian general Holofernes, then beheaded him with his own sword in order to protect her community from invasion.

REMBRANDT: THE PERFECTION OF LIKENESS From Leonardo on, the demand for portraiture increased in Europe. As years passed, rich and powerful households began to decorate their halls with the watchful eyes of departed ancestors. Perfect likenesses, which might also doctor up an unattractive wrinkle here or a weak chin there, brought newfound riches to artists who could master the skill of faithful—or nearly so—imitation.

The master painters of the **Dutch school** of the seventeenth century were able to reproduce faces, figures, and landscapes with the greatest accuracy possible until the invention of photography two centuries later. In fact, many casual and infrequent visitors to museums still respond most favorably to their work because of its startling realism.

Of all the Dutch masters, none surpassed Rembrandt Harmenszoon van Rijn (1606–1669). While he can be said to have mastered the art of perfect likenesses, he was also, like Leonardo, interested in what we may call **psychological realism**. Like many artists, Rembrandt often worked on commission, but he almost always looked for the challenge in his subject: the character behind the face, the pain suffered (even if he didn't know the cause), the longing for that something else that might have compensated for a disappointing life. He was fond of painting old people, whose faces bore the marks and burdens of many years of hardship and loss.

In seeking ways to further the technique of intense inner realism, Rembrandt was aided by the chiaroscuro effect that Caravaggio had used with such eloquence; so painstakingly did Rembrandt practice the effect that he has come to be identified with

Figure 5.21 Artemisia Gentileschi, *Judith Slaying Holofernes,* **c. 1612.**
Rabatti Domingie/Akg-Images/Newscom

Figure 5.22 Michelangelo Merisi, known as Caravaggio, *Judith Beheading Holofernes,* **c. 1598–1599.**
Do you notice differences in how Gentileschi (Fig. 5.21) and Caravaggio depict Judith's expression? What might explain these differences?
Scala/Art Resource, NY

Figure 5.23 Rembrandt van Rijn,
Self-Portrait, **1659.**
What do you find most interesting
or striking about this portrait of the
artist?
Peter Horree/Alamy

it. In the work reproduced here, only the face matters, bathed in light from a mysterious source. To look at many paintings by Rembrandt is to see such a contrast between light and darkness that it is tempting to believe the source of light must be external to the painting. Though the amazing light dominates this picture, we must not suppose that the darkness is unimportant to the total effect; the artist uses it to enhance the quiet drama of his own self-portrait (Figure 5.23).

A visit to a major museum will afford you the opportunity to look at many conventional portraits that are nearly perfect likenesses—but *only* of surface realism: expressions seem devoid of emotion; they offer no clue to what sort of life the person has led. It takes a supreme genius to accomplish that.

Rebellion Against Perfect Likeness

5.3 *What are the major art movements of the eighteenth and nineteenth centuries?*

The art world was well aware that Rembrandt and other masters of the Dutch school of intense realism had taken the imitative aspect of visual art about as far as it could go. So, as one would expect, new generations of artists would attempt to emulate their work. Well into the eighteenth century, on both sides of the Atlantic, landscape and portrait painting tended to be technically proficient—and, with rare exception, generally unexciting. One of the frequent characteristics of art, however, is novelty, so sooner or later this trend had to run its course. Someone was bound to come along and rebel against the tradition of perfect likeness. Francisco Goya (1746–1828), Spain's major artist of the late eighteenth century, was a decisive leader of that rebellion.

The Transition from Realism: Goya

Goya's early work, it is true, is characterized by realistic landscapes depicting the natural beauty of the Aragon countryside in which he was nurtured, as well as portraits of considerable vitality with finely detailed, nearly photographic likenesses of his subjects. The young Goya proved he could do (or almost do) what the Dutch had done. Though he was little known when he came to Madrid, the cultural center of Spain, he quickly became a star, gaining great favor among the aristocracy because of his talent for flattering portraiture.

Then something happened he had not counted on: The lifestyle of Madrid's fashionable elite became unbearable to him. He was appalled by the greed, hypocrisy, and constant jockeying for social position, realizing that, if his success were to continue, he would have to race through life churning out portraits for the aristocracy. Fortunately for posterity, the demands of artistic integrity were too great for Goya. Instead of doing the lucrative work of an official portrait painter, he wanted to paint what he *felt* about this society, in a style that would mock the pretentiousness of the lazy, unproductive, yet arrogant aristocracy. The negativity may have been partly influenced by a serious illness which left him totally deaf in 1792.

The artist became a thorough-going cynic, developing a hatred for the privileged and the things they did to hold their power. His style became increasingly dark, eventually bordering on madness.

The invasion of Spain by Napoleon during the first decade of the nineteenth century, bringing with it the ravages of war and demonstrating the brutal acts human beings were capable of committing, depressed him further. In two of his masterpieces, *The Second of May 1808* and *The Third of May 1808* (Figure 5.24), Goya used art to make an intense statement by dramatizing war's cruelty. In the latter work, reproduced here, we see the execution of several Spaniards by Napoleon's firing squad. The artist's focus is on the pleading looks in the faces of the condemned and frightened men. The figures are recognizable as men, but they embody the artist's powerful statement about war that gives the work its enduring relevance. Notice, too, Goya's superb

Figure 5.24 Francisco Goya, *The Third of May 1808,* **1814.**
How might our experience of this painting change if we saw the faces of the soldiers as well as their victims? Or if the central figure did not have raised arms, which may bring to mind Christ on the cross for some viewers?
GL Archive/Alamy

handling of chiaroscuro, and the influence of Rembrandt in the contrast between light and shadow.

Many of Goya's later works seem downright unpleasant, if not hideous, to many viewers. They raise even now, as they surely did then, questions about the sanity of the artist and the legitimacy of art that is intended to disturb, to externalize its creator's dismal view of existence—art that seems anything but aesthetic and provokes feelings of outrage and horror.

Still, contemporary art that intentionally disturbs the viewer is so commonplace that many of Goya's descendants would regard as impertinent the question of whether art always has to be beautiful. Or they would contend that art by virtue of its artistry always *is* beautiful regardless of subject matter. If one of the criteria for determining that a given work should be labeled as "art" is that the artist has conquered a challenging medium, breaking through steel-like limitations, then Goya's astonishing feat of capturing humanity's elusive passions must be called beautiful.

Impressionism

While Goya and others opened the door for the intensely personal in art, realistic landscapes and portraits continued to be popular. In some countries, there were rumblings among younger artists that the days of perfect likeness had run their course, but in art meccas such as France and England, art had come to mean the imitation of likeness in fine detail. Would-be artists were judged on how proficiently they abided by the rules. In Paris, particularly, new artists aspired to have their work exhibited at the annual Salon, a vast juried exhibition open to the public. The jurors who selected the works to be shown were by and large drawn from the ranks of so-called experts who had governed popular taste for decades. Paintings in unfamiliar styles were seldom welcome, and the few that slipped by were generally crucified by the critics.

For artists of the Impressionist movement, painting was viewed as an experience of color and light. The familiar world is the starting point for the Impressionists, but

Figure 5.25 Édouard Manet, *Le Déjeuner sur l'Herbe* (*The Luncheon on the Grass*), 1862.

The "meaning" of art may change over time. This painting, initially rejected by the Parisian art world and now considered priceless, was intended by the artist as an experience of color and light. Yet 21st-century viewers might see something more here—a message about cultural values. What do you think?

Peter Horree/Alamy

it becomes a world transformed by some of the most brilliant colors ever applied to canvas, a world in which the outlines of human beings and natural shapes are softened, less boldly distinguished one from the other, each playing an integral part in the total unity that is a subjective vision of the world at each moment.

Those who were affected by the Impressionists' rationale were also greatly influenced by the science of optics, investigating the phenomenon of sight that had originated during the Middle Ages in Islamic countries, notably Egypt. The new artists wanted to go further than their Renaissance predecessors in the attempt to recreate true visual experience. They wanted to experiment with how color strikes the eye. Philosophers were beginning to ask questions such as "Is color inherent in objects, or is it something that happens within the viewer?"

ÉDOUARD MANET   One artist who was regularly rejected from the great juried shows was Édouard Manet (1832–1883). Intent on painting in a style that was wholly his own, he did not follow the strict guidelines established by the panel of experts who selected the pieces for Salon showing. Accustomed to rejection, Manet nonetheless went ahead, convinced that eventually his methods would be recognized as legitimate. In 1862, he submitted the work that is now acknowledged as an early masterpiece of the Realist/Impressionist movement, but which was at the time the subject of scorn and derision. *Le Déjeuner sur l'Herbe* (Figure 5.25) features three figures seated on the grass in a modern Parisian park: two well-dressed men and a nude woman. Another woman is in the background, perhaps drying herself off after a skinny-dip in the lake. The nude on the grass may or may not have been bathing, but it really doesn't seem to matter. On one level, we may view the painting as a study in the way the eye sees. It is a sort of realism in its observation of the modern world, but perfect likeness is not its aim, as it flattens space and uses a stark lighting system that flattens the figures.

Manet advanced a comprehensive rationale for the new style. A painting, he said, should not imitate the superficial appearance of things. Nor should it be valued because it makes a statement. Instead, a painting should be an event, equal to nothing but itself, existing for itself—not for an issue and not as a souvenir of how someone looked.

The artist, for example, sees a group of people enjoying a picnic by a lake and decides to paint the event. But what is seen and must therefore be duplicated on canvas is a rush of light falling upon the eye in various hues and shadings, blending in with each other, and with brightness blending in with shadows. Rembrandt and Leonardo had done wonders with the effect of light on their subjects, but their technique was a way of giving drama to those subjects. For the Impressionists, light *itself* should now be central to art: the colors of the world carried to the marveling eyes of an artist by the amazing phenomenon of light. It would be many years before physicists would discover that light is made up of tiny particles called photons, but Impressionism revolutionized art by instinctively perceiving that light isn't just *there*: it is somehow a physical thing.

Figure 5.26 Claude Monet, *Impression, Sunrise,* **1872.**
What qualities about this painting make the label "Impressionism" an apt one?
Album/Art Resource, NY

CLAUDE MONET   The new style found its name in a haphazard manner. Claude Monet (1840–1926), whose name was often confused with that of Manet, had also been rejected for years by the experts, but he began to sell after many of his contemporaries, working in similar styles, gained recognition. Edmond Renoir, son of another Impressionist, Auguste Renoir, was in Monet's studio one day, browsing through some of Monet's new works, when he came upon an intriguing scene of fishing boats in the harbor at Le Havre. What attracted him was the vibrant color of sunrise flooding the canvas and the hazy indistinctness of the boats, the entire scene forming a subjective experience capturing a glorious moment in time. He asked Monet what he was going to title the painting. The artist merely shrugged and said, "Oh, you can just call it *Impression*." Renoir, thinking the work deserved a less generic label, wrote *Impression, Sunrise* (Figure 5.26). From then on, Monet and all of his close allies were identified (not always with a positive connotation) as the *Impressionists*.

BERTHE MORISOT AND MARY CASSATT   The Impressionist revolution in visual art fostered the careers of two major female artists of the nineteenth century: Berthe Morisot (1841–1895), Manet's sister-in-law, and the American Mary Cassatt (1844–1926). Morisot was the first woman admitted to the tight circle of French Impressionists, and her work, like theirs, shows an intense concern with the way light is seen. Interested in creating nearly true likenesses, she remained throughout her life on the outer rim of the circle. Morisot uses muted light and shadow, combining domestic realism with Impressionist techniques.

Mary Cassatt was influenced by the Impressionist use of light and by the Impressionist philosophy that, in painting, content is subordinate to the artist's technique. Because of her affluence, she was instrumental in keeping the movement alive and gaining acceptance for it in the United States. Her father, a wealthy businessman of French ancestry, who recognized his daughter's artistic talent, sent her to the

Figure 5.27 Mary Cassatt, *The Boating Party,* 1893–1894.
Cassatt was strongly influenced by Japanese art, which tended to use strong, clean lines, bold shapes, and fewer details (as in Fig. 5.28). Can you see any of that influence in this painting?
National Gallery of Art Chester Dale Collection 1963.10.94

Pennsylvania Academy of Fine Art and after graduation to live in Paris. There the young woman met many of the important artists of the Impressionist movement who influenced her later work.

The Boating Party (Figure 5.27) clearly shows that influence, especially Manet's, who painted a similar scene. Cassatt, like many of the Impressionists, also was inspired by Japanese art, an exhibition of which she had viewed in Paris. Japanese painters were fond of using bold shapes and fewer details (see Figure 5.28). The darkness of the oarsman's coat is in sharp contrast to the soft light on the figures of the mother and the child on her lap. These figures, much like Morisot's, are representative of Cassatt's interest in domestic subjects. *The Boating Party* was created in 1893–1894, a time believed to be when the artist's powers were strongest.

Figure 5.28 Kitagawa Utamaro, *Mother and Child Gazing at a Handmirror,* 1802.
Brooklyn Museum Collection

Post-Impressionism

The Impressionist movement took hold so strongly on both sides of the Atlantic that it eventually became as authoritative as the traditions it replaced. Newer artists emerged who became dissatisfied with paintings of optical effects of light and color and sought to use color to express emotion and symbolic meaning. The label **Post-Impressionism** was coined by art historians as a convenient way to refer to the work of a group of artists who came after the heyday of Impressionism and whose work, though influenced by it, does not clearly belong to the earlier school.

VINCENT VAN GOGH Of this group, Vincent van Gogh (1853–1890) was perhaps the most original. He differs from the Impressionists in a major respect: He had no real scientific theory of art. He loved color, especially bright yellow and intense greens and reds, which he sometimes juxtaposed to a jarring effect. He had no interest in consulting the science of optics so that he could accurately imitate the experience of seeing.

We know a great deal about van Gogh's approach toward painting from the letters he wrote to his brother, Theo, which record his ideas about his work at length. He used color as a means of expressing emotion, from pleasure and joy to loneliness and despair, rather than to accurately describe the physical world.

Van Gogh is the prototype of the artist who creates entirely for himself, although he did try to sell his paintings. His style was so unusual in its time that the few critics who ever took notice of his work were generally baffled. If his devoted brother Theo had not handled most of his expenses, chances are he

Figure 5.29 Vincent van Gogh, *The Starry Night,* **1889.**
This painting may be second only to the *Mona Lisa* in worldwide popularity. Why do you think that is true?

Brian Jannsen / Alamy

would have been hungry and homeless most of the time. But Theo believed in his genius and stood by him, even when his paintings were denounced and ridiculed. Only one of the artist's paintings was sold during his lifetime. Tragically, he committed suicide when he was only 37.

Van Gogh's life reinforces the romantic concept of the starving artist for whom art is the last outpost of being. Totally alienated, totally misunderstood by almost everyone except his brother, rejected twice as a suitor (once with a vehement cry of "No, never, never!"), hovering much of the time on the thin borderline between functional rationality and insanity (eventually to cross that border, never to return), he survived as long as he did only because of an often childlike delight in his private way of seeing and imitating the world.

VAN GOGH, *THE STARRY NIGHT*   Van Gogh's multiple depictions of sunflowers and his masterpiece, *The Starry Night* (Figure 5.29), are priceless. These and his many other paintings show a brushstroke method that has become utterly identified with its creator: a short, stabbing technique called *impasto* that makes the entire canvas seem to be throbbing with energy. Despite the indifference of the art world, van Gogh abandoned himself to the sensuous impact of life's forms and colors, absorbing them fully and converting them into a heightened reality—an explosion of pure feeling transferred to color, shapes, and paint textures. He also used intense flat color and thick paint-strokes to create meaning. For instance, he explains in his letters to Theo that his scenes of starry nights and cypress trees express his ideas about death and the afterlife.

We began this chapter by discussing the *Mona Lisa,* indicating that it is the world's most famous painting. Van Gogh's *The Starry Night* may well deserve the honor of being regarded as second only to Leonardo's masterpiece in popularity and critical adulation. Ironic for a man who took his own life before he was 40, never knowing what posterity had in store for him!

Art as Alteration

5.4   *Why is "art as alteration" an appropriate way to characterize twentieth- and twenty-first-century art?*

Though they painted the world as *they saw it,* we can still recognize on Impressionist canvases traces of the familiar world, even if drastically changed. Looking at van Gogh's *The Starry Night,* we recognize a sky, albeit one blending yellow with blue. At the same time, his work is moving in the direction of what has come to be called **modernism**. Many schools, movements, and techniques dating from about the last quarter of the nineteenth century to roughly the last quarter of the twentieth century have been linked by critics and art historians under that broad term. The style of the literature and visual arts from the late twentieth century to the present is often called **postmodernism**. What unifies modern and postmodern artists and makes them different from, say, van Gogh is *intention.*

Both van Gogh and the Impressionists give us the familiar world as altered by the emotions and the subjective experiences of light, color, and form. But when we speak of the art that follows them as **alteration**, we are speaking of artists *who do not even start with the familiar world*. Instead, they want to impose something new on that world, some secret part of themselves. With such an intent, they have no reason to be bound by an artistic tradition unless it suits their personality, unless it can be adapted to their imagination. Entering the world of modern art can be confusing at first. There may seem to be no rationale at all, no clear overall purpose, no rules.

When Marcel Duchamp (1887–1968) bought a urinal and submitted it, untouched, for an exhibition in 1917, he challenged all definitions of art. Critics of such "found art" ask: "How much work does an artist have to do? What is off-limits for an artist?" Modern artists impose their own rules upon their own work. They are out there creating new traditions, and most of the time they feel alone. Small wonder that they sometimes, like Duchamp, develop a sense of humor.

Some modern art—in fact, a good deal of it—does in fact resemble people, places, and things. But that is usually where its traditionalism ends. Francis Bacon (1909–1992), for example, offers canvases with *some* recognizable reality, but that reality might be somebody sitting on the toilet, or a slab of meat bleeding. You know what it *represents,* but you may ask: "Why would anybody want to paint *that*?"

The Sixty-Ninth Regiment Armory Show, 1913

Modern art made its way to the United States at the tail end of the *Gilded Age,* a name given to the last two decades of the nineteenth century. Some Americans who had made their fortunes in railroads, coal, or steel, for example, were becoming intensely art conscious. This was the time of elaborate mansions, incredibly luxurious ocean voyages, and the accumulation of what became priceless art collections. New York in particular had a burning need to be respected as a hub of modernism in art. Its collectors wanted to see all that was new and exciting. They had already opened their arms to Impressionism long before it was fully respected in Europe.

In 1913, the Sixty-ninth Regiment Armory in Manhattan was the site of an exhibition of new works by European artists that is still considered the most important single art show ever held in this country. Many American viewers saw for the first time the startling paintings of van Gogh, as well as the work of other artists whose styles seemed downright puzzling, if not laughable.

WASSILY KANDINSKY   The work of the Russian painter and art theorist Wassily Kandinsky (1866–1944) provides an excellent introduction to modern art. Though as a young artist he achieved technical competence in drawing the human figure, he set his eyes on other goals. Kandinsky came to believe that what mattered in a work of art is *form,* the pleasing arrangement of lines and color, existing for no purpose other than aesthetic experience. In other words, a painting should provide an experience of the beautiful. Kandinsky delved into his imagination, found a new world of pure shapes and forms, and imitated those in a style that came to be known as **abstract art**. However, "What's that supposed to be?" is often the first question viewers ask.

Like many other modern artists, Kandinsky distinguished between beauty and anything else one might see in a painting, arguing that

> … in order to speak directly to the soul and avoid materialistic distractions, it was preferable to use an art based solely on the language of color. Free from references to a specific reality, color could become like music, beautiful for its interrelationships of tones and intensities.[1]

Kandinsky's rationale made perfect sense to him, as well as to other exhibited artists, but not to all of the art critics and potential collectors who came to the Armory show in droves hoping to pick up some real bargains. In fact, not much of the show was received with open arms by either critics or the public. The shock of so much alteration was simply too devastating, confined as it was to one building. Canvases by Picasso, who would become the century's most celebrated artist, were widely denounced. The room in which they were displayed was nicknamed the Chamber of Horrors.

DUCHAMP, *NUDE DESCENDING A STAIRCASE*   The work that caused the biggest uproar and controversy, bringing instant notoriety to its creator, was Duchamp's *Nude Descending a Staircase* (Figure 5.30). One critic called Duchamp "the biggest transgressor" in modern art. Four years later, in 1917, Duchamp would further arouse the amused hostility of critics by submitting that urinal we mentioned earlier for an exhibit. (It was promptly rejected.) The artist did in fact start a movement known as "found art," which has won (perhaps grudging) acceptance.

In *Nude Descending a Staircase,* Duchamp developed his own brand of abstractionism in which he moved from an actual model through successive stages of reduction until all that was left from reality was the sense of descending movement and the hint of a human figure. Duchamp, in other words, abstracted from a real scene only those elements that interested him as an artist, excluding everything else. He had signed away his responsibility and obligation to make his work resemble something a viewer could instantly recognize. The controversy might have been less heated had the painting, with such a promising title, not disappointed viewers by giving them no hint of the reality they were expecting. Abstract art remains a popular form of expression among contemporary artists. Sometimes we can gain subject matter clues from the title, but more often the artist will call the painting or sculpture something purely descriptive, such as *Study* or just *Line and Color.*

Cubism and the Birth of Modernism

The enduring fame of the Armory show owes much to its having introduced America to the work of the most baffling, the most controversial, yet easily the most innovative of all

Figure 5.30 Marcel Duchamp, *Nude Descending a Staircase,* 1912.
Viewers at the Sixty-ninth Regiment Armory Show in New York in 1913 found this painting laughable, even offensive, perhaps because it did not fulfill the expectations suggested by its title. How much attention do you pay to titles when you look at art? Do titles matter?
SuperStock. Art © Succession Marcel Duchamp/ADAGP, Paris/Artists Rights Society (ARS), New York 2015

modern artists. Pablo Picasso's work, displayed in the "Chamber of Horrors," drew thousands who came to laugh, but many came away in admiration. He was to exercise more influence on a whole century of artists than any other we can think of, and he transcended his age so completely that some art historians rank him among the three or four greatest artists of all time.

PABLO PICASSO Pablo Picasso (1881–1973) lived the entire length of the modernist movement in art. Anyone seeing only his work and none by his contemporaries would nonetheless know what modernism is all about. In his youth, he was influenced by the Impressionists and their decision that, with the emergence of photography, imitative realism was dead. During the incredible span of his artistic existence, he worked steadily and impeccably in more modern styles than any other artist of his time. Traditionally trained, he could bring to the canvas a lifelike portrait, but he could also duplicate subjective visual experience, or create a wholly new style that was neither realistic nor abstract but derived from yet another way of seeing the world. This style, which Picasso invented with strong help from a fellow artist named Georges Braque, was **Cubism**.

Picasso was just 19 when he visited Paris for the first time and there saw and marveled at the colors of the Impressionists. He was particularly drawn to the color blue and quickly developed extraordinary skill at both imitation and alteration by painting mostly indigent types—such as prostitutes and homeless wanderers—all in distinctly blue tones.

From the outset, Picasso wanted to show more than a "mere" talent for perfect likeness, which he possessed in abundance. As he intended to mark the world with the stamp of his unique genius, so too did Picasso want to alter its reality. And indeed he did, working not only on two-dimensional flat surfaces but in sculpture, architecture, and scenic design for the theater. (He also wrote poems and plays in his spare time!)

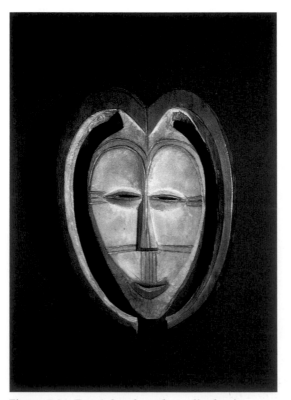

Figure 5.31 Ram's head mask on display in Kinshasa, Zaire.

Charles Lenars/Fine Art/Corbis

Figure 5.32 Pablo Picasso, *Les Demoiselles d'Avignon*, 1907
Picasso had seen an exhibit of African masks shortly before creating *Les Demoiselles*. How does that influence manifest itself in Picasso's painting?
Joseph Martin/Album/Newscom

Picasso's joy in using colors has something of the child about it, the child who refuses to grow up; as a matter of fact, as he aged, he was fond of advising young artists to do everything possible to avoid growing up. The child in Picasso led him into an obsession with the circus, where—still in his twenties—he embarked on a new period dominated by pink, orange, yellow, and gray and did portraits of clowns, trapeze artists, and other performers—portraits lifelike enough to be recognizable, but beginning to show the distortions of real forms that would characterize most of his mature work.

At an exhibition of African masks in Paris, he became excited by their colors and distortions of the human face. The influence of these masks was overpowering and immediate, leading him to his first major triumph, *Les Demoiselles d'Avignon* (1907). This large painting depicts five prostitutes whose body parts are reduced to geometric shapes, as in African masks, and shown simultaneously from different points of view, as in Egyptian sculpture, another important influence for Picasso. The figures are arranged in a space that is fractured and flattened, abandoning the Western tradition of naturalism and of perspective (see Figures 5.31 and 5.32). Early viewers found the painting startling—or, sometimes, amusing.

GEORGES BRAQUE   Georges Braque (1882–1963), a year younger than Picasso, saw *Les Demoiselles* in its initial showing and admitted that it changed his life and his artistic plans for the future. He made it his business to meet the genius who had opened his eyes to a wholly new way not only of painting but of *seeing*. Acting on advice from his "older" mentor, Braque began working in the new style. He would look at a scene that appealed to him for some reason, then leave it, allowing himself to forget the realistic details until he was ready to *deconstruct* it in his memory, then *reconstruct* it on the canvas as geometric blocks in bold, unshaded colors. He did a series of landscapes in this style, causing one critic to complain that Braque had taken beautiful subjects and reduced them "to cubes." After the critical article appeared, the label *Cubism*, meant derogatively at first, was applied to the work of both Braque and Picasso. In 1909, the two artists formed a close association and consciously devised a Cubist movement, providing for it a clearly articulated rationale.

In thinking critically about their art, the two friends theorized that nobody ever really sees an object or a figure. Rather, what is seen is an event extending over a period of time, no matter how rapid. The eye, moreover, is in continual motion and observes from continually shifting viewpoints. From where we sit or stand at any given moment, we are looking from one particular and fixed vantage point. Both realistic paintings and photographs foster the misconception that such a thing exists as a stable field of vision. Our language suggests that we see reality, but in truth what we really see is fragments reassembled by the mind.

Cubist works do not abandon an identifiable subject; their titles reveal themes that are familiar to the viewer. An example is Braque's *Man with a Guitar* (Figure 5.33), painted when he was just 30 and a signature work of Cubism. There are enough ties to the familiar world to orient the viewer: the vague outline of a standing man, and another of a stringed instrument. The picture exists as an illustration of the fragmented world of vision—and *that*, not the likeness of an actual musician, is the point.

Figure 5.33 Georges Braque, *Man with a Guitar,* **1912.**

What familiar objects can you identify in this painting? Do you in fact see a man with a guitar—or something else entirely?

Gianni Dagli Orti/The Art Archive at Art Resource, NY. Art © 2015 Artists Rights Society (ARS), New York/ADAGP, Paris

PICASSO, *GUERNICA*   In 1937, Picasso was invited to do a large painting for the Spanish Pavilion at the Paris World's Fair. Instead of simply choosing a visual event and breaking it into geometric shapes in the style that made him famous, Picasso made an impassioned statement against war. *Guernica* (Figure 5.34) is now considered not only Picasso's masterpiece but one of the great artworks of all time. Among other things, it silenced critics who were saying that modern artists were too wrapped up in their technique and their innovations to pay attention to what was happening in the world.

Using Cubist techniques, although he had abandoned the movement earlier when he and Braque went their separate ways, Picasso was able to deliver a message with one swift visual impact—a message that elsewhere had required thousands of words from reporters and innumerable pictures from photographers. The painting describes an event that caused worldwide revulsion: the German air force's infamous saturation bombing of Guernica, the cultural center of the Basque region in northern Spain and a stronghold of the Republican Army fighting against insurgent forces, who would ultimately win the Spanish Civil War. Francisco Franco, leader of the antigovernment army, had appealed to both Germany and Italy for support. The United States backed the Republican government, which had been duly elected, while Hitler sided with Franco. The bombing of Guernica was also a way for Germany to demonstrate its military strength to the world.

The bombing took place on April 26, 1937, and numbered among its casualties not only Republican soldiers but 2,500 civilians, including hundreds of children. Newspapers around the world published graphic images of the dead. Picasso, who had been undecided about whether he wanted to do a work for the Spanish Pavilion, saw the pictures and was so moved that he rushed home and immediately began sketching out what would become his masterpiece.

When it was unveiled at the New York World's Fair in 1939, *Guernica* received nearly unanimous critical acclaim and established Picasso's supremacy among living artists. There were, of course, detractors. The Marxist government in Russia said that only realistic art could bring about significant social change, and the Nazi regime, as expected, denounced it as "degenerate art."

A true masterpiece, *Guernica* continues to be frighteningly relevant. Wars such as those in Vietnam, Iraq, and Afghanistan, which also have scarred national and world consciousness, come to mind whenever one looks closely at the painting. It is not a

Figure 5.34 Pablo Picasso, *Guernica*, 1937.
Compare this to the painting by Goya (Figure 5.24) that also depicts the horrors of war and, for many viewers, carries a dramatic anti-war message. How do the approaches of the two artists differ? How are they similar? Which painting moves you more?

Oronoz/Album/Newscom. Art © 2015 Estate of Pablo Picasso/Artists Rights Society (ARS), New York

historical record of an event long past, but a living conscience. As such, it continues to generate profound emotional responses. The United Nations headquarters in Manhattan has on display a tapestry reproduction of the work. In 2003, when Colin Powell, then the U.S. Secretary of State, addressed the U.N. Security Council to advocate military action against Iraq, the tapestry, which would normally have been in full view, was covered.

Picasso's work became simpler in his later years, reflecting a retreat to an almost childlike innocence that makes as strong a statement in its own way as *Guernica* does. This is a statement of hope for the future in a world tamed by peace and love, a statement that will be needed as long as the horrors of a Guernican bombing repeat themselves. The artist painted doves on the ceiling of a tiny chapel in the southern French town of Valauris, near his home in Nice. With his friend and neighbor Henri Matisse, he developed **collage** into an art form, spending hundreds of hours cutting out tiny designs and pasting them onto large and colorful backgrounds. The 90-year-old Picasso was not "losing it"—as has been suggested by a few cynics; rather, he was showing that he had managed to do what few of us can: He had kept alive the child inside him. The art of being human needs the spirit of children.

"Unreal" Realism

One reason for any artist's huge critical reputation is the degree to which the work influences other artists. Future artists viewed Picasso as a revolutionary leader, encouraging others to follow their own bent, regardless of how the public might react. Picasso and his peers freed artists to follow their own leads in finding new styles and new voices, and art in twentieth-century Europe, and especially the United States, moved in many directions. Social realists like the Mexican muralist Diego Rivera created monumental works of social criticism honoring the working man. The surrealists, including Salvador Dalí and Rivera's wife Frida Kahlo, found inspiration in strange dream worlds, perhaps inspired by the emerging popularity of psychoanalysis. In the second half of the century, Andy Warhol, with his multiple portraits of Marilyn Monroe and Campbell's soup cans, was the most famous proponent of Pop Art. And some artists such as Georgia O'Keeffe seemed somehow to avoid being "typed" and followed their own paths.

SURREALISM: DALÍ AND KAHLO   A popular style during the first half of the twentieth century, surrealism employs recognizable shapes and forms put together in unrecognizable contexts. The best way to define **Surrealism** is to say that it imitates the world of dreams and the unconscious mind. It owes much to the psychological theories of Freud and Jung. Their explorations into the strange regions below consciousness excited visual artists, writers, and philosophers. Inner space was proving to be just as fascinating as recent discoveries regarding the physical universe.

The Surrealists wanted to imitate the geography of inner space, to make the unconscious mind a tangible part of the external world. At least this was the stated purpose of the movement, the major exponent of which was the Spanish painter Salvador Dalí (1904–1989). Unlike Picasso, who gives us fragments of things, Dalí creates a dream world made up of recognizable images that do not fit rationally together.

Dalí became as famous for his neurotic behavior as for the bizarre world of his canvas. His paintings are objects of fascination for psychiatrists and those art critics who interpret an artist's work in terms of psychological disorders, and some critics labeled his paintings as the work of a madman. But if Dalí was mad, he was also a highly commercial, carefully calculated artistic oddity, who produced art from the outset designed to capitalize on the popularity of Freud, to make the artist a center of widely publicized controversy—and thus to increase the price of his paintings.

Dalí's most famous work, *The Persistence of Memory* (Figure 5.35), is an obviously, and perhaps consciously, Freudian work. It shows a tree branch over which hangs a watch made of a soft, rubbery material. Another rubbery watch hangs limply from a table, on which also sits a solid watch, and another is draped over what ought to be, but

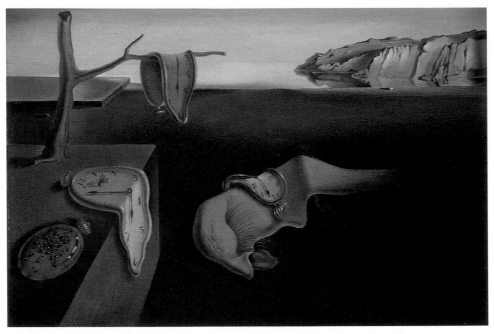

Figure 5.35 Salvador Dalí, *The Persistence of Memory*, 1931.
Where do you think these bizarre images come from? What do you think they mean?
M.Flynn/Alamy. Art © Salvador Dalí, Fundació Gala-Salvador Dalí, Artists Rights Society (ARS), New York 2015

is not, a wrist. Those who insist on a Freudian interpretation, as Dalí perhaps hoped they would, may recognize the limp watches as symbols of unresponsive male sex organs, and the undistorted pocket watch as a symbol of a happier sexual past. Was the artist forced to hide his sexual attitudes? Or was he deliberately giving his public the controversy he thought it wanted?

The Mexican artist Frida Kahlo (1907–1954) lived much of her life in the shadow of her famous husband, the muralist Diego Rivera; she also suffered debilitating pain after a bus accident that left her with multiple injuries and unable to bear children. Despite these challenges—or perhaps because of them—she created a series of work, much of it in the form of self-portraits (see Figure 5.36), that turned her into a feminist icon for her unsparing depictions of the complexities of the female psyche. Her work, which combines the naïveté of primitive folk art with the sophisticated psychological focus of Surrealism, was largely unrecognized during her lifetime. After her death at only 48, however, her reputation has grown, and she is now one of the most celebrated of twentieth-century artists.

Figure 5.36 Detail from Frida Kahlo's *Las Dos Fridas*, 1939.
What is going on in this painting? How does it make you feel? How is it similar to, and different from, Dalí's *Persistence of Memory*, another surrealist masterpiece (Figure 5.37)?
Album/Art Resource, NY. Art © 2015 Banco de México Diego Rivera Frida Kahlo Museums Trust, Mexico, D.F./Artists Rights Society (ARS), New York

GEORGIA O'KEEFFE   The paintings of Georgia O'Keeffe (1887–1986) present another form of "unreal" realism. She gives us likeness that is also abstraction, and perhaps a glimpse into her unconscious as well. The artist appears to have worked from deep impulses inside her which led her to reinterpret the familiar world. She maintained resolutely that all art can be analyzed only in terms of what is happening on the canvas, of what the artist is *doing*, not saying.

What O'Keeffe *does*, then, is usually to imitate one or two striking and colorful forms in the familiar world and transfer them to canvas with many details left out. O'Keeffe sees the world not as the Cubists did—broken down into geometric shapes—but as a place in which certain shapes leap out at the artist for whatever reason: the colors, the aesthetic appeal of the form itself, the textures, or, as some critics have said, the perhaps unconscious sexual significance to the artist of the form—what it *looks* like or *suggests*. Although O'Keeffe always protested against interpretation, many critics have found the sexual undertones in her work undeniable, and feminists have claimed her as one of them. (See, for example, Figure 5.37.)

Born in Wisconsin and educated at the Art Institute of Chicago, O'Keeffe moved to New York when she was just 20, and there she met and eventually married the photographer Alfred Stieglitz, at whose gallery the most fashionable artists of the day showed their work. O'Keeffe's early work was influenced by Asian art, as well as the Cubists and the Surrealists, but she quickly developed a style unique to herself, particularly after she moved to New Mexico, where she spent most of her life.

Much of her most famous work dates from after this move: flowers bursting from their stems; mountains, canyons, the infinite sky with its continually changing colors; the bleached skulls of dead animals. All of these forms she transferred to canvases that were first painted stark white, so that the electric colors and the proud shapes would stand out in sharp relief. As colorful as the Southwest surely is, O'Keeffe altered the landscape, giving it an electric vibrancy, offering back as much as she took from this land, something all artists claim the right to do.

AARON DOUGLAS While Dalí, Kahlo, and O'Keeffe were honing their craft, a young African-American artist named Aaron Douglas (1898–1979) was traveling from Kansas City for a stopover in New York before heading to Paris. During the 1920s and 1930s, the French capital was a magnet, luring artists from every country in the world and with every imaginable style. Ever since the heyday of Impressionism, it was recognized as *the* place to be for those intending to make a name for themselves in the art world. However, the stopover took far longer than he expected, for while Douglas was in New York, he discovered Harlem.

Douglas, born in Kansas of middle-class stock and a visual

Figure 5.37 Georgia O'Keeffe, *Ram's Head, White Hollyhock—Hills*, 1935.
O'Keeffe often painted objects she found in the surrounding New Mexico landscape. But frequently critics have insisted that the paintings reflect implicit female imagery. Do you think a painting's meaning is always intended? Or do viewers bring perceptions to art that the artist may not have intended?
Brooklyn Museum, Bequest of Edith and Milton Lowenthal
Georgia O'Keeffe (American, 1887–1986). *Ram's Head, White HollyhockHills (Ram's Head and White Hollyhock, New Mexico)*, 1935. oil on canvas, 30 × 36 in. (76.2 × 91.5 cm).

arts graduate of the University of Nebraska, at first lacked a sense of connection to African roots. The eventual uncovering of his African heritage made a deep impression on the young artist in search of a style and a statement. What Douglas responded to in Africa was something he had not found in the quiet, uneventful life of midwestern America: a sense of being able to express emotion without restraint, whether it was joy and exaltation or bitterness and sorrow. All around him, Harlem voices were giving vent to their feelings in poetry, jazz, dance, and drama. Some were seeking an appropriate visual arts language, and they encouraged Douglas to join them.

Douglas knew he wanted to go beyond art as strict likeness, but he hadn't an idea of *where*—and why. In the Harlem Renaissance and Cubism, he found that idea. Douglas liked the fact that Cubist paintings forced the viewer to reconsider how reality was viewed. He also knew that he did not agree with those African-American leaders who urged artists and writers to use their talents to make protest statements. He believed passionately that African American art should be its own movement and stand on its own merit. It, too, could show the world a new way to see.

The art of ancient Egypt gave Douglas his first encounter with Africa. What both shocked and excited him was that ancient Egyptian artists stylized the human figure in a way he knew Picasso would have understood. In the painting shown here (Figure 5.38), African dancers express themselves ecstatically, surrounded by tribesmen and drummers. The small ankh-like figure in the upper center seems Egyptian, but the form would have also been familiar to Picasso.

Douglas's style is the result of a deep-rooted belief that in trying to imitate the actual world, art-as-likeness was really falsifying the way we see that world. Figures

Figure 5.38 Aaron Douglas, *Aspects of Negro Life: The Negro in an African Setting*, 1934.
In what details of Douglas's painting can you see the influence of Picasso? Of Egyptian art?
Schomburg Center, NYPL/Art Resource, NY

such as the drummer enabled him to transfer to visual art the excitement he found in the African-American spirit, an excitement that was part of the way he saw things. Thus he was an imitator of both reality and his own emotions.

Abstract Expressionism

Perhaps the most significant of mid-twentieth-century art movements was **abstract expressionism**, a term that grew out of the German Expressionist movement but eventually became identified almost exclusively with post-World War II American artists such as Jackson Pollock and Mark Rothko, and sculptors such as Louise Bourgeois and Louise Nevelson. Abstraction was in some ways a reaction against the social realism that had found mainstream popularity during the early years of the twentieth century, but also a logical continuation of both Surrealism and Cubism, and the work of artists such as Picasso, Kandinsky, and Matisse. Shape and color were primary.

JACKSON POLLOCK Jackson Pollock (1912–1956) was born in Wyoming, raised in Arizona and California, where he was exposed to Native-American sand paintings, and studied with the American regionalist and muralist Thomas Hart Benton. After several years of working with the WPA Federal Art Project, Pollock settled in New York in the early 1940s and began experimenting with new techniques. He quickly abandoned the traditional easel and painter's brushes, using sticks, trowels, and even syringes to paint on huge canvases that he laid on the floor, so he could walk around all four sides (see Figures 5.39 and 5.40). His paintings, often referred to as *drip paintings* or *action paintings,* no longer portray identifiable

Figure 5.39 Jackson Pollock, *Number III Tiger*, 1949.
Album/Art Resource, NY. Art © 2015 The Pollock-Krasner Foundation/Artists Rights Society (ARS), New York

Figure 5.40 Buddhist monks making a sand painting.
Both of these works were created by artists hovering over them, rather than working on easels. How might this technique change the viewer's experience of the work?
Maria Grazia Casella/Alamy

subjects, but record the exuberance of the artist's energetic gestures, tapping into his inner psyche. Although Pollock's work drew a mixture of scorn and admiration, he influenced several generations of American artists. An alcoholic, Pollock died in a single-car crash at only 44. Eventually much of the work of Pollock's contemporaries, even that which strayed far afield from his techniques and style, was enveloped in the all-encompassing label of *modern art*.

LOUISE BOURGEOIS Sculpture became an increasingly important medium in the last half of the twentieth century. Abstract expressionism's focus on shape became fodder for minimalists such as David Smith and Isamu Noguchi, while others such as Duane Hanson and George Segal turned their backs on modernism and created works labeled *superrealism.* Louise Bourgeois (1911–2010), born in Paris but a longtime New York resident, was part of the coterie of abstract expressionists in the 1950s. She quickly established her own unique sensibility as a sculptor, however, often using her art to work through years of early abuse by her father, the death of her mother, and the problems of transition to a new country and language. Although she, like Georgia O'Keeffe, rejected the label of feminist, her works often are explicitly feminine, like her most famous piece, *Maman* (Figure 5.41), created when she was almost 90.

Figure 5.41 Louise Bourgeois, *Maman*, 1999.
Based on this work, would you call Bourgeois a feminist? Why?
Manuel Cohen/The Art Archive at Art Resource, NY. Art © The Easton Foundation/Licensed by VAGA, New York, NY

Pop Art

Influenced by popular culture, including comic books, movies, television commercials, and billboard advertising, **Pop Art** arose, perhaps inevitably, as a phenomenon of the mid-twentieth century. It has been described as "fun" art, for its exponents all seemed to have a sense of humor about much of what they did. They were sometimes making statements about the endless fads and superficiality of American culture and, in their focus on ordinary objects, sometimes offering the sly suggestion that American life has nothing more important to offer.

ANDY WARHOL Undoubtedly the biggest name in Pop Art, Andy Warhol (1928–1987) earned his reputation with subjects drawn from popular culture such as *100 Cans,* a painting that contains the apparently identical likenesses of row upon row of Campbell's beef noodle soup cans. The inspiration for this kind of art is clearly the popular ad, but the excessive repetition of the can is both amusing and frightening. Is Warhol ridiculing the stultifying conformism in American culture and its lack of imagination?

Yet Warhol is also in *love* with the culture he seems to find so tawdry, as we can see from his famous portrait of the movie star Marilyn Monroe (Figure 5.42). Derived from a publicity still from the 1953 movie *Niagara*, this portrait represents a heightening of the type of image that graced the covers of popular "movie magazines"—the

Figure 5.42 Andy Warhol, *Marilyn Monroe,* **1962.**

Warhol produced much of his art in multiples and sometimes had others in his studio do the actual work of reproducing his prints. Is this art? What defines art?

Akg-Images/Newscom. Art © 2015 The Andy Warhol Foundation for the Visual Arts, Inc./Artists Rights Society (ARS), New York

forerunners of *Entertainment Weekly* and *Star*. The colors are brilliant, suggesting the unreality of "tinsel town." But the artist, like so many others, was unable to resist the flashy sensuality that turned Monroe—once an unremarkable young woman named Norma Jeane Baker—into a modern Aphrodite. Yes, Warhol knew that the star was a studio-manufactured product, but he himself was a filmmaker who manufactured a whole bevy of unreal types for his bizarre movies, including a fleshy transvestite named Divine and an entourage that was a walking Pop Art statement.

Warhol's films were central to his art, and *Chelsea Girls* (1966) contributed to a new cinematic phenomenon, the "underground film"—films made on minuscule budgets, often unplotted, often in black and white—and typically arguing against (or satirizing) the dominant American culture. Warhol's film lasted more than three hours; apparently unconnected actions were shown simultaneously on two screens. The "plot" comprised fragmentary sequences but also strangely haunting images. In one five-minute sequence, we watch a young woman standing in front of a mirror, cutting her hair. Nothing else happens, yet the intense camera focus on her face and the sound of scissors create a mesmerizing effect.

Warhol's films were usually shown on special nights in art houses—theaters that cater to alternative tastes. Much of his film art is now hard to track down, but it remains an important link between what we might call "stationary" art, which is available in museums and galleries, and "impermanent" art, which occupies a brief moment in time and is not meant to last—a new direction in art that may have been an inevitable development in America, the land of short attention spans and people always on the move.

Performance and Installation Art

Performance art and **installation art** are art as event. Their exponents are looking for ways to be different in an art world that changes all the time—or perhaps they believe that art is more beautiful and more useful to the extent that it doesn't stay around very long. Performance artists ignore the goal of one day having their work part of a permanent collection in a prestigious museum; they prefer to do something that will be available for a time, perhaps create a storm of controversy, and then be seen or heard no more. Performances can be recreated, but they will never offer exactly the same experience twice. Installation artists create environments, sometimes in nature, sometimes within structures, that also are designed to be experienced for a relatively brief span of time, although installations can be re-created multiple times

MARINA ABRAMOVIĆ One of the twenty-first century's best-known performance artists is Marina Abramović, born in Serbia in 1946, whose presentations focus on confronting pain and testing the endurance of the body. She has variously allowed viewers to use scalpels and scissors to strip her of her clothes, stabbed her own hands multiple times, and ingested extremely powerful pills while gallery-goers watched her body react. In her most infamous performance, *The Artist Is Present* (2010, Museum of Modern Art, New York), Abramović sat motionless and mute for 736½ hours over the course of two months, while museum visitors waited in long lines, sometimes for hours, to sit across a small table from her.

CHRISTO AND JEANNE-CLAUDE Christo Javacheff (b. 1935), and his wife Jeanne-Claude Denat de Guillebon (1935–2009), who as artists are known only by their first names, do not imitate or perform; they literally alter the world briefly, creating a huge and highly publicized event. They claim the natural environment as their medium. Their projects have included wrapping over a million square feet of Australian coastline in plastic, installing a gigantic curtain between two mountains in Colorado, constructing a 24-mile fence made of 20-foot-high nylon panels across hills in northern California, surrounding an island in Biscayne Bay, Miami, with enormous sheets of

Figure 5.43 Christo and Jean-Claude, *The Gates*, Central Park, New York City, 2005.
Only photographs of this massive artwork remain for posterity. Many who saw this exhibit reported that Central Park was full of smiling, happy people. Others were outraged by the cost and effort that went into its brief existence. What do you think? Does temporary installation art have value?
Ilja Hulinsky/Alamy

flamingo-colored plastic (a feat that struck terror in the hearts of environmentalists, who attempted, unsuccessfully, to halt the proceedings), and an enormous installation of 7,503 wooden frames, from which hung orange curtains, six years in the making, which went on display in Central Park for 16 days in 2005. Titled *The Gates* (Figure 5.43), the last event was said to be the largest art project since the Sphinx.

Photography and Digital Art

5.5   *What impact does technology have in the creation of photographic and digital art?*

With the increasing popularity of photography since its invention in the nineteenth century, the roles of portrait painting and realistic landscape art were diminished. People argued that if they wanted something that looked like the real thing, why not go to a medium that could better provide it? Creative artists, fascinated by the new invention, almost immediately began experimenting with, and greatly expanded, its possibilities. In the twenty-first century, art produced through technology—what we now call **digital art**—has taken up more and more space in the art landscape.

Photography: Stieglitz and Sherman

One of the finest photographers working in the early twentieth century was Alfred Stieglitz (1864–1946), who was obsessed with the desire to establish photography as a distinctly American art form. Some of his most famous works are camera images of his wife, Georgia O'Keeffe. He became famous both for his portraits, in which he was bent on proving that the camera could capture the inner person as well as, if not better than, the eye of the painter, and scenes of big-city life, which provide us with a photographic record of what urban life in America looked and *felt* like. The New York of Stieglitz is already showing signs of the congestion and frenetic pace that would become signature characteristics. In 1897, he founded the journal *Camera Notes* (later

Figure 5.44 Cindy Sherman, *Untitled, Film Still #3,* **1977.**
What do you think Sherman is intending to "say" in this photograph? Or is it simply a photograph?
Courtesy of Cindy Sherman & Metro Pictures/LACMA

followed, in 1903, by *Camera Works*), the first periodical devoted to studying the art and science of photography, and he was influential as well in mentoring and providing gallery space to many young artists in the 1940s and 1950s.

New Jersey-born Cindy Sherman (b. 1954) is best known for using herself as the model in most of her photographs. Dressed in various costumes, she focuses on the role of women in American culture (see Figure 5.44), and in particular on the "male gaze"—the expectations that our society has for what women should look and behave like. Controversy has followed Sherman for her portrayal of "centerfold" women, which some critics label voyeuristic, but which Sherman contends simply brings American culture face to face with its preoccupation with women's bodies.

Digital Art

The rise of computers and digital technology has changed the face of art in the twenty-first century. Digital or multimedia art allows artists to manipulate reality in new and fascinating ways, to create works made of light and sound, and to build three-dimensional simulations of figures, objects, and dreamscapes. Computer-generated art is omnipresent in today's culture, from advertisements to video games to social media *memes,* and multimedia installations threaten to dominate the collections of contemporary art museums. Recently artists have collected Instagram photographs posted by others to create new "art"—a panel of sunset or sunrise photographs, for example. It's hard to anticipate what will come next, but surely we will see more and more technologically produced art, as technology becomes increasingly pervasive in our lives and our culture.

Architecture

5.6 *On what grounds do we call architecture art?*

Performance art is transitory by nature, limited to the time of presentation. This final section is concerned with a more permanent component of society: architecture, which serves a dual purpose. It provides for our many human needs: shelter, work, play, religious worship, and education. Of all the arts, architecture alters reality most noticeably. It gives many cities their distinctive look, and it adds an aesthetic dimension to life. Not all of it, of course, can be considered art. There has to be an aesthetic intent on the part of the architect. Major architects such as Frank Lloyd Wright, Frank O. Gehry, and Zaha Hadid have approached the design of buildings as a painter or sculptor would contemplate beginning a new work—that is, as a contribution to the aesthetic well-being of society.

The fundamental issue in determining whether a given architectural work can be labeled "art" is the interplay of *form* and *function.* The function of a building is to accommodate the needs of the inhabitants. An office building should provide employees with pleasing surroundings that will make working less of a chore, and it should allow employees easy access to spaces they will have to visit throughout the day. It must make doing business there simple and enjoyable, and it must be wheelchair accessible. A religious edifice such as a cathedral or a temple should be imposing and awe-inspiring both inside and out, so worshippers or meditators can believe for a time that they have left the familiar world and entered a different, some might say higher, mode of consciousness.

The form of a building—the general impression that it makes as a pleasing presence in a certain space—can be as important as its function. If designed by an architect-as-artist, it can also make a personal statement: *This form is what I consider beautiful, and I offer it for your use and your aesthetic pleasure.* Like all visual artists, architects seek to project themselves into space. They want to know that, because of them, a public area has been altered in some way that reflects their identity and may ensure them lasting honor. They know that architecture is art that alters for very long periods of time, and in some cases forever. The Taj Mahal in India, Saint Peter's basilica in Rome, and the Hagia Sophia in Istanbul are architectural masterpieces that have endured for centuries and have become symbols of their culture.

The debate over which is more important, form or function, has continued for centuries and will probably never be resolved. Those who want architecture primarily to serve a useful purpose argue famously that *form follows function.* Others, often called architectural purists, elevate form and the aesthetic experience it provides over what they call "mere utility." Still others ask, "Why can't we have both?"

Religious Architecture

Buildings created for religious worship or meditation are among the finest achievements in world architecture. The Parthenon in Athens, built to honor the goddess Athena, is one of the world's oldest architectural marvels and remains for many the symbol of Western classical civilization (see Figure 5.10). Angkor Wat, the largest of 70 temples in a complex in Cambodia, is not only a place of meditation for thousands of Buddhists but, as one of the wonders of the world, the main tourist attraction in that nation. Each year many thousands come for inspiration and an aesthetic experience that has been described as nearly without parallel.

Not many edifices have been cornerstones of two religions, but Angkor Wat, still the world's largest religious building, has been home to both Hinduism and Buddhism. Built originally in honor of the Hindu god Vishnu, it became in 1177 CE a Buddhist shrine after the Cambodian king converted to Buddhism. With five pineapple-shaped towers rising close to 200 feet against the sky, Angkor Wat became the most imposing temple in the holy city of Angkor (Figure 5.45). The temple contains innumerable passageways and alcoves, the walls of which boast ornate facades depicting both mythic stories and scenes from everyday Cambodian life.

Few works of architecture have cast the same sort of spell as Angkor Wat. The English novelist W. Somerset Maugham once observed that the vast temple "needs the glow of sunset or the

Figure 5.45 Angkor Wat temple, Cambodia, 12th century CE.
iSiripong/Shutterstock

Figure 5.46 Crystal Cathedral, Garden Grove, California, completed 1981.
Spires reaching skyward are common to houses of religion. Compare this one to the temple at Angkor Wat (Fig. 5.45). Which of these buildings do you think might inspire you more toward faith in the unknown? Why?
Gertjan Hooijer/Shutterstock

white brilliance of the moon to give it a loveliness that touches the heart."[2] Many have noted that merely walking its nearly 3-mile expanse is a transforming experience, leading to distinct (and for the better) changes in mood and attitude.

Modern cathedrals and other places of worship frequently break with tradition, and the results vary from praise in architectural journals to condemnations by the faithful. St. Louis Catholic Church in Miami looks like a flying saucer about to take off. The Crystal Cathedral in Garden Grove, California (Figure 5.46), has a neo-Gothic form, except that it is made entirely of glass and, according to some detractors, looks more like a luxury hotel than a church. A Lutheran church in Helsinki, Finland, was carved into the side of a hill and gives the illusion that one is entering a cave rather than a house of prayer.

Among the most admired and time-honored of religious buildings is the Blue Mosque in Istanbul, built between 1609 and 1616. Its function, like that of other religious buildings, is to make worship spiritually uplifting in a splendid setting. Its interior is made up of more than 20,000 ceramic tiles that lend a bluish aura. It also serves as a hospice for the dying. But the magnificence of the architecture and the extraordinary light inside have made it a must for tourists.

Secular Architecture

Whenever the desire is to combine function with the form that only a great artist can bring to architecture, conflicts inevitably arise between those who create and those who pay for or use the structure. The architect-as-artist often runs into difficulties with both the general public and the specific person or group that has commissioned a given structure. The artist's irresistible urge to self-expression can be accused of subordinating a building's primary purpose.

Even where architecture is viewed as a public art, those who finance it can only speculate on how to define the public interest. When a private corporation or city planners underwrite an expensive structure such as a performing arts center, they will expect (for their millions of dollars) one that satisfies both functional and aesthetic needs, but not exclusively the desires of the architect. They know their investment is going to result in an edifice that will be around for a long time, and they are in trouble if it meets with public disapproval! They suspect it is going to define their city—for better or worse—as Sydney, Australia, is identified by its daring, internationally admired opera house (Figure 5.47).

With its gleaming white, sharply pointed gables looking like sails, the Sydney Opera House opened in 1973 after 16 years of construction. The design was to allow for excellent interior acoustics and to create for the audience a pleasant environment

Figure 5.47 Jørn Utzon, Sydney Opera House, 1973.
How does the form of this building reflect its setting?
VanderWolf Images/Shutterstock

that would heighten the pleasure of the music being heard. The building was also intended to symbolize the city, so that people on ships entering Sydney Harbor for the first time would know they were about to visit a progressive, young metropolis very much involved in the arts and the new. An intense contest for the architectural commission resulted in the choice of a celebrated Danish architect, Jørn Utzon (1918–2008), who insisted on being able to express himself as an artist—to shape a certain space so as to embody his vision of the beautiful, not only to obey the functional requirements set forth by the city planners. The opera house, in short, was intended to be a meeting of the civic and the personal.

Not every taxpayer in Sydney agreed that the structure met either practical or aesthetic needs. As always happens when an environment is altered by a forward-looking artist who breaks with established tradition, there were many who decried his efforts and predicted that their city would be a laughingstock. World opinion, however, has been on the side of Utzon; now the Sydney Opera House is often singled out as one of the great architectural achievements of the twentieth century, an edifice that perfectly marries form and function.

FRANK LLOYD WRIGHT   There is by now widespread agreement over the innovations of a man considered the outstanding American architect of the twentieth century, Frank Lloyd Wright (1867–1959). He was born and raised in the relatively small Wisconsin town of Richland Center. Accustomed to open spaces, air to breathe, and panoramic landscapes, he must have become aware of a growing urban America with huge buildings beginning to reach for the sky and densely crowded city neighborhoods where residents seldom interacted with nature. The writings of American philosopher Ralph Waldo Emerson and his vehemently anti-city friend Henry David Thoreau also had a strong impact on Wright's architectural vision. Early on, Wright developed a strong rationale for his work: to link the functional demands of large buildings with the environmental demands of his own heart. His mission would be to provide for the practical demands of big business without the claustrophobia of crowded industrial complexes.

At the outset of his career, Wright designed what he called his "prairie house," a rambling one-story structure with plenty of windows and a low, overhanging roof. The idea was that the structure should blend into its surroundings—unlike the huge nineteenth-century mansions that many monied families insisted upon, with their ornate external carvings, statues, and stained-glass windows designed for the blatant display of wealth. Wright's aim was to create a balance among function, form, and the environment. He went on to conceive a dwelling that many critics have deemed the consummate integration of structure and surroundings: Fallingwater (Mill Run, Pennsylvania) is built into a cliffside; a natural waterfall flows around and under the house.

During the first decade of the twentieth century, Wright designed the Larkin Building in Buffalo, New York, and its distinctively sleek look brought him to the attention of European urban planners. By the 1930s, the term "streamlined" became fashionable and international in its appeal, and Wright was the acknowledged exponent of the new style, which used translucent glass brick, curved surfaces, spacious interiors, and in which unnecessary, purely decorative frills were noticeably absent. He believed strongly that form follows function. With Wright leading the way, many modern architects argued that no building could be considered beautiful if its basic function was impaired by "artistic" aims—such as installing a fountain ringed by statues to block its entrance.

In 1936, Wright designed the administration building and, in 1944, the research tower of the Johnson Wax Company in Racine, Wisconsin, achievements hailed as masterpieces of modern architecture. One architectural historian proclaimed them "the most profound work of art that America has ever produced."[3]

Money was never Wright's primary consideration. He wanted, first, to shield employees and visitors from the growing ugliness of the urban scene. Although he loved light and made extensive use of glass, he placed windows so that users of the buildings would not have to look out on parking lots and decaying streets. Instead, they were enclosed by solid brick walls at street level while light was provided from overhead. He wanted users to feel as though they were among the pine trees, breathing fresh air and sunlight. Wright was a visionary who helped create the look of the modern world, and he was an archenemy of overbuilding in that world.

Wright's final work—and for many, his crowning achievement—is the Guggenheim Museum on Fifth Avenue in New York (Figure 5.48). It is admired by some as the best possible example of modern architecture, and scorned by others who say it looks like a parking garage. The building is a series of circular stone ramps, which ascend in great swirls and serve as a thick barrier to the noise of the city. There are no windows; instead, light enters through the small spaces between the ramps. Inside, art works are illuminated by soft indirect lighting. The

Figure 5.48 Frank Lloyd Wright, Guggenheim Museum, New York, 1959.
Rafael Ben-Ari/Alamy

Figure 5.49 Frank O. Gehry, Guggenheim Museum, Bilbao, Spain, 1997.
What do the two Guggenheim Museums, shown here and in Figure 5.48, share? How do they differ?
Maremagnum/Getty Images

artist's first thought was to shut out as much light as he could and provide visitors with a quiet oasis, another world of human creativity.

FRANK O. GEHRY   A Canadian-American based in California, Frank O. Gehry (b. 1929) has taken modern American architecture to new levels. His work tends to put a great deal of emphasis on form without ignoring function. Gehry's genius lies in the ability to make form seem an inevitable result of function. Some of his critics call his style impractical, accusing him of subordinating function in the interest of artistic self-expression. A good many artists, however, defend his right to do just that.

As an "adopted" Southern Californian, Gehry enjoys the *funky* in modern art—those elements that incorporate whimsy into serious aims. He is fond of fish, for example, and is apt to put a fish sculpture where one would least expect it—in front of an elevator, perhaps. He makes furniture out of corrugated boxes, and he uses chain-link fencing unsparingly and, again, unexpectedly. He will stretch a chain-link fence across a courtyard where it serves no useful purpose except to be an object of art, similar to what Christo might do, except that Gehry's installations are permanent. To those critics who call such installations "frivolous" and "ugly," he replies that he is not sure "what is ugly and what is beautiful." Such a retort, a denial of absolute aesthetic standards in architecture, defends the right of artists to make personal statements with their work.

By almost universal consent, Gehry's masterpiece thus far is the Guggenheim Museum in Bilbao, Spain (Figure 5.49). Here he was commissioned by people who were already on the side of art, people who knew and loved the innovative, however daring and controversial, and people who wanted to call worldwide attention to the city they loved. This time there was no room for the frivolity that sometimes characterizes other Gehry works.

ZAHA HADID   Iraqi-born architect Zaha Hadid (b. 1950) was the first woman to win the prestigious Pritzker Architecture Prize, in 2004, and has broken barriers around the world for women in a profession long dominated by men. Her buildings are fluid and powerful, reflecting both the structure and the chaos of modern life. She has designed everything from a ski jump and soccer stadiums to museums and shopping centers; her first building in the United States was the Contemporary Arts Center in Cincinnati, OH. Hadid has ongoing commissions in various Middle Eastern countries, but her best-known work may be in China (see Figure 5.50).

Figure 5.50 Zara Hadid, Galaxy Soho (mixed-use complex), Beijing, China, 2012.
What influences do you see in this architecture? Is this a place where you would feel comfortable? Is it art?
View Pictures/Universal Images Group/Getty Images

If you never visit Bilbao or Beijing or New York, you may nevertheless be fortunate enough to live in a city large enough to support a museum or gallery where both a permanent collection and traveling exhibits are displayed. Seize the opportunity whenever it presents itself. You will be delighted at how much your range of consciousness will expand and grow. If museums are not available, public libraries and the Internet have the astonishing capability of taking you to galleries and museums all over the world. You can relive the classical past in Greece and Rome, the magnificence of the Florentine Renaissance, the Holland of Rembrandt and other seventeenth-century artists who perfected the imitation of likeness, or visit the world of van Gogh and see the treasures he left for us. You can virtually travel to the Louvre in Paris with its multitude of antiquities, or to Musée d'Orsay, with its priceless collection of Impressionist paintings. You can discover the rich legacy of American artists such as Cassatt, Douglas, O'Keeffe, and so many others.

You are also fortunate to have been born into a digital world, where you can not only view but also create art at the touch of a finger. If you have access to technology, try your hand. And if you don't, pick up a pencil and a piece of paper. Make a sketch. Make art. The world of art belongs to you, and it is our hope that this chapter has encouraged you to browse in it whenever your spirits need uplifting. Art never fails you if you come to it with an eager curiosity and an open mind. The visual effects can be stunning. Look carefully.

A Critical Focus: Exploring Adaptation

Artists often "comment" on one another's work, or adapt styles created by earlier artists to their own ends. For example, the African-American artist Kara Walker (b. 1969) often uses cut-outs, an artistic technique employed by the French impressionist Henri Matisse late in his life. Compare the two works below.

Figure 5.51 Henri Matisse, *Icarus,* **1947.**
RMN-Grand Palais/Art Resource, NY. Art © 2015 Succession
H. Matisse/Artists Rights Society (ARS), New York

Figure 5.52 Kara Walker, *Rebel Leader,*
2004.
The Museum of Modern Art/Licensed by
SCALA/Art Resource, NY. Art © Kara Walker/
Walker Arts Center

- What do you think the artists' intentions might have been in creating each work?
- What is the difference in your viewing experience?
- How important is the artist's intent in the viewer's experience?
- How important is cultural context in how we view art?

Now compare the two works below.

Figure 5.53 Johannes Vermeer, *Girl with
a Pearl Earring,* **c. 1665.**
Scala/Art Resource, NY

Figure 5.54 Awol Erizku, *Girl with
a Bamboo Earring,* **2009.**
Courtesy of Awol Erikzu

Chapter 6
Music

Learning Objectives

6.1 Define the basic elements of music.

6.2 Differentiate among varieties of musical experience including the fugue, the symphony, and the art song.

6.3 Discuss the emergence and impact of various forms of popular music, including folk, jazz, blues, gospel, rock and roll, and hip-hop.

Figure 6.1 Gerrit van Honthorst, *Musical Group on a Balcony*, 1622.
Why do you think music has played such an important role in cultures throughout history?
Digital image courtesy of the Getty's Open Content Program

We live in an audio environment that is most of the time unplanned. That is, we hear what happens to be around, whether it is a jet taking off, the squeal of brakes, a hair dryer, music from someone else's smartphone—or the conversation that someone is having on that phone. Noise has been around forever. Mammoths were probably sending forth bellows at the moment human awareness was first forming. The majority of the world's population still exists at the mercy of unwanted noise.

Music is the best of it. Created by instruments or human voices, music can be defined as *the shaped sound between silences*: the better the shape, the richer and more pleasing the sound. Just as visual art offers a wide variety of shapes and forms to provide an enriched visual environment, music has many sounds: Bach, Mozart, Gershwin, Armstrong, Sinatra, Johnny Cash, James Brown, Beyoncé. Limiting ourselves to one kind of music is as detrimental to growth as if we were never to set foot outside our houses and discover the unlimited life experiences waiting out there.

Many sounds in the natural world are like music: the song of birds, a mountain stream, gently falling rain, wind over the prairie. The desire to imitate pleasing natural sound seems to be intrinsic to our species. Whistling can remind us of bird song (and note how we refer to the sound of birds in musical terms). The soothing sound of a flowing brook has inspired many composers. In *Tapiola*, an orchestral work by the Finnish composer Jean Sibelius, the strings recreate the sound of wind in a forest. In *The Birds*, the Italian composer Ottorino Respighi has the orchestra imitating the various songs and calls of different species. Composers recognize the affinity between nature and music.

Most ancient cultures shared the belief that music was a vital component of the natural world, a gift from heavenly beings. One theory is that for very early people natural sounds were the voices of the gods, and human song was developed to imitate their voices. In popular idiom, we sometimes hear comments such as "She sings like an angel."

Whether or not one believes the mythology of musical origins, music appears to be vital to the human spirit. Is it possible to imagine what life would be like without it? Music is one of the endless treasures bestowed upon us by the humanities, and we are fortunate that, as this art form developed over the millennia, it divided into endless varieties.

The purpose of this chapter is to encourage you to explore the wide range of musical sound. Some of it is recognized as part of the world's artistic heritage. Some of it is still very new and may achieve that distinction one day. (It's fun to predict what *will*.)

We will first separate music into its component elements, then describe some of its major, and widely differing, forms, together with some suggested works from the past and present as well as from other cultures that may offer us a more well-rounded musical life. As in any introductory text, the process is necessarily selective. We attempt to open the door of musical recognition a little wider.

Figure 6.2 Native American dancers at a powwow on the National Mall in Washington, D. C.
These dancers are accompanied by rhythmic drumming. Can you imagine music without rhythm? What do you think of as the basic elements of music?

Dennis Tarnay, Jr. / Alamy

The Basic Elements of Music

6.1   *What are the basic elements of music?*

Credit for the development of formal music goes to the ancient Egyptians and their belief that the god Thoth gave humanity seven basic sounds, perhaps much like the seven-tone scale that would come later. Ancient Chinese philosophy, which believed all nature was ruled by a divine principle of order, saw music as the human connection to that order.

Along with laying the foundations of Western thought, art, and literature, the Greeks also created a profound theory of music. In *The Republic*, Plato writes about "the music of the spheres," a concept that has endured for many centuries. He describes the heavens as divided into eight spheres, on each of which a siren sings a note of astounding sweetness. The sirens in Greek mythology were long-haired, beautiful women who lured sailors to their deaths with glorious sounds; but, apparently, the sirens in Plato's heavens had no such destructive motives. Instead, their song represented the eternal order, or *armonia*, of the universe. That Greek term, which became the English word **harmony**, indicates a connection between music and the structure of the universe. Religions of the world have long claimed that through music one achieves union with the divine.

We see that music existed in many guises long, long ago. It became an art form in the West with the development of rules and guidelines.

Tone

The basic element of music is the **tone**, or note, a sound produced by the human voice or by a musical instrument that maintains the same frequency of vibration regardless of duration. Perhaps the imitation of a natural sound was then shaped to become pure and sweet. Or perhaps that pure and sweet tone just came from someone's imagination, and people nearby were astounded when they heard it. However it happened, the discovery of tones marked the beginning of the human victory over the unplanned audio environment. True music began when someone experimented with a variety of tones, some higher, some lower.

The Scale

People in the ancient world who discovered different tones through a natural instinct for song or a way to accompany dances and rituals could not have known that tone was caused by the frequency of sound-wave vibrations: the higher the frequency, the higher the tone, and vice versa. Yet nearly every culture, ancient and contemporary, recognizes the aural phenomenon of the **octave**, or the space between two tones that sound as if they are the same, although one is higher and one lower.

Different cultures have divided the octave in different ways, although most cultures typically employ between five and seven tones in an octave. After a time, someone must have happened upon a distinct progression of individual tones from low to high, and that was the beginning of Western music as we know it. This orderly progression of frequencies from low to high is the **scale**, which divides the space of an octave into a certain number of scale steps; a scale step is the recognizable distance (or interval) between two successive notes of the scale. All cultures that developed music used a scale, though they did not necessarily happen upon the same sequence of tones.

PENTATONIC, DIATONIC, AND CHROMATIC SCALES At first, the dominant scale in both non-Western and Western music consisted of five tones, known as a **pentatonic scale**. It remains the basis for most traditional Asian music. The Western scale was expanded to six tones by the sixth century CE and was first written down (or notated) by an Italian monk. With the later addition of a seventh tone, the Western, or **diatonic**, scale was complete. Notes were also given letter designations—ABCDEFG—and each sequence of seven could constitute a scale. Over time, the first note of each scale became the identifying **key** in which a given piece of music was composed. This first note—called the *tonic*—acts as a sort of center of gravity, a home base from which the music departs and to which it eventually returns. The basic scale in Western music can begin on any note, and the notes are often identified generically by the names *do, re, mi, fa, sol, la,* and *ti*—a system created by a sixth-century Benedictine monk to help singers remember the progression of tones in Gregorian chants.

Yet there is much more variety in Western music than seven simple notes. Although some cultures include more than 24 unique tones in any given octave, the Western musical system typically recognizes a 12-note division of the octave, with equal space between each tone. The addition of sharps and flats—or **half-ones**—to the letters A through G represents these other possible pitches in the Western musical scale. A scale that uses all 12 tones (imagine using all the white *and* black keys on the piano) is called a **chromatic** scale, and the space between each is called a half-step. To the list of musical keys we may thus include C-sharp, B-flat, and so on.

MAJOR AND MINOR SCALES   When we play or sing a seven-note scale that has an interval pattern of two whole steps (W-W), a half-step (H), three more whole steps (W-W-W), and one final half-step (H) to ascend one octave, we are using a *major* scale. A *minor* scale is more complicated. The *natural* minor scale is defined by the interval pattern W-H-W-W-H-W-W. The *harmonic* minor scale raises the seventh-scale degree (thus creating an interval of a step-and-a-half between the sixth and seventh tone), whereas the *melodic* minor scale does this when ascending but retains the natural minor interval pattern (W-H-W-W-H-W-W) when descending. Though the verbal definitions are complex, music in minor keys is easily recognized. Many songs of heartbreak and loss are written in minor keys, as is instrumental music that seeks to create a somber mood.

Traditional symphonic music is usually identified in terms of the key and type of scale (major or minor) in which it begins (composers can change either or both within a given work) and the *opus* number (that is, where it occurs in the composer's repertoire). Thus one might see this on a program: Beethoven, Symphony No. 9 in D Minor, Op. 125.

Beethoven: Symphony No. 9 in D Minor, IV

SCALES IN NON-WESTERN CULTURES   The music of most non-Western cultures is based on a scale of five tones that do not necessarily correspond to Western sounds. The Western preference for seven tones may have to do with the fact that Western listeners are accustomed to the narrower frequency intervals between the seven tones of the familiar scale. Hearing traditional Asian music for the first time and expecting the familiar scale, they are likely to find the sounds quite strange.

Africa has long been home to several musical traditions without formalized scales at all, many of which display extraordinary rhythmic complexity. Tones were, of course, fundamental as in other cultures, but these could change to suit the emotion of the musician or singer. Traditional African music has always made strong use of the human voice, and, when the voice is the primary way of preserving melody, much variation was and continues to be the rule. The music of Africa made possible the evolution of jazz and blues, two art forms that allow for maximum freedom of expression.

Rhythm

Early music throughout the world was probably monophonic—that is, limited to just the melodic line and sung or played without harmony. But rhythmic accompaniment would have been provided when appropriate, such as at ritual events like a funeral or a rite of passage celebrating the arrival of puberty.

We know rhythm was the underlying factor in early Greek ceremonies because we have written accounts of it. Certain rhythms were held appropriate for inspirational ceremonies because of their uplifting effect on the soul, while other rhythms—certainly those involved in the orgies held annually in honor of Dionysus—were deemed conducive to uncontrolled, licentious behavior.

Formal music might have begun with the discovery of tones, but rhythm by itself might well have preceded tone, scale, and the earliest instruments. It is the most fundamental element of music; our own bodies have their rhythms, as does the universe. Most likely, a rat–a–tat pounding of sticks and stones was an early factor in human development, used to mark occasions of great joy or solemnity. Later, drums accompanied such events (see, for example, Figures 6.1 and 6.2). The early instincts are still with us. We often see very young children rat–a–tatting with blocks or just with their hands, the beat becoming more pronounced and regular as they grow older. Rap and hip-hop today give clear indication that people are just as attracted to the hypnotic effect of steady rhythm as their ancestors were.

APOLLONIAN AND DIONYSIAN RHYTHMS   Moving to a beat—or, as it is better known, *dancing*—may be even older than singing. Even without specific tones to sing, people must have found pleasure in letting out their feelings at the insistence of loud beats from any number and kinds of sources. Of the two contrasting aspects of human culture and human personality, the Apollonian and the Dionysian, the Apollonian half enjoys order; the Dionysian half exults in unrestrained expressions of feeling. Neither side is sufficient by itself. Civilization advances with Apollonian order, but without Dionysian spontaneity, it can become rigid and uncreative.

Rhythm in music usually refers to the temporal organization of sounds—how long each tone lasts (its duration), how fast or slow the underlying pulse (or beat) of the music is, and how these beats are grouped into patterns. As in poetry, there is frequently an alternation between stress and unstress. Rhythm acquires its different forms according to the pattern of alternation used. The waltz, a once-popular rhythm in Western music, is created from a stressed beat followed by two unstressed beats. Also described as a "stately" rhythm, it is far more Apollonian than it is Dionysian, and it was thus suitable for the aristocrats of nineteenth-century ballrooms, though it had its Dionysian side in an era when touching someone of the opposite sex in public was otherwise frowned upon. Popular among aristocrats of the eighteenth century, the minuet was also based on Apollonian (that is, rigid and repetitive) rhythms. So are the marches used for funerals and graduations.

Plato approved of stately rhythms, which for him lent gravity to public occasions and affirmed order in the state. He disapproved strongly of rhythms that were there only to excite the emotions. People of today who enjoy letting go on a dance floor to the beat of rock bands or hip-hop evidently find Dionysian liberation a satisfying escape from the Apollonian demands of household duties, jobs, or schoolwork. Rhythm is the mortar that holds a work together, that gives coherence to a collection of sounds. A change in rhythm can be a major event, often very exciting to the listener. It opens up new possibilities, new directions.

When musical tones joined the ancient human passion for rhythm, a new force was born that provided a way for emotions to be expressed, released, and controlled. Once rhythm was discovered, it never left musical art. Even the plainsong, a chant sung by medieval monks and clerics, has a rhythm; it conforms to the natural stresses and inflections of spoken language. In the famous *Bolero* by the Impressionist composer Maurice Ravel, the underlying rhythm is so pronounced that it structures the entire piece.

Desiring to free themselves from the restraints that traditional rhythms impose, some composers attempt to be totally arrhythmic; that is, they avoid all regular alternations of stress and unstress, seldom repeating a pattern. The listener is kept off guard, presumably on edge, and the piece aspires to create a mood of agitation and emotional instability.

What is the magic that rhythm weaves inside us? We can speculate at great length, of course. Children are conceived in rhythm, born in rhythm; parents clap their hands in rhythm to keep them from crying. The universe itself throbs with rhythms: the rotation of the earth, the alternation of the seasons, incoming and outgoing tides, birth and death. How about order and disorder, Apollo and Dionysus, belief and doubt, joy and sorrow? Anthropologists studying early rituals have suggested that rhythmic effects were used to express the heartbeat of Mother Earth.

Rock percussionist Mickey Hart of the Grateful Dead once said, "Rhythm is at the very center of our lives." If you were to ask a number of people which musical element they could most easily dispense with, rhythm would probably not be the answer.

Melody

The art of music began with differentiated tones played or sung in certain patterns that might or might not have been repeated. One might have flowed into another. These patterns were melodies. Sometimes referred to as a "tune," **melody** is the part we remember of a song or a symphonic movement. If we remember nothing beyond a "babble" of instruments and a great deal of percussion, chances are many of us would ask, "What happened to the melody?"

The discovery of tone made melody possible. Melody can be defined in two ways: one, most familiar to Western ears, as *a significant sequence of musical tones that form a unity, like a sentence of prose, and are usually repeated later in the exact order or as a recognizable variation of the original;* or two, as found in many non-Western cultures, *an arrangement of tones in a flowing sequence that may or may not have a definite end.* Much of the "classical" music of the eighteenth and nineteenth centuries was designed, first and foremost, around melody.

Opera-goers, hearing a new work in its premiere performance, may at first find that "there are no melodies in it." Someone accustomed only to Western symphonic music may wonder why, at first hearing, there is no "beautiful melody" in sitar music from India, or may denounce a rock band for pounding out "just noise." Not every melody is beautiful in the sense of being played or sung often enough to be remembered.

ROMANTIC MELODY   Many are understandably drawn to what may be termed *romantic* melody, the melodic line that falls soothingly and repeatedly on the ears. Much of its emotional impact has to do with the instruments that play it: often, the violin, the piano, the guitar, and the flute, instruments that produce delicate sounds. Romantic melody tends to be "gentle," befitting the tender emotions it calls up. It is almost always slow.

A Romantic musical style was dominant during the nineteenth and early twentieth centuries. Composers including Brahms and Tchaikovsky were, and still are, called "masters of melody"—that is, they provide lush sequences of tones that are easily recalled and that evoke emotions within the listener. Brahms's *Cradle Song*, or "Lullaby," is known throughout the world and has become almost synonymous with treasured memories of an infant's earliest days. The main theme in Tchaikovsky's *Romeo and Juliet Overture-Fantasy* reminds people of the joys of first love. Translated into a popular song called *Our Love*, it contributed to Tchaikovsky's reputation as the king of melody.

Rhapsody on a Theme of Paganini by Sergei Rachmaninoff (1873–1943) offers excellent examples of romantic melody. The main theme is introduced at the beginning—a sprightly and graceful melody written by Niccolò Paganini, an Italian violinist and composer who lived a century earlier. Though Paganini's work has long been popular with violinists because of its intricate challenges to the instrument, Rachmaninoff's variations on his theme have become immensely more popular with audiences than the original—especially his Eighteenth Variation, in which, after a dramatic silence, the piano enters and plays a melody that is Paganini's lively theme turned around and performed at a much slower tempo. When the string section passionately repeats the theme, the listener cannot help experiencing a surge of emotion.

MELODIC VARIATIONS   Among jazz musicians, melody usually means the theme that begins their performance and on which the remainder of it is based. By the conclusion of the piece, the original theme is usually different from the melody we heard at the outset—*very* different. Jazz is complex, requiring an initial willingness to devote the time needed to explore its many treasures.

An effective way to increase your appreciation for what is often considered non-melody is to become a more attentive listener to jazz. In doing so, you will find variations on a melody performed by different instruments throughout a piece. From jazz, move on to **chamber music** (concert music written for a few instruments rather than a symphony orchestra). Once again you will hear clearly defined themes that are then developed through variations into ever more complex patterns of sounds. By extending your definition of melody, you will find yourself enjoying a broader range of musical experience.

Sometimes melody is a sequence of tones that seems to go on indefinitely without repeating itself. During the 1960s, sitar music achieved popularity in the West because of its extended melodic lines and its clearly non-Western, hence "anti-Establishment," sound. Some modern composers are drawn to non-Western sound in an effort to break away from the traditional. Philip Glass, a contemporary American composer, wrote music early in his career that was insistently repetitive, repeating a single pattern for an extended time. Some have called his work monotonous and endlessly repetitive, while others find it pleasantly hypnotic (Figure 6.3). Director Martin Scorsese recruited Glass to write the Asian-sounding score for the film *Kundun* (1997), the story of the Dalai Lama. Although Glass is Western, the music sounds unfamiliar to most Western ears and therefore is accepted by audiences as Tibetan. Listening to this music is a good way to explore alternative kinds of melody. We should remember that the so-called beauty of melody is a matter of historical period and cultural heritage. Not that all melody is beautiful—or that no melody is beautiful; rather, beauty in music has a lot to do with familiarity and the kind of instruments popular within a given cultural tradition.

DISSONANCE AND MINIMALISM Extreme departures from tradition have characterized modern Western music since the earliest years of the twentieth century, when composers reacted strongly against the romantic conception of melody. The aggressive **dissonance** in their music has had much to do with its deliberate lack of appeal to those who wanted music to sound romantic and were unwilling to tolerate anything else. Throughout the twentieth century, composers kept experimenting with

Figure 6.3 *Satyagraha*, **an opera by the American composer Philip Glass (1979).**
Satyagraha is based in non-Western musical traditions unfamiliar to most of us, including repetitive patterns that lack clear melody. Can you think of other kinds of contemporary music that lack melody? Do you look for a "hummable" melody in the music you like, or are other elements more important?

Jack Vartoogian/Getty Images/Getty Images

nontraditional scales and sounds. Sometimes they invented new kinds of musical notes that were not in any scale anyone knew but had to be half-sung and half-spoken. Composers have even included long stretches of silence in their music.

In recent years, a significant number of composers have reacted against modernism, especially what they consider "noisy jangling and crashing," a fierce determination to sound like nothing that ever came before. The new music can be called, like the new visual art, *postmodern*. The most frequently performed works of this genre come from a group of composers frequently called *minimalists*, although they themselves reject the term. Their goal is to divest music of modernism's unnecessary trappings and return to the basic elements, particularly rhythm. Minimalist music, such as that by Philip Glass and Steve Reich, is sometimes dismissed as coldly formal and unemotional, as well as monotonous, by unsympathetic listeners who also find it unmelodic. But, like all unfamiliar music, minimalist compositions can reward those willing to take the time to listen, and post-minimalist composers such as John Adams regularly incorporate moving melodies into their work.

It has been said that music is what emotion sounds like. The emotional life of an individual is exceedingly complex, is it not? To insist that music sound only a certain way is like saying that people can feel only a certain way. We can turn away, just as we don't have to welcome any stranger we think we don't want to know. But we also have the freedom to make friends.

Harmony and the Orchestra

In Asian music, tones are usually played by themselves, that is, without *harmony*, which is the simultaneous production of tones by voices or instruments. So accustomed are Westerners to hearing simultaneous tones that they tend to take harmony for granted, but like melody, harmony has historical and cultural roots.

During the first millennium, Christian churches incorporated music into the private services of monks and priests as well as public masses. Emphasis was placed on song as a means of communicating with God. Greatly influenced by ancient Hebrew chants, these sung prayers became known as *plainsong*. They were performed in unison by clerics acting as one voice praising God's glory and asking for mercy and forgiveness. Harmony created by units of voices singing different tones would have been out of place, a violation of the belief that all people were the same in the eyes of God. Beginning in the twelfth century in Paris, however, composers began experimenting with harmonies, creating new sonic textures that befitted the architectural grandeur of the Notre Dame Cathedral.

During the sixteenth century, as the Renaissance, with its rebirth of classical culture, moved from one European country to another, bringing with it a celebration of life on earth, music—secular music—was eagerly sought. Since the Renaissance emphasized enjoyment during one's brief stay on earth, music could fill leisure hours with many pleasures. The royal courts all had musicians on hand, and new instruments were invented to explore the richness and sensuality of secular music. In these venues, scarcely an hour of the day went by without the sounds of lute, recorder, or oboe, playing sometimes alone but often in small groups.

Renaissance composers explored the harmonious interweaving of instruments and voices, as if to say that music should be the contribution of a number of individuals, each adding to life's enjoyment, each with a musical statement to make. The Renaissance also celebrated the uniqueness of each human being. Harmony allowed for a variety of interweaving musical themes, each with its own melody, played or sung by individualized instruments or voices. Eventually the development of harmony would lead to the complexities of the **Baroque** style that flourished in Europe during the seventeenth century.

The invention of harmony also made possible the art form known as *opera* (the plural of *opus*, a Latin term meaning "work"), a collaboration of many distinct individuals—composers, orchestras, singers, poets who wrote their words, dancers, and that new species of artist, the scenic designer—with the whole becoming a rich and complex visual tapestry and festival of sound, all working together to give added meaning to the concept of harmony.

THE SYMPHONY   Orchestras grew in size and complexity, and, as they did, composers eagerly explored the range of the new instruments, each distinguishable from the other by the particular **timbre** (pronounced "TAM-bur"), or tone color, that they produced. By the eighteenth century, the **symphony**, a musical form in separate units, or movements, became a concert staple, combining families of instruments such as strings, winds, brass, and percussion. Major aggregations of musicians became known as symphony orchestras; these steadily increased in numbers as Haydn, Mozart, Beethoven, Brahms, and, late in the nineteenth century, Mahler wrote works that required more and more instruments. One of Mahler's major works is titled *The Symphony of a Thousand* because it involves literally that many musicians and singers. Tchaikovsky's *1812 Overture* requires, in addition to a massive orchestra, the firing of cannons as the music reaches its climax. Beethoven's Ninth Symphony is now performed by an enormous orchestra of at least 150 musicians in addition to a chorus of perhaps 200 voices.

In 1989, Leonard Bernstein, an American composer and conductor, was invited to present the Ninth Symphony at the site of the newly fallen Berlin Wall, which had, since the ending of World War II, separated East and West Berlin. On this occasion, more than 200 musicians and singers from the United States, the Soviet Union, Great Britain, and France participated. The theme of the final movement, a choral setting of the poet Schiller's "Ode to Joy," heralded a new dawn of freedom and friendship between the previously separated citizens of Berlin and also gave ringing hope that all oppressed peoples would triumph in their struggle against tyranny.

To open the 1998 winter Olympics in Nagano, Japan, conductor Seiji Ozawa led a performance of the "Ode to Joy" using choruses from four locations around the globe joined together by satellite. This time the music represented global unity, as athletes from diverse nations, unable to communicate with each other through words, could find in Beethoven's music a common bond.

Musical harmony, especially in the glorious complexities of the great symphony orchestras, has become a model of human society at its most ideal. It requires every musician to pull together for one common purpose. No one sound can be any more important than another, yet each one has its moment of prominence. If one tone is flat, the entire enterprise suffers.

Silence

Silence is the unpublicized ingredient that makes music possible in the same way that the empty space around a sculpture makes the sculpture possible, or the judicious use of wall space can make or break an art exhibit. Just imagine 25 original van Goghs crammed together: "Where is *The Starry Night*? Oh, there it is. I almost missed it. Funny, but somehow it's just not as exciting as I thought it would be." Fast-forwarding a video destroys all dramatic value. The acceleration erases the pauses, which are as significant as the words themselves. After all, if characters talked nonstop, how could a dramatic situation develop? In music the spaces—or silences—between notes can be equally important.

To deepen an appreciation of music, we need to hear and enjoy silence. Silence has been an integral part of many works. The pauses in the second movement, the "Funeral March," of Beethoven's Third Symphony are as famous as the themes that precede and follow them. They make possible the dramatic effect when the main theme of the movement returns for the last time. There is silence, then part of the theme, then more silence, then more of the theme. The effect reminds the listener of someone trying valiantly to hold back tears.

Tchaikovsky: *1812 Overture*

Think of the last time you were in the presence of someone struggling for self-control while obviously overcome by a powerful surge of emotion. Weren't the silences full of meaning? Great composers handle silences in the same way that great artists since Leonardo da Vinci have known how to handle shadows. Great stage actors owe something of their greatness to the mastery they have achieved over the words that they do *not* speak and to the silences before and after the words they do speak.

A famous solo theme for French horn occurs soon after the opening of the fourth movement of Brahms's First Symphony. The moment is heralded by a tympani roll, which is followed by the introduction of the French horn theme. Some conductors, recognizing the musical benefits of silence, make the orchestra pause briefly before the theme is heard. This silence dramatically intensifies the significance of what follows. The French horn enters like an actor making an appearance for which the audience has been eagerly waiting. In some interpretations, however, there is almost no pause at all, perhaps losing an opportunity for creating a thrilling moment.

The composer John Cage (1912–1992) is famous for having incorporated silence into his work and making it as important as the actual notes he wrote down for musicians to play. One of his compositions, *4'33"*, named for the 4 and a half minutes it takes to perform it, asks the artist to sit at the piano for that length of time. Cage insisted that the "notes are silent," but that they are there all the same; in effect, he encouraged his audiences to hear all sounds as potentially musical, and all of life as potentially art. One of his longer pieces for the piano combines both played and silent notes, and in yet another, the pianist performs a series of complex chords and difficult runs up and down the keyboard, and then sits perfectly still for about 15 minutes. Audiences, according to one critic, seem "almost afraid to cough." A strong influence on Cage's work was Zen Buddhism, an extremely austere and disciplined form of Buddhism, demanding long hours of meditation in absolute silence.

What ultimately distinguishes one musician from another is not only the ability to play the notes as written but the musical intuition that manifests itself. One way in which the critical ear can detect the presence of this intuition, or this "feeling for the music," is to listen to how the performer manipulates the silences that surround the tones. Three world-class pianists might record Beethoven's *Pathétique Sonata*, and though each plays exactly the same notes, the interpretation by each will have subtle touches unique to that musician. In almost every instance, the telling factor is the handling of silence. Here a pause is elongated; there, foreshortened. As with the space surrounding a sculpture, silence in music helps to define, to single out, to create individuality.

The most evident gift from great music is its sound. But the very absence of sound is just as important. Remember: *Music is the shaped sound between silences.*

Varieties of Musical Experience

6.2   *How do we differentiate among varieties of musical experience, including the fugue, the symphony, and the art song?*

There are so many styles, so many musical forms that singling out a few is difficult indeed. Within those parameters, however, certain kinds of musical experience—musical genres of the past and present—illustrate what music has to offer. Let's look at two such forms.

A Bach Fugue

Johann Sebastian Bach (1685–1750) was born in a Germany that did not regard music as an art form, but considered it either as court entertainment, composed and performed for upper-class amusement by hirelings paid to do a job, or as a subordinate adjunct to religious services. The music with which Bach is associated, which indeed he came to epitomize, grew out of religion but went beyond religion in its impact and influence on the future of music as an art. It became the very epitome of the Baroque, a highly complex style not only of music but of art and architecture as well. Historians of the humanities usually date the Baroque period from the middle of the seventeenth century to 1750, which happens to be the very year in which the composer died.

The Baroque period was characterized by architectural grandeur and an elaborate use of color and ornamentation. Civic buildings, such as those that still line the Ringstrasse, the main street of Vienna, were adorned with gilt, statuary, and other forms of embellishment, none of which was intended to be purely functional. The term *baroque* was taken from French and Portuguese words that meant "imperfect pearl" and applied to the new style, which was far from classical simplicity. Architecture made abundant use of curved rather than straight lines, and Baroque music is exceptionally intricate.

Catholicism found in Baroque architectural splendor one means of bringing people back to the fold. The German monk Martin Luther (1483–1546) had rebelled against Catholicism for what he considered its moral corruption. With other reformers, he had started a revolutionary movement known as the Protestant Reformation, which aimed to divest religion of its Catholic sensuality. In contrast to the stark, wooden churches of the Protestant Reformation, the Catholic Baroque houses of worship, especially in Italy and Poland, reintroduced the marble, brilliant colors, and statues of the Renaissance churches, perhaps in an effort to encourage defectors to return to a reinvented religion with an appeal to both the spirit and the senses. These churches, dating from the seventeenth century, are adorned with flying angels suspended from brightly painted ceilings and smiling gold cherubs resting near the tops of marble columns. They were for their time the epitome of opulence, offering both dramatic and aesthetic appeal without apology.

Despite the many reforms instituted by Luther and his followers, Lutheranism remained closer to Catholicism than would be true of the multiple Protestant sects that were to develop. While Lutherans generally shunned the impetus toward elaborate visual ornamentation of the churches, they felt differently about the ornamentation of their music. Music became especially important in the Lutheran service, for which Bach composed many of his works. As the era progressed, both religious and secular composers sought to outdo one another in the intricacy of their compositions. They made strong use of **counterpoint**, playing one melodic line against another, with two or more melodic lines being given equal value and independence.

Harmony, of course, had been standard in music since the early Renaissance, but Bach's counterpoint carried complexity a step further. Nonetheless, even though he had achieved considerable recognition for his music during his lifetime, after his death his church still considered him as primarily a great organist rather than a composer. When they first began to hear his compositions, congregations may have been slightly confused, if not overwhelmed, by what they heard.

When Bach (Figure 6.4) was first hired to play the organ, he was welcome to compose little pieces to accompany the service, which fed his insatiable appetite for experimenting with organ sound. Seeking to expand his musical horizons, Bach took a leave of absence and went in 1705 to study with the famous Danish-German organist and composer Dieterich Buxtehude, returning with new works of such intricacy and virtuosity that the church choir often could not sing them. By this time, however, word of the new music began to spread. Eventually he became musical director and choir director at St. Thomas's Church in Leipzig, where he remained for most of his productive life, scarcely traveling more than a few miles from the city.

His reputation expanded and blossomed, then began to fade as he grew older, even though the complexity of his work deepened. In some quarters, he began to be called old-fashioned. He had almost single-handedly brought Baroque music to its pinnacle and then was accused of not being modern enough. By mid-century Franz

Joseph Haydn (1732–1809) was learning his craft and soon would give birth to 104 symphonies, earning him the reputation he still enjoys as father of that musical genre. Haydn returned to the relative simplicity of classicism, and his tremendous influence helped to make Baroque complexity obsolete. In Bach's declining years, younger composers were already experimenting with the style that Haydn would make famous.

Through the new works, German music was attaining stature as an art form, and thus the great repertoire of Bach—the cantatas, the oratorios, and the magnificent displays of counterpoint known as **fugues**—were considered dated even before they were ever really discovered. Bach's music would have to wait a full century before it would take its place among acknowledged masterworks.

Confined both geographically and professionally, Bach found liberation in exploring the possibilities of musical language. The Baroque style required not only long, highly fluid melodies and countermelodies but also **improvisation**—a spontaneous variation or set of variations on a given theme. Through improvisation, Bach could take wings and soar into the endless skies of inner space.

BACH'S *TOCCATA AND FUGUE IN D MINOR* Music in the time of both Bach and Haydn was not expected to express a composer's innermost emotions; and indeed Bach's music is frequently labeled intellectual. It is, for example, greatly admired by mathematicians, who see in it a musical parallel to higher calculus. Nonetheless, there is indeed an emotional side to it. The great *Toccata and Fugue in D Minor* draws the listener into a vortex of sensations that are almost indescribable. The ear discerns the many melodic strands that play against each other, and the inner eye translates the sounds into patterns of light and lines that crisscross, engulf each other, and continually change into shapes never before seen or imagined. Surrendering to this music, we the listeners find ourselves visiting strange inner landscapes flooded with both thoughts and feelings.

A **toccata** is a freestyle musical form designed to allow the performer of Bach's day to display virtuosity; it is frequently, as in the case of the D Minor work, followed by a fugue, which is more strictly controlled by established musical laws. In a toccata, the composer or performer may improvise on the stated themes, taking them in a variety of directions.

This practice has definite counterparts in jazz. It is no coincidence that jazz players sometimes acknowledge a strong debt to Bach, particularly for his genius at improvisation, and often include variations on Bach melodies in their repertoire. The fugue allows for the simultaneous hearing of different melodies played or sung; it is a swift-moving form, stabilized by the laws of counterpoint—that is, the melodic lines heard simultaneously must complement, not conflict with, each other.

We need only listen to the D Minor performed on an organ to be astounded that one pair of hands and feet could master so difficult a composition. The idea behind the fugue is to demonstrate that what for the average person would be an impossibility is indeed well within the capabilities of the performer. It allows both composer and performer to display their virtuosity. At the same time, the intricacies of the form require strong guidelines as well as enormous technical skills. The result may sound free and unrestrained, but in actuality the music is rigorously disciplined. The major jazz composers and performers of our time are often highly trained musicians whose flights of improvisation follow definite rules, similar to the fugues of Bach.

A Beethoven Symphony

Sometimes the history of the humanities lopes along for many years, even decades, without producing an artist who rises to the highest levels of creative achievement. It can also happen that many artistic geniuses appear at or around the same time. The late fifteenth century in Italy, for example, saw three visual artists, acknowledged

Figure 6.4 Johann Sebastian Bach, 1746.
Bach, at first considered simply a church organist, eventually revolutionized the art of music. Listen to the *Toccata and Fugue in D Minor*. What does it make you feel?
Georgios Kollidas/Fotolia

 Bach: Toccata and Fugue in D Minor

to be perhaps the world's greatest, all contemporary with each other: Leonardo, Michelangelo, and Raphael. Germany and Austria can boast that they gave the world Beethoven and Mozart during the late eighteenth century.

In the Baroque musical tradition, composers worked in a limited range of musical forms to find their own way through the music. Bach achieved greatness by making the forms accommodate his tremendous musical intellect and imagination, mastering every known form with the exception of opera. Mozart easily rivaled Bach with his phenomenal output—and in a much shorter life span (1756–1791)—composing not only operas but symphonies, chamber music for inexhaustible combinations of instruments, several huge masses, a long list of songs, and concertos for both violin and piano. Mozart expanded the capabilities of the symphony orchestra and, in so doing, prepared the way for Beethoven, who would take it to new heights. In order to provide emotional release from a tormented life in which he gradually lost all of his hearing, Beethoven composed in new or greatly expanded musical forms; he caused fundamental changes in how music was perceived—as a subjective expression of individuality and personality.

Mozart: Symphony No. 40 in G Minor, I

Beethoven (Figure 6.5) composed for churches, concert halls, small salons, private performances, royal chambers, and, above all, for himself. When he lost his hearing during the peak of his musical career, Beethoven turned inward, and out of his complex and anguished soul came sounds no one had ever heard before. Even today, more than a century and a half after the composer's death, when every note written by him has been played and interpreted by thousands upon thousands of musicians and heard by millions, new listeners and new performers can find in the music some as yet undisclosed aspect of Beethoven's gigantic personality.

This new tradition combined secular, religious, and nationalistic trends into one, making the music of northern Europe the equal of Italian music, which had been for centuries the dominant musical tradition of the West. In particular, it created and then quickly broadened the scope of the symphony, which became for Germany what the opera was for Italy.

The development of the symphony cannot be measured in terms of quantity alone. Haydn wrote 104 symphonies, Mozart 41, and Beethoven "just" nine. (Later, Johannes Brahms, intimidated by the majestic symphonic creations of Beethoven, would spend 20 years working on his first symphony and would leave the world "just" four!)

BEETHOVEN'S *SYMPHONY NO. 3: EROICA*   Having given the world two symphonies in the tradition of Mozart, who had already stretched the limits of the form beyond anything yet known, Beethoven in 1804 came forth with his Third or E-flat Major Symphony, which is called *Eroica* ("Heroic"). The premiere proved to be an occasion for which the music world was still not completely prepared, even though the work had been preceded by Mozart's last symphony, the titanic *Jupiter*. After all, a symphony was originally a 20-minute concert diversion, consisting of four movements: the first moderately paced, the second slow and lyrical, the third rapid and light-hearted, and the fourth rousing and climactic. The four movements were related only in terms of a composer's characteristic style, but they were not expected to make a unified statement of any kind.

The *Eroica* was twice the length of the *Jupiter*. It was a work so huge in conception, so complex in execution, and so overwhelming to experience that by all rights it should have invited immediate comparison with Michelangelo's *David*, the Sistine Chapel ceiling, or the great tragedies of Shakespeare. Unfortunately, many of the first listeners could not accommodate the work's heroic dimensions or its daring innovations, particularly its heavy use of seventh chords, up to that time a musical taboo (most chords were built on three tones at that time), considered barbarically dissonant, unfit for civilized ears.

Figure 6.5 A romanticized image of Ludwig von Beethoven painted by Carl Jäger (1833–1887) in 1870, well after Beethoven's death.

Beethoven's symphonies may be the best known and most popular works of classical music in the Western world. Listen to the first movement of his Third Symphony, or "Ode to Joy," the fourth movement of his Ninth Symphony. What might account for the vast popularity of Beethoven's music?

Library of Congress, Prints and Photographs Division, LC-USZ62-29499

In the *Eroica*, the four movements constitute a unity, in that each succeeding movement sounds like a perfect complement to the one before it. It is clear that Beethoven did not finish one movement and then tack on another as though the preceding one had not existed. In the opinion of music historians, the most astonishing aspect of the *Eroica* is that it is not just big for the sake of bigness.

The first movement is on a grand, heroic scale, an epic style with noble themes and huge orchestration to be rivaled only by the composer's own fifth and ninth symphonies. The story is that Beethoven was inspired by the heroic image of Napoleon (Figure 6.6) as the liberator of Europe. He created in the opening movement music that paralleled his feelings and then dedicated the entire work to the man he perceived as savior of the free world. It is also widely believed that when word reached the composer that his hero had demanded to be crowned emperor, Beethoven rescinded the dedication.

Instead of glorifying an imperial leader, the work came to be identified with the common man movement hailing the heroism of ordinary citizens. It has the same fist-shaking thunder we find in the work of Michelangelo. A musical rebel, defying all tradition, plagued by illness that would eventually rob him of his hearing, misunderstood and criticized by many, Beethoven could readily identify with revolutionary movements in his native Germany, as well as in America and France.

🔊 Beethoven: Symphony No. 3 in E-Flat, "Eroica," I

One is tempted to hear in the second movement a musical parallel to Beethoven's profound disillusionment with Napoleon. Profound sorrow is certainly there, as indicated by the tempo notation: *marcia funebre* (funeral march). It is the slowest of all slow movements, dirgelike and heartbroken. We have already spoken of it in the section on silence as a musical element. Whether Napoleon was the direct cause of the sorrow or whether Beethoven, having exhausted the range of noble emotions, found himself exploring the depths of sadness, we cannot know; but we can say that the first two movements of the *Eroica* strongly suggest an experience common to nearly everyone: the passage from heroic, idealistic youth to maturity and its awareness of tragedy.

The third movement, by contrast, is almost shocking with its galloping pace and precise horns, all of it sounding like nothing so much as a hunting party. Out of place? Surely not. Listening carefully to every note of the funeral march shows that there is only so much emotional wrenching one can sustain. Life must go on. The depressed spirit must pull itself up from despair.

The finale begins with a graceful, dancelike melody suggestive of polite society: civilization restored, so to speak. This melody leads through an intricate development back into the same heroic mood that opened the symphony. We have passed from romantic illusion to the depths of tragedy and, through struggle, upward again to a more mature, sober, and deliberate affirmation. The composer of the *Eroica* captures the human soul in full range. It would not mark Beethoven's last glimpse of paradise.

Figure 6.6 A portrait of the Emperor Napoleon by French artist Jacques-Louis David, 1812. Beethoven originally dedicated his Eroica symphony to Napoleon. Listen to an excerpt from the symphony. Does the music suggest heroism to you? How?

Courtesy of National Gallery of Art/ Samuel H. Kress Collection

BEETHOVEN'S *SYMPHONY NO. 9* Beethoven's ninth, and final, symphony was composed around 1824, when he was totally deaf. It is easily four times the length of a late Mozart symphony, and twice that of even the *Eroica*. Not the journey of a young man's soul coping with the sobering realities of life, the Ninth Symphony is rather the final statement of a gigantic mentality that has struggled for years with both physical and creative suffering—of a person who has labored to find and capture it all, as Michelangelo, two centuries earlier, had sought perfection in marble, and as Einstein, a century later, would seek the ultimate equation for unifying the interactions among all the forces in the universe.

During the first three movements of the Ninth, Beethoven gives us one haunting melody after another, complex rhythms, intricate harmonies, and bold dissonance. He seems to be striving to find a musical equivalent to every feeling that can be experienced. By the fourth movement, he appears to have concluded that the orchestra alone was not enough to express the sounds he must have heard in the far recesses of his silent world. He needed human voices.

Other composers before him had written large choral works: Bach's *Passion According to Saint Matthew*, Haydn's *Creation*, and Mozart's *Requiem*, to name three supreme examples. But Beethoven pushes the human voice further than many have believed possible.

There remains considerable controversy about the final movement of the Ninth. Some critics say it takes us as close to the gates of heaven as we can get in this earthly lifetime. Some have called it a musical embarrassment, totally unsingable. One soprano, after attempting it, vehemently declared that Beethoven had no respect whatever for the female voice. Others have suggested that in his deafness Beethoven heard extraordinary sounds that were not contained within the boundaries of music and for which there were no known instruments, not even the human voice. Perhaps such sentiments over-romanticize the work. But perhaps not. No one will ever know what Beethoven was hearing.

Beethoven: Symphony No. 9 in D Minor, IV

The musical setting for Friedrich von Schiller's "Ode to Joy," the main theme of the fourth movement, has attained the stature of an international hymn. By far, the majority opinion about this music is that it transcends its own "unsingability" and any breach of musical taste it may commit. Asking whether one "likes it" seems beside the point. One can only feel humbled by its majesty. Listening to Beethoven's Ninth Symphony is discovering what human creativity really means.

The premiere performance of the work in Vienna, at that time the capital of European music, was attended by every Viennese musical luminary. By now fully convinced of the composer's genius, they were eager to discover what new sounds the great man could possibly bring forth from an inner world that was barred forever from the real sounds of humanity and nature. Beethoven was the co-conductor.

Witnesses to the event have left behind stories of the performance, especially of how the maestro conducted with sustained vigor, hearing his own orchestra no doubt; for when the "other" orchestra had finished the work and the enthusiastic applause began, Beethoven had not yet put down his baton. When at last he realized what was happening, he started to walk from the stage, perhaps feeling his music had not communicated. The other conductor caught up with him and turned him around in time to see the huge audience on its feet, shouting, crying "Bravissimo!" Beethoven simply bowed his head. No one will ever know what it was he had heard, just as he could not have known what *they* had heard. Nonetheless, that moment lives on in the history of the humanities as a rare meeting of souls in that strange space where the spirit of art lives.

Art Songs

So far we have discussed possible origins of music, the basic elements of music, two major musical forms, and composers who achieved distinction through making glorious musical history. For many of us, however, everyday musical experience comes from songs, much shorter compositions with easily remembered melodies and rhythms.

As children, we had nursery songs to teach or lullabies to soothe us. Most of us learned the alphabet by singing the letters. Some kind of song-making—if only the spontaneous chanting of a child—is innate to the growing-up process at every time and in every place. Like poetry and the other arts, song evolved into ever more sophisticated styles. Eventually it reached a point at which the composer's choices were rigidly defined by the rules of music.

The birth of song as art probably dates back to the classical period when epic poems such as the *Iliad* were sung by minstrels or bards as a means of being more easily remembered. In the early Middle Ages, monks sang their prayers as a regular part of the worship service. By the later Middle Ages, however, wealthy aristocrats demanded song as part of court entertainment, and the subject almost always was love. By the time of the great composers we have discussed, song was a recognized art form, expected in concert programs and performed by highly trained professionals. Their works have come to be known as art songs, as distinct from popular songs, which are not originally written as concert pieces. They mark a fusion of words and music, using the voice and—typically—piano to give added meaning to a poem.

FRANZ SCHUBERT   A genius of the art song was Franz Schubert, who, in his tragically brief life (1797–1828), composed more than 600! He wrote painstakingly for both singer and accompanist, his musical settings precisely suiting the words and fitting the mood of the poem. An excellent introduction to Schubert songs is "The Trout," with its sprightly melodic line and rippling fishlike accompaniment, and also "Death and the Maiden," with its agitated melodies and strangely peaceful accompaniment. The maiden of the title sees Death, a savage-looking skeleton, approaching and pleads with him to pass by and not touch her. But Death turns out to be friendly and promises that she will sleep gently in his arms.

Among Schubert's most famous works is the musical setting he gave to "Ave Maria." There is a legend that the composer, chronically poor, wrote the piece rapidly on a napkin or tablecloth and sold it to someone for the equivalent of 15 cents. True or not, the story does suggest what we know about Schubert: namely, that he was unsuccessful in his lifetime, though, unlike van Gogh, he had a small circle of friends who recognized his genius.

ALMA SCHINDLER MAHLER   Belated recognition for her art songs came to Austrian composer Alma Schindler Mahler (1879–1964). Early on, she was a wealthy Viennese socialite and hostess of glittering salons. Her warmth and nurturing spirit attracted numerous male artists to her. When only 17, she fell in love and married one of them, who neglected to mention that he already had a wife. Undaunted, and driven by her creative passion, she enrolled in a music school where she inspired fellow student Arnold Schoenberg, who would become a twentieth-century pioneer in the avant-garde, to compose music he heard inside him rather than what audiences would immediately accept. Alban Berg, another avant-gardist, also became a close friend and dedicated to her a masterwork, the opera *Wozzeck*.

Much given to amorous infatuations, she fell in love with Gustav Mahler (1860–1911), one of the great conductors and composers of the late nineteenth century. Her expectation was that they would nurture each other's careers, but he had other plans, demanding that she give up writing her little songs and live for him alone, as wives were expected to do. Mahler was already a recognized genius as both a composer and the conductor of the Vienna Opera, answering to no one except the emperor of Austria and God, to whom he dedicated his final symphony. Twenty years her senior, as her first near-husband had been, Mahler assumed the role of protective father, treating Alma as was expected of fathers in this time and in no way interested in encouraging her to develop her own considerable talents.

Exerting the same dictatorial attitude with which he directed the Opera, Mahler instructed his wife that she must nurse the children, create a quiet home with well-prepared meals, and, in her spare time, copy all of his manuscripts. But Alma was secretly in rebellion, writing to a friend that "the man who had to spread his peacock train in public wants to relax at home" and that this "after all is woman's fate. But it isn't mine!"

Finally, feeling perhaps a slight twinge of guilt, Mahler spent an afternoon with Sigmund Freud and admitted his marital problems. Freud's answer was to encourage him to look into his wife's work. After the session, Mahler returned home, played some of Alma's songs, then cried out, "What have I done? These songs are good," and insisted they would be immediately published. Unfortunately, Mahler died before he could follow through on his promised support. Alma lived to be 84, with a reputation only for being the nurturer of male genius. Belatedly, her songs have been rediscovered, but sadly only 17 survive.

The Musical Avant-Garde

Like their counterparts in visual art, innovators in concert music do not want to sound like anything that has gone before them; they do not wish to be confined by time-honored guidelines but seek to forge new directions. They are the **avant-garde**. Translated, the term says *advanced guard*, but this is a military phrase. Applied to the arts, *garde* can also mean *guardian* or *watchman*. In other words, the avant-gardist is one who looks after our best interests by protecting us from what has become dull, overly familiar.

The need to be free from restraint has always been a key factor, especially in works of genius. Beethoven, for example, expanded the range of music in creating his Third Symphony, forcing the music to accommodate his mighty passions. In the twentieth century, George Gershwin's *Rhapsody in Blue* combined jazz and symphonic music as had never been done before, and when the Beatles arrived on the scene, audiences could not have been prepared for the style and musical expertise the band brought to the rock genre. All of these composers did what they had to do: *express themselves in ways congenial to their temperaments regardless of conventions.*

The need to rebel is thus the need to be who you are, and if you happen to be an artist, your art will be rebellious. Some concert composers today are tired of the diatonic scale—sometimes *any* scale. One composer attacks a grand piano with her fists, then climbs up onto the instrument, stands upside down inside it and plucks the hammers; others have found in the synthesizer, and later the computer, the keys to uncharted inner worlds that enable them to produce sounds no one has yet heard.

🔊 Stravinsky: *The Rite of Spring*, "Danses des adolescentes"

Igor Stravinsky (1882–1971) is regarded by many as the father of the modern avant-garde in music. His revolutionary score for the 1913 ballet *The Rite of Spring* introduced sounds so unfamiliar that, combined with the provocative movements of Vaslav Nijinsky as well as his choreography, they sparked a riot at the Paris premiere. Though denounced by audience and critics alike (one critic called the music a "barnyard come to life"), Stravinsky would eventually win the day, and his unorthodox rhythms, dissonances, and timbres would prove seminal to the music that followed after him.

One of his contemporaries was Arnold Schoenberg (Alma Mahler's one-time classmate), born in Berlin and musically educated in Vienna. For his large-scale concert works, he reduced the size of the orchestra to 15 instruments, for which he provided dissonance in dizzying counterpoint and bizarre harmonic progressions. Embracing atonality, Schoenberg abandoned key altogether in many of his early works, notably *Pierrot Lunaire*, using human voices that don't always sound like human voices to produce the intended musical equivalent of mental disturbance. In this work, Schoenberg replaced the standard musical notes with notations requiring the "singers" to speak-sing at approximate pitches. At times they sound like lost souls seeking release from solitary confinement. His **atonality**—music that lacks a key, or tonal center—encouraged other avant-gardists to break away from bondage to familiar harmonies and structures.

In 1925, Schoenberg moved back to Berlin, where he came under the influence of the German avant-garde, which had strong counterparts in theater and visual art. This Berlin art scene was brimming with postwar cynicism and had an audience that saw only deteriorating civilization for its future. Here, Schoenberg composed his opera *Moses und Aron*, in which characters sing-speak of their inability to communicate with each other. Both *Pierrot Lunaire* and *Moses und Aron* remain stern tests of one's willingness to entertain the *extremely* unfamiliar. But we encourage you to give it at least a fair try. To no surprise, there are contemporary avant-garde composers who consider Stravinsky and Schoenberg old-fashioned.

Much of the music of the avant-garde, as we have said, is produced on synthesizers. Leading the way was the French composer Edgard Varèse (1883–1965). Starting out as a mathematics student, he found himself unable to resist the excitement of creating new musical sounds on a machine that seemed to be able to do anything the user desired. He declared boldly that he refused to submit to sounds that had already been heard, which could really be the battle cry of the musical avant-garde. Then he added that rules do not make a work of art. Encouraged by his friend and admirer Claude Debussy, he explored non-Western sounds, eventually combining them with his own reconfiguration (or discarding) of Western scales and tonal patterns.

In 1923, his *Hyperprism* premiered, and, like *The Rite of Spring*, it caused a riot in the theater. Some of the instruments he employed were sleigh bells, rattles, crash cymbals, an anvil, Chinese blocks, Indian drums, and a washtub with a hole in the bottom that allowed the player to reproduce the sound of a lion's roar.

At the age of 71, Varèse created *Déserts*, his response to atomic energy and the dangers it posed for the world. The piece, using both taped and synthesized sounds, drove the audience into a frenzy and nearly led to another riot. One critic observed that Varèse deserved the electric chair for composing such noise.

Music Beyond the Concert Hall

6.3 *How do we explain the emergence and impact of various forms of popular music, including folk, jazz, blues, gospel, rock and roll, and hip-hop?*

So far in this chapter we have talked about music that is most often listened to in a concert or recital hall—music that was composed, written down, scored, orchestrated, learned and performed by professional musicians. But for many of us, the more familiar experience of listening comes beyond the walls of a concert hall, through our smartphones or tablets, from our favorite movies, or at outdoor festivals and events. Often this is music just as complex and sophisticated, and as emotionally compelling for the listener, as that written for and played by orchestras, classically trained singers, or chamber musicians.

Folk Music

Unlike many art forms that have established traditions within the humanities, the folk song has followed few aesthetic rules. Some folk songs originated centuries ago, perhaps as a way of spreading news in isolated areas, perhaps as musical improvisations by people who had little else to entertain them. Folk songs didn't require expert musical accompaniment or trained voices. They were likely to be handed down from generation to generation and changed every time they were sung. That's why there are many versions of the same song.

Folk music enjoyed a wave of popularity in the mid-twentieth century, fueled by the work of Woody Guthrie and Huddie Ledbetter, known as Lead Belly, and then turned by accomplished musicians such as Joan Baez, Joni Mitchell, Bob Dylan, Judy Collins, and more recently, Ani DiFranco into something closer to art song. Yet it can still be a participant's art, an affirmation of group identity. In certain parts of the country, let a fiddler introduce the first few notes of "Turkey in the Straw" and almost immediately people are clapping their hands or dancing. During the civil rights movement of the 1960s, the song "We Shall Overcome" created—and even now can create—instant bonding among people who may never have seen each other before.

Songs sung spontaneously at rallies or sporting events are not exactly folk music, but they fulfill a similar purpose in promoting group solidarity. For example, during the 1980s, the rock group *Queen* released a song called "We Will Rock You" that is still sung by students all over the country, especially during football games, and "We Are Family," released in 1979 by Sister Sledge, became the rallying cry for Pittsburgh Pirates fans.

SONGS ABOUT REAL PEOPLE AND EVENTS   During the Middle Ages, troubadours kept people informed of heroic actions in battles and skirmishes through song. Maritime lore abounds with songs commemorating events that took place at sea, such as atrocities committed by a pirate captain or the sinking of a ship to its lonely, watery grave. Folk songs often memorialize individuals, ranging from heroes like the "steel-driving man" John Henry to otherwise forgotten ordinary people, like the murdered barmaid in Bob Dylan's haunting, rage-filled "The Lonesome Death of Hattie Carroll." The narrator of the commemorative song is rarely identified. A typical opening line is: "My name is nothin' extra/ So that I will not tell." The group, the event, or the individual that the song is about are always more important than the singer/ reporter.

Commemorative songs continue to be written. In 1968, the gentle hit song "Abraham, Martin and John" paid tribute to the victims of assassins' bullets, and Don McLean's "American Pie," composed in 1971, offered an infectious, and slightly mysterious, story written, many people believe, to commemorate the deaths of pop stars Buddy Holly, Ritchie Valens, and the Big Bopper in a 1959 plane crash.

Work songs are also highly durable, for it is hard to imagine a time when work will not be central to most people's lives. In some cases, the work song reflects great hardship and a state of tension between management and labor. Often, however, the music is jolly and full of bounce and joy, as though to help the original creator forget his tired limbs and meager salary.

> *I've been workin' on the railroad*
> *All the livelong day;*
> *I've been workin' on the railroad*
> *Just to pass the time away.*[1]

The nineteenth-century folk ballad "John Henry"—both a commemorative and a work song—reflects the conflict between worker and machine at a time when the steam drill was about to replace hammers swung by human arms. John Henry became a folk hero, mythologized as a superhuman individual who was stronger and smarter than a machine, for a while. In his effort to beat the steam drill through the mountain with his hammer and steel pike, John Henry's great heart finally failed him.

> *John Henry said to his captain:*
> *"You are nothing but a common man,*
> *Before that steam drill shall beat me down,*
> *I'll die with my hammer in my hand."*
> *...*

John Henry was hammering on the right side,
The big steam drill on the left,
Before that steam drill could beat him down,
He hammered his fool self to death.[2]

Another such worker was Joe Hill, a Swedish-born immigrant who, like so many others, came to the United States in the early twentieth century with dreams of success, only to be swallowed into a vast labor force, toiling for 40 or more hours a week and trying to survive on a minimum wage. A born folk poet and singer, Hill began to compose songs about the hardships endured by the workers and the obstinate refusal of management to meet their demands or even to offer a compromise. He became a modern folk minstrel, and his songs, simple, easily sung and remembered, soon spread from union hall to union hall, adapted to many kinds of labor problems.

Hill was also an activist, traveling throughout the country, speaking to larger and larger gatherings of workers; and he inevitably acquired the reputation of troublemaker and rabble-rouser. While he was in Salt Lake City addressing a union meeting, a murder took place and Hill was arrested and charged with the crime. In a still famous trial, the prosecution produced witnesses who placed Hill at the scene of the crime. After a short jury deliberation he was found guilty and sentenced to die by firing squad. While awaiting his execution, he wrote his final song in which he said that some people could find justice in Salt Lake City "but not Joe Hill."

Joan Baez, a folk singer who epitomized the human rights movement of the 1960s and 1970s, wrote a commemorative ballad about Joe Hill, one that has already achieved the status of genuine folk art.

From San Diego up to Maine,
in every mine and mill,
where working-men defend their rights,
it's there you find Joe Hill,
it's there you find Joe Hill![3]

SONGS ABOUT ROGUES AND OUTLAWS The *scoundrel song* celebrates the Dionysian personality—the perennial favorite of our hidden selves—the lawless, irresponsible, but charming rogue you couldn't trust or marry or put in charge of an important operation but who is always fun. A traditional Irish favorite is "The Moonshiner," which upholds a life of drinking, carousing, gambling, and avoiding work. The narrator proudly sings that "if you don't like me, you can leave me alone." Who can argue with that premise? He intends to

. . . eat when I'm hungry and drink when I'm dry,
And if moonshine don't kill me,
I'll live till I die.[4]

To be sure, society would perish if it depended upon wild rovers, but the singer of scoundrel songs was usually a loner who could not, *would* not, adapt easily to the demands of organized society and so could hardly have been expected to celebrate the morally upright, the hard-working, and the pious.

ACCUMULATION AND NARRATIVE SONGS The *accumulation song* is deliberately drawn out, with verse after verse and a refrain repeated after each one. Songs such as "The Twelve Days of Christmas" and "Old MacDonald" start off with one detail (one gift, one animal) and then add more and more as the song continues. Accumulation songs extend group solidarity for longer periods, prolong the high spirits of the gathering, and keep loneliness at bay. The warmth and hominess of accumulation songs is echoed in what is sometimes referred to as primitive, or folk, art, like that of Grandma Moses (Figure 6.7).

Figure 6.7 Grandma Moses, *We Are Coming to Church*, 1949.
How does this work by the mid-20th-century artist Grandma Moses provide a visual parallel to folk music?

Christie's Images Ltd./SuperStock

The *narrative song*, as its label implies, tells a tale, often at great length, answering, like the accumulation song, the need of listeners to stay together as long as possible. It was the folk version of the epic, usually filled with accounts of wondrous and miraculous events. The Scottish ballad "Binorie" recounts the sad story of a miraculous harp that was fashioned from the breastplate of a murdered girl and that sings as it plays. The harp reveals the events leading up to the girl's murder, then comes to the shocking climax: "My sister it was who did me slay." Quite possibly the song, like many others, was based on an actual event.

Country and western music has carried on the narrative tradition of folk music, adding its own unique tales to the repertoire. During the late 1960s "Ode to Billie Joe" was popular as a crossover song, topping country charts as well as the Top 40. Fans listened intently to the tragic story of a teenage boy who jumped to his death from the Tallahatchie Bridge. What was unique about the song was that it gave subtle suggestions about the "why" of the incident but never actually told us in so many words. Radio talk shows had hundreds of callers who gave their opinions, but the composer, Bobbie Gentry, refused to divulge the secret.

SONGS OF PROTEST AND SOCIAL JUSTICE   The 1960s, a period of widespread alienation in the United States, saw a significant revival of folk music. Young people, often far from home, got together for the night in hastily improvised camps or in communes with ever-changing members and became instant—if temporary—friends through the common bond of singing. Joan Baez, composer/singer of "Joe Hill," and Judy Collins attained huge popularity by reviving old songs, particularly those that still spoke to the rebellious spirit seeking freedom from restraint. But the main thrust of the folk revival was the tightness of the group. It could have a distinctly spiritual side. At concerts, Judy Collins sang the old hymn "Amazing Grace" and soon had 10,000 voices joining in with hands interlocked in a show of community. The hymn, once revived, has remained an integral part of our culture; it was sung by President Obama at a memorial service for nine murdered black churchgoers in South Carolina in 2015.

New folk minstrels emerged, using *protest songs* to make statements against war, pollution, and the corruption of the establishment. Bob Dylan's "A Hard Rain's A-Gonna Fall" and John Lennon's "Give Peace a Chance" were written and sung in protest, originally against the Vietnam War, but since then against other wars, or all wars. They are modern folk songs that attain the level of art. Lennon summed up the dream of a world without war, hunger, and hatred in what may be the most important folk song of the last century: "Imagine." Though composed and sung by a master musician, "Imagine" has all the simplicity and the passionate honesty of the folk tradition. These three songs will probably endure as long as there are troubled times. And when will there *not* be?

FOLK THEMES IN CONCERT AND BALLET   Folk music has inspired concert composers of the past and present. Beethoven was charmed by the Gaelic folk tradition and composed songs based on both Irish and Scottish melodic patterns.

The American composer Aaron Copland (1900–1990) was so delighted by his country's folk music, especially songs of the Old West, that his music has come to define America in sound. *Billy the Kid*, one of Copland's many ballet scores, utilizes the folk song "Goodbye, Old Paint" (sung by a cowboy to his horse) in a stirring theme and variations. *Rodeo* interweaves themes and rhythms from Saturday night barn dances. *El Salón México* is an orchestral suite woven out of traditional Mexican folk material and exuberant Latin rhythms, set against Copland's unique dissonance. Perhaps the composer's most famous score was written for the ballet *Appalachian Spring*, which employs a number of folk themes, notably the old Shaker hymn "Simple Gifts." The ballet itself celebrates time-honored rituals such as the raising of a barn by everyone in the community.

Folk themes such as those incorporated into this ballet often came from other cultures. Appalachian music, for example, has deep roots in the Gaelic folk music of Ireland and Scotland as well as the British folk tradition. The Israeli *hora* and the Italian *tarantella* are folk dances known throughout the world. *Polka* music was originally derived from Polish folk themes. We encourage you to pay attention to the many folk cultures brought to these shores from other countries and the rich musical experiences they provide.

Spirituals and Gospel Music

The **spiritual** had its beginnings in the need of African slaves to articulate and preserve their roots, to give meaning to their suffering, and to demand a rightful place in society. Taken—stolen—away from their homeland as far back as the seventeenth century, with no future except slavery, pain, and death, they took comfort in their relationship with God and an ultimate reward in a paradise where everyone was free.

> *Deep river, my home is over Jordan,*
> *Deep river, Lord, I want to cross over into camp-ground.*
> *I want to cross over into campground.*[5]

Spirituals emphasize God's personal concern for each person, however obscure that person may be in the eyes of other mortals. For instance:

> *I sing because I'm happy,*
> *I sing because I'm free*
> *For His eye is on the sparrow,*
> *And I know He watches me.*[6]

As the spiritual genre grew and developed, it was made more and more complex by church choirs and soloists, each of whom would add the mark of their individual interpretations. Often transported by religious ecstasy, they created the new genre of *gospel* music. Over the years this genre, while remaining as an indigenous part of church services, has also moved into the arena of popular music. It is characterized by giving the singer free reign to add enough notes to allow a fuller emotional expression.

Mahalia Jackson (1911–1972) became the best-known and highly influential exponent of the gospel genre. Born in New Orleans when that city was bursting at the seams with new music—ragtime, jazz, and blues—she grew up next door to a church in which music played a vital role. She heard traditional hymns played and sung with many rhythmic variations. In addition, the sounds of Mardi Gras music, street vendors, and the songs belted out from the barrooms with wide-open doors and windows seeped into her blood. Devoutly religious, Jackson blended spirituals and aspects of the New Orleans secular style into religious songs that became nationally famous when she moved to Chicago and married a businessman, who recognized her potential and launched her career. In 1954, Columbia Records signed her to a long-term contract, and gospel music was soon on the charts.

A civil rights activist, Jackson took part in the historic March on Washington in 1963, singing before thousands assembled on the Mall to hear Martin Luther King Jr.'s epoch-making "I Have a Dream" speech.

Ragtime

Ragtime music dates back to the turn of the twentieth century, to a period when the legendary fortunes of the Rockefellers, Vanderbilts, Goulds, and Astors were being amassed and when the American monied aristocracy, their acquaintances, and all those who emulated their Victorian manners were entertaining guests with salon orchestras playing stately waltzes. The aim was to establish European elegance on this side of the Atlantic.

Some of the less privileged, eager to take advantage of the freedom to pursue upward mobility, wanted to gain the social recognition already enjoyed by wealthy families, and they wanted to show everyone they were capable of creating elegance of their own. Ragtime emerged from the African-American community and its musical traditions, transformed by the influence of European styles. African-American musicians wanted to do more than play the minstrel-show type of music with which white audiences had come to identify them. Ragtime came along at just the right moment. The acknowledged master of the new genre was Scott Joplin (1868–1917), who began his career in backrooms and honky-tonks but became a national celebrity with the publication of "Maple Leaf Rag" in 1899.

Joplin heard the original ragtime tunes played by small African-American combos on riverboats. They may have been variations on old plantation songs, minstrel-show cakewalks, and banjo melodies, played at lively tempos. White audiences expected African-American music to be high-spirited, but **ragtime** would be different. Its label was coined to identify the syncopation that was the trademark of the new genre. **Syncopation** occurs when the melodic line of a piece is played against, not with, the accented beats of the rhythm accompaniment; the notes fall in the cracks between the beats. Syncopated pieces are usually difficult to play because the left hand and the right hand emphasize different beats or divisions of the beat. (For a perfect example of syncopation, listen to George Gershwin's "Fascinatin' Rhythm.")

Joplin was captivated by the new sounds, but he wanted to turn them into a legitimate, recognized genre that would be associated with African Americans but also prove the equal of the foreign imports. This meant imitating or at least coming close to European rhythm. He slowed down the pace to make the music even more stately. On the sheet music of his "rags" he would write: "Do not play this piece fast. It is never right to play Ragtime fast."

The waltz is always played in three-quarter time. Ragtime, played almost exclusively on the piano, is written in *two*-quarter time, its tempo also never changing. The primary influences on Joplin's music, in addition to riverboat songs, were the popular European marches as well as the waltz and the quadrille, a dignified French square dance.

The enormous popularity of "Maple Leaf Rag" and other Joplin hits made African-American musicians sit up and take notice, especially in New Orleans, which was a stronghold for the liberal acceptance of new music. Jelly Roll Morton (1890–1941) introduced Joplin to New Orleans but played him at a faster tempo, an innovation that would be integrated into yet another American musical genre: *jazz*.

🔊 Joplin: "Maple Leaf Rag"

Jazz

The musical roots of jazz are African. The music brought to this country by slaves was marked by what is known as a "call and response" pattern. Participants would sing or play a particular combination of tones, and this combination would be answered by singing or playing a variation on it. The original purpose was similar to that of the folk song: community bonding.

During the late nineteenth century, African-American musicians went to New Orleans where they studied European genres and rhythmic patterns. But they brought with them a knowledge of their own traditional sounds, derived from what were called "field hollers" as well as rhythmic songs sung by slaves as they worked, and the spirituals that were a profound part of African-American religious life.

The typical scale used in African music contains five tones instead of the European scale of seven. At first, the New Orleans musicians tried to combine the two without sacrificing the African scale. The result was that they added slightly lowered notes called *blue notes* to the diatonic scale. From ragtime they borrowed syncopation. The synthesis of all these strains made possible the evolution of jazz.

As the decades of the twentieth century rolled by, the form attracted a range of musical geniuses, some self-taught, some classically trained. They had—and continue to have—one thing in common: knowing how to maintain a balance between control and the need for soaring release. The call and response form had required that the responders change the original theme, adding their own variation. Even when jazz became a sophisticated art form, improvisation continued to be its major characteristic.

Whatever their training, jazz instrumentalists and composers admire Bach because he lifted improvisation, the art of taking flight from a set theme, to new heights. A typical jazz piece follows a disciplined pattern. The group, or the soloist backed by the group, will play the main theme once through, sometimes a well-known song, sometimes an original tune composed for the group. Then one instrument after another performs a variation of the theme.

Original jazz works often have titles that are specific to a place or time, like "Take the A Train" (referring to a New York City subway line that runs to Harlem), "One O'Clock Jump," and "Stompin' at the Savoy" (the Savoy was a Harlem dance hall that rivaled the midtown Roseland, which mostly catered to a white clientele). From the beginning, jazz has shaped and defined the "cool scene"—a late-night coming together of sophisticated people who want to lose themselves in the music and escape, if only briefly, from their problems, just as the performers seek to lose themselves in the music.

Following in the footsteps of Jelly Roll Morton, great jazz soloists such as Charlie Parker and Louis Armstrong became famous for going off on lengthy variations, often improvising for 10 or 15 minutes before returning to the theme. One motive behind jazz improvisation was to explore the potential of one's instrument and take it to places that no one else had ever found. In a life tragically interrupted when he was only 28, a phenomenal cornet player named Bix Beiderbecke is said to have been obsessed with the desire to find the perfect note beyond the normal range of other players. Presumably, he did not live long enough to reach his goal. Some who were fortunate enough to hear him report that, as he pushed his instrument beyond the ordinary limits of its capabilities, his face turned almost scarlet and all of his facial muscles threatened to break loose from his skin.

DUKE ELLINGTON   Musical histories that deal with jazz as a serious and major art form give preeminence to Edward Kennedy Ellington—known universally as Duke (1899–1974)—the person who did the most to bridge the gap between the concert hall and the intimate jazz club (Figure 6.8). A bandleader who had Manhattan society driving to the Cotton Club in Harlem during the late 1920s, Ellington sought to expand the range of jazz through continual experimentation

> *with what he called his "jungle effects." When the sounds of "growling" trumpets and trombones, sinuous clarinets and eerie percussion were recorded, the originality of the orchestration was immediately grasped internationally by music critics and record buyers. . . . As a jazz arranger his great gift was in balancing orchestration and improvisation.*[7]

Ellington brought jazz to Carnegie Hall, where it could be played and evaluated in a setting built for the performance of classical concert music. In so doing, he wrote out elaborate and complex orchestrations—something no one had done before him. He did leave room for solo flights (or else it would not have been jazz), but his own

Figure 6.8 Duke Ellington.
Some scholars label jazz America's
greatest contribution to the world of
music. Do you agree? What makes jazz
uniquely American?

Bettmann/Corbis

compositions, like "Mood Indigo," "Satin Doll," and "Sophisticated Lady," which he usually performed while wearing elegant evening clothes, display a classic sense of discipline and musicianship.

GEORGE GERSHWIN Another major American composer who brought jazz to Carnegie Hall in the early years was George Gershwin (1898–1937). He started his career as a Tin Pan Alley songwriter, but Gershwin, who had been classically trained, was hungry for greater things. He moved on to compose the scores for Broadway musicals of the 1920s and the opera *Porgy and Bess*.

In 1924, he found his chance. Paul Whiteman, a bandleader also hungry for serious recognition, commissioned him to write a concert jazz piece. The result was *Rhapsody in Blue*, which combined the textures of romantic works for piano and symphony orchestras with the pulsations, dissonance, and syncopated rhythms of jazz. Gershwin thus put an American art form on the international musical map. The *Rhapsody* became an overnight success and has sold millions of recordings. It remains in the standard concert repertoire of nearly every major orchestra.

Jazz has remained a major art form, studied in almost every school and performed regularly in concert halls throughout the world as well as in annual festivals devoted exclusively to both jazz classics and the very newest styles and musicians. The Newport Jazz Festival in Rhode Island and Jazz at Lincoln Center in New York are two notable examples producing important artists who are at ease in both the classical and jazz scenes.

MILES DAVIS One such performer was trumpeter and pianist Miles Davis (1926–1991), whose versatility led him to the forefront of innovators in many genres of jazz, including *bebop* and *cool jazz*. By the time he was 18, Davis had shown so much talent that The Julliard School offered him a scholarship, but he proved too impatient to wait for graduation. When he was 19, he made his first recording and joined the jazz quintet of Charlie Parker, the premier saxophonist of the period. Because of his youth and lack of professional experience, Davis was used as a *sideman*—a non-soloist who played back-up to the stars. It was not long before he stepped into the solo spotlight. In 1955, he created the Miles Davis Quintet, which took jazz to new heights.

In his earlier work, Davis experimented with bebop, which had become the rage in the 1940s. An offshoot of the parent form, jazz, bebop was almost totally improvised and therefore greatly favored by soloists who wanted the music to serve their unique showcase needs. The more mature Davis of the Quintet gradually eased away from the eccentricities of bebop and moved toward what became known as *cool jazz*, a form more disciplined, more faithful to the music, and less given to wild flights of musical fancy. By the late 1950s, Davis, who also played Carnegie Hall, was presenting jazz versions of concert music, and still later, he began integrating electric instruments into the mix, eventually producing what critics consider one of the greatest albums of all time, *Bitches Brew* (1970).

Blues

The term *blues* derives from the melancholy mood produced by music that made liberal use of expressively lowered tones, the so-called blue notes. The genre has permeated our vocabulary to such an extent that "blue" seems always to have meant "down in the dumps." Many jazz tunes are bouncy and lively, but the jazz repertoire includes its share of blues.

The genre had its origins, as did ragtime and jazz, in the songs sung by slaves after a grueling day in the fields. While they sometimes desired an upbeat mood, the workers must have, just as often, sought an outlet for depression. As the form became caught up in the entertainment industry of jazz, sophisticated composers and singers turned the old songs into haunting expressions of sadness that found ready listeners among audiences of varied backgrounds.

Blues songs are almost always about the empty aftermath of a once-burning passion. They are written from either a male or a female point of view. Men sing of women's faithlessness, and women return the compliment about men. Probably the most famous of all blues songs is "St. Louis Blues" by W.C. Handy (1873–1958), who also composed "Beale Street Blues." If jazz is associated with New Orleans, the headquarters of the blues was Memphis, and it is on Beale Street that many of the great blues clubs are located, attracting visitors from all over the world.

Many of the soloists who elevated the form to a high status had tragic lives themselves, caused by bad relationships, social discrimination, or substance abuse. Famous was Bessie Smith (1894–1937), believed by many to have developed the blues style imitated by countless others. Bessie immortalized many lines from blues lyrics, including "If it wasn't for bad luck, I wouldn't have no luck at all."

🔊 Handy: "St. Louis Blues"

One of the most versatile of all the blues singing greats—as well as one of the most tragic—was Billie Holiday (1915–1959) (Figure 6.9). Singer and songwriter, she excelled in jazz, jazz blues, torch songs, and swing. Nicknamed Lady Day, she was strongly influenced by jazz instrumentalists, developing a style that has never been imitated. The most famous of her own songs is "Lady Sings the Blues," and she is also remembered for a dramatic rendition of "Strange Fruit," a song about lynching.

Popular Song

During the 1930s through the early 1950s, the so-called big bands were all the fashion. To escape the downbeat mood of the Great Depression and then the World War II years, people flocked to supper clubs to hear and dance to the well-orchestrated music of full-scale orchestras led by Glenn Miller, Tommy and Jimmy Dorsey, Benny Goodman, and numerous others. Miller developed a whole new style, featuring tight harmony serving as background for his own trombone solos. Goodman became the leading clarinetist of the day, crossing over easily from the night club to Carnegie Hall. Many songs that have since become standards were written for these aggregations, and many singers, including Frank Sinatra, made their debut with the big bands. Sinatra was soloist with the Tommy Dorsey orchestra.

The big-band song, such as "This Love of Mine," the piece that vaulted a thin and wispy Sinatra into public prominence, had a very specific pattern. Usually about 3 minutes in length, it would be played once by the orchestra, then a soloist or group would sing it through once. Until Sinatra became a sensation and the main reason people came to hear the Dorsey band, most of the orchestras played so that couples could dance. But the lyrics to the songs were extremely important also because phonograph records (78 speed) were hot items in music stores.

The period was also the heyday of the movie musical as well as the Broadway show, which featured songs meant to be recorded and popularized as so-called hits. This necessity imposed stiff restraints upon lyricists who had to develop and conclude an idea in the usual 3 minutes, with words vaguely applicable to the film or stage context but able to tell their own story apart from any other context. A classic among these songs is Jerome Kern's "Smoke Gets in Your

Figure 6.9 Billie Holiday, c. 1940s.

One central myth of the humanities is that all great artists live lives full of pain. Do you agree? Or can happiness also inspire great art?

World History Archive/Alamy

Eyes," with lyrics by Otto Harbach, who really deserves to be labeled a poet. Harbach develops a very common theme, dating at least as far back as Roman poetry: that of love lost. At first, the narrator believes the beloved is faithful, though friends think otherwise, advising that "when your heart's on fire" you must realize that "smoke gets in your eyes." But the narrator scoffs, only to discover that his love has left him. The friends are now the ones who scoff, but the narrator, in an absolutely brilliant repetition of the song title in a different context, points out that tears come when the flame of a beautiful romance is dying out and "smoke gets in your eyes."

IRVING BERLIN   Irving Berlin (1888–1989) could not read or write down a note of music but compiled the greatest number of enduring twentieth-century popular works. His songs generally express simple, honest, and universal emotions. While he could define the everlasting joys of love, he had no peer at providing the bittersweet happiness of nostalgia. It's all over, but one is left with fond memories all the same. The nostalgia of "White Christmas" elevated a popular song written for a sequence in a movie to the status of a Christmas carol.

In 1938, the popular singer Kate Smith asked Berlin to compose a patriotic song with which she could conclude her broadcast celebrating the twentieth anniversary of the armistice that ended World War I. After several attempts proved futile, the composer remembered a song he had written for an Army camp show during that conflict, a song rejected for being "too jingoistic." He found "God Bless America" buried in an old trunk, polished it a bit, and then offered it to Smith. Its first performance on the broadcast of November 20, 1938, electrified both the studio and the vast national audience. The song contains ten short lines and, sung once through, probably takes less than 3 minutes. No one has to be told about the song's impact in all times and on countless occasions since. When Jerome Kern was asked to indicate Berlin's place in American music, he answered tersely: "Irving Berlin *is* American music."

FRANK SINATRA   The reputation of Frank Sinatra (1915–1998) not only outlived the big-band era but expanded until it may very well be claimed that he was the greatest vocal stylist of popular songs. Composers and lyricists jumped at the chance to write for him because he was without peer in delivering a song's message through his vocal flexibilities and his acting talent. Many of the songs with which he was associated have become classics, though almost no contemporary singer has been able to duplicate the power of the original performance, which crystallizes emotions all of us share and gives us comfort in the knowledge that we are not alone.

A Sinatra classic is "One for My Baby," in which the narrator is sitting at a bar very late at night with no one around except a bartender who may be, but is probably not, listening, having heard the story so often. Nonetheless, the narrator pours out his heart. He has been abandoned by his one true love, though he does not deny having been responsible for the breakup; now there is only the effort to escape the pain through drink. The refrain to which he keeps returning asks the bartender to give him two more drinks: "one for my baby" and "one more for the road." As both poems and songs do when they achieve art, this one captures a certain moment, an image in the flow of time with universal applicability—that of the loner in a bar late at night with no clear future and, obviously, no one to comfort him.

Rock and Roll

Rock is the most pervasive musical phenomenon of our time, having endured in its many forms for well over half a century. It is a major way of defining our culture in sound. **Rock** is a fusion of rhythm and blues, gospel, country and western, and rap styles. It has many complex facets, ranging from the conscious artistry of serious musicians to the out-of-control, body-bending shouting by athletic musicians prancing around a stage. Rock is first and foremost a celebration of the Dionysian spirit let loose and often exulting in a total disregard for rules. Lyrics often denounce the establishment (*any* establishment) and glorify the strident life of total freedom.

Some historians of popular culture trace the origins of rock to 1955, the year in which the film *Blackboard Jungle* leaped onto the screen with an explosion of music titled "Rock Around the Clock." With its overly pronounced and rapid beat, the song had film audiences jumping in the aisles and dancing—even as the rock concerts would be doing in a few years. The band that arranged and played the piece was Bill Haley and the Comets, and to them is given the credit for introducing the musical movement first called **rock 'n' roll**, although scholars and historians agree that the roots of rock reach back into the African-American music of the 1940s called rhythm and blues.

Rhythm and blues music had long been a staple in small African-American dance clubs in the South. Because of their confined spaces, these clubs could accommodate only small combos, which made a big sound in compensation. The new sound spread quickly in popularity wherever small clubs were located and eventually moved from the African-American community onto mainstream radio stations—generally, how-ever, adapted by white performers. The polite dances of the big band era no longer suited a postwar generation bogged down in academic studies or nine to five jobs and in need of weekend release. The beat of rock 'n' roll accentuated by the strings of a twirling bass fiddle met the new needs.

LITTLE RICHARD   Audience excitement generated by rock groups and rock con-certs within a few years was foreshadowed in the frenetic energy of Richard Wayne Penniman, who called himself Little Richard (b. 1932) and claimed that he was the founder of the entire movement. He was certainly one of early rock's most outlandish performers, dressing usually in formal attire that was a bit disheveled, or it became so as he accompanied himself on the piano, without sitting down, frequently jumping on top of the instrument, never letting up on the crashing chords. Rock historian Nik Cohn agrees that Little Richard was the true father of rock:

> *Dressed in shimmering suits with long drape jackets and baggy pants, his hair grown long and straight, white teeth and gold rings flashing in the spotlight, he stood at, and some-times on, the piano, hammering boogie chords as he screamed messages of celebration and self-centered pleasure.*[8]

In 1957, Little Richard, once more known as Richard Wayne Penniman, abruptly left the music world to become an evangelist preacher. But he did not find spiritual ecstasy incompatible with the music for which he was famous; and so he has gone back and forth between the two main areas of his life.

ELVIS PRESLEY   One year before Penniman's departure, a young singer from Mississippi named Elvis Presley (Figure 6.10) appeared on television's popular *Ed Sullivan Show*, the premier venue for showcasing new musical talent. Elvis (1935–1977) quickly became a cultural phenomenon, scandalizing older audiences with a gyrating pelvis while simultaneously making rock wildly popular with younger audiences.

The immediate musical influence on Elvis was gospel, particularly its exuberance. With his guitar, Elvis added the beat and chord progressions of the rhythm and blues being played in Memphis. He incorporated elements from country and western songs, injecting them with a high-powered aggressiveness that remains the signature of all rock. In some circles, his music became known as *country rock* or *rockabilly*.

In the opinion of rock historian Charlie Gillett, Elvis reached his peak as an artist in the early years when his songs delivered the passionate themes of the country-and-western genre—usually broken romance or condemnation of

Figure 6.10 Elvis Presley, 1957.
Often simply called The King, Presley
fused elements of rhythm and blues,
gospel, and country and western to
create a unique and powerful style.
What do you think accounts for
Presley's astonishing impact on music
and on this country?

Library of Congress, Prints and Photographs
Division, LC-USZ6-2067

infidelity—as well as rock's liberation of the spirit. His first hit song was titled, characteristically enough, "Heartbreak Hotel," which achieves near poetry in its metaphors, such as the hotel of that name located on Lonely Street.

In Gillett's opinion, however, becoming a superstar so quickly was the worst thing that could have happened to Elvis. He signed a multimillion dollar contract with RCA, which insisted on putting a high-powered slick gloss on the music. The singer's former emotional directness became lost against a background of "vocal groups, heavily electrified guitars, and drums . . . more theatrical and self-conscious as he sought to combine excitement and emotion, formerly generated without any evident forethought"[9]—in other words, with honest spontaneity. Other singers and combos followed this trend, and the simple term *rock* was given to a variety of styles, many with the ear-splitting amplification of Presley's later work.

THE BEATLES By the early 1960s, rock 'n' roll had become popular throughout the Western world and would soon spread even further. Now there is scarcely a corner of the globe where it cannot be heard. In England, particularly, it beckoned to a younger generation that was tired of the rigid mores and traditions of that country. They liked what they were hearing from the other side of the Atlantic. Yet what music historians consider rock's most important band did not emerge from the United States, where the genre was born, but in the economically depressed northern English port of Liverpool. In 1964, the Beatles made an indelible mark on American consciousness the moment they were introduced on the Sunday night TV variety show, *The Ed Sullivan Show*, which had showcased Elvis Presley eight years earlier. The Beatles were whimsically named and immaculately well-groomed, their songs were bouncy and exuberant, and as performers they were disciplined. Their harmonies were complex and increasingly sophisticated (admired by no less an expert than the composer and conductor Leonard Bernstein), but the clarity of the lyrics made it seem as though they were singing with one voice. That Sunday night performance is considered by many as the greatest debut of any singers, anywhere.

Like their predecessor Elvis, and before him Frank Sinatra, the Beatles were mobbed wherever they went. Sales of their records hit the stratosphere. Parents shook their heads in despair over what they saw as the decline not only of music, but of an entire generation. John, Paul, George, and Ringo, with their unfamiliar new style and a repertoire destined to take its place among the all-time classics, appealed almost uncontrollably to a rising subculture of "hippies," young people who championed freedom from all social and moral restraints. In all of its phases since the 1950s, rock has retained its revolutionary social battle cry, becoming the ultimate Dionysian music of our time.

The Beatles, charming and witty, might have attained enormous popularity even if their music had been second-rate, but of course it was not. Paul McCartney, John Lennon, and George Harrison created songs of such originality and beauty that many—songs like "Yesterday," "Eleanor Rigby," "A Day in the Life," "While My Guitar Gently Weeps," and "Let It Be," for example—rank among the best popular songs in Western culture. And the album *St. Pepper's Lonely Hearts Club Band* is generally considered one of the two greatest rock albums ever made, along with Michael Jackson's *Thriller*.

Both Lennon, whose life was cut short in 1980 by a deranged fan's bullet, and George Harrison, who played guitar for the group and who died in 2001, were strongly influenced by the culture and religion of India. All four Beatles briefly studied meditation at an ashram. Harrison studied the sitar with Ravi Shankar, a master Indian musician. His own songs, less well-known than those of Lennon and McCartney, are deeply felt poems set to very mystical, spiritual musical sounds. Ringo Starr and Paul McCartney, both now in their early 70s, continue to perform.

THE ROLLING STONES   If the Beatles were the good boys of rock, the Rolling Stones, another British group that emerged in the 1960s, were the bad boys. The Stones didn't dress alike; they didn't cut their hair alike; and they made no effort to be amusing or charming. If parents worried about the Beatles, they were driven to distraction by the Stones, whose lead singer, Mick Jagger, wagged his tongue and his hips lasciviously and sang songs with titles like "Sympathy for the Devil," and whose lead guitarist, Keith Richard, flaunted his drug habit. But like the Beatles, the Rolling Stones produced a series of extraordinary records and a long list of rock classics—"(I Can't Get No) Satisfaction," "Gimme Shelter," and "You Can't Always Get What You Want" among them. The Stones songs moved rock almost single-handedly from something fairly lighthearted to something densely dangerous. *Rolling Stone* magazine says this about "Gimme Shelter": "Like nothing else in rock & roll, the song embodies the physical experience of living through a tumultuous historical moment. It's the Stones' perfect storm: the ultimate Sixties eulogy and rock's greatest bad-trip anthem, with the gathering power of soul music and a chaotic drive to beat any punk rock."[10] And in the words of rock singer, critic, and poet Patti Smith:

> By 1967 they [the Stones] all but eliminated the word guilt from our vocabulary . . . I never considered the Stones drug music . . . they were the drug itself . . . thru demon genius they hit that chord . . . as primitive as a western man could stand. Find the beat and you dance all night.[11]

The Rolling Stones continue to tour, with three of their original line-up—Jagger, Richards, and drummer Charlie Watts, all now over 70—still playing. Their concerts—multimedia events in huge stadiums—continue to sell out quickly. They may not have invented the big-time rock concert, but they have certainly perpetuated the art, filling venues such as Yankee Stadium and the Los Angeles Coliseum. Enthusiastic fans are known to camp out days in advance in order to buy tickets, and that ritual continues undiminished. The rock concert begins where polite society left off. It cuts through the many layers of so-called civilized behavior that evolved to put a lid on untrammeled expressions of feeling, and it demands from the audience shouting, stamping, gyrating on their feet with cries of ecstasy—a return to the pleasures of the sheer act of living, unverbalized, unanalyzed, uncensored.

WOODSTOCK AND ALTAMONT   By the mid-1960s, promoters began to see the appeal of bringing multiple bands together for huge outdoor concerts, far larger than the theater and music hall concerts where rock and roll bands had been performing. The most famous rock concert ever held took place in a small village near Woodstock, New York, in August 1969, when performers ranging from Joan Baez to Janis Joplin, from the Grateful Dead to Jimi Hendrix gathered for a three-day celebration of love and freedom, and to protest the war in Vietnam. There were 32 acts in all, and about 400,000 young people filling the meadow in front of the stage.

The crowds were so unexpectedly huge—promoters had anticipated about 50,000, and eventually, unable to handle the crush, simply let everyone in for free—that the New York State Thruway, the main highway leading north from New York City, had to be shut down. Equally unexpected was the weather: Monsoon rains cascaded down, and thousands of screaming fans played in the mud, oblivious to the hardships and indignities they were enduring. The performances were memorable, but even more historic was the collective experience, which made a powerful statement that war as a means of settling human problems was not an acceptable expression of humanity.

Local residents, horrified by what was happening to their once pleasant neighborhood, denounced the concert as a blight on American history. In all probability, however, the annual rites in honor of Dionysus, which gave birth to the great era of Greek tragedy, also got out of hand. Dionysian revelry and human creativity are often closely paired.

If Woodstock was the high point of collective rock culture, a free concert the following December at Altamont Speedway in northern California may have been the low point. Headlined by (who else?) the Rolling Stones, Altamont took the collective joy of Woodstock and turned it to the dark side. Four people died—three in accidents, one stabbed to death by a member of the Hell's Angels, who had been hired as "security." The Grateful Dead, the original organizers of the concert, refused to play because the level of violence among the fans was so high. So in the space of six months, the massive "tribal gatherings" of rock and roll came and went. Today, festivals such as South by Southwest (known as SXSW in Austin, TX) and Coachella (in Indio, CA) are well-organized, well-disciplined—and cost hundreds of dollars to attend.

Although critics have long bemoaned the "death of rock and roll," the changes that its emergence wrought on the music scene in this country and the world are undeniable. The pulsating beat of rock has wound its way through any number of incarnations—disco, emo, punk, club and house music—but it does survive. Almost every country has given birth to a rock group of varying importance. Many are proponents of *progressive rock*, which includes an endless variety of experimental genres and subgenres. They tend to attract smaller legions of devoted fans and are glad they don't have to play the kind of music demanded by a mass market, thus freeing themselves to go in many new directions.

Hip-Hop and Rap

The broad term **hip-hop** defines an entire way of being (as rock really doesn't), and it has differing musical expressions as integral components. As one hip-hop critic points out, it "encompasses rap, baggy clothing, break-dancing, graffiti, vocabulary, and a general life style." The latter can be described as freewheeling and centered on the rights of individuals to declare their identity in any way they choose.

Rap, a major subgenre of hip-hop culture, is half-sung, half-spoken music with a pronounced and steady beat supporting rapid-fire rhyming words performed by singers with great verbal dexterity and extensive vocabularies. The subject matter is frequently social protest, but it can also range from philosophical cynicism about life to frank descriptions of sexual encounters. Rap enthusiasts insist that much of the material is sheer poetry.

Rap had its origins in the urban setting of the Bronx in the late 1970s with toasts, dub talk, and improvisational poetry delivered over music at weddings, proms, and other celebrations. Reminiscent of the call-and-response characteristic of the plantation songs, it would begin with a DJ, band leader, or master-of-ceremonies shouting in rhythm something like "Wave your hands in the air/ And if you got on clean underwear / Shout 'Oh yeah!'" The excited crowd would then scream "Oh yeah!" The first broadly successful rap album, *Rapper's Delight* performed by the Sugarhill Gang, appeared in 1979.

Some of rap's exponents have been called folk poets, like Lonnie Rashid Lynn (b. 1972), better known as Common (previously, Common Sense). His debut album *Can I Borrow a Dollar?* won him an almost instant cult following, and in the late 1990s he went mainstream. In 2003 he won a Grammy for his song "Love of My Life (An Ode to Hip-Hop)," and in 2006 was awarded a second Grammy for "Southside," a rap song performed with Kanye West. He has performed all over the world and, to the dismay of many conservatives, was invited to perform at the Obama White House.

Rap has also been criticized for glorifying violence and drugs and expressing intolerance toward women and gays—for not being "nice" or politically correct. Defenders counter that an artist is an artist, and that the history of the humanities is filled with examples of works that are not "nice," or were created by people who cannot be characterized as "nice," but are compelling and classic (and sometimes even masterpieces) nonetheless. They defend rap by pointing out that it does not exist to promote antisocial values, but instead honestly depicts the realities of urban life.

At its best, as in the work of Common, Jay Z, Eminem, and Kanye West, rap represents a virtuoso use of language and an incredibly spontaneous kind of poetry, an exercise in exciting creativity.

What We Listen to Today

The world of popular music has changed dramatically over the past ten years, with the advent of iPods and streaming. Albums, which used to sell millions of copies, are now fortunate to sell a few hundred thousand. Hot artists come and go almost daily—Amy Winehouse to Adele to Ariana Grande. Singers such as Taylor Swift and Beyoncé wield astonishing control over their creative output and their financial lives, control that early artists such as Little Richard, Chuck Berry and even Elvis Presley never came close to achieving. Hip-hop and rap musicians have become, in many ways, the aristocracy of our celebrity culture. Sean Combs (variously known as Puff Daddy and P Diddy), Jay Z, and Kanye West all have clothing lines, record labels, and various other corporate interests. What they do makes the front pages—and the business pages—of major newspapers. Jay Z and his wife Beyoncé (see Figure 6.11), are arguably the number one "power couple" in our country, and perhaps the world, today.

Is the music better now? Well, the range is wider in popular music than it has been in many years. There is room now for rappers and gentle singer-songwriters such as Ed Sheeran, belters like Adele, and calculating survivors such as Madonna. Lady Gaga moves easily back and forth between generational anthems like "Born This Way" and duets with the octogenarian crooner Tony Bennett. Some argue that the soul of popular music has been buried by corporatization. Do you agree?

Contemporary World Music

The diverse contemporary musical scene includes contributions from many other cultures, and we must always remember that one of the goals of humanities study is to raise our awareness that there are alternative modes of human creativity. A Chinese composer may be experimenting with new scales and new sounds on a synthesizer; a Cambodian equivalent of Lady Gaga may be recording her first CD with an equally crowd-pleasing verve but singing music that is not based on notes familiar to the West; an Islamic pop singer may be thrilling a café audience with a love song in a plaintive vibrato to the accompaniment of an instrument that is akin to but not the same as a mandolin or guitar; a vocal group in Ghana may be swaying as they chant an updated version of a much older song of welcome. Many non-Western sounds can be heard on the Internet, and, because of today's rapid-fire communication, they will influence tomorrow's musical styles in both hemispheres.

In China, popular music is no longer limited to the marches and patriotic songs approved by the Communist government before it opened its doors to the outside world. Some Western influences were there during the early twentieth century, but some musical forms, including rock, were judged to be a threat to the government because they encourage freedom of expression and were banned. A singer/composer named Cui Jian emerged during the student demonstrations of 1989, exuberantly singing daring lyrics denouncing government tyranny. Defecting to the West, where he found a strong welcome, he performed before thousands in a 1999 Central Park concert. Almost as popular in both Asia and the West is

Figure 6.11   Jay Z (Shawn Carter) and his wife, the singer Beyoncé Knowles, 2015.

Like Kanye West and his wife Kim Kardashian, Jay Z and Beyoncé are cultural icons, not simply performers. Does the celebrity culture we now live in influence the way you listen to music? In what ways?

Epa European Pressphoto Agency b.v./ Alamy

the Tang Dynasty, a Beijing rock band that blends the sounds of the Asian five-note scale with the more familiar diatonic, or seven-note, Western scale.

Traditional Chinese music is still prevalent, making liberal use of percussion, especially drums, tympani, gongs, cymbals, bells, xylophones, and triangles. String sections include the two-stringed violin, the dulcimer, the lute, and the harp. The woodwind section comprises flutes, pipes, and Chinese trumpets, which look but do not sound like oboes.

Islam has supported a variety of musical forms, including jazz. The highest selling Arab albums come from an Algerian musician named Khaled, whose output has gone diamond, platinum, and gold. In 2009, he was a featured performer at the Montreal Jazz Festival. In 2010, he performed his piece "Didi" at the World Cup opening ceremony in South Africa. Khaled has had to move to Paris because Islamic fundamentalists objected to his portrayal of women both dancing and dressed provocatively.

An afternoon can be well-spent in exploring these new sounds, now abundantly available online.

There is not space enough here to discuss all of the strange and wondrous new sounds that are being produced all over the world by both men and women. Our goal in this chapter has been to suggest how your life can be infinitely enriched if you are willing to listen—listen to the great classics of the past and the perhaps great-one-day experiments of the present. Don't forget that Beethoven was often considered too "modern" by some of his contemporaries. But with all the sound for you to hear, don't forget to spend a little time with your silences.

A Critical Focus: Exploring Claude Debussy's "Clair de Lune"

Claude Debussy (1862–1918), a French composer, created harmonies that were regarded as revolutionary in his day and that have been largely influential on modern-day composers. His best-known composition, "Clair de Lune," is the third movement of his *Suite bergamasque*, a piano piece published in 1905. The title "Clair de Lune" means "moonlight" and was taken from a poem by Paul Verlaine, a French poet of the Symbolist movement.

Listen to Debussy's "Clair de Lune."

Debussy: "Clair de Lune"

- Which of the basic elements of music, described in the first section of this chapter, can you identify in this piece? Which ones seem most important to your listening experience?
- Would you describe "Clair de Lune" as Apollonian or Dionysian? How would you characterize these terms as applied to music?
- Debussy's "Clair de Lune" belongs to a musical school known as Impressionism. How would you describe the similarities and differences between Impressionism as an artistic movement and as a movement in music?

Looking Back

In this chapter,

- we identified and discussed the basic elements of music,
- we explored the differences among classical forms, including the fugue, the symphony, and the art song, and discussed the ways in which the form influences our experience of the music, and
- we offered a brief history of popular music in the United States, including folk music, spirituals and gospel, ragtime and jazz, blues, rock and roll, and hip-hop.

Key Terms

atonality A characteristic of much avant-garde music composed without regard for key.

avant-garde Art forms that defy traditional guidelines; avant-garde music sometimes employs much dissonance and atonality.

Baroque Term applied to the artistic style of the mid-seventeenth to mid-eighteenth centuries; marked by elaborate ornamentation and complexity; original meaning: *irregular pearl*.

chamber music Composition for small ensembles, such as two violins, a viola, and a cello.

chromatic scale Consists of 12 tones; if played on a piano, a consecutive run using both black and white keys.

counterpoint Two or more melodic lines played against each other; characteristic of Bach's work.

diatonic scale Consists of seven tones arranged in a W(hole)-W-H(alf)-W-W-W-H interval pattern; the fundamental but not the only scale in Western music.

dissonance In music, two or more uncongenial notes sounded or sung at the same time, producing an unfamiliar and, for some, unpleasant effect.

fugue Lengthy musical composition or section within a larger composition in which two or more melodic lines are played against each other.

half-tone The interval between each note of a chromatic scale; the smallest interval in most Western music.

harmony Two or more tones, congenial or otherwise, sounded or sung at the same time.

hip-hop Contemporary style of music that includes rap; a lifestyle marked by DJing, sampling, baggy clothes, idiomatic speech, and graffiti.

improvisation Spontaneous set of variations on a stated musical theme; once performed, it may be written down and repeated by other performers.

key A particular scale that dominates a musical composition, identified by the first note of that scale and whether the scale is major or minor: e.g. C major, B-flat minor.

melody Any arrangement of tones in a definite sequence that constitutes a unity.

octave The space between two notes that sound the same.

pentatonic scale Five-tone musical scale that preceded the familiar seven-tone scale dominant in the West; remains the basic scale of much non-Western music.

ragtime Musical genre, forerunner of jazz, invented in the late 1890s by African-American composers, notably Scott Joplin; strongly influenced by slow and stately European dances.

rap Major subgenre of hip-hop in which rhyming lyrics are half-sung, half-spoken rapidly.

rhythm Alternation of stress and unstress in music, usually created by a percussion instrument.

rock Generic name covering a variety of styles that have a loud and insistent beat.

rock 'n' roll Style of music introduced in the 1950s and popularized by Elvis Presley; grew out of a fusion of rhythm and blues, gospel, and country and western styles.

scale An arranged pattern of tones within an octave.

spiritual A religious song associated with black Christians of the southern United States, and thought to derive from the combination of European hymns and African musical elements by black slaves.

symphony A major orchestral form from the late eighteenth century to the present, usually consisting of four separate sections, or movements, with contrasting tempos, sometimes constituting a unity, often not.

syncopation A rhythmic device in which the melodic line of a piece is played against, not with, the accented beats of the rhythmic accompaniment, as in Gershwin's "Fascinatin' Rhythm" and the Beatles' "Eleanor Rigby."

timbre The quality of a musical sound, as opposed to its pitch or intensity.

toccata Musical form perfected by Bach making liberal use of improvisation and allowing for an overpowering display of musical virtuosity by the performer.

tone A single sound produced by a musical voice or instrument; also called a note.

Chapter 7
Theater

Learning Objectives

7.1 Compare and contrast classic Greek tragedy and Elizabethan tragedy.

7.2 Differentiate among various forms of comedy, including satire, comedy of character, farce, and parody.

7.3 Discuss the key developments in nineteenth-century theater.

7.4 Describe the new theatrical directions and themes that evolved in the twentieth and twenty-first centuries.

Figure 7.1 The angel descends in *Part I: Millennium Approaches* of Tony Kushner's *Angels in America* (1993).
This powerful hit play was in part about the unacknowledged AIDS crisis of the 1980s. How effectively can theater take on social issues?
Photo by Joan Marcus/courtesy of the Everett Collection

Drama has always been a natural activity. Children play-act, often dividing themselves into totally good or totally bad white hats and black hats—characters rarely found in real life. Yet drama *is* closely related to real life. It is a way of clarifying experience, a way of making sense out of life by imitating it; it is also a way of enhancing and intensifying certain occasions, as in a parade, a ceremony, or an imposing entrance to signal an important event. Drama gives shape to events, adds spice to life, quickens the pace. It is as though the dramatic instinct was invented to charge our lives with electricity and give us the need to project ourselves into make-believe action, as well as the wisdom to accept pretense as reality. To become involved in theater is to have a greater share of experience.

Theater exists in every culture, but it takes many different forms. Like visual art, drama does not always pretend to be an exact replica of real life. (In fact, realistic staging was absent throughout most of the history of theater.) Even plays that seem to mirror real life as we know it really do not. The scenery is not real, and actors are saying lines that have been scripted for them. They may talk in verse or use language in an unusual, bizarre way. What happens on the stage depends on the *conventions* of theater, and these are not always the same. In Shakespeare, characters talk in verse. In musical theater, people sing their feelings. Conventions also reflect the period of time in which the play was written or is being performed.

The conditions governing the staging and performance of a play are known as theatrical **conventions**, or *the conditions which the audience agrees to accept as real*. Granted that the stage may be totally bare or clogged with furniture, and granted that the actors may look nothing like the characters they are portraying (for instance, the *Elephant Man*, universally acknowledged as repulsive-looking in real life, played by Bradley Cooper), habitual theater-goers cooperate by playing along, by suspending their disbelief. Conventions have changed throughout history, and modern directors often like to add flavor to a production by surprising audiences. Habitual theater-goers adjust immediately to the new rules. Indeed, doing so is part of the fun of going to plays.

Drama and Tragedy in Theater History

7.1   *How are classic Greek tragedy and Elizabethan tragedy similar? How do they differ?*

Theater typically divides itself into two main categories: the serious (including tragedy) and the comic. This is, of course, a much over-simplified statement. "Serious" and "comic" are broad terms that contain rich multitudes within them, and many performances blend comedy and drama effectively.

Greek Classical Theater and Elizabethan Theater: A Comparison

In order to explore the conventions of serious theater, or drama, let's begin with a contrast between the classical theater of ancient Greece and the very different Elizabethan theater of England. In classical theater, our representative playwright is Sophocles, author of many plays including *Oedipus the King* (430 BCE) and *Antigone* (440 BCE). In the Elizabethan theater, the representative playwright is Shakespeare. The vast difference between the theaters for which Sophocles and Shakespeare wrote their plays strongly influenced the conventions governing them. In the classical period of Greece, audiences would have been sitting on stone benches in an outdoor stadium accommodating 14,000 to 20,000 people (Figure 7.2). They would be seeing plays shown only once during an annual three-day festival, part of a religious celebration sponsored by the state. In the Elizabethan theater of London, audiences would have been sitting or standing close to the stage (Figure 7.3). Plays would have been available at almost any time of the year, and plays would have had no religious purpose. Entertainment and commercial success were the goals.

The major Elizabethan theater was the Globe, where most of Shakespeare's works were performed. It was an octagonal building, partly open at the top, because plays could be performed only in daylight. A platform featured a long balcony as well as trapdoors for the entrance of hellish demons such as the witches in *Macbeth.* To accommodate this space, Shakespeare and his contemporaries used a new set of conventions. Upper- and middle-class patrons were protected from inclement weather by a

Figure 7.2 The theater at Epidaurus, Greece, built c. 4th century BCE.
Javarman/Shutterstock

Figure 7.3 The New Globe Theatre, London, built as a replica of the original in 1997.
What do these two structures imply about the role of theater in their respective cultures?
Kamira/Shutterstock

roof, while the lower classes or **groundlings** stood under the open sky vulnerable to whatever the weather visited upon them. There was no scenery and a minimum of props, but the minimalist conventions allowed for swift-moving, fluid action that has been compared to today's cinema.

THE USE OF MASKS AND A CHORUS   In the early days of classical theater, there were no plays as such. Instead, those who attended the festival saw a Chorus of masked men singing and dancing to hymns in praise of the gods, especially Dionysus, who provided the harvest. During the sixth century BCE, a soloist named Thespis stepped out of the **Chorus** and engaged in some form of sung dialog with them, much as a priest celebrating a high mass might interact with the choir. Gradually the emphasis shifted from the Chorus to the actors—no more than three at any one time. Familiar myths were retold as transformed by the creativity of the writer. Emphasis was on what could happen if the gods were not obeyed. Drama was born.

A number of theories have been advanced to account for the convention of the mask. Its use may simply have been a hold-over from early rituals, or grotesque, over-size masks may have been useful in inspiring fear or dread in audiences, who were typically watching dramas in huge amphitheaters. The most prominent theory is that masks allowed actors to play multiple roles. In the smaller Elizabethan theater, masks were not employed, but males continued to play all the parts. Greek tragedies were based on well-known myths, though many in the audience must have assumed the stories were historically true. Elizabethan plays were not all based on myths, though Shakespeare took dramatic license with history in works such as *Julius Caesar, Antony and Cleopatra*, and the plays about various English kings.

Classical Greek theater had a Chorus of 12 or 15 men, praising the gods, providing background information, and making moral comments on the consequences of the central character's tragic mistakes. The Chorus typically all wore the same mask, since they were intended to represent a single presence. No Chorus was required for the Elizabethan theater, although Shakespeare occasionally chose to use a single actor to perform the same function, as in the opening of the fourth act of *Henry V*. Standing on a bare stage in daylight, this character's function was to make the audience believe they were watching a tense encampment of soldiers on the night before a great battle.

> *Now entertain conjecture of a time*
> *When creeping murmur and the poring dark*
> *Fills the wide vessel of the universe.*
> *From camp to camp through the foul womb of night*
> *The hum of either army stilly sounds.*
> *That the fix'd sentinels almost receive*
> *The secret whispers of each other's watch:*
> *Fire answers fire, and through their paly flames*
> *Each battle sees the others umber'd face....*
> *The poor condemned English,*
> *Like sacrifices, by their watchful fires*
> *Sit patiently and inly ruminate*
> *The morning's danger, and their gesture sad*
> *Investing lank-lean cheeks and war-worn coats*
> *Presenteth them unto the gazing moon*
> *So many horrid ghosts.*[1]

In the plays of both periods, the elevated verse language was in keeping with the gravity of issues involved. Shakespeare, a poet known for the quality of his verse, occasionally included prose dialog for characters of lower rank.

THE ROLE OF VIOLENCE   In the Greek theater, violence occurs offstage, never in front of the audience. We hear blood-curdling cries from the wings, then a Messenger enters to describe horrifying moments taking place elsewhere. In the original productions, actors wore not only masks but stilts to make them truly larger than life, especially for so vast a space. Such outfits would have made onstage violence difficult.

Roman tragedies, performed in smaller venues, showed violent scenes such as multiple stabbings in full view of the audience. Sometimes slaves were substituted for actors at the last moment and actually killed. The phrase *Greek elements* is sometimes used now to describe a play with much dialog and limited action, while *Roman elements*, staples of the film industry, mean that a work is full of violent action.

Although the Elizabethans on all levels of society were fascinated by poetry and intricate wordplay, they too adored action—lots of it—and the more violent the better. Shakespeare gave them unceasing action: simulated battles, sword fights, multiple stabbings, and poisonings. He wasn't even afraid to violate the gravity of a tragic work by injecting scenes of low-life comedy, combined with sexual humor, in the midst of great tragic moments. Just before her suicide, Cleopatra has an encounter with a clown in which both engage in what can only be described as suggestive "gags."

Acting styles were very different, as would be expected by the design of the performance spaces. In Greek and Roman amphitheaters, gestures were broad rather than subtle. Actors used exaggerated, sweeping movements to accompany their words, just as officials at an athletic event indicate penalties by using hand gestures as they shout the nature of the offense and penalties imposed. In Shakespeare's theater, far more naturalistic acting was beginning to be seen, no doubt because of the complexity of the characters.

THE UNITIES   Another classical convention, first developed in Aristotle's *Poetics*, is *unity of time, place,* and *action. Unity of time* means that everything happens in the course of a single day. *Unity of place* mandates that there be no shift of scene; and *unity of action* allows for no subplots. These rules are generally followed in classical tragedy. Audiences can concentrate on the single conflict unfolding before them, with no side issues involving minor characters.

The **unities** were not required by the conditions of the Elizabethan theater. Although Shakespeare in *The Tempest* did have all the action take place in one day (as if to prove he could do it!), he was able to have as much time pass as he chose. He was also able to write plays with subplots showing the fortunes of more than one character. In *King Lear*, the protagonist's relationship with his three daughters is paralleled by that of the Duke of Gloucester with his son.

SOPHOCLES, *OEDIPUS THE KING*   Classical **tragedy** revolves around a central character, or **protagonist**, in terms of whose fortunes we follow in the story. Plays and movies of today continue to include this character, often called the *hero*, but this term can be misleading. *Hero* suggests a person of virtue and courage, who usually triumphs over forces of evil. In the great tragedies, however, the protagonist seldom has these qualities. A flaw in his character leads to his tragic downfall. *Oedipus the King*, one of the masterpieces not only of Greek theater but of all time, has a central character who can serve as the very model of a tragic protagonist.

The play begins with relative peace (as tragedies often do—the calm before the storm). The state of Thebes is in good hands, or so it is believed. King Oedipus is powerful and wise, able to solve problems as no one else can. In the past, he saved the citizens from being devoured by a horrible monster. Now, years later, Thebes faces another threat. There is a plague, and the Chorus, representing the people of Thebes, entreats their king to find out why. The oracle sends word that the plague will continue until the murderer of the previous king is found and brought to justice.

Oedipus confidently agrees to solve the mystery, without realizing that he himself is the killer. A blind prophet tells him the truth, but Oedipus becomes enraged and denounces the man. He has saved the kingdom and cannot be a murderer. By the end of the play, he is forced to recognize that the man he killed years before in an unplanned skirmish had been the former king of Thebes—and his own father as well.

Disaster follows disaster. As if this news were not bad enough, he realizes he is married to that deceased king's wife, Jocasta, who has borne him four children, and who is in actuality his mother. After discovering the horrible truth of his past, he tears his eyes from their sockets. We hear bloodcurdling cries from offstage, then the messenger enters to describe the terrifying moment. So vivid is his telling of it that we feel we are actually *there*.

The Recognition Scene in Sophocles and Shakespeare

The great tragedies usually have a **recognition scene**, a moment when the protagonist fully understands what has brought about the disaster. First, there is a search for the meaning of what has occurred. This search may be followed by the attempt to justify the action and, finally, the acceptance of responsibility.

Is Oedipus responsible for what has happened? The fact that he would kill his father and marry his mother had been prophesied at his birth. The Greeks believed that fate ruled human life, so nothing could have changed Oedipus's destiny. Yet he *does* accept responsibility, perhaps wishing to show that he is a powerful man to the end.

A famous recognition speech is delivered by Creon in *Antigone*. Having inherited the throne of Thebes after the downfall of Oedipus, Creon has become a powerful and arrogant ruler. In the speech, he realizes his arrogance has caused the death not only of his son but also of his wife, who commits suicide because of it. He has lost those who were dearest to him, and his life now lies in ruins. He cries:

> *Lead me away. I have been rash and foolish.*
> *I have killed my son and my wife.*
> *I look for comfort; my comfort lies here dead.*
> *Whatever my hands have touched has come to nothing.*
> *Fate has brought all my pride to a thought of dust.*[2]

Although Shakespeare rarely followed classical conventions, he did include a speech of recognition in *Othello,* which is generally considered his most classically constructed work. In the final act, the protagonist has realized that he was tricked into believing his wife was unfaithful and he has murdered her without cause. At the point of his arrest, he says to his captors:

> *Soft you; a word before you go.*
> *I have done the state some service and they know 't.*
> *No more of that, I pray you, in your letters,*
> *When you shall these unlucky deeds relate,*
> *Speak of me as I am; nothing extenuate,*
> *Nor set down aught in malice. Then must you speak*
> *Of one that lov'd not wisely but too well.*[3]

At the conclusion of the speech, he removes a concealed dagger and stabs himself. The protagonist, having taken full responsibility, holds onto his dignity. Freedom to choose his own death is all that is left.

In all of theater, there may be no other moment that matches the power of the recognition scene in *King Lear*. The king, close to death, finally understands the terrible mistake he made in exiling his youngest and only loving daughter, Cordelia, from his kingdom. Because of his prideful blindness to reality, he has supported his older daughters, only to have them turn on him. The innocent daughter is captured and executed, and the old man, who has not always been in full possession of his faculties, finally understands what he has done and knows that he will never see again the one daughter who truly loves him.

For many theatergoers, the moment is unrivaled. Instead of vast eloquence, Shakespeare gives Lear relatively few words.

> *Why should a dog, a horse, a rat, have life,*
> *And thou no breath at all? Thou'lt come no more*
> *Never, never, never, never, never.*[4]

That last line, many argue, comprises the most tragic five words in all of drama. Actors who perform Lear are often unable to say them all before dissolving into tears.

Aristotle on the Nature of Tragedy

Thus far this chapter has dealt with the work of playwrights and the conventions of performance. We now turn to the world's first theatrical critic, the Greek philosopher Aristotle (c. 382–322 BCE), who established some of the most enduring standards for analysis of the purpose and the elements of tragic drama.

Looking around the amphitheater where the plays were performed, Aristotle wondered what moved people, *why* they were moved, what were the essential elements all tragedies must have, and finally, why some plays were more successful than others. He wrote his observations in *The Poetics*, which contains his famous and intact essay on tragedy and, it is believed, an essay on comedy of which all but the first line has been lost.

Aristotle analyzes how experiencing a make-believe story could have the same effect as it would if people were witnessing an actual tragic event. He realized that spectators were identifying with the characters and feeling almost the same pain as the actors, who pretended they were suffering. For this reason, he decided that the ideal protagonist for a tragedy must be someone who is mainly virtuous (otherwise people wouldn't care what happened to the character) but is not totally innocent either. The character has a tragic flaw that leads to his or her destruction. If a bad fate befell an innocent person, the audience would reject this outcome as being too cruel.

THE PARTS OF A DRAMA   Aristotle divided tragedy into six parts, arranged in order of importance: *plot, character, thought, poetry, spectacle,* and *song.* He then gave his famous definition of tragedy, which is

> the imitation of a good action, which is complete and of a certain length, by means of language made pleasing for each part separately; it relies in its various elements not on narrative but on acting; through pity and fear it achieves the purgation of such emotions.[5]

By "action," Aristotle is referring to the forward motion of the tragedy, which, through what the characters do, brings about a change of circumstances—a change for the worse—and thus the emotions of the audience grow more intense as the play leads to inevitable catastrophe. The aim is to stimulate an emotional response not for the sake of the emotion, but for the aftermath of emotion: the feeling of calm that follows it.

This calm, called **catharsis**, also comes after undergoing other kinds of aesthetic experience: after listening to Beethoven's Third Symphony, for example. To the question "Why put oneself through such a wrenching ordeal?" the Aristotelian answer is that *one derives strength from reacting to make-believe pain as if it were real.* The spectator slowly returns to the life that was left outside the theater, but with the rational calm that would follow an actual catastrophe.

The flaw of Oedipus is **hubris**, or arrogance. It is universal. Everyone knows people who insist that there is no other truth but theirs. Aristotle's analysis holds. Tragedy, he said, requires audience identification; only then will the downfall of the protagonist be emotionally devastating, and no one can achieve catharsis who is not profoundly moved. Small wonder that playwrights have continued to stretch for the heights of tragedy. No other theatrical art form has so much power to reach the viewer.

As if dramatically underscoring the passing of the golden age of classical Greek tragedy, the deaths of Sophocles and Euripides (c. 484–406 BCE) occurred in the same year. Although the plays of Euripides seldom illustrate completely the principles set forth in Aristotle's *Poetics*, although they lack the concluding speech in which protagonists recognize their responsibility for the catastrophe, and although his plots generally lack the tight structure Aristotle so admired in *Oedipus*, Aristotle nevertheless calls Euripides "the most tragic of all." Perhaps the philosopher meant that Euripides saw most deeply into the pain of being alive. This pain is his subject. In fact, the *Medea* of Euripides has proved to be, for modern audiences, the most persistently stageworthy of the Greek tragedies. Perhaps Euripides' work is closer in spirit to the modern temperament than that of his contemporaries.

EURIPIDES' *MEDEA*   What makes the plot structure of the *Medea* so tight and a principal reason for the work's popularity with modern audiences is the diminished role of the Chorus. The tragedy is driven by the terrifying inevitability of a jealous wife's revenge on her husband by murdering their sons. Scene after scene shows the wife's hatred growing and the effects of her decisions becoming more tragically irreversible at the same time that her maternal love intensifies. Euripides is more interested in the emotional and psychological turbulence that drives the work than in the moral and philosophical issues raised by a character's actions.

The play tells only the last part of Medea's story. We learn, though, that in the past Medea has used her magical powers to help her eventual husband, Jason, find the famous Golden Fleece and gain the stature of a hero. He has married her out of gratitude, not love. As the play begins, Medea is living in Jason's country, finding herself among people who have little regard for either foreigners or women. Jason tells Medea of his plans to marry a princess so that their sons will have the advantage of living in a royal household and be half-brothers to the royal children Jason will sire. He expects her to be pleased at the thought of their children's future. She is not, but pretends

approval so that she can take revenge. After using her powers to design a poisonous gown that kills her rival, she is not yet satisfied that Jason has suffered enough. In one of the theater's most powerful scenes, Medea struggles against what she knows would be the ultimate revenge: the death of Jason's sons (Figure 7.4).

As the innocent children play, their mother tries to stem the force that is driving her to do the unspeakable, but she cannot do so. She takes them inside and, after a terrifying moment of silence, we hear their agonized cries. Medea, their own mother, has slit their throats.

The ending of the play lacks the moral completeness of *Oedipus*. For Sophocles, even though the fate of Oedipus was prearranged, his arrogance was a defiance of divine law, and for this arrogance, he pays a tragic price. The suffering of Medea, however, does not spring from the violation of a moral law, but from natural passions: a loving mother, she should not have been brought to such a state by an insensitive husband; her passion for revenge has torn her apart. Nor does Medea go forth in ruins, as Oedipus does.

Figure 7.4 Lorna Haughton as Mediyah in *Pecong*, a 2010 updating of *Medea* by Steve Carter, set on a Caribbean island.
How might this change of setting and time period change a viewer's experience of the story of Medea?
Hubert Williams

With Jason grieving over the bodies of his slain children, Medea rides off in triumph on a chariot sent for her by a sympathetic neighboring king. Her last line as she looks up at the "unfriendly stars" is "Not me they scorn." If she will feel the pangs of guilt for the rest of her life, her grief will be private and no business of the gods—if indeed there *are* gods.

Euripides gives every indication that he has abandoned the effort to find meaning in obedience to the laws of the gods. There is a pervading cynicism in his plays, a fear that humanity is abandoned in a godless universe, or at least one in which the gods, if they exist, are cruelly whimsical and justice is never carried out. As if to underscore his cynicism, many of his plays have contrived, unbelievable happy endings. He seems to be saying that in an amoral world, a happy ending is a random accident. In the world of Euripides, moral responsibility does not exist; pain does.

The Genius of Shakespeare

Shakespeare created a wide range of characters who have achieved immortality, from Romeo and Juliet to Lear to Othello to Shylock. This may not have been his intention: He was certainly interested in providing entertainment and making money and indeed was very successful at it. But somehow he rose far above the level of his peers—and of those playwrights who succeeded him—and his works have lived through the centuries.

Because the Elizabethan audience was so close to the stage, they could see the faces of the actors and could also hear quiet speech. One of the foremost conventions developed by the Elizabethan playwrights is the **soliloquy**, in which an actor, alone on stage, speaks his thoughts aloud. Though it was widely used in other plays by Shakespeare and his contemporaries, the most famous soliloquy in all of drama is Hamlet's, which begins "To be or not to be."

In contrast to the soliloquy, the **aside** is a remark made by an actor when other actors are present. The audience hears what is said, but other actors are not supposed to. Sometimes it is a shortened version of the soliloquy, as when Hamlet, after listening to his treacherous uncle's insincere rhetoric, comments to the audience, "A little more than kin, and less than kind." In nine words, Shakespeare defines how Hamlet feels about the man who has married his father's widow almost immediately after the man's death. Most serious drama stopped using the *aside* by the eighteenth century, but it continues to be used in comedy and musical comedy today.

SHAKESPEARE'S USE OF VERSE Epic battles are fought in the plays of Shakespeare and his contemporaries, but Elizabethan conventions allowed the wounded to make eloquent speeches before dying. Except for lower-class characters, who speak in prose, most of Shakespeare's characters speak in elaborate poetry, revealing deep feelings. No effort was made to have them speak the way ordinary people, including those in the audience, would actually speak. No one complains, "Haven't had a thing to eat since last night" or "This rain is a nuisance." Everyone has a speech appropriate to the situation. *That* is a timeless and universal convention. Only on a stage do people always have the right words when needed!

The verse is written in iambic pentameter, a line of five feet (or poetic units), with rhythm sounding like this: da DAH, da DAH, da DAH, da DAH, da DAH. When skilled actors perform Shakespeare, the rhythm is often hard to detect, because they somehow—miraculously—fit the rhythmic words to the scene so precisely that audiences seldom know the rhythm is there. Except for the more obviously rhythmic ending of some scenes, the dialog sounds like elegant prose. (And if it didn't, think how monotonous the play would be!)

An amazing example of Shakespeare's genius for tying together iambic pentameter and the precise words for a dramatic situation is found in the final act of *Othello*. The protagonist, maddened by suspicion that his wife has been unfaithful, smothers her to death. Immediately after the deed, he hears a knocking on the door and an entreaty from Emilia, his wife's attendant, asking that she be allowed to enter. Othello shouts to Emilia that he will open the door soon, and then speaks to himself as the full horror of his deed becomes clear to him (Figure 7.5).

Part of Shakespeare's genius was his ability to write lines that scan almost perfectly but allow the actor to explore the full range of emotion.

> *Yes: 'tis Emilia. By and by. She's dead:*
> *'Tis like she comes to speak of Cassio's death,—*
> *The noise was here. Ha! No more moving?*
> *Still as the grave. Shall she come in? Were 't good?—*
> *I think she stirs again:—no. What's best to do?*
> *If she come in, she 'll sure speak to my wife:*
> *My wife! my wife! what wife? I have no wife.*[6]

Figure 7.5 Lawrence Fishburne and Kenneth Branagh in a 1995 production of *Othello*.
Have you seen a Shakespeare play? What was the experience like? How might modern alterations in staging change our perceptions of a Shakespearean play?
Everett Collection

The lines *scan* almost perfectly: that is, they can be read so as to emphasize the iambic pentameter. But they cannot be spoken that way by an actor. Consider the first line. "Yes" is directed to Emilia in a loud voice. "'Tis Emilia" is spoken to himself in a soft voice. "By and by" is loud and to Emilia again. Then an absolutely essential pause before "She's dead."

The word "no" in the fifth line stands all by itself, demanding that the actor speak it between two pauses; otherwise the line is exact iambic pentameter. In fact, the entire passage compels the actor to hesitate wherever Othello's manic thought processes require it. Shakespeare's genius allows the actor to have it both ways: to have a rhythmic underpinning to the poetry, and also to have the freedom to explore the character's emotions.

SHAKESPEARE'S USE OF IMAGERY Shakespeare's poetry is filled with **images**, words that create pictures in the mind of audience and reader. Perhaps he was trying to compensate for the fact that the plays were performed on a stage with no scenery. Lighting and sound systems would not come for hundreds of years. Perhaps no more famous dramatic image exists than the first two lines of the balcony scene from *Romeo and Juliet*:

> *But soft, what light through yonder window breaks?*
> *It is the east, and Juliet is the sun.*

The moon, by contrast, is "sick and pale with grief/That thou her maid is far more fair than she."[7] In the famous scene in Act III of *Hamlet*, taking place in the bedroom of his mother, the adulterous Queen and accomplice in the murder of his father, there are some bold and violent images in the exchange between mother and son. After he has renounced her for her crime, she cries out: "Oh, Hamlet, thou hast cleft my heart in twain." Hamlet answers with a really powerful image:

> *Oh, throw away the worser part of it,*
> *And live the purer with the other half.*[8]

The lines also illustrate the use of *verbal dynamics*, moving from slow to fast, from loud to soft. Hamlet's famous speech to the actors who have come to perform at the castle indicates that Shakespeare was highly critical of the melodramatic acting styles of the period and sought a more natural kind of delivery.

Speak the speech I pray you, as I pronounced it to you,
trippingly on the tongue....Nor do not saw the air too much
with your hand, thus, but use all gently; for in the very torrent,
tempest, and, as I may say, the whirlwind of passion, you must
acquire and beget a temperance that may give it smoothness.[9]

Shakespeare wrote the words for Hamlet to say, and it is likely that Shakespeare himself agreed with the advice. Still, it is a speech in a play, not in a handbook written for aspiring actors. This speech, like those of many other characters, may not represent Shakespeare's own beliefs after all. He loved words, he loved ideas, and he seems to have enjoyed creating characters adept at both words and ideas. Scholars have been tempted to discover a consistent Shakespearean philosophy that runs through all of his plays. Indeed many passages, especially in *Hamlet, King Lear*, and *Macbeth*, contain profound wisdom about the human condition, wisdom that will necessarily stimulate thought when it is read or heard. Whether or not it represents Shakespeare's personal philosophy is still a matter for scholarly discussion.

SHAKESPEARE AND THE ELEMENTS OF DRAMA: THEME, PLOT, SETTING Unlike classical plays, Elizabethan drama was under no obligation to deal with universal themes. Shakespeare may have been primarily interested in giving his diverse public a rich, many-layered entertainment. The profundity of the major characters also suggests that he was fascinated by human psychology (though the word did not exist in his time) and the challenge, in Hamlet's words, to "hold...the mirror up to nature."

If tightness of plot is generally not Shakespeare's strength, in his greatest plays character and thought are without equal in the entire realm of theater, whether he was educated in the formal sense or not. His major characters go from the particular to the general, finding broad moral principles that offer profound insights into the meaning of human life. These insights are often cynical. Many of his characters entertain a bleak vision of life. When Hamlet is challenged to a fencing match in which, unknown to him, the tip of his opponent's sword is dipped in poison, his friend Horatio has a grim foreboding and urges Hamlet to decline. Hamlet will not, his lines suggesting that death will come when it will.

. . . we defy augury: there's a special providence in the fall of a sparrow. If it be now, 'tis not
to come; if it be not to come, it will be now; if it be not now, yet it will come: the readiness
is all: since no man has aught of what he leaves, what is't to leave betimes?[10]

Macbeth, whose kingdom lies in ruins and whose enemies are closing in on him, responds to the news of his wife's death in lines that could be the pessimist's manifesto:

She should have died hereafter;
There would have been a time for such a word
Tomorrow, and tomorrow, and tomorrow,
Creeps in this petty pace from day to day
To the last syllable of recorded time,
And all our yesterdays have lighted fools
The way to dusty death. Out, out, brief candle!
Life's but a walking shadow, a poor player
That struts and frets his hour upon the stage
And then is heard no more; it is a tale
Told by an idiot, full of sound and fury,
Signifying nothing.[11]

The Elizabethan theater was free from the burden of moving heavy scenery about, and playwrights realized that a bare stage could be any place as long as their words could describe it vividly. Scenes could move from indoors to outdoors or from garden to palace or the imaginary tomb in which Romeo and Juliet meet their deaths. Elizabethan audiences quickly adapted to the rules governing their theater.

Shakespeare's audiences were challenged in another way, for the only way to tell night from day was to hear what the actors said. Plays were performed in daylight, so "night" occurred when actors mentioned it. Audiences saw the ghost of Hamlet's father wandering in the dark provided by their imaginations.

Neoclassic Tragedy

In the years following the Elizabethan era, theatrical conventions changed once again. In the latter half of the seventeenth century, drama, poetry, painting, and architecture saw a general return to classical principles of order and balance. The ensuing century and a half is appropriately called **neoclassicism** in the arts.

Neoclassic theater moved indoors. For the first time, plays no longer were performed in a vast amphitheater or confined to a courtyard depending on lighting from the sun. Instead, plays could be staged in elaborate rooms within a great house and could be shown at night through the use of lighting from elegant chandeliers.

Audiences changed, too. Instead of the many social levels that attended the Greek and Roman theaters and the Elizabethan playhouse, audiences were now made up primarily of well-educated, beautifully dressed aristocrats, whose preferences had to be considered. The demand was strong for a return to a theater less violent than Shakespeare's, with subject matter based on myth as it had been during the classical period, but with the stories altered to reflect the issues and moral values of the age. A nonclassical element was the appearance for the first time of women playing female characters. The new convention allowed playwrights to focus on tragic myths about the destructive effects of sexual passion and other dramatic conflicts between men and women.

Playwrights returned as much as possible to the classical unities of time, place, and action. If the plot demanded scenes in different places, the problem was solved by having one lavish but neutral set, such as a large room that could represent a number of locales. Furniture and props were carried on and off by stagehands.

In addition to the unities, neoclassical dramatists, like their ancient predecessors, employed a highly stylized, elevated stage poetry. The verse was even farther removed from natural speech than the iambic pentameter of Shakespeare. Language was ornate, geared to aristocratic taste. The word "air," for example, was avoided in favor of "ozone," and "cat" became "feline creature."

RACINE, *PHÈDRA* *Phèdra* by Jean Racine (1639–1699) was by far the major tragedy in either England or France during the approximately hundred-year span of neoclassical theater (1650–1750). The dialog is elevated in accordance with the acceptable style, and characters speak elegantly of their intense emotions without actually demonstrating them.

The protagonist is married to the mythical hero, Theseus, but feels a burning lust for her stepson, Hippolytus. She knows she must conceal that lust, but it builds to such intensity that the actress performing this challenging role is forced to find ways to externalize the torment she is suffering.

Phèdra thus adds to the theater the element of the inner life. In recent years, writers and directors have created characters who feel more than they speak, forcing the audience to focus on their sparse words, their facial expressions, and their body language in order to understand them fully. A theatrical experience is less satisfying the more emotions are verbalized and more satisfying when less is said.

Governed by the conventions of its time, *Phèdra* takes place entirely in a civilized drawing room, and, although the characters have Greek names, they look and sound like aristocratic contemporaries of the audience. Should Phèdra reveal to her stepson her burning desire for him? Of course not, it isn't done; strong feelings don't belong in public.

Phèdra steps over the bounds, however. She tells her stepson that the only way she can even bring herself to look at her husband is to see the facial resemblance to his son. She does the unthinkable by revealing her true feelings.

Her stepson's response would be more suited to a mild dispute about an assigned seat in a theater: "Madame, I fear there has been some mistake." He is, of course, playing the game. His manners are impeccable, but they set off lethal rage in Phèdra, who takes revenge for her humiliation by reversing the situation. She tells Theseus that she has been the victim of unwanted sexual advances by his son. Her husband impetuously pleads with one of the gods to whip up a storm and a sea monster along the shore and so have his son killed (Figure 7.6). That violent death is, of course, reported by a messenger.

> *Before our eyes vomits a furious monster.*
> *With formidable horns its brow is arm'd,*
> *And all its body clothed with yellow scales,*
> *In front a savage bull, behind a dragon*
> *Turning and twisting in impatient rage.*
> *Its long continued bellowings make the shore*
> *Tremble; the sky seems horror-struck to see it;*
> *The earth with terror quakes; its poisonous breath*
> *Infects the air. The wave that brought it ebbs*
> *In fear. All fly, forgetful of the courage*
> *That cannot aid, and in a neighbouring temple*
> *Take refuge—all save bold Hippolytus.*
> *A hero's worthy son, he stays his steeds,*
> *Seizes his darts, and, rushing forward, hurls*
> *A missile with sure aim that wounds the monster*
> *Deep in the flank. With rage and pain it springs*
> *E'en to the horses' feet, and, roaring, falls,*
> *Writhes in the dust, and shows a fiery throat*
> *That covers them with flames, and blood, and smoke.*
> *Fear lends them wings; deaf to his voice for once,*
> *And heedless of the curb, they onward fly.*[12]

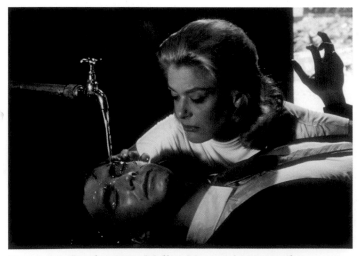

Figure 7.6 Greek actress Melina Mercouri mourns the death of her stepson and lover, played by Anthony Perkins, in a 1961 film based on the classic story of Phèdra.
Eugene O'Neill's mid-20th-century play *Desire Under the Elms* tells a similar story. Why do you think classical tales like this one continue to be adapted in contemporary theater and film?
Photos 12/Alamy

The return to classical myths told in their own aristocratic language impressed writers for the English as well as the French stage. The Messenger is describing a scene of unspeakable horror that he has actually seen, yet he does so elegantly and unemotionally.

Shakespeare, whose work is rife with passionate outbursts, died in 1616, and, although he had been admired during his lifetime, his work was rather too uncontrolled for neoclassic audiences. Within half a century, efforts to "improve" him had already begun; his plots were acceptable, but his emotional directness was considered vulgar. Playwrights had no hesitation about rewriting his work. For example, John Dryden (1631–1700) turned *Antony and Cleopatra*, Shakespeare's tragedy of tempestuous middle-aged lovers who destroy each other, into *All for Love*, "a polite" tragedy of aristocrats who overstep the bounds of propriety. A neoclassical play, like a neoclassical building, exalts balance, harmony, order, and it shuns out-of-control passion. Characters talk brilliantly—and in rhyme—about their emotions but do not *show* emotion except in death scenes.

Modern Tragedy

With only a handful of exceptions, Greek, Elizabethan, and neoclassical tragedies focus on fatal mistakes made by protagonists of high stature. Aristotle had been quite clear about the matter. The downfall of a nonaristocratic person was just not big enough to lead the audience to an emotional catharsis. Shakespeare was interested in the inevitable fall of the noble and powerful because he viewed power as a curse, something that corrupts and leads to ruin. Ordinary people had no power and so could not be brought to disaster on a grand scale.

Beginning in the nineteenth century, a new kind of tragedy evolved, first in Europe and then in the United States. Because most audiences were no longer well-educated aristocrats, a different sort of tragic protagonist was necessary, along with a different philosophy about the cause of the downfall. Playwrights seeking tragic themes turned to people with ordinary occupations.

GEORG BÜCHNER, *WOYZECK*   An early tragedy was *Woyzeck* (pronounced "voy-check") by Georg Büchner (1813–1837), left incomplete just before his death at 23. The play revolves around a lowly worker and his obsessive love for a girl who has given him a son, but whom he suspects of infidelity. In a violent confrontation, he plunges a knife into her throat, then later drowns when he attempts to retrieve the murder weapon. Büchner wanted to write for the theater but thrust aside all previous traditions. Büchner was a profound pessimist who believed that ordinary human beings were victims of a class-conscious society that denied them education and forced them to live in poverty, conditions that filled them with uncontrollable rage.

The manuscript of *Woyzeck* was lost until the early twentieth century. Long after his death, Büchner influenced whole generations of tragic dramatists who shared—and share—his view that the tragic protagonist does not have a flaw of character causing a catastrophe for which he or she is morally responsible. The real tragedy, for them, is that no moral order exists to be overthrown.

ARTHUR MILLER, *A VIEW FROM THE BRIDGE*   A century later, the American playwright Arthur Miller (1915–2005) would attempt to elevate lower-middle-class characters to the stature of tragic protagonists in a true classical tradition. Miller's intent was to replace Aristotelian requirements for tragedy with new standards appropriate for his middle-class subject matter. He gained international recognition with *Death of a Salesman* in 1949, the title of which suggests the ennoblement of a common man. While praising the work for its lyricism and dramatic intensity, many critics have insisted that *Salesman* falls short of tragedy because the protagonist remains deluded to the bitter end, never realizing his mistake. Indeed, playwrights of today often have difficulty providing recognition scenes because of our common belief that circumstances outside the individual almost always account, at least in part, for bad behavior.

In 1955, however, Miller wrote *A View from the Bridge*, with a protagonist who *is* aware of the mistake that leads to catastrophe (Figure 7.7). Without that awareness, the audience would not be able to share the character's pain and feel the intense pity that leads to catharsis.

Figure 7.7 Scarlett Johansson and Liev Schreiber as Catherine and her uncle, Eddie Carbone, in Arthur Miller's *A View from the Bridge*, 2010.
More and more "Hollywood" actors are taking star turns on Broadway. How might the presence of a Scarlett Johansson or a Hugh Jackman influence the audience's experience in the theater?
Joan Marcus Photography

At the outset, Eddie Carbone, a middle-aged longshoreman, lives happily with his wife and her young niece, Catherine, to whom he shows a fatherly, protective—perhaps a bit too protective—affection. Trouble begins when Eddie helps smuggle his wife's young cousins, Marco and Rodolpho, into the country and welcomes them into his household. Soon Catherine and Rodolpho, whom some consider effeminate, begin to date, and Eddie finds himself plagued by jealousy. He monitors the couple's every move, pacing the floor each night until they come home, and even plants a passionate kiss on Rodolpho in an attempt to prove to Catherine that her suitor is in fact gay. Finally, overcome by passion, Eddie secretly denounces the two young men to the immigration service, and they are arrested. Released on bail, Marco—who has a family back in Italy—comes at Eddie with a knife, and in the struggle, Eddie is mortally wounded. As he lies dying, Eddie feels the shame of his actions and acknowledges what he has done.

Miller created what he believed to be the ideal protagonist for modern tragedy. Not only can the audiences identify with a hard-working, basically honest and charitable human being, but they can also understand his human weakness. If a modern tragedy is to succeed in the classical tradition, two factors must be involved.

- First, *we have to feel that the mistake could have been avoided*. Eddie is advised to curb his passions: gently by his understanding wife, and firmly by his lawyer, a character who serves a function similar to that of the Greek chorus counseling the protagonist. Eddie, in short, knows better.
- Second, *the mistake not avoided must have been caused by a believable character flaw*. Eddie is defensive about a sexual attraction that his conscious mind believes to be morally unacceptable. Consequently, he buries it deep inside, a suppression that only makes the situation worse.

The influence of Sigmund Freud is clearly evident in many modern tragedies. The father of psychoanalysis has given playwrights insight into the hidden sexual causes of anxiety and irrational behavior. Unsatisfied lust and unshakable feelings of guilt over forbidden sexual encounters are plausible ways to explain character actions and motivations. Eddie's anger toward the young immigrant might also have been a sign of buried homosexual curiosity. Ultimately, then, the play is the tragedy of a decent man who refuses to acknowledge things about himself that he does not like and therefore denies. By turning on the young men, Eddie symbolically turns on his own unacceptable urges.

Melodrama and Tragedy: A Contrast

In tragedy, the protagonist, as Aristotle notes, is mainly virtuous but not totally innocent. In nineteenth-century **melodrama**, the hero or heroine *is* innocent and is beset by problems from external forces, never from an inner flaw that leads to destruction. Melodrama makes no huge demands on the mind, and, though it can be highly suspenseful, there is always the knowledge that everything will turn out as it should. Aspects of the genre are still with us, mainly in film or on television.

If he had lived into the early twentieth century and seen popular films such as *The Perils of Pauline* and *Orphans of the Storm*, Aristotle would have denied that these were tragic. Tragedy is not about a helpless heroine tied to a railroad track by a sinister villain or about poor people seeking shelter from the elements. Melodrama characters are easily separated into the totally good and the totally bad. When the villain is, inevitably and predictably, punished, the audience cheers, because "it serves him right." Traditional melodrama was not (and still isn't) big on examining the motives of a character. The stereotypical nineteenth-century villain who threatened the virtue of a pure heroine was simply bad because, well, that's what he was. When the heroine was rescued by the equally pure hero, again there was no troubling ambiguity.

Melodrama is the triumph of the righteous over the once powerful, but finally defeated, bad guys. It can also be lots of fun: a night out, popcorn, and back home untroubled by any new ideas.

One element of melodrama is a holdover from the Greeks: the **deus ex machina**—literally, "god from a machine." Not all the classical playwrights created characters like Oedipus, heading for an unavoidable doom because of a tragic flaw. Sometimes they wanted to provide a happier ending, so they invented the device of having an actor, playing a god, come down from the stage in a cart attached to a pulley, a god who would straighten everything out. The phrase *deus ex machina* is now used to describe any plot contrivance that violates the probabilities of human behavior and is introduced by the author for an expedient but implausible resolution: for example, a convenient bolt of lightning to kill the evil-doer.

Audiences became so accustomed to the suspenseful thriller formula that they stopped caring whether the artificial separation of people into good and bad violated their sense of what was real. The melodrama lives on as a source of pure entertainment, enjoyed by those who want to escape from the storm and stress of reality. Think about both the television soap operas of the twentieth century and the reality shows of the twenty-first century: How much do many of us enjoy watching the trials and tribulations of those housewives in New Jersey, with the villains and heroines clearly defined?

Comedy in Theater History

7.2   *What are the differences among various forms of comedy, including satire, comedy of character, farce, and parody?*

At the opposite end of the theatrical spectrum from tragedy is **comedy**, which encourages little audience identification with the protagonists—for otherwise how could we laugh at their foolishness? *We are not foolish, they* are. We must remain separate from them in order to enjoy the spectacle of their troubles, which are comparatively trivial and temporary.

Greek theater could consist of three tragedies presented in a single, long afternoon. To send the audience home in a happier state of mine, the Greeks invented the comic afterpiece, presented as a fourth play following the afternoon's tragedies. Though the plays contained mythical elements such as the costumes of the Chorus, the stories were not based on myth but rather made fun of greed and corruption in Athenian society. After a time, they became so popular that audiences wanted to go to the theater only to laugh. Thus was born the still thriving institution of the comedy.

The only surviving sentence from Aristotle's essay on comedy is this: *"Tragedy is life seen close at hand; comedy is life seen from a distance."* It remains as valid as ever. Many disasters in *slapstick* comedy—someone falling through an open manhole; an arrogant man who has insulted the hero turning and suddenly tumbling down a flight of stairs—could turn dark if we were allowed to see the characters actually suffer; but we are not, and so we are able to enjoy ourselves at their expense. Our own lives don't seem so bad anymore.

Comedy is often about situations in which trivial mistakes lead to hilarious consequences. A secret must be concealed at all costs; a couple is really married but their parents don't know; there is a mix-up in identities, perhaps between two identical twins. A chronic liar makes a vow that he will tell nothing but the truth for a full week and, of course, loses his friends who cannot bear his honesty. A really neat man becomes the roommate of a slob, and they fight unrelentingly. The people a family is trying to impress arrive for dinner on the wrong night, when the household is in utter chaos.

Comedy has evolved into many forms that have endured through the ages, and more than one kind of comedy can exist in the same play. Let's begin with comedy as performed in the Greek classical theater and follow the historical periods as we did in the previous section.

Satire

The comic afterpiece required of the Athenian playwrights was known as the *satyr* play, because it was performed by actors in costumes identifying them as the mythical creatures who were half man and half goat. The plays made fun of the tragedies the audience had just seen, as well as events and personalities in society that the playwrights considered ridiculous. **Satire** has come to mean a species of comedy that ridicules the problems of society—corruption in government, inequality, war as a solution to human problems, injustice, and hypocrisy. The satirical playwright is typically both a comic writer, interested in getting audiences to laugh, and a reformer, dedicated to the betterment of society. (Perhaps the finest satirist of the early twenty-first century is Jon Stewart, who took on the ills and evils of the present day for almost 20 years, from 1996 to 2015, on *The Daily Show*.) Serious criticism of society can be communicated in other ways, such as newspaper editorials or sermons, but people prefer to laugh, and the satirist obliges—writing with a stiletto.

ARISTOPHANES, *LYSISTRATA* The Greek playwright Aristophanes (445–385 BCE) used the stage both for comedy and as a plea for the improvement of the human condition. One of his enduring works is *Lysistrata*, with its perennially viable antiwar message and a basic situation that never fails to delight its audience.

During the unpopular war between Athens and Sparta, which lasted from 431 to 404 BCE, the women of both sides, tired of the senseless conflict and foolish loss of life, take matters into their own hands by uniting and establishing an all-female outpost on the Acropolis, the hill that dominates Athens. Not only are men barred from entering, but the women, under the leadership of the title character, go on strike. There will be no lovemaking for the men until hostilities cease.

An antiwar play in the midst of war? For the Athenians it was no problem. Although some political leaders argued that it was not the right time or place for such an unpatriotic attitude, most believed that the ability to express a point of view was more important than automatic obedience. Indeed, even today, the suggestion is occasionally raised—not always satirically—that women follow the lead of Lysistrata and combat the push toward war by exercising their own special weapons.

Satiric plays continue to be written (and satire reigns supreme on much of television—think John Oliver's *Last Week Tonight* or *South Park*), but the appeal is often limited to an appreciative audience that already agrees with the author. A prospective theatrical producer concerned about box-office receipts may be wary of writers who "preach to the choir." Politics, religion, and the extremely wealthy may offer convenient targets for ridicule, but advocates for the targets may fail to find any humor in the work.

Comedy of Character

Although Aristotle listed *character* as second in importance only to plot, he and the Greek audience may not have thought of *character* as we do today. Aristotle may have meant simply the actor playing a certain role, defined by certain traits. Thus Oedipus, for example, is a king, a man of power, arrogant about his power, and unyielding in his convictions.

Today's writers have been strongly influenced by psychology, a science unknown in Aristotle's day. A contemporary Oedipus might be portrayed as paranoid and defensive. His inner turmoil might be at least as important as the details of the story.

Euripides is probably the Greek tragic dramatist most accessible to modern audiences. In *Medea*, he concentrates on the inner passions of his central character and thus develops something much closer in spirit to the modern concept of character as a component of theater.

The term "character" meaning a figure in a play is quite different from the term "character" meaning a combination of traits we remember about a person, traits that make that person unique. All plays have characters of the first kind; not all plays have the second. Although the science of psychology was still nonexistent in Shakespeare's time, the playwright nonetheless created more memorable characters than any writer before or since. Indeed, many of his works continue to hold the stage less for plot than for memorable characters, many of whom are the standout figures in his comedies.

SHAKESPEARE'S FALSTAFF   The comic portrait of Sir John Falstaff (Figure 7.8) enlivens the history plays *Henry IV, Parts I and II*. A drunkard, a liar, and a con man, Falstaff's outrageous disregard for propriety makes Prince Hal—soon to become King Henry V—adore the company of this man, who urges Hal to sow his wild oats as long as possible. Shakespeare gave Falstaff so many identifiable human weaknesses that his audience must have adored him as much as the prince did, laughing *with* not *at* him. Falstaff is not only a rogue but also a great philosopher of fun and corruption—the perfect Dionysian. He scandalously praises the sins of excess that most of us commit but hate ourselves for committing. Nothing is worth repenting, as far as he is concerned. Nothing should be taken too seriously in our all-too-brief existence.

Falstaff not only consumes too much food and drink without concern for the morning after, he encourages the prince to do the same. He is neither honest nor patriotic. Given the assignment to buy uniforms for a group of recruits, he spends the allotment on himself. On the battlefield, when an enemy soldier expects to engage in hand-to-hand combat, Falstaff puts away his sword rather than fight and delivers a famous speech on the dubious value of honor. He observes that it "hath no skill in surgery" and cannot be felt or heard by those living or dead. He may be dishonest in misappropriating public funds meant for uniforms, but he is certainly honest about his own disinclination to be a wartime casualty.

He is poignant, too, in his misunderstanding of what he thought was the prince's friendship for him. Pretending to be dead, Falstaff hears the prince deliver a "eulogy" by making unflattering comments about his size. Even worse, when the prince finally does become king, Falstaff tries to benefit from their old friendship, only to be totally rejected with these words:

> *I know thee not, old man; fall to thy prayers;*
> *How ill white hairs become a fool and jester!*
> *I have long dreamt of such a kind of man,*
> *So surfeit-swell'd, so old and so profane;*
> *But, being awaked, I do despise my dream.*[13]

Do we then side with the new king and dismiss Falstaff? Literary scholar Harold Bloom, who has spent his life writing about and teaching Shakespeare, reports that one of his students denounced Falstaff by claiming that "the transformation of Prince Hal into King Henry V was exemplary . . . that Hal represented rule and that Falstaff was a lord of

Figure 7.8 Antony Sher as Sir John Falstaff in a Royal Shakespeare Company production of *Henry IV*, 2014.
Can you think of "bad" characters, in film or television as well as theater, who manage to charm the audience despite their flaws? How might the writer make such characters sympathetic?
Robbie Jack/Corbis Entertainment/Corbis

misrule," and Bloom "could not persuade her that Falstaff transcended her categories, as he transcends virtually all our categories of human sin and error."[14]

Professor Bloom's admiration for Falstaff was so great that he briefly deserted the classroom to play the role in a stage production. He sees Falstaff as complex, not merely a coward or a jester. In his encounter with the king, Sir John is courageous, aware that "Hal's ambivalence has resolved itself into a murderous negativity. … Time annihilates other Shakespearean protagonists, but not Falstaff. …"[15]

In his analysis, Bloom is at odds not only with his students but also with other critics who have argued endlessly about the relationship between Falstaff and the prince. Was he a rejected father substitute or a dishonored mentor, as some have claimed? The critical fights continue, just as they have about countless other Shakespearean characters. To those who argue that "it's just a play" and wonder how there can be so much dispute about characters who never actually lived, theater lovers know: Shakespeare's characters, along with so many characters created by other playwrights, did—and do—live in the minds of the viewers and readers of plays in which they are portrayed.

MODERN COMEDY OF CHARACTER Snobs abound in comedy and are usually laughable. More sympathetic are those characters who would resist the expectations of middle-class life in many twentieth-century plays. In *You Can't Take It with You* by George S. Kaufman and Moss Hart (1936), a family of extraordinarily unconventional characters live happily together. The daughter dances ballet badly, the grandfather makes illegal fireworks, and the mother is writing a play that will never be finished because she doesn't know how to get her characters out of a monastery. Except for one rational daughter who goes to work, the rest of the family does everything except hold down a 9-to-5 job. Conflict arises when the one employed family member falls in love with the son of a banker. They would like to marry, and she invites his family for dinner. In an effort to suggest that they are respectable folk, the hosts decide to conceal their idiosyncrasies. But there is a mix-up about the date, and the banker and his wife arrive on the wrong evening. Everything goes wrong that could go wrong, including an explosion of fireworks that leads to everyone's arrest. Happily, the encounter between the two families leads the banker and his wife to a more tolerant acceptance of the Dionysian side of life.

The clash between upright Apollonianism and Dionysian lack of organization is also chronicled in the Tony Award–winning *The Odd Couple* (1965) by Neil Simon (Figure 7.9). The carefree, disorderly sportswriter, Oscar Madison, allows his newly divorced friend, the overly neat Felix Unger, to move in with him. The roommates, who have very different ideas about cleanliness, clash in hilarious ways, including one scene in which Oscar, frustrated to the breaking point by Felix's unyielding neatness, dumps a whole plate of linguine on his head. While most audience members would probably not want Oscar as a houseguest, he is clearly the sympathetic focal point of a work that was remade multiple times: into a hugely popular movie, a long-running television series, and another, more recent less successful series.

Figure 7.9 Walter Matthau as Oscar and Art Carney as Felix in the original production of Neil Simon's *The Odd Couple*, 1965.
This play has been remade as a movie and two television series, one in the 1970s and one in 2014. What makes this theme of contrasting personalities so durable?
CSU Archives/Everett Collection Inc/Alamy

Farce

Farce is a genre of comedy that draws laughter from outrageous physical actions and improbably chaotic situations. Its characters are two-dimensional stereotypes easily described in a word or two. They are superficial, like dolls or animals in a cartoon.

Many are derived from the **commedia dell'arte**, an Italian pantomime street theater originating in the middle of the sixteenth century. Its plays were usually improvised from bare plot outlines developed by the actors, each of whom was assigned to a certain character, often for life. Some of the comic types—or stock characters—were so universal they are still around (for example, the doddering old man who really believes a beautiful young girl loves *him*, not his money). Each age adds its own types: characters who are foolish because they do not fit the definition of a normal, rational human being.

In the *commedia*, a central theme often concerned the interaction of two young lovers trying to get together but thwarted by a miserly father, or by another characteristic type, the pretentious boor who used unnecessarily long words and arrogantly thought himself a suitable mate for the girl, only to have scheming servants aid the lovers. Actors in early *commedia* wore costumes and masks that immediately identified the type portrayed. Audiences loved the repetition of familiar stories with minor variations and the pratfalls and physical abuse visited upon the fools, who were, after all, so silly that they could be safely laughed out of existence.

The list of fools inspired by the *commedia* and still around today is almost endless. Here are a few: the rich but stingy old man; the old man who tries to marry a beautiful young girl; the nerd; the bragging coward; the bigot; the clumsy, unpolished social climber; the brat; the completely self-absorbed actor (or beauty queen); the drunken, irresponsible husband; his (understandably) nagging wife; the innocent "hick" or "rube." More recent "types" that can be added to this list include clueless jocks, airhead rock musicians, and people who obsess about health or food fads. You could probably come up with a half-dozen more!

MOLIÈRE, *THE WOULD-BE GENTLEMAN* AND *TARTUFFE*   The *commedia* exerted strong influence on the work of the major neoclassical comic dramatist, Molière, whose real name was Jean-Baptiste Poquelin. Monsieur Jourdain, the protagonist of one of his greatest comedies, *The Would-Be Gentleman*, is rich but without the rank or social skills that would make him an acceptable guest at the court of King Louis XIV. His clumsy efforts to look like a titled gentleman, to learn fencing and the minuet, provided a hilarious target of ridicule for aristocratic audiences. When he initially rejects the man his daughter loves as a suitable husband for her, the couple trick him into believing that the young man, now disguised, has a title—and the father delightedly allows the wedding to proceed. As the curtain falls, everyone onstage and in the audience is aware of the trick played on Jourdain except the foolish social climber himself.

In farce, the recognition scene does not exist. Imagine if, before the curtain fell, the foolish M. Jourdain had realized he had been tricked and that his daughter had just married a man of her own class rather than a titled lord. Audiences might have felt sympathy for the duped Jourdain, and the laughter would have stopped.

Molière was a neoclassic playwright, contemporary of the tragedian Racine. His audiences would have included well-educated aristocrats, eager to laugh at the social climber M. Jourdain, as well as the title character of *Tartuffe*, his play about religious hypocrisy, controversial at the time in strongly Catholic France. In the scene pictured in Figure 7.10, Tartuffe, pretending to be a dedicated evangelist so that he may bilk his host, Orgon, out of thousands, is scolding the maid for showing too much cleavage. He hands her a handkerchief to cover herself. Of course, his eyes help themselves to what is being revealed by the cleavage.

Figure 7.10 A performance of *Tartuffe*, 1669.
Sexual innuendo continues to be a comedy staple (think of Judd Apatow's films). Why do you think this kind of humor has been central to comedy for hundreds of years? Does it make you laugh?
KML Gallery of Fine Art

Molière used rhymed couplets in the neoclassic style. Here Cleante, Orgon's brother-in-law, who serves as the voice of reason in the play, tries to communicate his doubts about Tartuffe's authenticity.

> *Brother, I don't pretend to be a sage,*
> *Nor have I all the wisdom of the age.*
> *There's just one insight I would dare to claim*
> *I know that true and false are not the same;*
> *And just as there is nothing I more revere*
> *Than a soul whose faith is steadfast and sincere,*
> *Nothing that I more cherish and admire*
> *Than honest zeal and true religious fire*
> *So there is nothing that I find more base*
> *Than specious piety's dishonest face—*
> *Whose impious mummeries and hollow shows*
> *Exploit our love of heaven and make a jest*
> *Of all that men think holiest and best.*[16]

OSCAR WILDE, *THE IMPORTANCE OF BEING EARNEST*   Like their non-comic counterparts, Victorian comic playwrights often dealt with real issues, and they also did so within the convention of verisimilitude, but the realism was often one of scenery and costumes, not speech. The dialog of Oscar Wilde (1854–1900), so witty and elegant, is rarely found except on the stage. In Wilde's plays, dialog is an idealized version of how civilized people *should* talk. It is far from being a transcript of everyday speech, and when a play is as consistently witty as *The Importance of Being Earnest*, we are grateful. We can hear plenty of familiar speech *outside* the theater.

Wilde's play, which has entertained audiences ever since it was written in 1895, has as its premise a familiar story: the effort of a suitor to win the approval of his girlfriend's mother. In the play the young man is living a double life; he is called Jack Worthing when he lives at his country estate and Ernest Worthing when he goes to London to court a young lady, Miss Gwendolen Fairfax, who has told him that she will only marry a man named Ernest. What stands in the way of the mother's approval is Mr. Worthing's inability to prove who his parents were. As a baby he had been "found" in a checked handbag at a London train station.

The story revolves around his identity and the need to meet the requirements of Gwendolen's mother, the formidable Lady Bracknell. When Jack as Ernest tells her about his bizarre origin, she answers curtly that neither she nor her husband would "dream of allowing our only daughter . . . to marry into a cloakroom and form an alliance with a parcel." In both its wit and its farcical elements, *The Importance of Being Earnest* is one of the funniest plays ever written in English.

In one of the many famous scenes, Gwendolen has discovered that Jack is not actually named Ernest, her main reason for having promised to marry him eventually, and has broken off their engagement. Jack's friend Algernon, who has just been rejected by his own fiancée, is helping himself to the muffins left on the tea table.

JACK:	*How you can sit there calmly eating muffins when we are in this horrible trouble I can't make out. You seem to be perfectly heartless.*
ALGERNON:	*Well, I can't eat muffins in an agitated manner. The butter would probably get on my cuffs. One should always eat muffins quite calmly. It is the only way to eat them.*
JACK:	*I say it's perfectly heartless your eating muffins at all under the circumstances.*
ALGERNON:	*When I am in trouble, eating is the only thing that consoles me . . . At the present moment I am eating muffins because I am unhappy. Besides, I am particularly fond of muffins.*[17]

Wilde chose comedy. Another playwright might have chosen to deal with the "horrible trouble" of the situation and allowed his characters to go on and on about what to do about it. Other characters could have been introduced to give their own opinions. The rejected suitors might have been given sentimental speeches. Instead, there are muffins. Because it is a comedy, everything turns out all right in a series of improbable coincidences and the curtain falls on the lovers happily embracing.

The play is farce, enhanced by wit that continues to cause audiences to howl with laughter, even at Lady Bracknell's insensitive remark on hearing about Mr. Worthing's background: "To lose one parent may be considered a misfortune. To lose both looks like carelessness."

Parody

The British playwright Tom Stoppard (b. 1937) is a master of many genres—comedy, serious drama, and, even the comic genre called parody. **Parody** makes fun of a particular work or genre—a film, a song, a painting, or a commercial—a work the author believes has been unjustifiably successful. The technique of parody is that it pretends to be the work it is ridiculing, except that the basic elements of the original are laughably exaggerated so that the audience (or reader) will see the absurdity of taking it seriously.

Stoppard's *The Real Inspector Hound* (1968) makes fun of the melodramatic thriller popular since the nineteenth century—a genre that Stoppard finds laughable. His play has the familiar plot of multiple murders in a remote English country house, complete with storms raging outside, a cast of characters, all of whom look suspicious, and plot entanglements impossible to understand.

What sets this work apart from the usual parody, however, is that Stoppard uses the tired old format to say something serious about the nature of reality. Two critics, sitting in a box and loudly denouncing the play, shatter the fourth-wall convention by climbing onto the stage when it appears the cast has deserted it. One critic answers the incessantly ringing telephone and thus becomes a character involved in the sinister proceedings. Soon he too disappears, and the other critic is murdered. Meanwhile, two of the characters, who have previously been "killed," take their seats in the box and become the critics. Stoppard thus investigates the often nonexistent difference between illusion and reality.

Parody tends to be of only temporary interest, unless the target continues to be relevant. As long as people flock to creaky melodramas, *The Real Inspector Hound* will be funny. But more likely its serious theme of illusion versus reality will keep it alive. When watching a parody, we need to ask ourselves whether it offers something besides passing entertainment.

The Nineteenth Century: The Roots of Modern Theater

7.3 *What are the key developments in nineteenth-century theater?*

Changes in the physical shape and structure of the theater in the nineteenth century, and the introduction of the proscenium stage, supported new directions in theatrical performance. Even more interesting, it's perhaps no surprise that the development of what we see as modern theater was paralleled by the development of psychology and psychotherapy. As humankind explored the interior of the human mind, plays became more and more realistic, and more and more focused on the world of ideas.

The Rise of Realism

During the nineteenth century, commonly known in the West as the "Victorian Era" in recognition of England's powerful and long-reigning monarch, a change took place in both society and the theater. An increasingly prosperous middle class patronized the theater and demanded to see their own lives and times portrayed as they were. Instead of classical myths, they wanted contemporary themes and characters very much like themselves. This held true on both sides of the Atlantic because the American middle class wanted to imitate the good manners and polite language of the English middle class.

In the Victorian theater, the audience sat in the dark and looked up at a stage lighted first with gas lamps, then electricity. People on the stage moved and talked to each other without noticing that what they did and said was being seen and heard by a large number of eavesdroppers. Their job was to pretend the audience was not there, and the audience's job was to pretend that they were not watching actors moving about a set made to look like a real interior. They walked up and down real stairs, opened a door and exited through it, presumably to go outside. The actor was only going backstage, but this was the era of **verisimilitude**, the convention of making everything look and sound like the real world.

The front of the stage—or **proscenium**—was supposedly the fourth wall of the room in which the action takes place. Actors were not supposed to "break" that wall—that is, to look at the audience. The convention, or rules, were clearly established. The play contained itself and only itself. These conventions are still with us. Despite all of the experimentation that has taken place in the last hundred years or so, realism is by far the dominant mode of much theater; and actors are trained in the techniques of realistic acting.

THE LIMITS OF VERISIMILITUDE   Still, a certain amount of license was taken in Victorian times and is still taken now. If the open proscenium is supposed to be the fourth wall of a room, why is furniture often facing that wall? Why do actors, talking to each other, frequently turn their faces casually toward that wall when the audience isn't supposed to be there? Is their dialog *actually* what we would hear outside the theater? The answer is that the convention is one of "as if," to use the famous two words of Konstantin Stanislavsky (1863–1938), founder of the Moscow Art Theater. Actors were meant to act "as if" they were really in that situation, and their language was "as if" real people really talked like that.

Yet when reading plays of the period, we are apt to wonder how on earth audiences of the time could have actually believed the dialog was authentic. Up to a point it was—for a time middle-class people observed the niceties of language that were stringently taught at home and in school. In today's theater and in films or on television, we still accept the "realities" of dialog, except that by now actors often talk in short, sometimes incomplete, sentences about food, trains, money, and sex. Much dialog is not allowed to be more insightful or profound than ordinary conversation. Even at moments of great love or great loss, characters can be as inarticulate as people without a gifted scriptwriter to tell them what to say. Sometimes instead of words there are grunts and sighs. This too is authentic—up to a point.

In Victorian theaters, time intervals were explained by a program handed to the audience, as is still the case. Lighting now indicated time of day or night. With the coming of electricity in the 1880s, actors were artificially lighted and their features heavily emphasized or even disguised by stage makeup. If a younger actor was cast as a middle-aged person, every effort was made to conceal the actor's youth; but, as theater companies grew and spread about the country on both sides of the Atlantic, actors began to be cast as they physically and vocally suited the part. Versatile actors, suitable for many roles, were able to demand high salaries. In the British theater, actors continue to train on the stage and tend to move fluidly back and forth between stage and screen. In today's American theater, however, the big stars tend to be those who have made their reputations in film but deign to return to the stage from time to time, working for far less money than they are used to, but finding satisfaction in plying their craft before live audiences and in the integrity they believe adheres to stage, as opposed to screen, acting.

The director also became a major figure. Before this period, plays were put together by the actors. Often the theater's manager would star in a production and inform cast members to give him center stage at all times. In the theater of verisimilitude, however, both movement and interpretation of lines were carefully supervised by a director.

THE "WELL-MADE" PLAY   If theater of verisimilitude were completely true to the claim that it was mirroring real life in the most honest way possible, its stories would not be as tightly knit as they are. Something else is at work, popularized by French playwrights earlier in the nineteenth century, something known as the **well-made play**. In this genre, objects and people mentioned in Act One *must* be important later on. Guns are mentioned and someone will be shot; someone who coughs slightly will be revealed to have a fatal illness; the casual mention of a letter having been mistakenly sent will lead to devastating consequences. Almost nothing is wasted as everything advances the plot. Even the set has to observe the rules of this convention. Every chair on the set has to be occupied by one or another character at some point; a lamp must be lit; a door must be opened; stairs have to be used. The latter convention still dominates in today's theater.

Important to the well-made play was **exposition**, the revelation through dialog of necessary background material, such as the past history and relationships among the characters. It remains vital to all realistic theater and has become a major problem for modern dramatists. In the hands of an inexperienced playwright attempting to sound realistic, exposition can sound silly. Families and friends in real life don't need to identify the people in a conversation. You already know that your best friend has a brother named Eddie who has been overseas in the Army. You therefore would not dream of asking, "How's your brother Eddie, who's in the Army?" Playwrights dealing with new characters, unknown to the audience, have to introduce information without sounding overly obvious, and they have to depend on dialog alone—no narrator, no chorus, no interior monologue to help explain.

Henrik Ibsen (1828–1906) revolutionized the theater of verisimilitude by writing plays about controversial social issues. Here we see how, influenced by the well-made play tradition, he adeptly and economically handles exposition—in this case, the nature of the relationship between husband and wife in the 1879 work *A Doll's House*, which exposes the sham that was, for Ibsen, the Victorian marriage.

HELMER:	(from the study) *Is that my little lark twittering out there?*
NORA:	(busy opening packages) *Yes, it is.*
HELMER:	*Is that my squirrel rummaging around?*
NORA:	*Yes!*
HELMER:	*When did my squirrel get in?*
NORA:	*Just now.* (Putting the macaroon bag in her pocket and wiping her mouth) *Do come in, Torvald, and see what I've bought.*
HELMER:	*Can't be disturbed.* (After a moment he opens the door and peers in, pen in hand) *Bought, you say? All that there? Has the little spendthrift been out throwing money around again?*
NORA:	*Oh. But Torvald, this year we really should let ourselves go a bit. It's the first Christmas we haven't had to economize.*
HELMER:	*But you know we can't go squandering.*

> NORA: *Oh yes, Torvald, we can squander a little now. Can't we? Just a tiny, wee bit. Now that you've got a big salary and are going to make piles of money.*
>
> HELMER: *Yes, starting New Year's. But then it's a full three months till the raise comes through.*[18]

"Lark," "squirrel," "spendthrift," "Christmas," a busy husband, a change in income in three months—we've learned a lot in those few lines of exposition. This exposition also hints at the wife's impending revolt. In the hands of a great playwright, exposition not only provides background for the audience but, more important, promises what will eventually happen. In a sense, most of the play is exposition. The past is exposed little by little and so is the shaky foundation of a Victorian marriage once thought ideal.

The Theater of Ideas

Related to satire in terms of dealing with social issues but generally presented in the convention of verisimilitude, *theater of ideas* came into prominence in the late Victorian period in the work of two playwrights who would use the stage to raise the consciousness of their audience. One was Henrik Ibsen of Norway, whose opening scene in *A Doll's House* was mentioned earlier as an example of adroit handling of exposition; the other was his Irish-born champion, George Bernard Shaw (1856–1950).

HENRIK IBSEN, *A DOLL'S HOUSE* At first this journalist-turned-playwright scandalized his staid Norwegian audiences with frank exposés of hypocrisy in all the major institutions of his time: marriage, business, government, the clergy, education. Although *A Doll's House* is now credited with having changed the whole course of Western theater, at the time of writing it was considered shocking, even obscene. One critic commented: "No self-respecting man would take his wife to see this play."

The husband and wife of *A Doll's House* are Torvald, a recently promoted bank manager, and Nora, the "doll" of the title. The secret in Nora's past is that she has forged her father's name on a promissory note in order to borrow money to take her sick husband to a warmer climate and thus save his life. The man who holds the promissory note is an employee in her husband's bank. He has threatened to make her crime public if she does not persuade her husband to give him a promotion.

So far this man fills the role of the villain in melodramas already familiar to audiences. The stereotypical villain often wore a black cape and twirled his mustache as he uttered threats to the helpless heroine, whom he called "my proud beauty." Ibsen is more subtle. His villain is a complex character with a need for love and acceptance. Ignoring efforts to intervene, Torvald has fired the man, an action that leads to a letter exposing her crime. Rather than rush to Nora's defense or take the blame himself (as she had assumed he would), Torvald denounces her, saying she is no longer a fit mother to their three children. However, she may continue to live in the house, giving the appearance of respectability (Figure 7.11).

Meanwhile, the blackmailer has found a woman willing to marry and nurture him. His spirits uplifted, he returns the promissory note to Nora's angry spouse. In a moment that stirred up a huge controversy, Torvald cries joyfully, "Nora, I'm saved!" There is a

Figure 7.11 Gillian Anderson as Nora in a 2009 production of Ibsen's *A Doll's House* at the Donmar Warehouse, London.
Why might this proto-feminist play have been written in 1879? How did it reflect cultural movement?

Photo by Geraint Lewis/Rex USA, Courtesy Everett Collection - (511463e)

profound silence, and then Nora asks quietly, "And what about me?" Eager to return the marriage to its former state, the husband tries to explain the rules of society: "No man sacrifices his honor for the one he loves." Nora's comeback shocked Ibsen's audience and remains one of the stirring lines in modern theater: "Millions of women have done so."

She has seen the truth, has seen the hypocrisy underlying their codified society, and now refuses to go back to where they were. Instead, she announces that she no longer consents to live a lie. Ignoring his protestations and promises to change the way he treats her, the newly liberated Nora quietly but resolutely informs him that she must first discover who she really is. She packs her bags, returns the wedding ring, and leaves, slamming the door behind her.

The slamming of that door is one of the most significant sounds in the history of Western theater. It caused a scandal so great that guests at dinner parties in respectable society were requested not to mention it. An actress playing Nora in Germany refused to play the final scene as written, so Ibsen wrote an alternate ending in which Nora realizes a mother cannot abandon her children.

GEORGE BERNARD SHAW, *PYGMALION*   Although attacked on both sides of the Atlantic wherever theater audiences were comprised mainly of genteel middle and upper classes fighting to hold onto moral absolutes they feared were slowly vanishing, Ibsen gained much stature with the publication of Shaw's *The Quintessence of Ibsenism*, which recognized in Ibsen a kindred spirit who also wanted to use the theater as an agent for significant social change. Shaw's own plays were aimed at shaking audiences loose from dangerous preconceived ideas, but for the most part his vehicle was comedy.

In *Pygmalion* (1912), he attacked the rigidity of the class system in Britain with an amusing story about the transformation of a Cockney flower seller into a well-dressed, well-spoken lady accepted by the very highest levels of British society. On the surface it is a Cinderella story: The poor grubby lass who can't speak English "properly" is eventually passed off as a highborn lady because she speaks so well. Beneath the surface, however, the play criticizes the sins committed by the British to preserve respectability at all costs. If Eliza Doolittle, it asks, can rise above her inherited lowly place in society by showing evidence of education, why are so many denied that privilege?

Eliza's father, a ne'er-do-well with a love of alcohol and a phobia against gainful employment, suddenly comes into money. Yet he is shrewd enough to know that if money also determines a person's social standing, it says nothing about the moral principles of the one who possesses it. He also knows that belonging to a higher class incurs certain unpleasant obligations, such as the need to be respectably married, which would deprive him of the pleasures that were his before anyone took notice of his existence. In *My Fair Lady* (1956), the Alan Jay Lerner–Frederick Loewe musical version of the play, Doolittle has two now classic songs: "With a Little Bit of Luck," a celebration of life without responsibility for upholding middle-class standards, and "Get Me to the Church on Time," in which he pleads for one more night on the town with his cronies before settling into a dull life of respectability.

IDEAS VS. PROPAGANDA   Neither Shaw nor Ibsen belabored one issue from play to play, nor did they have one speech per play which would have sent a too explicit message to the audience. Plays designed as propaganda do that. Propaganda lacks subtlety and is less interested in character than in producing a desired action: getting people to vote, to protest, to revolt.

In the more subtle Theater of Ideas, playwrights tend to present more than one side of an argument. Nora's final speech before slamming the door may be—and has been—taken as a rallying cry for feminism, but does Ibsen really recommend abandoning marriage and children as the only possible solution? Some scholars who have studied the play carefully maintain that it also can be presented as the tragedy of other human beings trapped in a social system that blinds them to the truth.

Naturalism

During the latter half of the nineteenth century, while Ibsen, Shaw, and their followers were forcing audiences to confront social problems once swept under the rug, other writers were experimenting with a new genre called **naturalism**. As its name implies, theatrical naturalism was an attempt to show life as it really was—without artificial-sounding stage dialog or the well-made play structure. Nor were (are) these plays concerned with conveying ideas or effecting changes in society. Their premise: This is life, this is human nature, it's all there is.

ANTON CHEKHOV   The pioneer in naturalistic theater was a Russian playwright and former physician, Anton Chekhov (1860–1904), who abandoned the play of one central figure in favor of the play that deals with a group of persons, their actions, and interactions. Almost every character in a Chekhov drama is at one point or another an object of sympathetic understanding. The plays are plotless in the usual sense of the word, without carefully crafted exposition or a relentless drive toward a climax. They reflect a dedicated physician's insights from having observed and listened to many patients, and his unwillingness to make moral judgments.

Chekhov's works were discovered in the first decade of the twentieth century and staged by Konstantin Stanislavsky at the Moscow Arts Theatre. The director noted that, since the plays lacked heroes and villains, there was no question of endorsing this character's behavior or condemning another's. It was really a matter of trying to understand why things happened. The author had spelled nothing out for the director. He seemed to have created certain individuals, set them in motion in certain situations, and allowed them to proceed according to mysterious laws of their own being. In order to present this new form of theater, Stanislavsky had to reinvent the art of acting, and his technique still pervades theater today.

Stanislavsky realized that an in-depth understanding of people in real life was the starting point. One had to know that when people did anything obvious reasons were not always accurate. Real people seldom behaved as one would expect, because all too often people were observed not as they were but in terms of preconceived notions. He came to see that Chekhov was being true to his own observations and knowledge of human nature, rather than to time-honored clichés that would be instantly understandable to theater audiences. If in real life a man were seen sitting by himself at a party, speaking to no one, someone might say of him, "He is antisocial." Someone else might observe, "Now there's an introvert" or "See that man? He feels guilty about something." Stanislavsky would say that we cannot ever fully understand another human being. We can only infer what is going on inside them by *what they are not saying*.

In developing his technique, Stanislavsky required his actors to use their imagination and project their characters into other times and places, determining what they might do or say under changing conditions. Gradually, he believed, the actors would put themselves inside the people they were playing, the only path to discovering the truth of a character; they would react to a given situation as if it were happening to them. The rehearsal process involved the actors' exploration of themselves—their past and present. In a very real sense, actors and playwrights were collaborators, and the director's function was to distinguish between what seemed true and believable and what did not. Hence the famous Stanislavsky definition of acting as *being truthful in imaginary circumstances*.

Chekhov's characters are often trapped inside their own feelings and longings, and his plays often deal with the gap between human desires and what reality provides. For this reason he knew that, though enormous social changes were underway in his native Russia, they would have no effect on people's behavior or their search for happiness. Yet he is compassionate toward those who delude themselves into insisting that progress is inevitable and that life will get better.

Figure 7.12 A 2010 production of Chekhov's *Three Sisters* in modern dress.
How might the audience's experience of this play change when the characters and settings are contemporary, rather than 19th century?
Drew Farrell/Lebrecht Music and Arts Photo Library/Alamy

CHEKHOV, *THREE SISTERS*

Chekhov's *Three Sisters* (1901), believed by many to be his masterwork, is also the most complex (Figure 7.12). Each of the characters, who create a tight ensemble on the stage, is dependent on what the others say and do, yet each is an individual whose inner drives must be explored by the actor, believed in totally, *lived*. No two performances of *Three Sisters* is ever exactly the same because to play Chekhov actors must continually seek new corners in their characters' inner lives.

The sisters in question are daughters of a general who had once lived in Moscow, a place to which they long to return, a place where they are certain happiness lies. Unfortunately, lacking the money to move from the country, they must endure the monotony of their everyday existence, finding brief moments of joy only in thinking of Moscow.

The oldest sister, Olga, is an unmarried school teacher who manages the household. She is afflicted with frequent headaches and fatigue from unrewarding work. Irina, the youngest sister, loves neither of the two men who want to marry her, but realizes she must settle for one of them and try to lead a life of useful work. The middle sister, Masha, is unhappily married to a dull and pedantic Latin teacher who probably would have been a good match for Olga. Their brother, at one time expected to have a brilliant career, has married a young woman from a lower-class family that enjoys living as if they were rich.

The arrival of a company of soldiers brings a brief excitement into their lives; then it departs. Other characters come and go. From time to time, small crises erupt: a fire, gambling debts, a duel in which one of the men who love Irina is slain. The brother's spendthrift wife begins to dominate the house. She dismisses a beloved family servant; she has an affair with a local official. Neither her husband nor his sisters know how to confront her. Their gentility has not taught them how to fight and win. Nor is Chekhov suggesting that they *should* know. They do what they must. Events are beyond their control. They react, they try, they cope. That is all anyone can do. Chekhov once remarked in a letter that it was a beautiful thing for people to hope that life will change and improve, but he knew it could not, because life just flows through and around people; and they have no way to control it.

In the hands of a romantic playwright, there might have been more overt drama, complete with impassioned speeches of love or denunciation. Far from romantic, Chekhov recorded reality as he found it, making riveting drama out of the everyday world.

A Century of Dynamic Change

7.4 *What new directions and themes developed in twentieth and twenty-first-century theater?*

During the twentieth century, the world seldom enjoyed prolonged periods of peace, and now the closing of the world into a global village has only intensified the unrest. Economic ups and downs have created social upheavals. The climate is changing rapidly and radically. It has become a world almost unrecognizable to people who have lived through the past half-century and longer. The endless problems of the twentieth century and beyond have had a huge impact on the theater. Many new genres emerged as playwrights struggled to approach the challenges of a modern world and reduce them to the size of a stage and to a few hours' duration. For many of them, it became clear that the realistic theater of the previous century was too confining. They also had to contend with competition from the new entertainment form, cinema, with the kind of storytelling that would make total realism possible.

Naturalism, the Theater of Ideas, and both classical and neoclassical drama continued to be respected and performed, especially by repertory companies and on university campuses. But audiences, growing accustomed to the continued acceleration of change, have been and continue to be eager for fresh approaches. In addition, gradual changes in the fabric of society—minorities and women demanding equal recognition, for example—quickly made obsolete the kind of problems Victorian writers had wrestled with. The theater has had to reflect the new reality.

Modern Genres and Conventions

The neatly plotted Victorian play, set in the well-furnished living room, inevitably struck younger writers as a cliché. Modern playwrights wanted to create theater that was not limited by the back-and-forth dialog of fourth-wall drama and the pretense that the audience was not there.

EXPRESSIONISM   In the early twentieth century, German theater exerted universal influence with a new genre known as **Expressionism**. Sets were no longer realistic, but symbolic. An American play called *The Adding Machine* (1923) had for a set a giant, early version of the calculator, on which the main character, named Mr. Zero, was eventually crucified. Stage sets were designed so as not to disguise their unreality, but often to convey a metaphor, representing society as a zoo, or a prison. Even in otherwise realistic drama, sets sometimes contained several rooms and levels all visible at the same time. Through increasingly sophisticated lighting techniques, audiences were trained to believe that, when a scene took place in a lighted part of the stage, the darkened part was not supposed to be there.

NEW WAYS OF STAGING   Theaters-in-the-round allowed audiences to feel closer to the actors and inspired playwrights to create works in which the visible presence of the audience was taken for granted. Even in proscenium theaters, stages could be bare of scenery to encourage audience imagination, a component of theater which many believed had been lost in the Victorian era.

In 1938 *Our Town* by Thornton Wilder (1897–1975) had a narrator walk out on an empty stage and create a small New Hampshire village in the audience's mind. Like other modern playwrights, Wilder wanted to return to the fundamental premise that audiences will accept anything as long as the rules are clearly spelled out in the beginning.

The theater introduced one innovation after another, sometimes more than one in the same play. American playwright Eugene O'Neill (1888–1953) wrote a modern tragedy called *Desire Under the Elms* (1924) in which a dramatic encounter between a son and his stepmother is taking place in an upstairs bedroom, while down below townspeople are doing a folk dance. So as not to detract from the intensity as the scene above nears its climax, the dancers are required to "freeze," though the audience is asked to assume the dancing is continuing. The climax of the scene shows the stepmother murdering the child sired by the stepson. Although the "frozen" dancers are in one sense not there, the still-visible figures serve as an ironic contrast: normal life going about its business even as tragic lovers are committing an atrocity.

NEW (AND OLD) WAYS OF SPEAKING THE SPEECH O'Neill also reinvented the Shakespearean soliloquy in *Strange Interlude* (1928), a 6-hour-long drama that meticulously and tirelessly dissects the complex thoughts of the characters. The play combines naturalistic dialog, a realistic set, and monologues spoken directly to the audience.

Even verse reappeared as playwrights sought ways to reach the heights achieved by the Greeks and Shakespeare. Except in a few instances, modern verse plays were ponderous and pretentious. Maxwell Anderson's *Winterset* (1935), for example, is about the son of an executed immigrant and his love for a girl who lives in a tenement; both speak improbable poetry. The playwright was more successful with historical dramas such as *Elizabeth the Queen* (1930) and *Mary of Scotland* (1933), characters for whom complex poetry was more believable.

That there are many new conventions does not mean that the older ones have been cast aside. Verisimilitude in setting, costumes, and makeup continues to dominate the professional theater. But dialog is evermore naturalistic as writers and actors work to approximate the way people actually do talk. There will always be an element of artificiality, however, since both drama and comedy are intensifications of reality. After all, a play is still a play. It is not real life.

Moments of silence often replace lengthy conversations. Instead of telling each other how they feel, characters are made to be as inarticulate as most of us can be. For one reason or another, there are constraints on expressing our deepest thoughts and emotions, and many of the new writers have become adept at writing dialog that isn't saying what characters are really talking about. British playwright and winner of the Nobel Prize for literature Harold Pinter (1930–2008), is a master of pauses and silences and is frequently baffling to audiences. At his best, however, Pinter is able to turn his characters inside out. His audiences may leave the theater discussing the play and its true theme long after other audiences have forgotten what they saw.

THE STORY IN REVERSE AND IN FLASHBACK Stories can be told in reverse rather than chronological order (as in Harold Pinter's 1978 *Betrayal*, which unravels a love affair from end to beginning). More common is the *flashback*, in which scenes from the past are dramatically enacted rather than merely spoken about as in the well-made play. With the emergence of so many convention options, writers can have a set that resembles a real place but is lacking in just enough realistic detail to permit characters to move back and forth in time. Arthur Miller's *Death of a Salesman* (1949) makes brilliant use of the flashback. We first meet his sons as they are in present time, not having fulfilled the dreams their father had for them. Frequent flashbacks to earlier and happier times make the contrast painful to see, yet necessary for Miller's intent.

Twentieth-Century Naturalism

Chekhov's naturalism influenced many subsequent dramatists, especially in the focus on the tensions that trap people within a family. Two American playwrights who acknowledged this influence were Tennessee Williams (1911–1983) and Eugene O'Neill. Although Williams's plays have a mysticism that removes them from being strictly defined as naturalistic, he probes the psychological depths of their characters, and his dialog is a blend of stark naturalism and poetic prose. O'Neill is more determinedly naturalistic in his challenging depictions of troubled family relationships. And the contemporary American playwright David Mamet (b. 1947) explores the difficult psychological reverberations of both family and workplace interactions.

TENNESSEE WILLIAMS, *THE GLASS MENAGERIE* At the outset of the play that established his reputation, *The Glass Menagerie* (1945), the narrator, Tom, all but apologizes for the artless kind of experience about to unfold. He calls it a "memory play" and admits that in memory things are not seen exactly as they were. His play will consist of relatively few scenes, most of which develop some aspect of family conflict. The work does not unfold as a chronicle of a lifetime crammed with incident, but it does remind us once again that the capacity for sharing the feelings of others is a major gift that great playwrights of today can offer their audience. It also makes us keenly aware that family ties creating obstacles to happiness all but impossible to surmount are the rightful descendants of Chekhovian drama. In the best of such plays there is never a happy, never a clear, conclusion.

The family theme has led to tragedy of a high order that differs in kind, but not emotional intensity, from the plays of Aristotle's time. The intensity that can be achieved from the often bitter confrontation between parents and children or between siblings becomes more profound and moving as the playwright delves further and further into the past, into the darkness that threatens to engulf and bring down the characters involved.

EUGENE O'NEILL, *A LONG DAY'S JOURNEY INTO NIGHT* Admitting that *Long Day's Journey into Night* (1941) was a personal document "born out of an old sorrow," Eugene O'Neill tells the story of a family torn apart by the mother's drug addiction, the father's bitterness over the passing of his glory days as a famous Shakespearean actor, the older brother's alcoholic compensation for his failure to equal his father's success on the stage, and the younger brother's futile efforts to make the family understand he needs treatment for consumption. The play, in fact, is *about* how people who love each other do not and cannot help each other.

Though O'Neill relives his painful youth in the character of the consumptive Edmund Tyrone, he does not make himself the central character. In Chekhovian fashion, each member of the Tyrone family shares that honor. In the fourth act, the mother, upstairs in her bedroom where she retreats from the world in morphine-induced fantasy, is heard walking back and forth. She will eventually surrender to her addiction and totally withdraw from all contact with reality.

Downstairs, the men confront each other in one scene after another of unbearable intensity. The father, a lifelong miser, is now hopelessly drunk and insists Edmund does not need to go into an expensive sanatorium. The older brother, Jamie, comes home, also drunk, having spent all his money on prostitutes, hating himself for his wasted life, confessing how jealous he is of his younger brother's genius and his secret wish that he will fail as a writer. In a powerful speech, he shows us how closely connected are love and hate.

> *Never wanted you to succeed, and make me look worse by comparison.... Always jealous of you. Mama's baby.... And it was you being born that started Mama on dope. I know that's not your fault, but all the same, God damn you, I can't help hating your guts.... But don't get me wrong, kid. I love you more than I hate you ... you're all I got left.*[19]

The play reaches its climax with the mother's sudden appearance, lost in her fantasies now, wearing her yellowed wedding gown believing this is the day of her wedding, her happiest day. The three men look at her with infinite sadness. The curtain falls on the four members of the doomed family in what has been hailed as a work that scales the height of tragic drama, not equaled in its profound effect on audiences since the days of the Greek masters.

DAVID MAMET, *GLENGARRY GLEN ROSS*   David Mamet is a Chicago-born playwright whose idiosyncratic dialog is marked by unusual emphases and pauses, similar to those employed by the British writer Harold Pinter. Mamet's early plays in particular were violent and mysterious. His best known work, *Glengarry Glen Ross*, follows the employees of a disreputable real estate sales group whose main occupation is selling bad deals to unsuspecting—generally poor and uneducated—targets. The agents are prepared to do almost anything—lie, steal—to get hold of the list of "good leads" that they are convinced will get them actual sales. The play calls for virtuoso ensemble acting from a cast where no character is really sympathetic.

The Modern Theater of Ideas

Early on, new playwrights realized that if they wanted to use the theater as a platform for their ideas they could no longer rely on the established traditions of Ibsen and Shaw.

BERTOLT BRECHT   A German playwright who came to prominence in the 1920s, after his disillusioned nation had lost World War I and was drifting into chaos, Bertolt Brecht (1898–1956) had a lot to say to audiences about the socialist system that he believed would stabilize his country. He believed deeply that the theater could be an important instrument of social change. Yet he recognized that audiences have a way of becoming so involved in a story being enacted that they overlook the ideas behind the story. His solution to the problem was **Theater of Alienation** designed to wrap ideas in a sparkling package, often resembling musical comedy, a highly popular genre attracting huge audiences on both sides of the Atlantic. In doing so, he believed he could prevent the viewer from identifying too strongly with the characters, thus missing the point being made. The undisguised unreality of the play would thus "alienate" the audience from the story and allow the playwright's message to be plainly heard.

In *The Caucasian Chalk Circle* (1944), written in America after Brecht had fled a Germany he perceived as cruelly suppressing human rights, he creates a fairy tale about a fabled kingdom in which a servant girl saves and cares for the child of a ruler during an uprising. After the conflict is over, the child's birth mother returns, expecting to be reunited with her offspring. The servant has, however, become to all intents the true mother. To resolve the issue, a wise judge draws a chalk circle on the ground, places the child inside, then informs the onlookers that whichever woman is able to pull the child from the circle will be declared the official mother and granted full custody. Each takes one of the child's arms and begins to tug, causing the child excruciating pain. The servant loves the child too much to continue and allows the other woman to win. The judge surprises everyone by announcing that the loser in this case has the rightful claim and gives the child to her. Legal rules about property and kinship by blood are, he says, less important than the willingness to care for the child.

TOM STOPPARD   We've mentioned the Czech-born British playwright Tom Stoppard several times—as a writer of parody and even farce—but his most lasting theatrical contributions are no doubt to the theater of ideas. The action in what some call his masterpiece, *Arcadia* (1993), includes lengthy (and often funny) discussions that lead to our deeper understanding of the role of time in human life and our inability to be certain of almost anything—all this while also exploring a number of dense questions of mathematics and physics which somehow entertain. We are intentionally confused about the timeframe as the setting moves, sometimes almost imperceptibly, between today and the early nineteenth century. We see both the similarities of the characters in both worlds—and the barrier of understanding between them.

Stoppard's most political play, *Rock 'n' Roll* (2006) follows a young Czech student in England in the days before Czechoslovakia's "velvet revolution," whose opinions clash with those of his mentor, a British professor who continues to believe in Stalinist communism.

CLIFFORD ODETS The playwright as propagandist belongs only nominally to the theater of ideas, but at its most intense, the *agit-prop* (agitation propaganda) play can stir an audience to an emotional frenzy, as happened at the final curtain of Clifford Odets's *Waiting for Lefty* (1935), a play about the plight of underpaid cab drivers in New York. On opening night, as the actors made the crucial decision "Strike!", the audience rose to its feet and echoed the call. Overcome with emotion, they rushed to the stage to embrace the actors.

Racial Themes

A Raisin in the Sun (1959) by Lorraine Hansberry (1930–1965) is a groundbreaking realist play that centers on the traditional theme of a family in conflict. The Youngers, an African-American family in Chicago, receive a large pay-off from a life insurance policy following the death of the family patriarch. The mother wants to buy a house in a previously segregated white neighborhood. Her son Walter wants to invest in a liquor-store scheme proposed by two street-smart friends; her daughter Beneatha wants to use the money, or some of it, for her education. Finally Mama puts a down payment on the house, puts some aside for Beneatha, and gives the rest to Walter—who promptly loses it to his erstwhile friends. Mama has chosen the house in the white neighborhood not from any political aspirations, but because it is cheap, and she maintains her will to buy against pressure from a representative of the neighborhood, who offers her money—which Walter initially wants to accept—not to move into "his" neighborhood. Despite their earlier opposition, the children eventually rally around her strength, and the family moves, ready to stand up to the hostility of their new neighbors.

The themes of *Raisin in the Sun*—family and racial conflict, the pursuit of the American dream (which is what motivates Walter)—continue to resonate: In 2011, *Clybourne Park*, by Chicago playwright Bruce Norris, took up the story of the Younger family after their move into the new, mostly white neighborhood, exploring the consequences of that move 50 years later, when the now all-black neighborhood is beginning to "gentrify," and the family once again faces pressures to move. And *A Raisin in the Sun* itself remains alive and well. In addition to a classic film starring Sidney Poitier and Ruby Dee in 1961, there have been multiple Broadway revivals: in 2004 starring Sean (P. Diddy) Combs (later broadcast on television), and in 2014 starring Denzel Washington, among others. More than half a century later, the play is still one of the most popular with collegiate groups doing African-American theater.

ATHOL FUGARD In 1976, the white South African playwright Athol Fugard (b. 1932), in collaboration with the black South African actors John Kani and Winston Ntshona, wrote *Sizwe Banze Is Dead*, an impassioned play condemning apartheid, the now outlawed segregation of the races. An illiterate man, seeking employment but finding he is unable to use the identity card issued in his own town, is persuaded by a friend to use one found on a dead man. Without a card, he will be sent back to the township restricted to his tribe. In a powerful speech, he demands the right to use his own name ("Am I not a man?"). But his determination to cling to his own identity, a mark of personal dignity, is thwarted. By the end of the play he has been forced to accept the dead man's name. In return he is given a job and a little money to send home to his family. He will survive if he can continue to be deferential to white authorities. Fugard's play stands as a stern reminder of racial prejudice and its destructive effects. The most recent play by Fugard, who has won a Lifetime Achievement Tony Award, is *The Painted Rocks at Revolver Creek* (2015), about the life of a black South African artist.

AUGUST WILSON   A subtle question of identity for African Americans is posed in *Fences* (1987 and revived in 2010), which won the Pulitzer Prize for its author, August Wilson (1945–2005). The ideas in this complex work touch on past and present racial inequities as well as the tangled relationships within a family. Wilson focuses on the psychology of his main character, a former Negro Leagues baseball player denied the opportunity to make real money in the major leagues, who becomes a symbol of the African American lost in a changing society. Every day, he experiences the slights and offenses that come with being an African-American man in 1950s American society. The building of a fence—a project undertaken by the lead character and completed before his death in the final act—represents both a boundary to mark the safe space in which these characters can live comfortably, without interference from the racist external world, and a barrier to hold off death. But the fence is symbolically a barrier between characters as well—between father and son, between husband and wife. The play responds to a question posed by the American sociologist and activist W.E.B. Dubois (1868–1963): How does it feel to be a problem?

Fences is the sixth in Wilson's cycle of ten plays about black life in Pittsburgh, his hometown, which has made him the most widely recognized black American playwright.

Gay Rights

Only in relatively recent times has theater addressed a subject that was once just whispered about. In the past, gay characters were not associated with the issue of rights but were more often given a comic treatment. Or, as in Tennessee Williams's *A Streetcar Named Desire* (1947) and *Cat on a Hot Tin Roof* (1955), homosexuality was made the unnamed source of failed marriages. The statement that homosexuality is tragic because of the suffering inflicted on gays by society had to wait for a more congenial social climate, a time when audiences were willing to confront once-taboo subject matter.

A very early treatment of that theme was found in a 1934 play, *The Children's Hour* by Lillian Hellman (1905–1984), which dealt with a woman's slow realization of her passion for another woman. Audiences accepted the shocking theme, probably because the friend does not feel the same way, and thus the play treats the woman's "condition" as a pathological tragedy. The play makes no plea for acceptance of a homosexual lifestyle; rather, it shows the pernicious effects of scandal as a malicious student deliberately spreads rumors about the women. The gay woman commits suicide, while the heterosexual woman is granted a happy ending in which she marries the man she loves.

More recently, the musical *Fun Home* (2014), based on the graphic novel of the same name by Alison Bechdel (b. 1960), creator of the ground-breaking comic strip *Dykes to Watch Out For*, traces the painful journey of a young lesbian as she confronts both her own sexual identity and the discovery that her father is also gay. *Fun Home* was a finalist for the Pulitzer Prize, received 12 Tony nominations, and won the Tony for Best Musical in 2015.

TONY KUSHNER, *ANGELS IN AMERICA*   Certainly one of the most stirring works to emerge from the newly found freedom of the stage has been *Angels in America: A Gay Fantasia on National Themes* by Tony Kushner (b. 1956), a 7-hour production divided into two plays—*Part One: Millennium Approaches* (1991) and *Part Two: Perestroika* (1992).

The first play was awarded the Pulitzer Prize before it ever opened in New York, and both won Tony Awards for Best Play.

Angels is a significant work of theatrical art for both its epic scope and its dazzling innovations in technique. Adopting a fast-moving, razzmatazz style clearly influenced by the plays of Brecht, popular musical comedy, music videos as well as the pacing of quick-action films, and requiring minimal scenery, the work is ultimately much more than a gay-rights statement. The author touches on gay rights, of course, but also political and religious corruption, the decline of the family, deterioration of the environment, and the need for a true spiritual awakening.

Despite its grim subject matter, the work is not pessimistic. As the title suggests, a miraculous turn of events is on the way, and this is foreshadowed through *Millennium Approaches* by feathers falling from the sky when least expected. At the conclusion of the play, the promised angel finally appears, descending in resplendent fashion, her white wings covering half the stage, and declares, "The great work begins." It is the angel's only line, but it is one of the most powerful moments in modern theatrical history.

Understanding the Experience: Beckett's *Waiting for Godot*

Sometimes plays in a totally unfamiliar style, such as *Angels in America*, lead to challenges for audiences and critics both. Although *Angels* was immediately and widely admired, there are examples in theater history of initial misinterpretation that led to disastrous openings. Stanislavsky's first production of Chekhov's *The Sea Gull* is one. Another is the 1956 American première of Samuel Beckett's *Waiting for Godot*. The play was advertised as "the laugh sensation of two continents" and starred two actors known for their comic roles in popular films: Tom Ewell of *The Seven-Year Itch* and Bert Lahr, the Cowardly Lion of *The Wizard of Oz*. Audiences and critics expected an evening of laughs. *Waiting For Godot*, since hailed by many as the greatest play of the twentieth century, bewildered the Miami critics and the opening night audience that clearly had never witnessed a play in which nothing ostensibly happens.

The play deals with two tramps in a park; they do not enjoy being there but for some reason they cannot leave until they have seen a mysterious man named Godot. After the successful second American production, one critic observed that the play was about "the anguish of waiting," but actually it is the thing itself. They wait. Nothing really happens. One decides to hang himself, but all he can use is the rope that holds his trousers up. When he removes the rope, the trousers fall. The bit was common in vaudeville many years before, but in this play it is poignant, not funny. They decide that perhaps they can hang themselves tomorrow. And perhaps Godot will come tomorrow. And perhaps, if they finally get to meet Godot, they will understand why they have been waiting. Or perhaps not. Or perhaps they ought to leave right now. The final stage direction is: *They do not move.*

As its critical reputation grew, the work was and continues to be revived and always serves as the topic for post-performance conversation and, sometimes, heated debate. It is studied in college courses. Scenes are popular in performing arts schools. The difference between *Godot* and other plays that have bewildered audiences is that the former is filled with possible meanings; and probing for meaning is part of its aesthetic appeal. In fact, the search for meaning can also be said to be the play's true theme. Does life in fact make any sense? And what do we do if it does *not* make sense? Like the tramps, who have only each other, maybe we are all abandoned in the park that is our world, hoping that somewhere there is someone named Godot.

This introduction to one of the world's most enduring art forms may encourage you to seek the pleasure of watching drama wherever it is found. Broadway is not the only place to look. Schools and colleges revive classic works, present new plays, and compensate for their limited budgets with innovative approaches. Many important theatrical productions, including the ground-breaking *Angels in America*, have been recorded on DVDs and shown on television. These media now offer a library of nearly all the modes and genres of theater discussed in this chapter, from tragedy and comedy to naturalism, the Theater of Ideas, and **avant-garde** masterpieces like *Waiting for Godot*. You can readily become a critical viewer if you choose.

A Critical Focus: Exploring a Scene from Arthur Miller's *Death of a Salesman*

First produced in 1949, Arthur Miller's *Death of a Salesman* won the Pulitzer Prize that year and launched Miller's career as the premiere American playwright. The play centers on Willy Loman, a salesman with aspirations of grandeur. Set while Willy is in his early 60s, the play frequently shifts through time with Willy to show scenes from his past. Slipping in and out of these daydreams, Willy's grasp on reality is tentative from the first scene and degrades throughout the play. Through his flashbacks, we see that Willy has long related the idea of success in the business world with popularity and has always forced his aspirations onto his sons, but mostly onto his oldest, Biff, who was a popular football player in high school.

The climax of the play occurs in a series of confrontations between Biff and his father. Having discovered Willy in an extramarital affair, Biff had become disillusioned with his father's idea of success at an early age. With time, his annoyance and frustration with his father's habit of incessantly (and falsely) boasting of Biff's successes grows. Biff and Happy meet their father for dinner, and while Biff is trying to gently explain the reality of his failures in the business world, Willy interrupts to inform them he has been fired. In reaction, Happy, who takes after his father and has always been more eager to play along with Willy's delusions, tries to comfort Willy with promises of Biff's success. Back at home, the confrontation re-erupts, ending with Biff in tears and Willy driving away to commit suicide convinced that with the $20,000 insurance payoff, Biff will finally achieve the success he is destined for. Below are a few lines from the final scene of the play, Willy's funeral.

CHARLEY: *(stopping Happy's movement and reply. To Biff.)*: Nobody dast blame this man. You don't understand: Willy was a salesman. And for a salesman, there is no rock bottom to the life. He don't put a bolt to a nut, he don't tell you the law or give you medicine. He's a man out there in the blue, riding on a smile and a shoeshine. And when they start not smiling back—that's an earthquake. And then you get yourself a couple of spots on your hat, and you're finished. Nobody dast blame this man. A salesman is got to dream, boy. It comes with the territory.

Figure 7.13 Dustin Hoffman as Willy Loman, with Steven Lang and John Malkovich as his sons, in a 1984 production of *Death of a Salesman*.
Everett Collection

BIFF:	Charley, the man didn't know who he was.
HAPPY:	*(infuriated)*: Don't say that!
BIFF:	Why don't you come with me, Happy?
HAPPY:	I'm not licked that easily. I'm staying right in this city, and I'm gonna beat this racket! [*He looks at Biff, his chin set.*] The Loman Brothers!
BIFF:	I know who I am, kid.

- Why do you think Happy is so angry with Biff?
- Do you consider Willy a tragic character? What is his tragic flaw? How does it lead to his downfall?
- How does *Death of a Salesman* fit the traditional definition of a tragedy? Compare *Death of a Salesman* to the traditional tragedies described in this chapter. How does *Death of a Salesman* expand the definition of tragedy?
- *Death of a Salesman* has often been described as a commentary on the American dream. What do you think Miller is trying to say? Do you agree? Why or why not?

Looking Back

In this chapter,

- we compared classical Greek tragedy with Elizabethan or Shakespearean tragedy and discovered both similarities and differences,
- we discussed the various genres of theatrical comedy,
- we explored the roots of modern theater in the nineteenth century, as proscenium stages became the rule

and psychological themes became more and more important, and

- we summarized the major movements in twentieth- and twenty-first-century theater.

Key Terms

aside Popular in Elizabethan drama, a remark made by an actor to the audience that other actors on the stage do not hear.

avant-garde French word meaning "vanguard" or "advance guard." In the arts, a movement constantly striving to break with convention and experiment with new forms. Used here to discuss theater, but also applicable to art, music, and literature.

catharsis According to Aristotle, the purging of pity and fear through our emotional responses to a tragedy.

Chorus In Greek tragedy, a group of masked actors who sing and dance as well as comment on the moral implications of the play; can be found in much contemporary theater in different forms and with different functions.

comedy One of two major genres to grow out of Greek theater. Originally, it was a short piece that followed a trilogy of tragic plays, the purpose of which was to lighten the mood of the audience. Now, any theater work with the primary intent of promoting laughter. Farce,

satire, parody, and comedy of character are forms of comic theater.

commedia dell'arte Professional acting and pantomime troupe that performed in Italian streets beginning in the Renaissance; famous for its stock repertoire of comic types, such as the doddering old man who pursues a beautiful young girl.

conventions Rules governing a given style of theater, such as fourth-wall verisimilitude or bare stage. These rules should not be violated, but often are, as when actors "break" the fourth wall by delivering a line directly toward the audience.

deus ex machina In Greek theater, an actor impersonating a god who descends to the stage on wires and resolves the action to the audience's satisfaction. Now, a contrived ending tacked onto a play (or story), intended to create a happy—or at least satisfying—ending.

exposition Dialog in a play that gives the background of the story and the relevant past history of the characters; problematic in the theater of verisimilitude, in which characters are supposed to talk as people do in real life—that is, without statements such as "As you know, dear, we have been married for 25 years."

Expressionism Form of avant-garde drama introduced by German theaters during the 1920s, in which characters and sets are symbolic. Best example of American Expressionism is the play *The Adding Machine*, with a giant calculator for a set and a central character named Mr. Zero.

farce Genre of comedy involving the actions of two-dimensional stock characters, improbable situations, much slapstick, and improbable resolutions of plot complexities.

groundlings Relatively poor people who loved theater in Elizabethan times and paid a penny for the privilege of standing on ground level to watch the plays; they were vulnerable when the weather was inclement.

hubris Greek term meaning "arrogance"—the common tragic flaw of Greek tragic protagonists.

image Poetic technique, used to great effect by Shakespeare, in which something that would otherwise need many words of explanation is communicated swiftly by being called something else that is easily understood and is usually visual as well.

melodrama Form of theater that resembles but is not legitimate tragedy dealing with a conflict between two-dimensional characters, often the very good and the very bad.

naturalism Technique of acting and writing based on the imitation of people as they actually are and talk in real life; naturalistic plays, like those of Chekhov, very often do not have well-structured plots, on the grounds that real life does not structure what happens.

neoclassicism A style of theater (as well as art, music, and architecture) which reinvents the pure geometric formalism that characterizes early Greece and Rome; abundant in the seventeenth century.

parody Exaggeratedly funny imitation of a person (usually a public figure or celebrity) or work of theater or literature that, according to the parodist, deserves ridicule; often it masks serious criticism.

proscenium In modern theaters, the front of the stage, usually framed and sometimes containing a curtain that can be raised and lowered, or drawn.

protagonist Central character in a drama (or literary work), the person in terms of whose fortune we view and respond to the action; not to be confused with "hero," who is generally someone without flaws, who triumphs over bad people.

recognition scene In tragic drama, especially that of the Greeks and Shakespeare, when the doomed protagonist understands that he or she is responsible for the disaster; often lacking in modern tragedy.

satire Genre of comedy that ridicules such things as war, political corruption, and religious hypocrisy. Tends to be less wildly exaggerated than parody.

scanning Reading a line of verse and exaggerating the rhythm so as to determine whether it underlies, without intruding upon, the words. Scanning helps us better appreciate a writer's skill when we see that a strict rhythmic pattern is maintained while the speaker or actor is also free to explore the emotions within the verse.

soliloquy Theatrical convention of Elizabethan drama in which an actor, alone on stage, voices private thoughts.

Theater of Alienation Dramatic genre associated with the work of Bertolt Brecht; its intention is to highlight the artificiality of the theater so as to prevent the audience from becoming too emotionally involved in the story and the characters and instead concentrate on the play's ideas.

tragedy One of the two major forms of drama focusing on the downfall of a protagonist due to a serious character flaw. In Greek and Shakespearean tragic drama, the protagonist is a high-ranking noble person, but not so in modern tragedy.

unities Convention of classical and neoclassical theater requiring the playwright to set the action in one place, have it occur during the time the audience is actually sitting in the theater, and limit the action to one central plot.

verisimilitude Technique of making scenery and dialog look and sound like real life; developed during the latter part of the nineteenth century but still dominant in today's theater.

well-made play Developed in the nineteenth century and using verisimilitude in scenery and dialog, but the tight, carefully crafted plot structure does not resemble the flow of real life.

Chapter 8
The Musical Stage: Opera, Musical Theater, Dance

 Learning Objectives

8.1 Trace the origins of opera and explain why the works of Mozart, Verdi, and Wagner are considered to comprise the "golden age" of this musical form.

8.2 Describe the role of operetta and "sung-through" plays in bridging opera and the musical theater.

8.3 Discuss the evolution of the Broadway musical from the "musical comedy" to the more common musical spectacular of today.

8.4 Analyze the differences between ballet and modern dance.

Figure 8.1 Kristin Chenoweth and Idina Menzel (costumed for their roles in *Wicked*) at the 2003 Tony Awards ceremony. *Wicked* explores the early friendship between Glinda and the Wicked Witch, before Dorothy's arrival in Oz, and includes themes of discrimination, bullying, and the right to be different. Why do you think *Wicked* has been such a success in the 21st century? Jeff Christensen/Reuters/Corbis

Theater and music have always been closely associated. It is hard to say if one came before the other, or if they were inseparable from the start. Essentially, musical theater history extends back to the rituals and ceremonies of very early cultures, which combined some form of dance and some kind of rhythmic accompaniment.

Cultural anthropologists have dated musical rituals as far back as 30,000 BCE. Cave paintings show human figures engaged in symbolic reenactments of the hunt, and there is ample evidence of the Dionysian festivals in early Greece that combined music, song, and dance. In *The Republic*, Plato approved of music that aroused national spirit but did not exist solely to stir emotion. We suspect that the dancing in the Dionysian rites not only stirred emotion but perhaps even drove spectators into a frenzy (an ancient version of the rock concert!).

The time of Shakespeare—late sixteenth to early seventeenth centuries—represents the Golden Age of English theater. If the bard did not write actual musicals, he certainly wrote many plays *with* music. Romeo and Juliet meet at a party in which there is masked dancing to an ensemble of musical instruments. At the beginning of the memorable final scene in *Othello*, Desdemona, the wife Othello suspects of adultery and will soon murder, has a premonition of impending doom while her maid is brushing her hair and expresses it in the haunting and melancholy *Willow Song*, for which both lyrics and music survive. In Verdi's opera version of the play, the scene is highlighted by the magnificent *Ave Maria*. In both scenes, music enhances the dramatic impact.

In Shakespeare's comedies, mirth and song as well as dance abound. *Twelfth Night*, in particular, named for the joyous celebration that marked the end of the Christmas season, comes close to being a musical play. The songs have been printed and reprinted thousands of times and are in the repertoire of both folk singers and opera stars. *A Midsummer Night's Dream* is frequently performed almost like a ballet, enhanced by the incidental music composed for the play by Felix Mendelssohn. Without music in the productions, Shakespeare's theater would be greatly diminished, though the poetry of the plays, when spoken by the best of actors, can be called unaccompanied music.

In 2015, a wildly ingenious musical called *Something Rotten!* opened on Broadway to widespread acclaim. It tells the story of two brothers, mediocre playwrights and contemporaries of Shakespeare, whose frantic efforts to find an innovation that will compete with Shakespeare's runaway success lead eventually to the creation of the very first musical!

Opera

8.1 *How did opera originate? Why are the works of Mozart, Verdi, and Wagner considered to comprise the "golden age" of this musical form?*

Audiences must have clamored for more and more music in theater. By the late seventeenth century, **opera** was already developing throughout Italy; during the eighteenth century, Italian opera became one of the world's premier art forms, and composers of other nationalities were forced to compose their operas in Italian if they hoped to get produced. An Austrian-born composer—Wolfgang Amadeus Mozart—would carry the genre to new heights that many believe have never been equaled, but many important composers paved the way for him.

The word *opera* is the Latin plural of *opus* ("work"), a label applied during the Renaissance to what was then a new musical art form combining the work of a playwright (librettist), a composer, an orchestra, singers, and dancers. The birth of opera was an inevitable byproduct of the Renaissance rediscovery of classical literature and art and the desire to create works that were elegant and noble enough to rival their ancient predecessors. Opera fitted nicely into the new striving.

Renaissance Opera

Renaissance music gloried in the invention of new instruments, making possible new sounds, and in the harmonies of different vocal lines played or sung at the same time. Opera arose as an attempt to re-create the emotional and cathartic power of ancient Greek drama; Italian musicians, artists, and poets suspected that the missing, magical ingredient might be music. But a problem quickly arose: How to reconcile the abundant use of music with the need to move a dramatic plot forward. Events in a play, unlike melodic lines, do not repeat themselves; and characters change as they are affected by experience. It seemed only logical, then, that the music in these sung dramas should keep changing as well.

The problem of melodic repetition versus dramatic change is still with us and may explain why the most popular operas are those with strong, memorable songs (*arias*) and duets—that is, melodic lines that recur. In Georges Bizet's opera *Carmen*, for example, tragic fate is represented by a particular theme (or recurring melody) that is heard again and again, always announcing disaster, which tends to elevate the drama.

CLAUDIO MONTEVERDI, *ORFEO*   The opera of the seventeenth century found a way to move the story forward while keeping the audience interested in the music. Claudio Monteverdi pioneered the development of the continuous musical line interrupted at regular intervals by a memorable aria. One of his great achievements was balancing solo songs, duets, and choruses—the more musically satisfying moments—with sections of **recitative**—speech-like singing that has little in the way of rhythm or melody but keeps the plot moving. His breakthrough work, *La favola d'Orfeo* ("The Fable of Orpheus"), appeared in 1607, seven years later than Jacopo Peri's *Eurydice*, which was based on the same tale and is credited with being the world's first opera.

In the legend, whenever Orpheus played his lyre, all those who heard him were struck dumb with wonder. Humans and animals alike would weep with joy at the sound. Even inanimate objects—rocks, trees—delighted in the music. Orpheus, the archetypal poet-musician, became the very symbol of glorious sound, a perfect union of words and music. How appropriate that his story would become the basis for the first major opera!

Orpheus falls in love and marries Eurydice, who dies in the flower of youth and is transported down into the underworld. Her abandoned lover plays such heartbreaking music on his lyre that Pluto, the god of the underworld, is moved to tears and promises to allow Orpheus to reclaim his wife and return to earth with her—on one condition: Eurydice will follow behind him, and he must never turn around to see whether she is there. If he does, she will be lost to him forever. Midway through the journey, Orpheus, unable to bear the strain of not knowing, disobeys the order and looks back. True to his word, Pluto reclaims Eurydice.

Monteverdi's opera, however, provides a happy ending to the myth. Eurydice is not lost. Apollo descends from heaven in response to Orpheus's grief and promises that husband and wife will eventually be reunited and live forever, for music cannot die.

Although Monteverdi used relatively few recurrent themes in his operas, later composers would employ repetition to heighten music's capacity for storytelling, using the music to represent specific characters, ideas, or places. This form of repetition would be made famous by Richard Wagner, who called a recurring musical idea a **leit-motif** (or "leading theme"). The *leit-motif* gives audiences melodic lines to remember and to recognize with pleasure when they hear them again; but, since the theme is tied to character, and character changes with events, the theme can be both recognizable and somewhat altered on each recurrence.

Classical and Baroque Opera

By the eighteenth century, European writers, artists, and composers started turning away from the robustness of the Renaissance and the decorative splendors of the Baroque period seen in its church architecture and heard in the complex harmonies and counterpoint of its music. European society settled into a time of polite behavior, elegance of dress, and the belief that excessive displays of emotion were rather vulgar and uncouth.

The Baroque musical style of Monteverdi's *Orfeo* both developed the drama of his characters and strove to maintain a solid musical structure. Other Baroque composers—notably Bach—displayed both Dionysian excitement and Apollonian structure. Early eighteenth-century opera, however, is on the whole marked by greater restraint and can properly be labeled *classical*.

GLUCK, *ORFEO ED EURIDICE*   A prime example of this classicism is found in yet another version of the Orpheus myth. In *Orfeo ed Euridice* (1762) by German composer Christoph Gluck (1714–1787), when Eurydice dies and is taken to the underworld, Orpheus is understandably grief-stricken; and what could be more appropriate for an operatic aria than the sorrow of a young man robbed of his only love? His aria beginning "So I mourn her death" contains one of opera's most unforgettable melodies, but it is precise and carefully rhythmic, allowing little room for tears or heart-rending emotion. In fact, it could almost be played without words as an aristocratic minuet. Yet the lyrics express the hero's broken heart.

There is still some Baroque complexity in the furious rhythms of the ballet danced by a chorus of furies (who were mythological demons, tormenting unworthy residents of the underworld). This is, however, immediately contrasted with the placid "Dance of the Blessed Spirits" and, later, with arias gently titled "These Meadows Are a Place of Blissful Peace" and "What a Clear Sky Decks This Place." The latter two arias represent a musical description that suggests the Christian concept of heaven, suited to the music of classical restraint.

The Golden Age of Opera: Mozart, Verdi, and Wagner

The eighteenth and nineteenth centuries saw a flowering of opera that most scholars and critics agree has not been matched before or since. Artists such as Handel, Gluck, Rossini, and Donizetti all contributed masterworks to the operatic repertoire, but three giants emerged: the Austrian Mozart, the Italian Verdi, and the German Wagner.

WOLFGANG AMADEUS MOZART   In the opinion of many, the art of opera was fully developed—and remains unsurpassed—in the work of Wolfgang Amadeus Mozart (1756–1791). Mozart (Figure 8.2) is considered by many to be the most naturally gifted composer who ever lived. In his operas, as well as in his many other astonishing achievements, Mozart represents a major transition from the classical to the *Romantic* style—an extremely melodic style that employed greatly expanded orchestrations and musical forms lengthened to accommodate the expressions of emotion. Yet Mozart's early training was thoroughly classical, modeled on the work of the greatest pure classicist of German music—Franz Joseph Haydn (1732–1809); and so we should

Figure 8.2 Wolfgang Amadeus Mozart.
Mozart died when he was only 35. We can only imagine what his musical legacy would have been had he lived a longer life.
Photos 12/Hachedé/Alamy

expect Mozart operas to display a blending of graceful, symmetrical arias and interludes as well as swelling, romantic sounds.

By the time this prodigy reached the age of four and his creative drives were already pushing him forward, opera had taken its place among Europe's premier arts. The great Italian opera centers—Rome, Florence, Venice, Milan, Bologna—beckoned wealthy tourists and aspiring composers. At the same time, other cities—London, Paris, and Vienna among them—were developing their own singers and orchestras; other composers of opera were eager to be heard, though Italian remained the dominant language.

Mozart was born in Salzburg, a city that boasted not only an opera house but a great musical environment in general. His father was an accomplished musician who quickly recognized his son's prodigious talents. By the time he was 13, Mozart had become concertmaster for the archbishop of Salzburg and been decorated in Milan by the pope himself. Having been a truly *serious* composer from the age of 6, when he wrote five pieces for the piano, he was probably not surprised that he was asked to write an opera for the Milanese audiences at the advanced age of 14. Before his 16th birthday, he had not only composed but directed *Mithridates, King of Pontus*. For the next nine years, however, he lacked the continuous patronage of a wealthy aristocrat, and he struggled for financial security. Despite this struggle, he gave the world what is arguably the most astonishing outpouring of great music ever received from one human being in so brief a time.

Opera intrigued him—the challenge of combining so many elements into one unified work. He mastered the complexities of orchestration and developed a distinctive style that was at once personal and characteristic of his cultural heritage. His first major opera, *Idomeneo* (1781), with an Italian text, was followed by *The Abduction from the Seraglio* (1782), a delightfully complicated comic opera that has become famous not only for its lilting and graceful music, but also because of two unique elements.

First, *The Abduction from the Seraglio* abandoned the Italian convention of alternating arias and duets with recitative, or sung dialog. Instead, Mozart drew on a particularly German form of opera called the **singspiel**. In place of recitatives, the singer-actors simply spoke their dialog, without music (much like the traditional musical comedy would several centuries later). Second, boldly—and shockingly to opera-goers of the time—the **libretto** or text of the opera (Italian for "little book") was in German rather than in the standard Italian expected by the aristocratic Viennese audience for whom Mozart was composing. Opera in German—at least for the wealthy—was revolutionary in 1782.

In 1786, Mozart met a clergyman named Lorenzo da Ponte, who was also a poet and dramatist. The collaboration resulted in three acknowledged masterpieces—*The Marriage of Figaro* (1786), *Don Giovanni* (1787), and *Così fan tutte* ("Thus Do They All," or sometimes, translated loosely, "Women Are Like That," 1790). Together, Mozart and da Ponte produced three of the greatest operatic works of all time—in only four years!

Mozart: "Dove Sono," *The Marriage of Figaro*

MOZART, *THE MARRIAGE OF FIGARO* Of all the Mozart operas, *Figaro* has arguably become the most popular with international audiences. But the work was coolly received in Vienna and found success only in Prague. Why did this masterpiece go unappreciated in Mozart's home country? There are several possible explanations.

One is that while the opera was sung in the acceptable Italian, the composer was nevertheless Austrian by birth. The official composer on the emperor's court was an Italian, Antonio Salieri. Although legend suggests that Salieri was obsessively envious of Mozart and may even have poisoned him, the facts appear to tell a different story. Salieri had no reason to wish Mozart dead. In fact, he was far better known and more widely respected, in high music circles, than Mozart. Vienna, it seems, preferred a *real* Italian to a local boy who was simply "borrowing" the language of opera.

In addition, it was probably a mistake to hold the première of *Figaro* in Vienna. The story—how two lowly servants outwit the aristocratic master of the house— could not have pleased much of the upper-class, indeed aristocratic, audience. The composer, an upstart from a little town of no consequence (at the time), already had a reputation for being a nonconformist. And indeed, Mozart was just that. Nonetheless, as often happens in the history of the humanities, the future was on Mozart's side.

The glorious arias in *Figaro* have made it one of the world's favorite operas. In it, Mozart has idealized human interaction. If Shakespeare's characters can talk to each other in verse, Mozart's characters can talk to each other in music. All theater, whether musical or not, depends upon a contract—the acknowledgment of conven- tions—between performers and audience. "We are going to do this and this," say the performers; and the audience replies, "We will believe you as long as you do it consistently." In a Mozart opera, characters sing the dialog between arias and duets throughout the opera.

For his libretto, da Ponte adapted a French farce concerning a Count who has grown tired of his wife and seeks fresh young conquests. According to custom, the Count has *le droit du seigneur*—the privilege of the master to bed his servant girl on her wedding night, before the groom may do so. The young bride-to-be is a beautiful girl engaged to marry Figaro, another servant. The Countess, weary of her husband's philandering, helps the unhappy pair outwit the *seigneur*, who denounces his profli- gate ways in time for a rousing and joyous finale.

Many elements justify the prominence now enjoyed by this opera in the standard repertoire. First, there is the genius of da Ponte, who, while retaining a lot of the farci- cal nonsense from the original, transforms the Countess into a character of depth: a lonely wife longing for the love she and her husband had once shared. In the tradi- tion of farce, the wife of a cheating husband was usually a nagging shrew, and the philandering husband a charming rogue. Da Ponte gives the Countess almost tragic dimensions, and, even though the aristocratic opening-night audience did not shout its approval, there must surely have been among them many women who understood the Countess's sadness.

The libretto with its unprecedented mixture of lively farce (the tricks played on the Count) and its unhappy Countess and its parallel plots of happy lovers and a trou- bled marriage gave the young Mozart a chance to reach into his amazing bag of musi- cal resources and put together a glorious score. What matter even long stretches of *recitative* when these are always followed by arias so beautiful that the listener *needs* some breathing space? Many operas contain two or three famous arias for which the audience patiently waits. In *Figaro*, the magic never stops.

For the Countess, a role to which dramatic sopranos aspire, Mozart wrote two of the greatest arias in the history of opera. In the first, *"Porgi, amor,"* she asks Love itself, which had once filled her life with joy, one final favor: restore her husband's affections or help her to find peace in death. In the second, *"Dove sono,"* she asks a question that people have been asking for centuries: Where have the golden moments fled? Why are happiness and love and youth gone before we know it? Why can't they last?

Many critics hail the final act of *Figaro* as the very summit of opera. The French play on which the libretto is based concludes with a farcical scene involving disguise, mistaken identity, hiding behind bushes, and so on, a scene that da Ponte copies faithfully. At first, everything seems rushed, as if the artists can't wait to ring down the curtain on happy people in a rousing finale. But then comes a moment when the injured wife forgives her husband. Da Ponte's libretto stays true to the spirit of farce, but Mozart's music transcends it. The philandering husband falls to his knees and simply sings "I ask for your pardon," to which the Countess replies "I consent." However contrived this ending may sound, the music makes it thrilling.

Mozart turns the moment into a soaring musical passage, an almost divine act of forgiveness from the soul of a woman who has been neglected but has never lost her love and understanding. The stirring melody is then repeated by full chorus with the voice of the Countess heard above all the others, reaching ever higher and higher. The moment suddenly has attained all the majesty of a solemn requiem sung in an enormous cathedral, filled at last with the joy of redemption.

In the 1984 film version of Peter Shaffer's play *Amadeus*, we watch Salieri, who is portrayed as obsessed by his jealousy of Mozart, as he watches the final act of *Figaro*. He listens to the countess sing her forgiveness, his eyes fill with tears, and a voice inside him acknowledges that if God could sing, He would produce music like this.

GIUSEPPE VERDI   Though portions of Mozart's operas have the grace and balance of the classical style, most of the arias and duets, in keeping with the emerging Romantic spirit, allow for a freer expression of emotion. The Romantic movement—political, artistic, literary, and musical—protested against restraint: political and social restrictions on human behavior, as well as Apollonian restrictions preventing poets, playwrights, and composers from being carried away emotionally. While French opera tended to be faithful to its classical roots, Italian and German opera embraced the new emotional freedom that Mozart had already shown.

The works of Giuseppe Verdi (1813–1901) offer major examples of the Romantic style. They are filled with glorious, melodious arias and rely less on sung dialog. Two of his operas—*Rigoletto* (1851) and *La traviata* (1853)—continue to rank among the world's favorites. They enjoyed international success almost at once. Without their music, Verdi's operas would have to be termed melodramas, with plots that overflow with scenes of heartbreak and self-pity. Yet when these moments are combined with soaringly beautiful melodic lines, audiences are transported into a realm that only great art provides.

Rigoletto (Figure 8.3), like Mozart's *Figaro*, contains so many familiar arias that audiences feel toward it as they would to a dear friend. The plot is typical of nineteenth-century melodrama. A court jester's daughter is seduced by her father's master. The angry father, hungry for revenge, plots to have the man killed. The daughter overhears that someone is to be murdered and deliberately walks into the trap, sacrificing her own life. The opera ends with the grieving father holding his dead daughter and singing one of Verdi's many glorious arias.

Figure 8.3 Verdi's *Rigoletto* in a 2014 Metropolitan Opera production set in Las Vegas.
Do you think this plot about revenge and corruption is a good fit for this new setting?

Mary Altaffer/AP Images

VERDI, *LA TRAVIATA*   Verdi insisted upon plots that would allow free reign to his genius for combining emotion and melody. In *La traviata* (literally, "the fallen woman") he found a perfect vehicle, a work that transcended period melodrama and could stand alone as a tragic play. Add to it the glorious music, and you have Verdi's masterpiece.

Based on a famous French literary success, *La dame aux Camélias* ("The Lady of the Camelias"), *La traviata* is the story of a courtesan named Violetta, a woman living in luxury provided by wealthy male companions. Her beauty attracts a handsome young man named Alfredo.

Although she struggles against falling in love and insists on living a free life (expressed in the aria "*Sempre libera*"—"Always free"), the suitor overcomes her objections, and they begin living together in the country.

Alfredo's father visits the courtesan and begs her to renounce his son, whose affair will, he fears, damage the family's reputation and prevent his son from marrying eventually into a respectable family. Violetta tearfully agrees to leave her lover; she writes him a note telling him that she is leaving him to return to her previous life in Paris.

In the final scene, Alfredo finds Violetta, intending to vow his everlasting love, but he discovers his beloved dying of consumption—a turn of events that allows Verdi to write some of the richest and most memorable music in all of opera. Violetta is another of the great roles for dramatic sopranos, not only because of the demanding score, but also because of the complex dramatic characterization of the heroine. In a sense, Violetta has sacrificed herself for her lover, a melodramatic convention—but in contrast to the daughter's sacrifice in *Rigoletto*, hers is motivated by real passion, an outgrowth of real character.

RICHARD WAGNER   Romanticism also fostered nationalism, especially among countries that had not yet found a prominent place in the world. Nineteenth-century-Germany was experiencing the initial excitement of world recognition. Beethoven, Mendelssohn, Brahms, and others had brought German music to the highest level. A showdown on the opera front between Germany and Italy was almost inevitable.

Mozart had written operas in German, including one—*The Magic Flute*—that is an unqualified masterpiece. Still, his Italian-language operas were better known and more successful. It was left to Richard Wagner (1813–1883)—born, coincidentally, the same year as Verdi—to lead the charge for German opera.

Wagner's works are enormous, epic, heroic, often noble and inspiring. Wagner (Figure 8.4) made the German language as powerful on the stage as Italian, and his masterpiece, *The Ring of the Nibelung*, is based on stories from Germanic mythology, which was until that time virtually unknown in the rest of the world. *The Ring*, consisting of four huge operas, made Germans proud that the world was now aware of a mythological heritage to rival that of the Greeks and the Romans.

Wagner went one step further than either Homer or Virgil. He added monumental symphonic music demanding full orchestral accompaniment and singers of extraordinary vocal power. To this day, the label "Wagnerian singer," and especially "Wagnerian soprano," carries prestige and critical respect, as well as the expectation that the voice will be powerful, large, and rich. Wagner added powerful dramatic confrontations and scenic effects, justifying his restoration of the label ***music-drama***. He made memorable use of the *leit-motif*, giving all of the major characters—as well as important objects and places—musical themes that were heard when they appeared or, in variations, that were included in their arias or in the symphonic introductions to scenes. The Wagnerian *leit-motifs*, running throughout the four operas, lend a unity to what might otherwise have been a sprawling, even chaotic, musical narrative.

In addition to being a composer, Wagner was a political radical, very much involved with various revolutionary ideologies sweeping Germany in the mid-nineteenth century. He took part in rallies and protest marches and translated into music his ideals of liberation. In *The Ring* cycle, the all-powerful gods—tyrants—are destroyed in the final act.

Wagner wanted to liberate opera from both its classical restraints and its Italian melodrama. He wanted to create true music-drama that could legitimately take its place beside the great works of Sophocles and Shakespeare.

Figure 8.4 Richard Wagner.
Wagner's music has been associated with German nationalism and Nazism. Should art be judged solely on aesthetic grounds, or should we also consider political context?
Library of Congress

He wanted characters that were larger than life: characters that were heroic and noble and met tragic destinies with courage and honor. An opera historian writes: "Wagner's essential standpoint was that opera should not be mere entertainment, but (and he drew on Greek tragedy to support this) a fundamentally educative and ennobling experience."[1]

Wagner believed Italian opera had made an aesthetic mistake in subordinating the drama to the music, beautiful as it might be. He wanted to reverse course and elevate drama to the position of dominance; otherwise, audiences would simply be there for a concert, not for the overwhelming emotional experience that he knew opera was capable of providing. In order to do this, Wagner realized that the composer must also write the libretto, ensuring that the creation would be a unified whole.

The composer turned first to the heroic figures of world mythology, to stories he thought worthy of his enormous talent. (Wagner was never modest about his genius.) As he was composing his first major opera, *The Flying Dutchman* (1843), he realized he was facing the same problem that both his classical predecessors and his Italian contemporaries had encountered: how to provide beautiful music and keep the flowing dramatic line from becoming uninteresting. In *Tannhäuser* (1845) and *Lohengrin* (1850), he found his answer. If the dramatic line were to be the dominating factor, the music that sustained it could never be less than glorious. He felt there was no choice but to conceive of an opera as a giant symphony, written for a full orchestra and singers with the vocal power to be heard soaring above the music. Orchestra and singers were to form a unity never before known.

WAGNER, *THE RING CYCLE* *Tannhäuser* and *Lohengrin* drew on Christian and Arthurian legends. Now the time had come to base an opera on Teutonic mythology, which bore a close kinship with the old Norse stories of gods and mortal heroes. In Norse tales, the king of the gods is Odin; in German, Wotan. The hero of *The Ring* cycle is Siegfried, who appears in the Norse sagas as Sigurd. Wagner took the old myths and turned them into an epic tale about the downfall of those who struggle for the power that a magic ring bestows upon the wearer. In true Romantic fashion, it is love that is ultimately greater than the lust for power.

The Nibelung are a race of elves, or dwarfs, who control a huge store of treasure, including a wondrous ring that has the power to make the wearer the supreme ruler of the universe—as long as he remains chaste. Wotan, wanting no one to be his superior, steals the ring, but the dwarf Alberich, who had forged the ring, places a curse on it that only the appearance of genuine love will lift. Disaster after disaster occurs as people destroy each other in the struggle for the power the ring holds, and Alberich remains confident that the horrors will never end, because true love will never emerge.

The four-opera cycle reaches a stirring climax when Wotan's daughter Brünnhilde, who loves the young Siegfried, rides her horse into the blazing funeral pyre on which the body of her beloved is being burned. The spectacular fire that results consumes Valhalla, the palace of the gods, who are destroyed along with Brünnhilde. Finally, the Rhine River overflows its banks to quench the flames, and the marathon cycle of operas comes to a magnificent close with a lyrical melody that represents the return of love to the world and the end of inhuman power.

The mythology of a magic ring is not limited to Norse and Germanic sagas or to Wagner's telling of the story. The fable of the ring of Gyges is originally found in Plato's *Republic*, and *that* ring also bestowed magical powers upon the wearer, who could, in this fable, become invisible at will, causing no end of damage. Many of us will think, of course, of the modern version of the story, Oxford professor J.R.R. Tolkien's *The Lord of the Rings* trilogy, which was made into three epic films. In Tolkien, the magic ring, like the one found by Plato's Gyges, allows its wearer to become invisible, and thus to rise above all human law. In Plato, Wagner, and Tolkien, the message is the same: Power corrupts, and only selfless love can save the world.

Wagner's achievements illustrate an interesting facet of the humanities. The writer Katherine Mansfield once said that a great poet must *be* a great poem, meaning that there should be no distinction between an artist's work and an artist's life. In Wagner's case, however, there was considerable disparity. His magnificent music dwells on themes of love and redemption, but the man himself was a total egotist who subjected his acquaintances to lengthy readings of new operas, borrowed money he never paid back, and cheated on his wife. Theoretically liberal in his political views, he was also strongly and vocally anti-Semitic. He was the center of his own universe. Genius, apparently, is unevenly distributed, but it cannot be ignored.

From Opera to Musical Theater: Operetta and the "Sung-Through" Play

8.2 *How do operettas and "sung-through" plays offer a bridge between opera and musical theater?*

Like all forms of music, not to mention the other arts, opera in the modern period has its own idioms and purposes. Italian is no longer the required language. Composers choose libretti written in their own tongue. If they do not, like Wagner, create their own libretti, they usually work closely with their authors. Wagner's ideal of opera as a unity of music and drama still applies, though by now the flow of the dramatic line is so completely dominant that audiences sometimes long for outbursts of melody. More and more, the aria is replaced with a musical underscoring of dialog to such an extent that listeners sometimes wonder "Why is this play set to music at all?"

Opera, among the summit achievements in the humanities, inspires modern composers to reach for its heights, just as modern playwrights seek to write tragedies that can rival those of the Greeks and Shakespeare. But the passage of time has affected musical styles. Many young composers consider melodious passages dated or hackneyed. Rarely do we hear an aria like those of Verdi or Wagner that stands out from the rest of a scene. To find one, we must often turn to the Broadway musical stage.

The antecedent to Broadway musicals was the **operetta**, a nineteenth-century European invention given worldwide fame by Austrian composers such as Johann Strauss II (1825–1899). In an operetta, like a *singspiel*, spoken dialog moves the action forward but is continually interrupted by musical numbers that are far more important than the drama itself. For many composers, the form solved the problem of how to keep the audience's attention during the spaces between songs: It allowed them to shorten the spaces.

Operettas include so *many* songs that audiences don't have long to wait for the next one. Typically the story line is either silly, complicated, and fast-moving, or filled with tear-jerking sentimentality. In either case, close listening is not really required. Characters in operetta tend to be two-dimensional, with singular identifying traits that remain unchanged throughout the proceedings. The songs do grow out of the context of a scene, but nobody complains if the two are not closely related.

Opera or Musical? The Sung-Through Play

By the early part of the twentieth century, musical shows that were largely "sung through"—that is, where music predominates over spoken dialog—began to focus on psychologically complex characters, and their creators offered more or less realistic settings and storylines. Several such works have become classics and are performed both in opera houses and as musical theater. These include *Show Boat*, *Porgy and Bess*, and *Sweeney Todd*.

KERN AND HAMMERSTEIN, *SHOW BOAT* *Showboat* (1927) with Jerome Kern's music and Oscar Hammerstein II's lyrics is important both for its songs, many of which remain popular to this day ("Ol' Man River," "Only Make-Believe," "Why Do I Love You?", "Can't Help Lovin' That Man"), and for the fact that it was really the first operetta to aim at a serious unification of music and story. Some historians of the musical stage have called *Showboat* the precursor of the musical play, as well as a link between Broadway and opera.

The story is embedded in nineteenth-century sentimental drama. The heroine, Magnolia, a sweet Southern girl, falls madly in love with a Mississippi river-boat gambler, Gaylord Ravenal. A handsome charmer, Ravenal sings divinely—and often—but we know that his addiction to gambling bodes no good. They marry, have a child, fight over his gambling, then separate. A reformed Ravenal eventually returns and, after a tear-filled scene with his grown daughter who fails to recognize him, persuades Magnolia that he has changed for the better. The finale, with the two reunited after many years of separation, is a glorious one.

Yet *Showboat* has much darker undertones. A secondary plot features the showboat's leading lady, a mixed-race singer named Julie who is passing for white, and her white husband, Steve. In a time when interracial marriage was not only illegal but dangerous, these two are discovered. As the sheriff comes up the gangplank to arrest them, Steve cuts Julie's hand and puts the blood to his lips; he can now claim that he, too, has black blood. The couple thus escape imprisonment, but they cannot stay with the show, and their lives deteriorate into alcoholism and tragedy over the years that follow.

The theme of racial strife is also echoed in one of the most memorable songs ever written for the stage. "Ol' Man River" is sung by an African-American dockworker with no future except for endless and exhausting toil. His few leisure moments are fraught with danger: "Git a little drunk, and you land in jail." He is "tired of livin', but scared of dyin'." *Showboat*, which dared to confront racism in America, was a sensational hit, and its success allowed the issues it raised to confront its huge—mostly white—audiences.

GERSHWIN, *PORGY AND BESS* George Gershwin shared the desire of many American composers to reach the heights of grand opera and achieve worldwide recognition. And why not? He had already proved that he was capable of writing rich symphonic scores. His brother Ira was a distinguished lyricist. All they needed was a subject that would allow them to keep their American roots and to create opera out of truly American sounds. They found the perfect subject in a novel called *Porgy* by DuBose Heyward, who was willing to write the libretto. So *Porgy and Bess* (1935) was born, a work that met initially with critical coolness, but has since been hailed as a supreme example of true American opera. "Disguised" at first as a Broadway musical in order to lure audiences, *Porgy and Bess* has more recently been performed at the world's major opera houses. Unfortunately, Gershwin, who died at 38, did not live to see *Porgy and Bess* hailed as a masterwork.

The setting for both the novel and the opera is a rundown section of Charleston called Catfish Row (Figure 8.5). Porgy, the unlikely hero, is crippled and gets around in a goat cart. He is high-spirited and optimistic despite his poverty. His first aria is the jaunty "I Got Plenty of Nuthin' and Nuthin's

Figure 8.5 Baritone Simon Estes as Porgy in a 1985 New York City Opera production of *Porgy and Bess.*
Porgy and Bess had its first run on Broadway but recently has been staged by a number of opera companies. What impact might the setting—Broadway theater or opera house—have on the audience expectations and experience?

Jacques M Chenet/Historical/Corbis

Plenty for Me." Bess, the stunningly beautiful heroine, is shunned by the residents of "the Row" because of her lax morals. She lives with Crown, a violent lawbreaker, who abuses her, but whom Bess finds irresistible.

When Crown is forced to flee the law, Bess finds herself abandoned and accepts Porgy's offer of a place to stay. Though at first Bess is just using Porgy until such time as Crown returns, she becomes aware that the man in the goat cart loves her with all his soul. Little by little, she responds to his love and affectionate kindness. "Bess, You Is My Woman Now," one of the glorious duets in modern opera, remains a concert favorite for singers and audiences, as does Bess's aria "I Loves You, Porgy" in which she pleads with her newfound love not to allow Crown back into her life.

Crown, however, does return—and Porgy kills him. The Catfish Row inhabitants—and the audience—believe the act is justifiable, and we appear to be heading for a happy ending. In the tradition of the greatest love stories such as *Romeo and Juliet* and *La traviata*, however, the curtain must fall on tragedy—this time brought about by a character called Sportin' Life, a gambler, a pimp, and a drug dealer, dressed out in glittery, expensive clothes. Sportin' Life exudes Dionysian charm, and he almost wins the audience over, but then his true nature is revealed when he exploits Bess's weakness for drugs. He promises her a lifetime supply if she will just go with him to New York. She struggles briefly with the dilemma, but Sportin' Life wins out. Though abandoned, Porgy remains optimistic about finding his lost love. He doesn't know where New York is, except that it's "over that way." The opera ends with Porgy setting off in his goat cart as he and the chorus sing the rousing but ultimately heart-breaking "I'm On My Way."

SONDHEIM, *SWEENEY TODD*   Stephen Sondheim (b. 1930) was still in his 20s when he wrote the lyrics for Leonard Bernstein's *West Side Story*. With songs such as "Maria," "Tonight," and "Somewhere," which have become classics, Sondheim quickly established a huge reputation for himself as a wordsmith. He became the dominant force in the American musical theater during the last quarter of the twentieth century, ultimately composing *both* music and lyrics and working closely with his librettists to ensure the unity of every component.

Thus far, most critics agree that his master-piece is a work with little spoken dialog, which is now being recognized as a genuine opera: *Sweeney Todd, the Demon Barber of Fleet Street* (1979), adapted from a creaky nineteenth-century melodramatic thriller (Figure 8.6). In the hands of Sondheim and Hugh Wheeler, who wrote the book for the musical, melodrama disappears, replaced by genuinely tragic dimensions, with a symphonic score of concert-hall importance.

When we first meet him, Sweeney Todd, a barber, has just returned to London after a long stretch in prison, where he was unfairly sent by a judge who wanted him out of the way because he lusted for Sweeney's wife, whom he has raped in Sweeney's absence. Obsessed by the need for revenge, Todd rents rooms upstairs from Mrs. Lovett, a pie-maker whose business is faltering because she makes, as a song suggests, "The Worst Pies in London." He opens a barbershop, and, when the hated judge initially eludes his grasp, falls into madness and begins a random

Figure 8.6 Johnny Depp as Sweeney Todd in the 2007 film directed by Tim Burton.
Although *Sweeney Todd* has been produced by opera companies, Burton chose to cast actors not known for their singing (Depp and Helena Bonham Carter) in the lead roles. What difference might this make to the way an audience perceives these characters?

Pictorial Press Ltd/Alamy

killing spree. As customers sit down for a shave, Todd slashes each man's throat with a razor and sends the bodies down a chute to the waiting Mrs. Lovett, who feeds them through a meat grinder and bakes them into pies. Everyone loves the resulting product: Her business skyrockets, and she becomes famous for serving up the *best* pies in London. Todd, of course, awaits the day when the villainous judge who destroyed his wife will come in for a shave.

The development of Sweeney Todd from wronged husband to cold-blooded killer is carried out with meticulous and chilling precision. In the final scene, the work approaches tragic heights when the crazed barber murders a haggard beggar woman, only to discover that she is the wife he thought was dead. His bloodcurdling cry of *"No!"* accompanied by crashing chords from the orchestra rivals the cries of despair often heard at the climax of great tragedies.

There are memorable and melodious songs along the way—notably "Johanna," about Todd's lost daughter; the haunting "Not While I'm Around," which Mrs. Lovett's young helper Tobias sings to her, promising to protect her always; and the grimly hilarious "A Little Priest," a duet in which Todd and Mrs. Lovett sing about the various professions to be found in her pies—but the emphasis is always on the inevitable rush forward of the drama. Much of the dialog is sung in an updated version of the mid-nineteenth-century operatic *recitative*.

The Broadway Musical

8.3 *What characteristics define the evolution of the Broadway musical from the "musical comedy" to the more common musical spectacular of today?*

If ragtime, blues, and jazz are established American contributions to the humanities, the same holds true for the Broadway musical, still popular after a century and a half, still dominant at the box office, and perhaps more widely performed throughout the world than any other theatrical genre. It has, of course, undergone a number of changes throughout its history.

The original heyday of the American **musical comedy** began after World War I and continued through the early 1950s. That original form—often almost plotless and full of expansive production numbers and beautiful showgirls—appealed to a public hungry to forget the devastation of war, later to a public seeking escape from the financial distress of the Great Depression, and still later to audiences living through yet another global war.

The typical plot—if one existed at all—was threadbare, the characters two-dimensional, the dialog unbelievable. The key was that these elements existed only as excuses for the songs that were often so bouncy that audiences silently moved their feet in accompaniment. Every now and then the pace slowed, and the audience was treated to a ballad with simple, easily remembered lyrics. The sheet music of the show's hits was typically for sale in the lobby, so that the songs could be played on pianos in parlors throughout the country. And if no one could play well enough, *piano rolls* could be inserted into *pianolas* (mechanical player pianos), which made the keys move as if by magic. The hit songs from musical comedies paralleled the opera arias that stood out from their context, and there was never a problem of how to keep the dramatic line going: Nobody really cared. But that began to change in the middle of the twentieth century.

The Musical Play

By the late 1930s, Hollywood was luring serious-minded audiences away from live theater by presenting films that confronted major social issues and that were peopled with characters of increasing depth and complexity. The lightweight Broadway show was starting to show its age. Works like *Show Boat* and *Porgy and Bess* were finding both critical and popular acclaim, and Broadway took note. Major show composers and wordsmiths recognized that the time was right for more serious work if the musical stage were to survive.

RODGERS AND HART, *PAL JOEY*   An important transition work of the Broadway theater is *Pal Joey* (1940), with music by Richard Rodgers and lyrics by Lorenz Hart (Figure 8.7). Still very much in the musical comedy tradition with peppy songs, tap dances, and ear-caressing ballads, *Pal Joey* also deepened the Broadway musical and deserves to be considered a pioneer **musical play**, a term sometimes used to designate a work in which music is more fully integrated into the story than is typical of musical comedies. It cast some dark shadows on the traditionally sunny landscape of the musical stage and provided the audience with a very *un*traditional hero who could sing and dance, but who was also self-centered and finally not very likeable.

Figure 8.7 Frank Sinatra and Kim Novak in the 1957 film of *Pal Joey*.
The genial and widely-liked dancer Gene Kelly played Joey in the original stage production of this musical about an amoral heel. Would watching Kelly in this role be different from watching Sinatra, whose own reputation was less savory? How much does an actor's public persona impact our perception of character?
Everett Collection

The authors were already established as major collaborators whose marquee names alone guaranteed the success of any venture, thus minimizing risks to the backers. The libretto was by John O'Hara, a leading author of serious fiction.

It all happened almost by chance. O'Hara, tired of the compromises a screenwriter was forced to make in order to satisfy studio executives, was determined to make a living by selling his stories only to *The New Yorker* magazine. Unfortunately, the editor of the magazine was not a fan. He rejected O'Hara's new work, declaring that he would never publish another of the writer's stories unless he understood it. O'Hara went on a drunken binge; when he recovered, he started work on a story about a ruthless heel, a master of ceremonies in a seedy nightclub. The character, Joey Evans, suited O'Hara's bleak mood. At first he had no idea where the piece was going, but "the more I wrote about the slob, the more I got to like him."[2]

The story became a series of stories. A close friend read them, fell in love with the charming scoundrel, and suggested that O'Hara write a play about him. O'Hara liked the idea but thought it should be a musical because of its nightclub setting and Joey's profession as a showman. Rodgers and Hart, who were looking for more challenging subject matter, became O'Hara's collaborators.

The work did not erupt overnight into a theatrical masterpiece. George Abbott, an experienced Broadway hand hired to direct the show, called the first draft of the libretto "disorganized." Abbott was also concerned that Joey might alienate the audience. But despite Abbott's worries, the collaborators forged ahead.

Rodgers and Hart insisted on retaining some musical comedy lightheartedness. They decided to exploit the nightclub for all it was worth, introducing a chorus line of broken-down, no-talent singers and dancers who, according to reviews, kept the audience in an uproar. They also wanted to characterize in song one of the leading characters, a spoiled socialite who ventures into the club, seeking escape from a dull and loveless existence. Although she sees through Joey instantly, she can't resist his charm and sexuality. For her, Rodgers and Hart wrote one of their greatest songs—"Bewitched, Bothered, and Bewildered"—which became an anthem for all those lovers obsessed with absolutely the wrong person. The affair is a disaster, of course. Joey will never change, but she will always love him. O'Hara refused to violate his plot so that the audience could go home happy.

The biggest *coup* of the enterprise was finding just the right person to play Joey. Gene Kelly, who later became a Hollywood legend as one of the greatest dancers ever to hit the screen, could overwhelm audiences with his complex choreography, but also seduce them with his velvet singing voice. Kelly had an outgoing personality filled with the charm, without which the show could not have succeeded.

Audiences kept filling the theater, and the show's box-office success encouraged others to strive for greater depth in the genre. Rodgers, Hart, and Abbott resisted O'Hara's efforts to some extent and tried to keep the show within the parameters of musical comedy, but what they had started with *Pal Joey* couldn't be put back in the bottle. As the scholar and critic William Hyland writes,

> Although the excellent music . . . was integral to the spirit of the play, for once Rodgers was overshadowed by the character, the lyrics, and the play itself. Because of the harsh and realistic story and the biting lyrics, the show became a landmark . . . a milestone in the liberation of the musical from the stale forms of the 1920s and 1930s.[3]

RODGERS AND HAMMERSTEIN, *OKLAHOMA!* The irresistible tide moving the Broadway musical away from frivolity and toward a more serious depth finally swept up Richard Rodgers himself. He remembered a play he had seen in 1933, which he thought would make a good musical. He suggested the venture to Hart, who read the script and said it wasn't suited to his brand of worldly-wise lyrics. But Oscar Hammerstein II, librettist of *Showboat*, was also seeking more challenging material and found the project to his liking. The libretto and lyrics for *Showboat* had displayed his abilities as a poet and his potential as a serious dramatist.

Green Grow the Lilacs was a folk play about the rivalry of two cowboys for a sweet and innocent young woman. One of the cowboys was handsome and honorable, the other villainous. On the face of it, it was a tired old plot, reminiscent of nineteenth-century melodrama. Yet Rodgers was charmed by the folksiness and relative simplicity of it.

Not only was *Green Grow the Lilacs* different from anything Broadway had ever seen but, the collaborators thought, it might also satisfy audiences' need for an escape from concerns over the war in that year of 1943. The play was set in the late nineteenth-century Midwest, when tensions could arise over which young man would offer the highest bid for a girl's picnic basket and win the right to be her companion for the festivities.

The first version of the musical was given a tryout in Boston, as was customary in those days. Called *Away We Go!*, it received lukewarm critical notices, and the producers feared they couldn't raise enough money to bring the show into New York. They did, however, eventually find an "angel"—someone willing to invest the necessary $50,000 (a sum that eventually grew into millions). The collaborators spent long nights in a Boston hotel room reworking every scene while trying to retain the show's down-to-earth honesty and simplicity. They knew it needed a great opening and a rousing choral finale, without which a show could not survive. The final number had to explode on the stage and send the audience home in high spirits. Since the setting was the Oklahoma Territory just prior to its achieving statehood, the authors realized they needed to give prominence to the huge event. What better way to end the show than singing of the promise that statehood brings, the promise of a better life in a better world?

Rodgers and Hammerstein named both the number and the show *Oklahoma!* and opened it in New York to ecstatic reviews and the largest post-opening box office any show had seen up to that time. Ticket scalpers were charging as much as $50.00—at a time when $3.50 was the reigning box-office price for an orchestra seat! On a radio sitcom, one character promised his beloved tickets to *Oklahoma!* if she would marry him. Her answer was, "And where would you get them?"

From the moment the curtain rose, audiences saw something completely new. Instead of a chorus line of scantily-clad beauties, there was a single figure—an older (fully dressed!) farm woman churning butter on her porch. From offstage came the sound of a cowboy singing, at first without accompaniment, "Oh, What a Beautiful Mornin'." Audiences in 1943, accustomed to the flashy musical comedies of earlier decades, must have been amazed.

The story is both sweet and frightening. The cowboy enters, finishes the song, and tells the woman that he is in love with her niece, who first seems not just uninterested but annoyed by his attentions. He returns her jibes. Instead of the usual love-at-first-sight sentiments, each demands that the other refrain from showing any sign of affection in front of others because "People Will Say We're in Love."

Everything about the story works to musical stage advantage. The settlers in the territory make up the chorus. The picnic auction allows for folk dancing. The crux of the drama comes when Laurie, the heroine, has to decide between the handsome Curly and the farmhand Judd. The conflict is dramatized in a spectacular dream ballet called "Laurie Makes Up Her Mind," for which choreographer Agnes DeMille (1905–1993) cast highly trained dancers performing against surrealistic backgrounds rich with Freudian symbolism. The introduction of ballet started a trend that lasted for decades; after that, musicals often incorporated ballet along with other forms of dance more typical of the genre.

Oklahoma!, which is still credited with having taken the musical stage in a startling new direction, was followed by one huge success after another for Rodgers and Hammerstein: *Carousel* (1945), *South Pacific* (1949), *The King and I* (1951), and *The Sound of Music* (1959). The death of Hammerstein in 1960 brought to an end the most productive collaboration in musical theater history.

BERNSTEIN AND SONDHEIM, *WEST SIDE STORY*   Given the increasing number of dance elements in musicals after *Oklahoma!*, the arrival of *West Side Story* (Figure 8.8) in 1957 was almost inevitable. The show is a musical play dominated by intricate ballets, modern dances, and a symphonic score that has become standard in the repertoire of great orchestras. An updated version of *Romeo and Juliet*, it also relies heavily on the drama of the doomed love affair. Because of the story's Shakespearean origins, the audience readily accepts the tragic ending.

West Side Story is a product of upscale collaboration. The idea of making Shakespeare's tragedy into a modern tale of two lovers caught in the feud between rival New York street gangs belonged to Jerome Robbins (1918–1998), a choreographer famous in the world of modern dance and ballet. Leonard Bernstein (1918–1990), the composer, had been classically trained at Harvard and was destined to become one of the world's leading conductors and composers.

Robbins and Bernstein had collaborated in 1944 on a sprightly musical comedy called *On the Town*, which chronicles, largely in dance, the adventures of three sailors on a 24-hour leave in New York City (and which was revived to great success in 2015). The new project, *West Side Story*, comprised what some critics called a "dance opera," but the play itself was never subordinated to the other components—at least in part because the libretto was written by Arthur Laurents (1917–2011), a recognized playwright not known

Figure 8.8 The "balcony scene" from a 2003 production of *West Side Story*.
Do you think that having seen Shakespeare's *Romeo and Juliet* would deepen a viewer's experience of watching *West Side Story*? Or does a strong piece of art stand on its own, no matter what its origins?
Rudi Blaha/AP Images

as a writer of musicals. The elements of the work are so rich individually that they are often performed separately: the dance sequences by international ballet companies, the music by symphony orchestras and solo artists. *West Side Story* has been revived multiple times both on Broadway and in opera houses, and theater companies have performed love scenes from Shakespeare interspersed with Bernstein songs (or arias).

The third member of this extraordinary collaboration was a young lyricist named Stephen Sondheim, a protégé of Oscar Hammerstein and, as Broadway later discovered, a composer in his own right. The *West Side Story* lyrics have a simplicity not characteristic of Sondheim's later work, but they occasionally display his wit—and they are eminently suited to the tragedy of the tale.

In *West Side Story*, Romeo is Tony, a New York teenager of Polish descent and a reluctant member of a street gang called the Jets, who respect his sensitivity and idealism, but nonetheless expect him to fight when they say the need arises. Their archrivals are the Sharks, young Puerto Ricans battling to own the neighborhood turf and rid the streets of non-Hispanics. The gang members on both sides were all played, in the original production, by seasoned ballet dancers.

Juliet is Maria, the sister of the Sharks' leader Bernardo, and therefore a sworn archenemy of the Jets. She and Tony meet at a school dance, even as Romeo and Juliet meet at a masquerade ball. The famous balcony scene of Shakespeare is transformed into the duet "Tonight," sung by Maria on her fire escape and a lovesick Tony in the alley below. Meanwhile, the Sharks invite the Jets to take part in a "rumble," an all-out street fight, with the victors laying claim to the "turf." Tony is reluctant, aware that the Sharks' leader is Maria's brother. But gang loyalty forces him to take part. Bernardo keeps daring him to strike the first blow. Tony holds back, but when Bernardo draws a knife and kills Riff, the Jets' leader and Tony's best friend, the anguished hero kills Bernardo in revenge, even as Romeo slays Juliet's cousin Tybalt in a sword fight.

In Shakespeare, the tragic climax is brought about by a quarantine that prevents Romeo, in exile, from getting a letter assuring him that Juliet is alive and waiting for him. In *West Side Story*, Tony is deceived into believing Maria has been killed by her jealous boyfriend. Bereft of all hope, the hero rushes into a darkened street and pleads to be shot. Hearing his voice, Maria runs joyfully to meet him, but the boyfriend shoots him before Tony can see her. She cradles her dying lover in her arms as a police siren is heard in the distance—too late to prevent the tragedy.

Many of the arias from *West Side Story* have become classics. In addition to "Tonight," they include the jazzy "Jet Song," the haunting ballad "Maria," and the main theme of the dream ballet, "Somewhere," which tells of a happy land where there is "a place for us, somewhere a place for us."

The Rock Musical

The rock musical and the rock opera have become increasingly ensconced in the Broadway scene since their debut in the 1960s with the "tribal" celebration *Hair*, which featured hippies and nudity but very little real rock music, and the Who's remarkable *Tommy*, which was introduced initially as a record album and later performed both on stage and in a film version. More recently, Broadway has seen a surfeit of shows dubbed "jukebox musicals," based on the music and careers of various artists, including *Dreamgirls* (which roughly chronicled the Supremes), *Jersey Boys* (the life and times of Frankie Valli and the Four Seasons), and the Tony-winner *Beautiful* (the experiences of Carole King).

Spring Awakening (2007, music by Duncan Sheik, book and lyrics by Steven Sater) may be regarded by historians of the musical stage as a consummate achievement in blending serious, even tragic drama with a rock score (Figure 8.9). Its source is a darkly tragic 1906 German play by Frank Wedekind (1864–1918), a dramatist and poet who, in this work, exposed middle-class moral rigidity as Ibsen had done in Norway. *Spring Awakening* adheres closely to its roots, changing very little of the story and, of special importance, not providing an unbelievable happy ending. This indeed is a tragic musical play. A forced happy ending would have destroyed a work many consider a masterpiece in its own right. Adaptation to the musical stage was risky; adding a rock score even more so. The time period of the play is 1891. So what is rock music doing in a German prep school of more than a century ago?

The music, so completely out of place for the time and setting, is an externalization of the suppressed emotions, especially sexual desires, of teenage students raised with no knowledge of where babies come from and no one to assure them their hormonal awakening is natural and not to be denied. Since,

Figure 8.9 Lea Michele and Jonathan Groff in the original Broadway production of *Spring Awakening* (2006).
What might the use of crashing 21st-century music bring to the audience's experience of this 19th-century story of adolescent angst?
Joan Marcus Photography

in this society, parents never discuss sex, either pro or con, the children grow up obsessed with the subject and filled with wrong information passed from one student to another in fearful whispers.

Melchior, the hero, is academically gifted and intent on probing the mystery of life, hiding forbidden books under his mattress and reading them late at night. Gradually he achieves an understanding of sexual intimacy as a natural rite of passage, dangerous if suppressed (much as Sigmund Freud theorized, shocking that same society). The result of his awakening is that he writes an essay explaining the sexual process in minute detail and then distributes it among the student body. He is painfully aware that his close friend, Moritz, has been so obsessed with misunderstood sexual urges that, unable to study, he has failed his exams. Moritz eventually commits suicide rather than face his family as a failure.

Melchior's girlfriend is the innocent Wendla, who at first resists his protestations of passionate longing for her and his assurance that their sexual coupling would be both natural and beautiful. Wendla, so much a victim of sexual denial and the subconscious need to throw off her moral shackles that she can think of nothing else than being alone with Melchior, finally allows the young man access to her body. They sing one of the show's memorable songs, a slow rock duet called "The Word of Your Body," in a scene tender and beautiful but filled with grim foreboding.

Their joy doesn't last long. The authorities discover that Melchior has written the shocking essay. He is sentenced to solitary confinement in a reform school, a sequence dramatized in the symbolic style of early twentieth-century German expressionism, with Melchior tied to the backstage wall in a crucifixion tableau. Wendla becomes pregnant, though she does not understand what is happening inside her. Her desperate parents send her to a doctor who supposedly specializes in handling these delicate matters; he diagnoses the pregnancy as a disease and gives her a fatal overdose of medicine.

Amazingly, the rock score balances the tragic bitterness of the play. The chorus of students can both sing and dance, as they break into rock affirmations of sexual attraction and rebellious denunciations of society's repressiveness. Like many important works in the humanities, this one awakens not only spring, but thought.

The Spectacular

The 1960s introduced not only the rock musical but also the stage spectacular—blockbuster shows that truly flourished in the 1980s such as *Cats, Phantom of the Opera*, and *Les Misérables*—which employed movie-like special effects (the falling chandelier in *Phantom*) and huge operatic set pieces (the construction of the barricade in *Les Mis*). The genre was more or less invented by the British composer Andrew Lloyd Webber (b. 1948), whose early partnership with the lyricist Tim Rice produced hits such as *Jesus Christ Superstar* and *Evita*, and whose *Cats*, which put poems by T.S. Eliot to a musical background, became the longest-running show on Broadway in the 1980s and 1990s. Webber's success inspired others to create huge musical spectaculars including *Les Mis* and *Miss Saigon* that were, more often than not, critically disparaged but beloved by audiences.

More recently, the Disney Company has taken Broadway by storm, creating long-running hits out of a number of their successful animated films, including *The Lion King, Beauty and the Beast*, and *Tarzan*. At least one of these shows, *The Lion King*, with a cast of massive puppets created by the director Julie Taymor, is recognized as a masterpiece. Taymor went on to epic failure and serial lawsuits, however, when she directed another huge musical spectacular, *Spider-Man: Turn Off the Dark*, in 2011, with music by U2's Bono.

WICKED   In 2003, the musical that has turned out to be this century's biggest blockbuster had its first tryouts in San Francisco. Based on a book of the same name, *Wicked* opened in New York in the fall of that same year, swept up three Tony awards, and immediately became the sold-out show that it remains—the hardest ticket to get on Broadway. *Wicked* takes a new look at a familiar story, managing to be both funny and moving along the way. It focuses on the two witches of *The Wizard of Oz*—Glinda, the good witch, and the green-skinned Elphaba, who becomes known as the Wicked Witch of the West (see Figure 8.1). We first meet these two when they are young, long before the arrival of Dorothy, and we see their friendship develop and then fall apart, as they wrestle with their own differing personalities, their love for the same prince, and their disillusionment with the great Wizard. Taking characters and a story that almost every American is familiar with and giving it a twist—and adding a solid score by the veteran Broadway composer Stephen Schwartz (who also wrote the music for *Godspell, Pippin*, and the film *Enchanted*)—has turned out to be a recipe for success rarely matched on Broadway.

Dance

8.4   *What key differences exist between ballet and modern dance?*

Pianist Leon Fleisher, rank-ordering the elements of music, puts rhythm first, followed by harmony, and then melody. His rationale appears to be that, although music can and indeed does exist without harmony or melody (in the romantic sense of that word), it has to have a rhythmic underpinning or else it becomes random sound. Music historians have indicated that rhythm came first, probably as an accompaniment to rituals of birth, coming of age, planting and harvesting, death, and burial. These rituals thus can be considered early forms of dance, which has been traced back 30,000 years.

The Early History of Dance

The Egyptians are known to have taken part in highly elaborate dance ceremonies in which they imitated the movement of heavenly bodies. Pharaohs required slaves to entertain them with dances that involved unusual gyrations and acrobatic skills. Around the same period, the Hebrew Bible refers to dance as an expression of joy as when Miriam, sister of Moses and Aaron, dances to celebrate the Red Sea escape from Pharaoh's soldiers.

In Greece, beginning around the sixth century BCE, the art of the dance became an official form of public entertainment. Dancing became a respected profession, and those with sufficient strength and suppleness of limb were trained from an early age. During the Middle Ages, dancing was banned by the church because it was associated with pagan rituals and religions. Folk dancing, however, was practiced despite the ban, and remnants of it survive to the present time.

The Maypole ritual dance (Figure 8.10), perhaps originating in ancient Ireland, continues to be practiced on both sides of the Atlantic. Circling a pole decked out in (usually) crepe paper of varied colors and chanting words such as "May party, May party, rah-rah-rah," the dancers, often young children, probably do not realize that their joyful activity dates back to an annual but forbidden spring mating ritual: for young people, a symbolic rite of passage.

During the Plague of 1348 known as the "Black Death," a terrified population of Western Europe released their fears by performing a "dance of death," usually led by a dancer dressed as a skeleton. Children today still do this dance and chant:

> *Ring around the rosey,*
> *A pocketful of posey.*
> *Ashes! Ashes!*
> *All fall down!*

Today's dancers probably do not know the original meaning of "rosey"—a reference to the reddish boils on the skin of those afflicted with buboes (hence "bubonic" plague). Today's young dancers fall on the ground giggling with excitement, unaware they are reenacting a catastrophe.

In the thirteenth century, an Islamic spiritual leader named Mevlana Rumi established a religious sect, the Mevlevi Order, whose members took part in a ritual still

Figure 8.10 Dancers around a Maypole in Blekinge, Sweden, during a midsummer celebration in 2014.
Why do you think a tradition like the Maypole dance has persisted in many cultures?
Piotr Wawrzyniuk/Shutterstock

practiced today. Known as whirling dervishes, they turned ever faster and faster until they achieved a trancelike state, which they believed liberated their souls from earthly bondage and allowed direct union with Allah.

In the late Middle Ages, as major cities grew in size and sophistication, dance became a highly refined art form for which only the graceful few were suited. Mimes, such as those in Italy's celebrated *commedia dell'arte*, studied dance to give their bodies the flexibility to execute their seemingly nonsensical movements, including sudden pratfalls that seemed painful but were in reality skillfully rehearsed movements. Pratfalls are still a mainstay of circus clowns.

In the early eighteenth century, the *kathak* dance was integral to the entertainment of a royal court in northern India. Originating as a stylized method of telling stories and educating viewers about their mythology, it became a highly professional art form with elegantly swirling movements, lightning quick pirouettes, sudden poses, rapid stamping of feet, and subtle gestures capable of expressing a wide range of emotions. Dancing has long been indigenous to Indian culture.

Dancing satisfies a universal human need, whether everyone assembled takes part in it or simply sits and watches. Seated audiences empathize with the motions and rhythms on stage, so that they too are in a sense participants. Dance awakens the Dionysian spirit in all of us, a spirit that longs to be free.

Ballet

Acknowledged as the premier form of Western dance art, ballet developed from Italian street mimes before it became a court entertainment for aristocrats. Ballet is fundamentally a series of controlled bodily positions and combinations that require years of arduous training to perfect, yet must seem effortless to an audience. Ballet dancers seem to float across the stage, and viewers forget the unnaturalness of the motion. Ballet forces the body to do things the body is not basically equipped to do. In the daily training exercises (even required for the stars!), a basic position is to have the feet turned outward with the heels touching. Most of us could manage that. But the dancers are then required to turn each foot horizontally in opposite directions, heels still touching. Try that one!

Females must stand on their toes for unnaturally long periods. Males must be strong enough to lift and then hold the ballerina with one hand. They must be muscular and lithe at the same time, their bodies resembling classical statues.

To the French and the Russians in the nineteenth century must go the credit for having formalized the art of the ballet, the French having been first in establishing the rigorous training exercises as far back as the seventeenth century. Ballet positions and movements still bear French labels. A *plié* is a lowering of the torso while keeping the feet turned outward as described above. A *jeté* is a leap, executed so lightly that the landing is almost silent (unless you're in the front row). A **pirouette** is performed standing on the toes of one foot as the body spins around and around, faster and faster. Classical ballet often tells a story, but it need not, since viewers don't come for the plots. Story or otherwise, classical ballet follows a traditional and expected format. There is an ensemble of males and females as well as a male and female soloist. The ensemble performs intricate combinations, then exits as the ballerina enters on her toes (**en pointe**) performing a complex combination, with complex design, especially if she is a major personality in the ballet world. She whirls offstage, still *en pointe*, as the male lead leaps onto the stage with many pirouettes, athletic jumps, and body spins high in the air. The great dancers—Nijinsky, Nureyev, and Baryshnikov—are famous for the amazing heights they could reach. Finally, the ballerina returns, holds out an arm to her partner, and the two perform an exquisite *pas de deux* to a slow, melodious accompaniment.

FRENCH BALLET: *GISELLE* Since ballet terms are all French, we should not be surprised to learn that the art form originated in France. When Louis XIV danced the role of Apollo, the sun god, at the age of 13, he thereafter was nicknamed "the Sun King"! By the late seventeenth century, French operas had to include a ballet, whether relevant to the story or not. By the following century, French ballet had become an internationally recognized institution.

By the nineteenth century, the spirit of Romanticism, with its less restrained emotionalism, became popular in France, and the blending of classical movement and Romantic music gave the ballet world one of its enduringly popular works, *Giselle* (1841), with music by Adolphe Adam (1803–1856). The ballet has an appealing story line, as well as traditional components such as the *pas de deux* and a *corps de ballet* executing complex movements *en pointe* (Figure 8.11).

Figure 8.11 A rehearsal for *Giselle* by the South African Ballet Theater in Johannesburg, South Africa, in 2012.
In this era of hip-hop culture, do you think ballet is still a relevant art form? Why?
Gallo Images/City Press/Alamy

The story centers on the love of a young maiden for an aristocrat named Albrecht, who has courted her disguised as a suitor on her social level. Eventually, shocked by his deception, Giselle dies from a weak heart and is destined to join the ranks of the Wilis, the souls of young women jilted before they reached the altar; their mission is to torment the men responsible. While mourning at Giselle's grave, Albrecht is visited by the Wilis, who sentence him to death by dancing. In true romantic fashion, however, Giselle's love for Albrecht overcomes the power of the Wilis, and she joins Albrecht in one last *pas de deux*. We leave the theater, knowing their love will last forever.

RUSSIAN BALLET: TCHAIKOVSKY AND DIAGHILEV Russia has proclaimed itself the dominant force in ballet since the nineteenth century for a number of impressive reasons. The first is that Peter Ilyich Tchaikovsky wrote some of the greatest scores in the ballet world: for *Swan Lake* (1877), *Sleeping Beauty* (1890), and *The Nutcracker* (1892).

In the first of these dances, a prince, melancholy at being forced to select a bride from among the eligible young ladies approved by his parents, goes out to hunt swans. As he is about to shoot one of them with his arrow, the Swan Queen intervenes, informing him that she and the other swans are women transformed by an evil sorcerer. He falls in love with her and promises marriage. During a ball sequence at the palace, the sorcerer enters with his beautiful daughter made to look like the Swan Queen. The prince announces that she is to be his bride, but he catches sight of the real queen outside the window. Rushing to the lake, he arrives just in time to hold her, dying of grief, in his arms. The story, typical of nineteenth-century sentimental melodrama, is more than overshadowed by the music and dazzling choreography, always evident in major productions.

Sleeping Beauty is based on the popular fairy tale of a girl who is cursed in revenge by an evil witch, furious at not being invited to her christening, and is fated to die when she is 16. The evil prophecy comes to pass, but the Lilac Fairy alters the curse, so that the princess—along with the kingdom—will sleep for 100 years. Later, when a handsome prince hears of her, he journeys to the castle, falls in love instantly, and kisses her lips. The kiss breaks the spell, and they live happily ever after.

The Nutcracker, performed during the holiday season in hundreds of theaters, often gives children their first exposure to ballet; and adults, perhaps having shared

Looking Back

In this chapter,

- we briefly explored the origins of opera and discussed the contributions of three of opera's premier composers: Mozart, Verdi, and Wagner,
- we traced the emergence of operetta and "popular" opera, or sung-through plays,

- we identified key moments in the development of the Broadway musical theater, and
- we discussed the major elements of dance, including ballet and modern dance, and looked briefly at the importance of dance culturally and artistically.

Key Terms

en pointe Ballet term for standing on one's toes.

flamenco Style of dance originating in Andalusia, involving precise foot movements and hand clapping, accompanied by guitar.

jeté Ballet term for a leap.

leit-motif Musical theme associated with Wagnerian opera identifying a particular character or a force, such as fate or a curse, repeated throughout the work.

libretto The lyrics of an opera, or the book and lyrics of a musical.

music-drama Name given by Wagner to his works.

musical comedy Genre of the musical, prevalent in the 1930s and 1940s, featuring songs that often have little to do with the plot, or what there is of one.

musical play Genre dating back to *Pal Joey* in 1940 and *Oklahoma! in 1943* with strong plots, much dialog, developed characters, and songs that spring from the situation.

opera The plural of *"opus"* (Latin for "work"), a genre with all, or most, of the dialog sung, and often interspersed with melodious arias, duets, and ensemble numbers.

operetta Lighter version of opera, featuring melodious arias and duets that often have only a thin relationship to a scene; libretto is usually just an excuse for having the music.

pas de deux French phrase meaning "step of two," a usually slow dance duet set to melodious accompaniment.

pirouette Spinning movement executed by the dancer balancing on one foot.

plié French ballet term for a basic position in which the dancer squats down, keeping the feet extended horizontally with heels touching.

potlatch Native-American community gathering to celebrate significant occasions such as marriage or birth.

powwow Dance performed by Native Americans of the Plains as a means of community unification.

recitative Sung dialog in an opera.

singspiel German term for an opera that included spoken, rather than sung, dialog.

Chapter 9
Film and Television

Figure 9.1 Orson Welles as Charles Kane in his 1941 film *Citizen Kane*.
Welles uses both innovative film techniques and a fragmented narrative structure in this masterpiece. Which do you think matters more in making a film a classic—the use of creative techniques, or storytelling?

AF archive/Alamy

Like other disciplines of the humanities, film, television, and video are vehicles of creative expression—perhaps the most collaborative of all creative endeavors (think about those endless lists of closing credits!). And these are also the most lucrative and popular of creative endeavors. Every Monday we can read box office rankings for current movies and viewer counts for television shows. We don't see those numbers for art gallery openings or premières of new operas. We even watch (albeit sometimes impatiently) the Academy Awards segments devoted to editors, sound mixers, costumers, and others who work behind the cameras. We recognize that screen art is not created solely by the actors with the familiar faces (although their contributions are surely critical) but by writers and directors and "showrunners" and cinematographers.

We live in an age when performances on screen are more readily accessible than ever before. First on tape, then DVD, and now streaming through our televisions, computers, tablets, and smartphones, the possibilities for watching are virtually limitless. This chapter briefly explores the early history of filmmaking, cinema's major genres, the careers of several prominent "auteurs," and the emergence of television and online streaming as the home of compelling new dramatic formats. The chapter begins with an explanation of some basic conventions of filmmaking, and it ends with some guidelines for critically evaluating what you see.

Conventions of the Moving Image

9.1 *What are some key conventions of filmmaking?*

In film and video, as on the stage, **conventions** are the techniques and conditions that audiences agree to accept as real. Beginning readers learn the "rules" for print—read left to right, top to bottom, capital letters, periods, etc. Similarly, critical viewing is helped by knowledge of the conventions of filmmaking.

Sound

Before the introduction of *sound* in 1927 (perhaps the most revolutionary of all the conventions), silent movies had printed cards inserted to indicate necessary dialog or information. Although we may consider silent films old-fashioned, in reality remarkable performers such as Buster Keaton, Mack Sennett, and Charlie Chaplin developed pantomime to a fine art. Music underscoring the action was at first played by a pianist in the theater and was later imposed on the film itself, leading the way to "the talkies."

Sound in film is divided into two categories: the sounds that clearly derive from the actions we see on the screen, like conversation and sound effects (called **diegetic sound**); and the sounds that are imposed from outside, like music scores and narrative voiceovers (called **non-diegetic sound**). Sound can be used to create suspense, to trigger emotions, to direct our attention to certain characters or actions. And silence can also be evocative, especially in a world where we are used to being surrounded by sound virtually all the time.

Music is almost as omnipresent as the camera—it is a rare film that doesn't have a musical soundtrack—and we are meant to forget that in real life music does not suddenly come out of nowhere. Sometimes pounding music underscores violent action, but imaginative directors may often use music as ironic counterpoint to what is being shown. In Oliver Stone's 1986 antiwar film *Platoon*, for example, a particularly violent death scene is played out against the slow and melodic sounds of Samuel Barber's "Adagio for Strings," and in Stanley Kubrick's 1971 classic *A Clockwork Orange*, a whimsical "Singin' in the Rain" accompanies a horrifying rape.

The Camera

Usually audiences are simply unaware of where the camera is and how it is being used, but the choices of the director and cinematographer can play a distinct role in the viewing experience. Critical viewers often "disobey" the rules and pay careful attention to what the camera is up to.

CAMERA POSITION, SHOTS, AND ANGLES   An ever-expanding variety of resources is available to contemporary directors. Standard shots—long shots, medium shots, close-ups, **pans**, zooms, tracking shots—allow directors to establish context, focus the audience's attention on single characters or objects, or follow the progress of characters or action through an ever-widening landscape. Techniques that include handheld cameras and Steadicams offer a suggestion of realism, a **documentary** feel. More recently, computer-generated video has opened an almost infinite array of possibilities. For his 2013 film *Gravity*, the Mexican director Alfonso Cuarón spent close to five years developing new computer techniques that would allow him to create the illusion that his heroine, played by Sandra Bullock, was free-floating in space. And in 2015, a film shot entirely on an iPhone 6, *Tangerine*, directed by Sean Baker, was released to critical acclaim.

Point of view is the positioning of the camera so it is clear which character or mind is experiencing the action. In the 20-year run of the television series *Law and Order* (1990–2010), for example, every single shot was from the detectives' or lawyers' point of view; the audience was never permitted to see anything that was not also available to the lead characters. Directors may also choose shots and angles that mirror the reality of an outsider's view, and certainly they make camera choices that encourage specific responses from their audiences—anticipation, sympathy, horror.

Some shots are particularly useful. The **close-up** allows the director to guide the audience to concentrate on a hand gesture, eyes that reveal hidden secrets, or a letter left lying on a desk, signaling that it will prove crucial later on. In the early days of film, when cameras were much less sophisticated than they are now and directors had only one or two cameras to work with, a film was often basically a photographed play, without close-ups. Nowadays a director who chose not to employ close-ups—to shoot an entire film in long shots or medium shots—would be considered highly experimental.

Tracking shots allow directors to follow characters through landscapes, or to move toward or away from an action. Some tracking shots provide emotional jolts, like the astonishing one in the 1939 classic *Gone with the Wind* that shows Scarlett O'Hara rushing wildly into an Atlanta street to find the family doctor and blundering into a field of wounded soldiers and unburied corpses (Figure 9.2). As Scarlett slowly realizes what she is seeing, the camera backs away from her horrified face, and the scene opens wider and wider to reveal hundreds upon hundreds of bodies. Sometimes tracking shots are such virtuoso feats that they can distract the audience's attention from the action at hand, however. The 5-minute tracking shot of the Dunkirk evacuation beach in the 2007 film *Atonement*, for example, is so intricately choreographed that the viewer begins to wonder how it was accomplished, rather than being drawn into the actual experience in the film.

Figure 9.2 A reverse tracking shot from *Gone with the Wind* (1939).
In this shot, the camera pulls back to reveal hundreds of bodies and corpses as Scarlett O'Hara (in red) makes her way among them. What does this shot accomplish that a straight long shot of the same scene might not?
AF archive/Alamy

SCENES AND *MISE-EN-SCÈNE*   Directors make choices about camera placement, shots, and angles, often in cooperation with cinematographers and other members of their crews.

Similarly, directors make choices about how to shape scenes, which operate somewhat like paragraphs in a short story—that is, to advance a single action or idea. What we actually see within each scene—the props, costumes, scenery, lighting, landscape, where the actors are placed—is called the *mise-en-scène*, a French term meaning literally "placing on stage."

Scenes may consist of many shots (watch the tent-raising scene in Disney's *Dumbo* for a masterful sequence that includes some 60 cuts) or a single one. Both Alfred Hitchcock's *Rope* (1948) and Alejandro Iñárritu's *Birdman* (2014) were edited meticulously to appear as if each film consisted of only one single shot.

Color

Color—or the lack of it—is an important element in **cinematography**. Some of the best films ever made (*Citizen Kane, Casablanca*, 1940s *film noir,* the comedies of Keaton and Chaplin) derive much of their power from the contrast between light and shadow that black-and-white film makes possible. Contemporary filmmakers may recognize the benefits of black-and-white, but they very rarely use it except to recreate an earlier world, as was the case with 2011's Oscar-winner, *The Artist*, about the days of silent film. But the colorization of classics such as *Casablanca*, at one time seen as a great innovation, stopped after a general outcry from fans and film scholars, who argued that the artists' originals had been defaced.

Time

The convention of *time* is as flexible as the director chooses to make it. An action meant to last a minute can be prolonged on screen for several minutes, as the camera focuses on separate objects or people—and returns to them again and again. The introduction of the sophisticated handling of time is found in the work of great pioneers such as D.W. Griffith and Sergei Eisenstein.

Deliberately *slowing down* the film can signal a lyrical, dreamlike scene, perhaps a beautiful memory or fantasy. Shutting it down completely results in a series of still photographs or **freeze-frames**, a technique used by François Truffaut at the beginning of *Jules and Jim* (1961) and later by Martin Scorsese in his gangster film *Goodfellas* (1990).

Deliberately *speeding up* the film makes the characters either comical, like Mack Sennett's Keystone Cops of the 1920s, or surreal and mechanical, like the thugs in *A Clockwork Orange* fighting each other in fast, jerky movements—all to the music of an equally fast Rossini overture. The unnatural speed produces a sense of machines rather than human beings, with no more lasting effects than the violence in an animated cartoon.

Narrative

What draws us to screen entertainment? Often it's not the camera-work or the director's choices but the story—the narrative arc that keeps us engaged from beginning to end. Many films and television episodes follow a relatively standard three-act structure—the complication is set up in the first act, expanded in the second, and resolved in the third. The ability to tell a story well, through visuals and sound, may be the most critical skill that Hollywood (and later television) developed.

Film writers face one particular challenge: keeping an audience engaged for somewhere between an hour and a half and two hours. For television writers, the challenge is different. Until fairly recently, television shows were written within rigid time restrictions—22 minutes for a half-hour show; 45 minutes for an hour show (with time out for commercials), and 26 episodes per season. Until the pattern was broken in the 1980s by the innovative series *Hill Street Blues*, which wove together various narrative threads and continued some of them from episode to episode in narrative *arcs*, most series were comprised of episodes that each had a beginning, middle, and end; each one could stand independently on its own. And since show creators never really knew if a show would be renewed from one year to the next, characters tended to stay pretty much the same from year to year.

As cable stations emerged and network dominance faded in the late 1990s and early 2000s, things became more fluid. The demands of the story began to dictate more and more the structure of the program. Seasons could be six episodes, or nine, or 12, and story arcs could begin and end at any time. Episodes could run under an hour or well over, depending on how much time the particular story needed. And showrunners could, on occasion, simply say from the start: This show will run for six seasons; then we're done.

Challenging Conventions

No one minds when a character defies gravity by dancing on the ceiling, as Fred Astaire does in *Royal Wedding* (1951). Asking how he does it would spoil the fun. We react in much the same way to the unrealities served up to us by new technologies. Do we really care how special effects designers turn Wolverine's fists into blades? Or how Daenerys's dragons in *Game of Thrones* breathe fire? We only know that we enjoy watching it happen. With so much technology available to them, directors continue to build on the "new" traditions, creating films in 3-D and combining advanced computer-driven animation with human characters. Theatrical release movies have become, as we move headlong into the twenty-first century, more and more the realm of special effects and Marvel comics heroes and plots. At the same time, what we might call serious storytelling—more or less real characters in more or less real situations—has begun to find a more comfortable home on the smaller screens of televisions and computers in programs such as *The Sopranos, Breaking Bad, The Wire,* and *True Detective*. Even video games tell stories now.

Early Milestones in Film

9.2   *What is the importance of these early milestones in film history?*

Film historians trace the impetus for motion pictures as far back as 1824, when Peter Mark Roget (of Roget's *Thesaurus*) published *The Persistence of Vision with Regard to Moving Objects*, a theory about why we continue to see when we blink our eyes rapidly. From Roget's theory about continuous vision—that is, the eye's ability to retain an image for a split second after vision is blocked—came the theory that vision actually consists of a series of frames, which combine to create one fluid motion. And from that idea came flipbooks—collections of drawings in successive states of motion that can be shuffled rapidly to appear as if a figure is moving—and eventually stereopticons, machines for viewing slides or photographic still images in narrative sequence. From there, it wasn't far to the moving picture.

The invention of the motion picture camera and projector is attributed to Thomas Edison (1847–1931), who patented the Kinetoscope, or "peep show," in 1891. A machine with a slot for the eyes and a crank handle for turning the pictures inside was a resounding entertainment hit. For the first decade or so, as technology slowly developed, movies consisted almost exclusively of single shots, most not more than a few minutes long. The best-known of these were made by the Frenchman Georges Méliès, who built his own glass-roofed studio in 1897 and produced more than 500 short films, including the breakthrough classic *A Trip to the Moon* (1902), which, at 18 minutes long, is widely considered one of the most important films ever made, with multiple shots, science fiction sets, and an iconic moment when a rocket launched from earth lands in the eye of the Man in the Moon. (The story of Méliès' life and work are woven through Martin Scorsese's beautiful 2011 3-D film *Hugo*.)

The Pioneers: Griffith and Eisenstein

Early films were novelties and were often shown as brief interludes between live song and dance performances. But the turn of the century brought more sophisticated technology and the ability to make longer films. "Chase films," which tended to show single actions, gave way to more complicated narratives. Grand palaces were built in which to show these new entertainments. Thomas Edison's studio produced almost 1,200 films between the 1890s and the 1920s, mostly forgotten, but two early giants in the field emerged, one in America and one in Russia.

D.W. GRIFFITH   In 1915, when the huge, elegant Strand Theatre opened on Broadway, D.W. Griffith (1875–1948) gave *The Birth of a Nation*—all three hours of it—to a dazzled public. The film, which deals with the American Civil War and the Reconstruction period in the South after the war, established movies as a mass medium. Many critics praised the film's cinematography, marvelous for its time, and its epic sweep, hailing Griffith as the first genius of the new art form. The content of the film was less admirable, however. There is no denying that Griffith imposed his own point of view on history, one that most now find offensive (and some no doubt did even then). His film is sympathetic to the Ku Klux Klan's attacks on the money-seeking Northern politicians and scam artists known as "carpetbaggers," who came south after the Civil War with false promises of rebuilding shattered homes and cities. Griffith's film suggests these attacks were justified but ignores the Klan's heinous activities in torturing and murdering not only carpetbaggers but freed African Americans.

The Birth of a Nation was the first film to exhibit a definite directing style. Griffith's camera moves in for a close-up at a climactic moment, then **cuts** to a scene that moves at a different tempo. His work has been called rhythmic, because the editing does not simply tell a story but actually controls the pace at which the story is experienced by the audience.

The film also introduced the **lingering take**, which became Griffith's trademark. During one famous moment, a young Confederate soldier rushing across a battlefield stops at the sight of a corpse lying on the ground. He realizes that the dead Union soldier had been his closest friend before the war. The Southern soldier's grief is short-lived: His own body is suddenly pierced by a bullet, and he falls across his friend. Instead of dissolving the scene, Griffith allows the camera to hold the moment silently. There they are, two friends, both dead, two young lives never to realize their human potential. In summing up the contribution of Griffith to the history of movies, critic and film historian Gerald Mast wrote, "The film remains solid as human drama and cinematic excitement, flimsy as social theory."[1]

SERGEI EISENSTEIN   A very different, but no less innovative, style was offered in 1925 by the Soviet director Sergei Eisenstein (1898–1948). His film *Battleship Potemkin*, about an unsuccessful revolt against the Russian Czarist regime, features a sequence that allegedly recreated a horrifying event. The scene shows a massacre by Cossack troops loyal to the czar of hundreds of innocent civilians on a staircase in the city of Odessa (Figure 9.3). In truth, the massacre never happened, but the film is so artfully edited, and this sequence in particular is so powerful, that *Battleship Potemkin* is required viewing in film schools today.

Why did Eisenstein invent the massacre? The 1905 Bolshevik attempt to overthrow the czar failed, but a renewed revolution in 1917 succeeded. Vladimir Lenin, the first leader of the Soviet Union, recognized the power of film to persuade. He chose Eisenstein to commemorate the failed uprising of 1905, and Eisenstein, a loyal Communist party member, used the massacre to depict the brutality of the Czarist regime and its

Cossack troops. But Eisenstein was also an artist, and he used film in an innovative way that went well beyond mere propaganda.

The sequence, over six and a half minutes long, required the splicing of 157 shots. It begins with 57 quick-cut shots that show an assortment of happy, unconcerned townspeople on the steps. Carefully, Eisenstein introduces key figures to whom he will return again and again while the atrocities are being committed. Most significant of all is a young mother wheeling her baby in a carriage.

Then the soldiers on horseback come thundering to the top of the steps, splattering carnage as they ride. A little boy is separated from his mother and crushed to death in the stampede. The mother, finding her son's body, lifts him in an appeal to the soldiers—who gun her down in response. The focus returns to the mother with the baby carriage. We watch as she is cut through by Cossack sabers. A close-up shows the abandoned carriage rocking back and forth dangerously on the edge of the steps and pulls back to reveal the mother, bleeding to death, leaning against it for support—and unknowingly pushing it over the brink. A close-up shows the innocent child inside the careening vehicle as it hurtles down the steps, over and around hundreds of corpses.

Figure 9.3 The famous massacre-on-the-steps scene from Eisenstein's *Battleship Potemkin* **(1925).**
What impact does the presence of the careening baby carriage have on the way we view this scene?
World History Archive/Alamy Stock Photo

Another character, an apparently cultured woman wearing fragile reading glasses, is also returned to again and again throughout the sequence. Each time, she is splattered with more blood. Finally we see a Cossack rider slashing at something out of our view, followed by a rapid cut to the woman's face. She has been mortally struck in the eye. We do not actually see the saber strike her. Instead, Eisenstein offers a close-up of the glasses lying on the steps, broken.

We might say that Eisenstein was led to art through some inner urge. The film is propaganda—but it is nevertheless, undeniably, art.

Major Film Genres

9.3 *What are the characteristics of the major film genres?*

The film **genre**—whether a farce or a three-hankie sentimental melodrama—was born almost as soon as film moved beyond short sequences and began to tell stories. By the mid-1920s, the tastes and preferences of the movie-going public were already in control, and studios gave them what they wanted: comedies, Westerns, and gangster films, with mainly predictable stories designed for quick and easy production, as well as *filmed plays*—language-oriented stories often centering on affluent marriages or tearful betrayals.

Slapstick Comedy: Sennett, Chaplin, and Keaton

Mack Sennett (1880–1960) was the father of movie **slapstick**—rapid and violent farce in which people got struck in the face with pies, crashed their cars into each other, and wound up getting doused with water. Sennett's world is one of total chaos kept in disorder by a band of idiotic, incompetent, bungling lawmen known as the Keystone Cops.

Today we tend to think that the speeded-up, jerky movements of the Sennett films were unplanned consequences of early technology. Nothing could be further from the

Figure 9.4 Charlie Chaplin in costume as the Little Tramp.
Chaplin wore the same costume in many of his films, no matter what character he was playing. How might this consistency of costume have influenced his audiences?
Moviestore Collection/Alamy

truth! Sennett became obsessed with the sight gag and the potentially unlimited resources of film to provide it. After all, a director could control the speed at which motion was viewed on the screen. He photographed action at an average of ten frames per second, but ran the film through the projector at an average of 18 frames per second—almost twice as fast as it really occurred in the studio. The effect was to dehumanize the characters so that the violent catastrophes—Sennett's stock in trade—could not be taken seriously.

CHARLIE CHAPLIN   While working for Sennett, an aspiring young comic named Charles Chaplin (1889–1977) put together a funny costume to wear in a crowd scene, probably as a means of getting a little attention. That costume—baggy trousers, shoes much too big for him—became Chaplin's signature, and Chaplin became the Little Tramp, the prototype of the social misfit (Figure 9.4). Chaplin's developing interest in character, not sight gags, as the main source of comedy led him to leave Sennett and strike out on his own. The result: Charlie Chaplin became the first truly big international star. The ongoing myth in Chaplin films is the eternal triumph of the underdog, a myth with universal appeal.

Chaplin continued to make films through the 1960s, but his acknowledged masterpieces are his silent films. Even after the introduction of sound, his films depended largely on his ability to tell a story through mimed actions. *The Gold Rush* (1925) includes iconic sequences in which a hungry Tramp cooks and eats his own shoe, delicately twirling the shoelaces on a fork and dabbing at his mouth to wipe away the imaginary gravy, and his perilous exit from a cabin teetering on the edge of a cliff during a blizzard.

CHAPLIN, *MODERN TIMES*   In what many consider his masterpiece, *Modern Times* (1936), Chaplin tells the story of a Depression-afflicted society in which thousands have been replaced by machines, and those lucky enough to have jobs are treated like animals. In the opening sequence, the screen is filled with sheep all headed in the same direction; the next shot replaces the sheep with a horde of men exiting the subway. The implication isn't subtle.

In the factory, Charlie works on an assembly line, where his job requires him to tighten the screws on products that come down the line faster and faster. (You may have seen a similar episode in the classic *I Love Lucy* television show, where Lucy and her friend Ethel try to keep up with a conveyer belt of chocolate candies.) In another sequence, to make the workers' lunch break more efficient, the boss tests an automatic feeding machine so that the employees don't have to stop working. And in the most famous scene, Charlie is caught in the gears of a giant machine. As usual, there is a girl who loves him, as well as an idyllic dream sequence showing how life ought to be, with love and respect for each individual. And as usual, Charlie is ever gallant, courting his girlfriend and swaggering in his ill-fitting but clean clothes.

Chaplin's career was interrupted when, in the 1940s, he was accused of Communist sympathies by FBI Director J. Edgar Hoover, hit with a series of legal suits from a disgruntled ex-girlfriend, and, in 1952, banned from re-entering the United States after attending a première of his film *Limelight* in London, where he had been born. The great Chaplin lived out the rest of his life in Switzerland, returning to the United States only in 1972, five years before his death, to accept an honorary Academy Award.

BUSTER KEATON   The other genius of early comedy was Buster Keaton (1895–1966). Unlike Chaplin's, Keaton's movies were determinedly unsentimental. Like Chaplin, Keaton headed his own production company, writing and directing all his films. The abused son of vaudevillians, Keaton was an astonishing acrobat, performing physical feats that no leading man would ever consider doing today, including, in a famous sequence from *Sherlock Jr.* (1924), climbing from a moving train onto a stationery water tower, literally breaking his neck (fracturing a vertebra) in a fall to the ground—and getting up and finishing the scene. Keaton's best-known stunts occurred in his 1928 film *Steamboat Bill, Jr.*, in which he plays the slightly dandified son of a rough-and-tumble steamboat caption. Here Keaton, among many other things, stands in front of a building as it collapses around him, and is blown down a street by a cyclone-force wind machine. Film critic Roger Ebert said of Keaton:

> The greatest of the silent clowns is Buster Keaton, not only because of what he did, but because of how he did it. Harold Lloyd made us laugh as much, Charlie Chaplin moved us more deeply, but no one had more courage than Buster. I define courage as Hemingway did: "Grace under pressure." In films that combined comedy with extraordinary physical risks, Buster Keaton played a brave spirit who took the universe on its own terms, and gave no quarter.[2]

Keaton's mastery was not just in stunt work but also in using film in ways that had not been seen before, employing innovative techniques including double-exposure, over-exposure, multiple images, and split screens. Keaton's greatest achievement, *The General* (1926), was over-budget and not particularly well received at the time; as a result, the studio he had signed on with, MGM, removed creative control from him after only one more film (*The Cameraman*, 1928), and his career and life both went into tailspins. Fortunately, prints of his early films survived, and Keaton was eventually acknowledged, in the mid-twentieth century, as one of the true greats of American cinema.

Farce: The Marx Brothers

The Marx Brothers—Groucho, Chico, and Harpo—dominated the comic scene during the 1930s into the war years of the early 1940s. Usually on the wrong side of rules and regulations, they manage never to be caught, thus still delighting those who cheer for the underdog. Whether it's their inability to pay a huge hotel bill or stowing away on ocean liners, they never play it safe, never walk the straight and narrow. Yet audiences always know that the rules they break are somehow unfair, or else codes of behavior that only snooty aristocrats would approve.

Their masterpiece, one of the screen's most memorable comedies, is *A Night at the Opera* (1935). In an early scene, Groucho, always the suave con man, and Chico, always the seemingly dumb but actually clever purveyor of his own brand of common sense, are negotiating a legal contract for the services of an unemployed tenor. The scene is a hilarious satire on legalese language, as the two tricksters keep tearing out what is incomprehensible until there is nothing left.

One of the most famous scenes takes place in the tiny stateroom in which the three brothers and the tenor are supposed to be living (Figure 9.5). Into the narrow space pour repairmen, maids, crew members, visitors—on top of several huge trunks—until the space is entirely filled with bodies. Finally the door is opened one more time, and everyone cascades into the hallway.

The thing about a masterpiece is that when creative inspiration is rolling it becomes unstoppable. The climactic episode of *A Night at the Opera* is the most uproarious in the entire film. At a performance of Verdi's *Il trovatore*, both the tenor and the soprano he loves have been unfairly excluded, according to the brothers, who then wreak havoc on the

Figure 9.5 The stateroom scene from the Marx Brothers' *A Night at the Opera* **(1935).**
Do you think this scene would make you laugh? Does what's funny change over time? Or are some things funny no matter what?
Everett Collection

opera with their shenanigans. Harpo (a classic mime, never speaking in any Marx Brothers film) inserts the music of "Take Me Out to the Ball Game" as part of the overture, and the orchestra dutifully plays it. As detectives and police raid the back of the theater, Harpo evades them by climbing up the ropes that change the backdrops. The villainous tenor on stage continues his aria as scenes of New York street vendors and Grand Central Station appear and disappear behind him. After Harpo is knocked unconscious backstage, the sympathetic tenor and soprano are urged to finish the opera, and all ends happily—something that can always be depended on to happen in a farce.

Farce still thrives on the big screen. The British *Shaun of the Dead* (2004) and many of the movies written, directed, or produced by Judd Apatow since 2000 (including various Will Ferrell vehicles, *Superbad, Get Him to the Greek*, and the huge hit *Bridesmaids*) can rightly be labeled farce.

Film Noir

During the 1920s, after Congress passed legislation prohibiting the sale and consumption of alcohol and illegal drinking establishments called "speakeasies" appeared, the cynical antihero gangster became a film archetype. Equally appealing was the hard-boiled private eye, a pay-for-hire investigator, sometimes a former gangster himself, who knew every dark corner of the city and every murderer lurking in the shadows. The private eye shot just as straight as the criminals and, like them, could kill without a moment's reflection. He operated just outside the law, but was forgiven, even admired, by the audience, because he was finally a moral being; he never killed for money or for personal reasons, only for principle. Identifying with him was easy and unambiguous. He was hired to find the bad guys, and did so, even if his methods were straight out of the gangster's handbook.

Like many of his gangster counterparts, the private eye projected a deep-rooted cynicism about the corrupt world. Both knew that ruthlessness was necessary for survival. He paved the way for a new film genre, labeled *film noir* by French film critics and characterized by "its dark, somber tone and cynical, pessimistic mood . . . [The label] was coined to describe those Hollywood films of the '40s and early '50s which portrayed the dark and gloomy underworld of crime and corruption, films whose heroes as well as villains are cynical, disillusioned, and often insecure losers . . . [It] characteristically abounds with night scenes . . . with sets that suggest dingy realism, and with lighting that emphasizes deep shadows and accents the mood of fatalism."[3]

JOHN HUSTON, *THE MALTESE FALCON* The private eye proved an apt hero for *film noir*. He usually worked alone or occasionally with one partner, had no family ties, and was good at his trade because, operating on the fringes of society, he knew the underworld and could easily pass for a gangster. At the head of the class in this genre still stands John Huston's *The Maltese Falcon* (1941), which created the powerful screen **persona** of Humphrey Bogart (1899–1957). Bogart had often played a ruthless gangster, but in *The Maltese Falcon*, his character added a moral streak to tough-minded realism, and this addition would give depth to Bogart's most memorable screen creations.

Here, Bogart plays Sam Spade, who has no illusions about the world and the kind of people who inhabit it. But he has his own principles, his own code of ethics, even if others have none. The death of his partner involves him in a labyrinth of dangerous intrigue, murder, and deceit as he seeks to solve the murder because, as he tells us: "When your partner is killed, you're supposed to do something about it."

Throughout the film, Spade is in trouble with both the police and a conspiracy of international crooks, who are among the evil-doers seeking the mysterious but clearly valuable bird statuette of the title. Like a warrior of old, he is equal to any task, despite being threatened, deceived, cheated, and knocked unconscious. But he has something else: vulnerability. He becomes romantically involved with an attractive woman, a client, who may or may not be worthy of his trust. Yet, love notwithstanding, he never allows emotion to override either his reason or his ethics; instead, he remains a principled realist to the end. In a world like this, he seems to say, you cannot afford to be anything else.

In *film noir*, women rarely reach such a principled vision, nor do the villains pretend that what they do is morally right—it's "necessary." Totally absent from the genre are sincere smiles and long discussions of feelings. Typically, the point of view is first-person, forcing the audience to identify with the hero's dark view of the world.

The term *film noir* is sometimes applied to contemporary films that are imbued with the same sense of darkness as those of the 1940s, including Martin Scorsese's *The Departed* (2006), about cops and gangsters in Boston, and *Shutter Island* (2010), about a crazed former federal agent. Even the *Batman* films, in particular the early Tim Burton films and 2008's *The Dark Knight*, seem to fit the label, with their shadowed Gotham, the isolated hero Bruce Wayne, and the principled law enforcement officer, Inspector Gordon. And television has embraced *film noir* more recently in cable series such as *True Detective* (first season 2014).

The Western

No film genre is more historically associated with Hollywood than the Western tale of good and evil. As in gangster and detective films, Westerns typically pit one principled good guy against an array of vicious bad guys, who are often menacing an entire town. Frequently, that town was located on the same studio back-lot set, complete with horses, a stagecoach, the jail, the general store, the saloon, and a dusty main street, the scene of a thousand shootouts.

FRED ZINNEMANN, *HIGH NOON* Fred Zinnemann's classic Western *High Noon* (1952) rises to the level of screen art. Will Kane (Gary Cooper), who is retiring from the office of marshal, plans to leave town with his bride Amy (Grace Kelly), whose Quaker faith opposes the use of firearms. But as he prepares to go, the town is threatened by the reappearance of a killer, just released from jail, who, with his brothers, seeks revenge against Kane, who was responsible for his conviction. The film examines a legitimate moral dilemma: Kane must decide whether to stay and defend both himself and the law-abiding citizens of the town or to head out of town with his wife, away from violence, to a life of peace.

The clock ticks away toward noon. Kane seeks help from the other townsfolk who, though united in their moral denunciation of the villains, are unwilling to fight. The bad guys are after Kane, they reason; it isn't really their problem. Kane's pacifist wife gives him an ultimatum—leave town with her, or she will leave alone. Torn between his love for his wife and his loyalty to his duty as marshal, Kane must decide alone whether to fight against overwhelming odds or to flee, knowing none would blame him if he did.

In the quintessential climactic shootout, Kane takes down three brothers, but the original killer remains. As the villain lifts his gun to shoot Kane, who stands in the middle of the street with an empty gun, a shot rings out: Amy, the Quaker pacifist, has picked up gun and brought down the killer.

Much has been made of the fact that *High Noon* was released at the start of the Korean War. Is this film an argument against pacifism? In the tradition of much high art, *High Noon* is content to remain ambiguous, perhaps understanding that it has posed questions for which there are no easy answers. But in the manner of the very best myths, it does tell us that, when a hero is needed, a hero will be there, because *somebody has to be there.* It doesn't guarantee that "being there" is necessarily its own reward. In the famous last scene, as the townspeople suddenly reappear to congratulate him, Kane bitterly removes his badge and drops it in the dust.

As Westerns fell from favor after the culturally chaotic 1960s, the hugely popular *Butch Cassidy and the Sundance Kid* (1969), directed by George Roy Hill, brought us another kind of Western hero: the charming rogue. The bank robbers, played by perhaps the two biggest stars of the era, Paul Newman and Robert Redford, commit crime after crime but, like Robin Hood, somehow seem to be on the side of the people. Identifying with this handsome, smart-talking Dionysian duo is much more appealing than siding with their humorless pursuers. The humor never entirely disappears. Even when Butch and Sundance are ultimately trapped by Bolivian police, they chat light-heartedly about running off to Australia. They head out to certain death—we see only a freeze-frame of their attempted escape—without a shred of remorse or self-pity.

Westerns also found a home in early television. Long-running series such as *Gunsmoke* (1955–1975), *Bonanza* (1959–1973), and *The Virginian* (1962–1971) kept the genre alive and well for many years, and introduced stars like Clint Eastwood (*Rawhide*) and Steve McQueen (*Wanted Dead or Alive*) to audiences. More recently, the relaxed restrictions on language and violence that accompanied the rise of cable networks have brought with them free-wheeling series such as *Deadwood* (HBO, 2004–2006), in which the central character is morally complex, and even programs on non-pay channels like the contemporary Western *Justified* (FX, first aired in 2010).

Although traditional Western films are few and far between in the twenty-first century, an argument can certainly be made that the mythology of the Western has morphed into the blockbuster—although our comic book heroes are less likely to show vulnerability or charm than their cowboy ancestors. But Mad Max and Iron Man, loners (at least initially) like the characters played by Gary Cooper and John Wayne, as well as teams of "good guys" like the Avengers and X-Men, confront the massed forces of evil very much as their predecessors did, protecting the world from bad guys—even if the bad guys often are now computer-generated and wear stainless steel masks rather than black hats.

Romantic Comedy

A movie theater used to be the perfect place for romance, on screen and off, ideal for a Saturday night date, when couples sitting in the dark could look at other couples on the screen, secure in the knowledge that no matter what has kept them apart for most of the film, they will surely end in each other's arms.

The man and woman on the 1930s or 1940s screen were apt to be better looking, better dressed, and richer than the couple on a date. For Depression-era audiences especially, looking at the luxury in a film offered welcome, if temporary, escape. The sets were often authentic recreations of Art Deco, and the costumes worn by the actresses were products of world-famous designers. Even today, people in romantic comedies tend to look good, live in attractive houses or apartments, and dress well.

Characters in these films often "meet cute"—find each other under embarrassing or witty circumstances—and then become enmeshed in a ridiculous series of circumstances that very nearly, but not quite, brings the relationship to a crashing end. After all, if Boy Meets Girl, and Boy Gets Girl, the film wouldn't last more than a few minutes. Instead, Boy must Lose Girl through misunderstandings, jumping to incorrect conclusions, refusing to listen to facts. Wisecracks often substitute for sentimental admissions of affection, and true love is hidden rather than spoken of until the end. Audiences know where we're headed—even if things don't necessarily turn out that way in real life. But then, who needs a reminder of what real life is like?

FRANK CAPRA, *IT HAPPENED ONE NIGHT*   In Frank Capra's *It Happened One Night* (1934), we follow the misadventures of an extraordinarily wealthy young woman (Claudette Colbert) who jumps overboard and swims ashore from her father's yacht off Miami, intending to marry a fortune-hunting playboy of whom her father disapproves. We know she is pursuing the wrong mate, and we don't have to wait long for the right one to arrive—in the person of a reporter (Clark Gable). Gable recognizes the heiress but promises (for his own reasons) to keep her secret, and he offers to help her travel back north by bus to meet her intended.

A spoiled and coddled heiress, our heroine at first seems to lack basic survival skills. She needs repeated rescues, which our hero is happy to provide. It turns out, however, that she can give as good as she gets, and in a famous scene, she uses her wiles to flag down a passing car when the pair are reduced to hitch-hiking. Despite the fact that the heiress seems remarkably irresponsible in the early portions of the film—and in need of a strong man to guide her—she gradually proves to be the strong man's equal (Figure 9.6). Our hero delivers the heiress to her father—and, finally acknowledging how smitten he is with her, gives up a promised bonus from his editor to write about his adventure, in order to protect her good name. In the satisfying ending, the about-to-be bride runs way once again, this time from the playboy—into the arms of the reporter, who has proven himself a principled and deserving mate.

Figure 9.6 Clark Gable and Claudette Colbert in Frank Capra's *It Happened One Night* (1934).
1930s and '40s comedies like this one often included women who were every bit the equal of their screen partners in wit and strength. Is that true in today's films? Why or why not?
Pictorial Press Ltd/Alamy

The romantic comedies of the 1930s and 1940s featured women who held their own with men in every way. The battle-of-the-sexes comedies featuring real-life lovers Spencer Tracy and Katharine Hepburn and fast-talking comedies such as *Bringing Up Baby, His Girl Friday*, and *The Lady Eve*, all allowed actresses including Hepburn, Rosalind Russell, and Barbara Stanwyck to dominate the screen. These films joyfully liberated women from earlier stereotyping.

MODERN ROMANTIC COMEDIES   The last half of the twentieth century brought great romantic comedies such as Woody Allen's *Annie Hall* (1977), Rob Reiner's *When Harry Met Sally* (1989), and Nora Ephron's *Sleepless in Seattle* (1993) and *You've Got Mail* (1998), both starring Tom Hanks and Meg Ryan. But in the twenty-first century, true romantic comedies, with men and women of equivalent strengths and vulnerabilities, have become few and far between, and for the most part, less than impressive. In many films, the male is depicted as hapless, adolescent, and very much in need of female guidance; and the woman is either an object appreciated mostly for her physical attributes or the only adult in sight—but not a particularly welcome one. In a *New Yorker* article, film critic David Denby uses the 2007 comedy *Knocked Up* to analyze the shift from earlier male-female screen relationships.

> *There they are, the young man and young woman of the dominant romantic comedy trend of the past several years—the slovenly hipster and the female straight arrow. The movies form a genre of sorts: the slacker-striver romance. . . . For almost a decade, Hollywood has pulled jokes and romance out of the struggle between male infantilism and female ambition.*[4]

The Musical

The stories in musical films, hugely popular from the 1930s through the 1950s, resemble those in romantic comedies of the period: The lovers are kept apart until the final embrace—except when they sing and dance together. This formula was gold for Fred Astaire and Ginger Rogers, whose characters had different names from picture to picture, but who always played essentially the same people. Clothing and sets were lavish. Impeccably-garbed Fred, with top hat and tails, and sleek, satin-gowned Ginger, adorned with sequins and feathers, dance up and down stairs, on tabletops, and even on miraculously cleared dance floors in intricately choreographed routines—despite the fact that they have, according to the story, just met. No matter what minor misunderstandings separate them, when the band begins to play, narrative logic disappears as they tap, waltz, and swirl in breathtaking dance routines.

The master choreographer of Hollywood musicals in the 1930s was Busby Berkeley (1895–1976), who placed beautiful women in designs that only cameras could capture. Audiences loved synchronized dancing (Radio City Music Hall's high-kicking, long-legged Rockettes continue to draw audiences today), and Berkeley arranged his dancers in intricate configurations, photographed them from above, and used lighting and elaborate moving sets to allow them to swirl into kaleidoscopic patterns.

Singin' in the Rain (1952), co-directed by Stanley Donen and Gene Kelly, is considered by many the epitome of the Hollywood musical. The plot, more realistic than most musicals, focuses on the transition from silent movies to talkies. Gene Kelly, who choreographed and starred in the film as well as co-directing it, dances in joyous abandon on every kind of surface, including, famously, a rain-soaked street. In the title number, Kelly twirls on a lamppost and splashes and dances his way through puddles, umbrella in hand, as he sings about the joys of being in love—a scene that can be separated from the story and viewed with delight as an expression of pure joy. *Singin' in the Rain* is both glorious escapist entertainment for the public and true to the integrity of plot and characterization.

Although musicals fell from favor after the glory days of the 1940s and 1950s, an occasional film breaks through. Rob Marshall's *Chicago* (2002) used every cinematic technique in the book to differentiate itself from its stage ancestor—fast cuts, overlays, special effects. The result was an Academy Award for Best Picture and big box-office numbers. Similarly, the 2012 film version of the hit Broadway musical *Les Misérables* found a wide audience, partly by casting big-name stars (Hugh Jackman, Russell Crowe, Anne Hathaway) and making them sing "live" (as opposed to over-dubbing their songs onto the finished film) as the cameras rolled (Figure 9.7). But where music plays the biggest role in contemporary film may be in animation. *Frozen* not only broke box-office records in 2014 but spun off one of the top songs of the year in "Let It Go."

Figure 9.7 Aaron Tveit and Eddie Redmayne as the young heroes on the barricades in *Les Miserables* (2012).
Why do you think the popularity of musical films comes and goes? What would bring you into the theater to see a musical?
Pictorial Press Ltd/Alamy

Science Fiction

Although what some consider the very first "real" motion picture, Georges Méliès' *A Trip to the Moon*, is a science-fiction film about the building and launching of a rocket ship, science fiction for most of film history was a low-budget, B-movie option. Audiences loved scream-fests like *War of the Worlds* (1953) and *The Blob* (1958), which introduced Steve McQueen to the big screen, but artful science-fiction films were few and far between. Fritz Lang's *Metropolis* (1927) masterfully depicts a world split in two, with workers toiling away in heavily mechanized underground factories while owners rule from high-rise towers above. The stylized, futuristic look of the film remains impressive today. And *Invasion of the Body Snatchers* (1956) offered a serious message about the dangers of conformism. On the whole, however, science fiction did not come into its own until the 1970s.

GEORGE LUCAS, *STAR WARS*   On May 25, 1977, audiences sat in darkened theaters, were engulfed by the opening chords of a compelling symphonic theme, and watched as giant words scrolled away from them on the screen: "A long time ago in a galaxy far, far away . . ." And they knew: Things had changed. Some film scholars and critics will argue that *everything* changed (and perhaps for the worse)—that movies have never been the same since the release of the first installment of George Lucas's *Star Wars*. Certainly *Star Wars* ushered in the era of high-end special effects, blockbuster franchises, and the centrality of science fiction and fantasy in our movie world.

But special effects alone, no matter how advanced, do not account for the impact of the *Star Wars* films. What does account for it? Let's look at the elements of these movies. A hero—Luke Skywalker—born of royalty (although unaware of his ancestry), goes on a quest. A series of obstacles—temptations, challenges—blocks his path. He is lost and defeated, finds a mentor who teaches him to trust his special powers. And eventually he completes his mission, defeating his "dark side" by—shades of Oedipus—killing his own father. Along the way, there is comic relief in the form of robotic sidekicks (R2D2, C3PO), and a princess to save. Both Luke and Han Solo, his initially reluctant colleague (shades of *Casablanca's* Rick Blaine), begin as egotists and learn the value of living for the greater good. Do we detect something mythological here? Of course we do.

If *Star Wars* special effects begat *Thor, Iron Man*, and *The Avengers*, the franchise also brought a serious exploration of psychology and myth into science fiction on the screen. *Star Wars* led to *Lord of the Rings* which led to *Game of Thrones*. For the emergence of mythological themes on screens big and small, audiences can be grateful.

Superheroes and "Comic Book Movies"

The 1970s and 1980s also saw the introduction of the comic book superhero onto the big screen. Comic books had long provided inspiration for movies and early television, beginning with the weekly serials such as *Flash Gordon, Superman, Captain America*, and *Buck Rogers*, episodes of which were shown at Saturday afternoon matinees in the 1930s and 1940s to bring children into movie theaters. But it wasn't until *Star Wars* suggested that audiences would flock to science fiction and special effects that the real rush to the screen began. *Superman* begat three movies (1978, 1980, and 1983) starring Christopher Reeve; Tim Burton cast the comic actor Michael Keaton as *Batman* (1989) in a dark *film noir*; and the *Robocop* franchise made it clear that big-name stars were irrelevant, if the effects were good enough. In the 2010s, the success of *X-Men. Iron Man, The Avengers*, and their various spin-offs threatens to overwhelm theatrical film. The *X-Men* franchise (Figure 9.8) has now spawned seven films, including three sequels, two "prequels," and a spin-off focusing on the Wolverine character played by Hugh Jackman—and four more films are already on the drawing board.

Figure 9.8 Hugh Jackman as Wolverine and Halle Berry as Storm in *X-Men* (2000).

X-Men follows the adventures of a band of "mutants"—beings endowed (or cursed) with special powers, who are seen as dangerous by the "normal" world. What might account for the popularity of this series, beyond special effects and big-name casts?

Everett Collection

The Social Issue Film

Very early in screen history, some directors recognized the power of film as a medium for social criticism. Such works made a statement about institutions and economic policies that are the root causes of human problems. In 1909, the one-reel silent movie *A Corner in Wheat* took on the stock market and the tragic results of human greed. Like most early films, it exaggerated its case: In one scene, newly-made millionaires lifted champagne glasses in celebration; a quick cut showed miserable-looking crowds on a bread line. Similarly, Lang's *Metropolis* showed graphically the differences between the haves and the have-nots.

The master of romantic comedy, Frank Capra, also created films about bigotry, political corruption, and the abuse of workers' rights featuring attractive, plain-talking heroes. An immigrant himself, the son of a fruit-picker, Capra had firsthand knowledge of poverty, but he also had profound respect for America, the land of opportunity. His films almost invariably end in optimism—perhaps naively simplistic solutions to insoluble problems, but box-office magic. In films like *Mr. Deeds Goes to Town* (1936), *Mr. Smith Goes to Washington* (1939), and *It's a Wonderful Life* (1946), small-town heroes played by Gary Cooper and James Stewart fight forces of corruption and evil in the world around them. The message of these films—that people's worth is measured by the amount of good they do, and that every individual matters—has elevated them to almost mythic status.

A 1958 black-and-white film called *The Defiant Ones* took on racism in the midst of the Civil Rights movement, casting Tony Curtis and Sidney Poitier, America's first black movie star, as escaped convicts bound together by handcuffs, who found they had to work together to accomplish anything. Much more recently, of course, films such as *Django Unchained* (2012), *12 Years a Slave* (2013), and *Selma* (2015) have also confronted the long history of racism and slavery in the United States.

SPIKE LEE The African-American filmmaker Spike Lee (b. 1957) has made straight-up commercial films (including *Inside Man*, 2006), but he has typically used his art to confront social issues, even in his most light-hearted ventures. In his first assignment at New York University's film school in 1983, Lee made a 10-minute film that ridiculed the stereotypes of African Americans found in films such as *The Birth of a Nation* by substituting *white* stereotypes in their stead; this was the first student film ever to be included in the prestigious New Director's Series at New York's Lincoln Center.

The desire to shake up cherished beliefs has never left him. Lee has continued to tackle themes including racism, interracial romance, and prejudiced police. His biography of *Malcolm X* (1992), starring Denzel Washington, is considered by many critics to be his finest film so far. Lee had to fight for the right to make the film, lobbying against a studio decision to put it into the hands of a white director and arguing that only a black director could understand the implications of the story. But when he was finally offered the job by a major studio, he turned it down, because he felt the budget was inadequate. Instead he went out and raised private funds and made the film on his own.

Lee's *Do the Right Thing* (1989) won critical acclaim for his use of an unusual film convention, essentially a revival of the Greek Chorus—in this case a group of men sitting on the front steps of a house and commenting on what's happening in the neighborhood. This story of racial unrest in a Brooklyn neighborhood centers on a pizza parlor where the character played by Lee works (Figure 9.9). Although *Do the Right Thing* drew large audiences, Lee was disappointed that less attention was paid to it than to the much more sentimental and traditional film about race relations, *Driving Miss Daisy*, which was released about the same time and won an Academy Award for Best Picture.

In recent years, Lee has alternated between powerful documentaries (*4 Little Girls*, 1997, about the bombing of a church in Birmingham, AL, in 1963; and *When the Levees Broke*, 2006, about Hurricane Katrina) and more commercial ventures.

Animated Film

By the early 1930s, "going to the movies" generally meant sitting through a full afternoon or evening of films—two features (the main feature and the "B-movie," a shorter secondary film, often a science fiction, horror, or gangster film), a newsreel, a short subject like a travelog, and of course the required cartoon (Figure 9.10), typically a 5 to 7 minute strip with Mickey Mouse, Bugs Bunny, or Donald Duck. In 1937, Disney released the first of a different kind of "cartoon": a full-length animated feature, *Snow White and the Seven Dwarfs*, with color, innovative artwork, and an unforgettable musical score. *Snow White* was an instant classic.

WALT DISNEY AND DISNEY STUDIOS Walt Disney (1901–1966) began making short cartoons in the 1920s in Kansas City. When he lost the rights to his popular creation, Oswald the Lucky Rabbit, to Universal Studios, he invented another character, based on a pet mouse, and called him Mickey. The first Mickey Mouse cartoon, *Steamboat Willie*, was released by the Disney Studios in 1928, and this time, Disney was careful to retain the rights to the character himself. (Although Disney eventually left the animation to others, he continued as the voice of Mickey through 1947.) Disney's vision—that animated characters could populate full-length features—drew scorn from most Hollywood hands, who thought it would spell the end for Disney Studios. Instead, *Snow White* became the highest-grossing film of 1938.

Disney's output became more and more sophisticated as the technology (and the talents of the animators) improved. Both *Pinocchio* (1940) and *Dumbo* (1941) are now recognized as animation masterpieces and are widely taught in film schools, and *Fantasia* (1940), a collection of animation *tour-de-forces*, remains the gold standard.

Disney Studios continued to release animated features, although Walt himself turned his focus away from pure animation to the development of theme parks in the 1950s, and then to the production of a combined live action–animation feature, *Mary Poppins*. After his death in 1966, the studio released a series of ever-more popular features, including

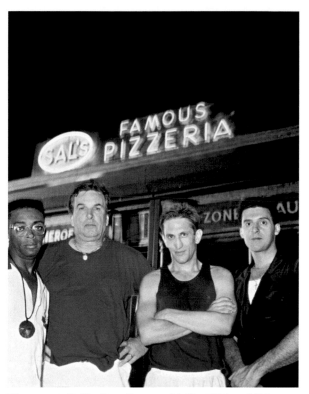

Figure 9.9 Spike Lee, Danny Aiello, Richard Edson, and John Turturro standing up against a gathering mob outside Sal's Pizza in Brooklyn, in Lee's *Do the Right Thing* (1989).
Can film influence social policy? Have you ever changed your mind about something because of the power of a movie?
Moviestore collection Ltd/Alamy

Figure 9.10 A still from *Gertie the Dinosaur*, a 12-minute short made by the American cartoonist Winsor McCay (1914).
This is one of the earliest animated films in existence. What might account for the continuing popularity of animated films in an age when the lines between live action and animation seem more and more blurred?
Ronald Grant Archive/Alamy

The Little Mermaid, Beauty and the Beast, Aladdin, and *The Lion King*. In 2013, *Frozen* became Disney's highest-grossing film of all time. In the early 2000s, the studio also began producing live-action Broadway shows based on their successful films.

PIXAR Disney remained pretty much the only player in animation until the late 1980s, when Pixar Studios, a division of George Lucas's LucasFilm and his special effects division, Industrial Light and Magic, and backed by Apple's Steve Jobs, began using computers to create sophisticated, innovative animated features. Pixar had begun as a computer software company, developing programs to create special effects and animation—but their only customer was Disney. Eventually, the company decided to make its own movies, releasing them through an agreement with Disney. Pixar's first release, *Toy Story* (1995), was both a critical and a box-office success, and the films that followed— *Finding Nemo, Cars, WALL-E, Up*, and *Inside Out*, among others—were also hits.

Animation technology has become so sophisticated that the simplicity of the first feature, *Snow White*, makes it appear dated. Its dialog and songs are never in close sync with the mouth movements of the characters, though the everlasting charm of the story still delights youngsters and allows adults to enjoy a brief excursion back to their youth. But because of animation's sophistication, the lines between animation and live action continue to blur. What, for example, is the Hulk, in the *Avengers* films? The character is played by a live actor, and in his incarnation as Dr. Bruce Banner, he is clearly human—yet what is that 50-foot high green monster he turns into but a cartoon? For that matter, when does Spider-Man pass from live to animated? Or any of the high-tech heroes we now watch endlessly on the big screen?

Documentaries

The very earliest films—one-shots of real events, like a train coming into a station or a medical procedure—were documentaries. They recorded actual events; they didn't seek to tell stories. The novelty of watching the event on film was enough. Now, however, viewers are more demanding. Simple recorded events are not enough. There must also be a story, or at the very least, some compelling characters: two eccentric socialites who happen to be related to Jackie Kennedy Onassis, living in a cat-filled, rubbish-strewn house on Long Island (*Grey Gardens*, 1975, by Albert and David Maysles); Bob Dylan's first concert tour, as he copes with emerging fame (*Dont Look Back* [sic], 1968, by D.A. Pennebaker); or even a mumbled off-camera confession, by the millionaire and suspected multiple murderer Robert Durst (*The Jinx*, shown on HBO television in 2015, by Andrew Jarecki). What is our fascination with "truth"? And, for that matter, what is "truth"? Nonfiction factual films, or **documentaries**, are often respected for their efforts at authenticity but, at the same time, films claiming to be documentaries have aroused opposition because of the possibility that reality has been doctored in order to make a case—or a more exciting film.

FREDERICK WISEMAN One of the influential exponents of this genre is Frederick Wiseman (b. 1930), who specializes in showing familiar institutions in unique ways. Over the years, he has made films whose titles suggest their content: *Hospital, Welfare, Racetrack, The Store, High School, Meat, Domestic Violence*. Unlike some documentary makers who add biting social and political commentaries to their work, Wiseman refrains from making comments or using interviews. His films have no narrative; he allows what is being filmed to speak for itself. As he told an interviewer in 2002:

> *I have no idea what the themes or the point of view are going to be until I get well into the editing. I don't have a story in mind in advance and I don't set out in these movies to prove*

a thesis. I discover what the themes are as I put the film together, as I edit the sequences and study the material.[5]

Wiseman's best-known work, *Titicut Follies* (1967), exposes the brutal treatment of inmates in a Massachusetts hospital for people labeled criminally insane; the work was banned in that state until just recently. Wiseman continues to make movies, although he is now in his mid-80s. His most recent work, *National Gallery* (2014), explores London's National Gallery, letting curators and docents talk about the remarkable paintings in their care, watching over their shoulders as restorers bring new life to works of art, and simply resting a camera's eye on masterworks by Caravaggio, da Vinci, Turner, Vermeer, and others—one discipline of the humanities portraying another.

MICHAEL MOORE   The documentaries of Michael Moore (b. 1954) leave no doubt about his sympathies. His first film, *Roger and Me* (1989), attacked the closing of Flint, Michigan's main industry when General Motors moved factories out of the country. The "Roger" of the title was GM's CEO, Roger Smith, whom Moore pursues throughout the film in an effort to get answers about the corporate decision. When his requests for interviews are repeatedly turned down, Moore instead talks with laid-off workers and their families and orchestrates a confrontation at GM headquarters with security guards.

Bowling for Columbine (2002), about two Colorado high-school students on a murderous rampage in 1999, makes a plea for tough gun control laws (and won the Academy Award for Best Documentary). *Fahrenheit 9/11* (2004), which was selected as the best film shown at the Cannes Film Festival in that year, gathered an enormous amount of footage to demonstrate what Moore considers the government's lax handling of the World Trade Center attacks, as well as the wars in Afghanistan and Iraq. *Sicko* (2007) investigates medical problems in the United States, especially the managed health care and pharmaceutical industries. So powerful has this filmmaker become that several major pharmaceutical companies refused to allow their employees to grant him interviews.

Moore's most recent films—*Slacker Uprising* (2008) and *Capitalism: A Love Story* (2009)—take on the apathy of young voters and the capitalist economy, respectively. In all of his films, Moore's narrative voice guides the audiences toward specific reactions and conclusions.

Moore's critics, and there are many, contend that what Moore is making are not documentaries but rather propaganda—films that manipulate reality so heavily to the left that they leave no room for opposition. But no one denies that these films are powerful, despite their basis in the director's own sensibility. And throughout history, what powerful voices in the humanities have not incited controversies?

CONTEMPORARY DOCUMENTARIES   We may be living in the golden age of the documentary. Although masters of the craft have always been around, hardly a day passes now without the appearance of a new and acclaimed "truth-telling" film, and these films are drawing audiences larger than ever before. Perhaps it's our addiction to "reality" television, which whets our appetite for more authentic reality in serious film-making, or perhaps it's the increasing polarization of our society, which offers opportunities for "preaching-to-the-choir" explorations of political and social issues. Whatever it is, we have rarely seen so many film-makers working as documentarians.

The popular success of nature documentaries such as *March of the Penguins* (2005), the climate change awareness raiser *An Inconvenient Truth* (2006), and 2014's *Citizenfour*, about the whistle blower Edward Snowden, demonstrate how powerful the documentary voice can be.

Two American Film Classics

9.4 *Why are Citizen Kane and Casablanca considered film classics?*

On almost everyone's list of classic American films are two masterpieces that appeared within a year of each other: *Citizen Kane* (1941) and *Casablanca* (1942). The timing may not be a coincidence. The history of the humanities is filled with such chronologies. Masterpieces, as well as the artists who produced them, have a way of appearing close together. Perhaps creativity is highly contagious. Remember that three of the greatest artists of all time—Leonardo, Michelangelo, and Raphael—all lived and worked at the same time in Florence.

Citizen Kane

Here was a relatively low-budget film, consigned to an amazing 26-year-old named Orson Welles. Several years before, Welles had done a radio adaptation of H.G. Wells's *The War of the Worlds* that had created panic throughout the United States. After the furor and subsequent notoriety for Welles, Hollywood gave him free rein within the confines of a modest budget. The resulting film, *Citizen Kane*, was far from a box-office sensation. Its techniques were too unfamiliar at the time, but its reputation as the best film ever made has grown steadily with each passing decade.

Welles's title character embodies the American dream in this rags-to-riches story of a supremely ambitious and energetic man who makes a great fortune as the head of a newspaper empire, influences public opinion, collects great treasures, and dies—fulfilled? His fame is so great that newspaper reporters seek an explanation for the mystery of his dying word: "Rosebud."

The plot, which centers on one reporter's attempt to unravel that mystery, unfolds in a technique innovative for its time and part of the reason for the film's acclaim. The story is told from several points of view. One is the director's objective presentation of the facts, such as the opening: Charles Foster Kane, a man who has interested the public for decades, is on his deathbed in his legendary mansion Xanadu. We hear the unseen protagonist whisper his final word; then we see his hand release a snow globe he has been holding. The snow globe falls and smashes on the floor.

CITIZEN KANE: **THE STORY** The retrospective of Kane's life begins as a voice-over narration by the reporter who is investigating the meaning of the word "Rosebud." Knowing that the camera cannot photograph what is inside a human being and that the audience can only guess at what lies hidden, Welles makes the investigating reporter—and not, in the *film noir* convention, a detective—the central character. The camera becomes his (and our) eyes.

Testimony comes from several sources, as the reporter interviews everyone who knew Kane. In the shadowy catacombs of the public library, he studies old newspapers in an attempt to recreate every incident in the life of a famous and incredibly wealthy man who started out as a carefree little boy, a boy who inherits a great deal of money and must leave home to collect his fortune.

The investigation centers on documents and eyewitness accounts that can assist the search. One sequence is told from the point of view of a man who knew Kane as a boy; one from a longtime associate in the newspaper business; another from his best friend who became disillusioned by Kane's unethical behavior; and the last by the woman, an untalented singer named Susan, who became Kane's mistress and then his second wife. Some incidents appear more than once, but they are told in different versions.

As the reporter pieces together the fragments, we follow the success of Kane's first newspaper venture, the opening of his vast chain, his increasingly gaudy lifestyle, his developing megalomania—the total self-absorption of someone who has everything but is never satisfied. Kane wants to be governor, then perhaps president, but with enough money and power, one can become almost *royal*. (See Figure 9.1.) His political progress is stopped by scandal, when, as a married man, he is uncovered having an affair with the younger Susan. After a divorce and remarriage to Susan, Kane tries but fails to manipulate a successful career as an opera singer for his new wife. Eventually, the couple retreat to a mansion surrounded by statues and other art objects Kane has imported. Susan, bored, does jigsaw puzzles, complains, and abandons him. Kane dies, alone.

The mystery of "Rosebud" is finally understood by the audience in a famous final close-up that reveals a seemingly worthless remnant of his lost childhood in snowy Colorado. (Can you find out what "Rosebud" means?) Even so, neither we nor our on-screen counterpart, the reporter, ever learn the complete truth about the man. The film captures the ambiguities in human nature and offers as profound an analysis of power-seeking as Hollywood has ever achieved.

CITIZEN KANE: **THE STRUCTURE**   Welles's reputation rests both on his storytelling and on his innovative use of film technique: deep focus, overlapping dialog, montage. Individual scenes in *Citizen Kane* are as compelling as the overall innovative narrative structure. In one, the disintegration of Kane's first marriage is indicated in a rapid montage of shots showing the couple at the breakfast table, at first sitting next to each other, then sitting farther and farther apart until, in a few seconds of screen time, the wife is shown at the opposite end of a very long table reading a newspaper published by Kane's rival.

In another scene, Kane's second wife, Susan, the would-be opera star, is shown on the stage, shrieking an aria for the small audience of Kane's friends and employees. As the lady trills on and on in uninspired cadences, the camera slowly ascends from stage level, up through the massive riggings that raise and lower the backdrops, finally coming to rest on a gridwalk hundreds of feet above the appalling desecration below. As one stagehand looks on in amusement, the other pinches his nose with two fingers to signify his critique of the performance.

Another shot illustrates an innovative technique known as *depth focus*, made possible by the wizardry of Welles's cinematographer Gregg Toland, who subsequently became a star in his own field. In the scene, Kane's friend Jed, the music critic for Kane's paper, is sitting at his typewriter finishing a scathing review of Susan's "performance." He is shown in the foreground as Kane enters the large room and stands in the background. An obvious rift is implied by the relationship of the figures. Kane is kept in the background so that we can only guess at what he is thinking.

Citizen Kane was widely believed to be based on the career of the real-life William Randolph Hearst, a newspaper publisher famous for manipulating the news and sensationalizing events that might otherwise have gone unnoticed. Hearst did initially try to prevent the studio from advertising and distributing the film. Unlike Kane, however, Hearst was happily married and entertained lavishly at his art-filled mansion, San Simeon, on the California coast; he was far from the lonely recluse shown in the movie. But the reality was less appealing to Welles than the opportunity to create a film of vast, shadowy complexity that continues to fascinate. *Citizen Kane* is not at all the same as a deliberate distortion of historical fact, nor a Hollywoodized decimation of a great literary work. It is a great work of cinema standing entirely on its own.

Casablanca

Casablanca (1942) became immortal almost in spite of itself. (See Figure 9.11) Originally envisioned as a fairly ordinary action-adventure film and entrusted to the reliable action director Michael Curtiz, the script was revised daily, with rewrites handed

Figure 9.11 Humphrey Bogart and Ingrid Bergman in *Casablanca* (1942).
Why do you think this movie is so popular—its stars, its story, its camera work? Or some combination of these? Does "popular" always equal "good"?
AF archive/Alamy

each evening to the cast, who would regularly make fun of the whole venture. No one seemed to know how the film should or would end, and almost everyone thought it would be a disastrous failure. For one thing, the United States had just entered World War II, the outcome of which was by no means certain. War movies abounded in Hollywood, filled with scenes of artillery fire, bombings, mine explosions, and Allied successes on the battlefield. *Casablanca*, despite its wartime background, had none of that. But somehow, through revision after revision, it became a powerful story about one man's ethical dilemma and his conflicting moral values.

Part of *Casablanca*'s continuing appeal is undoubtedly the screen personae of its stars, Humphrey Bogart—fresh from success in *The Maltese Falcon*—and Ingrid Bergman, the Swedish beauty whose career was just getting underway. In this film, Bogart transcends the *film noir* stereotype he had already perfected and becomes a three-dimensional, fully-realized human being. Bogart's portrait, in a white dinner jacket, with a drink in one hand and a cigarette in the other, has been reproduced many times over, and his toast to Bergman, "Here's looking at you, kid," rates right up there with Romeo's speeches to Juliet in the annals of romance.

In *Casablanca*'s Rick Blaine, the studio found the perfect Bogart role. An expatriate American, Rick runs a small café—a "gin joint"—with an illegal gambling operation in its back room in the capital of French Morocco, a "neutral" territory during World War II, and a destination for refugees from war-torn Europe looking for an escape route to America. Nominally under French control, the city is patrolled by both French police and German soldiers on the lookout for people trying to buy exit visas. Rick, hard-boiled but basically tenderhearted, helps them out by letting them gamble for the money, as the French police captain, Louis, looks the other way. Still, there's always a gun in Rick's pocket, just in case. The ingredients for melodrama are all there. They had to be—or the film would never have been made.

CASABLANCA: **THE STORY**   The film follows the best Hollywood narrative tradition. It spends the first 20 minutes or so establishing the character and the dramatic situation—we learn that Rick was essentially jilted by a girl he loved passionately in Paris, and that's why he is in Casablanca. Then we get the turn: His lost love Ilsa arrives—but accompanied by a husband Rick never knew existed, the Resistance leader Victor Laszlo. In what is essentially Act Two, Rick deals with the conflicts and obstacles caused by Ilsa's arrival. And finally, he resolves to do what he has to do, and Act Three offers us the resolution we didn't quite anticipate—but somehow we knew would happen all along.

This story—perfect as it is—didn't spring full-blown from the screenwriters' heads. Rather, it was the product of allegedly almost endless rewrites, during which the complexities of Bogart's character began to take center stage. Rick begins as an unemotional realist, concerned about the refugees but unwilling to become involved in their lives. He was desperately hurt in Paris, and he cannot afford to put his emotions on the line again. He refuses to take sides in the war. He shares nothing with anyone about his private life. When Louis, the police chief, coyly attempts to find out why he has come to Casablanca, Rick deadpans that he came for the waters.

When Louis points out that they are in a desert with no "waters" in sight, he replies calmly, "I was misinformed."

Slowly, however, the screenwriters show us his character softening. A desperate young wife comes to him for advice. Louis has offered her a substantial amount of money—enough for letters of transit for her husband and herself—if she agrees to sleep with him. She doesn't want to be disloyal to her husband, but she asks Rick: Would it be wrong to accept the offer? He suggests she gamble at the roulette wheel instead—and then covertly directs the croupier to let her win. Louis, who clearly understands what has happened, smilingly accuses Rick of being "a sentimentalist" at heart.

Inevitably, Rick's armor is pierced. His lost love, Ilsa, unaware that Rick is in Casablanca, appears at the club with Victor, seeking those elusive exit visas. Victor represents the biggest possible catch for the Germans in Casablanca; turning him over to them could make Rick's fortune. But we know that won't happen.

Later, when the club is empty, the director uses flashbacks to show us the Parisian love affair that has left Rick so damaged. Ilsa had agreed to leave with him on the last train out of Paris to escape the advancing German troops, but he had waited at the railway station in vain; she never appeared. Embittered, he departed on his own. Only when Ilsa reenters his life does he learn her secret: She had been married to Victor all along. But during the time in Paris, she had believed that her husband was dead, and that she was a widow. She had let her passion for Rick carry her away. But when she had discovered the truth at the last minute—that Victor was still alive—she had returned to him rather than leaving Paris with Rick.

THE EMERGENCE OF A MORAL CHOICE Back at the café the following night, Ilsa's husband asks the café orchestra to play the French national anthem to drown out the singing of Nazi soldiers at a nearby table. The orchestra leader looks to Rick for permission; he nods. That brief nod signals to all of us that Rick has turned a corner; perhaps moved by his memories, he will begin making the right, the principled decisions. We knew it all along, but we breathe a small sigh of relief. As the refugees stand and join the café entertainer singing *La Marseillaise*, Rick makes no effort to stop them. From that point on, he cannot remain uninvolved.

The Nazis seem ready to capture Victor, and he and Ilsa understand that only Rick's exit visas can save them. Gun in hand, Ilsa confronts Rick, demanding the visas. He acknowledges to her that he still loves her, and he offers to provide the exit visa for Victor—but only if she will stay behind with him. Struggling with her loyalty to Victor but clearly still in love with Rick, she decides she cannot leave him a second time, and she agrees. They head for the airport, where a plane awaits to take Victor and Ilsa to freedom.

Legend has it that the scriptwriters did not know how this scene would run until the night before it was filmed. Through the mysterious, often chaotic labyrinth known as the creative process, their dilemma suddenly turned into Rick's famous moral choice. That choice in that scene—and the line that caps it—has made film history.

Casablanca premiered in December 1942—almost exactly a year after the Japanese attack on Pearl Harbor that brought America into World War II. This film, which merges a hard-boiled hero into an immensely touching romance, also manages to reflect the central concern of its audience. By finally giving up his nonchalant and selfish independence, Rick effectively joins the team. He allies with the "good guys" in a war effort that, at that point, no one could be sure would be a winning one.

Telling a Good Story

Citizen Kane and *Casablanca* have much in common. Both begin with exposition provided by a news broadcast. Both employ dialog sparingly. Neither central character reveals himself through what he says. Both use the screen medium to create a complex reality that we must interpret, because neither makes a direct, easily phrased statement about people or existence.

There are also significant differences between the two films. *Citizen Kane* was consciously designed to be a "quality" film, made by an independent young director with no previous ties to Hollywood, using innovative techniques. *Casablanca* was the product of a studio paying high prices to its stars and directed by a man who specialized in action-adventure movies rather than artistic masterpieces.

What the two films share most obviously may be their most important element: They tell good stories. They set up fascinating characters in challenging situations; they complicate the narrative with obstacles and choices; and they resolve everything to our satisfaction. *Casablanca* tells its story in straightforward narrative from a single omniscient point of view, with attractive, established performers and no tricky camera-work; *Citizen Kane* cuts rapidly among several points of view, uses innovative cinematography and obtrusive editing, and employs actors who were barely known.

But the narrative in both cases is compelling—the characters are intriguing; the relationships are moving; there is drama, and there is humor. In each case, the filmmakers demonstrate that they know how to use the conventions of filmmaking to put a good story onto the screen. Two opposite roads led to the same destination: a secure niche in the history of classic films.

The Film *Auteur*

9.5   *What does* **auteur** *mean when applied to filmmakers? Why do these directors qualify as* **auteurs**?

The French word ***auteur***, or "author," has been applied to the most significant directors, those whose special style and themes are so evident that their work is instantly recognizable. "A film by . . ." usually means the director rather than the scriptwriter (although they may be the same person). The work of the *auteur* bears signs of individual technique—like an author's unique use of language or an artist's unique brushstrokes. It can be recognized in camera angles, overlapping dialog, swift transitions, and a personal view of reality. Occasionally, more recently, cinematographers, film editors, and even costume designers with distinctive, recognizable styles have been acknowledged as auteurs.

On television, the *auteur* may be even more prevalent. Each of the major dramatic series that have moved audiences and blown away critics over the last 10 or 15 years has been associated with one person, a creative "engine" who came up with the vision, wrote many of the scripts, and, often, played the critical role of **showrunner**, at least for the initial season or two. This has been the case for network shows such as *The West Wing* (Aaron Sorkin), which follows the presidency of liberal Jed Bartlett; *Scandal* (Shonda Rhimes, who also created *Gray's Anatomy*), which focuses on a Washington "fixer" who happens to be a beautiful woman; and *Lost* (Damon Lindeloff), a sometimes confusing fantasy adventure about a plane crash on a mysterious island. And it has been even more true for the plethora of ground-breaking series on cable: *The Sopranos* (David Chase), *Breaking Bad* and *Better Call Saul* (Vince Gilligan), *Mad Men* (Matthew Weiner), *True Blood* (Allan Ball, who also created *Seven Feet Under*), and *Orange Is the New Black* (Jenji Kohan), among others.

Federico Fellini

The young Federico Fellini (1920–1993) learned his craft from Italian neorealistic directors like Vittorio De Sica and Roberto Rossellini who, in the aftermath of World War II, had little money to work with and often used untrained actors to tell stories of ordinary people amid the streets and buildings bombed out during that war. Fellini, however, wasn't satisfied photographing only external reality as it unfolded; he saw other possibilities for the camera. He wanted to uncover the true potential of the camera, to unlock the haunting imagery it could film. He sought to combine realism with poetry.

FELLINI, *LA STRADA* In *La Strada* (1954), Fellini tells the story of Gelsomina, a simple-minded young woman (Giulietta Masina, who was also Fellini's wife) working in a traveling carnival as assistant to Zampanò (Anthony Quinn), billed as the world's strongest man. Secretly in love with him, Gelsomina becomes his virtual slave (Figure 9.12). Zampanò's enormous ego doesn't allow him to treat her humanely: He rebukes her for every little mistake and eventually deserts her altogether, leaving her penniless in a world she can never hope to comprehend. The only tenderness she is ever shown comes from a musician, also a victim of Zampanò's brutality, who teaches her to play a simple tune on a trumpet. In the final scene, as Zampanò heart-rendingly recognizes that for all his strength, he is nothing, he recalls Gelsomina's devoted smile and the sound of her music. He weeps.

Figure 9.12 Giulietta Masina in Fellini's *La Strada* (1954).
Have you watched a film in another language? With subtitles? What impact did that have on your experience as a viewer?
Moviestore collection Ltd/Alamy

La Strada leaves an ambiguous message: Is love the answer? To what question? The girl's love for Zampanò bore no fruit, and the strongman is left with no one to love him. Is love just another myth, sweet and poetic but, sadly, nonexistent?

As Fellini continued to experiment, his work became more and more complex. He turned inward, focusing on what happens when an artist's creativity wanes—and perhaps fearing that this was happening to him. In what many consider Fellini's masterpiece, *8½* (1963), the protagonist is, like Fellini, a film director who has made eight films and is now struggling to finish his ninth. But early commercial success, fame, a restless sexual appetite, and the continual pressures exerted by Hollywood-influenced studio executives all conspire to keep him from focusing sharply on his goal.

In the opening shot—a memorable one—the hero is inside an automobile on a ferry, windows shut tightly, so that sounds of reveling passengers cannot be heard: The artist is alone and alienated. Yet there is no comfort in that inner space, only more confusion. In a few breathtaking seconds, Fellini sums up the plight of the artist in an indifferent world. The final scene, a fantasy-like sequence in which various kinds of artists are shown dancing in a ring, gives hope that somehow the creative imagination will survive—but it might also mean that true art is simply going in circles within itself and can never reach an audience.

The French *Auteurs*: Godard, Truffaut, Resnais

Mid-twentieth-century French filmmakers belonged to a school that acquired the label *nouvelle vague*, or "New Wave." New Wave directors, especially those associated with the iconic magazine of film criticism, *Cahiers du Cinéma*, put style above all else. Like Fellini, they experimented with the possibilities of the camera. They were less interested in startling, symbolic images than in refining brilliant new techniques in editing and controlling the pace at which the audience experiences the story. Many New Wave films are fast-moving—so fast that audience understanding often lags behind the action; the result is a need to concentrate that forces viewers to put aside their popcorn and pay attention. Others, particularly those of Alain Resnais (who disassociated himself from the *Cahiers* directors), moved slowly, making every minute last a long, long time.

JEAN-LUC GODARD   Jean-Luc Godard (b. 1930) achieved fame with his version of the traditional American gangster film. *Breathless* (1960) would not have been possible without the shoot-to-kill violence of the 1930s and 1940s gangland B films. In *Breathless*, we are less concerned with outcomes than with what we might call the "poetry of violence." Free from the constraints of the Motion Picture Production Code in the United States, which set "moral" standards for film, Godard uses murder and mayhem as a means of stirring up screen excitement. His style of rapid cutting continues to influence directors including Oliver Stone (*Natural Born Killers*, 1994), Quentin Tarantino (*Reservoir Dogs*, 1992, and *Pulp Fiction*, 1994), and the Bourne films (*The Bourne Identity*, 2002; and especially *The Bourne Supremacy*, 2004, and *The Bourne Ultimatum*, 2007, both directed with rapid-fire cuts by Paul Greengrass).

FRANÇOIS TRUFFAUT   François Truffaut (1932–1984) started out as a film critic, a career choice that may have led him to believe that he could do better work than some of the directors be wrote about. Seeing so many movies also made him knowledgeable about film styles and techniques, and he was able to "borrow" from the best while creating his own personal style. The term "eclectic" is often used to describe that style, meaning that it is wholly original but composed of bits from many sources.

Truffaut is a genuine *auteur* in that his primary subject, like that of Fellini, is himself: his own philosophy, emotions, fears. His first major work was *The 400 Blows* (1959), the story of a troubled boy at odds with school authorities and with his mother. Truffaut's own childhood was an extremely troubled one, and this haunting film was apparently his way of escaping from its hold on him. While less renowned for imagery than Fellini, Truffaut has nonetheless left us his own visual poetry. In the final moments of *The 400 Blows*, the protagonist, who has been running away, reaches the sea. Unable to run any farther, he turns and faces the camera in a close-up of despair and confusion that sums up certain teen experiences better than volumes written on the subject.

Jules and Jim (1962) offers an apparently conventional sequencing of events, but this story of a love triangle involving two close friends and the extremely eccentric woman whom they both adore exists not only for its story but also for the imagery with which it is told, and even the background music that, in its lighthearted mood, provides a counterpoint to the tragedy of love betrayed. In one of the screen's unforgettable performances, Jeanne Moreau as Catherine creates the prototype of a new woman in convention-bound society: a free spirit whose crazy antics are infectious, and whose off-center dazzle arouses ardent longings in men. Loved by Jules, a morally upright German, she tries unsuccessfully to avoid becoming infatuated with his best friend Jim. Catherine is both restless and rootless, incapable of fidelity, a person who will never find herself or be at home in this world. She has no options but suicide, and in the final moments of the film, she drives her car off a bridge, taking Jim with her. The film is a perfect expression of postwar European despair. It is an artistic whole, with a beginning, a middle, and an inevitable tragic end.

ALAIN RESNAIS   A contemporary of Truffaut and Godard, Alain Resnais (1922–2014) belonged not to the tightly knit *Cahiers du Cinéma* group but to a loose affiliation of more politically driven filmmakers called the Left Bank. While *Breathless* and *Jules and Jim* require close watching, their plot lines bear some recognizable relationship to the familiar world. Not so in Alain Resnais' *Last Year at Marienbad* (1961). In *Marienbad*, there is no conventional handling of time and space. We never know exactly where we are; past, present and future intertwine without regard for logical sequencing. People open doors, for example, that appear to lead from outside in, only to find themselves in another exterior space, perhaps in another era. Resnais' message to audiences appears to be that a film does not need to make sense as long as it is itself a sense experience. Like Godard, Resnais was anti-interpretation. He felt that if a film *did* something to you, nothing more needed to be asked of it.

Alfred Hitchcock

Unlike the American master Orson Welles, who came to Hollywood determined to create film art, British-born Alfred Hitchcock (1899–1980) was imported to make scary melodramas and only gradually acquired the critical reputation his work continues to merit. Known first as a man who made thrillers about spies and murders among highly civilized people, Hitchcock was dubbed the "master of suspense" in the late 1930s. The plots in his films were filled with unexpected twists, and always there was a breathtaking and surprising finale with a new and ingenious kind of danger. Hitchcock's heroes are typically ordinary, decent—if often flawed—people whose lives are disrupted by evil only after we have come to know, and like, them.

Famous for sketching out every shot on story-boards before the first day of filming, Hitchcock was a technical master who rarely deviated from his initial plan. He used the technical tools of filmmaking—sound, camerawork, *mise-en-scène*, color—skillfully, to make our hearts pound faster. Janet Leigh's murder in the shower in *Psycho* (1960), probably the most famous scene Hitchcock ever filmed (and one of the most famous in the history of film), uses (according to some sources) over 75 camera angles, more than 50 separate cuts, and a soundtrack full of screeching violins to achieve its effect.

The director believed implicitly that we live in a fundamentally amoral universe in which good triumphs only by accident, and in which, despite the civilized façade we erect, chaos is the law of nature. In *The Birds* (1963), that chaos comes frighteningly to everyday life in a peaceful northern California village. Without warning and without any known motives, the birds—masses and masses of them—take over the town, killing some of its inhabitants, injuring others.

The most memorable scene is typical Hitchcock: the juxtaposition of danger and normal activity. A woman waits outside an elementary school, totally unmindful of a grim scene taking place behind her, where hundreds of blackbirds are massing in the schoolyard. From inside the schoolhouse comes the joyful sound of young voices singing. Suddenly the calm erupts into a scene reminiscent of the **elongated moment** in Eisenstein's Odessa steps sequence in *Battleship Potemkin*. The woman, the children, and the teacher are running down a steep hill, holding up their arms to shield themselves from the shrieking onslaught as the birds swoop and peck. Hitchcock cuts from one fleeing person to another in a montage so rapid that we actually *see* very little of the devastation but *think* we see it all.

ALFRED HITCHCOCK, *PSYCHO* Hitchcock had already used this rapid montage technique in *Psycho* (1960), considered by many critics to be his masterwork. The film may well be the scariest movie of all time. Here evil assumes the form of a shy, lonely young man named Norman Bates (played by Anthony Perkins), who runs an out-of-the-way motel in rural Arizona.

In *Psycho*, the Hitchcock vision of the world is fully realized. As usual, he brings ordinary people into what turns out to be a twisted and evil world. An attractive young woman, Marion (Janet Leigh), has embezzled $40,000 from her Phoenix employer in order to run away with her boyfriend. Marion is not, obviously, entirely innocent—but still, we understand and sympathize with her. Driving through the night to get away, she is caught in a blinding rainstorm, takes a wrong turn, and seeks shelter at the Bates Motel, where she is the only guest. She happily accepts the hospitable offer of sandwiches from the young owner, who gives every appearance of being sweet and helpful, although she is taken aback when she overhears him arguing loudly with his mother. After the slightly uncomfortable meal, Marion heads to her room and steps into the shower—but only after regretting what she has done and deciding to return to Phoenix with the money in the morning.

We do not (or at least, before *Psycho*, we did not) expect terrible things to happen in our showers. What surroundings could be more conventional and uncharacteristic of a horror film? As Marion washes away her guilt and enjoys the warm stream of water caressing her face, a silhouette appears against the shower curtain—what appears to be a woman, holding a knife. Against a terrifying score of violins imitating discordant screams, the figure repeatedly stabs the naked Marion. We think we are seeing every moment of her agony, but in fact, the cuts and edits are so masterful, so quick, that we are actually watching only a collage of camera shots: the water, the shower head, the woman's hands to her face, blood swirling into the drain. Finally there is only ominous silence—and the close-up of a dead face, eyes open in horror. We have not seen the murderer, nor, despite what we may think, have we seen knife touching flesh. The scene lasts 45 seconds and took seven days to shoot, and led an entire generation to hesitate before getting into the shower.

Akira Kurosawa

The Japanese film *Rashomon* (1950), which shows a single event from multiple points of view, catapulted its director, Akira Kurosawa (1910–1998), into the forefront of internationally recognized filmmakers and brought new audiences to an appreciation of non-Western cinema.

Though he had studied Western techniques very carefully, learning the wizardry of a camera, Kurosawa was also dedicated to recreating his country's past and bringing it to the attention of a worldwide audience. His masterpiece *Seven Samurai* (1954) introduced that audience to the code of feudal Japan's warrior class, their nobility, their sense of honor and decency, as well as their super-swordsmanship, which they were always prepared to demonstrate in a good cause (Figure 9.13). In some sense, the *samurai* were the equivalents of King Arthur's Round Table knights.

Seven Samurai strengthened Kurosawa's already growing reputation and caught the attention of Hollywood, always eager to jump on a new bandwagon. In 1960, director John Sturges brought forth *The Magnificent Seven*, a Westernization of feudal Japan, in which a band of roaming gunfighters with no allegiances finds itself fighting against an army of bandits terrorizing the innocent inhabitants of a Mexican village. The blazing and dangerous shootout turns the previously lawless bunch into righteous crusaders. The film was hailed by critics as an ethical Western with a solid sense of values.

Kurosawa's films are visually glorious, often using sweeping long shots and intense color for effect. He is also noted for his meticulous approach to filmmaking; he often held up production if something about the set was not quite right. On one occasion, during the filming of *Seven Samurai*, he insisted that the painstakingly constructed sixteenth-century fortress—a set costing over a million dollars—be

Figure 9.13 A scene from Kurosawa's *Seven Samurai*, 1954.
Kurosawa's film about a band of rogues who come together to save a small town from bandits was remade in English as *The Magnificent Seven*. What might the appeal of this story be?

World History Archive/Alamy

completely torn down and rebuilt because the carpenters had used steel nails, which didn't exist at that time. When someone objected, asking "Who'll know there are steel nails holding up the set?" he answered, "I will."

Stanley Kubrick

An American director whose films were sometimes funny, even when his themes were death and the destruction of the planet and the cosmos, Stanley Kubrick (1928–1999), in the best tradition of satire, lashed out at self-deception and hypocrisy. He always did the unexpected, refusing to turn out formula work designed for the "blockbuster" market (even though one of his most popular films, the 1960 *Spartacus*, certainly qualifies as a blockbuster). He made only 16 films in his lifetime, but almost all earned awards, and four earned Academy Award Best Picture nominations.

Kubrick's influence on a generation of filmmakers is obvious from the admiration he draws from directors with such diverse styles as Steven Spielberg, Woody Allen, Martin Scorsese, Terry Gilliam, and George Romero. He was an early user of Steadicam (in *The Shining*, 1980), reverse tracking and wide-angle panorama shots (in *Spartacus*), and innovative use of color and light (especially in his masterwork, *2001: A Space Odyssey*, 1968). His use of music has been widely imitated. He took many chances in an industry where risk-taking is increasingly expensive and not necessarily admired. Very much in the tradition of Orson Welles, the earlier bad boy of Hollywood, Kubrick attained worldwide recognition as a true *auteur*.

STANLEY KUBRICK, *DR. STRANGELOVE*   *Dr. Strangelove or: How I Learned to Stop Worrying and Love the Bomb* (1964) continued Kubrick's interest in antiwar, antihypocrisy themes, but this time in a blatantly satiric style. The film concerns the effort of a general named Jack D. Ripper to start a war by ordering American pilots to drop a nuclear bomb on the Soviet Union. When word reaches the Pentagon, the president and his staff are able to rescind the order, but one bomber crew continues flying. Kubrick parodies World War II movies by making the bomber crew the customary cross-section of geographic and ethnic backgrounds. The music accompanying the bomber as it flies over Soviet territory is the Civil War song "When Johnny Comes Marching Home Again." The pilot, wearing a ten-gallon hat, discovers that the bomb bay door will not open; but, undaunted, climbs on the bomb himself and, uttering a triumphant "Yee-haw," rides it gleefully to the destruction of both himself and thousands of civilians below.

The president of the United States puts in a call to the leader of the Soviet Union. In an effort to be fair, he suggests that, since an American plane has bombed Soviet territory, perhaps the Soviet leader would like to retaliate by bombing only one place in America. But that solution is impossible, he learns; a Doomsday Machine designed by the Soviets to rid the planet of all life for the next 99 years has already started its countdown. Nothing can stop it. As politicians and military strategists on both sides prepare to take shelter deep underground (accompanied by lovely young women who will breed future generations), they look forward to a time when their descendants will be able to continue the hostilities, once the earth has breathable air again. The final scene shows an airplane being refueled by another plane in mid-air to the tune of "We'll Meet Again."

The "Small Screen": Television

9.6   *Why are the 2000s referred to as the "new golden age" of television?*

Although the technology of television developed to some extent in tandem with that of motion pictures, television didn't really come into its own until the 1940s and 1950s, when television sets began to appear in homes across America. A number of inventors filed patents in various countries for early versions of the television; the widely acknowledged breakthrough was September 7, 1927, when the American Philo Farnsworth transmitted the first electronic image. For the next two decades, the process was refined, and the "hardware"—the actual television sets—became more widely affordable.

For much of its history, television was not considered an artful medium. Indeed, in 1962, Newton Minow, the chairman of the Federal Communications Commission made history by calling it a "vast wasteland."

> *When television is good, nothing — not the theater, not the magazines or newspapers — nothing is better. But when television is bad, nothing is worse. I invite each of you to sit down in front of your own television set when your station goes on the air and stay there, for a day, without a book, without a magazine, without a newspaper, without a profit and loss sheet or a rating book to distract you. Keep your eyes glued to that set until the station signs off. I can assure you that what you will observe is a vast wasteland.*[6]

Consider the first sentence in those comments, however: "When television is good, nothing is better." The fact is that television has gone through several creative "golden ages." The first, in the 1950s, saw the small screen as a repository of high culture—live and taped original dramas written by the likes of Arthur Miller and William Inge on prestigious programs such as CBS's *Playhouse 90*; nature and science specials on ABC's *Omnibus*; and Leonard Bernstein's concerts for young people. For the more popular taste, Alfred Hitchcock produced a weekly mystery show, Rod Serling created the classic science fiction series *Twilight Zone*, and of course there was comedy: the classics *I Love Lucy* and *The Honeymooners*.

By the 1960s, television programming showed the direct influence of our favorite movie genres: Westerns, detective stories, and cops-and-robbers dramas dominated. Variety shows, on which everyone from operatic tenors to acrobats juggling plates appeared, mimicked not film but an even older form: vaudeville. And the half-hour situation comedy, often focused on the adventures (and misadventures) of a family, was king. Early **sit coms** were typically benign: Father knew best, the kids cracked wise, and mother took care of the house. Later, groundbreaking series such as *All in the Family* and *Maude* confronted issues including racial tension, abortion, rape, and homosexuality within a context of family comedy that made liberal viewpoints somehow palatable to all of America.

The New Golden Age: Contemporary Television Drama

When we ask where serious drama has gone, now that it has been largely chased out of movie theaters by the likes of Thor and Iron Man, the answer is simple: It has gone to television. When thoughtful and visionary writers are looking for a home now, they more often than not look to the small screen—although the "small screen" seems to get ever bigger (with wall-hung televisions now ranging up to 90 or even 102 inches in diameter) and ever smaller (down to tablets and 2- by 3-inch phone screens!).

The fact is that the "new golden age" of television is now. Brought into being by the rise of premium (nonadvertising) cable distribution channels such as HBO and Showtime, nurtured by the new streaming possibilities of Netflix and Amazon, and welcomed even on advertising-supported channels such as FX and AMC, shows produced in the early 2000s began to cast off the restrictions long endured by network television—restrictions on language, violence, and sexual content, as well as restrictions on timing and scheduling.

The first to make the breakthrough to classic status was HBO's *The Sopranos* (1999–2007), a complicated story of an insecure New Jersey mob boss whose fears and dreams send him into therapy—but don't seem to prevent him from murdering more than the occasional enemy. Tony Soprano is clearly a criminal, and not a particularly likeable soul, and yet he is a complex enough human being for us to find him intriguing and even sympathetic. He has some of the same troubles we do (rebellious teenage children, a difficult mother, a wife who feels ignored and seeks solace from her parish priest)—and a number we don't (how to dispose of a corpse).

Following in the footsteps of *The Sopranos* have come a torrent of compelling dramas featuring complicated, fully realized characters: Walter White, the mild-mannered chemistry teacher turned meth manufacturer in *Breaking Bad*; the incarcerated women of *Orange Is the New Black*; the handsome, mysterious, outrageous Don Draper in *Mad Men*. The unrestricted possibilities for scheduling (no more 22-minute or 44-minute episodes to allow for commercials; no more rigid 26-episode seasons to fill) allow creative minds like Vince Gilligan (*Breaking Bad*) and Matthew Weiner (*Mad Men*) freedom to explore as deeply as their visions will let them. Even network show creators like Shonda Rhimes (*Grey's Anatomy, Scandal*) have followed suit to break precedents in casting and narrative structure. It's not clear which (if any) of these series will endure as classics, or even masterpieces; only time will tell.

DAVID SIMON, *THE WIRE*   Many critics have deemed HBO's *The Wire*, a five-season (2002–2008) exploration of the city of Baltimore created by former *Baltimore Sun* reporter David Simon, one of the best television series in the contemporary era. *The Wire* used each season to dig deeply into the web of relationships among Baltimore's communities, some hidden, like the children and drug dealing networks of an African-American housing project and the longshoremen of the Port of Baltimore, and some on the surface, like the city government, the schools, and the leading newspaper. Characters who are central in one season become peripheral in the next, and then re-emerge as the story shifts back and forth among the city's neighborhoods and institutions.

Much of what we see in *The Wire* seems almost foreign—some viewers use closed captioning to understand the dialog—but it is overall an indictment of the institutions of capitalism and democracy: the failure of the education system, the political system, the economic system to care for everyone, to lift the fortunes of everyone. The one set of characters who thread through every season—a small team of police officers—are more honest than corrupt, but even they fall into bad habits when they feel under attack.

What makes *The Wire* compelling is both the realism of the settings (it was filmed almost exclusively on the streets of the city it portrays) and the authenticity of the characters, many of whom are played by veteran character actors and even nonactors drawn from the city milieu. These people are not likeable, many of them, but they are real, and the more we watch them and learn about them, the more we understand why they do what they do.

The "new" television and video not only has become a home for quality drama (and comedy, for that matter) but also has changed the way we watch things. Programs can now be produced and released all at once, and we can "binge-watch" through the night if we find the narrative and the characters compelling enough. Nothing will ever replace the experience of viewing movies on the big screen among an audience of like-minded souls, but we can also say now that the intimacy and depth of a long-form television drama can rarely be matched by a two-hour theatrical movie.

A Word on Critical Viewing

9.7   *Why is critical thinking important to the experience of viewing and evaluating film or video?*

Throughout this book so far we have stressed the primacy of critical thinking in your life and the role played by the humanities in helping you to develop the skill. The critical viewing of films is a way to bring the pleasure of movie-going to a new and higher level. Recognizing the choices made by filmmakers and showrunners is akin to learning more about the craft of a poem or a painting. Screen performance comes in a variety of themes and styles. Here are some questions to pose in evaluating the merit of a film or a television show.

- **Is the style used unique to the art of video?** No other medium can so skillfully show quick cuts, overlapping dialog, and sweeping visuals to tell a story. The *Bourne* films use rapid-fire editing to keep us on the edge of our seats. The *Game of Thrones* producers film in far-flung locales to emulate the exotic world they are portraying. Does what you're watching use the available techniques artfully?

- **Do the characters have complex inner lives?** The best films and television programs, like the best novels and plays, reward close attention of viewers willing to listen carefully and concentrate. Rick Blaine in *Casablanca* is both the hard-boiled realist of *film noir* and a tender-hearted romantic who would like the world to be a better place; Don Draper of *Mad Men* is haunted by a chaotic and abusive childhood. Are the characters you are watching authentic? Do they have complex histories and visions?

- **Are the actions on the screen relevant to the times?** Both documentary and fictional films and videos are sometimes responses to social conditions in need of reform. Chaplin's *Modern Times* illustrates the dehumanization of the working class during the Depression; *The Wire* explores the dysfunction of contemporary social communities. Does what you're watching feel relevant? Does it move you?

- **Is the integrity of the audience respected?** Films that present serious problems should respect their audiences enough not to hand them unbelievable solutions. Tony Soprano should not live happily ever after. Michael Corleone, who initially wants no part of his father's "business," must succumb to the pull of family in *The Godfather*. Does the show you're watching assume your intelligence as a viewer?

- **Does the action follow the rules of probability—or at least possibility— within the context it has set up?** Biographical pictures (biopics) often distort the events of the subject's life for dramatic effect, and we accept that. But results should be justified; endings should seem reasonable within the context of the film. Even *Game of Thrones* must live by the rules it creates. Once upon a time, we always expected—and Hollywood almost always gave us—a happy ending. That changed dramatically with Roman Polanski's 1968 film *Rosemary's Baby*, which insistently demands our sympathy for an ever more terrified heroine who is trapped into carrying the devil's baby. When the baby is born, we anticipate the heroine's victory (finally) over the forces of darkness—and then watch in horror as her maternal instinct instead kicks in. The "happy ending" is her agreement to care for her satanic child, a twist that we did not expect from a Hollywood film, although such surprises have become more commonplace since then.

- **Are depictions of gender roles realistic and equal?** The graphic novelist Alison Bechdel created a now widely-cited "gender test" for movies in her comic panel "The Rule," part of her cartoon strip *Dykes to Watch Out For*: "One, [the movie] has to have at least two women in it who, two, *talk* to each other about, three, something besides a man."[7] Use it the next time you watch a movie or television show.

This chapter has discussed many works on both large and small screens. If you have viewed the ones we singled out for praise, you may disagree with our assessments. Nothing could be more harmonious with the spirit of the humanities than disputes among critical thinkers giving serious consideration to a work that aspires to be art. Often the dispute itself is more important than the work.

A Critical Focus: Exploring Tony Soprano and Omar Little

Figure 9.14 James Gandolfini as Tony Soprano on *The Sopranos*.

Pictorial Press Ltd/Alamy

Figure 9.15 Michael K. Williams as Omar Little on *The Wire*.

Nicole Rivelli/HBO/Everett Collection

Vince Gilligan, who created the AMC show *Breaking Bad* (2008–2013), has said that he wrote the protagonist, Walter White, with the specific intention of garnering audience sympathy for an apparently good man pushed into doing bad things by circumstances of fate, and then seeing how long that audience would remain sympathetic as it became more and more clear that Walt was anything but a good man—was, in fact, a monster in his very soul, and had been all along. Similarly, the serial killer and blood-spatter expert at the center of the Showtime series *Dexter* is an evil man, struggling always with his "dark passenger."

Pictured above are James Gandolfini as Tony Soprano on *The Sopranos* (1999–2007), garroting an old enemy while visiting colleges with his daughter (Figure 9.14), and Michael K. Williams as Omar Little on *The Wire*, staring mournfully into the distance (Figure 9.15). Both these men are criminals; both have murdered more than once. In other ways, they are very different from one another: Tony is a middle-aged family man, a mob boss, with a strong network of support (including a therapist!). Omar is in his 20s, a lone gun, a Robin Hood of sorts, with virtually no close connections in the world around him. Yet both are admired— and not only by the communities in which they live. They are admired by *us*—by the audience that views them. How does that happen? How can we possibly feel compassion for the Tonys and Omars of the world? How can their creators—David Chase of *The Sopranos* and David Simon of *The Wire*—draw us into their lives so completely?

- What strategies can filmmakers and television showrunners use to create sympathy for characters who do unsavory things?
- How might camera work or the use of visuals be employed to balance an act of criminality or even evil in a story line?
- Do characters need to be complex to draw our sympathy? Is our acknowledgment of some kind of common "humanity" a key to our feelings?

Looking Back

In this chapter,

- we identified some key filmmaking conventions,
- we discussed some important early milestones of film history,
- we identified the characteristics of major film genres,
- we looked closely at two film classics, *Citizen Kane* and *Casablanca*,

- we discussed what characterizes an *auteur* and explored the films of some important *auteurs* of the twentieth century,
- we explained why television shows in the 2000s constitute a "new golden age," and
- we emphasized the importance of critical thinking when evaluating films and television.

Key Terms

auteur French term for author, used by film historians in reference to certain directors who develop a reputation as serious artists whose imprint is found in almost every film they make because of recognizable camera styles, rhythms, themes, and symbols.

cinematography The way the camera tells a story.

close-up In film, when the camera moves in to enlarge the image of one character on the screen.

conventions Elements of filmmaking often unnoticed by audiences, e.g. the presence of the camera and its variety of shots.

cut A director's command that the shooting of a scene must stop; also, when the camera moves from one character to another or from one scene to another.

diegetic sound Sounds that arise from within the world we see on the screen (characters' speech, sound effects).

dissolve When one scene fades out to be replaced by another; or when the camera, instead of cutting from one scene to another, superimposes the next scene on the present one, then gradually fades out.

documentary Nonfiction film that usually has a narrator but not a structured storyline.

elongated moment Technique associated with Eisenstein in which an action that may be brief in real time is broken into component details and thus lasts longer in screen time.

film noir French term for a genre of film known for dark settings, cynicism, and emphasis on the seamy side of human nature; the story usually centers on crime in the city investigated by an alienated tough-guy hero.

freeze-frame When the camera suddenly stops in mid-scene and the image becomes a photograph.

genre A category of film, such as romantic comedy, Western, or *film noir*; recognizing genre helps filmgoers know what to expect about style and content.

lingering take Technique associated with Griffith in which the camera lingers on a face or an object to underscore a dramatic effect or a significant moment.

mise-en-scène The overall visual look of a scene, including placement of actors and props within a space, lighting, costumes, and background.

non-diegetic sound Sounds that come from outside the world we see on the screen (soundtrack music, narrative voiceovers).

pan When the camera travels from one character to another, from one object in a room to another, and so on without pausing on anyone or anything.

persona A characterization identified with a certain actor, such as Humphrey Bogart, often to the point where the public comes to believe the actor and the character are the same person.

point of view The vantage from which the camera is filming a scene so the audience knows whether it is supposed to be inside a character's consciousness or sharing the director's objectivity.

showrunner The person responsible for the day-to-day operation of a television series, often also the series creator and sometimes its chief scriptwriter as well.

sit com Short for *situation comedy*, a regularly televised show that follows the comic adventures of a group of characters, often friends, co-workers, or members of a family.

slapstick An enduring style of physical comedy in which characters often suffer mock violence; the term comes from the practice of hitting two sticks together to create the sound of a punch or a slap in early films.

tracking shot The camera on rollers or rails moving in for a close-up or moving outward to display a wider area, such as the gradual revelation of the hundreds of dead or dying soldiers in the railway depot scene from *Gone with the Wind*.

Themes of the Humanities

Chapter 10
Religion

10.1 Explain why religion is important to the study of the humanities.

10.2 Identify the major *polytheistic* religions and describe their key characteristics.

10.3 Identify the major *pantheistic* belief systems and describe their key characteristics.

10.4 Identify the major *monotheistic* religions and describe their key characteristics.

10.5 Explain why the question of good and evil challenges religious thinkers.

10.6 Identify and describe the key characteristics of *agnosticism* and *atheism*.

10.7 Discuss some examples of the role religion has played in the humanities.

Figure 10.1 A bronze figure of the Hindu god Shiva, India, ca. 16th century.
Most major religions have inspired art through the centuries, like this Hindu representation of Shiva and the vast array of Christian art. Islam, on the other hand, forbids the depiction of sacred figures such as the prophet Muhammad. What role might art play in a faith community?
Photos.com/Getty Images Plus/Getty Images

Religion is integral to daily life for billions of people around the world. They read books, wear sacred symbols, eat or don't eat certain foods in holiday observances, and are born, married, and laid to rest in accordance with the requirements of a given faith. Because religion is so prevalent and because religious themes appear so frequently in the arts, philosophy, and literature, recognition of the enormous influence of this powerful force is indispensable to a study of the humanities.

In this chapter, we will consider some of the many ways in which religion affects us and the humanities. Religion is presented here as a phenomenon found in all cultures and all periods of time, as a recognition of the need to believe in a higher order, as a response to fears about death and to unanswerable questions—such as how to account for evil in a world created by a benevolent God, and as an investigation into various pathways to divinity.

We begin with a brief overview of the role religion has played historically in literature, art, and the other disciplines of the humanities. After that, we divide the chapter into studies of religions that believe in more than one god (*polytheism*); those that see deity as a universal, spiritual order, but not a person (*pantheism*); and those that believe in one god only (*monotheism*). We conclude with a sampling of religious themes in the humanities.

The Importance of Religion in the Humanities

10.1 Why is religion important to the study of the humanities?

Most religions of the world are based on sacred books—books that provide origin stories for the world and for the religion itself, responses to fears and questions about death and suffering, and guidance for how believers should behave on earth. Often, these books are not only religious documents but also works of great literature, with passages of prose and poetry that equal or surpass the best of secular writing. Among the sacred books of the world are the Hebrew and Christian Bibles, the Qur'an (Koran) of Islam, the Vedas of India, the Buddhist scriptures, and the *Tao Te Ching* ("The Way of Life") of China, all of which offer explanations about the past and guidelines for living in the present.

In addition, of course, religion has long demanded the attention of artists and sculptors, writers and musicians. For thousands of years, the creative among us have depicted the gods or a single God, the afterworld (both good and bad), and innumerable supernatural beings, both demonic and angelic. Religion and religious questions underlie some of the great works of literature: Dante's *Divine Comedy* (c. 1302–1321), with its descriptions of Hell, Purgatory, and Heaven; Milton's *Paradise Lost*, with its interpretation of the Adam and Eve story and its solution to the age-old dilemma of how to account for evil in a world created by a benevolent God; St. Augustine's *Confessions*, widely seen as the first autobiography, which traces Augustine's conversion from a life of sin to Christianity. And faith underlies some great modern works as well, including the stories and novels of Flannery O'Connor and Thomas Mann, and C.S. Lewis's Narnia series.

Questioning of traditional belief is also a major theme in many literary masterpieces. Almost all the novels of Fyodor Dostoevsky (1821–1881) portray struggles with faith (although Dostoevsky eventually decided, after much soul-searching, that Christianity is the answer to the world's troubles). Ahab, the fanatical captain of *Moby-Dick* by Herman Melville (1819–1891), reflects the Biblical Ahab, who "did evil in the sight of the Lord" (1 Kings 16:30), raising his fist to God as he seeks vengeance against the white whale. And the final sentence of *Tess of the D'Urbervilles* by Thomas Hardy

(1840–1928) suggests intense frustration with an uninterested God. After the heroine is executed for having murdered her seducer, the narrator comments: "The President of the Immortals had ended his sport with Tess."

Religion has aroused a great deal of discussion and has led, as we are all aware, to devastating wars. The passion of belief, for some, outweighs everything else. Religion continues to spur heated debates between those who believe in the literal interpretation of their sacred text and those who view such writings as allegorical and metaphoric and therefore not literally true; between those who believe the religion they follow is fixed for all time, and those who accept belief as flexible and are willing to explore and discuss. Even those who find themselves somewhere in the middle, or who generally live their lives outside the religious community, find it hard to ignore when religion becomes central to national debates over public prayer or contraception or abortion, or to private ones about a family member's unexpected choice of marriage partner.

The Belief in Many Gods

10.2 *What are the major polytheistic religions? What are their key characteristics?*

Early religions practiced **polytheism,** with ceremonial rituals honoring different gods, who often represented various aspects of the natural world, the underworld, and the afterlife. A considerable body of mythology was created around the many gods of early religions. Some, such as Thor, the iron-fisted god of thunder in Norse mythology, were fierce and terrifying, wielding enormous power over the human race. The Greek goddess Aphrodite, on the other hand, brought love to the world, and the Greek god Apollo brought enlightenment.

Egypt

Beginning at least 7,000 years ago, religion and daily life were inseparable in Egypt. The king ruled as the son of Re, the sun god; he was also closely identified with Horus, the sky god, and others. Kings were believed to mediate between the Egyptian people and the gods, and great cities and monuments were built for Egypt's pharaohs. Ordinary people were surrounded by reminders of their god-rulers. This secular religion fostered an extraordinary early civilization. Giant statues, stone busts, heads made of precious metals, temples adorned with elaborate stone carvings, and, of course, the pyramids and tombs built to provide a luxurious afterlife for the pharaohs all came into existence because the principle of the king as god demanded it. Little remains of the cities, but because the great tombs, containing so much artwork and so many artifacts, have stood supremely independent of time, we can piece together an understanding of what ancient Egypt was like.

The walls of the tombs are inscribed with hieroglyphics—carved pictures and symbols representing words and ideas, functioning, as far as we know, as the Egyptian alphabet; and from deciphering them, we have learned that Egyptians thought of life as a continuous, orderly process governed by a succession of king-gods who passed their divinity to the next generations. The period of time in which a given family held power is known as a *dynasty*.

The history of Egyptian art is divided into dynasties. Each has its particular art style, although for thousands of years pharaohs were depicted in similar ways as idealized versions of human beings, always noble-looking. Traditional Egyptian art probably influenced the techniques used by Greek and Roman artists to create visual images of their own gods. Since the pharaohs were deities who would live forever in their tombs, there could be nothing "simply" human about the way they looked in stone or metal.

THE INTRODUCTION OF MONOTHEISM IN EGYPT   In the late fourteenth century BCE, a change took place. The pharaoh Amenhotep IV (c. 1400–1334 BCE) declared that the universe was ruled by one supreme god, Aton, whose visible appearance was the sun's disk. Amenhotep changed his name to Akhenaton, or son of Aton. He said that pharaohs were the earthly representatives of this god and argued that they commanded adoration and worship even though they were no longer to be regarded as gods. After their deaths, kings would enjoy the pleasure of eternal existence; their tombs were to be built and decorated as before. Akhenaton's **monotheism**, the worship of a single deity, was highly controversial at the time in Egypt, and it replaced traditional polytheism for just a short time: the religion ended with Akhenaton's death.

Figure 10.2 Relief heads of Akhenaten (left) and Nefertiti (right), probably made as a sculptor's model, c. 1352–1336 BCE.
Are you aware of the influence of Egyptian religion or art in contemporary culture?
Ancient Art & Architecture Collection Ltd/Alamy Stock Photo

The style of Egyptian art, however, was altered during the reign of Akhenaton, as Figure 10.2, a photograph of a **bas relief** (a stone wall carving), clearly shows. The profiles are far from idealized; the jaws are so prominent that the profiles might almost be caricatures.

Akhenaton was succeeded by his son-in-law, Tutankhamun (c. 1341–1323 BCE), who, despite his death at 18, readily overturned the radical monotheism of his predecessor. King Tut, as he is familiarly known, was buried, like the pharaohs before him, amidst vast riches; his tomb, discovered completely intact in 1922, was filled with some of the world's greatest treasures. An exhibition of the tomb's contents at museums in London, Chicago, and New York in the 1970s attracted millions, who marveled at the magnificent pottery, rich jewelry, ornate carvings, and, above all, at the solid gold casket with its reclining statue of Tutankhamun, arms crossed, each hand holding a scepter of kingly power.

The wonders of Egyptian art arose largely from the need of powerful men to be enshrined and adored, and this need in turn arose from a religion that conferred godhead over and over to a continuous line of god-rulers.

Greek and Roman Religions

Ancient Greek religions—there was no single form of belief—generally centered on the worship of a hierarchy of 12 gods and goddesses derived from earlier myth, with Zeus at the head. These deities inhabited Mount Olympus and were far from perfect beings; they had to obey the whims of fate, just as humans did, and they often interacted directly with humans, fathering or giving birth to the occasional semidivine immortal. The gods were thought to control certain aspects of nature and life—Zeus, for example, could create thunder and lightning; Poseidon could manufacture storms at sea—but they were not all-powerful. If Odysseus' fate was to return home, the gods could not prevent it; they could only make the journey longer and more difficult.

Early Greek beliefs were eventually influenced by those of various regions with whom they fought or interacted. The Egyptian god Isis was worshipped for a time, and the Greek pantheon of gods was heavily reflected in that of Rome. Alexander the Great (356–323 BCE) introduced the Egyptian belief in king as god, moving the rulers into the pantheon of deities. And Greek philosophers challenged religious beliefs as well. Plato, for example, discarded the notion of multiple deities and argued instead for the existence of a single universal spirit, the Good. Plato's student, Aristotle, posited the existence of a single creator, the Prime Mover.

Greek and Roman gods and goddesses have long intrigued Western artists and writers, from Botticelli to the pre-Raphaelites, and from Petrarch to Shakespeare to James Joyce. Contemporary filmmakers draw on the legends of Hercules (Disney made an animated feature about him) and, in the *Percy Jackson* franchise, all the Olympian gods.

Hinduism

The primary belief system of most of India and Nepal and, after Christianity and Islam, the third largest religion in the world, Hinduism is unlike most other major faiths in that it did not coalesce around a single historical figure like Muhammad or Jesus. Rather, Hinduism grew by accretion, gathering in a wide variety of traditional practices and beliefs, and it remains open to and tolerant of many different beliefs, with a "complex, organic, multileveled and sometimes internally inconsistent nature,"[1] according to religious scholar Wendy Doniger. Scholars have assigned the date of 1500 BCE as the beginning of the long Hindu tradition, because it was around this time that the *Aryans* (the word means "noble") took over, brought the Sanskrit alphabet, and established a national religion.

Diyaus Pita was the Aryan equivalent of Zeus; Prithivi was the earth mother; Indra, the god of storms and war; and Varuna, the god of the sky, responsible for the order in the universe. One of the principal rituals was that of sacrifice (probably human in its earliest phases), for the belief—which occurs in almost all early religions—was that the gods needed constant appeasement and would come to earth to help those who had performed the sacrifice.

THE SACRED TEXTS OF HINDUISM   The sacred documents of Hinduism are the *Vedas*, of which the *Rig-Veda* is considered the most important. It contains poems and hymns used in rituals, as well as the names of the various gods to whom the rituals were directed. The Vedas are the sacred words revealed to mortals, and in this respect, they are similar to the Hebrew and Christian Bibles and the Islamic Qur'an. Closely related to the *Vedas* are *The Upanishads*—not revealed religious truths, but rather philosophical dialogs between holy men and their students. These contain strict guidelines for living and are therefore also considered sacred. One of the most beloved texts is *The Bhagavad-Gita* ("Song of the Lord"), a still widely read epic poem, which, like *The Upanishads*, offers philosophical views on both human and divine existence.

In addition to these writings, Hinduism offers literary works that depict the heroic deeds of ancestors, as well as more philosophical arguments about the meaning of life and the responsibilities of human beings toward the gods. The earliest of these is *The Mahabharata* ("The Epic of the Bharata War"). The Bharata was one of the Aryan tribes, and the epic—the longest poem in the history of the world, running to more than 100,000 stanzas—provided descendants with a proud history, much as did the Roman epic *The Aeneid* of Virgil. The hero is Krishna, a god who could also become mortal and assist in a just cause.

Equally cherished is *The Ramayana*, which describes the heroic exploits of Rama, another mortal who is also a deity—in this case the god Vishnu. In addition to the heroic acts, the poem contains passages of advice to mortal beings on how to lead a happy life despite the pain and suffering that abound in the world. The work continues to be held in the highest esteem, and its teachings are still followed by the devout Hindu.

THE EMERGENCE OF BRAHMA, SHIVA, AND VISHNU   As time passed and cultural strains crisscrossed, the religious tradition of India underwent many changes, and a threesome of deities emerged at the forefront: **Brahma**, the Creator of all that exists in the visible universe; **Shiva**, the Destroyer, who makes sure everything eventually passes out of existence, making way for the new; and **Vishnu**, the Preserver, who balances the two forces of creation and destruction so that the continuity of existence is assured.

As time passed, Shiva and Vishnu assumed greater and greater prominence in the pantheon of gods. Vishnu is especially important as the bringer of stability. In the Hindu view of life, the individual, on a day-by-day basis, is aware of continual change, but change is only an illusion. The failure to see the eternal nature of existence is the cause of human suffering. Shiva (see Figure 10.1) is the god of change. He is often shown in Hindu statues and paintings doing an elaborate dance with his multiple arms and legs. The dance represents the continual movement and changing nature of the visible world, and learning to accept it without being overwhelmed is one of the fundamental goals of Hindu thought.

Beyond the constant dance of life, with its comings and goings and daily commerce; beyond wealth, poverty, hard work, love won and lost; beyond pain and death . . . beyond all these is a universal, unchanging soul, **Brahman**, of which everything and everyone are parts. The three gods Brahma, Vishnu, and Shiva are godlike embodiments of this universal, unchanging soul, defining its workings: creation, destruction, stability. Brahman transcends the separate gods, but it can be known only through them.

Indigenous Religions

Religions that grow up among native populations and are generally constricted to a relatively compact geographic region are often termed indigenous. Although the term might also apply to major world religions such as Hinduism and Buddhism, it typically is used to refer to those belief systems created by ethnic groups like Native-American or African tribal societies.

NATIVE-AMERICAN RELIGIONS   Native-American culture and the various religions practiced within it are as diversified as any in the world. Some anthropologists believe that various North American groups can be traced back to migrations from northern Asia over 10,000 years ago, when it would have been possible to walk from Siberia to Alaska. But some Native-American tribes maintain that their culture has always existed in the Americas, having originally emerged, according to powerful "origin" or "creation" myths, from beneath the earth's surface.

Whatever their beginnings, Native Americans long ago divided into groups migrating throughout both American continents, establishing early civilizations wherever they settled, developing their own languages, and practicing their own religions. Cultural anthropologists who have made a careful study of the many groups found certain common beliefs and values as well as many differences.

These belief systems are overwhelmingly polytheistic. However, like the Greeks and Romans, the various groups tended to think of the gods and their world as an extension of this world. For the Hopis of the American Southwest, for example, Tawa, the sun god or creator, mediates with his people through Spider Woman, who leads mortals from one world to the next. For the Inuits of Alaska, who depended on the sea for their bounty, the central goddess is Sedna, who is part human and part fish and lives underwater. Sedna keeps a watchful eye on the daily lives of her people, allowing the good to haul in as many fish as they need.

Native-American belief systems, like Hinduism, infuse everyday life. In fact, some argue that these systems are not religions at all, but simply the rules of existence. In almost all Native-American communities, belief in the sacred nature of the earth and its bounty is paramount, and the reality of the spiritual world is simply a given.

The arrival of Christianity around the sixteenth century created massive changes for Native Americans in belief, lifestyle, and religious practice. In many cases, the new was blended with the old. The Christian God became the Great Spirit who controlled the entire world—but with many helpers who oversaw the hunt, the planting, and the harvest. These transitions did not come easily. Often there were terrible clashes between Christian settlers and Native Americans, including massacres and kidnappings, events that only intensified the European perception of Native Americans as "savages." Nevertheless, many North American tribal societies maintain the dances, festivals, and celebrations of their ancestors, sometimes allowing visitors to observe, but often closing off access to pueblos and towns during these events.

AFRICAN RELIGIONS As in Native-American religions, the need for humans to live in harmony with nature and with the spiritual world is at the center of most African ethnic or tribal-based beliefs. Also like those of Native Americans, most African religions maintain elaborate legends about the creation of the world, of humankind, and of the spirit world. However, African indigenous religions may fit less well into the category of polytheism, since most center on a single supreme being, who is aided by an array of secondary spirits more akin to the semidivines of the Greeks and Romans than to actual gods and goddesses. Ancestor worship is also relatively common, as is a belief in reincarnation within a family.

As is true in the Americas, Christianity and Islam have spread throughout the African continent, causing a process called **syncretism**, or the blending of traditional beliefs with those of the new religion. Thus even though Christianity and Islam are now the majority religions in Africa, scholars estimate that over 100 million Africans in 43 countries continue to practice their traditional belief systems in some form. In addition, the African diaspora has led to new outposts for traditional African religion, primarily in Latin America and the Caribbean.

Belief in an Amorphous or Universal Divinity

10.3 *What are the major pantheistic belief systems? What are their key characteristics?*

Some belief systems do not suggest the existence of one god or of many gods, but instead include a belief that, as Plato posited, there is an all-encompassing spirit or soul that is synonymous with nature or with the universe itself. As Hinduism evolved and the principle of Brahman emerged, for example, a belief in the universal soul became its central tenet. **Hinduism** does not include a belief in a personal God promising freedom from pain. True, it gives a name to the universal soul, but Brahman is not a conscious being; Brahman is universal order. Brahman is what believers mean by "it" in the sentence "It is raining." Rain is in the nature of things, and Brahman *is* the nature of things.

Are suffering and pain also part of that nature? Or are they, like change, an illusion? The devout in India believe that suffering, if not intentionally imposed by some god, must be part of the universal order. Somehow there must be a reason for it, and therein the hope of tolerating it. *The Upanishads* ask the question of whether life is worth living. The answer is in the affirmative, and this fact means that eventually there will be emancipation from pain.

The Concepts of *Moksha* and *Nirvana*: The Attainment of Bliss

This condition—the achievement of oneness with the universe and emancipation from pain—was called *moksha* in Hinduism, and later, in Buddhism, *nirvana*. To reach *moksha* or *nirvana*, a person must suffer. Without pain, there can be no such thing as bliss—for how could anyone recognize bliss if it were attained without a struggle?

Reaching *moksha* is extremely difficult for most of us. We are angry or frustrated by life's tribulations, and so we do bad things: We lie, we cheat, we rob, we even murder in attempts to make our own life better. But these wrongful deeds necessarily lead to further misfortunes, since punishment for immoral behavior is in the nature of things. Transcending desire—for more things, for a better life—must therefore be the primary human goal, even for those who are poor and desire a better life. But freedom from desire cannot be accomplished overnight.

Karma is the name given to the cumulative moral consequences of actions. *Good* karma means an accumulation of good deeds; *bad* karma, the accumulation of sins. At the end of each of our lives comes the summing up. A preponderance of bad karma results in having to be reborn into a lower social class and attempting once again to lead a virtuous life regardless of suffering. Good karma results in reincarnation in a higher social class with better living conditions and less suffering.

Still, the temptations of this world are great, and so the cycle of death and rebirth can be expected to continue for a very long time. Eventually, however, perhaps after many thousands of years, the individual will attain *moksha*, the reward of eternal release from pain—not heaven, just peace at last. Within such a state, the rightful order of the universe will be understood; we will achieve **enlightenment**, the total union of Atman, the individual soul, and Brahman, the universal soul, and the cycle will end.

According to the sacred books, on very rare occasions, an individual will lead a perfect life and achieve enlightenment without ever having to be reborn. This person is called a **buddha**, or "enlightened one." The coming of a buddha occurs perhaps every 25,000 years.

Buddhism

Although the term "buddha" is found in Hindu sacred books, it was not associated with a separate religion until the birth and life of one man who lived sometime around the fifth century BCE. The one who was called the Buddha has become, for millions of Buddhists ever after, a godlike figure, although he would not have thought of himself that way. Hailed by his followers as Jesus would later be hailed by his, the Buddha was originally an unlikely candidate for the honor. Siddhartha Gautama (c. 564–c. 483 BCE) was born a prince in India, surrounded by luxuries beyond imagining. He married a beautiful woman, who bore him a handsome son. The family lived in the gorgeous palace he inherited from his father. He was the envy of all who knew him. Yet he became restless and unhappy. Something kept telling him he did not belong where he was, leading a life that was filled with sensual pleasure but essentially meaningless. He would grow old and die, he worried, leaving behind mementos of a wasted life.

One day, according to legend, Siddhartha went for a walk through his village and encountered three things that were new to him. The first was *poverty*. Everywhere he looked, he saw beggars reaching out their bony hands for alms. The second was *sickness*. He saw people who could no longer even sit up and beg, but could only lie back and waste away from malnutrition and disease. Finally, he saw *death*. A man in the prime of life had just died, and his relatives were preparing the body for cremation right there on the street. Siddhartha was appalled by the fact that for the poor people outside the privileged confines of his palace, life amounted to nothing more than a desperate attempt to survive, and the "reward" for the struggle was death and rebirth into what traditional belief suggested would likely be an even more wretched existence.

SIDDHARTHA'S CONVERSION Siddhartha experienced a sudden conversion, like Paul of Tarsus, the Emperor Constantine, and Muhammad after him. On that very day, he went home, threw off his royal apparel, dressed himself in cast-off garments and rags, bade farewell to his wife and son, and, abandoning the comforts of the palace forever, set out on a quest for another way to live.

Like the beggars he had seen, he sank into abject poverty. The stories tell us that he denied himself food, except for one sesame seed a day, until he grew so weak that he knew he would die before he discovered the secret of a truly meaningful and virtuous life (Figure 10.3). He was so obsessed with the search for a life opposite to the life he had formerly led that he was killing himself in the process. One day he said: "If the string is too tight, it will snap."

Finally, in a state of near total exhaustion, he found a large *bodhi*, or rose-apple tree, and flung himself down under it. He sat there, cross-legged, not resting against the trunk, because he found that by sitting perfectly upright, with his back straight, he could remain wide awake. In that state, Siddhartha suddenly began to see everything and everyone around him with a clarity he had never known. Putting his ego to rest, Siddhartha engaged in the first recorded instance of the **meditation** practice that is almost synonymous with Buddhism today.

Buddhist scripture tells us that storms howled and rivers flooded during the 40 days and 40 nights that Siddhartha remained sitting beneath the tree. Those who gathered around were amazed that he never moved or reacted in any way to the pounding of the elements. Evil demons attempted to distract him, sometimes disguised as beautiful women holding out large baskets of food, but Siddhartha was not to be swayed. At length the storms and the demons went away, and there was peace, not only there but all over the world. Lotus blossoms and golden water lilies fell from the sky, and the world "became quite quiet, as though it had reached full perfection."[2]

Siddhartha had attained enlightenment, an important step on the way to *nirvana*. In the West, enlightenment means cognitive understanding. In **Buddhism**, an enlightened person loses all consciousness of ego and, utterly detached from participation in the stream of life, sees everything as it is, with total objectivity, understanding everyone's thoughts, motives, joys, and sorrows. Since it is freedom from the emotional strain of living within one's ego, enlightenment in Buddhism is the gateway to achieving total peace—*nirvana*, which is not death, but peace without end.

SIDDHARTHA'S MINISTRY After 40 days, Siddhartha finally rose from his meditation and embarked on a mission he considered greater than remaining in the blissful state of enlightenment. He would first advise those who would listen that they must find a middle way between the extremes of total self-denial (as when he had denied himself food

Figure 10.3 The starving Buddha, a statue outside a temple in Japan.
The central figures of three major religions—Christianity, Islam, and Buddhism—all went through periods of desperate suffering. What role might this play in their importance as figures to be worshipped?

Melpomene/Fotolia

and money) and a total mystical withdrawal from life. One should, he taught, conduct oneself like a string that is neither too tight nor too loose. (In many statues of Buddha, the fingertips are lightly touching, perhaps suggesting the analogy with the string.)

As he walked through the villages of India, Siddhartha paused to speak to anyone who would listen. Gradually, he attracted followers who trudged beside him, and, from time to time, he would stop to share with them the insights that kept flooding his mind. The long meditation had sharpened his rationality. Eventually he arrived at what were to him the four basic truths of life—that life is filled with pain; that pain is caused by unfulfilled desires; that there is a way out of pain; and that the way out is to follow the Eightfold Path.

Siddhartha's Eightfold Path has become the Buddhist guide to a life of peace and harmony, a life that can, as death nears, be recalled happily, in the knowledge that one has brought goodness into the world. The Path is built around the concept of *righteousness*—acting, reacting, and thinking relative to things as they are, not as we would like them to be or as we pretend to ourselves that they are. It means walking in a constant state of wakefulness so that all actions are appropriate and not based on narrow self-interest. The eight paths are:

- Right views—opinions based on a knowledge of things as they are.
- Right intentions—decision to act on such views.
- Right speech—saying what is appropriate, guarding one's statements so that they do not provoke anger and defensive behavior in others (but not saying what is false in order not to offend).
- Right conduct—behaving toward and interacting with others in accordance with things as they are, not as you want them to be.
- Right livelihood—earning what is needed to survive and help others to survive, but never earning for its own sake and for unnecessary possessions earning makes possible.
- Right effort—striving to do what needs to be done, not to advance one's own cause or prestige.
- Right mindfulness—maintaining the sitting or meditative attitude anywhere, whether in solitude or in society.
- Right concentration—focusing unwaveringly on reality without the intrusion of ego and the idle chatter that floods the mind.

The Buddhism of Siddhartha was never intended to be a religion. Its practice was intensely personal. Instead of commandments, it offered advice for leading a life of goodness. As the centuries passed and followers numbered in the millions, Buddhism acquired many different aspects.

ZEN BUDDHISM *Zen Buddhism*, a strain of Buddhism that developed in China (where it was known as Ch'an, and subsequently Zen in the West) but spread to Korea and Japan, is an austere, monastic philosophy requiring many years of practicing detachment and a continuing regimen of lengthy meditation sessions, often with an experienced mentor. **Zen** may reflect the influence of Chinese traditional religions, particularly Taoism and Confucianism, on the Buddhism imported from India.

A thousand years after Siddhartha's enlightenment, a Hindu monk named Bodhidharma traveled to China with missionary zeal to win converts to Buddhist teachings. Now, the rigorous meditation practices emphasizing self-observation, conscious breathing, and mindfulness are practiced in Western as well as Asian societies. Zen masters and their students engage in dialogs in which questions are asked that cannot be answered through logical reflection. Confused at first, the student gradually becomes adept at answering intuitively with what is called the *non-mind*.

The most famous Zen question—*What is the sound of one hand clapping?*—has been traced to the teachings of an eighteenth-century Zen monk named Hakuin Ekaku

Figure 10.4 Bodhidharma, Japan, 1836.
Does the concept of meditation appeal to you? Why might meditation, yoga, and other practices that originated in Buddhism and Hinduism be appealing in today's world?
Gift of Leslie Prince Salzman/LACMA

(1686–1769), who was also an artist. The aim of this question-and-response training is to clear the mind of the traditional reasoning process, which separates the individual from reality. In Zen Buddhism, reality has no words and thus cannot be understood rationally. The aim of meditation is to confront the void that is reality, thus losing ego and its fantasies.

Zen art has many facets, ranging from quick pen-and-ink drawings produced rapidly after a lengthy period of meditation, to sophisticated portraiture, such as the depiction of Bodhidharma in Figure 10.4. The wide-open eyes suggest a state of total wakefulness, which is the goal of Zen; and the absence of eyelids is derived from the legend that Bodhidharma pulled them off in order to remain awake.

Though the schools of Buddhism are varied, the common thread is to trust the workings of the universe. Just as "it" knows when to rain, when to grow and yield the harvest, people must learn to walk in step with "it." If they do, they will behave righteously toward others, they will be treated righteously by others, and they will be at peace. Common to Hinduism, Buddhism, and the Chinese belief system of Taoism is belief in a central intelligence—called *Brahman* in Hinduism, **dharma** in Buddhism, and the **Tao** (Dow) in Taoism. A common definition is "the Way." Morally right actions are aligned with the Way. The individual who follows the Way lives in harmony within society and the environment, and both of these live in harmony with the individual.

Taoism

Of Chinese origin, Taoism can be traced to the writings of Lao-tzu, who is believed to have lived some time during the sixth century BCE, but about whom little else is known. The name Lao-tzu, simply meaning "the old one," may have been shared by a number of writers who contributed to the little book called *Tao Te Ching* ("The Way of Life"). Reprinted continually, it is a slender volume of short poems, often cryptic, seemingly simple, but at the same time extremely profound, containing the view that the Way is an impersonal divine order that rules the universe. Taoism is a religion only in the sense that its followers are obligated to live their lives in accordance with this order. It is expressed through the health of the body's system, the mind's harmonious processes, ethical dealings in all human interaction, respect for elders, and hospitality toward strangers.

The philosophy grew out of a Chinese civilization that was rapidly advancing and was proud of its urban culture. In India at approximately the same time, the era of Siddhartha, there was a great disparity between the poor and the affluent. Siddhartha, a prince, saw no reason to be proud of luxury and left his place in society. Taoism, on the other hand, tells us we are all part of that society, with all of its prejudices and double-dealing, and teaches us to conduct ourselves honorably and ethically within it.

Fundamental to Taoism is the belief that the Tao operates through the continual interactions of opposites: joy and pain; birth and death; male and female; day and night; cold and heat; success and failure, and so on. We cannot embrace life without being prepared for death. The fear of death—or for that matter, of anything opposite to what we hold dear—leads to suffering. If youth, vigor, and unwrinkled good looks are all-important, we must know they cannot last and we must therefore feel no anguish with the onset of age. Success and failure are implicit in the way the world goes. Today's failure might be tomorrow's brilliant achiever.

The universe was created by the entwinement of the fundamental opposites: **yin**, the passive element, and **yang**, the active energy (Figure 10.5). In Chinese art, yin and yang are visually represented as a circle with a white crescent and a black crescent, each side containing a smaller circle of the other's color. The white crescent, yang, is the sun, the source of all life, and is traditionally known as the masculine principle. The black crescent, yin, is the moon, the passive and traditionally feminine principle. The passive yin requires the driving force of the active yang to bring forth the variety of things that go to make up the world.

WU WEI   Central to Taoist teachings is the concept of **wu wei**, which is difficult to translate exactly into English. Perhaps the closest definition is *to do without doing*—allowing the Tao to work freely, rather than trying to manipulate reality. If we do without doing, we are following our true nature, and we will be successful no matter how insignificant our accomplishments may seem to others.

Figure 10.5 The yin-yang symbol.
In Taoism, *yin* (passivity) and *yang* (energy) are cosmic opposites. Why do you think each is depicted as containing a part of the other?
Borislav Marinic/Getty Images

Does *wu wei* mean that we should remain passive while others manipulate us? Does it mean that our goal is to sit back while others suffer pain or injustice? Not at all. Taoism teaches that we must take appropriate action whenever necessary and possible. The Tao is ethical in all things, and our true nature is ethical as well. If we become aware that a close friend is guilty of wrongdoing, it is our obligation not to turn away or say "I really don't want to become involved." We must act to prevent the wrong from happening or, if it has already happened, to see that the action does not go unreported. Putting friendship before ethical responsibility may be deeply rooted in our natures, but these natures are distortions of the Tao, acquired from a long history of living within complex society and adopting its values.

Some Western scientists find Taoist philosophy profoundly meaningful and hardly limited to Chinese culture. In 1976, for example, Fritjof Capra published *The Tao of Physics*, in which he shows parallels between the Taoist concept of yin and yang and the basic forces in nature that involve the interaction of opposites, as in the magnetic force that binds protons and electrons to form the nucleus of the atom.

Socrates and Plato

The great Athenian civilization of the fifth century BCE witnessed a surge of philosophy, including that of Socrates and Plato, that did not further the cause of polytheism in Greece. Socrates (469–399 BCE) specialized in the **dialectic**, an analytical method of thinking. Instead of merely presenting an idea, he arrived at it by revealing the flaws of its opposite. Though his contributions to human thought are recorded in no writings of his own, his esteemed follower, Plato (427–347 BCE), did leave behind some of the greatest works of the humanities, most of them written as dialogs in which Socrates debates with his students on philosophical matters. One of these, *The Republic*, offers a profound vision of the ideal society and the importance of the well-ordered soul.

Socrates was arrested on charges of preaching atheism and corrupting the youth of Athens. Historians of philosophy, however, believe that the true "crime" that condemned him to imprisonment and execution was that he taught his young followers to think for themselves, a goal that makes many governments uneasy. Socrates even referred to himself as "gadfly to the state," and he said it with pride.

According to Plato, Socrates refers both to "gods" and "a god," and it is not clear whether he is making metaphoric use of the terms. In his famous speech to the assembly of citizens who have just condemned him to death, a speech Plato records in

The Apology of Socrates, he tells them that he harbors no ill will toward them and that they are not to pity him. Rather, they should

> be of good cheer about death, and know of a certainty that no evil can befall a good man, either in life or after death. He and his are not neglected by the gods; nor has his own approaching end happened by mere chance.[3]

The polytheistic reference does not extend to the considerable body of Socratic thought written down by Plato and may simply have been intended to show the citizens that he was in the good hands of a higher authority, that they had not in fact won a victory over him. That authority was probably his own virtuous existence guided by the principle of reason. Socrates concludes the speech by saying that

> the hour of departure has arrived, and we go our ways—I to die, and you to live. Which is better God only knows.[4]

The singular "God" here should not be taken as a sign of an emerging monotheism. Nothing about the thought of Socrates and Plato suggests faith in any force except the inherent rationality of the universe and in the individual willing to think. Rationality was divinity to them. In *The Republic,* they created a vision of the ideal state, governed by a philosopher-king, not a god-king like that of the Egyptians.

Aristotle's *Unmoved Mover*

Plato opened the first official university in the West, the *Academy* (named after the public groves of Academe, in which Socrates walked with his followers), and there he influenced his star pupil, Aristotle (384–322 BCE), who would later open his own school, the *Lyceum*. Aristotle formalized logic as a method of thinking. In his *Metaphysics*, he pondered the problem of how the universe got started. His conclusions came close to the monotheism of Judaism, and Christianity later embraced him as the pagan who anticipated Christian doctrine.

Aristotle believed that the universe, an orderly system of sun and planets, always existed, but in the beginning it was cold, lifeless, and without motion. Motion by definition always has a cause. Logic impelled him to conclude that the whole system must have been *set* in motion, far back in the past, by something that was not in motion itself. If it were, we would then have to determine the cause of *its* motion, and so on into infinity.

The result was the principle of the **Unmoved Mover**, to be thought of as a cause that led to the first effect, which was motion, but not as a causer. This distinction is all-important. Causers can become personalized, and that is precisely what happened later. For Aristotle, the cold and lifeless universe was not created. It just *was*. But his system required a mover, one that was a principle of motion—a *potentiality* for motion that was always there. He could not fathom how what existed, including the principle of motion, could ever have been nonexistent.

> For if it had ever come into existence, we should have to suppose an original constitutive element "already there" for it to come out of. But this character of being "a subject already there as a basis of change" is precisely the thing we have just been inquiring about; hence, if the matter of what changes were itself to change, it would have to exist before its own coming into existence.[5]

The three religions that were to dominate the Western and Middle Eastern worlds would make a separation between what creates (God) and what is created (the universe). Lacking a theory of God the Creator, Aristotle had to explain just what the Unmoved Mover was and where it was found.

He envisioned the universe as a sphere, the outer two rims of which were the circle of the sun and the planets and the circle he called the Prime Mover. Beyond this sphere was the *Empyrean*, the abode of the Unmoved Mover. Whether he knew it or not, Aristotle was getting close to monotheism or, at least, to a philosophical foundation that would support monotheism.

The Belief in One God

10.4 *What are the major monotheistic religions? What are their key characteristics?*

Monotheism is a powerful religious concept central to three major religions in the world today: Judaism, Christianity, and Islam. The first appearance of monotheism can be traced back over 3,000 years to the short reign of the Egyptian pharaoh Akhenaton, but his idea of one god did little to eclipse the overwhelming polytheism of early cultures. The monotheism that would eventually dominate Western religious thought had many obstacles to overcome.

Judaism

The religion of early Semitic tribes who traced their ancestry to the patriarch Abraham, Judaism introduced the first powerful vision of one almighty deity, a vision later shared by Christianity and Islam. Of the original 12 Hebrew tribes, the tribe descended from Judah, a son of Jacob, became dominant; *Judaism* derives its name from Judah.

THE HEBREW BIBLE   The Hebrew Bible (the text that Christians refer to as the Old Testament) is presumed to have been collaboratively written over a period of many centuries, sometime after the exodus of Hebrew slaves from Egypt in the thirteenth century BCE. Much later, it is believed, Hebrew scholars, desiring to gather together the history and literature of their people, organized and wrote an early version of Judaism's sacred book. Because the text has been subjected to so much scrutiny and so many interpretations, almost any statement about evidence or meaning can be open to debate.

There is disagreement about the origin of the book; whether the writers were putting down the literal word of God; how certain words should be translated; and whether the book is to be read as history, legend, or literature. At one extreme are fundamentalists who continue to seek evidence of biblical truth, such as a piece of wood from Noah's Ark. Others look to biblical stories and characters for lessons to use in today's world. Still others prefer an anthropological investigation into what the development of the Bible tells us about the changing nature of divinity. And for many, regardless of their beliefs about a deity, the Hebrew Bible, like the Christian Bible and the Qur'an, is a source of solace and wisdom.

The first five books of this Bible, traditionally attributed to Moses, are known as the **Torah** or Pentateuch. The Torah begins with Genesis, one of the most remarkable documents in the history of the humanities, describing in elegant, compact prose the creation of the universe, the expulsion of Adam and Eve from the Garden of Eden for disobedience, and the covenant made between God and Abraham, in which the Promised Land is given as a reward for obedience. The Book of Genesis can stand on its own as an epic, rivaling the *Iliad* and the *Aeneid*, and has served as an inspiration for countless artists and writers through the ages.

The second book of the Torah, Exodus, tells the story of the liberation of Hebrew slaves and their flight from Egypt into the desert under the leadership of Moses, who receives the Ten Commandments on Mount Sinai. The last three books are less poetic but still significant: Leviticus explains priestly laws about temple rituals; Numbers contains a census of the Hebrew population and the story of an attempted rebellion against Moses; and Deuteronomy recounts the farewell speech of Moses, who died before reaching the Promised Land.

Other books of the Hebrew Bible tell stories of kings, generals, judges, and prophets, of war and treachery, family betrayals, and reconciliations. The central figures are human, with human flaws; they struggle to learn about God and to maintain their communities.

Beginning about the tenth century BCE, the biblical texts suggest changing attitudes about the nature of God, who is perceived not only as the supreme ruler but also as a father and comforter. The Psalms, lyrical poems attributed to David, the second king of Israel, who succeeded Saul around 1000 BCE, contain contrasting views of divinity: Some are pleas for God to strike down an enemy, and some reflect a gentle, loving God who cares for his people—or his "flock," as in the well-known Twenty-third Psalm.

During the sixth or seventh century BCE, the age of the Hebrew prophets began, and the books of the prophets, which could be attributed to specific writers, were added to the Bible. Some of these works corresponded to actual events, such as the fall of Jerusalem; others were tales with a philosophical and moral purpose. During this time, Judaism underwent a profound change, becoming more complex, more concerned with justice for the widowed, the poor, and the helpless. Later works also question the wisdom of the Hebrew laws as set forth in earlier books.

The books of the later biblical period reveal a God who can be both awesome and wrathful. He has set down absolute laws for human conduct and severely punishes those who violate them. He is a shepherd who restores the soul, but who also controls all the forces of nature, which he can unleash upon humanity. This dual nature of the deity led to the famous question with which theologians and the devout of many faiths and sects have struggled and still struggle: *"If God is good, why is there so much evil in the world?"* The answer that evil is punishment does not satisfy everyone.

Figure 10.6 Francesco di Antonio del Chierico, *Job*, c. 1475.
In this illuminated manuscript page, Job is seen covered by canker-ous sores. Do you understand Job's patience in the face of such challenges? Can you explain his continuing faith?
Digital image courtesy of the Getty's Open Content Program

THE BOOK OF JOB The agonizing puzzle of God's true nature is examined in the book of Job, considered by many to be the masterpiece of the later period, and the only book in the Hebrew Bible in which Satan appears. The work of a profound and gifted writer, the text, which rivals the greatest works in Greek tragedy, tackles perhaps the most important question raised by monotheism: Why must the good suffer?

And Job does suffer—the death of his children, his servants, and his livestock, the ruination of his livelihood, and finally physical disfiguration. What he does not know is that all this is the result of a challenge to God from Satan (*Satan* is Hebrew for "the accuser"). When God singles out Job as the very model of a good and pious man, Satan argues that Job's piety comes solely from the fact that God has never allowed anything bad to happen to him. "But stretch out your hand now, and touch all that he has," Satan challenges, "and he will curse you to your face" (Job 1:11). In response, God agrees to test the pious man's faith.

At first Job is resolute, as news comes to him of the deaths of his animals, his servants, and finally his children. All that he has comes from God, he argues, so God has the right to take it away. When God allows Satan to cover Job with painful boils (Figure 10.6), Job's wife urges him to curse God. The afflicted man refuses—but he does curse the day he was ever born. He grieves over his lost sons and wonders why he was created with intelligence, only to be torn apart by questions he cannot answer: "Why is light given to one who cannot see the way, whom God has fenced in?" (Job 3:23).

A famous debate follows between Job and his friends, reminiscent of dialogs between Socrates and his followers. They question everything, and Job refuses to yield up his faith, though holding onto it has become increasingly difficult. Finally a mighty whirlwind comes upon them, and God speaks to Job—and rewards him for his patience, his piety, and his refusal to curse his fate. In addition to herds of livestock, Job receives a new family (seven sons and three daughters) and lives long enough (140 years) to enjoy great age and prosperity.

Both the wager with Satan and Job's "compensation" of a new family seem naive to some scholars, unlike the main body of the story. Rabbi Joseph Telushkin comments:

> The angel Satan makes his only appearance in the Hebrew Bible, and God is cast in the morally dubious role of wreaking havoc on Job's life just to show off to Satan.

But, he adds, the ending of the story does not overshadow the stature of the work as a great allegory "about the problem of God and evil."[6]

THE INFLUENCE OF THE HEBREW BIBLE Perhaps no other single work in history has had as much influence on art, literature, thought, drama, and, especially, popular idiom as the Old Testament. Much of the accepted wisdom of Western morality derives from its text. To get a small sense of the importance of this work, we need only look at the wide array of titles—novels, films, poems—derived from it, including *Paradise Lost*, *The Grapes of Wrath*, *Adam's Rib*, and *East of Eden*. For art lovers, no matter what their religious affiliation, a knowledge of biblical persons and events adds to the enjoyment of a Rembrandt painting or a Michelangelo sculpture, as well as countless other masterpieces.

Composers of past and present have been inspired by biblical themes. Mendelssohn's nineteenth-century *Elijah* is one notable example, as is Leonard Bernstein's twentieth-century *Lamentations of Jeremiah*, based on the book that reflects deep despair over the fall of Jerusalem to an invading army, a fall permitted by the Lord because "Jerusalem sinned grievously." Here God is regarded as the supreme ruler of the universe, the creator of that universe, the administrator of punishment to those who break his commandments.

> The Lord has done what he purposed, he has carried out his threat; as he ordained long ago, he has demolished without pity....
>
> Lamentations 2:17

The stories and characters in the Hebrew Bible have provided poets, philosophers, and artists with subject matter, plots, and profound questions for thousands of years; and, as we can see from the examples above, its influence strongly continues.

Christianity

Even as the followers of Siddhartha believed he was the promised Buddha of the scriptures, so too did the followers of Jesus believe that he was the Messiah foretold in the Hebrew Bible by the prophet Isaiah: "Therefore the Lord himself will give you a sign. Look, the virgin is with child and shall bear a son, and shall name him Immanuel" (Isaiah 7:14).

The historical Jesus, walking among the Jews at a time when their land was occupied by the Roman Empire, was a source of controversy. Some hailed him as the Messiah, the Promised One of the prophecy, the bringer of a philosophy that would end oppression and bring peace to the world. Others refused to accept him or his teachings. That difference caused the separation of Judaism and what became Christianity, a religion spread by Paul of Tarsus based on the teachings of Jesus and the belief that he was sent by God to save the world. Jews who did not accept his divinity, and Romans who saw him as a fanatic and a troublemaker, both protested against him. After a trial officiated by Pontius Pilate, the Roman proconsul of Judea, Jesus was crucified and, according to Christian belief, rose from the dead and ascended into heaven.

CORE BELIEFS AND PRACTICES   Most knowledge about Jesus is derived from the Four Gospels at the beginning of what Christians call the New Testament of the Christian Bible. The Gospels are attributed to four of Christ's followers: Matthew, Mark, Luke, and John. Biblical scholars have long discussed the differences and similarities between the four accounts, which vary in their portrayals of both Jesus and the events that surround him. The well-known nativity story, for example, is found only in the gospel according to Luke, and the Sermon on the Mount, in Matthew, appears in a different form in Luke as the Sermon on the Plain. These discrepancies suggest that the Gospels are not eye-witness accounts, but that they, like the books of the Hebrew Bible, were composed by others after the fact. Their influence, however, cannot be minimized.

The Gospels all agree that Jesus was the son of God. Christians point to the word "son" in the prophecy. But the son is also referred to as the "everlasting Father." Ultimately the Christian church adopted the belief that Jesus was both Father and Son, as well as a spiritual being they called the Holy Spirit. The Trinity—the idea that the one God existed as three divine persons—became mandatory for Christians to accept. Central to Christian belief and practice are two biblical guidelines, one from the Hebrew Bible and one from Matthew, in the New Testament. The first, "You shall have no other gods before me" (Exodus 20:3) posits the need to worship one and only one god. The second, "In everything do to others as you would have them do to you" (Matthew 7:12), comes at the end of the Sermon on the Mount at the Sea of Galilee. Often called the Golden Rule, *Do unto others as you would have them do unto you* appears in some form in almost every major religion. It is often phrased in the negative ("Hurt not others in ways that you yourself would find hurtful," for example, in Buddhist texts, and "No one of you is a believer until he desires for his brother that which he desires for himself" in the Qur'an). Jesus may have been the first to be credited with a positive version of it.

QUESTIONING BELIEF   Christianity swept over the Western world after the fall of the Roman Empire in the fifth century CE and now is the belief system of over 30 percent of the world's population. Christianity initially demanded absolute acceptance of its teachings, imposing severe penalties on those who questioned. Early Christian philosophers, however, struggled to reconcile Christian mysticism with human logic. For example, the model of the creation of the world posed in the book of Genesis (which Christianity adopted, along with the rest of the Hebrew Bible) troubled some minds:

> *In the beginning when God created the heavens and the earth, the earth was a formless void and darkness covered the face of the deep, while a mighty wind swept over the face of the waters. Then God said, "Let there be light"; and there was light.*
>
> Genesis 1:1–3

This passage implies that God existed before there was a world and created that world out of nothing, a concept that has become known by the Latin phrase *creatio ex nihilo*. Plato had taught that knowledge preexisted the creation, however, and Aristotle that the Unmoved Mover must have existed in order to set things (things that already also existed) in motion. The concept of nothingness made classical thinkers uneasy. (The Greeks, for example, did not recognize zero as a number.) Yet now the idea of *creatio ex nihilo* was obligatory for believers. God had created everything; nothing but God preexisted the creation.

The *creatio* would not be the last monotheistic idea to cause consternation. Like others, it had to be taken on *faith* rather than by *reason*. But it was difficult for Christian philosophers to abandon the right to question, especially in the centuries before official doctrine came into being. Many of the questions they wrestled with continue to challenge Christians today. Here are some of the many problems they encountered.

- *Can this world have been the extent of God's creation?* If the ability to create matter out of nothing is intrinsic to God, then did creation stop with this one achievement? Is there life elsewhere?
- *Could God have had any purpose in creating the world?* How could an all-powerful God be so limited as to have had a purpose? Purpose implies need. What could God need?
- *Does God think?* This question was debated for centuries. If it is assumed that human beings engage in thought in order to know something that was not known before, what could a perfect God not know?
- *Does God feel?* Christianity, Judaism, and Islam all insist that human sinfulness offends God. The Hebrew Bible's stories of God's wrath against humanity, such as those of Noah and the terrible flood or the destruction of Sodom and Gomorrah, imply emotion. But emotion is a response to what is beyond control. Were there things God could not control?
- *If God does not think or feel, how can he respond to human need?* What was the use of praying to a God who neither thinks nor feels and therefore must be oblivious to us? Was it not futile to believe that God would intervene in human affairs?

As the centuries rolled on, questions increased. It did not take much for anyone to realize that the world was filled with corruption, depravity, and cruelty. If God knew in advance that these would come about, why did he not prevent them? Why did he not prevent maritime disasters or volcanic eruptions? If God knew about catastrophes *before* they happened, did failure to prevent them indicate indifference, or callousness?

AUGUSTINE   The major Christian philosopher of the early Middle Ages, Augustine (354–430) would ultimately conclude that philosophical questioning and analysis could not take Christians where they needed to go. Analysis could lead only to a weakening of belief and even to atheism, a destination unthinkable for Christians. But before he found an answer that satisfied him, he had to wrestle with his own doubts.

Like Paul of Tarsus, who preceded him by several centuries, Augustine became a convert during his adulthood. As a young man without any religion, he lived for pleasure. His Christian mother despaired over her son's wanton ways and kept urging him to reform and find God. Though Augustine eventually renounced his life of sin and entered the Christian fold, he did not do so easily.

Augustine's *Confessions*, one of the most personal and candid works ever written by a philosopher, deals with the intellectual difficulties facing him upon his conversion. One of his first concerns was reason itself. Why was it given to us by God when it was of no use in trying to comprehend God or the universe? The doctrine of *creatio ex nihilo* puzzled him. In this passage he speaks directly to God:

> Nor in the whole world didst Thou make the whole world; because there was no place to make it before it was made, that it might be. Nor didst Thou hold anything in Thy hand, whereof to make heaven and earth. For whence shouldest Thou have this, which Thou hadst not

made, thereof to make anything? For what is, but because Thou art? Therefore Thou spakest, and they were made, and in Thy Word Thou madest them. But how didst Thou speak?[7]

THE PROTESTANT REFORMATION   As Christianity spread and gained millions of converts during the Middle Ages, it became Catholicism, from a word meaning "universal." It was a powerful empire in itself and would command the faithful to refrain from sin or face the fires of hell. Among the greatest of sins was that of **heresy**, words or deeds interpreted as being anti-Christian. During the late Middle Ages, a tribunal of church officials conducted the **Inquisition**, a high religious court in which heretics were tried and, if found guilty, imprisoned or even burnt at the stake.

There were rumblings of discontent. Dissidents in private complained about the growing wealth of the church as well as the continuing poverty of most worshipers. They also took exception to the church doctrine that salvation was impossible without the intervention of priests. They believed that God listened to each of his children, who could communicate with him privately. They called this principle "the priesthood of the true believer." They also condemned the church for its giant, expensive cathedrals (such as Notre Dame in Paris), with their artifacts of gold and silver, their expensive frescoes and statues. Such extravagant displays in the name of religion amounted to idolatry, which horrified them.

Ultimately the quiet questioning flared into an open rebellion led by Martin Luther (1483–1546), who made a list of 95 proposals for religious reform and nailed it to the door of the church at the University of Wittenberg in 1517. The result was the great division in Christianity between the protesters (later called Protestants), who wanted to simplify religious worship and divest it of its bureaucracies and worldly power, and the Catholics, who held tenaciously to the belief that the pope was the one true representative of God on earth and that priests were chosen to carry the word of God to the people and the prayers of the people to God. Lutheranism was thus the first Protestant sect. But Protestantism would eventually give rise to further disputes and the formulation of other sects.

Islam

The second largest—and fastest growing—of the world's religions is Islam, founded by the prophet Muhammad (570–632), who is considered by Muslims to be the last in a long line of prophets that includes Abraham, Moses, and Jesus. A respected leader, a husband, and a father, successful in all aspects, Muhammad was visited by the angel Gabriel, a messenger from Allah ("the one god"), while stopping in the city of Mecca, in present-day Saudi Arabia. Gabriel commanded Muhammad to deliver God's word and his laws to the world, because previous iterations of God's message—the Ten Commandments delivered to Moses, for example—had been misinterpreted.

THE PROPHET MUHAMMAD   Muhammad first thought he must be going mad. He told his wife, who suggested that he visit a wise relative and ask his opinion. This man assured Muhammad that he was blessed among all men and had been clearly chosen to restate the laws of God. The hearing of a divine voice convinced Muhammad that his relative was right. The voice told him he must devote his life to teaching. His teachings are compiled into the Qur'an, the sacred book of Islam and the central component of the faith.

As Muhammad grew older, he wanted to do more than preach the word of God. He wanted to help fashion a society of brotherhood, peace, and ethical dealings—all based on Allah's laws. He became a political consultant and an agent for social reform, unlike Siddhartha, who taught the Eightfold Path and believed reform would come about by itself as more and more followers heeded his message and incorporated it into their daily lives. Muhammad's vision of the ideal world is still the basis of government in Islamic nations; that is, the function of government is to implement the laws of God. There have, historically, been disagreements over how those laws should be interpreted.

After the death of Muhammad, there was considerable disruption in Islam, a profound division between those who believed Muslim leadership belonged to Muhammad's close friend Abu Bakr and those who wanted Muhammad's cousin and son-in-law Ali. Abu Bakr emerged victorious after a long struggle between the two parties, but followers of Ali insisted that the command had been wrongfully taken from him. At length, those loyal to Abu Bakr became the Sunni Muslims, while those loyal to Ali became the Shiites. Both parties, living in Iraq, Iran, India, and Pakistan, continue to believe that control of the Islamic faith is rightfully theirs.

CORE BELIEFS AND PRACTICES At the heart of Islam is a life lived in service of Allah. (The word *Islam* has roots in the word "submission.") The Muslim God is a very personal one, who intercedes to help individuals as help is needed; there are no clergy to mediate, although some individuals may lead the prayers. The term *imam* refers to such worship leaders, as well as to scholars and wise men who are students of the faith. Imams function not only as prayer leaders but also as community leaders and, when Islamic governments are established, as heads of state.

The central practices of Islam include an unquestioning belief in the creed, or the Qur'an (*shahadah*), prayers offered five times each day (*salat*), charity, or the giving of alms (*zakah*), fasting during the period called **Ramadan**, and making a pilgrimage to the holy city of Mecca (the *hajj*), where Muhammad was visited by the angel Gabriel, at least once during one's lifetime. The existence of God is a given; doubt simply cannot exist, although some may turn their backs on God because of temptation. As religious scholar Karen Armstrong tells us:

> *The existence of God is not in question . . . In the Koran an 'unbeliever' . . . is not an atheist in our sense of the word, somebody who does not believe in God, but one who is ungrateful to him, who can see quite clearly what is owing to God but refuses to honor him in a spirit of perverse ingratitude.*[8]

Since there is no intermediary between the individual and God, confession is not made to a priest, as in the Catholic faith, but directly to God. Worshipers speak their daily prayers sometimes alone but, as often as possible, in groups, reflecting Muhammad's insistence on community. Fasting, taught Muhammad, builds discipline, necessary if one is to resist the temptations of the world. During the sacred month of Ramadan, Muslims are required to fast each day and to refrain from all sexual activity from sunrise to sunset. Ramadan commemorates the communication of the Qur'an to Muhammad. It occurs during the ninth month of the Muslim calendar, which is based on the revolution of the moon, and advances ten days each year according to the Western calendar.

Unlike the other major religions, Islam is considered a political as well as a spiritual path and includes a system of laws and economic rules, derived mostly from the *hadith*, the reported and gathered sayings of the prophet Muhammad, which Muslims see as clarifying the Qur'an. The two branches of Islam, Sunni and Shiite, look to differing versions of the *hadith* based on their beliefs about the reliability of the narrators who wrote these down, all of whom lived well after the death of the prophet.

ISLAM AND CHRISTIANITY: DIFFERENCES AND SIMILARITIES As in most religions, Islam has its fundamentalists—believers in the very letter of the law—as well as those who support greater flexibility. The separation has grown stronger over the centuries. In the beginning, Muhammad as spiritual leader allowed Christians and Jews living in Islamic communities to practice their own faiths openly and commanded his followers not to persecute or try to convert them. He told the people that Arabs, Jews, and Christians all prayed to the one God and that they were entitled to heed the word as passed down in their own sacred books.

The Qur'an bears striking similarities to those books. The commandments given to Muhammad by Allah are very much like those given to Moses and accepted, with modifications, by Jesus. In fact, Moses and Jesus were accorded much honor by Muhammad, who declared that they were pious and honorable men, much beloved by God, who had also spoken to them. Muhammad argued, however, that the messages that had been transmitted to previous prophets by God had been distorted over the centuries, and that the Qur'an represented the true interpretation of the word of God.

Like Christianity, Islam believes there will be an inevitable ending of the world, followed by a Judgment Day, in which the good will be rewarded with eternal life in heaven, and the bad will suffer the torments of hell. Heaven and hell are vividly described in the Qur'an.

Strict Islamic law forbids gambling and drinking alcohol at all times. Instead of stressing redemption, the forgiveness of sin, Islam seeks to make its followers morally perfect. Redemption is thus unnecessary.

ISLAM AND MYSTICISM   Like Judaism and Christianity, Islam produced its questioners. One in particular, Al-Ghazali (1058–1111), was trained in both law and theology. He taught at the University of Baghdad and was eventually caught between worldly matters and the austere discipline of the Muslim faith. He had problems with both extremes.

The Arab world was becoming a center of culture and erudition, rivaling those of the great Western cities such as Paris and Bologna. There were many temptations that could easily lead one to forego, for example, the daily prayers or the fasting. Al-Ghazali realized he had to make a choice: either total immersion in the pursuits of the material world or total submission to the will of Allah.

He also found Islamic tradition too demanding for its followers, with its emphasis on discipline, and too remote from God. Wherever he looked, he could see people disobeying the laws set forth in the Qur'an. He realized that, if he were to practice total submission, he could not do so and lead a secular existence as well. Then he discovered the *Sufi*, Islamic mystics who practiced meditation in their efforts to achieve total unity with God. In this they resembled some of the monastic orders of Christianity and the Hasidic branch of Judaism, whose members gave free rein to song and dance as a means of transcending cold reason. After his conversion to Sufism, he again took up his teaching duties, but this time he taught his students that God must be an active force in their lives, not a distant figure in whose name they went without emotion through their daily practices.

All of the religions discussed in this chapter are still very much with us. Some have strict rules that are binding on their followers, while others encourage the faithful to seek their own path to God, arguing that what matters in the long run is the development of a moral human being.

Understanding Good and Evil: The Problem of Faith

10.5 *Why has the question of good and evil challenged religious thinkers?*

Philosophy, ancient and modern, has had as a major concern the nature of the good. The hedonists of ancient Greece defined the good as a life filled with all possible pleasures. Socrates and Plato use *good* in an ethical sense, referring to actions that are performed not for the sake of personal enjoyment or gain but for the sake of what reason decrees is right and just. *Evil* in ancient thought is the pain and suffering that are part of life, often rained down upon human beings by the gods or by the whimsies of fate. Socrates is famous for having said, "No evil can befall a good man." The statement was made in his speech, already mentioned in this chapter, to the assembled citizens of Athens who were to judge him guilty or innocent of corrupting their youth. What he meant by "evil" was the pain of death should the jury of citizens reach a guilty verdict. In other words, evil was a synonym for disaster, or what most people would consider disaster. It did not imply malicious intent.

Figure 10.7 The Garden of Eden and the Temptation of Eve, by a local muralist, British Virgin Islands, date unknown.
This scene has been portrayed by hundreds of artists through the centuries. What do you think makes it so powerful, and so appealing to artists?
John Ferro Sims/Alamy

The myth of Pandora was one explanation for how evil came about. Locked in the box that Pandora was not supposed to open were war, plagues, and all natural disasters such as fire and floods. In this myth, there is no implication that people are *born* evil. Evil is something that *happens* to them. Even the brutal killing of Hector by Achilles, as recounted in the *Iliad*, is less the action of a truly evil person than it is the fulfillment of a warrior's obligation to show his superiority in battle.

The Hebrew Bible gives a clear explanation of both good and evil. In Genesis, God creates Eve from Adam's rib and is satisfied that he has created two innocent human beings, whom he places in the Garden of Eden to be fruitful, to multiply, and to act as custodians of the earth. He also warns them about the Tree of Knowledge, the fruit of which they may not eat; if they do, they will learn the difference between good and evil, but it will be too late. They will be punished for disobeying God.

Adam and Eve are thus not born evil. They are born good—that is, without sin, the tendency to disobey God's commands. What changes them? A talking serpent that entices them to eat the forbidden fruit (Figure 10.7). At first they are afraid because God has told them that if they disobey him they will surely die. The serpent tells them this is a lie. He gives this as the real reason for the command:

> For God knows that when you eat of it your eyes will be opened, and you will be like God, knowing good and evil.
>
> Genesis 3:5

Good and Evil in Christianity

Early Christianity accepted the Hebrew Bible as an accurate account of the beginnings of humankind, though it modified and expanded the range of the Ten Commandments. Christianity also transformed the serpent into the Devil, an embodiment of pure evil and one of the most influential of all archetypes. Pitting God against the Devil, Christianity thus utilized the concept of the eternal conflict between absolute good and absolute evil, a concept leading in turn to the agonizing question asked by early Christian philosophers and by Augustine: *If God is good and all-powerful, why does evil exist?*

In Genesis, the attitude of an angry God toward the sin of Adam and Eve is accepted as being appropriate for a supreme being. God curses the ground on which they walk and invents death for them but only after Eve brings forth progeny in utmost pain. Things only get worse. By the time of Noah, God is so disgusted with the race he has created that he sends down a flood to destroy it—all except Noah, the one good man, who pleases God with his piety and his burnt offerings:

And when the LORD smelled the pleasing odor, the LORD said in his heart, "I will never again curse the ground because of humankind, for the inclination of the human heart is evil from youth; nor will I ever again destroy every living creature as I have done."

Genesis 8:21

Thus God became a supreme being and an angry father who was quickly offended by human sinfulness but pleased by piety and goodness.

Yet by the time of the early Christian philosophers, it was becoming difficult for those who questioned things to be content with the conflicting ideas that evil was inherent in humankind but that the choice of being good was always there, the choice of not being tempted to disobey. Did not God create the serpent? Had he done so deliberately to throw temptation into his children's path? Why would God do such a thing? Why not create a perfect race to begin with—without serpents?

Good and Evil in Islam

The concepts of good and evil are central to Islam, as they are to virtually every belief system. Evil results, for Muslims, from the interference of Shaytan, or the devil, who tempts individuals to choose evil over good. The moral Muslim must use *free will*, which Islam argues is a natural instinct, to resist such temptations.

Islam shares its origin story to some extent with Judaism and Christianity: There is an initial paradise, within which Allah creates Adam and Eve, or *Hawwa*. Adam is not created first in the Qur'an, however; rather God created "one soul and created from it its mate and dispersed from them many men and women" (*Surah* Al-Nisa 4.1). (Similarly, Eve is not solely responsible for the first sin. Instead, the Qur'an states that both Adam and Eve ate the forbidden fruit.)

After the creation of humanity, God orders all the angels and spirits (called *jinn*) to bow down to Adam, and one *jinn*, Iblis, also known as Shaytan, refuses. God casts Iblis out of paradise and rejects him until the Day of Judgment. In angry response, Shaytan vows to tempt humanity with evil and to turn them away from God.

Because individuals have free will and can make choices, Shaytan is sometimes successful in luring them into evil. The Islam God does not impose moral character on anyone; rather, free will is the foundation for the constant testing that each Muslim faces. Through following the practices of Islam—prayer, charity, fasting—Muslims will be led (but not coerced) into making right choices, into choosing good over evil. And for those who follow the wrong path, God will always forgive those who are truly repentant. God's greatest virtue is forgiveness.

The Concept of Free Will

By the time of Augustine, the problem of evil was well-known and widely discussed. To the philosopher, it proved just as puzzling as that of creation. To a thinking person it seemed evident that evil happened *despite* God. Traditional Christian belief was that the universe was divided into two distinct substances: one material; the other immaterial. It was unthinkable to Augustine that evil should exist in the immaterial world. But God was also the creator of the material world, was he not? And the material world was the abode of evil. If one denied that God was responsible for evil but *was* responsible for the material world, then it followed that evil was neither material nor immaterial. Evil, then, could not exist!

Augustine reasoned that what we call evil must be *the absence of good* in the same way that disease is the absence of health. Evil was, then, moral disease. When a person sins, moral perfection departs. The world, like the human body, was perfect when created and returns to perfection when the disease is gone.

Yet why do people sin? If they were created perfect, where did moral disease come from? Here Augustine further developed the idea of *free will* that is part of most major belief systems and remains with us—not just in religion, but in philosophy and psychology as well. Augustine concluded that people sin because God allows them to choose between good and bad actions. He knew this had to be the case, because God exacted penance from sinners and doled out punishment to the unrepentant. The Tree of Knowledge was put there in the Garden as a test, and so freedom of choice made perfect sense.

Or did it? The matter of God's nature crossed Augustine's mind. An all-knowing God must be aware in advance of what our choices will be. Before we are tempted to appropriate the money carelessly left on a table by a departing guest, must not God know that we will or will not take it? In God's eyes, the deed has already taken place. Where then is the element of choice? And without choice, how can there be responsibility?

Augustine advanced the idea of **predestination**, which states that, before birth, the course of a human life is already determined. The philosopher believed that the concept of an all-powerful, all-knowing God made predestination mandatory for mortals to accept. There could be no argument about God's foreknowledge of human choice; at the same time, humanity could not be absolved of responsibility for sin. It was unthinkable that God should be blamed for human evil. Otherwise, what incentive was there to be good and to win God's approval?

Free will offered a way to make the two beliefs compatible. An all-powerful God could choose to bestow on humanity the *gift* of freedom. An all-knowing God could tell what our choices would be *without having willed those choices*. Thus freedom was real on the human level; predestination was real on the divine level.

If reason was too weak to reach these conclusions, then faith must be stronger than reason. How could humanity expect to understand God? Reason could take us to a certain point at which the paradox of fate and free will must be accepted. Faith, which was the answer in the Book of Job, stepped in to make acceptance possible. But again the matter did not end there. Some religious thinkers would not be satisfied with Augustine's conclusion that faith was all. Why did we have reason if we weren't supposed to use it? They would eventually say that reason *can* lead to an understanding of God, though critics of religious logic often point out that it only shows why a God must exist, not what *kind* of God.

Proving God's Existence

As we have seen, early philosophers had many concerns about the doctrines they were being asked to accept. In the Book of Job, the central character is told by the voice from the whirlwind that the running of the universe is not humanity's business. Faith in God has to convince us that God has his reasons for everything. In the twelfth century CE, a Jewish rabbi emerged who was also a profound philosopher and scholar, and he would show how logic and faith were not incompatible.

MOSES MAIMONIDES   Moses Maimonides (1135–1204) was born in Spain of Jewish ancestry. Threatened with persecution, he moved to Egypt, where he became physician to the Muslim ruler Saladin. Trained in medicine, he decided that philosophy and theology were as important as healing the body. Besides, in the world of both Jewish and Muslim scholars, if a man wished to be considered learned, he was expected to demonstrate knowledge in many areas.

At first Maimonides was appalled at the Muslim philosophical acceptance of the philosophy of **materialism** that had been advanced centuries before Socrates and Plato, maintaining that only matter existed and so-called spiritual experiences were solely in the mind. A devout Jew himself, he maintained that the material world was created by God out of nothing, but he was enough of an Aristotelian to realize that he would have to use logic to defend his belief. Although many of his Jewish contemporaries were content to accept the Bible as mystic revelation, Maimonides was also a scientist living among Muslims who had inherited and further developed the logical and mathematical theories of the classical world. They were fully acquainted with Aristotle, Euclid, and the work of mathematicians in India. His mission was to show his contemporaries that a belief in God was not only desirable but logically, not just mystically, inevitable.

Since he was familiar with Aristotle's theory of the Unmoved Mover, it made sense to him that nothing can be in motion uncaused by something else, but cause and effect cannot be traced back into infinity. Sooner or later there has to be a causer that is not in motion itself. What Maimonides did was to give the name of God to the Unmoved Mover. The perfection of God made the Unmoved Mover plausible. God was thus defined as *that which cannot be caused*. Depending for his existence on a prior cause would make God imperfect. A perfect being cannot be dependent. If there *were* a prior cause that created God, then that cause would be God. No matter how far back you went, you would always find God waiting.

Some Hebrew scholars and theologians denounced the writings of Maimonides on the grounds that his so-called logic was founded on a strong belief in God to begin with and consequently was unnecessary—not only unnecessary, but an affront to the traditions of their forefathers for whom revelation was sufficient. Hadn't God told Job that it was not the place of humanity either to understand or to question the nature and ways of God? If, in fact, you needed proof, you were not truly religious.

THOMAS AQUINAS   The world of Christian thought was also influenced by mathematics, stirrings in science, and the work of Aristotle. Thomas Aquinas (1225–1274) never doubted his own faith, but he was imbued with the spirit of inquiry that became widespread during the later Middle Ages. Educated by Benedictine monks and having become a Dominican, he moved to Paris, which was already an intellectual center, a place where bright young students met exciting teachers and where even the clergy were not afraid to question established beliefs.

Here Aquinas came into contact with Aristotelian logic and was responsible for creating a system of thought designed to persuade nonbelievers that God must exist. Once introduced, his theories gradually found their way into Christian tradition. Even today, students in Catholic seminaries are thoroughly trained in *Thomism*, the name given to the philosopher's logical methods of proving God's existence.

Aquinas gave five proofs of God's existence, all based, as were the theories of Maimonides, on Aristotle's Unmoved Mover. The first, *Argument from Motion*, is a restatement of that theory, as is the second, *Argument from Causation*. The third, *Argument from Being*, is cited by many philosophers as the strongest. Here is a paraphrased summary of that argument:

> *Though we have only to look around to see that things* are, *it is indeed possible to imagine that they should not be. On the other hand, though it is conceivable that nothing should be, it is clear that this is not the case. Hence there must be a principle of necessary being which cannot be imagined as not existing. Only God can be so imagined.*

The fourth, *Argument from Gradation*, asserts that wherever we look we see greater or lesser amounts and qualities. We cannot conceive of "better," for example, unless we can also conceive of "best," for it stands to reason that we cannot go on into infinity finding "better" things. Eventually there has to be a "best" beyond which the mind cannot go. God is therefore the fullest realization of "best."

The fifth, *Argument from Design*, is probably at once the most famous and the most hotly debated. It asserts that since there is clear evidence of order in the operation of the universe, it cannot have been put there by accident. If there is a design, it follows that there was a designer. Countless millions continue to use this argument. Others say that a universe governed by laws that have been experimentally verified is not equivalent to design. There is no universal agreement.

Doubt

10.6 *What are the key characteristics of agnosticism and atheism?*

Nonbelievers and those who dared to dispute the mandates of an organized religion have been imprisoned, tortured, or executed. There are still places in the world where the harshest penalties are imposed upon those persons whose lifestyle and mode of dress deviate from prevailing religious requirements. The strict enforcement of religious law runs counter to widespread philosophical positions that question or openly deny the existence of God. As philosophy has been and continues to be an instrument for the logical proof of God, so too can it be used for the opposite purpose.

Agnosticism

An **agnostic** (from a Greek word meaning "unknown" or "unknowable") is a person who does not patently disbelieve in God but who asserts that nothing about God, including his existence, can be known for certain. Agnostics are sometimes accused by the faithful of being too lazy to bother with religion. They are challenged to prove that God cannot be proven.

Yet agnosticism is a valid philosophical stance, often arrived at after much soul-searching. William James, a late-nineteenth-century philosopher who will be discussed in the final chapter of this book, was an agnostic with compassion for those who relied upon religion to see them through difficult times. Sometimes called the father of modern psychology, James counseled innumerable people who were trying to make sense out of life, who had suffered grievous losses and were desperately seeking reasons. His advice was that if religion is essential to happiness, who is to deny someone the right to believe? Carl Sagan, a widely read popularizer of modern science, once remarked, "Absence of evidence is not evidence of absence."

In the arts, one finds many who are "God-obsessed." They are angry because reason prevents them from believing in God yet offers nothing to take God's place. The American poet Edwin Arlington Robinson (1869–1935) concludes his great work "The Man Against the Sky" with these lines that attack the rational denial of faith.

> *If after all that we have lived and thought,*
> *All comes to Nought,—*
> *If there be nothing after Now,*
> *And we be nothing anyhow,*
> *And we know that,—why live?*
> *'Twere sure but weaklings' vain distress*
> *To suffer dungeons where so many doors*
> *Will open on the cold eternal shores*
> *That look sheer down*
> *To the dark tideless floods of Nothingness*
> *Where all who know may drown.*[9]

For the confirmed agnostic, it makes sense not to burn bridges or to risk drowning in Robinson's "floods of Nothingness."

Atheism

Unlike the agnostic, the **atheist** takes a bold negative stand. Instead of shaking their heads and saying, "I don't know," atheists challenge believers, especially those who use logic to prove God's existence. They sometimes take that very logic and use it to prove that the nonexistence of God is logically necessary, but sometimes people who call themselves atheists do not do so on logical grounds.

One method, which can be called "*informal*" logic, is to point out that the very question "Does God exist?" is meaningless since its subject has not been shown to have a valid identity. Consequently, all answers to that question have to be disregarded. Atheists are fond of the poem by Lewis Carroll (of *Alice in Wonderland* fame) called "The Hunting of the Snark," which concerns a dangerous sea voyage in search of the Snark, a creature no one has ever seen. The voyagers have been warned to be careful because there are rumors that the Snark may really be a Boojum. At length, in a hilarious conclusion, which could be a parody of *Moby-Dick*, the Snark, finally encountered, destroys the ship, and we are left with the mournful final line: "The Snark was a Boojum after all."

CHARLES PEIRCE   A foremost American proponent of atheism was Charles Sanders Peirce (pronounced "purse," 1839–1914), who was deeply involved in a philosophical movement known as **pragmatism**. According to pragmatism, no philosophical question is important if it makes no difference to the actual conduct of life. Like William James, Peirce realized that religion did indeed make a great deal of difference to a good many people. In a pivotal essay called "How to Make Our Ideas Clear," he turns the notion of belief inside out. He analyzes it in terms of three properties:

> *First, it is something we are aware of; second, it appeases the irritation of doubt; and third, it involves the establishment in our nature of a rule of action, or say, for short, a* habit.[10]

One difficulty with belief, Peirce argues, is that we are likely to seize on any sort that will appease the "irritation of doubt." We cannot stand not to know or be able to explain, and for the majority of us, it is important that a belief be *good* rather than necessarily true. In his opinion, religious beliefs are notoriously successful in appeasing the irritation of doubt. Indeed, they are held more often for this reason than for any other, no matter what claims for their logical necessity may be made. They are particularly difficult to dislodge from people's lives (or habits) because, if they cannot readily be proved, the believer is confident they cannot be disproved.

> *Thus if it be true that death is annihilation, then the man who believes that he will certainly go straight to heaven when he dies, provided he has fulfilled certain simple observations in this life, has a cheap pleasure which will not be followed by the least disappointment.*[11]

The passage has become famous, not least because of its wit. Peirce is throwing down the gauntlet. He is saying: *If you don't believe me, prove that there's an afterlife.* Such reasoning employs the philosophical technique of *reductio ad absurdum*, by which you prove your point by postulating that its opposite is an absurdity. Take as example the statement *There can be no afterlife*. To say that *there is* such a thing is pointless and meaningless. The opposite of *There is no afterlife* is *There is an afterlife*; but the latter statement cannot possibly have any validity since no one has ever visited an afterlife and returned to tell of it. All one can say is "I believe there is an afterlife," but this automatically rules out logic.

The philosophy of Peirce is staunchly rooted in science. Nothing is true that cannot be observed or experimentally verified. In another famous passage, he attacks the Catholic belief in *transubstantiation*, which holds that, through the mystical powers invested in the priest celebrating the mass, the communion wafer actually becomes the body of Jesus and the communion wine the blood of Jesus. Peirce noted:

> . . . we can consequently mean nothing by wine but what has certain effects . . . upon our senses; and to talk of something as having all the sensible characters of wine, yet being in reality blood, is senseless jargon.[12]

Whether to accept this argument as a logical one is a personal decision, but, if nothing else, it makes clear the fact that the scientific and religious outlooks are on different wavelengths. The atheist is much closer to science, while the devout believer must be willing to accept even the miraculous on faith. Another American atheist, H.L. Mencken, defined faith as "an illogical belief in the occurrence of the improbable."

ATHEISM IN PHILOSOPHY AND THE ARTS   A number of other atheistic philosophies have become prominent. Friedrich Nietzsche, the German philosopher, made the famous statement "God is dead"—that is, the very question of whether God exists or not is a dead issue. The implication is that religion had its day, but by the late nineteenth century, the time of Nietzsche, that day was over.

In the same time period, a number of writers and poets expressed disillusionment over what they considered to be the unfounded optimism of the late Victorian age, particularly the use of religion to justify the unstoppable accumulation of wealth and property. John D. Rockefeller, one of the world's richest men, wrote in his autobiography that his wealth showed he was favored by God.

Author Stephen Crane (1871–1900), who wrote *The Red Badge of Courage*, a biting antiwar novel, was also a poet whose moods swing from stark pessimism about a world from which God is notably absent to a belief that humanity will somehow pull itself up from the dark pit of chaos. (His poem "I Saw a Man Pursuing the Horizon" closes this book.) In the following poem, Crane's pessimistic side turns grimly humorous.

> *God fashioned the ship of the world carefully,*
> *With the infinite skill of an All-Master*
> *Made He the hull and the sails,*
> *Held He the rudder*
> *Ready for adjustment.*
> *Erect stood He, scanning His work proudly,*
> *Then—at fateful time—a wrong called,*
> *And God turned, heeding.*
> *Lo, the ship, at this opportunity, slipped slyly,*
> *Making cunning noiseless travel down the ways.*
> *So that, forever rudderless, it went upon the seas*
> *Going ridiculous voyages,*
> *Making quaint progress,*
> *Turning as with serious purpose*
> *Before stupid winds.*
> *And there were many in the sky*
> *Who laughed at this thing.*[13]

Religion and the Arts

10.7   *What are some examples of the role religion has played in the humanities?*

Given the impact of religion on cultures, societies, and individuals throughout the world for hundreds of years, it isn't surprising that religious beliefs and stories have played major roles in the various disciplines of the humanities.

Figure 10.8 Interior of the Masjide Elman Mosque (formerly the Shah Mosque), Isfahan, Iran, 1629.
Because Islam prohibits the depiction of sacred beings such as Muhammad and God himself, much Islamic art takes the form of calligraphic mosaic and elaborate architecture. Does this building and its decoration inspire awe? What have the builders and artists done to help create that feeling?

Robert Harding World Imagery / Alamy Stock Photo

Composers, choreographers, artists, writers, philosophers—all have found it a rich source of content for their work. During some periods of history and in some parts of the world, religion has been central to an overwhelming majority of the artistic works produced. From the intricate mosaic work of the mosques of Isfahan to the soaring buttresses of French and English Gothic cathedrals, from the massive stone Buddhas of Myanmar and Japan to the elaborate illuminated manuscripts of Scottish monks, from Michelangelo's pietàs to the delicate calligraphic works of Muslim artists—our culture would be much the poorer if not for these outgrowths of religious beliefs. Consider a world without the Sistine Chapel ceiling, or *The Last Supper*, or mosaics like those shown in Figure 10.8.

Religion in Literature and Philosophy

Western philosophers and writers have long been influenced by the Hindu concept of a unifying spirit behind the universe and have given it various names. The German poet Johann Wolfgang von Goethe (1749–1832) called it the "world-soul." The American philosopher Ralph Waldo Emerson called it the "over-soul" and wrote a famous essay by that title. In John Steinbeck's *The Grapes of Wrath*, the hero, Tom Joad, explains to his mother that he cannot remain with the family working only for their survival when so many others are hungry and homeless. He believes all people are part of "one big soul," and, now that he has realized this truth, he has no choice but to work for others, even if it means sacrificing his own safety and the possibility of a happier future.

Some of the great works of Western literature are reaffirmations of religious teachings, such as Dante's *Divine Comedy* and Milton's *Paradise Lost* (1667), written to "justify the ways of God to man." Both works greatly influenced the way artists, other writers, and millions of worshipers think about God and the spiritual world beyond.

But writers often have their own relationship to religion and give us unorthodox but no less uplifting visions. "Batter my heart," the sonnet by John Donne, speaks of religious ecstasy in highly sexual terms but strongly communicates the idea of submission to God's will in an unforgettable way.

WALT WHITMAN Walt Whitman, an American poet also greatly influenced by the religious thought of India, entitled his most famous work *Leaves of Grass*. Grass, like Brahman, is a totality that exists only through its individual leaves. If you have just one blade of grass, you have grass. If you have one drop of water, you have water. If only one person is left on earth, humanity has survived. Any individual is as important as all others, and no one individual is more important than the rest. Whitman's famous opening lines should not be interpreted as egotism.

> *I celebrate myself, and sing myself,*
> *And what I assume you shall assume,*
> *For every atom belonging to me as good belongs to you.*[14]

On the other hand, one solitary leaf would be lost in the universe, and so would one lone individual isolated from the human family. Whitman's idea of democracy and the relationship between the private citizen and the whole population is a political extension of an ancient religious philosophy.

THE ROMANTICS During the Romantic movement in the last part of the eighteenth century and the first half of the nineteenth, Western artists and writers encountered a new kind of religious vision founded on nature and the natural rights of all people.

A major voice in romanticism is that of William Wordsworth (1770–1850), one of whose masterpieces is "Lines Composed a Few Miles Above Tintern Abbey on the Banks of the Wye." Here is a famous passage from the poem. It is indeed religious, but not in a traditional sense. For Wordsworth, God is the soul of nature, a belief that brings him close to Hinduism.

> *And I have felt*
> *A presence that disturbs me with the joy*
> *Of elevated thoughts; a sense sublime*
> *Of something far more deeply interfused,*
> *Whose dwelling is the light of setting suns,*
> *And the round ocean and the living air,*
> *And the blue sky, and in the mind of man;*
> *A motion and a spirit, that impels*
> *All thinking things, all objects of all thought,*
> *And rolls through all things.*

Religion in the Visual Arts

Without religion, the visual arts would have a shorter history. Art and religion have maintained close relations since the beginning. The Egyptians saw painting and statuary as a means to immortality. Polytheism led the Greeks and Romans to erect masterpieces of art and architecture. Greek drama was associated with worship of Dionysius and the festival held each year in his honor. In addition to the moral laws on which most societies, regardless of their religious orientation, are based, Judaism has given the world masterpieces of literature, poetry, and philosophers. The medieval church brought into the world countless paintings, statues, and frescoes in which heavenly beings and biblical incidents were visualized. The theater of the Western world had its beginnings in the medieval mass. Islam frowned upon the production of artificial images, but, as we have seen, many of its buildings remain as very models of architectural grandeur.

Islam's influence on the art of Western civilization has been strong, largely because of the artistic bent of the Moors, a Muslim sect living in northwestern Africa that invaded Spain during the eighth century CE. In occupying much of Spain for a number of centuries, they were responsible for a good deal of Spanish architectural design, such as that of the Alhambra (Figure 10.9), built as a palace for Moorish kings during the thirteenth and fourteenth centuries and located outside the city of Granada. It is considered the epitome of Moorish art, with slender columns miraculously supporting complex arches and a colorful interior of stucco and mosaic tiles in an infinite variety of patterns and designs. Visitors to the palace may feel as though they have been transported into an *Arabian Nights* fantasy. Though the building is a secular one, its architecture is an outgrowth of the richly designed and decorated mosques, which, like Christian cathedrals, are meant to bring the worshiper into closer touch with the next world.

The great artistic works of the Vatican, including Saint Peter's Cathedral and the Sistine Chapel, were deliberately monumental, designed to overshadow and replace the polytheistic art that at one time had been pervasive throughout Rome. The art of Leonardo, Michelangelo, Raphael, and many others gave a vivid and visual reality to religious stories familiar to the public: Adam and Eve, Joseph and the wife of

Figure 10.9 Alhambra, Granada, Spain, 1338–1390.
The Moors, an Islamic people, ruled Spain during this period. How does this building reflect Islamic influences?
Shaun Egan/Digital Vision/Getty Images

Potiphar, Moses, David, the Prodigal Son, the Virgin and Child, the Annunciation, the Crucifixion, the Resurrection, Judgment Day—the list is almost endless.

During the Protestant Reformation, beginning in the late fifteenth century, church architecture became simplified; but this change led indirectly to the flowering of the Baroque art and architecture of the seventeenth century. Baroque churches were elaborately decorated in what may have been a strong effort to win back worshipers who felt that religion had lost its inspiring grandeur. The complex counterpoint of Bach was another great gift from the Baroque period.

Religion cannot possibly be exhaustively treated in only one chapter of one text. We have presented an introductory outline of the major religions of the world, as well as major philosophical opposition to religion. We have given some consideration to the role played by religion in the humanities. As always, the purpose has been to stimulate your thoughts and encourage you to think about your own position relative to these matters.

Many people become uncomfortable when religion is analyzed as a human phenomenon, as if discussing it threatens sincerely held beliefs. Discussion should not have this effect. If engaged in intelligently and with an open mind, religious discussion can strengthen your beliefs. Knowing the *why* of belief is far better than expressing allegiance to it without understanding. Full awareness of your commitment and your responsibilities after having *made* the commitment is all-important.

Looking Back

In this chapter,

- we explained why religion is important to the study of the humanities,
- we explored the major polytheistic religions, including the religions of Egypt, Greece, and Rome; Hinduism; and indigenous religions, and their key characteristics,
- we discussed the emergence of pantheistic belief systems such as Buddhism and Taoism, as well as the beliefs of Plato, Socrates, and Aristotle about the nature of the divine,

- we explored the major monotheistic religions, including Judaism, Christianity, and Islam, and described their key characteristics,
- we discussed why the question of good and evil has long challenged religious thinkers,
- we described the thinking of agnostics and atheists, and
- we discussed some major examples of the role religion has played in the humanities through the ages.

Key Terms

agnosticism Belief that one cannot possibly know for sure whether God exists.

atheism Belief that God cannot logically exist.

bas relief Stone wall carving, found in many ancient tombs.

Brahma In Hinduism, a godlike personification of the creative principle in the universe.

Brahman In Hinduism, the name given to the spiritual force that governs the universe; the universal soul.

Buddha Sanskrit term for "the enlightened one"; used in Hindu prophecies as a reference to a special being who comes along once in 25,000 years and attains enlightenment without having to be reborn;

as the Buddha, a reference to Siddhartha Gautama, who taught that anyone is potentially able to reach enlightenment.

Buddhism Lifestyle, meditation practice, and religion based on the teachings of Gautama.

creatio ex nihilo Latin phrase meaning "creation out of nothing"; used in Judaism, Christianity, and Islam to describe the universe that God made.

dharma In Hinduism, the moral structure underlying existence; in Buddhism, the equivalent of Brahman, the universal soul; Chinese equivalent, Tao.

dialectic The philosophical method used by Socrates involving question and answer.

enlightenment In Buddhism, the state achieved by Gautama of total detachment devoid of ego, in which one sees things as they really are.

heresy Here, belief held or statement made that challenged medieval Christian teachings.

Hinduism Generic term for religion of India dating back to c. 1500 BCE, based on the honoring of numerous deities and a belief in reincarnation.

Inquisition High Christian court assembled beginning in the thirteenth century for the trial and sentencing of those convicted of heresy.

karma In Hinduism, a moral summing up of one's deeds that determines where one will be in the next lifetime.

materialism A philosophy that says only matter is real.

meditation In Buddhism, the practice of sitting until one achieves a state of detachment from ego.

moksha In Hinduism, Sanskrit term given to the state of eternal bliss achieved after having successfully gone through many rebirths.

monotheism Religion based on one supreme god.

nirvana In Buddhism, a state of bliss attainable to those who devote their lives to meditation and a transcendence of ego; adapted into English to mean a totally stress-free condition.

pantheism The belief that the universe, or nature, encompasses divinity, rather than a belief in a personal or anthropomorphic god or gods.

polytheism Religion based on more than one god.

pragmatism Philosophy developed in America which holds that the truth of an idea is measurable by experiment and practical outcome.

predestination The belief stated by Augustine that one's entire life, including moral and immoral choices, is already determined before birth; in Calvinism, the belief that one is born either for salvation or damnation.

Ramadan The ninth month of the Muslim calendar, determined by the phases of the moon; held sacred because of the belief that this was the month in which Muhammad received the Qur'an from Allah in the city of Mecca.

Shiva In Hinduism, a personification of the principle of change, of destroying what Brahma has created in order to make way for the new; the second god in the Hindu trinity.

syncretism The blending of traditional beliefs with those of a new religion.

Talmud A collection of writings that interpret the Torah and provide a clarification of biblical laws.

Tao Chinese name, adopted into English, for the moral order that rules the universe.

Torah The first five books of the Hebrew Bible: Genesis, Exodus, Leviticus, Numbers, and Deuteronomy; attributed to Moses.

Unmoved Mover What Aristotle called the force that always existed and was responsible for setting the entire universe in motion but was not in itself set in motion by anything preceding it.

Vishnu In Hinduism, a personification of the force balancing creation and destruction.

wu wei Phrase used in Taoism that translates as "to do without doing"; means that people who live their lives in tune with the moral order of the universe will always do the right thing.

yang In Taoism, the active component of existence, symbolized in art as the white crescent of a circle which also contains a small black circle. Both of the small circles symbolize the necessary working together of active and passive elements.

yin In Taoism, the passive component of existence, symbolized in art as the black crescent of a circle which also contains a small white circle.

Zen Austere and monastic form of Buddhism centering on the highly disciplined practice of meditating for very long periods of time; from the Chinese *ch'an*, meaning "meditation."

Chapter 11
Morality

Learning Objectives

11.1 Identify the major queries of moral philosophy.

11.2 Discuss the key arguments for accepting the contention that morality is always based in self-interest.

11.3 Identify and discuss the key arguments of utilitarianism, Kant's categorical imperative, and altruism.

11.4 Explain the relationship between religion and morality.

11.5 Discuss the impact of the arts on moral beliefs, and the impact of moral beliefs on the arts.

11.6 Analyze the arguments supporting moral relativism and the dangers that relativism implies.

Figure 11.1 Lady Justice, St. Veil, Carinthia, Austria, 16th century.
Justice is typically portrayed blindfolded, implying that everyone is equal before the law, and only truth matters. Do you believe this? What are your reasons?

Fiore/TopFoto/The Image Works

Two of the first words most babies learn are "good" and "bad." Whether the words are used with a smile or a shaking finger, they are soon integral to an early understanding of the world. As a child grows, the terms become the basis of approving others' behavior. Those two words—good and bad—are with us for life, though applied in many different ways.

Because **moral** problems arise every day of our lives and because artists and philosophers are so often concerned with questions of right and wrong, morality is a major theme in the arts. It is, of course, central to religious thought, philosophy, and law (see Figure 11.1).

In this chapter, we will explore how morality has been defined through history, especially by those philosophers who have concerned themselves specifically with it. We will look at various systems of morality, in particular those focused on self-interest and on behavioral utilitarianism, and on the categorical imperative proposed by Immanuel Kant. We'll briefly discuss morality and the arts and morality and religion. Perhaps the most significant development in the study of morality for our times is moral relativism: Our recognition that what comprises moral behavior may be fluid rather than written in stone.

Defining Morality

11.1 *What are the major queries of moral philosophy?*

Morality is the basis for differentiating between actions that are "good" or right and those that are "bad" or wrong when we are making choices among *significant options*. If we're just deciding on an ice cream flavor, morality is not in play; but if we are deciding on an action that impacts our life or the lives of others, it is. The opposite of morality is immorality, which is often (but clearly inaccurately) defined as *what others do wrong*. This definition eliminates considerations of all sides of an issue and restricts moral acts to the choices that other people make. This chapter is about moral problems that concern us all—choices that have concerned thoughtful people through the ages.

Samuel Butler, a nineteenth-century novelist, defined morality as "the custom of one's country, and the current feeling of one's peers." But which custom? Which country, and which section of that country? Which peers? In centuries past, if one person killed another in a duel fought according to agreed-upon norms of conduct, nobody called it murder, although it would certainly be called that today. If a young woman of social stature and marriageable age spent unsupervised time alone with a man, her actions would have been considered immoral, and her reputation would have been ruined. Not so anymore. It is hard for us to accept that only a few hundred years ago, acceptable moral behavior included *owning* other people. Context drove morality; moral questions were decided by those in authority (usually men, usually clergy or governments) and accepted without question.

Today, context continues to frame our definitions of *moral* and *immoral*. Violations of marriage vows by a celebrity tend to be waved away, but such violations by a candidate for political office are condemned as "immoral." We indulge in an "us-versus-them" culture, where loyalties to sports teams, political parties, and religions divide us and lead us to view behaviors as immoral or wrong that we might otherwise, in an earlier time, have ignored. Family traditions, education, and agreed-upon social norms all influence our definition of morality, as do fairy tales, literature, plays, movies, and television.

Morality and Philosophy

If morality can be defined as the basis for a choice among significant options, philosophers have wrestled through the ages with what these options might be. Certain questions arise again and again in the study of morality. Here are some thorny ones to which many great thinkers have tried to respond.

1. *Does the end justify the means?* Put another way: If the overall goal is considered beneficial, is it morally right to do *anything* to get there—including certain acts that on their own would be regarded as wrong, criminal, or even evil? Machiavelli, a Renaissance philosopher (see pp. 315), says yes. Others maintain that any moral transgression, even telling a lie, is wrong under every circumstance.

2. *Are punishment and the fear of punishment the only things that keep us from doing wrong?* The question of whether to obey the law when we can get away with breaking it is at the heart of a famous debate between Glaucon and Socrates in Plato's *The Republic* (see pp. 309).

3. *Do the needs of society outweigh the needs of the individual?* Some philosophers argue that the needs of the individual should always take precedence over those of society and suggest that anything else is unnatural. Altruism (see pp. 317 and 322–323) maintains that we should be more concerned for others than for ourselves.

4. *Should economic resources be controlled by individuals or communities?* Some political and economic leaders defend the free market, as defined by Adam Smith, while others insist the free market system does not work in quite the way Smith described (see pp. 313). Others say that whether we perceive totally free enterprise as moral or not depends on our economic status.

5. *Are results all that matter, or do intentions also count?* Jeremy Bentham (see pp. 317) argues that moral decisions depend on outcome rather than motives.

Moral Systems

A network of related values on which moral choices are based is called a **moral system**. Most religions share the belief that a divinity has set down certain rules that must be followed whether or not they interfere with an individual's personal desires. Often those rules are found in a sacred book. Accepting these rules thus involves both faith in the existence of the divinity and faith that the sacred book was written by people in a position to record accurately the words of that divinity.

Alternate moral systems are based on reason, not faith: One does what is right because reason determines that it is right, and therefore doing wrong is irrational. It can, however, be argued that this view really depends on faith as well, faith that reason is the correct decision-maker in all matters.

People who have a hard time making up their minds when faced with a difficult choice may wish to consult a moral authority, such as a well-known and trusted philosopher, a spokesperson for religion, or even a close friend with a reputation for making intelligent decisions. Yet here's a question that inevitably arises: *In the event that two sources offer sharply divergent opinions, which one do we follow?* Will we follow our intuition? Will our decision in the end come down to self-interest? Or will we lack confidence in our own reasoning and find it easier to follow a moral authority (provided we don't find ourselves torn between two opposing authoritative views)? And if we *do* settle on one choice or the other, how will we ever know that we made the *right* choice? As you can see, the ever-present problem of right versus wrong can lead us into a vortex of questions that never seem to stop.

The terms *should* and *should not* are constantly cropping up, especially in commentaries by religious moral authorities. The words also abound in rules of the military, the family, schools, sports, and games.

People who feel uncomfortable with an absolute *should* are apt to reject the word in favor of *moral relativism*: "Who's to say what's right?" "People are different. What's good for one may not be good for another." "Times have changed; there are no more universals." A popular maxim has been, "As long as you don't hurt anybody and it makes you happy, do it!"

Life pushes us into so many quandaries that doing the right thing in every instance is exceedingly difficult. That is why the humanities are sensitive to the pain that can be caused by moral dilemmas and the often tragic results of what we thought were the right choices.

The Morality of Self-Interest

11.2 What are the key arguments for accepting the contention that morality is always based in self-interest?

When young siblings angrily dispute who owns what, a parent will remind them not to fight. Instead, they are urged to share. In school, children are taught to obey rules, not to be selfish, and to cooperate with others. Public praise for philanthropy reminds us that charity is good, that acting out of self-interest is wrong (except, of course, when it was self-interest that allowed the donor to amass the fortune being donated). Yet free societies are also based on the principle that free enterprise, which benefits the *entrepreneur* (a person who operates a business) first, also helps employees and their families. Getting ahead is a recognized goal, with its implied corollary that some must win while others have to lose.

Is acting out of self-interest such a bad thing? Is selflessness necessarily good? If everyone acts out of self-interest, does it breed a self-reliance that is better for society as a whole? During the nineteenth century, self-interest came to the fore as the most desirable characteristic of a human being. Even before that, the term was often preceded by the adjective *enlightened*, conveying the belief that self-reliant people, realizing their full potential as human beings, would enrich, not damage, society. Other theories, however, tell us that, in a choice between self-interest and the general good, self-interest must always prevail.

This question is more cogent than ever in today's world, where income inequality has grown beyond anything imagined even 50 years ago, and where the wealthiest 1 percent in the United States control almost half the wealth of the country—more than the total owned by the bottom 90 percent. The way we acquire and divide wealth—the system of capitalism—may be the most important moral dilemma of the twenty-first century. But it is not a new one.

Glaucon versus Socrates

Early in Plato's *The Republic*, a series of philosophical dialogs between Socrates and his students as chronicled by Plato, a confrontation occurs between Socrates, who is always on the side of reason, and Glaucon, a student described by Plato as "that most pugnacious of men," who is a firm believer that everyone does the right thing out of motives that have nothing to do with reason or innate goodness. (Glaucon was also Plato's older brother.) To strengthen his case, Glaucon tells the story of a shepherd named Gyges, who discovers that the ring he has removed from a corpse has the power to make him invisible. Taking full advantage of his newfound power, Glaucon reports, Gyges

> contrived to be one of the messengers who were sent to the court, where, as soon as he arrived he seduced the queen, and with her help conspired against the king and slew him, and took the kingdom.

An argument then ensues in the class over whether a basically honorable and just man would have done the same thing. Glaucon continues:

> Suppose now that there were two such magic rings, and the just [man] put on one of them and the unjust the other; no man can be imagined to be of such an iron nature that he would stand fast in justice. No man could keep his hands off what was not his own when he could safely take what he liked out of the market, or go into houses and lie with anyone at his pleasure, or kill or release from prison whom he would and in all respects be like a God among men.[1]

Socrates replies that if the just man decided not to take advantage of the magic ring, he would die in peace, content that his had been a good life. Glaucon quickly counters by asking the group to suppose that somehow the just man had developed a reputation for being unjust, while the unjust man enjoyed the opposite reputation. Would the just man not decide he would be a fool not to use the power of the ring? What would be the satisfaction in doing the right thing if nobody knew it? Furthermore, what if he was made to suffer excruciating torture because of his supposed lack of goodness? (Socrates was, of course, famous for teaching that nothing bad can happen to good people.) It would not be long, concludes Glaucon, before the just man realized that the *appearance* of goodness is all that matters. Doing the good, if nobody knows it, is futile.

Having a reputation for being truthful, hence trustworthy, the unjust man, according to Glaucon, goes on to enjoy all the benefits that come with social approval.

> *With his reputation for virtue, he will hold offices of state, ally himself by marriage to any family he may choose, become a partner in any business, and having no scruples about being dishonest, turn all these disadvantages to profit.*[2]

Society, so goes Glaucon's argument, expects virtue to be only an appearance, the result of pressures brought to bear on each of us, not of the human capacity to determine through reason what is right and what is wrong.

SOCRATES' REBUTTAL   Yet reason is precisely what Socrates relies on, and his counterargument stirs up as much controversy as his opponent's: He maintains that the virtuous act is *done for its own sake*. Rational humans live according to the law, even if the law is harmful to them. Periclean democracy, or the direct rule of citizens, was still new, and many expressed doubts that the ordinary citizen would have enough sense not to take advantage of so much freedom. Socrates firmly believed that the rationality of citizens would give rise to laws that were fair, just, and moral. Plato attributes to Socrates one of the most ringing (and still controversial) declarations in all of philosophy: *To know the good is to do the good.*

Socrates' meaning, which may at first seem naive, is actually awesome in its simplicity and ultimately hard to refute. What he says is that people cannot claim to be deliberately choosing the wrong action despite knowing the right one. If you do the wrong thing, then that is what you know. Acting is part of knowing. In other words, anyone can pretend to know something, but the only proof of that knowledge is action. If your deeds are bad, then there is no evidence that you knew what was right. We may disagree, but the force of the argument is powerful.

Socrates paid with his life for his trust in reason (Figure 11.2). After being found guilty of trumped-up charges—corrupting the minds of young Athenians and teaching atheism—he was jailed and threatened with execution. He refused the offer of a lighter sentence if he were to agree never to teach again. Doing that would have meant no longer seeking the truth, and without possessing the truth, he would be no better than Glaucon's shepherd.

Socrates does observe that the opinions of others are important—but *only* the opinions of knowledgeable good people. Why should one care what ignorant bad people think? If one lives so as to win the respect of the good, then obviously one is leading a good life. Then he gives one of his final lessons before committing suicide by drinking the hemlock that will end his days: "Not life, but a good life, is to be chiefly valued."

THE RELEVANCE OF GLAUCON AND SOCRATES IN THE TWENTY-FIRST CENTURY   Fortunately, on a daily basis, most of us make much smaller choices than the ones debated by Glaucon and Socrates—and we don't face a cup of hemlock for making what we think is the right choice. Still, even without the ring of Gyges, we are

Figure 11.2 Jacques-Louis David, *The Death of Socrates*, c. 1787.
Socrates chose to die rather than to be forced to stop seeking the truth as a teacher. Are there moral issues that you consider "life or death"?
The Metropolitan Museum of Art. Image source: Art Resource, NY

often invisible. Consider the opportunities you have to test the theory to do what you know is right.

- When, driving late at night, without a policeman anywhere around, do you automatically stop the car at a traffic light? What about a stop sign?
- At a gym, do you obey the posted rules to wipe down your machine and take a shower before entering the pool? But what if nobody else is around?
- How many customers call attention to a billing mistake in their favor which they notice once they leave the store?

As "invisible" citizens, all of us can rationalize failure to do what we would do if others were around to observe us. We can rationalize by telling ourselves that a minor mistake in our favor by a cashier or a mechanic will compensate for previous visits when a product or service was faulty, or we were overcharged. Students who work two jobs may claim that they need to get advance copies of a test by any means possible, or that they must purchase a paper online rather than writing their own, in order to compete with classmates who have more time to study and write. The choice in each instance is not between life-or-death options, but the ring of Gyges is still around.

Nowadays it is easy to find billionaires who succeed even without that ring by following the path of self-interest. They offer huge sums to charity, for which they are generally admired—but pay the workers in their businesses very little. Their success is equivalent to Glaucon's idea of a good reputation. Also in the Glaucon camp are those who quote with admiration the cynical adage of baseball manager Leo Durocher: *Nice guys finish last*.

What guided the Athenians who voted for Socrates' death sentence? Socrates was convicted not by a jury as we know it today, but rather by an assembly of every eligible male citizen who wanted to participate. Reason may not, finally, have been *their* guiding principle. Political factors appear to have been involved. Socrates was known to have been friendly to someone considered an enemy of the state, and the philosopher's teachings often challenged the state. Did the self-interest of the state, in the care of the male citizenry (which comprised only 5 percent of the entire population), finally triumph? Can a governing body ever be expected to survive in the name of reason alone?

THE PHILOSOPHER KING   Later in *The Republic*, Plato admits that the majority of people—both the governing and the governed—will generally be driven by self-interest unless held in check by one supreme ruler—a man not out for himself but rather one motivated solely by reason in every instance. A man who rules with a clear vision of a state in which justice prevails. A man, perhaps, like Socrates. Plato calls this ruler the *philosopher king*. Whether such a being has ever existed or could ever exist is a matter of long debate. A number of rulers have made claims about their wisdom and no doubt have earnestly believed they and their methods were best for their state. But history has not always confirmed their claims.

Plato's plan has many problems. The first is determining who would judge the credentials of someone who applied for the job. Reason says only the wisest person is qualified to make the decision. Because there can, by definition, be only one "wisest person" in a society, choosing him (Plato doesn't say *her*) would seem to be impossible. Only the wisest person can do that, and we're right back where we started. Glaucon would probably say the struggle for the power of this ruler would result in all manner of underhanded magic-ring ploys on the part of ambitious people who would cheat, even kill, to win the job.

Government and Self-Interest

What is the moral role of government? Without the services of Plato's philosopher king, it's hard to know just what government should and shouldn't do. In fact, that is one of the central questions being debated today. Should government play as small a role as possible, allowing individuals (and corporations) free hand in finding their own paths and following their own moral standards, with the assumption that individual (and corporate) self-interest is the right choice and (if this is our concern) will benefit all in the end? Or should government provide support for those citizens who are suffering or struggling, perhaps by placing restrictions on things such as individual accumulation of wealth? Should government regulate the ownership of weapons for the good of society? Should government regulate access to drugs? What about access to abortions? Where does government's moral role begin and end?

Historically, many of the major moral changes have happened as a result of citizens pushing their governments to act in the face of moral inequities. Think, for example, of the sit-ins in the South that provided a foundation for this country's civil rights movement, and the eventual legislation that ended legal segregation (although not racial conflict, as we see almost daily). Think of the roles played by Mahatma Gandhi and Nelson Mandela in the huge upheavals in their home countries of India and South Africa that resulted in expanded rights for all citizens. Think of the Suffrage movement in this country, which earned women the right to vote. We think of these movements as socially beneficial—but weren't they, at heart, actually born of self-interest? Out of individual desires for equality, for the vote, for better treatment? What do you think?

CIVIL DISOBEDIENCE: HENRY DAVID THOREAU   Henry David Thoreau (1817–1862) begins his famous essay *Civil Disobedience* (1849) with this declaration:

> *I heartily accept the motto—"That government is best which governs least," and I should like to see it acted up to more rapidly and systematically. Carried out, it finally amounts to this, which I also believe,—"That government is best which governs not at all . . ."*[3]

He implemented this belief by refusing to pay a tax levied for a war against Mexico, which he opposed. He then announced that he was seceding from the Union and moved to a woodland cabin, away from the pressures of civilization. In *Walden; or, Life in the Woods* (1854), an account of his life in the cabin (where he lived for about two years), Thoreau says his one room was furnished with three chairs: one for solitude, two for friendship, and three for society. He refused to go beyond three.

His friend Ralph Waldo Emerson (1803–1882) had inspired Thoreau's uncompromising individualism, as Emerson has similarly inspired countless readers for generations. In his essay "Self-Reliance" (1841), Emerson delivers the manifesto of individualism. He advises us to be ourselves, never to imitate others, never to conform if doing so is in conflict with our own will ("Who so would be a man, must be a nonconformist"), and never to be fearful of behaving unpredictably ("A foolish consistency is the hobgoblin of little minds, adored by little statesmen and philosophers and divines"). Among his most dramatic utterances is this: "[I]f I am the Devil's child, I will live then from the Devil."

Except for Thoreau's refusal to pay the poll tax, neither man committed acts against government. Their strong individualism was confined to their explosive writings. In these they showed themselves to be part of a sweeping nineteenth-century movement in which self-interest would come to the fore as the most desirable characteristic of a human being. There is no evidence that either man championed the cause of aggressive greed and the destruction of others in a single-minded quest for a secure foothold in this world.

Economics and Self-Interest

Another area besides government where morality raises its head frequently is economics. Economical philosophers for at least three centuries have tried to find moral systems that govern the accumulation of wealth. Now, in the twenty-first century, we are seeing the largest inequalities of wealth distribution that have existed in well over a hundred years. What actions are moral when it comes to making choices about money? What systems are the fairest?

ADAM SMITH The Scottish economic philosopher Adam Smith (1723–1790) believed the perfect society was one in which all people were free to pursue self-interest. Like Karl Marx, who would come later, Smith observed that economic well-being was the guiding force in human life. People were interested in making money, in getting ahead, in providing the most comfortable standard of living for themselves and their families. Greed itself was not necessarily a bad thing, as long as one did not break the law or harm others in the process of accumulating wealth. Far from being immoral, greed was the natural condition of humanity (see Figure 11.3).

Smith's theory that people should have the freedom to pursue wealth became the basis for the capitalist system of today. To those who argued that unlimited freedom of economic activity would yield a society of constant conflict and dangerous competition, Smith's answer was that *without* such freedom, only those in power would enjoy the pleasures that rightfully belong to everyone.

Smith's policy is called **laissez-faire** (literally, "allow to do") and is based on the principle that businesses should be free to charge whatever they want for their goods and services, and that the public's response to those charges, not government controls, should regulate the process. Smith's ideal society has a built-in system of checks and balances that prevent the accumulation of wealth in just a few corporations.

According to Smith, manufacturers and other entrepreneurs perform a service for the public by seeking to make a profit for themselves. Salaries paid to employees increase the money supply,

Figure 11.3 Leonardo DiCaprio in Martin Scorsese's *Wolf of Wall Street* (2013).
"Wall Street" is often used as a metaphor for personal greed. Do you agree that greed is the natural condition of humanity? Are there ways in which personal greed benefits society?
Mary Cybulski/Paramount Pictures/Everett Collection

which keeps circulating throughout the economy, guaranteeing more employment for everyone. Without their being aware of it, says Smith, all people who live in a free-market system are joined together by what he termed "an invisible hand." It is in the best interest of the entrepreneur, Smith argued, to manufacture a product that people actually need. Continuing to produce an unneeded product would result in bankruptcy. (Once the automobile displaced the horse and carriage as the primary means of transportation, who wanted to buy buggy whips?)

Problems develop when entrepreneurs become too greedy (though greed is still what drives the free-market economy). If a product is successful and large numbers of people buy it, the supply dwindles and prices go up. When the price gets too high, people stop buying, supply outweighs demand, and companies are forced to bring the cost back down. The laws of supply and demand always apply and regulate the economy. When the product is cheap enough, people start buying again, and the price goes up again. The cycle would seem to be infinite. But is it?

SUPPLY AND DEMAND: THE NEW REALITY   In the real world, we have learned, the laws of supply and demand may fall short. Our wants appear to be insatiable—but some resources are limited. Crude oil, for example, is nonrenewable. Finding it and getting it ready for market has proved more and more difficult, as supplies run low and we turn to more and more challenging locales (offshore, where drilling is expensive and dangerous, or in troubled countries). Recently, the development of a process called *hydrofracking* has provided a wide range of new sources for obtaining oil—but perhaps at the cost of contaminating water supplies or introducing dangerous chemicals into the earth. What is the "good" moral choice here? To extract the oil we need, or to concern ourselves with the impact that process might have? Who decides?

The next crisis, experts predict, will center on an even more valuable resource: water. As the climate warms (as most scientists agree is happening), drought is anticipated in much of the world. Water is necessary for life itself. What is the moral choice for those countries or regions that still have ample water? Should they guard it for their own citizens? Sell it at a high price? Or share it and risk running low themselves?

Smith could not have predicted today's global economy, in which nations do not fend for themselves but rather participate in a network of mutual dependence. A bank collapse or a credit crunch in a once-powerful nation that had attracted much foreign investment can create chaos all over the world. Economists agree that there is no such thing as an ideally self-regulating market, and therefore Smith's theory that self-interest is in the best interest of humanity is now hotly debated.

Most of us who live in free societies continue to depend on a (more or less) free market and believe (more or less) in Smith's theory. We must admit, however, that it poses problems that may never be resolved.

AYN RAND   For novelist Ayn Rand (1905–1982), **capitalism** was essentially a religion. She preached complete reliance on a free market, which she believed encouraged the strong and self-reliant to make the most of their talents without spending a lifetime helping others, who only grow weaker and lose the incentive to help themselves. Born in prerevolutionary Russia, Rand as a teenager witnessed the sweeping changes and promises of a glorious future in a classless society. She resisted indoctrination after thoroughly examining communist ideology, rejecting Karl Marx's claims about the benefits society would receive once the bourgeoisie (middle class) was eliminated.

Rand inevitably defected to the West, where she started to write. In one of her famous essays, *The Virtue of Selfishness*, Rand says people of vision should have unlimited opportunities to follow their own laws. In her philosophy, the strident loner does help others, but not out of the belief that it is moral and honorable to make sacrifices for them. The rest of us profit because a strident loner like Howard Roark, the hero of *The Fountainhead* (1943), can use his genius to build great cities and make the world a better place (Figure 11.4). There isn't an ounce of sentiment in him. He proudly asserts, "No man is worth five minutes of my time." But his arrogance and self-assuredness, Rand believes, only increase his value to the rest of us.

"Enlightened" Self-Interest

While humanism has historically been opposed to self-interest as a way of life, some philosophers who would consider themselves to be humanists have espoused the theory that self-interest alone is not only rational but also in the best interest of society.

MACHIAVELLI, *THE PRINCE*   *The Prince* (first distributed 1513; published 1532) is the great work by Niccolò Machiavelli (1469–1527), a prominent Florentine Renaissance philosopher. The book is dedicated to Lorenzo de Medici, head of a famous family, a man of extreme wealth and power, patron of many artists, and both loved and feared by hundreds. Lorenzo, as we might expect, had many enemies and critics. Persons with his kind of power and influence usually do.

Figure 11.4 Gary Cooper (right) as Howard Roark in the 1949 film of Ayn Rand's *The Fountainhead*.
Do you think we all profit from individual self-interest, as Ayn Rand argues?
Everett Collection

Machiavelli, however, swore staunch allegiance to Lorenzo. To defend his patron, he composed *The Prince*, which contains advice to all aspiring rulers. Effective leaders, he claims, must never assume their followers would seek a justice inconvenient to themselves. He therefore concludes that the wisest course for a true leader is to curb the self-interest of the population by inspiring in them a sense of awe. Leaders must present an intimidating appearance, both in extravagant dress and in imperial behavior, to let the populace know that someone regal is in charge. They should exhibit signs of their power, such as by riding in magnificent carriages followed by a large retinue of influential friends, security personnel, and important local politicians. This advice has been followed by modern heads of state who fly from country to country in gigantic official planes and arrive at their destinations in police-escorted stretch limousines, long motorcades, and with a parade of bodyguards.

Machiavelli's political philosophy is a continuation of earlier beliefs, such as those held by Plato and Aristotle, who did not trust ordinary citizens to be rational enough to make intelligent decisions. They advocated strong rule from the top in order to guarantee stability and justice. Plato had his philosopher king, while Aristotle believed the ideal government had three major components: the king, the aristocrats, and groups of outstanding citizens known for their wisdom and fair dealings.

All three philosophers—Machiavelli, Plato, and Aristotle—were against ruthless self-interested dictatorships and the whimsical rule by people whose wealth enabled them to buy their way to power. All three were concerned for the welfare of the total society, but they could not recommend direct rule of the populace. Instead, they believed wise rulers best served both their own and their country's interest by imposing rules based on a carefully considered political philosophy of **enlightened self-interest**: serving the self in order to make an effective government that provides for people better than they could provide for themselves.

The term **Machiavellian** has unfortunately become a reference to cynical individuals who scorn the masses, considering themselves superior to all others and therefore entitled to exert power over them. Literature offers a gallery of characters that critics have labeled—and always negatively—*Machiavellian*. These characters are usually villains who prey on unsuspecting goodness.

Machiavellianism, as understood by the founder of the philosophy, emerged from the Renaissance focus on individualism. In a sense, Machiavelli's ideal ruler typified the new age, for such a ruler was not encumbered by the restraints of the Christ-like existence demanded of (but not necessarily realized by) rulers in the Middle Ages.

THOMAS HOBBES, *LEVIATHAN* Thomas Hobbes (1588–1679) was a British political philosopher who believed that tight autocratic control was necessary, because the masses of people were innately evil and solely out for themselves. He believed egoism was the natural condition of humanity and denied that such a thing as a noble purpose could exist. With this pessimistic view of the individual, Hobbes wrote his most famous work, *Leviathan* (1651), recommending a political system based on absolute monarchy. He employed the term *commonwealth* to describe the ideal state, one in which each subject must willingly turn over his rights to the sovereign for the mutual protection of all people from each other. He advises that

> *every man should say to every man, I authorize and give up my right of governing myself, to this man* [i.e. the Leader], *or to this assembly of men, on this condition, that thou give up thy right to him, and authorize all his action in like manner.*[4]

Although this may sound like a democratic social contract whereby each citizen willingly gives up individual rights for the good of all, Hobbes makes no pretense of democracy, reasoning that power invested in the monarch could not, by definition, be challenged by the people. If it were, the monarch would not be feared, and if he were not feared, order would disintegrate. The monarch, backed by an invincible army, would protect his subjects from each other as well as from attacks by other nations. Hence the term *Leviathan*, which for Hobbes meant "*mortal god*, to which we owe under the *immortal God*, our peace and defense." The commonwealth would then flourish peacefully—an impossibility if each citizen were allowed to think and act for himself. Without the Leviathan, every person would distrust every other person, with the result that no person or property would be safe. Hobbes states in *Leviathan* that, without the absolute strength of the leader, "every man has a right to every thing, even to one another's body. And therefore, as long as the natural right of every man endureth, there can be no security to any man."

We can see that Machiavelli and Hobbes both favored nondemocratic government as the only way to prevent self-interest from destroying society. Hobbes, further influenced by the rise of rational philosophy during the seventeenth century in reaction to the otherworldliness of the Middle Ages, maintained that reason alone, not a sentimental faith in the inherent goodness of human nature, could allow humanity to live in peace and harmony. Tough-minded as his political philosophy was, Hobbes insisted that it represented the only rational course if the human race were to survive its cutthroat instincts.

Satire and the Morality of Self-Interest

Not surprisingly, the clergy of various faiths warn their congregations against excessive emphasis on self. One clergyman, Jonathan Swift (1667–1745), was dean of St. Patrick's, an Anglican cathedral in Dublin, and also a satirist who could be bitterly cynical behind his façade of humor. In his famous 1729 treatise, published anonymously, on the brutalities of self-interest, "A Modest Proposal," he assumes the persona of a well-bred—and well-fed—English gentleman, who appears to have a perfect solution to the problem of Irish poverty, especially the fact that poor Irish children are forced to subsist on a near-starvation diet. His solution? Dispose of the children by having them served up as delicious meals for the rich, and by so doing, raise the economic level of the parents.

I have been assured by a very knowing American of my acquaintance in London, that a young healthy child well nursed is at a year old a most delicious, nourishing and whole-some food whether stewed, roasted, baked or boiled, and I make no doubt that it will equally serve in a fricassee, or ragout.[5]

The narrator, in a passage that is prophetic of what Utilitarian philosopher Jeremy Bentham would propound seriously some years later, calmly computes the mathematics of the enterprise: 20,000 would be spared for breeding; of these only one-fourth need be males, "more than is usual for livestock." A child of one "will make two dishes as an entertainment for friends, and when the family dines alone, the fore or hind quarter will make a reasonable dish . . . seasoned with a little pepper or salt."

He goes on to itemize the consequences, including the value to the breeders of getting rid of needless expenses. Taverns would have a new dish, and "a skillful cook who understands how to please his guests will contrive to make it as expensive as they please." Marriages would increase, and mothers would be treated more tenderly as they fattened up their children. His proposal, he adds, is not based on any desire on his part for profit: "I have no children by which I can propose to get a single penny, the youngest being nine years old, and my wife past child-bearing."

As can be imagined, "A Modest Proposal" has aroused indignation among those who don't catch on to Swift's humane purpose. Some literalists took him at his word and denounced what they called his "savagery," not recognizing that he was really attacking smug self-interest as the only goal in life.

Moral Alternatives to Self-Interest

11.3 *What are the key arguments of utilitarianism, Kant's categorical imperative, and altruism?*

It is hard to deny that self-interest is sometimes necessary. But most of us recoil to some extent at the thought of living our lives governed entirely by self-interest—even if it calls itself "enlightened." What alternatives have been proposed through the centuries? Three important ways of looking at morality are *utilitarianism*, developed and modified by the British philosophers Jeremy Bentham and John Stuart Mill; the *categorical imperative* posited by the German Immanuel Kant, historically perhaps the single most important thinker about good and evil; and *altruism*, the belief that social good always outweighs self-interest, which is enjoying a resurgence of attention in the twenty-first century, particularly in the works of British philosopher Peter Singer.

Utilitarianism

Jeremy Bentham (1748–1832) was unwilling to say that self-interest was wrong, though its pursuit was contrary to the rigid morality taught him as a child. Why were moral laws so unreflective of true human nature? Accordingly, he formulated the theory that since self-serving pleasure is the natural goal sought by everyone, all people ought to have an equal chance of attaining it. He rebelled against the moral codes set forth by religion and traditional philosophy, as well as those that became laws binding on an entire population. What, he asked, gave anyone the right to tell anyone else which pleasures to enjoy and which to avoid? But must there not be guidelines? Surely everyone could not wantonly pursue pleasure if this meant interfering with the right of others to do the same. *Unrestricted* self-interest made no sense to him.

As a philosopher, he was attracted to science and mathematics, for those fields offered methods of achieving certainty. Accordingly, mathematics became the basis for a moral system that allowed self-interest to be both defended and restricted. He called it **utilitarianism**.

BENTHAM'S MORAL MATHEMATICS   Bentham declared that numbers were the key to moral certainty: A formula would decide the right course of action in every instance. For him, the goal was a society in which the maximum number of people achieved the maximum amount of pleasure *without* impinging on the rights of others. He denied the validity of *moral absolutism* and formulated his famous definition of a moral action as one that provides *the greatest good for the greatest number*.

In Bentham's system, before choosing an action with consequences that will affect others, a person assigns a plus or minus numerical value to the degree of pleasure or pain the action might cause for the most people. Let us say that, in a modern example, the question is whether to allow a giant resort complex to be built along a lakefront. So many plus points go to the contractors, builders, construction workers, and service personnel, all of whom stand to profit from the enterprise. For all of them, the construction offers positive pleasure. Additional plus points are awarded to vacationers, who will benefit from having a place in which to relax and relieve stress. Points are subtracted by environmentalists concerned about the inevitable pollution and the extermination of fish and waterfowl, and by residents who see the resort as destroying the neighborhood, thus bringing down the resale value of their property. The calculator (an invention Bentham would have loved) tells the story. Plus points for those who benefit, minus points for those who don't. Assign your own points, do the simple arithmetic, and get the moral answer.

Bentham's **moral mathematics** also adds or subtracts points based on "intensity" and "duration." In the example of the resort, we must consider the annoying sounds and air pollution of road expansion, not to mention the fact that, once the resort is in place against the wishes of many who gave it minus points, it isn't there for a short stay. May points be determined strictly by the number of individuals involved? If so, the displeased residents might outnumber the owners and the contractors. But what if the builders insist that the number of possible vacationers is almost infinite, and so might be the terrific boost to the economy of the region?

MOTIVES AND RESULTS   For Bentham, the measurable results tell all regardless of motives. Few would imagine that the owners of the resort complex are concerned only for the economic welfare of the residents. Nonetheless, if they "win" the numbers game, the resort is morally right. But critics of Bentham's morality see many problems.

Suppose the builder of the proposed resort had a longstanding feud with the head of the Environmental Committee, a feud that had nothing to do with business or pollution. What if anger and revenge are his true motives? He has proposed the entire scheme just to embarrass the environmentalist in front of his supporters. Bentham's calculation yields only external results and pays no attention to motives *unless* there is a chance that a motive, once discovered, might cause pain to a lot of people—unlikely to happen in this hypothetical case.

Another example of a numerical question that sidesteps motives is: Is it better to give $10 to a cause you vehemently believe in or $10,000 to the same cause because you want to see your picture in the paper along with a caption praising your philanthropy? For Bentham (and probably for the fundraisers), the larger amount would be preferable and its moral virtue assured.

What might be Bentham's mathematical calculation for a decision on abortion? Or on the right of homosexuals to marry? Abortion might be considered right or wrong depending on whether an underpopulated country needed more pregnancies carried to completion. As for homosexuality, the question would be whether the practice of it harms the general population. What if the population believes, for example, that there will be fewer babies born in a society that allows same-sex marriage, since a marriage between two men cannot produce children? (This argument, of course, ignores the possibility of adoption or surrogate parenthood, as well as the ability of one or both partners in a lesbian relationship to become mothers.) Even though Bentham was essentially a political radical, to be consistent with himself, he would have to approve of a ban on homosexuality if the greatest number in a given society decided the practice would lessen the population, depriving the future of artists, philanthropists, scientists, dedicated physicians, and so on. In such a society, homosexuality would be mathematically immoral, yet moral in another society that placed the highest priority on human rights.

Bentham believed in various definitions of the good, depending on particular circumstances. The lakeside resort, for example, might bring wealth to its town but also draw tourists away from another resort 20 miles distant. And what happens when calculations do not agree (which is frequent)? My pleasure, in other words, is your pain—and vice versa.

Bentham proposed that the government would have to step in and be responsible for providing the greatest good for the greatest number. He even organized a political party called the Philosophical Radicals in order to campaign for moral reform based on his mathematical system. The name was eventually changed to the Utilitarian Party, suggesting a practical approach to moral philosophy, basically democratic in that it recognized the equality of all individuals in the matter of decision making, with majority rule holding sway. A countryman who also wanted moral reform was not, however, as generous as Bentham.

UTILITARIANISM MODIFIED: JOHN STUART MILL   Also a utilitarian philosopher, John Stuart Mill (1806–1873) came along a half century after Bentham. His father, James Mill, had assisted Bentham in the development of his political party. James Mill was also an elitist when it came to the education of his son. The boy was allowed to associate only with friends of whose intellectual capabilities the father approved. But he was also taught a Socratic brand of rational liberalism—that is, almost unlimited freedom for those responsible enough to use it for purposes other than the gratification of sexual desires.

As Mill matured, becoming a writer and philosopher, he expressed approval of Bentham's views on government's responsibility to guard the rights of the private citizen, but he disagreed that majority rule is always the proper course. Bentham's mathematics implied that decisions were numerically variable, but what about matters of taste? Followers of Mill continue to question the wisdom of the majority in all decisions. What if, for example, a proposal to erect a new museum or an opera house were put to a popular vote and it had to compete with a new sports stadium? The greatest number might well opt for the stadium, thus depriving opera-goers of the pleasures they sought. Imposing "low art" on everyone regardless of preference was, for Mill, as immoral as imposing absolute standards. Yet would not the rule of the majority (an absolute in itself) deprive the opera lovers of *their* moral rights?

Our present-day society's preoccupation with winners—blockbuster movies, sports rankings, bestsellers, awards, and scorekeeping of every kind—causes regret in critics concerned that numbers can overlook quality. The negative accusation of elitism always lurks in the background for those urging criteria other than popularity.

THE ROLE OF GOVERNMENT IN UTILITARIANISM   Mill recognized that government was needed to balance irresponsibility on the part of the general population. This fact, however, did not give government the right to legislate morality for the responsible few. In defending the rights of enlightened citizens, Mill proved to be more radical than Bentham.

One of Mill's famous essays, "The Tyranny of the Majority," in his book *On Liberty* (1859) maintains that letting the majority rule in all decisions is just as bad as the autocratic rule of monarchs in previous centuries. Mill writes that his objective

Figure 11.5 William Hogarth, *The Enraged Musician*, 1741.
Hogarth, a satiric artist, shows a violinist angered by the chaos created by presumably lower-class musicians outside his window. Should the majority rule in all cases, even when their actions conflict with those of more educated and wealthier individuals?

Library of Congress Prints and Photographs Division[LC-USZ62-78249]

. . . is to assert one very simple principle, as entitled to govern absolutely the dealings of society with the individual in the way of compulsion and control, whether the means used be physical force in the form of legal penalties, or the moral coercion of public opinion. That principle is that the sole end for which mankind are warranted individually or collectively, in interfering with liberty of action of any of their number, is self-protection. That is, the only purpose for which power can be rightfully exercised over any member of a civilized community, against his will, is to prevent harm to others. His own good, either physical or moral, is not a sufficient warrant.[6]

The English artist William Hogarth (1697–1764), famous for paintings and engravings that poke fun at all levels of English society, gave us *The Enraged Musician* (Figure 11.5), displaying both sides of a conflict. The musician in question sits by his open window, his work interrupted by an extremely noisy crowd. We ask ourselves: What if the musician were to call the police on the grounds that his right to work in privacy had been violated? What if the case ended up in court? Would the judge rule that the crowd has a right to cavort as it pleases as long as no one is physically harmed? Or that the musician is right in objecting to the crowd on the grounds that his artistic work is more important than their fun? What do you think Mill would say?

The Categorical Imperative: Immanuel Kant

Born in East Prussia and a resident there for most of his life, the German philosopher Immanuel Kant (1724–1804) was, like Bentham, impressed with the certainties that science was able to achieve. As a University of Königsberg faculty member, he read insatiably in a number of fields, becoming so adept he was given courses to teach in mathematics, physics, anthropology, logic, metaphysics, and ethics. This impressive background made Kant feel comfortable with both science and philosophy, and he would merge the two into one of the most influential systems of thought ever devised.

The various branches of Kant's philosophy are like the spokes of a wheel radiating from a central belief, adopted from science, that truth is arrived at through experience. He differed, however, from kindred philosophers who took the extreme position that experience is strictly what our senses tell us.

Kant's view was that the input of the senses does not constitute experience until it is interpreted by our inborn rational capacity. He believed that we are born with mental **categories**, into which sensory data are filed—much as a postal worker takes an armful of random mail and flips each letter into an appropriate box. We know, for example, that the chair is next to the table because we categorically understand "nextness." If we did not, the spatial relationship would be meaningless: If someone asked us to go fetch the chair next to the table, we would return a blank stare.

Kant also turned his attention to moral concerns. His theory stated that the sense of right and wrong was also inborn. True, we hear "yes" and "no" from our parents, but no learning can take place unless we are able to attach approval and disapproval—first to specific actions, then to the abstract concepts of rightness and wrongness. For Kant, the average person has no trouble reaching those abstractions because the inborn moral sense gradually unfolds in the same way that a bud gradually opens into a flower. He labels this inborn faculty the **categorical imperative** or "sense of ought": an intuitive classification of actions and choices as morally acceptable or unacceptable. Experience teaches us which specific actions are right, but first we must know rightness or wrongness—and that cannot be taught. It resides inside us.

THE MORAL IMPERATIVE   The actions that we take based on our internal knowledge of right and wrong are compelled by what Kant called the **moral imperative**. Kant argued that this imperative was based solely in reason. (Later thinkers, particularly religious thinkers, attributed the principle to the conscience or the soul, and suggested that it was divinely inspired.)

Kant was a dedicated opponent of slavery. He argued that regardless of the number of people who held slaves and justified their actions for a variety of reasons, including religious ones, the fact remained that slavery was morally (hence universally) wrong. That slaveholders had to search for justification clearly indicated a secret knowledge that what they were doing was reprehensible. Socrates believed that those who *know* what is good will *do* what is good. Kant did not believe this was true. Each of us is born with a knowledge of the good, but some disregard it later if it proves inconvenient. He admitted that self-interest all too often suppressed the moral imperative.

Kant's ethical philosophy is a powerful way of knowing in advance whether a proposed action is morally right. It does not depend on consequences, and it is not relative to varying circumstances. All it requires is that we hesitate before we act and ask ourselves one vital question: *Would it be okay for everyone else to do this*. If this sounds familiar, it may be because it resembles the principle found in the sacred texts of almost every religion: *Do unto others as you would have them do unto you*.

KANT'S IMPERATIVE AT WORK   A person temporarily down on his luck sees a drunken man weaving his way down the street. A wallet falls out of the man's pocket without his noticing; he continues on his way. The first man immediately picks it up and sees that it contains a considerable amount of money. The drunken man cannot, however, walk very fast, so it would be a simple matter to catch up with him and return the wallet.

The finder of the wallet is now like Glaucon's shepherd. He is invisible as far as the owner of the wallet is concerned. The temptation is strong to wait until the owner is well out of sight and then to disappear with the money. Why not? Who would return the money under those circumstances? Suppose now the finder of the wallet convinces himself he has been unjustly treated by society and deserves whatever he can get. It's a dog-eat-dog world, is it not?

If faced with this example, Kant would surely not assume that the finder of the wallet, knowing deep down inside that keeping it is wrong, would shout for the owner to stop so he could return it. If he keeps the wallet, he is in fact making a definite choice between two options; he is deliberately choosing the immoral one.

But, you ask, how can we be certain that it *is* immoral? Just because the man has been taught by his family and church that keeping what does not belong to him is stealing? Suppose he does not accept this view. He has already convinced himself the world is amoral and anything goes. And so the wallet is not returned, and no one is the wiser for it.

The story, however, does not end there. Having decided to spend some of the money for a sumptuous dinner and a comfortable hotel room, the man is walking down a deserted street and is accosted by a thief who, brandishing a weapon, demands his wallet. The man complies, the thief disappears, leaving him once more homeless and hungry. Would he be bitter? Would he denounce the thief? Or would he say to himself, "It serves you right"?

In Kantian terms, the latter response is possible, but not probable. The chances are good that the finder of the wallet would be furious about the theft. Translating his anger into philosophical terms, he would, in effect, be saying to himself: *It was all right for me to keep the wallet, but wrong for the thief to steal it from me. I am special.* If we agree that keeping the wallet is stealing, then what is the difference between the first and second thefts? The answer: nothing. The first thief's reasoning strikes us as absurd. Kant tells us that before we commit an act we need to ask ourselves whether it would be universally acceptable for everyone to do so. If we regard ourselves as the only exception to a moral law that applies to everyone except us, we are swept away in a vortex of nonlogic.

Kant's theory is ingenious, we must admit. In all probability none of us leads a morally perfect life, but that does not excuse us from willing that everything we do is universally acceptable. And this is a tough act to carry off.

Altruism

The word **altruism**, or selflessness—the opposite of self-interest—was coined by the French philosopher Auguste Comte (1798–1857) and comes from the Latin *alter*, meaning "other." The principle of acting out of concern for the greater good, rather than out of self-interest, is an old one. Some version of it appears in most religious belief systems, and while we rarely hear the term in ordinary conversation, it has long been viewed as a noble—if almost impossible to achieve—ideal.

Can there be a place in our world for altruism? Some argue that no such thing exists, because human nature simply does not allow for it. Every act, they suggest, is selfish, even if reason requires us to place others before ourselves, since what *appears* to be an altruistic or selfless act really springs from secretly selfish motives.

There is no doubt that we regularly witness examples of altruistic deeds that require no questioning of motives, as when a firefighter loses his life in a daring rescue attempt, or when a teacher shields the body of a child in a random school shooting and receives a fatal bullet. In such instances, the cynics are quiet, perhaps observing later that the number of people willing to die for others is trivially small. Still, the deaths of 343 firefighters and 71 police officers in the disaster of September 11, 2001, may have changed the attitude of many such cynics. We cannot know their motives, but it seems almost indisputable that they were altruistic.

In the everyday world, altruism does exist: People do donate an organ to save a stranger's life; people do dive into the sea to try to rescue someone in distress. During the ongoing insurgencies in the Sudan, with millions of innocent women, men, and children slaughtered in acts of "ethnic cleansing," and during the Ebola epidemic of 2014 in West Africa, Doctors without Borders, humanitarian medical personnel, worked tirelessly to save as many lives as they could, even though they faced being shot for their efforts or becoming infected with disease themselves.

In the corporate world of today, where workers may become aware of defective auto parts, unsanitary food preparation, or the advertising of products they know carry a health risk, cases of altruistic whistle-blowing exist. Workers who see that their fellow workers are overworked or underpaid risk losing their own jobs to demonstrate for higher wages and more regular working hours. There are no easy moral victories here. If nothing else, we learn from them that doing the right thing takes not only courage but the willingness to stand quite alone.

The ideal notes that human beings are all connected—and by more than DNA. The stirring words of John Donne's *Meditation XVII* (1623) are emblazoned in the history of idealism:

> *No man is an island entire of itself; every man is a piece of the continent, a part of the main. If a clod be washed away by the sea, Europe is the less, as well as if a promontory were . . . Any man's death diminishes me, because I am involved in mankind. And therefore never send to know for whom the bell tolls; it tolls for thee.*[7]

EFFECTIVE ALTRUISM: PETER SINGER The Australian moral philosopher Peter Singer (b. 1946) is perhaps the strongest voice arguing for altruism today. Singer's 1975 book, *Animal Liberation*, condemned the treatment of animals as a prejudice in favor of our own species, when in fact (to greatly oversimplify his argument), great apes are much closer in every way to humans than they are to, say, an oyster. But Singer has gone on, in his books *Practical Ethics* (1979) and *The Most Good You Can Do: How Effective Altruism Is Changing Ideas about Living Ethically* (2015), to lay out clear arguments for behaving in ways that reflect what he calls "effective altruism"—ways that will truly help change the world without seriously harming the donor. He suggests giving away half or more of our incomes to others in need, or donating organs anonymously, for example. Singer's position is based on Bentham's utilitarianism—that more of what's good is better than less—and built on science and numbers. The problem comes, as always for both utilitarianism and altruism, in determining what constitutes "good." Is it more beneficial, for example, to donate $100,000 to a museum (which might, based on numerical calculations, enhance the aesthetic lives of 100,000 people over 50 years) or to use that same amount to cure blindness in 100 people? Singer responds without hesitation that we should be curing blindness. Others might have different ideas.

Morality and Religion

11.4 *What is the relationship between religion and morality?*

Immanuel Kant's parents were deeply religious, teaching that moral laws were set forth by God and could not be altered. As Kant grew older and learned about new theories in science and philosophy, he used reason rather than religion to justify moral principles. For many, however, religion remains a strong moral force. Though some of us may have subsequently entertained moral alternatives, we probably hear the whispers of those early teachings whenever we are faced with a moral evaluation of an act.

The major world religions—Hinduism, Buddhism, Judaism, Christianity, and Islam—provide moral orientation for over 70 percent of the world's population. They differ in many respects. All of them, however, share moral precepts:

- Their followers believe that the world was not created for human beings to do with as they please.
- Their followers believe that human beings owe an obligation either to a personal God or to the moral order governing the universe.
- Their followers believe that none are free to behave irresponsibly toward themselves (since they did not create themselves), toward others, and toward the earth (which they did not create either).

The Biblical Moral Code

Basic moral codes for most of Western society derive wholly or in part from the Ten Commandments, delivered by God to Moses as he led his people out of slavery in Egypt and recorded in the Hebrew Bible. The Commandments

1. require the recognition of one God
2. forbid the making and worshiping of any graven image
3. forbid the taking of the Lord's name in vain
4. require that the Sabbath be kept holy
5. require that parents be honored
6. forbid killing
7. forbid adultery
8. forbid stealing
9. forbid the bearing of false witness against another
10. forbid the coveting of another's wife and of another's goods

The first four commandments are not found in law books (although some U.S. communities still have so-called *blue laws* requiring businesses to be closed on Sunday, or preventing the sale of beer and liquor in the morning, when people are expected to worship). Nor are there universal rules for how to honor one's parents.

Most of the other commandments, however, have parallels in moral codes throughout the world. Rules against adultery are often legally enforced—sometimes with the death penalty. Rules against killing and stealing are part of a virtually universal criminal code. It is taken for granted that everyone lies for one reason or another, but it is hard to imagine any society in which lying itself is not condemned.

From its beginning, Hebrew moral law served to remind the powerful that they were not exempt from obeying God's commands. Biblical prophets were not afraid to confront sinners no matter how exalted their rank, as when Nathan denounced King David for doing away with the husband of Bathsheba, whom David wished to marry. Biblical scholar Huston Smith describes the democratizing effect of the Commandments:

> *The prerequisite of political stability is social justice. . . . Stated theologically the point reads: God has high standards. Divinity will not put up forever with exploitation, corruption, and mediocrity. . . . One thing is common to all [the prophets]: the conviction that every human being, simply by virtue of his or her humanity, is a child of God and therefore in possession of rights that even kings must respect.*[8]

Much of Hebrew moral law is concerned primarily with actions based on principles. It places limitations, for example, on what an injured party may demand for revenge. The principle of "An eye for an eye and a tooth for a tooth," which is sometimes perceived as a brutal response to crime, in fact prevents restitution from being more than what was lost in the original crime—you cannot kill a man for putting out another's eye. This principle is not original to Hebrew law. It appears first in the Code of Hammurabi (c. 1734 BCE), a set of laws developed by the Babylonian king which is the earliest known such document.

Christianity accepted Hebrew laws and added restrictions against evil intents, not just acts, and harboring ill will toward others. The Sermon on the Mount tells us:

> *You have heard that it was said, 'An eye for an eye and a tooth for a tooth.' But I say to you, Do not resist an evildoer. But if anyone strikes you on the right cheek, turn the other also.*

Matthew 5:38–39

The commandment to turn the other cheek was already foreshadowed in the Buddhist moral treatise *Dhammapada*: "'He abused me, he beat me, he defeated me, he robbed me'—in those who harbor such thoughts hatred will never cease. For hatred does not cease to be hatred at any time; hatred ceases by love—that is an old rule."[9]

In general, Islam requires its followers to observe the biblical laws, for Muhammad declared that both Moses and Jesus were true prophets. He stressed especially the doctrine of brotherhood and placing the interests of others before one's own. He also warned enemies of God not to attack or persecute the devout.

PUNISHMENT AND REWARD Punishment for disobedience to scriptural laws varies from religion to religion, as do promised rewards for leading a virtuous existence. Hebrew morality focuses on family and community. Disobedience can result in ostracism; leading an exemplary life brings inner peace as well as good repute in the community. After death, the good person lives on in the happy memories of friends and family or, for some believers, in the world to come.

Islam fosters the belief that after death the virtuous children of Allah will be with him in paradise, a sentiment echoed in Christianity. Christian concepts of heaven for the blessed and hell for the damned evolved slowly. The Christian Bible's Gospel of Luke reports the dialog between Jesus and one of the thieves who were also being crucified. The thief refers to the "kingdom" to which Jesus will go after death: "Then he said, 'Jesus, remember me when you come into your kingdom.' He replied, 'Truly I tell you, today you will be with me in Paradise.'" (Luke 23:42–43).

"Paradise" is variously interpreted. Does it mean a state of freedom from pain, similar to the Hindu moksha and the Buddhist nirvana? The promise that the thief would be "with" Jesus, however, may indicate that the reference is to continuing life in a definite place.

The morality set forth by religion is exceedingly complex and always open for discussion and debate, but nevertheless remains a powerful force that helps many understand the agonizing questions in the world today.

Morality and the Arts

11.5 *What impact have the arts had on moral beliefs, and what impact have moral beliefs had on the arts?*

It isn't surprising that the great questions of morality have been central to much Western literature and art. More surprising is the role that the arts have played in influencing moral attitudes and thought, past and present.

The Influence of Dante and Milton on Western Morality

As Christianity developed and spread, the promise of joy for the virtuous in heaven and eternal torment in hell for the damned became increasingly ingrained in Western religious minds. Vivid images of heaven and hell in Dante's *The Divine Comedy* strongly influenced how many people thought—and still think—of rewards and punishments for sin. (The term "comedy" in the title is used in the sense of "not tragic"; the work ends on a note of joy when the poet-narrator finally sees God.) Similarly, John Milton's poems *Paradise Lost* and *Paradise Regained* have played a big part in our understanding of moral ambiguity.

DANTE, *THE DIVINE COMEDY*   In his masterwork *The Divine Comedy*, written between 1307 and 1321, the Italian poet Dante Alighieri (1265–1321) pictures hell, or the Inferno, as a deep pit in which the souls of sinners endure degrees of endless pain, depending on the gravity of their offense. Punishment takes place on seven separate circles, not all of which are fiery. Though in the popular mind hell is associated with flames, in actuality the lowest circle in Dante's hell, home of Satan—the worst offender of all—is described by the poet as a lake of thick ice representing a total lack of feeling and a total absence of love.

Purgatory is a mountain on which live those guilty of less grievous sins, those who will eventually ascend to Paradise, the abode of God, the angels, and the souls of the righteous. Paradise consists of nine circles of heaven arranged in a hierarchy of blessedness—from ordinary good people to martyrs and saints. The abode of God is the tenth heaven (ten being considered a perfect number), only glimpsed by the poet, who is unable to describe in detail his mystic vision.

Naturally enough, this drama of sin, punishment, and redemption has inspired writers, artists, and philosophers for centuries. The thought of hell's torments incites as much anger as fear and perennially gives rise to the age-old question of why humankind must be punished for sins that were predestined. In addition, the sinner has proved a more durable figure for writers than the virtuous person, even as in popular entertainment the bad guys tend to be more interesting than the good guys.

MILTON, *PARADISE LOST* The classic example of moral ambiguity is the treatment of Satan, called Lucifer in John Milton's epic poem *Paradise Lost* (1667). Milton (1608–1674) declares at the outset that his purpose in writing the poem is to "justify the ways of God to men." Like Nathaniel Hawthorne after him, he was raised in the strict Puritan faith, which painted a portrait of a God perpetually angry at his sinful children yet required a belief that their sins were predestined. The three main characters are Adam, Eve, and Lucifer (see Figure 11.6). We learn that before creation Lucifer had been one of the angels in closest attendance to God, and that he had become jealous of God's power and organized an unsuccessful rebellion. He and his cohorts were banished from heaven and allowed to live in a dark palace called Pandemonium. There Lucifer becomes a powerful ruler, exulting in his authority and embodying many admirable traits of the defiant individualist. Shaking his fist toward heaven, he cries out that he would rather "reign in Hell than serve in Heaven." Scholars and historians of the humanities continue to debate whether Lucifer is really the hero of the poem.

The argument that Milton intended Lucifer to be despicable does not convince everyone, even though as the serpent in the garden he eventually loses his heroic qualities. Nor is everyone convinced that the poet entirely makes his point when he tells us that God gave Lucifer free access to human beings in order to tempt them into sin. Milton's God said he wanted no more rebellion in Heaven and so created the race of mortals capable of either sinning or choosing virtue. In this way, only the good would live eternally with God. Milton described the fall of humankind as "fortunate," for the disobeying of divine law required the sacrifice of Jesus. Without original sin, in other words, the path to redemption would never have been revealed.

Figure 11.6 William Blake, *Satan Watching the Endearments of Adam and Eve*, c. 1816–1825.

In Blake's illustration for *Paradise Lost*, Lucifer (Satan) watches the innocent affection between Adam and Eve before the temptation. Do you believe, like Kant, that we all have internal knowledge of right and wrong?

Huntington Library/SuperStock

The Problem of Censorship: Who Decides What Is Right?

The belief that art ought to be sincere and "infectious" to encourage morality was held by Count Leo Tolstoy, who opposed art as mere entertainment. He wrote:

> *Formerly people feared lest among the works of art there might chance to be some causing corruption, and they prohibited art altogether. Now they only fear lest they should be deprived of any enjoyment art can afford, and patronize any art. And I think the last error is much grosser than the first and that its consequences are more harmful.*[10]

There are still those who would urge censorship "for the good of society."

One of the works deemed scandalous and *not* for the good of society was Édouard Manet's *Olympia* (Figure 11.7), which depicts a reclining nude woman. Not only was she obviously a courtesan, but her bold gaze was accused of staring shamelessly at the viewer. Exhibited at the Paris Salon of 1868, *Olympia* provoked one critic into writing that Manet had sunk to an incredibly low level and that his ugly portrait of a disgusting whore was brazen and offensive to all decent-minded people.

NATHANIEL HAWTHORNE, *THE SCARLET LETTER* Published earlier in the century, Nathaniel Hawthorne's novel *The Scarlet Letter* (1850) suggests that the individual citizen does not have to be bound by a community's moral rules. Hester Prynne, the heroine, who lives in an austere community of rigid religious conservatives, finds herself trapped in a loveless marriage. While her husband, aptly named Chillingworth, is away, she succumbs to her passion for a handsome young man, who cares for her in

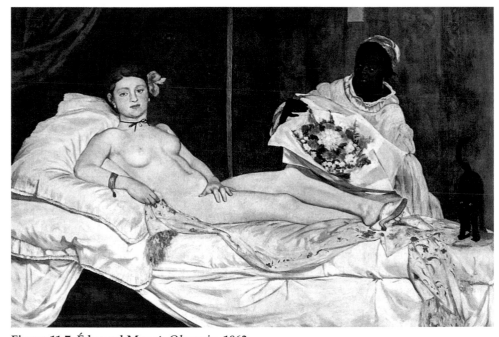

Figure 11.7 Édouard Manet, *Olympia*, 1863.
Nudes have always been featured in art. Why do you think this particular nude was considered
scandalous when it was first exhibited?
The Protected Art Archive/Alamy

a tender way she has never known. When a child is born and Hester refuses to name
the father, the outraged community, led by the elders of the church, force her to wear
a scarlet *A* (for adulteress) and to endure the scorn of the citizens. Though Hawthorne
himself was brought up as a strict Puritan, the growing liberal side of him came to
believe that an inflexible moral code was more sinful than the adulterous relationship,
which had, after all, grown out of sincere love. Even though *The Scarlet Letter* was
written more than a century and a half ago, the question of whether genuine love
supersedes a community's moral values is still with us, especially if the transgression
is in the neighborhood.

JAMES JOYCE, *ULYSSES*   The Irish novelist James Joyce (1882–1941) faced much disapproval for his pioneer effort to create fiction that truthfully mirrors the workings
of the human mind, including its forays into forbidden sexuality (see Figure 11.8).
Ulysses (1922), eventually cited by a panel of literary critics as the greatest novel of the
twentieth century, was initially banned in Britain (for 14 years) and the United States
(for 11 years). It also became the subject of a famous court case. In 1933, an American
judge named John M. Woolsey was asked by booksellers to decide whether the sexually explicit language of the book was so morally offensive that the public should not
be allowed to read it.

   After two careful readings, the judge stated that the book was difficult but not
pornographic; rather, the author had made one of the most objectionable characters express feelings that would have been appropriate for a woman of her station
in the time frame of the story. The character in question was Molly Bloom, Joyce's
modernized version of Penelope, the wife of Ulysses in Homer's *The Odyssey*, who,
like Penelope, was waiting for her husband to return home from his wanderings.
Joyce revolutionized fiction by taking the reader inside Molly's mind to show what
was really going on. In doing so, he shocked many readers as well as many more who
joined in the moral crusade against the novel without having read it.

   Embedded in the final stream-of-consciousness passage, which runs 40 pages
without punctuation, are language and images many found highly improper for an

Figure 11.8 James Joyce and the bookseller Sylvia Beach in Paris, c. 1922.

Joyce's novel *Ulysses* was banned for years but is now considered one of the great masterworks of literature. Who gets to decide what is great and what is immoral? What standards are available to us to judge works of art?

Lebrecht Music and Arts Photo Library / Alamy Stock Photo

 Beethoven: Symphony No. 9 in D Minor, IV

author to put into the mind of a woman. Nobody said Joyce was being untrue to human nature—only that such truths had no place in fiction. In lifting the federal ban, Judge Woolsey struck a blow against those who believe the purpose of art is solely to improve society. The struggle is far from over.

Outrage over Moral Wrongs

The disciplines of the humanities offer powerful tools for showing us the horrors of wrong moral choices. Pablo Picasso's *Guernica* (Figure 5.34) remains one of the most potent statements ever made about the horrors of attacking an enemy city and killing hundreds of innocent civilians, including women and children. This outrage has been echoed more recently by opponents of the wars in Iraq and Afghanistan, in both Christian and Muslim communities. Oliver Stone's 1986 film *Platoon* showed the burning of a Vietnamese village, with Samuel Barber's mournful *Adagio for Strings* as background music. Similarly, the 2008 Academy Award winner for Best Picture, *The Hurt Locker*, showed us a lone soldier, encased in protective gear, disarming bombs on the streets of Iraq while children play nearby. The director, Kathryn Bigelow, used silence to emphasize the chaos of the scenes. Supporters of these conflicts often argue that a just cause can result in terrible disasters, but nonsupporters ask whether any cause can excuse acts of inhumanity.

Beethoven's gigantic later works are in part fist-shaking denunciations of what he saw as the cosmic injustice that turned him totally deaf—he of all people, whose life was devoted to creating wondrous sounds. He expressed his rage in the *Heiligenstadt Testament* of 1802, in which he says, "What a humiliation for me to be standing next to someone who . . . heard a shepherd singing . . . and I heard nothing." All of his life he had been a champion of individual rights. In his *Symphony No. 9*, created from the depths of his despair, Beethoven nonetheless achieves a glorious affirmation of the joy of creativity, the joy of living, probably because the act of venting his feelings caused him to hear sounds no one had ever heard before. The fourth movement, utilizing a huge chorus in a musical setting of the poem "Ode to Joy" by Friedrich von Schiller, is a statement, by implication, that all people must be free to experience this joy.

The symphonic work *La valse* by Maurice Ravel (1875–1937), written in 1919–1920, has been interpreted as a musical vision of the chaos of Europe after the devastation of World War I. Beginning as a disciplined, politely played waltz, then gradually reflecting increasing chaos with crashing dissonance and electrifying rhythmic effects, the work may be heard as the product of an artist mourning the passing of an age in which moral values were clear and straightforward—and musical compositions followed strict guidelines.

HUMOROUS OUTRAGE   Moral issues can also be treated humorously. A *New Yorker* cartoon (July 18, 1988; Bernard Schoenbaum) shows a prisoner explaining to his cellmate: "All along I thought our corruption fell within community standards." Don't many business tycoons found guilty nowadays often believe they are violating no moral principles?

But what is intended as humor can also go terribly awry. In January 2015, a dozen staff members of the French humor magazine *Charlie Hebdo* were gunned down by Muslim fundamentalists in response to a series of cartoons they had published depicting the prophet Muhammad, an act that Islam prohibits. We can never condone murder. But where does the right to free speech end? Are there moral limits to the creative impulse? Is it a moral act to intentionally violate the religious principles of others? The questions are difficult.

Moral Relativism

11.6 *What are the key arguments supporting moral relativism, and what dangers does relativism imply?*

If the opposite of *relative* is *absolute*, it is easy to understand the appeal of the former, a term that promises flexibility and tolerance, versus the latter, which connotes rigid certainty and judgment against nonbelievers. Moral relativists point out that prison, torture, and even genocide have been inflicted by those who are sure that there is only one truth, and that they (and often they alone) know what it is. The temptation is great to reject theories that place unwavering restrictions on us. According to moral relativists, beliefs about right and wrong have no universal meaning. It is therefore possible to make (and hear) remarks such as these:

> "Well, who has the right to tell another what to do? A lot of trouble has been caused by people who were sure they *had* this right."
> "It all depends on the situation, the culture, and the times in which a choice is made."

Many of the moral philosophers we have studied helped build a case for absolutism. Socrates believed right and wrong were the same for everyone. Kant believed in an inborn moral imperative. Even Bentham's moral mathematics are not relative to the wishes of the minority who don't belong to the "greatest number" in an important decision. Moral relativists, on the other hand, maintain that right and wrong must be defined within a given context that may or may not include the greatest number.

That context could be the workplace, the community, the family, the educational establishment, or a person's religion or community. Each of these areas governing human behavior may impose absolute standards, but the standards are not always harmonious with each other. Bitter clashes result when two absolutes refuse to give ground: religious laws and those of the community at large, for example.

The Global View: Cultural Clashes

A major factor in the rise of **moral relativism** is the globalized concept of society. New communication technologies continue to shrink the size of the world, and exposure to the customs and values of cultures different from our own inevitably widens the issue of morality. Many cultural observers now argue that the appeal to absolute reason by Socrates and Kant, among others, was narrowly Western. It isn't that other cultures are thought of as not being rational; rather, it is the recognition that, while reason itself may be universally shared, ideas and values arrived at rationally are also influenced by culture, traditions, and circumstances.

Still, some people argue that aboriginal natives, for example, would be better off learning to succeed in the dominant culture, learning its ways and following its rules of behavior. The relativist, on the other hand, points out that the imposition of dominant-culture values causes breakdowns in both individuals and families. In 1959, American novelist James Michener wrote *Hawaii*, a fictionalized account of what actually happened when missionaries from the United States told native Polynesians their sexual morality was unacceptable to civilized people. They condemned immodest clothing, premarital sex, and incest, assuring the "guilty" that they were damned forever. (One "guilty" man felt such shame that he ended his life.)

In an example from another part of the world, "The schools took us from our parents and taught us that the ways of our people were shameful and wrong," claims a Cree Indian in a lawsuit alleging cultural abuse in a church-run boarding school supported by the Canadian government. She argued that efforts to make natives assimilate into "white" Canada were wrong, that being forced to learn English, adopt Christianity, and acquire "suitable" job skills led to heavy drinking and domestic disharmony and to the loss of her native tongue and traditions.

The problem offers no easy solutions. Some principles taught in early childhood are so deeply ingrained that they motivate actions throughout life and conflict with those in a different society. An American living in Japan once held a birthday party for her 5-year-old son; many of the invited children were Japanese. During a game of musical chairs, the American father noticed that when the music stopped a little Japanese girl stood next to an empty chair but did not sit down.

> So Gregory scrambled into her seat, and Chitose-chan beamed proudly at her own good manners. Then I walked over and told her that she had just lost the game and would have to sit out. She gazed up at me, her luminous eyes full of shocked disbelief, looking like Bambi might after a discussion of venison burgers. "You mean I lost because I'm polite?" Chitose-chan's eyes asked. "You mean the point of the game is to be rude?" Well now that I think of it, I guess that is the point. American kids are taught to be winners, to seize their opportunities and maybe the next kid's as well. Japanese children are taught to be good citizens, to be team players, to obey rules, to be a mosaic tile in some larger design.[11]

In a real-life incident involving the moral gulf between cultures, the mother of an Asian visual arts student in an American school refused to give permission for her 16-year-old son to attend a life-drawing class in which nude female models posed. The department head later reported attempting to "reason" with the woman, who obstinately held her ground, insisting that her son was being unfairly forced to violate a strict moral principle. Given the ultimatum that the child take the required course or leave the school, she withdrew the boy and enrolled him the next day in a neighborhood school that offered no arts courses. A moral relativist might have wondered whether the art world had been thus deprived of a potential talent.

Another source of dispute is a school ban on students wearing head coverings indicating religious affiliations. In order to have a cohesive student body, school officials in some European countries forbid the distinctive Islamic scarf but are often inconsistent about other religious symbols such as those worn as jewelry. Immigrant students who abandon public school secularism for religious school may be encouraged to accept further separation from the dominant culture of the host country through a different set of heroes, villains, and explanations for historical events. In many cases, objectivity is indeed an elusive goal.

Cultural traditions and generational differences exist uneasily side by side: an "assimilated" child impatient with a grandparent's old-world cooking; young people unwilling to accept traditional matchmaking; a religious teenager clashing with agnostic parents. Can the relativist position solve all conflicts by claiming that universal right and wrong are outmoded concepts? Are some moral issues simply a matter of taste, like one's preference for chocolate ice cream?

Moral relativism is attractive to those who believe in tolerance and avoidance of authoritarian excesses, which can take the form of judging foreign customs and religions according to one's own standards. Almost every part of the world is now available to travelers and Internet users, and this increased contact with other cultures may lead to the rejection of a belief that indisputable morality is the exclusive property of one group. Tolerance for the customs of the Cree, for example, would have prevented the conflicts described earlier.

The Slippery Slope

An offshoot of cultural relativism is that what used to be respect for the values of others can turn into the belief that there are *no* absolute values, that no truth can be accepted the world over. In our personal lives, we can see how we view events differently as we mature and age. What frightens children seems benign to adults, just as some of the scandals of one age seem harmless in later times. If a good many moral viewpoints inevitably change, do we then abandon the idea of universal values altogether? What happens to those who stand firm in their belief that they have found the one, the only, the unchanging truth? For them, the suggestion that they respect competing beliefs is heresy! Or does "democratic society" mean places must be found for diametrically opposed beliefs?

Travelers may be delighted to observe cultures different from those in their home country—otherwise why travel at all? If nothing else, the strange customs provide one more story for travelers to tell when they return home. One may be charmed by unexpected hospitality or a gift offered by a merchant at a bazaar, or intrigued by meeting a man accompanied by more than one wife. One is less charmed by seeing brutality and abuse, no matter how traditional the custom is said to be. Child prostitution, genital mutilation, and abandonment of unwanted family members (including those who have lived beyond an age considered reasonable by a given community) are among the practices that horrify observers suddenly unwilling to be moral relativists.

A prime example of moral relativism in action is found in the prize-winning novels by Hilary Mantel, *Wolf Hall* (2009) and *Bring Up the Bodies* (2012). The books, adapted into both a PBS television series and a Broadway drama, follow the life of Thomas Cromwell (1485–1540), who was born in poverty and became the right-hand man to King Henry VIII of Britain. A "fixer," Cromwell is skilled at survival; he manages to find and articulate moral rationales for everything Henry wants to do—divorce a first wife, behead a second, put an admired clergyman, Sir Thomas More, to death. Cromwell finds ways to make all these acts fit within an ever-changing moral system—until he finally miscalculates and loses his own life.

Moral relativism, of course, has a few absolutes of its own. The whole institution of the defense attorney in our society rests on the assumption that everyone deserves a fair trial. The attorney's personal opinion about the guilt or innocence of his client is immaterial. Presumably, a person does not take on such a role without believing in the relativity of right and wrong. This, for the attorney, is an acceptable absolute.

Gender and Moral Relativism

Moral relativism of a different sort has arisen during the past four decades from philosophers and cultural historians all over the world who point out that cultural, religious, and literary traditions—whether expressing absolutist or relativistic values—have been dominated by the male viewpoint. In some cases, this aligns with the female viewpoint, but all too often it does not. The discrepancy is especially obvious in the low esteem accorded to women in many areas of the globe. Restrictions on dress, education, travel, and even expressions of personal feelings continue to exist, though old rules are gradually eroding in many cultures.

We have said from the outset that being human is an art, and nowhere is that assumption more crucial than in moral matters. You can decide that you are a fully realized human being if you get everything you can from life regardless of how others are affected. You can also decide that moral integrity—doing what you know is right regardless of how you do or don't profit—is the mark of a fully realized human being. There are risks involved, to be sure. The risk of running afoul of someone else's moral code, enforced by bully tactics, is and has always been there. But a ringing declaration in the humanities is that moral integrity is worth the risk. Gambling on integrity may be basic to the human condition in its finest hour.

Looking Back

In this chapter,

- we defined "morality" and identified the major queries of moral philosophy,
- we discussed the concept of moral self-interest and explored the key arguments for accepting the argument that morality is always based in self-interest,
- we explored alternatives to self-interest as the basis for making moral choices, including utilitarianism, Kant's categorical imperative, and altruism,

- we discussed the relationship between religion and morality,
- we looked at the impact of the arts on moral beliefs—and the impact of moral beliefs on the arts, and
- we analyzed the arguments supporting moral relativism and the dangers that relativism implies.

Key Terms

altruism The quality of acting out of concern for the welfare of others rather than one's own.

capitalism Economic system based on Adam Smith's philosophy that if people are allowed to make as much money as they can, others will profit also.

categories According to Immanuel Kant, mental "compartments" that we are born with which allow us to interpret data from the senses; an inborn sense of reason makes it possible to understand spatial relationships (nextness) as well as the morality or immorality of actions.

categorical imperative In Kantian philosophy, the inborn capacity to understand certain concepts, including the difference between right and wrong when faced with moral decisions.

laissez-faire French phrase meaning "allow to do"; an economic policy fundamental to Adam Smith's philosophy that allows businesses to operate with little or no government control.

Machiavellian Now a negative term, pertaining to the manipulation of others through duplicity; derived from Machiavelli's theory of government that, to ensure order in society, advocates a leader with almost unlimited power.

moral An adjective indicating a choice between significant options, based on principles derived from reading, family teachings, education, religion, or law.

moral imperative The internal principle that compels a person to act, based on a categorical understanding of right and wrong and, according to Kant, dictated by reason alone, although later thinkers suggested it originated in the conscience and might be divinely inspired.

moral mathematics A scientific system of moral choice, advocated by Jeremy Bentham, based on projected quantifiable positive or negative results.

moral relativism The belief that moral standards are not universal, but rather depend on time, culture, and situation.

moral system A network of beliefs that can form the basis on which a moral choice is made, e.g., religion, laws, or Socratic reasoning.

morality The system by which significant choices are made; in popular usage, the user's sense of right conduct, so that a given person is said to be or not be "moral."

utilitarianism Moral philosophy that can revolve around the greatest good for the greatest number or what makes the most sense to rational people, regardless of whether or not they constitute a majority.

Chapter 12
Happiness

Figure 12.1 Caravaggio, *Self-Portrait as Bacchus*, 1593.
Bacchus is another name for Dionysus, the Greek god of wine, merriment, fertility, and religious ecstasy, among other things. What else makes us happy besides the traditional Dionysian pleasures? What *is* happiness?
Artepics/Alamy

The search for happiness is high on the list of themes in the humanities. There aren't many works about people richly satisfied with their lives. The majority of literary, dramatic, and cinematic works deal with unhappy people and either end sadly, all happiness denied, or conclude with a manipulated happy ending so that viewers or readers may see the world as it should be, not as they know it is. Some of the most memorable characters have been rich people; and even if they are left with their fortunes, they may be regretting the loss of something or someone they hadn't realized was so important to them.

In addition to its concern for defining good and bad actions, moral philosophy also engages in exhaustive analysis of what makes life good and therefore happy. For most of us, analysis seems beside the point. Doesn't everyone want to be happy? Yet how easy is it to attain? Would we know it if it came our way? What *is* happiness, anyway?

The word "happy" dates back to our earliest memories. It is written in cake frosting, shouted at midnight on New Year's Eve, and invoked during wedding receptions. Are we using the right word when we claim to be happy for friends when they make decisions we disagree with, perhaps to cancel a wedding or leave school? We say, "Oh well, as long as you're happy," as though that's all there is to it.

What is the best route to happiness? Is pleasure what makes life good (Figure 12.1)? Or is the good life based on the observance of principles, obeyed even when to do so means a loss of pleasure? Are we happier when we are praised by others—or when someone we envy suddenly falls on hard times? Is joy the same as happiness? Can we be happy *without* feeling joy? Do we need to feel pleasure in order to be happy? The humanities suggest many alternatives.

Hedonism: Happiness Is Pleasure

12.1 *What is hedonism, and what are its key assumptions about happiness?*

The Greek philosopher Aristippus (435–356 BCE) declared happiness to be the *sum total of pleasures experienced during one's lifetime.* He thought of pleasure in purely physical terms: taste, sexual excitement, touch, and so on. He admitted that a certain amount of satisfaction comes with the knowledge, for example, that one's country is faring well, but nothing mental compares with physical comfort. Bodily pain is far worse than mental pain, and therefore bodily pleasure is better than mental pleasure. People, he said, are by nature selfish animals, concerned solely with their own comfort. He asked the question that has been around for centuries: *Is anything greater than being happy?* He said no, and added that if happiness were not pleasure, saying you were happy would mean nothing.

The writings of Aristippus have not survived, but a historian named Diogenes Laertius, living in the third century CE, has provided a detailed summary of his philosophy of pleasure. He pointed out that Aristippus proved his argument by noting that from the time they were capable of making choices between available options, people always selected the one that provided the most pleasure and the least amount of pain. Home and society might try to teach less selfish values, but instinct prevailed in the end.

Thus, if Aristippus is right, people prefer not to work, but do so because what they earn can provide them with pleasure. There is no satisfaction in work for its own sake. As a matter of fact, Aristippus believed there was no satisfaction in even the memory or anticipation of pleasure. Nothing counted except what could be experienced at the moment.

Hedonism (from the Greek for "delight") is the name given to the philosophy that happiness is equivalent to physical pleasure and to the possession of things that provide us with pleasure. Hedonism has survived for thousands of years, substantially unchanged from its inception.

The artist Diego Velázquez (1599–1660) has given us one of the best visual representations of hedonism in *Los Borrachos*, or *The Drunkards* (Figure 12.2). The laughing figure on the left is Bacchus, whose associate is bestowing a garland of grape leaves on the kneeling figure. The work seems to make comic reference to the traditional honoring of a hero with a laurel wreath. Even so, the painting allows viewers to place their own interpretation on the scene. To the dedicated hedonist, the pleasure obviously being experienced by the men may be all that is necessary for achieving the highest state of happiness.

Figure 12.2 Diego Velásquez, *Los Borrachos*, 1629.
This image seems to suggest that pleasure equals happiness. Why might this interpretation of happiness appeal to artists?
Interfoto/Fine Arts/Alamy

The Greek society in which Aristippus lived may have produced Socrates, Plato, and Aristotle, who spent their lives in thought, but it was also highly receptive to the idea that hedonism was based on human nature. In fact, both Plato and Aristotle addressed the subject, disagreeing with the views of Aristippus but acknowledging the popular appeal of his ideas. In his famous analysis of love, Plato does not discredit the pleasures of sex but elevates nonphysical love to a position of greater importance. While Aristippus excludes intellectual pleasure, Plato and Aristotle believe it is one of the defining graces of a fully realized life. Aristotle developed a philosophy of happiness vastly different from that of Aristippus.

Literary Hedonism

Between the austere Middle Ages and the time of the militantly rigid Puritans—both periods of strict moral codes—poets, including Shakespeare, celebrated the "eat, drink, and be merry" life of the hedonist. One of the most famous declarations is this widely welcomed piece of poetic advice from the poem "To the Virgins, to Make Much of Time" by Robert Herrick (1591–1674):

> *Gather ye rose-buds while ye may,*
> *Old time is still a-flying*
> *And this same flower that smiles today*
> *Tomorrow may be dying.*

Another name given to the hedonist view is **carpe diem** (from the Latin for "seize the day"). While the advice is rooted in Aristippus, it has had numerous applications through the ages. For some, it means doing the most with their potential; it means reaching for the stars. For others, such as Omar Khayyám in *The Rubáiyát*, it means, as it does in Herrick, have all you can during your brief lifetime.

A contemporary of Herrick, Andrew Marvell (1621–1678), makes a plea to a special person he is intent on seducing in a poem called "To His Coy Mistress":

> *Had we but world enough, and time,*
> *This coyness, lady, were no crime.*
> *We would sit down, and think which way*
> *To walk, and pass our long love's day.*

If he had forever to woo her, the poet adds, he would spend a hundred years praising her eyes, two hundred for each breast, and "thirty thousand to the rest."

> *But at my back I always hear*
> *Time's wingèd chariot hurrying near;*
> *And yonder all before us lie*
> *Deserts of vast eternity.*
> *Thy beauty shall no more be found;*
> *Nor, in thy marble vault, shall sound*

My echoing song: then worms shall try
That long preserv'd virginity:
And your quaint honour turn to dust;
And into ashes all my lust.
The grave's a fine and private place,
But none, I think, do there embrace.

Many people are proud to call themselves hedonists, boasting of their income and their possessions. They assert that with only one chance to live, they should deny themselves nothing and try to have it all. A bumper sticker proclaims: "He who dies with the most toys wins." Another boasts: "We're spending our grandchildren's inheritance." A current restatement of *carpe diem* is "Life is not a rehearsal. This is it!"

Hedonist Assumptions

For a hedonist, there never seem to be enough pleasurable moments in life. There seems to be so much undeserved pain. "Why me?" is a frequent question both openly and silently asked. "When am I going to get *my* chance to be happy?"

So the first hedonist assumption is that *everyone deserves as much pleasure as possible*. A variant of this assumption is that *people never really get as much pleasure as they deserve*. Other people always appear to have more. Those believed to have more may communicate—even exaggerate—their pleasures, especially unexpected raises, which point out how truly deserving they really are. Those without raises perpetuate the myth that the undeserving are getting more from life.

A second assumption, vitally related to the first, is that *pleasure is automatically good*. In unprosperous times, when some are barely eating enough to get by, those who can eat anything they want are undoubtedly envied. No one feels sorry for the affluent people who might overeat and overdrink!

Hedonists recognize that people cannot have pleasure every moment of their lives, but still they think they should. A third assumption, therefore, is that *no amount of pleasure is ever too much*. There may be a submerged feeling of guilt about gorging oneself in an "All U Can Eat" restaurant or downing one drink after another at somebody's open house, but the typical hedonist response is, "There will be time enough later to cut down; don't bother me now." Besides, overindulgence in moments of plenty supposedly makes up for past disappointments.

A fourth hedonist assumption is that *the absence of pleasure is a misfortune for which compensation is due*. Many who attempt robbery believe they are only getting even with society. Those who carry the hedonist viewpoint through life find themselves plotting continually. "Just wait until *I* have the upper hand!" Since moments without definite feelings of pleasure are an abomination, they entertain themselves by thinking of the time when they will finally gain "rightful" pleasure.

This particular mindset stems from the **big earnings theory**. An "earning" is considered the pleasure owed to a deserving person for services rendered or unpleasant chores completed. In the ledger that many hedonists carry inside themselves, there is a strict accounting of pleasures owed them; eventually a vast number may accumulate. Unless something happens to change their philosophy of happiness, these hedonists may become obsessed with thinking about pleasures due. If they are paid off, life is good; if not, life is bad. Life is evaluated strictly in terms of total payments received. An excellent life is one in which no big earning is left unrewarded.

Hedonism Reconsidered

The glories of hedonism are displayed throughout our culture today, in movies such as *The Wolf of Wall Street* and television shows such as *Keeping Up with the Kardashians* or the *Real Housewives* series. But finally, we need to ask: Is that all there is?

Hedonism has been subjected to ongoing critical appraisal by philosophers and cultural historians alike. The crux of their argument is whether the hedonist definition of pleasure is too limited. Fundamental hedonism is clear: Pleasure is experienced through the five senses. People who spend time in thought are denying themselves that much pleasure and, therefore, that much happiness. People who devote their lives to working in a clinic a thousand miles from civilization, who expose themselves daily to the risk of disease without even the reward of outside recognition, are supposedly doing without pleasure. But how can we assume that such people are deliberately perverting their own natures to follow a calling that requires them to labor in the interest of others? Are those whose happiness is not derived from hedonism wasting their time or being cheated of the pleasure they secretly desire?

Mystics and members of religious orders who spend hours in prayer or silent meditation lose contact with the self in ways that the hedonist could never understand. Are they robbing themselves of the pleasure that their natures crave? Is it accurate to say that celibacy is necessarily a sublimation of normal sexual passion, as many contend? Or is human nature such that it cannot be narrowly defined? May sensory pleasure be all-sufficing for some and less fulfilling for others?

If, as some, called existentialists, maintain, no such thing as human nature exists at all and humanity is indeed a self-defining, self-determining species, then there is ample room for alternate ways of defining pleasure. Those who choose to do so are free to relegate pleasure to a low priority, in fact, without being "unnatural."

Epicureanism: Happiness Is Living Moderately and Avoiding Pain

12.2 *What is epicureanism, and what are its key assumptions about happiness?*

In a musical comedy some years back, the heroine, trying to explain to the audience in song why she adores the hero, compares her love to a number of familiar pleasures, including the smell of bread baking and the feeling she has when a tooth stops aching. In the first instance, she is a hedonist, directly sensual in her values. In the second, however, she turns to a different philosophy of happiness: **epicureanism**. The sudden cessation of a toothache brings happiness, according to this philosophy—*the happiness of not being in pain.*

Epicureanism is named for the Greek thinker Epicurus (c. 341–270 BCE), who first formulated its precepts (Figure 12.3). Aware of Aristippus and his beliefs, Epicurus was highly critical of a philosophy he believed weak in logic and, more than that, impossible to follow.

Epicurean Assumptions

Epicurus accepted the initial premise of hedonism, that pleasure is a great good, but he added that it was not the only good. He refused to say with the hedonists that the more pleasure we have, the happier we are. "And since pleasure is the first good and natural to us, for this very reason we do not choose every pleasure, but sometimes we pass over many pleasures, when greater discomfort accrues to us as a result of them."[1]

Epicurus was particularly critical of those who recommended pleasures in excess, for these, he knew, would always be followed by both physical and moral pain. "For from prudence are sprung all the other virtues, and it teaches us that it is not possible to live pleasantly without living prudently and honourably and justly."[2]

Figure 12.3 Bust of Epicurus, 3rd century BCE.
Have you ever experienced the feeling that comes with the cessation of pain? Would you call it happiness?

Sam Spiro/Fotolia

For Epicurus, hedonism was a time-conscious, death-ridden philosophy. If happiness increases with the quantity of physical pleasure, then logically no life could ever be long enough. We are here for an uncertain amount of time, true, but all of us are subject to the infirmities that come with age—if indeed we do not burn ourselves out before age ever becomes a problem. Therefore hedonists are fundamentally insecure and unhappy, unable to escape the inevitability of age and death, always worrying about the loss of pleasure. Thus the major assumption of epicureanism is that nothing lasts forever, and we must accept that fact cheerfully. If we are to define the good life, it is the wiser course of action not to believe that it consists only of pleasure.

Another epicurean assumption is that no one can sustain pleasure over prolonged periods of time. We cannot indefinitely gorge ourselves on delicious food, indulge in sex, stay drunk. Why saddle ourselves then with a philosophy of life that is so limited from the very outset? Unable to satisfy our pleasure-seeking instincts perpetually, we do the next best thing: seek material possessions or fame, both of which *symbolize* happiness without *bringing* happiness. Money and fame are constantly in the hedonist's thoughts. They are the compensations of having to die. They are the only possible tangible embodiments of a successful life. When age makes physical pleasure less attainable, people turn to the accumulation of wealth. But Epicurus also recognized that the pursuit of wealth was self-defeating, futile. The same is true of insisting on fame: The wealthy or famous person feels insecure and distrustful of others, certain that others are envious and scheming.

THE REQUIREMENTS FOR A HAPPY LIFE Why, asked Epicurus, burden ourselves with a philosophy of built-in frustrations, disappointments, and inevitable pain? Why not rather change the requirements for the good life? Epicurus assumed people of reason had free will and could control their desire for pleasure, and therefore they could reduce the amount of pain that always follows pleasure. Complete happiness is a moderate amount of pleasure with freedom from pain—an unlikely scenario for most people, but one that can be more nearly realized as we exert our will not to suffer. To those who would ask, "Why may I not agree to the suffering as long as I have the pleasure?", the epicurean answers, "The anticipation of pain, if it is intense, detracts from the pleasure."

Insofar as it recognizes the importance of pleasure in our lives, epicureanism is not so much an all-out attack on hedonism as a modification of it. Admitting that unpleasantness is part of life, the epicurean plans strategies to ward it off as much as possible rather than march forward in the blind hope that things are going to be fine. The worst that can happen when we anticipate pain is that we will not be disappointed. But clearly, we have a good chance of doing something about life's pain before it occurs *if* we apply ourselves conscientiously to the task.

Exerting control and enjoying pleasure in moderation, epicureans share with hedonists delight in the taste of exquisite food—but epicureans, anticipating the pain of overindulgence, stop themselves before reaching their limit. They will drink, but never to the point of drunkenness, and not at all if they are certain their health will suffer.

A character in Ernest Hemingway's story "In Another Country" fully illustrates the epicurean outlook. Before going off to war, a major in the Italian army marries a beautiful woman considerably younger than he. He discovers she was unfaithful while he was fighting. Now, injured and confined to a hospital, he learns his wife has died of pneumonia. "She had been sick only a few days. No one expected her to die." The lesson he gleans from the tragedy is a lesson about how best to live. A man, he explains, should not marry.

"He cannot marry. He cannot marry," he said angrily. "If he is to lose everything, he should not place himself in a position to lose that. He should not place himself in a position to lose. He should find things he cannot lose."[3]

Confirmed epicureans avoid excess, seeking out many nonphysical pleasures. They are lovers of art, theater, books, and music, perhaps realizing the humanities represent treasures one "cannot lose." After all, intellectual and aesthetic pleasures do not lead to pain. Epicureans are typically lean and trim, exercising their bodies to keep in the best possible shape. They are mentally agile and aware of the latest development in many fields. They are good workers, and the one who finds a marital partner with a similar outlook is likely to build a reasonably happy relationship.

Pure hedonists, however, warn epicureans that they sell themselves too short and may often settle for less than they have a right to expect from life. The hedonist maintains that unless you work aggressively at being happy, you will give up too easily, spending too much time running away from pain that might not be there. Why not go for all you can and take your chances? The pure epicurean, however, might well answer with an old French song that says "the joys of love are but a moment long; the pain of love endures forever."

Epicureanism Reconsidered

One objection that can be raised to epicureanism is that it is as firmly rooted in self-interest as the philosophy from which it departs. It has been accused of being hedonism in a disguised form. In seeking to avoid pain, it may be saying indirectly that pleasure is really the goal. Does it merely redefine pleasure? In addition to the good feeling one gets from the absence of pain, are not the pleasures of reading and spending one's life with the arts ultimately selfish?

Thus another objection is that epicureans are more interested in their own peace of mind than in causes that help others. If not wishing to lose means detaching oneself from life as much as possible, any form of activism is off limits. Concern for one's neighbors, stressed in all of the world's major religions, is generally absent from the traditional epicurean outlook. To be sure, Aristippus and Epicurus belonged to the classical world, and most classical theories of happiness focus on the individual, as though happiness by *definition* were a matter of how one's own life is faring.

We cannot rule out the possibility that happiness can be achieved only by working to combat pain wherever it is found, and sometimes the battle incurs personal suffering, which is accepted as the high price of success. After all, there are people, seldom mentioned in history books, who have voluntarily devoted their lives to nursing the sick in parts of the world ravaged by plagues, like the Ebola epidemic of 2014, and earthquakes, like the one that ravaged Nepal in 2015. Maybe the new epicureanism seeks not only to avoid pain oneself, but to do everything possible to help *others* avoid pain.

The cataclysmic events that befell New York and Washington, D.C., on September 11, 2001, and took over 3,000 lives had an effect quite different from the total chaos the terrorists may have planned. Instead of scattering to save themselves, hundreds of police and firefighters gave up their own lives in an attempt to rescue as many victims as they could. It is clear from cell phone calls made to loved ones before the collapse of the Twin Towers that a number of those who might have escaped stayed to help others, forfeiting their lives to do so. There are further indications that some of the passengers aboard Flight 93, which crashed in a Pennsylvania meadow, overpowered the hijackers and gave up their own lives in order to save perhaps thousands who might have died had the deadly mission been completed. Who is to say that dedicated epicureans would not, in moments of extreme crisis, forego all thoughts of self-interest? If someone survived by not trying to save another, would that individual lead a peaceful and contented life from that day on?

The cynic might say that social consciousness is only an extension of a principle stated by Epicurus that the just man enjoys the most peace of mind. That is, happiness consists of an undisturbed conscience; if you want tranquility, you must sometimes labor in the interest of others.

Stoicism: Happiness Is Survival

12.3 *What is stoicism, and what are its key assumptions about happiness?*

A famous poster shows a cat holding tightly to the knotted end of a rope and just hanging there in empty space. The caption reads: *When you come to the end of your rope, tie a knot and hang on.* This, in capsule form, is the philosophy of **stoicism**. It operates under even fewer illusions about life than does epicureanism. It tells us neither to plan ahead for a life of unlimited pleasure nor to expect to avoid pain through discipline and moderation. Stoicism asserts pain is intrinsic to living. The best possible course is to prepare for the worst and develop a technique for dealing with it. *Epicureans avoid pain; stoics cope.*

Stoicism was born over 2,000 years ago. Like hedonism and its modified offspring epicureanism, it is the product of Greek intellect; it lays heavy stress on human reason and the belief that humankind is the superior form of animal life. The philosophy of Zeno (335–264 BCE), its first major advocate, is close in spirit to that of Plato and Aristotle. The school founded by Zeno was located in a columned portico called a *stoa*—hence the name of the philosophy.

Stoic Assumptions

Stoicism sees the will as the means through which each of us can control our response to external events. Despite the disasters that may befall them, stoics believe in human reason. They believe it is reasonable to know that disasters—natural, social, personal—inevitably happen. Life just occurs. We make plans, but we cannot include happiness in those plans. As someone once said, "Life is what happens while we are making other plans." Nor should we believe that all is chaos in the universe. If there is order in the human mind, there may be order in the universe as well, and the unpredictable things that happen may be *part* of that order. Recognizing this, we can see to it that the will is in tune with events as they occur. The sometimes despairing question "How can terrible things be part of any order?" may be irrelevant. Stoics contend disasters are possible to accept without emotion.

Central to stoicism is the belief that true happiness is not a matter of circumstance, or good fortune, or of what happens to us, but rather a matter of *how we respond to what happens*. Happiness, like sorrow, is an idea, an attitude, not an object or an event. If no one welcomes the first day of spring, how can it be said that spring is a time of hope and joy? If in some remote civilization with unusual customs and mores the birth of a child were considered a dreadful curse, then the inability to produce offspring might be regarded as a happy stroke of luck.

RESPONDING POSITIVELY TO SUFFERING   To find the roots of unhappiness, we must look inward. Nothing is under our control except the way we think about things. Natural disasters, social upheavals, wars, revolutions, outbreaks of disease, rising crime rates—all happen as a result of either accidental or highly complicated causes. Our happiness should not depend on their *not* taking place. We cannot alter external circumstances, but we can decide not to feel negatively about them.

One of the best-known stoic teachers was a Greek named Epictetus (50–130 CE), who was captured and enslaved by the Romans. His brilliance was eventually recognized, and he was allowed to conduct classes. But prior to that, Epictetus was tortured and oppressed in his captivity. On one occasion, his leg was broken on his master's whim. During this period of extreme suffering, Epictetus was faced with the choice of surrendering to despair or finding some means of enduring. He chose the latter course, recognizing that nothing, not even torture, was unbearable unless one wished to find it so. After his liberation, he dedicated his life to spreading the stoic creed, which had kept his spirit intact for so many years.

Stoicism later found ready acceptance among the Romans and became a sort of unofficial state philosophy. Its emphasis on reason and the control of negative emotions accorded well with the Roman ideal of the perfect human being. Rome was an empire-building civilization requiring a superbly disciplined military machine to carry out its conquests. It therefore found a meaningful application of stoic teachings: The rigors of military training as well as the hardships of war itself must never depress the human spirit. Good soldiers, with feelings well under control, must become indifferent to their own suffering.

STOICISM AND CHRISTIANITY When Christianity began to spread throughout the Roman Empire, many of the converts had already been exposed to stoic beliefs. The by-then ancient and honorable philosophy meshed with the outlook and needs of Christians, who had to face untold suffering including ongoing persecution, flight, starvation, and separation from loved ones. The stoic doctrine of inner control blended perfectly with the Christian belief about the interconnection between body and soul. One could endure all manner of pain and still be serene.

Christian martyrdom was deeply rooted in stoic principles, especially the directives to love one's enemies and to turn the other cheek. A famous martyrdom is that of Thomas à Becket (1118–1170), the Archbishop of Canterbury and, as such, the pope's representative in England, sworn to carry out papal decrees and uphold Christian dogma. By the twelfth century, however, England was becoming a major world power, and the English monarchy assumed more and more authority, even in matters of religion. King Henry II, once Becket's friend, passed laws in direct violation of Church canon. The pope was displeased and Becket, of course, sided with him, causing a dangerous rift between monarch and prelate. Late in 1170, Becket urged the pope to dismiss several bishops known to be on the king's side. The king then sent four knights to Canterbury with the king's command to restore the deposed bishops, but Becket refused. Knowing that he had probably signed his own death warrant, the archbishop went into the cathedral to pray.

While he was there, the knights returned, this time with an armed band. Becket's attendants saw them coming, shut the heavy doors and were about to lock them when the archbishop cried out, "God's house must be closed against no man." The assassins, thus given unchallenged entry, rushed to the altar, whereupon Becket made a ringing stoic declaration: "For the name of Jesus and for the defense of the Church, I am ready to embrace death." They fell upon him with their swords, and he was murdered on the altar (Figure 12.4). The scene was memorably recorded in the verse play *Murder in the Cathedral* (1935) by the American poet T.S. Eliot and later in French playwright Jean Anouilh's *Becket* (1959), which was adapted as a film in 1964.

Whether religiously oriented or not, stoicism remains as pervasive as ever and offers to many a genuine alternative to hedonism. In a period of ever-accelerating change, of being wary of violence as a condition of life, of the realization that prosperity does not last forever, small wonder that many are asking less for pleasure than for inner peace. Although weekly pilgrimages to analysts continue, some principles of stoicism may be at work here also. After all, self-knowledge is vital to psychoanalysis. Analysts contend that people will be able to transcend negative feelings once they understand what is making them unhappy or ineffective. This may be the same as saying that happiness is really within our power to create and preserve. Not everyone agrees.

Stoicism Reconsidered

Stoicism in modern dress is, for its advocates, still a viable theory of happiness. Its basic assumption remains much the same as always: Tranquility is worth any price. Stoicism has something to offer the chronically poor or

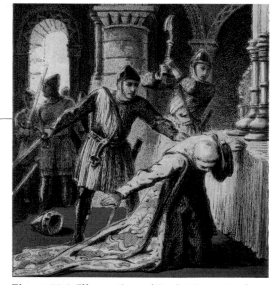

Figure 12.4 Illustration of Becket's martyrdom, date unknown.
Thomas à Becket stoically accepted his death rather than closing the doors of his church to shut out his assassins. Do you consider yourself stoic in the face of pain? What, if anything, would permit you to face death stoically?

Mary Evans Picture Library/Alamy

the dispossessed, and those who suffer from low self-esteem and cannot see that they deserve any better fate. Even the most zealous social worker might agree that in some cases a stoic attitude is better than false hope for a better tomorrow.

Yet a negative aspect of stoicism is its convenience. If you're down and out, abandoned by family and friends, with no prospect that things will turn around for you, why not become a stoic? Surely the distance is short from "Things are pretty bleak" to "There is no reason to believe things should be otherwise." Does this view mean simply coping but *doing* nothing? Many of the characters in television's *The Wire* seem stoic in accepting their inability to move up in society; in fact, the one character who strives for upward mobility, a drug dealer named Stringer Bell, learns quickly that such efforts will lead only to further disappointments.

STOICISM IN THE FACE OF GOOD FORTUNE   Suppose, however, that the ad hoc stoic—the person who adopts the philosophy out of sheer desperation—suddenly experiences an unexpected reversal of fortune, say, winning $5 million in the state lottery or, more modestly, finding a good-paying job. Or suppose, as actually happened in the wake of a television newscaster's human-interest documentary about the homeless in New York, a couple randomly singled out for an interview found themselves swamped with offers of money, jobs, shelter, even a film contract! What happens to stoic doctrines then? Can one embrace stoicism one day and abandon it the next?

Some might respond "Why not?" If adversity can be endured because the rational control of emotion makes endurance possible, dropping stoicism when it is no longer working is not necessarily unreasonable. Others could object to this line of thought, claiming that reason, which justified the initial adoption of the stoic philosophy during bad times, also requires us to believe that good fortune may not be permanent.

There is an old fable about a tyrannical king who, finding himself plagued by bad fortune, kept asking various wise men to give him grounds for hope. If they could not, their heads were chopped off. Finally, one clever sage gave him a plaque to hang on his bedroom wall: *These Things Shall Pass*. The king, deriving much comfort from the plaque, rewarded the sage handsomely until the king's fortunes took a turn for the better. The maxim, which had once buoyed up his spirits, now angered him, and he ordered the once-favored philosopher to be beheaded.

A frequently raised objection to stoicism is that its advocates secretly want everyone else to be as miserable as they are, yet they don't realize it. Is adversity more bearable when no one around you is having a run of good luck? Loving the company of the miserable may be a fundamental human trait. Enjoying nothing so much as the sad tales of others may be as universal as secretly resenting a friend's prosperity. The German word *schadenfreude* describes the pleasures derived from the misfortunes of others. Radio and television programmers assume there's a smaller audience for good news than for accounts of grisly murders and natural disasters happening to other people.

Yet another objection is that what passes for reason in stoicism should really be called rationalizing, a process by which we find satisfying rather than logical reasons for believing something. The possibility exists that control for the stoic actually means manipulating thoughts so that reality becomes tolerable. When loved ones stop calling, do we endure their absence by entertaining the possibility that they have transferred their affections or have ceased to be interested in us for this or that reason? Or are we more likely to believe whatever makes us feel good? We pick and choose among comfortable versions of reality. In this way, say the detractors, what masquerades as stoic acceptance is a false sense that reality is being fearlessly confronted. We accept what we *want* to accept, rejecting everything else. The trouble, they warn, is that rejected reality can strike back at any time, delivering a crushing blow.

DOES "ACCEPTING FATE" EQUAL PASSIVITY?   Classical stoicism emerged from two cultures, the Greek and the Roman, with their strong belief in fate. The universe was run by all-powerful deities who intervened in human affairs whenever they chose. The gods and goddesses were capricious and unpredictable, but human reason could counteract heavenly whimsy by expecting ill times before they occurred. In other words: The universe was predictably full of disaster. (This may explain why the Romans were strong on building a well-ordered state.) Critics of stoicism have said the universe does not make even that much sense. Perhaps disasters are no less certain than continuing success. They argue that the uncertainty invites debilitating passivity. Expecting to fail has kept many a potential winner from even getting started.

There is also the passivity of the fortunate, especially when it comes to turning away from the fact that people the world over are suffering and that they are in a position to help. "I'm a stoic and believe those who are suffering poverty or the ravages of war would be happier if they would only follow my example" can be an excuse for enjoying a comfortable existence without the nagging of conscience.

Harriet Beecher Stowe's novel *Uncle Tom's Cabin* (1852) opened the eyes of many who were unaware of the wretched poverty in which slaves were forced to live without any hope of liberation. The title character, however, adopts a stoic acceptance of his lot and has since lent his name as the very icon of nonresistance. Looking at the novel from over a century and a half removed, one might become infuriated by conditions that forced those without hope to embrace stoicism. In contrast, one character, Eliza, also a slave, is indeed desperate enough to endanger her life in a flight from the plantation. Modern readers sometimes criticize the passivity of Tom and praise the courage of Eliza.

Aristotle on Happiness

12.4   *What is Aristotle's theory of happiness?*

For Aristotle, Plato's star pupil and founder of the Lyceum, an early version of the liberal arts college, happiness is the purpose for which we live. In analyzing this most complex of phenomena, Aristotle concludes that happiness is not a moment-to-moment experiencing of pleasurable things but a way of characterizing how one's life is being conducted. Happiness is living and having lived a good life. It is not measured in momentary eruptions of joy. *Complete* happiness is the final summing up of one's life. If we are leading a good life along the way, we know we are on the right path. Then the philosopher goes on to tell us what makes life good along the way.

In his great work on the conduct of living, *The Nicomachean Ethics* (named for his son Nicomachus), Aristotle lists the things that make life good, including the *highest possible good,* the one that is valued for its own sake, the one that, when (or if) it is reached, leaves nothing else to be desired.

In the final season of the acclaimed television series *Mad Men*, the lead character, Don Draper, an advertising executive with a mysterious and chaotic past, asks those around him what their goals are for the future. One after another, his colleagues tell him they want to land a big ad account, or come up with a catchphrase that captures the public's attention. When he persists—"What else?" he keeps asking—they respond with either bewilderment or anger. They just aren't thinking—or perhaps don't want to be pushed to think—about the larger notion of what makes a happy life. Don is left, as we all often are, with the wistful question: Is that all there is?

When people are asked what would make them happy, the standard answers include loving relationships, family, health, money, a good job. Sometimes the responses include peace, or justice for all. Aristotle concludes that the reason we want money, health, love, and everything else worth striving for is that they *provide* happiness. Therefore none of them by itself can *be* happiness. The person who delivers your mail is not the mail. Individual goods, in other words, are means to the end, but none can be the end in itself—although some people often make the mistake of believing that is possible. For example, a poor person might dream of someday inheriting great wealth from a distant relative. "If I had all that money, I would ask for nothing more." Want to bet?

In identifying happiness with any particular state or possession, we could always think of something else that would be even better and therefore our life could be *more* happy at that moment. Just as Einstein told the world that at the speed of light, time stops, so too can it be said that in a state of complete happiness, desire and need stop. But only then.

Aristotle therefore defines happiness as the highest, or final, good. Since all of us continually strive for greater goods than we have at any particular time, it follows that reaching the final good is the goal of life. It also follows that what affords us pleasure or joy at any given moment cannot be the same thing as happiness because it is always possible at any given moment to think of something that would be better. Winning gold medals in the Olympics leaves athletes in a state of extreme joy, yet two medals are better than one, and three even better than that. Michael Phelps, who may possibly be the greatest swimmer ever to compete in the Olympics, would never have been satisfied with only one or two medals.

Reason and Virtue

Aristotle's theory has enormous implications for how we can best live. It assures us that life can be good without our having everything we thought we wanted. Every so often we can stop and take inventory and then decide how our life is going and what the final summing up is likely to be. Is it headed in a direction that can be summed up as "Yes, this is a good life—so far"?

Further, do we want things that make happiness more difficult to attain than need be? The answer, according to Aristotle, is staring us in the face. If happiness is the same as the good life, why not simply *live* the good life and make sure the final summing up will be a positive one? He believed there was one good which stood out above all, one good which was better than all the others that promote happiness, and that was *reason*. If we allow reason to be our guide in making all decisions, we will always do the right thing. By doing the right thing in every circumstance—not the most profitable or immediately pleasurable—one can be sure the summing up will be on the side of the good life.

Aristotle equated reason with virtue. The virtuous course is also the perfection of a particular action. To act out of self-interest, ignoring others, can never be excellence. Too many others can be hurt by the action, and pardoning oneself to avoid guilt means lying. Of what action is lying the perfection? Do we judge a lie to be a perfect action if nobody finds out? Or do we persuade ourselves that no one has been hurt? How can we know? And even if we could be assured that the lie is a harmless one, might we not be encouraged to choose lying over the truth in another, or perhaps even *every*, case? A life built on lies is bound to crumble like a house of cards.

Aristotle believed the path to happiness was a life lived in accordance with reason and virtue. This cannot be said for a life that achieves only *some* of the goods that are possible: recognition without love, for example, or money without health, or health without fulfilling any other purpose. A life that has displayed reason and virtue in all actions and decisions can be one that is free of care, free of guilt, free from wishing that much more could have been done. In today's topsy-turvy world, however, such freedom could be construed as overpassivity.

A person who lives a totally virtuous life may in the end regret that all goals have not been reached: the pay hike never received, the novel never written, a reconciliation never reached. But—and this is crucial—such regret is not a sign that the life has not been a happy one. In other words, according to Aristotle's theory, life can be good, hence happy, even though you are not always aware of it, by asking every so often, *"What am I doing that makes my life good?"* Not *"What is missing in my life?"* If the missing is also the attainable, then you have willfully blocked the road to happiness. Are there people who need your help? Are you in a position to help? Even if *present* conditions depress you, this does not mean you are not on your way to a final, positive summing up of your life.

Happiness: A Government's Responsibility?

Aristotle proposed that the purpose of government was to see to it that citizens were happy. Having deduced that the purpose for living is the attainment of the happy life, the philosopher believed nothing should be allowed to hinder the quest. The institutions of society exist to promote the happiness of all and therefore the means to that end.

The drafters of the Declaration of Independence apparently agreed with Aristotle. Starting from John Locke's argument that the purpose of political society was to protect "life, liberty, and estate," by which he meant property, Jefferson and his colleagues made the fundamental American revision to "life, liberty, and the pursuit of happiness." That single change underlies much of what we now call "American exceptionalism"—the pursuit of the American dream, the right of every individual to be "happy." And yet American political society—by which is meant not only government but also the economic system it upholds—often operates in opposition to that.

Aristotle argues that law and order in the well-regulated state are necessary; otherwise the happiness of all cannot be guaranteed. People must be protected against their own baser natures, as well as against those who wish them harm. For many critics of this theory, questions remain: How much power should the state be given before it contradicts its avowed purpose, which is to promote the happiness of all? May not some harm be done to the innocent? In this age of DNA testing, many long-time prisoners have been exonerated and released from prison, having given up as many as 30 or 40 years of their lives for crimes they did not commit. Some justify this by saying that the system works overall, and the imprisonment of a few innocent individuals is a small price to pay for keeping many criminals off the street. This argument does not satisfy those who would support the view that the happiness—and therefore the rights—of all must come first. How, they ask, can happiness be guaranteed when freedom is denied?

GOVERNMENT AND REASON Aristotle held fast to the belief that the road to happiness was through the exercise of reason and virtue and government must not stand in the way of reason. Government itself should be the very model of rationality. (Alas! Can this ever be the case? It's a tough proposition to believe in this age of Congressional dysfunction.) Therein lies the great dilemma. How can government *reasonably* protect the state if it sometimes uses *unreasonable* methods?

One of the great literary instances of this problem is in Herman Melville's *Billy Budd*. Billy, a young and innocent sailor, unwittingly antagonizes the master-at-arms, Claggart, who (perhaps jealous of Billy's popularity) accuses him of instilling a mutiny. At a hearing overseen by the ship's captain, Claggart states the untrue and unfair charges, and Billy, who suffers from a severe stutter, is unable to respond. Frustrated, he strikes Claggart and kills him. Although everyone on board the ship, including Captain Vere, knows that Billy's act was a morally innocent accident, Vere nevertheless insists that the letter of the law be followed—and martial law calls striking a superior office a capital crime. Billy is hanged, mourned by all around him.

But Vere believes that the law must be followed for the greater good of all; not to do so would lead to moral chaos.

There is a further dilemma. What happens when the government's supposedly rational view of happiness differs from that of the majority? In *The Republic*, Plato reports a famous debate over whether the best interests of the government can coincide with the best interests of the governed. Socrates believed there was only one rational course in every decision that had to be made, and that if the government truly followed reason, then it would automatically serve the interests of the people. That belief was the foundation of Socrates' decision not to escape from prison, though he questioned the "justice" that brought him there. What he did not question was the logic of having law itself. He was found guilty, however unjustly, and therefore the law required the extreme penalty, death by drinking hemlock. He argued it was unreasonable to assume anyone had the right to escape who thought he had been unjustly imprisoned. Aristotle had a very limited faith in the ability of the average citizen to be rational, but this only made him insist that those who governed *must* be reasonable at all times. Whether this has ever or will ever happen is open to endless debate.

Aristotle Reconsidered

There are always going to be limitations on happiness. Many millions have no choice but to wait and hope for a miraculous change of fortune, people who live under oppressive governments or in places where drought and other natural disasters create famine and the spread of fatal disease, people who have never had or maybe never will have anything that can be called a good. It is almost impossible to tell them their lives are happy without their knowing it. Aristotle would probably not have even tried. Recognizing when one is fortunate in comparison to many others can be a severe limitation on one's own progress toward a happy life. And helping those in need may be the only way to find the path again. Until one does find it and until no further help is necessary (an unimaginable condition), complete happiness is unreachable.

The economic disaster of the Great Depression was addressed by the administration of Franklin D. Roosevelt, which began in 1933 promising what it called the "New Deal." Based on the economic theories of John Maynard Keynes, an English economist, the New Deal was intended to stimulate economic growth. Financed by the government, the Works Progress Administration (WPA) and the Civilian Conservation Corps (CCC) put the unemployed to work building and rebuilding infrastructures. The New Deal proclaimed that the government's responsibility was to look out for the welfare of all citizens. In theory at least, everyone capable of working would have a job. Making a fair wage and putting food on the table equated to happiness.

Today, with the vast growth of income inequality in the United States, workers are once again faced with challenging circumstances. Wages for most people have grown very little or even have gone down in the last 20 years; unions—long the protectors of the working class—have been systematically dismantled. Some state governments have begun trying to raise the legal minimum wage, and workers themselves have begun to organize and demonstrate for fairer treatment, but the federal government seems paralyzed in this arena, as well as many others. The happiness of many seems a less attainable goal than the wealth of a few.

Aristotle assumed that a society with citizens' welfare as the sole concern of government would be on its way to happiness. Since his time, it is clear that all societies have become much more complex and government actions tangled in webs of red tape. Can anyone in any society rely solely on government to provide happiness? Is happiness attainable under a *repressive* government? Is happiness really possible in the strict Aristotelian sense?

Models of the Happy Life

12.5   *Why are some tragic lives also considered happy ones?*

One might ask how true happiness can be achieved in a world where we are continually facing the suffering of the less fortunate. And yet some individuals manage to live good—and presumably happy—lives despite the challenges around them. In fact, good lives are sometimes the result of facing those challenges directly, thoughtfully, and with optimism.

History is filled with remarkable examples of how good lives managed to overcome horrible barriers. Consider this passage by Austrian psychiatrist Viktor Frankl, who was a prisoner in a Nazi concentration camp. It illustrates how life can be good even in the shadow of death.

> *The size of human suffering is absolutely relative . . . It also follows that a very trifling thing can cause the greatest of joys. Take as an example something that happened on our journey from Auschwitz to the camp affiliated with Dachau. We had all been afraid that our transport was heading for the Mauthausen camp. We became more and more tense as we approached a certain bridge over the Danube which the trains would have to cross in order to reach Mauthausen. . . . Those who have never seen anything similar cannot possibly imagine the dance of joy performed in the carriage by the prisoners when they saw that our transport was not crossing the bridge and was instead heading "only" for Dachau.*[4]

The Aristotelian moral of this story is that the rational course was for the prisoners to put themselves into the hands of a two-pronged fate: Mauthausen or Dachau—certain death or a chance to live, even if imprisoned. Knowing the two possibilities in advance, it was rational to be prepared for either eventuality, not to wish for luck. Had liberation been the only possible good that would have satisfied them, the fact that the transport did not cross the Danube would not have been enough to fill them with optimism. Instead, they made their own "luck."

Anne Frank

Anne Frank (1929–1945), a young Jewish girl, was hidden, along with her parents and others, in the attic of an Amsterdam office building during the Nazi occupation. She had been given a diary on her 13th birthday, a few weeks before the family went into hiding, and she kept a record of her thoughts and feelings throughout her years in the attic—a work that was subsequently found, published, and read by millions.

Not the dewy-eyed idealist portrayed on stage, film, and television, Anne Frank was a girl with an adult mind who knew what she was doing at each moment. In 1944: "I have made up my mind now to lead a different life from other girls and, later on, different from ordinary housewives." The "different life" was that of the calm, reflective writer. "I can shake off everything if I write, my sorrows disappear, my courage is reborn." After the war she hoped to write a work of great significance, but if this goal were denied, "my diary will be a great help."[5]

Remarkably able to transcend what would have been an understandable fear for her own safety and that of her family and friends, Anne takes the larger view, thinking sadly of those who have already been captured and sent to camps. "If it is as bad as this in Holland, what ever will it be like in the distant and barbarous regions they are sent to? We assume that most of them are murdered. The English radio speaks of their being gassed; perhaps that is the quickest way to die."[6]

Anne's strength may have come from the fact that she knew herself to be innocent of any wrongdoing, and also from an acceptance of the conditions under which she and the others hiding in the attic had to live. She became the mainstay of the entire group. On the occasion of Hanukkah, she made presents for everyone out of old materials she found in the attic.

Her writing consistently reveals a person of resolve, one who has her emotions generally under control and, like the stoics, one whose spirit refuses to be broken. She admits to being afraid of death, but can that be called irrational? At the same time, she is not obsessed with fear. "When I sat in front of the window this morning I suddenly realized that we have had a great, great many compensations. I mean inward compensation."[7]

She proudly admits to believing nobody is all bad, despite the suffering she and her family have been forced to bear and the possibility of even more dreadful consequences to come. In the context of her brief but intensely rational life, her forgiving attitude seems more the triumph of the happy person (in Aristotle's sense) than the sentimentality of a young romantic. Observations like hers are not the result of a momentary, on-the-spot impulse, a sudden flurry of passing joy unjustified by the circumstances; rather they persist in one form or another throughout the diary, evidence of a mature mind that knows what Aristotle reasoned a thousand years ago: *Life is good for one who is good*. Though Anne Frank was eventually captured and died in a concentration camp, we can say, in Aristotelian terms, that hers was a happy life tragically foreshortened.

Martin Luther King, Jr.

Martin Luther King, Jr. (1929–1968), winner of the Nobel Peace Prize in 1964, devoted his own foreshortened life to nonviolent protest against racism and the denial of civil rights to African Americans. An ordained Baptist minister, King was often in the midst of police brutality, urging victims to stay calm and not reciprocate in kind when force was used. Considered by many as the greatest American orator since Abraham Lincoln, he gave hope with his stirring rhetoric to millions of the poor and oppressed. He made numerous memorable speeches, but the most memorable of all was his "I Have a Dream" oration, delivered before thousands on the Washington Mall, August 28, 1963 (Figure 12.5).

In this speech, which is available at many online sites, King confronted the bitter truths of injustice, discrimination, school and housing segregation, and widespread joblessness. Without giving hollow protestations of hope, he gave what he surely must have considered rational reasons for hope, but always stressing nonviolence.

It is impossible to think that Dr. King was unaware of how dangerous it was to stand by his uncompromising principles and to take his powers of oratory into the most segregated parts of the country, knowing full well how many enemies were lying in wait. Five years after giving this speech that now belongs in the history of the humanities, he was assassinated by a man who spent the remainder of his life in prison, never admitting guilt or showing remorse.

Figure 12.5 Martin Luther King, Jr., speaking on the Washington Mall, 1963.

A happy life, by Aristotle's criteria, is defined by an unwillingness to abandon reason and virtue even in the face of death. How do you respond to that definition? Do you agree that Martin Luther King's life was a happy one?

Anonymous/AP Images

Mahatma Gandhi

A sterling example of the Hindu path to bliss, or *moksha*, is provided by the life and death of Mohandas Gandhi (1869–1948), who also devoted his life to promoting the cause of nonviolence (Figure 12.6). He attained a huge following, who anointed him with the title **Mahatma**, meaning "one who is wise and good."

Like Siddhartha (see Chapter 10), Gandhi wanted to do more than simply save himself by becoming detached from all participation in the world. He wanted to save the world by persuading all those who would listen that a serene and happy existence could come about only through nonviolence and love.

Hindu doctrine teaches that the divine spirit dwells inside each person, that the soul of each person is part of Brahman, the great soul, and therefore is fundamentally good. Unfortunately, the world is filled with luxuries, in plentiful supply to the rich, and with handsome and beautiful human beings who arouse sexual longings that must be fulfilled. The desire to possess both objects (including land) and other people leads to frustration and despair, because, as epicureans well know, there can never be enough pleasure if pleasure is the only goal. The thwarting of burning desire causes people to become violent, to seize what they want by any means.

Gandhi realized that when frustration was multiplied by the entire population of an oppressed land or by an ethnic group subjugated by a stronger power, revolutionary uprisings were inevitable. The endless cycle of violence, war, and death (often of the most innocent) made life bitter. He knew that, for many, the only way to reach serenity was to back off and do nothing. But for himself, there could be no bliss, no serenity in a world ruled by hate. Thus he became, as King would become, an activist determined to make nonviolence a potent counterforce.

SPEAKING TRUTH TO POWER As a native of India, Gandhi lived under British colonial rule and suffered the pain of discrimination. Speaking out against British imperialism, he acquired considerable notoriety and was frequently denounced in churches and meeting halls. He carried his message to South Africa, where he found the same sort of prejudice and resistance to change. Exhausted and frequently ill from hunger strikes, he persisted, obsessed with the need to convince those who gathered to hear his speeches that there was only one way for people to live a good life: to lay down all weapons and talk to each other. He was convinced that through dialog everyone would discover the basic oneness of all humanity. How could you hate someone who was really *you*?

Figure 12.6 Mahatma Gandhi, c. 1940s.
A lawyer by training, Gandhi put aside a potentially easy life to offer resistance to the ruling authorities in India—to "speak truth to power," in a phrase first used in a Quaker pamphlet offering alternatives to violence in the mid-1950s. Does speaking truth to power enable happiness?
Bettmann/Corbis

Gandhi was painfully aware that the greatest threat to peace in India, even more than British sovereignty, was the irreconcilable divide between Hindus and Muslims—each practicing a different religion: Hindus with their Brahman, the soul of the world but not a personal god, and Muslims with their father-god Allah. To Muslims, Hindus were godless infidels. But often Hindus held the upper hand.

Gandhi stepped into the bitter conflict, seeking to convince each side they could live in peace, tolerate their differences, and respect each other's right to believe as they wished and practice religion as they saw fit. In 1947, India became an independent nation with self-rule, a tremendous step forward for which Gandhi was partly responsible. Yet he was not satisfied. The internal conflicts had to be resolved.

Gandhi's dream, like that of Martin Luther King, Jr., decades later, would remain unrealized. On January 30, 1948, as he was about to enter a temple for a period of meditation, he was shot and killed by a Hindu fundamentalist, who apparently hated Muslims and could not tolerate the idea of peaceful coexistence.

Once again we have evidence that if perfect happiness is to be anything more than momentary joy, it has to be recognized as a distant goal that can probably never be reached but can be approached through unceasing effort. One may conclude that Gandhi was a really happy person, who may not have taken the time to think about the matter. If Aristotle's spirit had followed him about like a guardian angel, he might have decided Gandhi was a shining example of the happy life. He did not have health or wealth, two components, but not the equivalents of Aristotelian happiness, though he surely possessed reason and virtue.

Buddhist Paths to Happiness

12.6 *What is the Buddhist path to happiness? What implications does it have for contemporary life?*

For Buddhists, bliss, or nirvana, has a twofold nature. Historians of Buddhism explain that over the centuries the practice divided into two schools, both leading to nirvana. One is **Hinayana**, which means "little ferryboat." It developed first, and its purpose was to formulate the teachings of Siddhartha into a systematic practice of the Four Noble Truths, which are

1. *life is filled with pain*
2. *the cause of pain is frustrated desire*
3. *there is a way out of pain*
4. *the way out is the Eightfold Path*

The last has to do with how we think, speak, behave toward others, and above all how we find peace through meditation (see Figure 12.7).

While Hinayana Buddhism involves moral conduct, which is automatic if we follow all of the recommended steps, its practice was seen by those who came after Siddhartha as too narrow, too limited. It was a wonderful means of self-help, of lifting the spirits of the depressed, but not a way to help others who may have lost their way.

Gradually the school known as **Mahayana**, "big ferryboat," developed by adding a larger perspective and a more expansive concept of bliss. Tibetan Buddhism is Mahayana in scope, continuing the legacy of Siddhartha and teaching that nirvana is attainable in one lifetime by the fully enlightened person, who then becomes a buddha renouncing bondage to the pleasures of this world and doing whatever is necessary, wherever it may be. It can mean something as simple as collecting clothes, food, and other supplies for victims of a devastating fire, storm, or earthquake, or joining a group of volunteers and helping to rebuild damaged homes. Or it can mean becoming a world-renowned person, carrying a message of peace and tolerance to millions. In Buddhism, both meanings have equal importance.

There is nothing self-congratulatory about the Mahayana path. One does not pat oneself on the back and bask in the glow of satisfaction that comes with knowing one has done a good deed or made a tremendous sacrifice. Mahayana Buddhists say it is the logical next step after one has practiced the narrower way. The idea is that, having reached enlightenment after long years of meditation, one has no choice but to live in and through others, just as Siddhartha, having reached enlightenment after sitting under the bodhi (rose-apple) tree for 40 days and nights, declined to remain in nirvana, feeling he must share his bliss with everyone else and teach them how to be as serene as he was (Figure 12.8).

In the time of Siddhartha, the world had many troubles, but there were no global conditions of today's dimensions, no continual outbreaks of terrorism, no everyday fears that disaster is omnipresent

Figure 12.7 Monk meditating in Cambodia with Angkor Wat temple in background, 2014.

Do you think meditation can bring happiness? Or does happiness result from acting in the world? Or some combination of both?

Heritage Image Partnership Ltd/E&E Image Library/Alamy

and waiting to happen anywhere, anytime. Were he alive today, he would very likely have been at Ground Zero on September 11, 2001, asking what he could do to help. For most of the rest of us, doing what is necessary may have a narrower definition: obligations to family, friends, and work. There are children to meet at the corner school bus stop, an aging parent or other relative to care for, and a host of personal tasks to be done, such as pursuing a degree, learning a new trade as a means of rising above tough economic times, supporting a family. Most of us cannot become buddhas or live as Siddhartha did, wandering from place to place without a family, eating very little, paying scant attention to personal needs. Yet Mahayana Buddhism does not expect quite this much. However far you go on the Path is better than not taking that first step. This is the Buddhist view of happiness.

The Dalai Lama

The Dalai Lama, the acknowledged leader of Tibetan Buddhism, is a role model for thousands who seek to emulate his serenity as well as his Mahayana efforts to help bring about world peace. Those who admire him and flock to his lectures often are curious about what it means to do without many of the pleasures that others of his stature and following usually enjoy—particularly pleasures of the flesh.

Figure 12.8 Shakyamuni Buddha attaining Parinirvana. Central region, Tibet, or Eastern Tibet. Late 19th to early 20th century.
Is there such a thing as pure happiness?
John Bigelow Taylor/Art Resource, NY

> *I am sometimes asked whether this vow of celibacy is really desirable and indeed whether it is really possible. Suffice to say that its practice is not simply a matter of suppressing sexual desires. On the contrary, it is necessary to fully accept the existence of those desires and to transcend them by the power of reasoning. When successful, the result of the mind can be very beneficial. The trouble with sexual desire is that it is a blind desire and can only give temporary satisfaction. Thus, as Nagarjuna said: "When you have an itch, you scratch. But not to itch at all is better than any amount of scratching."*[8]

The Dalai Lama's writings are full of wise sayings and aphorisms in short entries that remind one of the *Tao Te Ching* of Lao-tzu. And with their publication and dissemination around the globe, the Dalai Lama must, of course, hope that he will lead thousands, even millions, to the path of serenity. Knowing how to live a serene existence would make a good many people desist from doing their utmost to spread terror and hatred and continually renew the cycle of war and broken peace accords. He cannot, however, wish that the peace (and hope for happiness) of the entire world would come about only when all sides are of one mind.

> *All the waters and rivers of different lands and climes have their ultimate meeting point in the ocean. So, too, the differing viewpoints of society, the varieties of economic theories, and the means to their attainment benefit mankind itself. There is no point in indulging in dissension-creating discussions on differing ideologies. No possible result has accrued from attempting to convert all men of different temperaments and likings into one common ideology and mode of behavior.*[9]

In his view, serenity—or, as he calls it, tranquility—has to be achieved through acceptance of, not the burning need to change, everyone else.

> *The essence of all spiritual life is your emotion, your attitude toward others. Once you have sincere and pure motivation, all the rest follows. You can develop the right attitude toward others on the basis of kindness, love, and respect, and on the clear realization of the oneness of all human beings.*[10]

Whether we call it bliss, moksha, or nirvana, or go with the hedonists and insist that it is having as much as possible of life's pleasures—plenty of money, sex, fast cars, a showcase for a home—the nature of the good life remains open to debate. This chapter has not promised an easy solution, a neat summing up. Happiness is but one of the colors we apply to the canvas of "human."

The terms *winner* and *loser* are strong in our vocabularies. Frequently they lead us to an either–or approach to living. Blithely we describe someone as a loser and resolve that only *winner* will ever apply to *us*. But if a loser is someone who fails at everything, must a winner be the exact opposite? Is it possible to win continually? Do we always know what it *means* to win? And what is *loss*? The absence of money, health, love? Can these be absent continually?

We do not wish to leave you with the impression that Aristippus, Epicurus, Aristotle, or Siddhartha discovered the best and only road to happiness. Our advice is to carefully map out your requirements for the good life, bearing in mind some of the options discussed in this chapter. Once you recognize that you are in control of defining happiness and can make it mean what is possible for you, not what you can never hope to achieve, then you may experience a measure of contentment.

Happiness (and Unhappiness) and the Arts

12.7 *How are happiness and unhappiness portrayed in the arts?*

We tend to think of happiness as comedy and unhappiness as tragedy. The standard motif for comedy from the Greeks through Shakespeare and even to the present day is the movement from a world of chaos to one of order—from mismatched lovers, misunderstood intentions, and misperceived identities to a "happy ending," often involving dancing or marriage. Shakespeare is, as usual, the master at this; his *Midsummer Night's Dream*, with its series of comic mix-ups that finally untangle themselves, allowing each character to find the appropriate mate, provides the archetype for comic performance. This model—chaos sorted out to end in order—is also the model for most contemporary television situation comedies, as well as for hit comic movies such as *Bridesmaids* (2011).

Is happiness the return to order, then? And if so, does that mean that happiness is always, at heart, a denial—a running away from the chaos of darker truths, including, most dramatically, death itself? Certainly that is the theme of many of the great masterworks of literature. Melville's *Moby-Dick*, for example, gives us both the "happy" character of Ishmael, who observes the action and comments on it—and ultimately survives—and the "unhappy" or tragic character of Ahab, obsessed with finding the white whale. Ahab both seeks happiness, which he assumes will come with killing the whale, and denies it, because he thinks succumbing to happiness will necessarily seduce him off the path he wants to follow.

Cervantes provides another model of happiness in *Don Quixote*, a novel that offers perhaps the first instance in literature of a comic acceptance of the foibles and failings of real human beings. In *Don Quixote*, we are led to a communal understanding of what it means to be human; we embrace the dark and the light that are brought together in the comic quest of one mad man and his devoted friend. Following Cervantes, the British novelists of the eighteenth century created a series of comic novels that followed lovable central characters from disorder to happiness, including Henry Fielding's *Tom Jones* (1749) and Daniel Defoe's *Moll Flanders* (1722).

Tragedy can also teach us about happiness—and sometimes the lessons it teaches are difficult to accept. Arthur Miller's classic play *Death of a Salesman* (1949) shows us all too vividly what happens when the American dream—the pursuit of happiness—is taken literally. Willy Loman, the salesman at the center of the play, confuses happiness with success in business. He pays too little attention to his family—his loving wife and two troubled sons—and too much to trying to gain a foothold in a business where his skills no longer bring success. When he fails, we feel his failure, and that failure is much more tragic for having been preceded by Willy's grand dreams of success and happiness.

The journey from unhappiness to happiness—or, for that matter, from happiness to unhappiness, as in Tolstoy's classic *Anna Karenina* (1877)—is most readily portrayed in literature or the theater, but the other arts often play another role: the bringing of happiness, even sheer joy, to the listener or viewer. Check out the whimsical cut-out art of Henri Matisse, for example, or the contemporary works of Christo and Jean-Claude (Figure 5.42). If you walked through New York's Central Park when *The Gates*, Christo's installation of huge panels of orange fabric, lined pathways for miles, you would have seen nothing but smiles on the faces of other strollers. Or find a video of the dance *Revelations* by the choreographer Alvin Ailey (see Figure 8.13). It's hard to deny the happiness that such works can inspire.

Portraying Unhappiness

Of course, any theory of happiness is finally just that: a theory. People whose circumstances are deplorable, who live in fear, hunger, and ill health, whose lifespan is often considerably shorter than it could be, who can rightfully say they never did harm to anyone, yet suffer, cannot be blamed for feeling they deserve a better fate. Misfortune is, unfortunately, inherent in this business of living. The amount of suffering in the world is for many a permanent roadblock to a happy life.

The humanities have not turned a deaf ear to human misery. The sometimes futile attempt to escape from poverty is the subject of much great art and literature. For example, Victor Hugo's *Les Misérables* (1862) called powerful attention to the plight of the poor in France. The hero, Jean Valjean, steals a loaf of bread for his hungry family, is sent to prison, and after his release gets into trouble again, before going on to lead a remarkably moral life. He is pursued relentlessly by Javert, a police inspector obsessed with punishing anyone who breaks a law, regardless of circumstances. The pursuit continues for hundreds of pages, resulting finally in Javert's suicide because he cannot reconcile his duty to the law with the mercy shown to him by Valjean, who is reunited with his adopted daughter as an old man near death—and all because of a loaf of bread!

Conditions in the modern world have not conspired to bring about rosier views in the literary and artistic depiction of life. A popular Egyptian novel in recent years, Alaa Al Aswany's *The Yacoubian Building* (2002), revolves around the tenants of an apartment house in Cairo. To one extent or another, all of them long for prosperity. The central character is Taha, son of the building's janitor, who aspires to become a policeman and then marry the woman he loves. When he is turned away from the police academy even after scoring high on the entrance examination, he enrolls in college, where he is snubbed by the wealthier, better-dressed students but welcomed by those as poor as he. They introduce Taha to a charismatic leader promising change and declaring the way to bring it about is to disrupt the status quo through well-placed bombs. What stands out in the novel is the fact that his solution is not described as a misfortune, but simply a sad commentary on the modern world.

Looking Back

In this chapter,

- we discussed hedonism and its key assumptions about happiness,
- we explored the epicurean approach to happiness and its key assumptions,
- we looked at the teachings of Zeno and the key assumptions of stoicism,
- we summarized Aristotle's theory of happiness, including the role of government and law in creating a greater good,

- we provided some models of good lives and explained why a tragic ending does not necessarily mean that a life was unhappy,
- we discussed the Buddhist paths to happiness and how the lessons taught here might apply to contemporary life, and
- we described some ways in which happiness and unhappiness are portrayed in—and inspired by—the disciplines of the humanities.

Key Terms

big earnings theory From the hedonist view that people who work hard or who make sacrifices for others deserve material rewards.

carpe diem Latin phrase meaning "seize the day"; a major hedonist creed advising us to live for the moment and amass all the pleasures we can.

epicureanism Based on teachings of Epicurus, the belief that happiness is freedom from pain.

hedonism From the Greek for "delight," the belief that happiness consists of the sum of all the pleasures we can experience.

Hinayana One of the two major schools of Buddhism; from the Sanskrit meaning "little ferryboat," the narrow path to personal happiness attained by serenity through meditation.

Mahatma From Sanskrit meaning "great soul," a title of love and respect for one known to be wise and good; applied to Gandhi.

Mahayana One of the two major schools of Buddhism; from Sanskrit meaning "big ferryboat," the wider path to happiness, attained by helping others find the way.

stoicism Belief that happiness consists of coping rationally with sources of unhappiness.

Chapter 13
Love

Figure 13.1 Pablo Picasso, *The Lovers*, 1923.
How do you define love?

Bridgeman Art Library, London/Superstock. Art © 2015 Estate of Pablo Picasso/
Artist's Rights Society (ARS), New York

We can scarcely overestimate the importance of love, yesterday and today, in our lives, in the world, and in the humanities. One of the world's most beautiful buildings, the glorious Taj Mahal mausoleum in Agra, India, is evidence of the love of one man, Shah Mumtaz, for his favorite wife. Without the theme of love, all of the arts would be diminished. Even the successive marriages of the frequently divorced suggest that people believe so strongly in love that they keep looking for it—and that, no matter what their other achievements, they probably believe that finding love is what makes living worthwhile. In countless poems, novels, operas, films, and plays, love is shown as the source of both pleasure and pain, often at the same time.

Scientific evidence suggests that what we call "love" is the result of the release of successive waves of chemicals in our body: first the gender hormones of testosterone and estrogen; then adrenaline, dopamine, and serotonin, which give us bursts of energy and sleeplessness and cause us to think nonstop about the person to whom we're attracted; and finally the "cuddle" hormone oxytocin and its partner vasopressin, which promote long-term attachment. But despite all this, we really can't explain love. As the hero in the Rodgers and Hammerstein musical *South Pacific* sings in "Some Enchanted Evening," fools give you reasons, but wise men never try.

Nevertheless, this chapter will analyze ways in which humanity has been affected by the myth or the mystery of love as it has been depicted in different cultures and different times. We note that artists are not united in their depictions of love: Some have glorified it; others have emphasized its pain; some have even tried to imagine a society whose leaders ban it entirely. Recognizing this obsession and its possible impact on our beliefs is crucial to the art of being human.

Eros

13.1 *What is the history of the term* **eros**? *What are some examples of its meaning through the ages?*

Love has a history. Human perception of what love is has changed dramatically over the centuries. And how love is defined differs from culture to culture. Cultural anthropologists once discovered that people in a certain remote area of Africa had no word that translates as "love." Parents undoubtedly showed affection for their young by teaching them how to survive in a hostile environment; their vocabulary was filled with words that relate to survival strategies, all with favorable connotations. They seemed, however, to have little need for words that refer to tight family bonds, and none for words indicating romance between adults.

Imagine the difficulty of having a meaningful discussion about love between people from totally different backgrounds, whose cultural conventions were at opposite ends of the spectrum—one waiting for romance and passion, with a wide choice of partners, the other preparing to marry a stranger in a match arranged by parents.

The one aspect of love that emerges again and again, both in anthropological studies and in the arts, is physical passion. The pleasures of the flesh have found their share of glorification in almost every culture, from the ancient world to the twenty-first century (think *Fifty Shades of Grey*). The Hebrew Bible, for example, contains the Song of Solomon (Song of Songs), which, though variously interpreted, appears to be a lyrical idealization of physical ecstasy. Its inclusion among sacred writings suggests that, to the Hebrews, passion was a glorious experience, not at all inconsistent with the love of God. In this work, the lover speaks to his beloved in sensual terms. Her physical splendors fill him with joy; he compares her breasts to clusters of fruit and her breath to wine.

In the classical world of Greece and Rome, the word *love* can be found in poetry, philosophy, and mythology. The Greeks made a distinction between **eros**, or love as physical lust (named after the god of passion), and **agape**, or a spiritual and intellectual relationship that is more important than a strictly physical one. Though the Romans are famous for their wine-filled orgies, they recognized the distinction as well, and that distinction is still with us.

Lust in Classical Myth

In the classical world, passion was dangerous. Love could be responsible for endless misery. This poem by the Roman Petronius Gaius (c. 100 CE) offers a warning about lust and an invitation to something better.

> *Doing, a filthy pleasure is, and short;*
> *And done, we straight repent us of the sport:*
> *Let us not then rush blindly on unto it,*
> *Like lustful beasts, that only know how to do it:*
> *For lust will languish, and that heat decay.*
> *But thus, thus, keeping endless holiday,*
> *Let us together closely lie and kiss,*
> *There is no labour, nor no shame in this;*
> *This hath pleased, doth please, and long will please; never*
> *Can this decay, but is beginning ever.*[1]

The destructive, often tragic, effects of physical desire have been the source of some long-lasting stories emerging from classical mythology. Typical is the account of someone—mortal or divine—caught in the grip of uncontrollable passion. In Roman myth, the figure of Cupid is often the mischief-maker as he aims his arrow at some unfortunate creature who is no longer able to think rationally.

THE STORY OF VENUS AND ADONIS   One of Cupid's victims is his own mother, Venus, the goddess of love, who, after being wounded by his arrow, is overcome by attraction to a mortal, Adonis. After enjoying passion with a divine being, Adonis announces his intention to go hunting. Venus pleads with him not to go in search of dangerous game. Such advice is distinctly un-Roman, and Adonis predictably ignores it—and is promptly killed by a wild boar. To perpetuate his memory, Venus transforms his blood into a dark red flower called the anemone. But like passion itself, the anemone is short-lived. The wind blows the blossoms open and all the petals disappear.

The story of Venus and Adonis lives on in powerful words and pictures. Many artists, especially the Flemish painter Peter Paul Rubens (1577–1640), have been inspired by the myth of an impossible love between a mortal and the immortal goddess who could not follow him to the grave (Figure 13.2). This story would not be the last to show that physical desire has a very brief existence and that death alone can insure what human beings dream of and sing about: love that never ends.

In Shakespeare's dramatic poem about the pair, Venus is very definitely the aggressor, pursuing and seducing the reluctant Adonis:

> *Thrice-fairer than myself, thus she began*
> *The field's chief flower, sweet above compare,*
> *Stain to all nymphs, more lovely than a man,*
> *More white and red than doves or roses are;*
> *Nature that made thee, with herself at strife,*
> *Saith that the world hath ending with thy life.*[2]

Figure 13.2 Peter Paul Rubens, *Venus and Adonis,* **mid to late 1630s.**
Do you believe that the passionate aspect of love is necessarily short-lived?

Akg-images/Newscom

After the young man dies, according to Shakespeare, the goddess puts a curse on love. Henceforth love will never make *anyone* happy. Love will be passion unfulfilled—passion turned bitter. And what's more, it will be the cause of war and dire events. Fathers and sons will fight each other over the same woman. If any lovers are lucky enough to escape the decay of their passion for each other, that passion will nevertheless make them miserable.

Adonis was not alone in being radically changed following an erotic misadventure. Other mythic mortals who attracted the attention of Olympian gods and goddesses either died or were changed into vegetation or heavenly bodies. In one Greek myth, it is a woman who must suffer because of a god's attraction to her. Persephone, daughter of Demeter, the earth mother, is so beautiful that Hades, god of the underworld, desires her, then captures and transports her to his dark kingdom. Demeter so grieves over her loss that Zeus, king of the gods, takes pity on her and allows her to share custody of the lovely daughter. During the months that Persephone is gone, the earth mother mourns—and thus winter comes to the world. When Persephone returns, however, the earth is reborn in spring.

In classical mythology, human beings are not responsible for their tragic passions. Outside forces, personified as the gods, toy with them for amusement or the satisfaction of their own physical needs. Occasionally, the afflicted mortal is rewarded for having been the target of a god's lust, but only after undergoing physical and mental torment.

Medieval Lust

During the late Middle Ages, though Europe was strongly Christian, secular and erotic themes began to creep into poems and songs, often written by young men studying for the priesthood.

If they did not turn from their faith, they could nonetheless be irreverent in their praise—or at least defense—of sexual pleasure. Groups of rebellious students known as **goliards** frequented the taverns in their leisure hours singing the praises of secular life. The most famous of these is "Gaudeamus Igitur" ("Let us rejoice while we are young"), which is still played at countless college commencement ceremonies minus the lyrics that urge people to eat, drink, and be merry before the inevitable happens: "Then the dust shall claim us." Many of the goliard songs as well as others have been discovered within the past century, including "In Trutina . . ." ("I am suspended between chastity and lascivious love"), which, along with other student songs, was given a modern setting by composer Carl Orff and recorded by innumerable artists including Sarah Brightman and Barbra Streisand. The narrator of the poem is probably a novitiate about to take her final vows—and wishing she were not.

The most famous secular author of the fourteenth century was Geoffrey Chaucer (c. 1342–1400), who was fond of creating lusty stories and characters that shocked church authorities. In his masterpiece, *The Canterbury Tales*, he recognizes the weakness of the flesh in both laypersons and clerics. Among the lust-driven men and women is his most unforgettable character, the aging Wife of Bath, married five times (but always "at church door") and as lusty a creature as can be found in the pages of literature. She sings the praises of youth and glorious sex, culminating with a misty-eyed recognition that as we grow old and unattractive we bid farewell to the joys that have made life rich and happy.

> *But lord Christ! When I remember*
> *My youth and joyful times,*
> *It tickles me to my heart's roots.*
> *Even now it does my heart good*
> *To know that I have had my world*
> *In my own time.*[3]

The Canterbury Tales notwithstanding, whatever indiscreet acts may have been taking place in the privacy of cloisters, monasteries, and rectories, medieval writings generally steered clear of the subject of lust. As the Middle Ages waned, however, and the Renaissance began to spread over much of western Europe, bringing with it the lost glories of the classical world, the ancient theme of lust awakened a sympathetic response from writers. Some treated it compassionately as a human tragedy, and others, like Shakespeare in his sonnets, ardently wished their lady friends would be a bit more obliging.

Lust on the Shakespearean Stage

Romeo and Juliet, probably the most popular love story ever written, quite clearly shows that physical desire initially attracts the pair. This desire makes Juliet fearful. Before encouraging Romeo's suit, she warns that such an attraction is "too like the lightning," because it "ceases to be ere one can say it lightens." Their sexual attraction causes them to forget family duty, forget the fact that Juliet is promised to someone else—in short, to commit themselves to each other with total abandon. Though their love is couched in the language of pure romance, they too are destroyed by the curse of Venus.

The darts of the mischievous Cupid are a popular plot device, whether for ill or good; and with or without him, we still have stories of people stricken with sudden, blinding passion—as if they *were* sporting arrows in their chests. Shakespeare also saw the humorous side of the affliction in his comedy *A Midsummer Night's Dream* (1594), when Titania, Queen of the Fairies, finds herself irresistibly drawn to a man she would never have looked at if she were in her right mind. But she is far from being in her right mind, because a magic love potion has been administered to her that causes her to desire the first creature she looks at—in this case, a bumbling rustic would-be actor wearing the head of a donkey and responding to the queen's passionate endearments with a typical donkey's bray, a sound that drives her into absolute sexual frenzy (Figure 13.3). This scenario is the comic flip side of the "love coin" for Shakespeare. Whether you laugh or cry, passion doesn't bring much good fortune.

Nonetheless, Shakespeare's time was one in which passion took center stage. In England, the philosophy of hedonism, discussed in the previous chapter, enjoyed much favor. It urged people, as the songs of the medieval goliards had, to enjoy life to the fullest because who knew what lay beyond the grave? The time of Queen Elizabeth I, who reigned until the very beginning of the seventeenth century, was the heyday of celebrating the pleasures of the flesh, but usually with the darker implication that death can strike at any time. The Greek philosopher Epicurus denounced hedonism on the grounds that its underlying obsession with death was more than enough to offset the fleeting pleasures of loving.

Eros in Middle Eastern Culture

A Thousand and One Nights is usually—and inaccurately—referred to simply as *The Arabian Nights*. In truth, however, this vast collection of more than 400 tales, put together from the ninth to the thirteenth centuries, came from India and Persia as well as from Arabia and so represents a blending of different cultures. In the decade of the 1880s, the stories were finally translated into English by Sir Richard Burton (1821–1890), an author and explorer, and have remained classic ever since.

Figure 13.3 Marc Chagall, *Midsummer Night's Dream*, 1939.

How big a part does physical attractiveness play in love? Could you love someone to whom you are not attracted? Are love and physical attraction two different things, or parts of a whole?

Scala/Art Resource, NY, Marc Chagall/Artists Rights Society (ARS), New York/ADAGP, Paris

The central character is Scheherazade, the latest wife of a much-married sultan who looks upon women as sexual playthings, with no other function than to be available at any time of the day or night. Because he is all-powerful and can have any woman he desires, he has each bride executed after the wedding night. Scheherazade faces the same fate as her predecessors unless she can find a way to entertain the sultan—other than through the customary lovemaking, which would guarantee her death.

The resourceful heroine decides to start telling stories, and they prove so engrossing that she dazzles her husband for 1001 nights, by which time we can presume that the sultan begins to see her as a human being rather than as a temporary bed partner. We can never know whether the long book was hugely popular with Victorian readers because the ending satisfied the moral standards of the time or because the ending was overlooked in favor of the exotic tales of harem intrigues. Perhaps it offered the perfect escape into an imaginary land of brilliant colors, fragrant spices, scrumptious feasting, and nights of delirious sex. Its musical counterpart, the symphonic poem *Scheherazade* by the Russian composer Nicolai Rimsky-Korsakov (1844–1908), remains a standard in the repertoire of all major orchestras and continues to enthrall listeners with its lush and sensuous tones.

The Rubáiyát (which means quatrains, or four-line verses, in Persian) was translated by the English scholar Edward Fitzgerald (1809–1883). Attributed to Omar, called Khayyám (tent maker), a Persian poet and philosopher who lived around 1100, it is a collection of verses that celebrate both the glory and the short-lived pleasures of life, especially those of physical love. The poems tell us that this love is at once the thing that makes life exciting and the thing that, because it cannot endure, makes life ultimately a sad, futile enterprise.

> *Ah, Love! Could you and I with Him conspire*
> *To grasp this sorry Scheme of Things entire,*
> *Would we not shatter it to bits—and then*
> *Re-mould it nearer to the Heart's desire.*[4]

Though a philosopher, Omar appears to have abandoned the life of reason in favor of the life of the senses. Making love and drinking steadily were far more satisfying than spending sleepless nights trying to understand existence.

> *You know, my Friends, with what a brave Carouse*
> *I made a Second Marriage in my house;*
> *Divorced old barren Reason from my bed,*
> *And took the Daughter of the Vine to Spouse.*[5]

The twelfth-century Sufi poet Rumi, while recognizing and praising physical delight, is also subtle and internal:

> *When I am with you, we stay up all night,*
> *When you're not here, I can't get to sleep.*
> *Praise God for these two insomnias!*
> *And the difference between them.*[6]

Adultery

The eighteenth century, on both sides of the English Channel, was a time of polite society. Manners were extremely important, but under the surface the lusty life continued to be celebrated. One historian of the period observed that though the drawing room was elegant and proper in all respects, behind the gilded bedroom door the rules were abandoned. Infidelity was rampant. It was expected that every well-bred gentleman of means would keep at least one mistress. Though religion kept denouncing flagrant immorality, even pious church-goers could look the other way, especially at their own behavior.

Bygone though these eras may have been, the fact remains that the theme of masculine domination and women-as-playthings—servants of Eros, if you will—has never gone entirely out of fashion. Two Mozart operas that center on roguish adulterers remain hugely popular. The countess in the 1786 *The Marriage of Figaro* is the long-suffering wife of a philandering husband who claims the right to take to bed a female servant on her wedding night—*before* the servant's husband does! The countess is, however, rewarded for her patience by getting to sing glorious musical laments—and by obtaining a promise from her philandering husband that he will be faithful, at least until the curtain falls.

Mozart's *Don Giovanni* (1787) is actually a glorification of perhaps the most famous serial seducer of all time, Don Juan. One of his victims, Zerlina, is engaged to marry someone of her own station in life and has sworn fidelity to him, a fact that makes little difference to the Don—and presumably the audience. Though the hero dies at the end and is consigned to hell, we cannot imagine that the intent of Mozart and his librettist, Lorenzo da Ponte, was to make a strong case against male promiscuity.

Adultery, once the primary basis for divorce in the United States, has become less and less an issue as "no-fault" divorces have become the norm. In many circles today, sexual encounters are assumed to be of brief duration, and relationships with numerous partners are accepted standard behavior. Freedom to engage in such relationships does not, however, mean that ending them is always painless. The early songs of the pop singer Taylor Swift almost all concern themselves with break-ups—and with, essentially, getting public revenge on her series of celebrity boyfriends. It is tempting to conclude that, during the eighteenth and nineteenth centuries, tales of philandering outside of marriage were popular *because of*, not despite, the rigid moral codes prevailing. The relaxation of moral codes notwithstanding, physical passion and the pain of lost love remain dramatic subjects.

Agape

13.2 *What is the history of the term* **agape**? *What are some examples of its meaning?*

We should not think *eros* in the humanities has always meant uncontrollable passion that makes people tragic victims or fools. In fact, its opposite, *agape* (ah-ga-pay), is a Greek word meaning simply "love." In the classical world, then, *eros*, or lust, was not considered to be love at all, but something else altogether.

The most famous discourse on the subject came from Plato (427–347 BCE); thus *agape* is often called **Platonic love**. In popular usage, the term "Platonic" has come to mean not only the opposite of lust, but a synonym for a totally nonphysical relationship. As you will see, a truly Platonic friendship involves much more than, say, having a classmate who studies with you while both save other relationships for the weekend!

The Platonic Ideal

In point of fact, Plato's ideal love may indeed include physical union with another, but the philosopher also believed the pleasures of the body can never be the highest possible good. There is no reason to believe he did not enjoy those pleasures, but he saw them as only the first rung on what we may call a ladder to the ideal.

In Platonic philosophy, each of us is born with a soul, the rational capacity for comprehending all of the eternal truths. The soul eventually discovers that it is imprisoned in a body, which is subject to deterioration, pain, and death. The soul, however, is immortal and will find a new home after the present body dies. The constant longing of the soul is therefore to escape from the body.

In his 1629 play *The New Inn*, Ben Jonson (1572–1637) defined Platonic love as "A spiritual coupling of two souls/ So much more excellent as it relates unto the body."

For Plato, a human being's attraction to another on a strictly physical level is at least a step in the right direction because it represents a preoccupation with something other than the self—our temporary home, which, being short-lived, is of no great importance. Besides, the goal of bodily attraction is reproduction, the generation of another life; such generation is likewise closer to immortality than being trapped in the trivial, everyday details of the self. Bringing into existence another life offers us a glimpse of the eternal, because we have for the time being substituted a fresh young life for a decaying, older one. Plato believed, therefore, that physical love can be construed as a good when it is an expression of the need for contact with what is *not* the self. It is not a good when physical attraction becomes obsession with the need to own, to possess, to make the other a part of oneself.

After a time, the soul glimpses higher visions. It longs for contact with other minds, with ideas, with art. One can therefore be in love—Platonically—with another person's mind, a painting, a sculpture, a symphony. One can fall in love with the face of another because it represents a perfect arrangement. In short, one can fall in love with anything as long as it provides aesthetic pleasure and is desirable for its own sake, not for the sake of possession.

One can find a painting in a museum that strongly attracts the soul and sit before it for a long time, wanting only to remain in its presence, even as one might have, at another time, longed to remain in the exciting physical presence of another person. The difference? Why is one said to be a higher good than the other? The answer is that the painting will always be there. The painting is a window through which one sees a little piece of the eternal. With the painting, the soul revisits its home beyond physical reality, where one is in the presence of pure beauty that cannot be tarnished like the things of the material world. Platonic love is a ladder that leads past physical pleasure and upward toward the experience of pure beauty, an experience that cannot be expressed in words, but only felt by the soul.

> [T]he true order of going, or being led . . . to things of love, is to begin from the beauties of earth and mount upwards for the sake of other beauty, using these as steps only, and from one going on to two, and from two to all fair forms, and from fair forms to fair practices, and from fair practices to fair notions, until from fair notions he arrives at the notion of absolute beauty, and at last knows what the essence of beauty is.[7]

For Plato, the highest form of love is the love of the beautiful: in a mind, in art, in life itself.

Christians during the Middle Ages preferred Plato to Aristotle mainly because of his theory of *agape*. Christians believed the Platonic ladder leading from physical desire to a vision of the ideal was in actuality a ladder to God. Platonic love thus became God's love for humanity and, conversely, human spiritual, or holy, love divorced from base passions. Whether Christian-based or not, this idea continues to influence vast numbers and forms the basis for the popular notion that to love Platonically means to refrain from sexual contact.

Platonic Love Reconsidered

Almost none of us can fail to be affected by this idealism that love transcends passion. During a long separation, lovers may imagine each other as they once looked, but in a reunion years later, they can face disappointment. Consider the major ideals of Plato's world: The Good, The True, and The Beautiful. Then consider how the world of the flesh conspires against them. To be alive, to be human, is to change, eventually to be different from before, just as a flower only briefly achieves its potential. The beautiful smiling child in a photograph is for its time the epitome of how a child should look. Part of the pleasure of seeing it is the knowledge that the child has the potential to become something else—larger, smarter, more agile—but different. The separated lovers may compare present reality with old photographs, noting with sadness how the actual person is no longer the ideal person.

Platonism carries with it an ideal worth striving for and yet intrinsically disappointing, even antilife. (An example is the famous song "The Impossible Dream" from *Man of La Mancha*, the 1965 musical version of *Don Quixote*, in which the virtuous knight declares that he will devote his life to pure and beautiful causes. But we note that even he admits his dream is "impossible.")

For the confirmed Platonist, a price must be paid for attempting to live in a world higher than the physical plane. In John Keats's "Ode on a Grecian Urn" (1820), the poet envies the inanimate lovers pictured on the urn as being superior to human lovers because they will not suffer the pains of aging and death: "All human passion far above/ The burning forehead and the parching tongue." The pictured lovers will stay the same: "Forever wilt thou love and she be fair." The poem is just one of many, many works to make the Platonic statement that art is better than life because it does not change; it is one of many works to view the love of art as equivalent to the highest form of love.

The Platonic concept that love in its highest form takes us to the realm of pure beauty that rules supreme at the top of Plato's ladder may have sounded inspiring to lovers and the artists who depict them, but they have also been quick to recognize that few can withstand the rigors of the climb.

In his short story "The Birthmark," Nathaniel Hawthorne recognizes the impossibility of reaching pure perfection, of experiencing ideal beauty. In the story, a husband frequently remarks that his wife is beautiful, almost perfect in fact, except for the small birthmark on her cheek. He thinks he knows a way to remove it, but there may be danger. The wife begs him to try. She wants to appear completely beautiful for the man she loves. With the aid of his assistant, the husband performs an experimental operation and manages to take away the ugly blemish. As the birthmark disappears, the wife dies. Hawthorne is saying that we cannot expect perfection in this world. Humankind is born naturally flawed and can never attain an ideal state in which love is pure and untainted and beauty lasts forever. But is the Platonist injured by striving for it?

Family and Friendship

13.3 *What is meant by love in the context of family and friendship?*

The majority of us take for granted having siblings, cousins, and aunts. These are the close kin who sign letters, cards, and e-mail "with love," hug and kiss us at family gatherings, and expect loyalties and favors from us—even as we expect such in return—without asking why. And most of us have a circle of close friends—people who will help us move, drive us to the airport, and listen when we want to share our deepest thoughts. All these actions are performed under the rubric of the word *love*.

Family Love

Calendars are filled with reminders to demonstrate the kind of family-love once called "togetherness." Advertisements exhort us to "show how much you care" with elaborate gifts and greeting cards. Supermarkets like to show a happy assemblage of relatives around a festive table, the implication being that if we would only shop at Food Stuff somehow all family ties will be restored and all guilt washed away.

Still, we know the truth is rarely as pictured. The French satirist and social reformer François-Marie Arouet, better known as Voltaire (1694–1778), once defined the family as a "group of people who cannot stand the sight of each other but are forced to live under the same roof." The American poet Robert Frost (1874–1963) in his narrative poem *The Death of the Hired Man* has one character observe

> *Home is the place where, when you have to go there,*
> *They have to take you in.*[8]

To be sure, this is not the final word on the subject in the poem, but these lines have become famous and are often quoted as if they did indeed express his philosophy. Sometimes they express the thinking of those who quote them!

How important are blood ties? The concept of family love has changed over time. Once we watched nuclear families, with a working dad, a homemaker mom, and two or three perfect children on television in shows such as *Father Knows Best* or *Ozzie and Harriet*. Then we moved to shows such as *Married with Children* or *Everybody Loves Raymond* (or, for that matter, *The Simpsons*—currently television's longest-running show), where Dad tends to be a bumbling idiot, Mom solves the problems, and the kids are rebellious smart alecks. And a more recent favorite show, *Modern Family*, focuses on three branches of one family—an older dad married to a hot young wife (who often proves smarter than he is), a gay couple with an adopted Asian daughter, and a traditional family with, yes, a bumbling dad *and* a bumbling mom, and three kids who are, more often than not, the problem-solvers (Figure 13.4).

A report from the U.S. Census Bureau tells us that only about 20 percent of the families in this country in 2012 consisted of married couples with children. Almost as many—about 18 percent—of the households with children were comprised differently: single-parent households, nonmarried parents or partners; grandparents raising children. It seems almost impossible, in light of this data, to continue to define "family" as a mother, a father, and children. Indeed, children nowadays easily master complicated family trees consisting of stepparents, grandparents, same-sex partners and spouses, adopted and surrogate-born children, and an array of other members.

Even before the current fluid state of marriage and family, the humanities dealt extensively with family love and its discontents, if only because people enjoyed reading about or watching stories about unhappy, dysfunctional families. One college instructor of playwriting told her class that "if you come from a happy home life, you may never be able to write a play."

Figure 13.4 The cast of *Modern Family* picks up an Emmy for Best Comedy Series in September 2013.
What defines a family?
Elizabeth Goodenough/Everett Collection

Family Conflicts

Think of the many unhappy children in literature and drama, eager to escape parents who don't appreciate them or stepparents who abuse them. Many of the fairy tales familiar to us from childhood, including Cinderella, Snow White, and Hansel and Gretel, focus on evil stepmothers and dysfunctional families. (Indeed, Snow White takes it upon herself to create a new family structure, functioning as the sensible mother in a "family" of seven messy and sometimes difficult dwarf-children.) Similarly, much romantic fiction occupies itself with unhappy couples who we know are meant for each other, but who are kept apart for reasons we often cannot quite understand.

In popular fiction, there is often a happy ending. The runaways return; the couple fall into one another's arms. In more serious work, however, especially on the stage, happy endings are rarer. Theater and literature feature a host of disappointed husbands, wives, fathers, mothers, and offspring who never manage to find themselves or reconcile with one another. And even when the reconciliation does occur, as in the best-selling novel *Gone Girl* (2012) by Gillian Flynn, made into a hit film by David Fincher, happiness is hardly guaranteed. Having framed her husband for her abduction (and having brutally murdered a friend who is protecting her), the cold and calculating wife returns home, and the husband, who has deep flaws of his own, accepts her. Both realize that they are damaged people, deserving of one another.

The humanities are full of epic struggles for family fortunes and hatred between brothers who have had nothing to do with each other for years. The challenges that are almost inevitable as families gather for holidays or in times of crisis are portrayed over and over again in films (*Home for the Holidays*, 1995, and *Four Christmases*, 2008, for example) and theater (the Pulitzer Prize-winning drama *August: Osage County*, 2008, by Tracy Letts, which was made into a 2014 film starring Meryl Streep). Although television commercials show Grandma setting a Christmas turkey on the table to the applause of her loving family, it's the rare family that comes together in this way in the twenty-first century.

Unhappy families are rampant in the arts, from the American theater classics *Death of a Salesman*, by Arthur Miller, and *The Glass Menagerie*, by Tennessee Williams, to the Muggle family of Harry Potter on page and screen. Perhaps some people find solace in reading about and seeing portrayals of families a lot less loving than theirs—or perhaps families, a context that all of us share in some form or another, are simply universally acknowledged settings for both drama and comedy.

The Family in Religion

The ancient Hebrews may have given the world its first idea of the family unit, the one that has survived for so many centuries. In developing the father–children relationship between God and humanity, Judaism also created a model for earthly existence. First came the tribe, the larger group comprised of interrelated families and governed by a patriarch, an older and presumably wiser man with great powers of judgment over all the members. The prominent biblical patriarchs Abraham and Moses are examples. Such an arrangement was logically paralleled by the idea of God the father with the same power over human children. The family circle became sanctified as a means of protecting the larger unit, the tribe. Rules against worshiping false gods or marrying outside the tribe helped to maintain coherence and unity.

Love for God, which included fear and respect, was also demanded for the father of the earthly family. Without obedience there would be no order, and without fear, awe, and respect there could be no obedience. Fear was the means by which the children of a patriarch—and of humanity, as children of God—showed their love. The sometimes wrathful imposition of discipline and punishment (as well as unexpected forgiveness) from both fathers was in turn *their* way of showing love.

Two biblical women, Ruth and Naomi, however, changed the traditional view of the family when, after the death of Ruth's husband, she chose not to return to her original roots but to remain instead with Naomi, her husband's mother, thus forming the basis for a new family.

> *But Ruth said, "Do not press me to leave you or to turn back from following you! Where you go, I will go; where you lodge, I will lodge; your people shall be my people, and your God my God."*

> Ruth 1:16

Even though the giving of the Ten Commandments to Moses is regarded as pivotal in Hebrew history, they have since been perceived as binding on all humanity, not merely those of the lineage of Abraham and Moses. One of the commandments—honor your father and your mother—is a restatement and an enlargement of early tribal requirements, but it has become universally accepted, whether acted upon or not.

Matriarchs and Patriarchs

Two plays by Federico García Lorca (1898–1936) illustrate the tragic consequences of strong parental control. In both, mothers claim the right to steer the destinies of their daughters and to have the final say about when and whom they marry. In *Blood Wedding* (1933), the bride, promised to a man she does not love, runs off with someone else, a solution that cannot end happily in the repressed, traditional Spanish society of Lorca's plays. *The House of Bernarda Alba* (1936) explores the tragic effect of a fiercely dominating matriarch over her daughters in a cheerless household dominated by unbreakable rules of endless mourning, forced chastity, and waiting without joy for an arranged match to materialize.

In a similar vein, a dominating mother in Laura Esquivel's 1989 novel *Like Water for Chocolate* (made into a film in 1992) demands that her daughter marry no one at all in order to continue to cook and otherwise take care of the household. All she can anticipate in life is becoming the caregiver of an aging parent.

John Steinbeck's *The Grapes of Wrath* gave the world one of the most memorable portraits of a matriarch, Ma Joad, who keeps her family together during the Great Depression (Figure 13.5). In the 1930s, the Joad family suffers bank foreclosure on their farm in Oklahoma and joins hundreds of other displaced families, scornfully labeled "Okies," on a grueling migration to the Promised Land of California, only to discover that the promise of abundant field work and high pay was a scam. Because there are so many of them, the impoverished Okies are forced to pick fruit from sunup to sundown for paltry wages. The four men of the Joad family are paid *collectively* one dollar for a day's work. Ma buys a dollar's worth of hamburger from the store operated by the company and watches as her men devour the few scraps of meat. When one of the sons asks if there is any more food, she says in a voice that tries to sound pleasant and hopeful but nonetheless tears at the heart: "No, son, they ain't." They made a dollar, and they ate a dollar's worth of meat. No one noticed that Ma ate nothing. The novel has attained the status of a classic, and Ma Joad, who has taken her place among the great archetypes of the family protector, is heroic in the best sense of that word.

HENRY JAMES, *WASHINGTON SQUARE*   All strong parents in American literature are not as self-sacrificing as Ma Joad. One of the most overbearing fathers is the creation of Henry James (1843–1916) in his 1880 novella *Washington Square*, which inspired a play and film of the 1940s, both called *The Heiress*. This father makes little attempt to conceal his disappointment in his daughter, reminding her that she is less attractive in every way than the mother who died giving birth to her. The daughter is told that she lacks grace and charm and the feminine ability to flirt and make small talk. In an age when a proper marriage is the only suitable future for a physician's daughter, she is continually reminded of her sad deficiencies.

Figure 13.5 Jane Darwell as Ma Joad, along with Henry Fonda as Tom and Russell Simpson as Pa, in *The Grapes of Wrath*, 1940.
Ma Joad is the archetype of a strong matriarch. Some societies are *matriarchal*, and children inherit through the female line. What arguments might support this?
Bettmann/Corbis

At length a suitor appears, a handsome, charming young man, who woos her respectfully and begs her to be his wife. After meeting the man and appraising both his income and career aspirations (or lack of them), the doctor decides the suitor is nothing but a fortune hunter. Why else would such a handsome person take an interest in his daughter? He will, he announces, bequeath all his money to charity if the marriage takes place. The daughter is confident that her suitor will marry her anyway, and the two plan an elopement—but the heroine is left broken-hearted, waiting for the man who claimed to love her and who never comes for her.

Years later, the absent suitor, now full of apologies and renewed declarations of love, reappears. Again she agrees to an elopement—but this time she leaves him pounding at the front door, begging her to forgive him. (The movie version strays somewhat from James's novella.) As his cries fill the empty street, she lights a lamp and goes upstairs to bed. When her aunt asks her how she can be so cruel, the heiress replies with a stony face, "I have been taught by masters."

CONFUCIUS AND FAMILY   For the Chinese sage Confucius (551–479 BCE), *filial piety*, respect for one's parents, is the fundamental value. Confucius provided specific instructions on all aspects of living, but none in greater detail than his rules for honoring one's parents and in-laws. Assuming that most households included several generations, Confucius instructs children to eat whatever food is left over after their elders have finished. They must constantly inquire after the comfort of their parents, whether they are too warm or too cold, whether they have an itch that needs scratching. There are prescribed visits morning and evening, and always obedience is foremost.

> *When sons and wives are ordered to do anything by their parents, they should immediately respond and reverently proceed to do it. In going forward or backward, or turning around, they should be careful and serious. While going out or coming in, while bowing or walking, they should not presume to belch, or cough, to yawn or stretch themselves, to stand on one foot, or to lean against anything.*[9]

The rules set down by Confucius may sound quaint to viewers brought up in a child-centered home and nurtured with the idea that individual happiness is more important than tradition or loyalty to the family. Audiences and readers cheer when the obedient (and therefore repressed) young adult leaves home to seek a fortune far from the restrictive rules of the tribe. Nonetheless, respect for the wisdom of the strong patriarch or matriarch remains alive and well in cultures throughout the world.

One of the reasons for the enduring popularity of the 1964 musical *Fiddler on the Roof* seems to be that its subject matter—the strength of the family unit and its ability to survive oppression—appeals to many who might accept the weakness of family bonds but secretly wish it were otherwise.

Friendship and Love

Unlike his teacher Plato, Aristotle does not speak about love—but he is a strong believer in friendship. He includes it among the highest goods of the happy life. For him, friendship is a strong bond between individuals sharing common interests and moral values, and it is thus suspiciously like Plato's ideal of the perfect nonphysical relationship, except that Platonic love may have as its object something nonhuman, like a work of art.

If *kinfolk* is the traditional word for people related by blood, there ought to be a designation for the friendship that replaces the bonds of family—"super-kin," perhaps, or "kin by choice." The ground-breaking stage hit *Hair* (1967), subtitled "The American Tribal Love-Rock Musical," ushered in the era of the family with a common bond that is not biological, focusing on a spontaneous family of young men and women bonded by a mutual hatred of the war in Vietnam. This family was also environmentally sensitive, singing a warning about the imminent death of our planet unless active measures are taken to save it. At a performance on Earth Day in Chicago in 1976, the audience, customarily invited to join the actors at the curtain call in a dance celebrating life and love, was inspired instead to pour onto the street and help the actors dispose of litter. Well-dressed ladies and gentlemen were photographed on their hands and knees picking up candy wrappers and cigarette butts. The dancing continued on the street for hours, tying up traffic and attracting police officers, many of whom joined this impromptu family in the common cause.

The television sitcom, once the domain of family tales, by the 1970s had also made room for what we might call "manufactured" families. Comedies set in the workplace such as *The Mary Tyler Moore Show* (1970–1977), *M*A*S*H* (1972–1983), and *Cheers* (1982–1993) or among groups of friends like *Seinfeld* (1989–1998), *Friends* (1994–2004), and *How I Met Your Mother* (2005–2014) attracted millions of viewers of all ages year after year. Clearly, these shows struck a responsive note—perhaps because they allowed us to feel less alarmed about the gradual erosion of the **nuclear family**.

Once considered the foundation of our society, the nuclear family, comprising parents, children, and often one or both sets of grandparents, has given way to the *extended family*, which may include blood relatives like aunts, cousins, and stepparents, but may also include lifelong friends and even recent acquaintances with whom quick bonds are established. Shows like *Cheers*, *Friends*, and *How I Met Your Mother* represented the kin-by-choice family in which blood relationships are beside the point. (Even the two related characters in *Friends*, brother and sister Ross and Monica, made little of that tie.) Perhaps the enormous popularity of these family-based shows in which the families are not actually related is evidence that Americans secretly fear the isolation that a swiftly moving, rapidly changing society can bring.

In times gone by, friendship may not have been as desirable as it now seems to be in our fragmented society. In *Hamlet*, for example, Polonius gives his son Laertes some advice before the young man sets out to discover his place in the world: "Neither a borrower nor a lender be;/For loan oft loses both itself and friend. . . ." This advice is tough-minded, isn't it? The implication is that friendship won't withstand either borrowing or lending. If the loan isn't paid back, chances are neither will ever speak to the other again.

Far more cynical is the recommendation made in the novel *Tom Jones* by Henry Fielding (1707–1754) that "when you have made your Fortune by the good Offices of a Friend, you are advised to discard him as soon as you can." In other words, what is a friend if not someone you can use to better your own station in life? One wishes that particular definition were indeed a thing of the past!

BEST FRIENDS   Close in spirit to the super-kin idea of family is the buddy relationship, extolled in two classic novels: Cervantes's *Don Quixote* and Mark Twain's *Huckleberry Finn*. In both cases, the authors create a close bond between two characters, both male, whose bonds seem almost unbreakable.

In *Don Quixote*, the buddies are the Don and his faithful servant, Sancho Panza, who knows exactly how inappropriate his master's acts are but who deeply loves his idealism, however misguided it may be. If love is sometimes defined as caring more for another than for oneself, Sancho Panza, in dedicating his entire life to a man who has lost all sense of reality, nurturing and protecting him from the jeers of the crude world, is the veritable icon of selfless devotion. Whether or not it can exist between friends in the real world, readers may decide for themselves. Sancho is, of course, a servant in the eyes of both the Don and the society around them. The servant's love for the master is the more admirable when we consider that the master is too far gone to appreciate it, and it may actually be that the fragile health of the master makes it easier for the servant to devote his entire being to him.

That relationship has a more recent parallel in Alfred Uhry's 1988 Pulitzer Prize–winning play and Academy Award-winning movie, *Driving Miss Daisy*. The master in this case is a feisty old woman who belongs to Atlanta's moneyed class. The servant is her African-American chauffeur, who understands and accepts the racial barriers separating them but, like Sancho Panza, has a deep-rooted loyalty toward and genuine love for the woman. He does all he can to protect her from the knowledge that she is close to senility and will soon be utterly incapable of even feeding herself. The popularity of both the play and the movie version may be a testament to audience nostalgia for a vanished past in which such unquestioning devotion might have existed. Some argue, however, that the story reflects a highly sentimentalized view of the real world of black and white relationships.

Huckleberry Finn begins with a continuation from Twain's *Tom Sawyer* of the buddy adventures of Huck and Tom, but the author must have realized that Tom was too middle-class, too much of a conformist to fully understand the rebellious Huck—or, perhaps, to fully engage his readers. That friendship is replaced by the much more complicated bond that develops between Huck and Jim, a runaway slave. Once more we have discrepancy in rank and ethnicity; Huck, a white boy who is the ragged, uneducated son of a drunkard and ne'er-do-well, is nevertheless seen by society as superior to Jim, a black man. Jim is the stronger of the two, teaching Huck how to survive the hardships of life on the Mississippi River. The great epiphany of the novel is the moment that Huck, on the verge of reporting Jim's escape in a letter to his owner, tears the letter up, fighting off all the strictures of society that he has been taught. If accepting a black man as an equal and a friend means he is doomed to hell, well, "All right, then, I'll go to hell." This is friendship, but it is, inarguably, also love.

Romantic Love

13.4 *What do we mean—and what has been meant historically—by the term romantic love?*

Most probably, when you first looked at the title of this chapter, you thought of one kind of love in particular, one that has yet to be discussed: **romantic love** (see Figure 13.1). For many, the words *love* and *romance* are synonymous. Perhaps we like to think that the need for such love is inborn. When friends advise that a current suitor is not the right man or woman for you, the implication is that such a person—the right one—must surely exist and will come along eventually. How many people have become lost in self-pity because Mr./Ms. Right has never shown up?

The "right" person is a mythic archetype indigenous to our culture, but not necessarily universal. The prototype of romantic love is, undeniably, Shakespeare's *Romeo and Juliet*, performed almost continuously throughout the world. It is the first work that comes to mind when someone is asked to name a great love story.

Still, as we have pointed out, the famous star-crossed lovers *are* smitten by passionate physical desires in the classical tradition. Near the end of the balcony scene, Juliet tells Romeo she must go inside now, and the anguished young man cries out, "O, wilt thou leave me so unsatisfied?" There is no mistaking what he means. Juliet answers, "What satisfaction canst thou have tonight?" The key word is *tonight*.

But there is more. Shakespeare wrote at a time when women, at least of the upper classes, were no longer mere commodities. Yes, Juliet is destined for an arranged marriage, and yes, its purpose is her financial security as well as the social advantages of uniting two prominent families; but Romeo, after all, is willing to have Juliet despite the fact that if they were to marry both would be cut off without a penny. Hence Juliet is not property in his eyes. The play tells the world there is something more important than financial security or social approval. And that has come to be called romantic—or true—love. The language of the lovers is the language of romance as far as subsequent eras have been concerned. Nobody is saying that romance is an experience entirely separate from sexual passion, but most of us would agree that romance has something more that transcends obsession with sexual union alone. Shakespeare's lovers indeed seem to believe in that something more, and to give up their lives for it (Figure 13.6).

Figure 13.6 Claire Danes as Juliet and Leonardo DiCaprio as Romeo in the 1996 film directed by Baz Luhrmann.
Why do you think *Romeo and Juliet* is considered the archetypal story of romantic love?

Moviepix/20th Century Fox/Getty Images

Love versus Lust: The Language of Romance

Cynics believe the language of romance is all a façade, and that lust is always the reality. Yet the idea of romantic love still exerts such a strong influence on our lives that one must be cautious about calling it a lie or a delusion. Why would romance novels constitute a billion-dollar industry? Why would so many readers be lost without those heroes and heroines who think of nothing but being with each other? Poetry and songs are filled with accounts of the all-consuming emotion defined by the word *romance*, with hearts being won, lost, broken, and crushed. The despairing lover in the classic Cole Porter song "What Is This Thing Called Love?" cries, "You took my heart and threw it away." The heart, not some other part of the body, is the location of romantic feelings.

Romance continues to be talked or written or sung about in terms that exclude all mention of physical desire. Lovers long for one glance, for the touch of a hand, for an ascent to paradise. Romeo and Juliet elevate their passion through verse. The *West Side Story* lovers in their version of Shakespeare's play do so by thrilling audiences with "Maria" and "Tonight." Even if so many of the pop tunes of today deal with the torments of finding that one's true love is cheating, even if romance is considered a *tragic* state, the fact remains that it is the basis of hopes and dreams for millions, the thing most worth striving for. It must therefore be a real force. And, if it comes from the humanities, why, what better testament to the power of myth, art, and literature? Where would we be without them?

The language of romance is exactly what we do not find in the writings of the Greek and Roman philosophers. Except for Plato, they were strictly earthbound; they saw love as an affliction, often terrible, that drives people into desperate fires of longing. Love may be fun for a time, but unless one is willing to suffer, one is better off without it. Plato, with his ladder that leads to the ideal, paved the way for the eventual emergence of the belief that ideal love transcends the flesh.

The notion of the love that transcends lust and lasts through and beyond time may have been glimpsed by Plato, but it grew firm roots in the Middle Ages. We can cite these sources for its growth and spread, and its continued hold on our emotions:

- The cult that grew up around the poets and artists who celebrated the glory of the Virgin Mary;
- The *romance* itself, a sophisticated genre of literature about a (usually highborn) young man or woman for whom physical union is not allowed; one partner may be married or have obstinate parents;
- The code of chivalry, a set of generally elegant actions performed by a knight to honor his lady fair including, if need be, laying down his life for her in jousting tournaments, and its offshoot, the game of courtly love.

Mariolatry

The writings of the Christian Bible do not say much about Mary, but as the religion spread and the Christian tradition grew during the Middle Ages, the subject of the mother of Jesus became a matter of increasing fascination. Madonna and Child were favorite subjects for medieval and, later, Renaissance painters and sculptors. Poets waxed eloquent about Mary as the perfect woman, and particularly about her chastity. Though the virgin birth was not always easy to comprehend, no one doubted the purity of Mary; and since Mary was mortal, not divine, her purity and glory encouraged reverence for other women as well, women deemed to be superior to men— virtually "above" them, as if they were on a pedestal, or in a tower, from which they could wave and provide inspiration to the adoring men below. Of course, such status deprived women of any serious engagement in the world of work or government.

Idolatry of Mary, or **Mariolatry**, led to innumerable kinds of artistic expression, and it carried over into secular literature as writers borrowed the idea of the virginal heroine, worshiped for her purity as the poets worshiped Mary. Earthly love was thus presented in spiritual terms, even if lust were secretly there as well.

The same period saw a rebirth of interest in Plato's theory of love. It now became readily understood as the pursuit of an ideal love—pure, chaste, true, and undefiled by lust—that cannot be destroyed, even in the grave. This ideal continues to color the relationships between men and women to this very day.

The Knight in Shining Armor

The **romance** is a literary genre that emerged in the eleventh and twelfth centuries. The word itself derives from the French *roman*, a long fictional narrative. Today the word is translated as "novel." Early romances were transmitted orally, rather than being written down; there was no printing press, and storytelling had by then become an art form. Though they usually revolved around a man-woman relationship, the stories were not always about love but might include perilous journeys to distant lands in search of a treasure such as the Holy Grail. Told from the Christian point of view, they often spoke of the dangers lying in wait for noble knights in combat with "infidels." Many of the best-loved romances from this period were stories about King Arthur, Lancelot and Guinevere, Camelot, and the knights of the Round Table. These Arthurian tales were gathered into a single volume, *Le Morte d'Arthur*, by Sir Thomas Malory and first published in 1485, and they have since provided inspiration for writers such as the Victorian poet Alfred, Lord Tennyson (*Idylls of the King*, published between 1859 and 1885) and T.H. White (*The Once and Future King*, 1958).

THE RULES OF CHIVALRY   The word *chivalry* also had its origin in France, coming from the word *cheval* (horse). The dashing knight on his horse had many admirable qualities, including a willingness to fight to the death in the name of his lady. All that was required of her was that she allow him to risk his life, perhaps while wearing a scarf she had given him as a token of the honor she bestowed. Thus was born the tradition of placing the lady on a pedestal and of expecting nothing in return, should she be disposed to offer nothing. Chivalry, the knight's code, was the ancestor of the polite gestures that are often performed and expected, such as opening doors, pulling out chairs, and in general placing the lady first in any order of events. (The gentlemanly practice of walking nearer to the curb is a latter-day version of chivalry, originally meant to spare the lady from being splattered with mud from carriages racing by.)

In many of the stories, even if the lady were willing to offer herself to the gallant gentleman, they could not form a lasting union because one of them was already married or otherwise unavailable. Typically such marriages were arranged by families more interested in property and financial gain than in the happiness of the offspring. Perhaps the loving couple experienced a few moments of physical gratification in secret, but on the surface was the assumption that love denied was nobler than a loveless marriage.

A second assumption was that true love was made in heaven and was therefore elevated above earthly concerns such as bodily pleasure and marriages of convenience and the wealth they brought. The belief that heaven destines each of us for someone else and that this someone is the right and only mate has persisted through the centuries. Even if no union ever takes place between two right people, the rightness lasts forever.

Courtly Love

During the twelfth century, Queen Eleanor of Aquitaine, wife of France's Louis VII and later England's King Henry II and mother of Richard the Lion-Hearted, inaugurated a form of entertainment that eventually spread to other royal courts and became known as **courtly love**. In order to amuse themselves, Eleanor and her circle of aristocratic friends would hold mock trials in which the defendant, a young man who had declared his passionate longing for a reluctant young woman, was given a series of difficult tasks to perform in order to win her approval. The "jury" would hear the case—that is, the young man's account of all he had done to win the lady's favor—and then decide whether such favor should be granted. Most of the time it was not, an outcome that was in no way expected to diminish the plaintiff's devotion.

Becoming known more precisely as a set of rules for the proper conduct of courtship, courtly love was based on the recommendations of Eleanor and others as they developed this "harmless" diversion. The idea that a high-bred woman was born to be adored and a man to be her virtual slave was implicit, if not directly stated, in the romances so that by the time rules were actually set down, there was little objection from the masculine side.

In *Don Quixote*, Cervantes created his own version of courtly love. The mad hero, who imagines himself to be a courageous knight, mistakes a peasant girl named Aldonza for a fair lady of his own invention, whom he calls Dulcinea. In his delusion he imagines she is pure and unreachable, and he makes himself her slave. The Don invites her to ask anything of him, even his very life.

In 1507, the long-standing rules of courtly love were altered in a book called *The Courtier* by Baldassare Castiglione (1478–1529), in which the tempering effect of the Renaissance begins to be felt. Though still powerful, the woman is now less cruel; instead, she is well-educated, charming, witty, and sophisticated, and she requires a suitor to be her match—or nearly so. She still refuses to lose control no matter how much she secretly admires the man, and while he is expected to sue for a physical encounter, she is not supposed to grant it. The rules, however, have changed. To surrender to him would coarsen what was thought to be an entirely civilized relationship. She anticipates some of Shakespeare's wittiest and most independent heroines, who adore privately but hurl insults publicly!

Romance and the Game of Love

The Roman poet Ovid (43 BCE–18 CE), who specialized in writing about the subject, defines love as "a game of seduction." Whether readers of Castiglione agreed and privately enjoyed physical encounters behind bedroom doors, we cannot be entirely sure. During the seventeenth century—again, among the highborn and well-bred—the game of seduction became quite fashionable, often as a way of making the satisfaction of lust more delicious. Courtship began as a verbal match between educated and witty partners and ended in a physical or physical-romantic union, only if preceded by stylish playfulness. The game of love has provided us with some of literature's most memorable dialog and charming characters. (Whether it will continue to do so depends on the willingness of authors, playwrights, and scriptwriters to provide clever talk—and whether audiences and readers will have the patience to listen.)

In England, especially during the period known as the Restoration (beginning in 1660, when monarchy was reinstated after 20 years of unsuccessful democracy), the sexes reached an equality exceeding even that of the late Middle Ages. Charles II adored women and encouraged them to show their strength. In this period, women took two steps forward—before the nineteenth century would take them three steps back.

CONGREVE'S *THE WAY OF THE WORLD* Eighteenth-century English theater sparkled with plays about the game of seduction. The most glittering couple to grace the stage at that time were Mirabell and Millamant in *The Way of the World* (1700), written by William Congreve (1670–1729). Like Benedick and Beatrice in Shakespeare's *Much Ado about Nothing*, the couple hide their intense feelings for each other behind a dazzling display of linguistic skill.

"Rules of the game" are observed by the couple, who openly scorn sentimentality and sincere vows. They speak curtly to each other and throw challenges back and forth designed to keep observers unaware of the game they are playing. Millamant sounds downright cruel when she laughs at her lover's serious face and talks of using his letters to roll up her hair. She will not entertain a proposal of marriage, despite her yearning to do just that. Rather, according to the fashion of the day, she declares that she will not surrender her cherished solitude.

For his part, Mirabell is no saint. His multiple affairs have led, in all probability, to his fathering a child. Nor is he foolish enough to suggest to Millamant that they elope without the approval of her aunt and guardian, who controls Millamant's fortune. Instead, he uses his wits and ingenuity to both embarrass the guardian and gain her approval—and Millamant's riches. Neither Millamant nor the audience would

Figure 13.7 Spencer Tracy and Katharine Hepburn in *Adam's Rib*, **1949.**

Can romance be enhanced by competition? How important is gender equality to true love?

Digital Press Photos/Newscom

have expected Mirabell to be morally perfect. In this sophisticated society, toughness was required for survival, and true love exists only as part of a high-stakes game.

The lovers in *The Way of the World* do finally come together, after signing what we would now call a prenup agreement laying out expected behaviors (he has to ask respectfully for her sexual favors; she has to cut back on her alcohol consumption). After three centuries, Millamant and Mirabell still stand as icons of how sophisticated people can hold their own in an unsentimental environment and yet not forego the pleasures of romance.

TRACY AND HEPBURN   A somewhat newer version of love-as-a-game was popular during the late 1940s, in a series of classic films starring Spencer Tracy and Katharine Hepburn, who were off-screen lovers and whose screen chemistry has perhaps never been equaled. One Tracy-Hepburn classic is *Adam's Rib* (1949) (Figure 13.7). Their married characters play successful lawyers—he as a prosecuting attorney, she as a defense attorney—who are arguing opposite sides in the trial of a woman who has shot and seriously wounded her unfaithful husband. Tracy's character insists that, despite his wife's efforts to convince the jury that the woman was only defending her home, no one has the right to violate the law and therefore the defendant must be sent to prison. The married lawyers go at it stormily in court (but in one priceless scene, they wave to each other under the table). Hepburn wins, and Tracy is furious with her *on the surface*. Underneath, both are modern Mirabells and Millamants, closet romantic lovers.

Yearning for the Unattainable: *The Divine Comedy* and the Tale of Tristan and Isolde

One of the enduring romantic and unconsummated relationships in the Middle Ages was that of the poet Dante Alighieri and the woman he called Beatrice, whom he first saw when he was 9 years old and whom he later immortalized in *The Divine Comedy*:

> *At that moment, I say most truly that the spirit of life, which hath its dwelling in the secretest chamber of the heart, began to tremble so violently that the least pulses of my body shook therewith; and trembling it said these words "Here is a deity stronger than I; who, coming, shall rule over me . . ." I in my boyhood often went in search of her, and found her so noble and praiseworthy that certainly of her might have been said those words of the poet Homer, "She seemed not to be the daughter of a mortal man, but of God."*[10]

Dante's overwhelming attraction toward Beatrice was, he said, the inspiration behind the hundred **cantos** of *The Divine Comedy*. His love is the reason that he, as narrator of the poem, is willing to undertake the arduous journey through the Inferno and Purgatory before reaching Paradise. It is understood that he will never be able to enjoy Beatrice's love in any mortal way.

In Canto V of his poem, Dante visits the second circle of hell (the Inferno) in which exist the souls of carnal sinners, who must suffer eternal punishment for their unsanctified lust. Because illicit passion had swept them off their feet, they can now find no rest. Still, in the tragic tale of Paolo and Francesca, two of the doomed lovers, the poet, while not justifying their sin, nonetheless is compassionate toward them. In fact, the reason he does not place them in lower circles where punishment is far more severe is that, even though they were misguided, at least they *loved*. The lowest circle is reserved for Satan, who represents the total absence of love.

Paolo is the brother of a man in an arranged marriage to Francesca; he is sent to inform the lady of the parents' wishes. One day, however, they are so strongly affected by reading about the passion of an Arthurian knight that they fall into each other's arms, unable to keep from enjoying the strong sexual feelings that overwhelm them. Francesca explains to the poet-narrator:

> *We were alone and without any dread.*
> *Sometimes our eyes, at the word's secret call,*
> *Met, and our cheeks a changing color wore.*
> *But it was one page only that did all.*
> *When we read how that smile, so thirsted for,*
> *Was kissed by such a lover, he that may*
> *Never from me be separated more*
> *All trembling kissed my mouth . . .*[11]

TRISTAN AND ISOLDE   Yearning and aspiration toward an unreachable beloved is a frequent feature of romantic love. Domesticity is not. Stories about romantic love tend, rather, to feature not wedding anniversaries and visits from in-laws and grandchildren, but the death of one or both lovers. Lovers of music are the beneficiaries of their suffering, as, for example, in the erotic yet also spiritual "Liebestod" (Love-Death) from the opera *Tristan and Isolde*, composed between 1857 and 1859 by Richard Wagner to celebrate his love for a married woman. As in the story of Paolo and Francesca, Isolde, the heroine, has been promised to another, in this case King Mark, and is escorted to the wedding by the king's nephew Tristan (Figure 13.8). On the ship, they unwittingly drink a love potion that creates feelings too powerful to resist.

Like much romantic art, the opera carries the implied message that illicit love is short-lived but wonderful enough to make early death worthwhile. Ordinary mortals who adhere to the rules are shown to have safe but dull lives. True love is therefore often combined with death. In the final scene, Isolde kneels by the body of her lover and sings the "Liebestod," perhaps the most sexually explicit as well as passionately romantic music ever written. Its rising melodic line and crescendo, its sonorous chords becoming a musical parallel to the sex act itself (according to many interpretations) reach a glorious high note of ecstasy before resolving in a serene aftermath, which brings peace and death to Isolde as she rests on the body of her lover.

If, as cynics like to say, romantic love is pure balderdash, we must be proud of a human tradition that can so nobly celebrate and create its reality.

Love and Marriage

13.5 *How has the concept of love in marriage evolved?*

You may have noticed that we haven't talked much about marriage thus far in this chapter. Marriage deserves its own special treatment, because sometimes convenience or pre-arrangements outweigh love as the reason to marry; sometimes romantic love is present at the outset but diminishes as time goes on; and often, quite often, differences of opinion about **gender roles** interfere with the course of true love. And, yes, true love can remain throughout the course of a lifetime. Clearly, no institution, especially in modern society, is quite so complex.

The Victorian Model

A strong moral code emerged on both sides of the Atlantic during Queen Victoria's reign (1837–1901). The Victorian era was the heyday of the upper-middle

Figure 13.8 Illustration from *Tristan* by Goffredo of Strasbourg, 13th century: King Mark exiles Tristan and Isolde (top), and later discovers Tristan and Isolde dead in a cave (bottom).

Do you think "forbidden" love is somehow more intense than love that can be easily achieved? Why?

DEA Picture Library/De Agostini Picture Library/Getty Images class, which decided to forget its humble past and start living "correctly" in what it believed to be the manner of the aristocracies of old. It created the most stringent code of behavior any society had ever known.

The Victorian model saw marriage as not only the goal but the duty of respectable men and women, the prime—really, the only—source of true happiness. Specific gender roles were assigned. The husband was the breadwinner. The status of men was thus elevated, and women saw their importance diminished—even when the wife's inheritance was the source of a family's income. If you watched any of the British hit series *Downton Abbey* (broadcast in the United States from 2011 through 2016), for example, you will be aware that the wealth of the American heiress Cora, which keeps the family afloat, was the reason Lord Grantham proposed to her—although love eventually grew between the lord and his lady.

Even though Victorian England was ruled by a woman, the husband was clearly the dominant figure in every household, making the big decisions about where the family would live, what kind of education the children would receive, and, of course, when and whom the children would marry. If daughters were likely to be married off to promising future executives, sons were frequently earmarked for wives who would bring with them generous dowries.

The wife's job was to run a household successfully. She dealt with the servants, chose the menus (always with an eye to pleasing her husband's tastes), and, on appropriate occasions, showed off her husband's net worth. The still prevalent phrase **conspicuous consumption** was coined in 1901 by economist Thorstein Veblen (1857–1929) to describe the spending habits of this money-conscious society, which included the wife's costly apparel and display of fine jewelry as demonstrations of her husband's success.

One of the best visualizations of the Victorian middle class can be found in *A Sunday Afternoon on the Island of La Grande Jatte* (1884), painted by Georges Seurat (1859–1891) in what was considered a revolutionary and controversial style known as *pointillism* (Figure 13.9). Instead of brushstrokes, the artist creates his images by dabbing at the canvas with the tip of a tightly rolled brush dipped in the desired colors. The effect gives the scene an almost unearthly appearance that can suggest the lack of substance in this stiff society in which proper manners were everything.

The Double Standard

Out of Victorian society emerged a **double standard** that haunted gender relationships for many years: The woman, but not the man, was expected to remain a virgin until the wedding night. The groom had the right to wed a bride untouched by other men, regardless of his own past (or present) escapades. An adulterous wife was ostracized forever from polite society, but a husband suspected of indulging in extramarital affairs usually incurred only mischievous winks from other men. Wives were not supposed to mention the subject. Novel after novel, play after play during the Victorian age showed the disasters that befell women who broke the moral code.

Remnants of the double standard remain today in varying degrees of acceptability. They continue to be influential, even admired, especially among those who value traditional institutions such as carefully specified gender roles that provide clear rules about the obligations of each member of the household. Such conventional double standards should not be confused, however, with religious inhibitions that also set clear rules about gender roles. In many societies today, a patriarchal system

Figure 13.9 Georges Seurat, *A Sunday Afternoon on the Island of La Grande Jatte*, 1884.
How does this painting reflect the mores of Victorian society?
Erich Lessing/Art Resource, NY

remains, marriages are arranged for toddlers, educational opportunities are minimal or nonexistent for girls, women are prevented from showing their faces in public, and in custody disputes, children are expected to remain with their father.

Marriage Today

When U.S. Census statistics suggest that the number of married couples with children is steadily shrinking and the numbers of single-person households and non-married-couple households are steadily growing, how important is marriage today? We might say, less important than it used to be. But how, then, to account for the massive political and social movement pushing for same-sex couples to enjoy the benefits—whatever they may be—of legally approved marriages? And what changes are we seeing in the institution of marriage? In many countries, including the United States, marriage is now available to all couples regardless of their sex. How are previous norms reflected—or not reflected—in twenty-first-century marriages?

Certainly most of us are freer to choose than we have ever been—to choose mates of differing ethnicities, races, social classes; to choose mates of the same gender; not to choose mates at all. Many of us live together for years before getting married; many of us marry multiple times (serial marriages, these are called) or marry too young and find ourselves eager to get out (starter marriages, we call these). The traditional rationale for marriage—to reproduce—is tossed to the winds by celebrities who produce multiple children from multiple relationships, in and out of marriage, or by those who choose not to have children at all (a rising percentage in the United States, according to Census records). Let's look at some of the changes that are occurring now, in this country and to some extent globally, and are changing the way we think about love.

Variations on a Theme

13.6 *How has our notion of love changed in the twentieth and twenty-first centuries?*

Despite current cynicism about the way family life used to be shown, differing attitudes toward love that we have reviewed in this chapter, including the Victorian model, continue to influence our hopes and expectations. Many of us still await that "knight in shining armor" created by stories of chivalric love, or the virginal wife required in the Victorian age. The double standard too often still applies: men who play around are admired; women who do the same are not. We still look for passion (*eros*), it seems, even while we acknowledge that deep friendship (*agape*) may actually be the key to a long relationship.

But large societal changes have also brought changes to the way we think about love itself. These include the feminist movement of the mid-twentieth century, the gay rights movement of the late twentieth century (and especially the efforts to legalize same-sex marriage in recent years), and the concerns generated by an aging population.

Feminism

Feminist movement leaders in the 1960s called for the abolition of marriage, an institution that they saw as supporting gender inequality and rigged against women. Many women who came of age in the early days of feminism were reluctant to marry, and many more married but retained their own names and identities within their marriages. Women—some who are now hesitant to label themselves feminists—continue to advocate for equality within marriage, including the Facebook executive Sheryl Sandberg, whose 2013 book *Lean In* guides women to a more aggressive presence in the world of business.

Feminist thinking sees no reason not to be frank and open in matters of intimate relationships, even if it means denying that love alone makes life complete. The heroine of Wendy Wasserstein's Pulitzer Prize–winning play *The Heidi Chronicles* (1988), revived in 2015 with the *Mad Men* star Elisabeth Moss in the lead, learns that love need not be *the* pivotal event in anyone's life. After several disappointing relationships, including one with a gay doctor, Heidi, in a final scene that is anything but poignant, feels totally free to continue her life without a long-term commitment to anyone—except the child she has decided to adopt on her own.

The myth that feminists have found perhaps most difficult to shake is the Cinderella fantasy that somewhere out there is a prince for a potential princess. Like the knight-on-the-white-horse myth, the Cinderella fantasy has led many women to wait for the perfect man—who very likely does not exist. A 2011 book, *Marry Him: The Case for Settling for Mr. Good Enough*, by Lori Gottlieb, sparked a continuing conversation about the problems of setting one's sights on that ideal man.

Perhaps the most influential peddler of the Cinderella myth over the years has been Disney Studios. After 50 years of creating princesses whose only goal was to find an appropriate prince, Disney released *Beauty and the Beast* in 1991, the story of a free-thinking young woman who rejects one suitor and, yes, does find true love, but does not define her life solely by that relationship. Later Disney films have continued to focus on brave, independent heroines (*Pocahontas*, 1995; *Mulan*, 1998; *Brave*, 2012; *Frozen*, 2013). Despite their ability to fend for themselves, however, in the earlier movies the heroine eventually, inevitably, ends up in the arms of a man—one who is deserving of her, to be sure, but still, a man. With *Brave* and *Frozen*, Disney finally lets go and shows us heroines who don't fulfill the romantic dream.

Gay Love

The fastest-moving civil rights movement of the twenty-first century has been the push for marriage equality. Indeed, just as we finished revising this book, the Supreme Court of the United States ruled that the Constitution guarantees a right to same-sex marriage, bringing marriage equality to all 50 states. Throughout the world, almost 20 countries perform or recognize same-sex marriage, ranging from Argentina and Brazil to Ireland, Israel, and South Africa. What does it suggest about the institution of marriage? It suggests that the institution is flexible, that it allows for change, and that marriage is considered by most people as a basic human right, one that should be available to all.

Gay love has made itself known explicitly or, more often, been hinted at in the humanities since time immemorial. Although Homer doesn't say so, later writers have been quick to suggest the close friendship between the hero Achilles and his fellow soldier Patroclus was something more. Legend has it that the emperor Hadrian (76–138) had a homosexual relationship with his young (and beautiful) Greek protégé Antinous, and the emperor Nero (37–68) certainly had gay lovers. In the nineteenth century, Walt Whitman's *Leaves of Grass* (1855) celebrated sexuality and in particular "the manly love of comrades" explicitly enough that scandalized readers burned the book. And *Moby-Dick's* Ishmael finds himself, while waiting to board his whaling ship, sharing what he calls the "matrimonial bed" with his soon-to-be shipmate Queequeg; in the morning when they wake, Ishmael discovers that Queequeg has thrown an arm over him in a "most loving and affectionate manner. You had almost thought I had been his wife."

LOVE IN THE TIME OF AIDS The pairing of love and disease has a long history in the humanities—especially in opera, in the likes of Verdi's *La traviata* and Puccini's *La bohème*—and pairing came to the fore during the 1980s, with the emergence of the AIDS epidemic. AIDS had a tremendous effect on the entertainment world; many actors and dancers succumbed quickly to the disease in its early days, when medical treatments were less advanced than they are now. Writers gave us plays and films about love that strengthens and deepens under the shadow of inevitable death, about dying men cared for by lovers who might otherwise have never shown the ability to care more for another than they do for themselves.

Larry Kramer's play *The Normal Heart* (1985), revived in 2011 and televised in 2014, contains a powerful and heartbreaking scene. The caregiving lover of a man near death from AIDS returns home with a bag of groceries, hoping to induce his dying partner to eat something, only to find him on the floor shaking from an unstoppable fever. The caregiver's profound grief suddenly erupts into anger at death, at his lover for leaving him, and at the whole complacent society that pretends none of this is happening. In his rage, he hurls groceries at the pitiable figure on the floor, screaming invectives through his tears. An equally memorable scene occurs at the end of Craig Lucas's *Longtime Companion* (1989) when a man holds his dying lover in his arms and gives him permission to "let go," even though it means leaving him forever.

Being Old and in Love

If thousands upon thousands of younger people have been lost to AIDS, thousands of older people have found their life spans greatly lengthened with the emergence of once unavailable drugs and medical treatments. In addition to experiencing unexpected and continued health, many senior citizens now face a different kind of problem: how to overcome society's (and their own) stereotyped notions of what is and is not acceptable behavior for people past 60—say, to go on dates.

According to Colombian-born Nobel Prize winner Gabriel García Márquez (1928–2014), one is never too old to love and be loved. His 1985 novel *Love in the Time of Cholera*—made into a 2007 film of the same title—deals with both disease and aging. In the beginning of the story, Florentino Ariza, a rather gangly and awkward young man, is overwhelmingly attracted to Fermina Daza. The lady, however, marries a successful doctor, partly because she finds her relentless suitor Florentino peculiar, if not repulsive. Nonetheless, the ardent admirer remains unmarried and loyal to his lady love for over 50 years. When at length Fermina's husband dies, Florentino renews his suit, though by now both have reached an age when there should be no question of sexual attraction.

Nonetheless, Fermina agrees to marriage, if only out of weariness from having repelled Florentino's advances for so long. At first she has no intention of sharing her body with him as they set sail on a long voyage to escape the cholera epidemic that is ravaging the country. One night, however, Fermina submits to his ceaseless demands:

> Then he looked at her and saw her naked to the waist, just as he had imagined her. Her shoulders were wrinkled; her breasts sagged, her ribs were covered by a flabby skin as pale and cold as a frog's. She covered her chest with the blouse she had just taken off, and she turned out the light. Then he sat up and began to undress in the darkness, throwing everything at her that he took off, while she threw it back, dying of laughter.[12]

So what is love in this instance? We cannot say the word is inappropriate or has no sexual connotations, for this geriatric couple indulge in passionate sex incessantly after their wedding night. It is their saving grace. Their love is not Platonic, for, having lost touch for over half a century, they know almost nothing of each other's mind. What they have, however, is assuredly good and seems to be the author's almost mystic answer to the world's problems.

It certainly beats hate, doesn't it?

Imagining a World without Love

Warnings about separating love and sex are evident in three works of fiction that attack **utopianism**, the belief that there are ideal ways to plan and run a society. This belief goes all the way back to *The Republic* of Plato, who describes a society in which parents give their newborns into the care of the state, which will raise them to become rational human beings, free of emotional ties, understanding that marriage is for reproduction only.

In Aldous Huxley's novel *Brave New World* (1932), there are no emotional quandaries that cannot be solved by popping a pill called "soma." Sex is easily available for pleasure alone, without guilt or responsibility. Couples get together briefly, enjoy themselves, and move on to other partners. This behavior is not only condoned but demanded by the state. Skilled scientists take care of reproduction through in vitro fertilization. Children are thus conceived and born in the laboratory. The babies have no connection with parents; they all immediately become wards of the state, to be carefully conditioned and monitored as productive citizens of the future.

The only taboo is affection for another person: in other words, sex yes, love no. In a world carefully engineered for efficiency, love would only get in the way. Something inside Huxley's main character, however, tells him that there is more to life than this, that he is missing out on something. He manages to escape this utopia and wanders far away, where he finds and joins a group of people living as a nuclear family. For the first time in his life he is happy.

In George Orwell's *1984* (written in 1949), love is again forbidden on grounds of being contrary to the interests of the state ruled by the unseen Big Brother, who watches everybody constantly. The novel gave rise to the immortal phrase "Big Brother is watching you," now used to describe surveillance technology in public buildings, the monitoring of protest marches, and the proliferation of bugging devices. Two of the citizens break all rules by falling in love and indulging in sexual relations, only to have their most intimate moments and private conversations discovered and exposed. Their punishment is to be sent for brainwashing at a rehabilitation center, called ironically the Ministry of Love. When Orwell wrote the novel, World War II had just ended and Soviet communism was being declared the next great enemy of the West. The book remains a powerful anti-utopian statement, but more than that, a powerful warning against government intrusion into the right of individual privacy.

In Margaret Atwood's novel *The Handmaid's Tale* (1985), all rights have been taken from women. They are denied education, careers of their choice, and the ability to choose a mate based on love. The handmaid of the title is a slave who must always wear an identifying garment; her name, Offred, means she is owned by a man named Fred. When they have sex, as is required when a handmaid is in her fertile period, Fred's wife is present to oversee the process. The child will then belong to the husband and wife. Atwood shows that the powers of the state, even in a democracy, can be used as instruments of oppression against those deemed undesirable.

The theme that runs through these three novels is that love is a natural instinct and cannot be denied or controlled by outside forces. Some may argue that *this* version of love is ultimately based only on the sexual drive. Or is there more to it than that?

The Freedom to Choose

One of the major lessons the humanities teach us is that all of us are free to choose, and that includes the freedom to define love in a way that is most meaningful for us. Will chivalry be an important component of our love life? Or a video on eHarmony? Will love be defined as a return to the stability of unbreakable family ties? Or as a game that is not expected to last?

We may choose to remain single without feeling the need to travel with or arrive at a social event with a lifetime partner. We may be comfortable behaving according to the traditional rules requiring us to marry someone from a background acceptable to our family and friends and fitting into accepted gender roles. We may make our own rules, unconcerned about which partner earns more money, which one is considerably older or younger than the other, or even whether a relationship that seems so right at the moment will or must last a lifetime.

Or we may decide love is not to be defined, only to be experienced, as the poet Hannah Kahn would have us believe.

SIGNATURE

If I sing because I must
being made of singing dust,

and I cry because of need
being made of watered seed,

and I grow like twisted tree
having neither symmetry

nor the structure to avert
the falling axe, the minor hurt,

yet of one thing I am sure
that this bears my signature

that I knew love when it came
and I called it by its name.[13]

Looking Back

In this chapter,

- we discussed the history of *eros* and offered examples of its meaning,
- we did the same for the term *agape*,
- we looked at love in the context of both family and friendship,
- we explored the long history of *romantic love*, including chivalry, courtly love, and love as a game,
- we examined love in the context of marriage, and
- we discussed some major social change movements that have impacted the way we look at love in the twenty-first century.

Key Terms

agape Greek term defining actions of the spirit or soul (in an intellectual or aesthetic sense) including love for another's mind; adopted by Christianity as love for God and one's fellow beings; generally understood as the opposite of sexual love.

canto A division of a long poem, such as in *The Divine Comedy*, corresponding to a chapter in a book.

conspicuous consumption Phrase coined by Thorstein Veblen to explain the economic habits of the Victorian-era middle and upper classes, connoting the desire to make a public display of one's wealth.

courtly love An artificial and codified set of rules governing the mating behavior of the upper classes during the late Middle Ages and the Renaissance; principal among these was the right of the lady to make

any demands she wished in order to test the loyalty and devotion of her suitor.

double standard Originally a reference to the right of the husband, but not the wife, to have had sex before, and often outside of and during, marriage.

eros Greek term used as the opposite of agape, referring to the appetites of passion and the flesh.

gender role The way society defines the rights and responsibilities of each sex, especially within marriage.

goliard A medieval troubadour, usually a young man training for the priesthood, who sang songs extolling the hedonistic life and encouraging others to enjoy themselves before entering austere holy orders.

Mariolatry The idealization of the Virgin Mary as practiced by a late medieval cult of poets and painters; not only did the practice ennoble the life and characteristics of the mother of Jesus but it also tended to elevate the status of upper-class women and women in holy orders.

nuclear family The traditional family unit of father, mother, and children; once including grandparents but less apt to now.

Platonic love Originally an ideal relationship between two compatible minds, one that may have begun as physical passion but moved to a higher plane that includes mutual intellectual and aesthetic interests; it can also define one's love for an idea or work of art or the physical beauty of another divorced from any desire to possess it; in popular usage, it connotes simply a relationship without sex.

romance A genre of fiction originating in the Middle Ages, then featuring the exploits of a dashing knight and his pure love for a lady fair for whom he is willing to die—and often does.

romantic love A relationship that may or may not include sex; most important are tender feelings and a desire to be with the other person for the sake of that person, not for the satisfaction of personal desires.

utopianism A belief that the ideal society can be planned and rationally administered.

Chapter 14
Life-Affirmation

Learning Objectives

14.1 Describe the ways in which death is imagined and celebrated.

14.2 Discuss the ways in which death is portrayed in the popular arts, and explain why these portrayals are often so compelling to audiences.

14.3 Explain the various strategies people use to affirm life and deal with the fear of death.

14.4 Describe ways in which literature, music, and philosophy help humanity understand death and affirm life.

14.5 Analyze various models of life-affirmation.

Figure 14.1 Mourners at a funeral procession in New Orleans, where exuberant music is often a critical part of the ceremony.
Is death a cause for sadness or celebration? On what might the answer to this question depend?

Philip Gould/Corbis/Documentary Value/Corbis

Many of us seek confirmation in art that "life is good." Even if the story is filled with vampires and villains, the ending for the heroic characters must be what we would want for ourselves. After all, why read, view, or listen to material that is depressing? Others, however, argue that art should reveal the truth of human experience—some of it life-affirming, and some of it not—and suggest that we harm ourselves by hiding from the truth, which is that we all, eventually, die. Insisting on never-ending optimism and refusing to acknowledge mortality may bring temporary comfort, but we cannot go down this path forever.

In this chapter, we explore how death has been portrayed in the arts through the centuries, both literally and symbolically; the stories we have created about what happens after death; how the arts have capitalized on both our fear of and fascination with death; and the strategies we have developed for dealing with those fears and fascinations.

Being Mortal: How We Portray and Celebrate Death

14.1 *In what ways is death imagined and celebrated?*

How do we benefit from the ways in which the arts use death, and the affirmation of life, as subject matter? In at least two ways: First, we benefit because experiencing intense creativity is in itself life-affirming for *us*; and second, we benefit from the reminder that we too may face problems as our lives unfold, and that ignoring them is a life-denying act. Once recognized and accepted, our mortality loses some of its terror.

Inconsistency of belief is one kind of death-in-life. Some beliefs are at cross purposes with each other: For instance, a belief in the happiness to come in an afterlife struggles against the belief that one cannot bear to leave the pleasures of *this* life. Many of us would not mind having both a rich, exciting life with fame and wealth and then an eternity of bliss.

One reason for despising the thought of life's termination is the importance placed on the self. It seems impossible that there should ever come a time when that self is nonexistent. For some people, the next best thing to immortality is the thought of their own funerals. In their fantasy they are actually present, listening to what is being said about them. Facing up to the reality that each of us is only a temporary resident of this world and that the world will continue without us may be difficult at first but more and more acceptable once we get used to the thought.

The idea that life is temporary, however, can be another form of self-preoccupation. Asked whether growing old was unpleasant, one person said, "*I don't mind getting old and facing death when I think about the terrible things to come on this earth.*" This sentiment can be rephrased to read, "*The one compensation for my death is that I won't be around to face the awful future. I'll leave that to the people who keep on living.*" This statement is not an example of the courage to face life. It is a comment by someone who allows death to cast its shadow each day and who tries to escape from fear by believing that life for the survivors will be worse than death.

It is our hope that this consideration of death in the humanities will encourage you to take stock of where you are at present in the matter of life-denying thoughts and actions. You may discover that death is not always an event that happens only once. Unfortunately, many people needlessly die over and over.

Images of Death

Death can be thought of in a number of ways. It may be an enemy out to get us; a force that makes us all equal; a glorious finale to the lives of the pious and the brave; a preordained end destined for everyone (but not until our "number is up");

a beautiful woman or a handsome man, welcoming arms extended, inviting us to a haven of peace and joy; or a natural event, part of the universal cycle.

Death is often portrayed by pictures of candlelit tombs, skulls, masked killers, and the black-hooded Grim Reaper holding a long scythe (Figure 14.2). Businesses thrive on such images, believing that if we didn't enjoy being safely frightened, we wouldn't look at them or attend Halloween parties where many are wearing ghoulish costumes. The thought of possible death provides excitement for people who love to raise their hands high when riding roller coasters or who love boat rides through dark tunnels with skeletons popping up unexpectedly and bodies emerging from coffins.

Celebrations of Death

Sometimes death is celebrated in a life-affirming fashion to honor the memory of those who have departed. In Mexico and Puerto Rico, the Día de los Muertos, or Day of the Dead, is an annual occurrence (Figure 14.3). Originally an Aztec custom that took place earlier in the year, it was moved to the beginning of November to coincide with the Catholic All Saints' Day. The holiday is now more often celebrated in rural areas than in the big cities, but wherever it is observed, people tend and decorate the graves of loved ones, after which there is a fiesta with large quantities of food, including cakes and candies in the shape of skeletons.

In a different way, Shakespeare's King Henry V, in the history play of that title, celebrates death in a speech to his troops by suggesting the possibility of heroism—of dying bravely on the battlefield. Henry encourages his outnumbered English soldiers as they await battle with the French and is defiant in the face of complaints about the larger French forces:

> . . . he which hath no stomach to this fight,
> Let him depart . . .
> We would not die in that man's company
> That fears his fellowship to die with us. . . .
> We few, we happy few, we band of brothers;
> For he to-day, that sheds his blood with me
> Shall be my brother; be he ne'er so vile,
> This day shall gentle his condition;
> And gentlemen in England now-a-bed,
> Shall think themselves accurst they were not here,
> And hold their manhoods cheap whiles any speaks
> That fought with us upon Saint Crispin's day.

[IV: iii, 35–39; 60–67]

But poet Wilfred Owen (1893–1918) describes military sacrifice in far less glorious terms. In one of the most famous poems written about war, Owen details the suffering he witnessed on a World War I battlefield and ends with a line by the Roman poet Horace—*Dulce et decorum est pro patria mori* ("it is both sweet and right to die for one's country"), which Owen calls "the old Lie."

Figure 14.2 Aubrey Beardsley, *The Pestilence*, c. 1890s.
Beardsley's Victorian image of Death shows blackness spreading across the land beneath the figure's feet. Do you picture death as a tangible, like the figure in this image, or as an abstract?

Aubrey Beardsley

Figure 14.3 A skeleton made of beans with marigolds at an altar for Day of the Dead, or Día de los Muertos, celebration. San Miguel de Allende, Mexico.
How might celebrations like Day of the Dead provide succor for the living?

John & Lisa Merrill/Photodisc/Getty Images

DULCE ET DECORUM EST

Bent double, like old beggars under sacks,
Knock-kneed, coughing like hags, we cursed through sludge,
Till on the haunting flares we turned our backs
And towards our distant rest began to trudge.
Men marched asleep. Many had lost their boots
But limped on, blood-shod. All went lame; all blind;
Drunk with fatigue, deaf even to the hoots
Of tired, outstripped Five-Nines that dropped behind.

Gas! Gas! Quick, boys!—An ecstasy of fumbling,
Fitting the clumsy helmets just in time;
But someone still was yelling out and stumbling
And flound'ring like a man in fire or lime . . .
Dim, through the misty panes and thick green light
As under a green sea, I saw him drowning.

In all my dreams, before my helpless sight,
He plunges at me, guttering, choking, drowning.

If in some smothering dreams you too could pace
Behind the wagon that we flung him in,
And watch the white eyes writhing in his face.
His hanging face, like a devil's sick of sin;
If you could hear, at every jolt, the blood
Come gargling from the froth-corrupted lungs,
Obscene as cancer, bitter as the cud
Of vile, incurable sores on innocent tongues,
My friend, you would not tell with such high zest
To children ardent for some desperate glory,
The old Lie: Dulce et decorum est
Pro patria mori.

Death in the Popular Arts

14.2 *How is death portrayed in the popular arts? Why might these portrayals be so compelling to audiences?*

The subject of death informs some of the most glorious of human accomplishments: works of visual art, music, drama, and literature. The reason? Because the omnipresence of death, even at its most tragic, can enhance our appreciation of being alive. Death and life-affirmation are often complementary parts of the same work. An unexpected source of life-affirmation may be the way death (including all acts of violence, of murder, suicide, and other kinds of self-destruction) is treated in popular arts and entertainment. The public that lines up to buy tickets for horror movies, murder mysteries, and even automobile races may not *know* these events are life-affirming, but in fact they are—in part because they turn death into an unreality.

In the nineteenth century, the popular arts consisted of magazines, pulp fiction, stage melodramas, and tented spectacles such as the circus and Wild West shows. Monthly journals with mass circulation ran serialized horror tales. Sentimental tear-jerkers featuring the deaths of young children and frail maidens were the staples of melodramas. (Audience members were advised to bring three or four hankies with them.) Pulp fiction—cheap, lurid novels called "penny dreadfuls" in Britain and "dime novels" in the United States—told tales of horror, crime, and evil often set in haunted houses, dreary castles, the grimy underbellies of cities, or remote inns. Spider webs blocked doorways, bodies hung on closet hooks, distant shrieks of terror filled the air, and thunderstorms raged outside. Damsels were never out of distress.

Audiences continue to enjoy the portrayals of death offered up by writers and film and video makers. Perhaps because such renderings keep us a safe distance from the real thing, we seem eager to experience the deaths, or near-deaths, on screen and even at actual spectacles like auto races; such adventures may allow us finally to heave a great sigh of relief: That could have been me—but it wasn't.

Glorifying the Undead: Vampires and Zombies

Bram Stoker's *Dracula* (1897) seized hold of the public imagination, and its subject matter has never let it go. We continue to be fascinated by stories about the walking dead stalking the living. The vampire novels of Anne Rice (b. 1941), including *Interview with the Vampire* (1976), revolve around the centuries-old vampire Lestat and have sold millions of copies. Her protagonist's insatiable thirst for blood has even led him to Miami Beach, where he jumps out of dark alleys and kills innocent old people—a subject one would *think* would be too horrible for readers to enjoy. More recently, we have been enthralled by the television series *True Blood* (2008–2014), based on *The Southern Vampire Mysteries* by Charlaine Harris, and the *Twilight* books and films, based on the young adult novels of Stephenie Meyer, which offer up every young girl's romantic fantasy of being courted by a pale, sexy vampire—not to mention by a werewolf competing for her affections.

What is it that attracts us about vampires? They are typically portrayed as smart, slick, and elegantly dressed. But more important are their methods. They do not kill; rather, they bring their victims over to the dark side through that most erotic of techniques: a bite on the neck. No wonder we have found them so appealing.

Vampires are not the only "undead" in our popular culture. In fact, zombies rival vampires as our number-one menace in television shows such as *The Walking Dead* (first aired in 2010) and movies such as George Romero's series (*Night of the Living Dead*, 1968; *Dawn of the Dead*, 1978; and *Day of the Dead*, 1985), as well as *World War Z* (2013). For a bit of humor mixed in, the American film *Zombieland* (2009) takes the cake. Zombies, unlike vampires, are generally neither attractive nor sexy (Figure 14.4). They are typically almost unstoppable. And yet they must serve some psychological purpose for us. In fact, zombies often re-emerge in popular culture during times of cultural or political unrest or fears about the future—which may explain their current popularity! Critics often suggest that zombies, which are terrifying and usually operate in hordes, represent real evils that cannot be controlled, like plagues (the Ebola virus or AIDS, for example) or terrorism.

Watching Danger at a Distance: Real-Life Spectacles

We undeniably enjoy watching horror and even death on the screen, whether from the couch at home or in a darkened movie house. But many of us also enjoy going out to real events that appear to—and sometimes actually *do*—put lives at risk. Circuses, rodeos, and similar spectacles continue to lure crowds, at least in part because of the element of danger faced by performers. Magicians from Harry Houdini to David Blaine fascinate us by taking what appear to be huge risks with their lives and their health.

Figure 14.4 A scene from the television series *The Walking Dead*, Season 5, 2015.
Why might zombies be a pop culture figure right now?
Gene Page/AMC/Everett Collection

Auto races, where drivers literally put their lives on the line, are equally popular. Crowds watch as drivers push their cars to death-enticing speeds—and await the unacknowledged but always present possibility of a fiery crash. Even when a driver is trapped inside a burning vehicle, spectators are at such a remove that they can readily distance themselves from the actual horror.

Confronting death at a safe distance, whether at a racetrack or in a movie house, can make us feel that we are strong enough to withstand the real thing. Nonetheless, we tend to glamorize the real thing, endowing it with exotic terrors it usually lacks in order to give us the illusion that we have faced death fearlessly.

Confronting Catastrophe

Some popular novels herald the near destruction of the world and the salvation of the good. These tend to balance apocryphal books and movies in which the earth is wiped out by meteors or comets. Both spring from the same source: the assurance that death can be overcome, either because it is happening on the screen rather than in real life, or because a last-minute rescue is possible for those who are more or less pure of heart.

Hugely popular, also, are novels, films, and television programs about the disasters awaiting humanity from global warming and the unpredictable effects of climate change. The Austrian horror movie *Blood Glacier* (2013) tells the story of a melting glacier that threatens a group of scientists and, by extension, the world. It is probably just a matter of time before we are treated to a succession of tales about people huddled together in seacoast communities, waiting to be engulfed by monstrous waves caused by sea levels rising to unthinkable heights.

Why would people seek escape from their fears by immersing themselves in stories in which life seems cheap? The answer is that, in stories and films involving global disasters, deserving people are usually not the ones who die. In one early disaster film, *Earthquake* (1974), a street suddenly opens and swallows hundreds of people (including a gay couple)—except the hero and heroine.

VISIONS OF AN APOCALYPTIC FUTURE George R.R. Martin's hugely popular series of epic fantasies called *A Song of Ice and Fire*, adapted into the equally popular television series *Game of Thrones* (first broadcast in 2011), envisions a world ruled by warring families that is rife with political plots, murders, assassinations, incest—and dragons (Figure 14.5). The planet on which all this takes place is slowly moving away from its sun and will eventually, we have to believe, freeze over. Until then, we are content with watching the mayhem, including the unexpected beheading early on of a hero, Ned Stark, whom we assumed would continue as a leading character throughout the series. The post-apocalyptic vision of the future offered by *Game of Thrones* has been called a fantasy for grown-ups.

Warnings about the end of the world are not new. Most major religions prophesy a day of judgment, when the world will end and the righteous and the sinful will be separately dealt with. Some descriptions of this end are terrifying,

Figure 14.5 Peter Dinklage as Tyrion Lannister in *Game of Thrones*.
Why might people enjoy watching or reading fantasies about the end of the world?
Macall B. Polay/HBO/Everett Collection

some less so. But we continue to be drawn in by the notion that the world as we know it will end—perhaps by the coming of climate change, as in the 2004 film *The Day After Tomorrow*; perhaps by the arrival of a meteor or asteroid, as in the films *Deep Impact* and *Armageddon*, both from 1998; perhaps by the invasion of disease, as in the video game *The Last of Us* (2013) or films like *Contagion* (2011); or perhaps by takeover by other species (the various versions of *Planet of the Apes*) or aliens (the list is too endless to recount).

Disaster films seem to have one thing in common regardless of the period in which they were written or produced: Deadliness is not random. Climate-change thrillers offer the "comforting" underlying message that reasonable people can still do something to avert the tragedies that engross audiences for two hours before the message is delivered. Various catastrophes are survived by the good-hearted heroes. A skilled video-game player can avoid "death."

The eternal fascination with lurking terror and sudden, violent death, and the reassurance that it is not random or personally threatening, allow us to confront and, in some psychologically satisfying way, defeat it. But these experiences may not completely strengthen us for the hard chore of facing up to reality. If we are to be strong and skillful in being human, we must still explore meaningful ways to say *Yes* to life without trying to escape from truth.

Strategies for Dealing with Death

14.3 *What are the various strategies people use to affirm life and deal with the fear of death?*

How do we cope with the knowledge that we will all die sometime? Humanity has developed a variety of responses: We deny it exists by believing in an afterlife; we accept it as our inevitable fate; we avoid talking about it; we laugh at it; we look at it as a clinical event. According to Sherwin Nuland, a physician who wrote a best-selling book called *How We Die* (1993), death is

> . . . not a confrontation. It is simply an event in the sequence of nature's ongoing rhythms. Not death but disease is the real enemy, disease the malign force that requires confrontation. Death is the surcease that comes when the exhausting battle has been lost.[1]

Artists, and writers in particular, have brought us multiple accounts of facing death. One such account is available in Randy Pausch's "Last Lecture," which can be found on YouTube. Pausch (1960–2008) was a professor of computer science at Carnegie Mellon University. In his video, aware that he faces imminent death from pancreatic cancer, Pausch does push-ups (one-armed at that!) and announces that he probably can do exercises better than most of his audience. With a twinkle in his eye, Pausch's message is basically *keep on keeping on*. His heads-up approach to death seems to have helped countless numbers facing a similar destiny.

Christopher Hitchens (1949–2011), an Anglo-American political writer who died of cancer at age 62, offers a very different message. Having garnered more attention for his writings about his illness than for his earlier works, Hitchens finally insists that there are no lessons to be learned from facing a death sentence.

> Of course my book hit the best-seller list on the day that I received the grimmest of news bulletins, and for that matter the last flight I took as a healthy-feeling person (to a fine, big audience at the Chicago Book Fair) was the one that made me a million-miler on United Airlines, with a lifetime of free upgrades to look forward to. But irony is my business and I just can't see any ironies here; would it be less poignant to get cancer on the day that my memoirs were remaindered as a box-office turkey, or that I was bounced from a coach-class flight and left on the tarmac? To the dumb question "Why me?" the cosmos barely bothers to return the reply: "Why not?"[2]

In his recent book *Being Mortal* (2014), the neurosurgeon and author Atul Gawande explores the way we deal with aging and death in the United States and suggests that everyone should have "the conversation"—that we should all think about what our trade-offs might be when facing death or a severely limited life. Gawande's father, he reports, when he was facing multiple illnesses, said that he wanted to be kept alive as long as he could eat chocolate ice cream and watch football on television. When he could no longer indulge in those two pleasures, he would welcome death. For Gawande and his siblings, this became a guiding principle for caring for their father. What are your trade-offs? What is life-affirming for you?

Belief in the Afterlife

The most prevalent strategy for dealing with death is, of course, a belief that it doesn't really exist—that life continues beyond the grave. Several religions offer concepts of an afterlife, a place where the dead retain their earthly identities and will one day be reunited with loved ones. Immortality has a different meaning for those who define it as living on in the memory of family and friends or achieving eternal life through the works they leave behind.

An argument against believing life continues beyond the grave is that it prevents us from accomplishing all we might during this one chance given to us. Another is that belief in an afterlife is simply a weak excuse to minimize our failures in this life.

THE CHRISTIAN AFTERLIFE   Christianity speaks of heaven as a reward for virtue and hell as a punishment for sin, but the Christian next life has always had an ambiguous nature. Is it an actual place with a geography of its own? Or are the Inferno and Paradise, so vividly described in Dante's *Divine Comedy* (written between 1302 and 1321), purely *literary* inventions? An afterlife is implied, if not defined, in the Christian Bible. On the cross, Jesus promises one of the thieves that he will be in paradise that same day, but "paradise" can have many meanings, including a state of release from pain rather than a place of eternal life. Many believe that Jesus appeared to the disciples after his resurrection. This story may be partly responsible for the idea that physical identity continues beyond death. The idea is reinforced by reports from those who have attended séances and claimed to have actually seen their loved ones. A popular element in films of the 1930s was the after-death appearance of the departed, looking just as they did in life, except for being transparent.

The Christian vision of the afterlife is often accompanied by feelings of apprehension and fear. In the Book of Revelation, the Christian Bible contains vivid, even frightening imagery of the world's end and tells about the violent war against the Antichrist and the terrible suffering that awaits the sinner. Hell, especially as described by Dante, has a tenacious hold on the human imagination. If the perpetuation of the body in heaven is often a vague concept, not so Dante's accounts of the physical torments to be endured in hellfire. The sermons of early New England Puritan ministers are particularly filled with flesh-crawling warnings of the agony to come.

THE AFTERLIFE IN ISLAM   The Qur'an speaks often about the afterlife. Souls continue to exist after death, and on the Last Day, all people living and dead will be raised, and judged, and divided between paradise, or the garden (*janna*), and hell (*jahannam*). Most Muslims do not anticipate going directly to either destination—only warriors who die in the act of defending the faith will be ushered directly to the presence of Allah—but rather they will rest in their graves after death until the Last Day. Hell, from an Islamic perspective, has seven levels (Figure 14.6). In both paradise and hell, Allah can instruct people on how to become better—those in hell, to eventually leave hell, and those in paradise, to advance to higher states of knowledge and perfection of the faith.

THE HINDU AFTERLIFE   In the Hindu faith there is not only *moksha*, the blissful state the soul attains when it is released from the cycle of death and reincarnation, but also a heavenly paradise enjoyed by the souls of those who died with a preponderance of good karma but who must still undergo at least one more stay on earth. They are allowed to remain in this paradise for a certain length of time before revisiting the earth. When they achieve perfection, however, they are not in paradise but become reunited with Brahman, the soul of the universe.

An eighteenth-century illustration from India depicts Krishna, believed to have been the god Vishnu (second in the Hindu trinity) in his mortal incarnation. Krishna continues to have many followers who see him in much the same light as Christians see Jesus: as a mortal incarnation of God. He is the god-hero of the Hindu epic the *Mahabharata*. In illustrations, Vishnu is shown in a geographical paradise, dancing to music played by three young women. Buddhism has no such concepts of a physical afterlife.

THE JEWISH AFTERLIFE   In Judaism, the afterlife is traditionally the memory of a good person who lives on in charitable works, in his ancestors, and the broad impact of a life well-lived. The ancient Hebrews were a realistic, survival-bound people, and in their bible is the hope of a better life *here*, free of persecution and despair. Canaan, the Promised Land of Abraham and the covenant, is a real place in a highly desirable fertile area over which violent struggles are still being waged. In contrast to the arid desert, it offers green pastures and may possibly have influenced agricultural images of the next world. The depiction of God as a shepherd providing green pastures for his flock reinforces the image.

Figure 14.6 A Vision of Hell, from an Arabic manuscript, *The Tales of Luqmann*, 1583.
Does the possibility of an afterlife help us overcome a fear of death?
Dea/G.Dagli Orti/De Agostini Picture Library/Getty Images

ENVISIONING THE AFTERLIFE IN THE HUMANITIES   The need to believe that life is somehow, if not some*where*, perpetuated beyond death is deeply ingrained in the human tradition. In the humanities of many periods, we keep finding the theme of survival through love. If two people are so close that they consider themselves to be one person, then death cannot take away the identity of *that* person. It matters not who dies and who lives on: The survival of one ensures the survival of the other.

John Donne (1572–1631) was death-conscious throughout his life, the more so as love for his wife deepened with each passing year. The thought that so ideal a relationship could end was unbearable to him. In 1612, he was asked to accompany his patron, Sir Robert Drury, to the continent, despite strong protests from a wife who feared that something tragic was going to happen during his absence. Her premonition was accurate: While Donne was away, his wife gave birth to a stillborn child. To reassure her before leaving, Donne wrote one of his major poems, "A Valediction Forbidding Mourning," giving posterity the gift of an amazing metaphor for life beyond death.

> *Our two souls, therefore, which are one,*
> *Though I must go, endure not yet*
> *A breach, but an expansion.*
> *Like gold to airy thinness beat.*

> *If they be two, they are two so*
> *As stiff twin compasses are two;*
> *Thy soul, the fixed foot, makes no show*
> *To move, but doth if the other do.*

Other artists have found that art itself is the gateway to immortality. John Keats (1795–1821), like Donne, was death-conscious throughout his life. It was a very short life, marked by ill health and the fervent need to believe that death would not be final. In one of his sonnets, he links death (his own?) to the rebirth of life in the spring—in three startling and immortal words that close the poem.

AFTER DARK VAPOURS

> *After dark vapours have oppress'd our plains*
> *For a long dreary season, comes a day*
> *Born of the gentle South, and clears away*
> *From the sick heavens all unseemly stains.*
> *The anxious month, relieved of its pains,*
> *Takes as a long-lost right the feel of May;*
> *The eyelids with the passing coolness play,*
> *Like rose leaves with the drip of Summer rains.*
> *And calmest thoughts come round us; as of leaves*
> *Budding—fruit ripening in stillness—Autumn suns*
> *Smiling at eve upon the quiet sheaves—*
> *Sweet Sappho's cheek—a sleeping infant's breath—*
> *The gradual sand that through an hour-glass runs—*
> *A woodland rivulet—a Poet's death.*

Belief in Fate

Fatalism—the belief that all events, including the nature, time, and place of one's death, have been predetermined—is found throughout history, religion, and literature. It is a popular way of thinking about and accepting misfortune and death. It was the foundation of Greek mythology in which great and powerful families are doomed by events beyond their control. Without the concept there would have been far less tragic theater in ancient Athens.

Greek myths saw fate as a mysterious, universal force that preceded the birth of the gods and the creation of the world. Sometimes fate was represented as three women spinning, measuring off, then cutting the thread of life. The snipping of the scissors appears arbitrary and capricious. On the other hand, with the coming of urban society and the establishment of law, people (even the Greeks) were held responsible for their actions, no matter how much they insisted their deeds were preordained.

The opposing forces of fate and free will have been a source of confusion for thousands of years. Fatalism in the courts nowadays takes the form of arguments that defendants were driven to commit crime because of a bad family background, a bad neighborhood, or temporary insanity that has robbed them of free will. Fatalism is also involved in religions that stress God's omnipotence as we wrestle with the unresolvable question: Does the fact that the deity knows in advance what will happen mean that it *must* happen? Does God therefore *will* it to happen?

For some, fatalism is the inevitable conclusion that must be drawn from the belief in God's omnipotence. But people of faith adopt different attitudes toward fatalism:

1. depression, because a disaster can be just waiting to happen and nothing can be done about it;

2. willingness to accept the inevitable no matter how unsettling, because if what happened *had* to happen, then it's really nobody's fault, is it? Nothing could have changed the outcome.

ACCEPTING FATE   Still, it is difficult, and for some impossible, to accept dreadful calamities, especially the death of the young, with serenity. In his popular book *When Bad Things Happen to Good People*, Rabbi Harold Kushner has a personal reason for discussing the subject; he himself lost a young son to incurable disease. In his search for answers, he considers possible errors in the way people think about and attribute motives to God. Perhaps fatalism is a human construct not in any way connected to God. Kushner suggests that instead of asking "Why me?" we say "Why *not* me?" In this, he echoes what was written long ago in the Book of Job: God gives and God takes away, and humanity must accept either action without complaint.

A popular brand of fatalism is one that can be accepted or rejected as circumstances dictate. A believer in free will may explain sudden death in terms of fate ("It was his time"). Some may say they don't mind flying because "if your number is up, there's nothing you can do about it." (The reply may be, "Suppose the pilot's number is up, not yours?") Yet the same fair-weather fatalist might avoid taking unnecessary risks, such as refusing to undergo a delicate operation with a 50-50 survival rate, on the grounds that the odds are not favorable enough.

Islam has traditionally maintained a strong belief in the will of Allah, allowing for the peaceful acceptance of all that happens. Asian thought has its own versions of fatalism. Hindus believe karma determines the circumstances of the next cycle of life, but they also believe the individual is responsible for leading a better life and proving worthy of a brighter future. This outlook surely implies that the will is free to accumulate good or bad karma, but, once the choice is made, there is no escaping the consequences.

To the Buddhist and the Taoist, the Dharma or the Way is a controlling force that operates through the choices people make. There is no conscious deity arranging the future. The universal order is a dynamic, flowing force that changes as people change. The death of anyone is part of the natural way of the universe and is to be accepted without anger.

Avoiding Death Talk

For most of us, having the conversation that Atul Gawande recommends in *Being Mortal* is almost impossible. We avoid the word "death" at all costs except for purposes of exaggeration: "I was so embarrassed I thought I'd die!" Directly confronting even the *idea* of death is considered "morbid." Life insurance sales people employ euphemisms such as "In the event that something happens to you. . . ." Married couples are urged to make out their wills as soon as the first child is born, but attorneys will tell you how seldom they do so. The very words "death" and "die" are considered poor taste in conversation. Instead, we speak of "passing on" or use other evasions.

Among those who avoid talk of death are people who believe they have plenty of time before they must be "serious" about such matters. Audiences that munch their popcorn, entranced by a screen full of blood, love the terror of anticipating what is going to happen to the innocent walker on the lonely street. They must certainly have a fear of death concealed in their unconscious even as the vampire is concealed in the doorway—but it is a fear that can wait a little while before it is realistically confronted. And the younger the audience, the less real the fear. That's why young people are sent off to fight wars; their sense of immortality has not yet been tested by real life. Those who are a little older and therefore apparently less immortal may enjoy the spectacle of violent death, or the many films and television shows about terminal illness, because the disaster is happening to *other* people.

Affirming Life through Humor

Would-be funeral directors studying for state boards that will license them as embalmers often exhibit a sense of humor about their profession.

> A woman golfer is asked why her husband is not playing with her that day.
> "He died," she replies.
> "Oh, I'm sorry. When was the funeral?"
> The woman looks up at a procession of cars passing by the course.
> "That must be it now."

> A son asks his dying father, "Pop, what can I do for you? Is there anything you want?"
> "Yes," replies the father. "I'd like a piece of your mother's apple strudel. I can smell it baking."
> The son leaves the room and comes back empty-handed.
> "Ma says it's for after the funeral."

The classic 1971 film *Harold and Maude* tracks a young man who has decided life is not worth living and attempts, time and again, to kill himself. He meets a 79-year old woman who is not just enchanted by life but exuberantly enthusiastic about it. She convinces Harold to abandon his quest for death and teaches him to live each day to its fullest—and the two eventually become unconventional lovers. A more recent movie, *Bernie* (2011), based on a true story, features Jack Black as a naïve and empathetic Texas funeral director who befriends a wealthy but cranky widow (Shirley MacLaine). For years, Bernie puts up with her abusive treatment, but eventually he cracks: He shoots her and hides her body—and then sets about using her money to fund benevolent projects throughout the town. When the crime is finally discovered and Bernie is arrested, he is so beloved that townspeople (some of whom are interviewed for the film) refuse to serve on a jury, and the trial has to be moved to another town.

Is it better to confront death in a humorous story than to suppress not only the fear but the very mention of it? Suppressed, the idea of death becomes magnified, and the more terrible is the anticipation of it. Laughing—when appropriate, of course—may be better than becoming addicted to the murder tales that actually *deny* the truth of death, despite the multiplication of corpses and the darkened streets down which the unsuspecting walk to their doom.

Magnifying and Beautifying Death

Most of us want to be recognized, singled out for special achievements. We want to leave our mark on the world. We find early deaths tragic, representing lives unfulfilled. And so few of us can think of death in casual terms as a natural event to be accepted whenever it comes. To magnify death—to mark it as a special event that happens only after a person has achieved high status—is to create a mythology for ourselves.

We mask our fears about our own mortality in the importance we place on the death of celebrities. Perhaps many of us, consciously or otherwise, identify with the pomp and majesty surrounding their funerals. The state funerals of the assassinated U.S. President John F. Kennedy and of Britain's Diana, Princess of Wales, glued much of the world to their television sets. Thousands turned out to watch the train carrying Abraham Lincoln's coffin from Washington back to his home state of Illinois. Noted personalities, revered authors, and heads of state pay eloquent tribute to the lifetime achievements of the deceased. We are moved; funeral eulogies often stand as the ultimate summing up of an individual's worth and can—at least for a time—dispel our own secret insecurities and doubts about our value to the world.

In magnifying the role of death, we also become aware of the pain of death, the stroke of the scythe, and so we need to invent strategies for shielding ourselves. The best thing we can say of someone who has just died is that the end was peaceful or that death came during sleep; these represent everyone's fondest hopes.

DYING A BEAUTIFUL DEATH   Greek mythology offers two versions of finality. One is well known as the dark place ruled by Hades, god of the underworld. But the Greeks also had their own kind of paradise: the Elysian Fields, a bright and sunny land of eternal happiness, where heroes who fall in battle are spared pain in death. (Parisians, wanting to make their major thoroughfare seem like a place of perfect joy, named it the *Champs-Elysées*; significantly enough, it leads to the tomb of the Unknown Soldier.)

The passing of a hero in myth is unlike that of other mortals. Typically, the hero does not suffer physical pain, but rather passes beautifully into a mysterious, non-threatening realm. Frodo, the tiny hobbit hero of J.R.R. Tolkien's popular trilogy *Lord of the Rings*, faces grave dangers in order to save others. When his quest is complete, he returns to his home in the Shire for several years; then, when he is ready to move on, he outfits his own little ship and sets sail for the Grey Havens.

Of course, there is nothing like opera to beautify death. Mimi, a beloved operatic heroine in Puccini's *La bohème*, dies beautifully as the magnificent music enhances our pleasure. In *La traviata*, Verdi's opera based on Dumas's *La dame aux camélias*, the dying heroine nobly extracts a promise from her lover that he will one day marry someone else and know she is observing and blessing them from the heaven she will soon inhabit. Again, the music eases the heartbreak.

But the question remains: Even if magnifying or beautifying death helps to diminish, temporarily, our fear of it, are we better off facing it as the natural termination of our time here and not masking it in mythology?

Attempting to Stay Young

Many of us try hard to stay young, working out at the gym, running, eating right, even indulging in plastic surgery to retain the unwrinkled appearance of youth. The brilliant twentieth-century comedian Jack Benny insisted on always giving his age as 39, right up until the day he died at age 70; his age—or rather his denial of it—was part of his act. Rather more drastically, the late comedian Joan Rivers poured money and energy into plastic surgery designed to make her *look* 39; her efforts, like Benny's, became part of her *shtick*, her comedy persona.

The classic literary treatment of the burning need to stay young is provided by Oscar Wilde in his 1891 novel *The Picture of Dorian Gray*. The hero is a slim, incredibly handsome young aristocrat who is totally committed to a life of sensuality, leisure, and extravagance. In the opening scene he is observing his portrait, just finished by a major artist of the day:

> How sad it is! . . . How sad it is! I shall grow old and horrible and dreadful. But this picture will remain always young. It will never be older than this particular day of June. If it were only the other way! If it were I who was to be always young, and the picture that was to grow old! For that—for that—I would give everything! Yes, there is nothing in the whole world I would not give! I would give my soul for that![3]

Like Faust, another famous character who barters his soul, Dorian has his wish granted by a mysterious power. He thus remains young while the man in the portrait grows older, but he loses his innocence. He becomes cruel and sadistic, develops an addiction to every conceivable pleasure, knowing he cannot do harm to his body, and ultimately, he even commits murder. The possession of eternal youth suggests he must be immortal—and perhaps out of the law's reach. In a grisly finale, however, the hero, both sickened by the knowledge of what he has become and now despising the portrait with its wizened face that shows every evil action he has ever committed, seizes a knife and plunges it into the heart of the painting. His servants find him "withered, wrinkled, and loathsome of visage." He has become the very thing he feared most; on the wall, however, the servants see a splendid portrait of their master in all the wonder of his exquisite youth and beauty. Immortality exists in art, but not in life.

For the young who have not yet learned how life works, who are involved in day-to-day struggles to find a secure place for themselves, each day brings new knowledge; and with new knowledge comes tension and bewilderment. The older person gains wisdom by realizing that everything passes. Since this is so, what makes that person think he will not also pass? The tragic mistake is to hold out for what is impossible.

Medicalizing Death

The medical profession has made the conquest of death a priority. Medical research has devoted itself to finding cures for cancer, diabetes, and other still-unconquered afflictions, and much progress has been made in prolonging life and making it as pain-free as possible. For this reason, most physicians are not only saddened but *outraged* when patients die. Doctors believe they have a duty to save lives at all costs. Sometimes this sense of responsibility continues even when a patient is beyond medical help or when death might in fact be preferable to the available medical options.

Medical shows on television have enjoyed almost unbroken popularity since the early years of the medium, when Dr. Kildare, Dr. Gillespie, and Dr. Welby were always ready to put aside their personal lives and sit by the bedside of the sick and dying. Images of death were abundant, but they were usually gentle; we rarely saw what it really means to die.

More recent medical shows have been somewhat less romantic. One of the longest-running shows of recent years, *ER* (1994–2009), showed us a staff under pressure, where mistakes were made, egos wounded, and conflicts erupted over proper procedures—all in an attempt to make the stories more real and less sentimental. A good many episodes revolved around the torment and guilt experienced by doctors who do not always triumph over death. Nonetheless, the show aimed to reassure, not depress, us.

The artistic success of a different kind of hospital show, *House M.D.* (2004–2012), indicates that the time had come for an antihero kind of doctor. Gregory House is described by a television critic as

> *an almost sociopathic genius who is given to muttering bitter comments such as "Humanity is overrated." He's a mess of a man, filled with open disdain as well as Vicodin, which he takes to stop the pain of "muscle death" in his leg. And yet he is a brilliant diagnostician, a last-ditch doctor who cures people the rest of the medical world has written off.[4]*

Gregory House is, in a sense, a medical detective; he is also, much like the cynical antiheroes of the *film noir* school, a hard-nosed realist, obsessively unsentimental. But a good many fans of this dark show would rather have a serious illness treated by someone like him, who may have no bedside manners whatever but can be depended on to find a solution—no matter how obscure. This is life-affirmation at a high price, but perhaps worth the money.

Some critics point out, however, that shows like *ER*, a pioneer in deromanticizing hospitals, and even the more intellectually appealing *House M.D.* are always going to be *seemingly* but not *actually* real. If we recognize, as we often do, that a famous actor is doing a cameo bit as a dying patient, we know in the back of our minds that he or she will be revived in a different show. The wise course is to approach the viewing in the knowledge that the story isn't real but the subject matter *is* real, and we are preparing ourselves for the truth by "practicing" with the fable.

Life-Affirmation in the Humanities

14.4 *How do literature, music, and philosophy help humanity understand death and affirm life?*

As we have seen, it is only human to be attracted to images of death as they appear in the popular arts. Mortality is also central to more serious works of art—and such works can enable us to transcend our own fears. In literature, books for both children and adults confront the terrible experience of children coping with death. Music is often associated with the rituals of death, but music also underlies our belief that the great achievements of humankind prove that life is worth living. And finally, the writings of philosophers such as Socrates help us understand and transcend the fear of death.

Literature: Children and Death

Death may generally be easier to take on the printed page because it is supported by neither skilled actors nor realistic scenery. Yet some of the most potent insights into the meaning of death have come from novelists and poets. It would take many volumes to do justice to the vast literature. Here is one: death and children.

JAMES AGEE, *A DEATH IN THE FAMILY*   *A Death in the Family* (1957) by poet and novelist James Agee (1909–1955) is an American classic that should be read by anyone concerned with the effect of death on children, especially now that death has been almost completely removed from home to hospital. Years ago, the viewing of a body (or wake) always took place in the living room, with neighbors and friends coming by to pay their respects and offer support. The sight of death was thus unavoidable for even the youngest family members. The book shows how a child approaches death when its reality is not kept hidden.

Rufus, the young protagonist, has not yet had death explained to him when his father is killed in an auto accident. Agee analyzes every detail of Rufus's thoughts, feelings, and confusion. At one point, we realize that the child is actually feeling a sense of pride and achievement because he is experiencing something special, something denied to the other kids on the block. A memorable passage (among many) is this account of Rufus's first sight of his father's body laid out in a casket in his grandparents' living room.

> *Rufus had never known such stillness. . . . Rufus had never seen [his father] so indifferent; and the instant he saw him, he knew that he would never see him otherwise . . . an indifference which would have rejected them . . . in this self-completedness which nothing could touch, there was something else, some other feeling which he gave, which there was no identifying even by feeling, for Rufus had never experienced this feeling before; there was perfected beauty. The head, the hand, dwelt in completion, immutable, indestructible: motionless.*[5]

It could be argued that what a mature writer feels about death is not what an actual little boy would feel. But we can trust the instincts and compassion of a poet and trust his assurance that children are able to handle early tragedy in their own way and that the exposure will only fortify them for the pain of loss in later years.

KATHERINE PATERSON, *BRIDGE TO TERABITHIA*   A powerful and popular children's book, *Bridge to Terabithia* (1977) by Katherine Paterson, explores the intense friendship between a young girl, Leslie, and Jesse, a slightly cranky outcast. The two create a magical kingdom that they call Terabithia beside a creek in a nearby woods. When Jesse accepts an invitation for an outing with a beloved teacher without telling Leslie, she heads for their secret place, swings from an overhead swing—and falls to her death. Jesse is left with feelings of guilt and loss, and he must work out on his own how to go on with his young life. The book is often banned from school libraries, but it is a cherished favorite of many children. Why do you think this is so?

SUZANNE COLLINS, *THE HUNGER GAMES* The best-selling young adult *Hunger Games* series (*The Hunger Games*, 2008; *Catching Fire*, 2009; and *Mockingjay*, 2010) by Suzanne Collins brings death front and center. In this dystopian world, what was once North America has been divided into 12 regions ruled by the Capital, somewhere in the Rocky Mountains. In an annual televised contest, a boy and a girl are chosen randomly from each region and pitted against each other to the death in a video game-like environment created especially for the event. As horrified but intensely engaged readers (or viewers, for the equally successful films made from the books), we watch as these teenagers hunt one another down and murder in order to survive. The exercise is seen by the Capital as a way of keeping the other regions in line. Of course, our heroine, Katniss Everdene, not only survives but inspires a rebellion that eventually brings down the Capital—but in the meantime, the spectacle of children killing children is a chilling one.

Other books both for children (like Maurice Sendak's *Where the Wild Things Are* and *Brundibar*) and for adults (like Dickens's *Oliver Twist*) confront children's fears of and experiences with the threat of death. Asked about when a child is ready to learn the facts about death, psychologists generally advise that children can deal with loss when they fully understand the concept of time: not how to *tell* time, but time as the unending agent of change. And children may be more sophisticated than we suppose, even though they may not have the words to express their knowledge.

Music: Ritual and Transcendence

We associate certain kinds of music with life's final moments and the rituals that follow: hymns played slowly on an organ; a somber march played in drawn-out cadences; a solo voice solemnly assuring the mourners that the deceased is at rest in a better land. The effects of the music vary, depressing some listeners, uplifting the spirits of others.

Sometimes music seems to be an exact translation into external sound of the way we feel inwardly; and sometimes it seems to impose a mood of its own. The jazz funeral, still conducted in New Orleans, has a dual personality (see Figure 14.1). On the way to the cemetery, mourners follow the casket and walk in time to a slow and sad march; but the return trip absolutely *defies* those in attendance to be consumed with sorrow. The musicians throw off the mantle of grief and break out into joyous jazz. What this performance says is that the deceased is better off now, is free of life's pain, worries, debts, tangled relations, and the pettiness and hypocrisy of others. The jazz funeral echoes Milton's famous line from *Samson Agonistes:* "Nothing is here for tears."

Great composers have explored through music the tangle of conflicting emotions that all must experience when the end is in sight, when no escape is possible other than to transcend the fear of losing a personal identity and merging with what is timeless.

RICHARD STRAUSS, *DEATH AND TRANSFIGURATION* Richard Strauss (1864–1949), one of those responsible for the transition from romantic to modern opera, is equally famous as the composer who brought the genre of the symphonic poem to new heights. The symphonic or tone poem is an elaborate work that tells a story through sound, belonging to a category known as **program music**, in which the composer has a definite scenario in mind. Repeated melodies represent major characters and events, as in the operas of Wagner. At the age of 26, Strauss contributed *Death and Transfiguration* to the permanent concert repertoire, showing a premature concern for what happens as a person dies.

In the opening section, the pulsating rhythm of muted strings suggests the ticking of a clock, as a sick man lies dying. Flutes suggest the flicker of candles, and strings suggest soft moans. A brief oboe melody represents a stirring of consciousness and, perhaps, the recollection of childhood happiness. In the next section of the music, the dying man rebels against the coming of death and asserts the will to live. Two melodic lines—one representing the fierce demands of death, the other a desire for life—struggle against each other in a massive and richly textured orchestration, out of which emerge the strands of what will be the beautiful Transfiguration theme played on cellos, trombones, and horns.

As these fragments of the final theme begin to come together, the protagonist slides peacefully into what we presume to be a coma, in which he returns to his childhood and then his young adulthood, revisiting as well the trials he undergoes as he matures, the pangs of lost love, the anger that wells up when one crisis after another begins to overwhelm him, leading to the worst of all—the onslaught of his final illness. The figure of death finally appears as the strings tremble and fade slowly away and the dramatic stroke of a gong is heard.

The Transfiguration theme now begins, building from near silence to a majestic musical statement of the human spirit freeing itself from the pains of the flesh and the tribulations of the world and ascending into what we have been taught to call the Unknown. But through the great gift that music is able to give us, the Unknown is heard while visual imagery floods the mind of the listener. If the fear of dying is indeed present in the unconscious of most of us, great works of the humanities, such as those we have been dealing with, can support and comfort.

Philosophy: The Concept of Selflessness

Unforgettable images of how some actual people faced death can be as life-affirming as the tone poem of Strauss. Exemplary lives are as much a part of the humanities as works of art. They are in fact *living* works of art, even as death neared. This aspect of the humanities offers shining images of people who endured the continual presence of death without the natural instinct to save themselves at all costs. What all of these people had in common is the ability to bear the thought of not existing. Preoccupation with the loss of personal identity can underlie the fear of death. An old folk song expresses an attitude shared by many people:

> *Nothing was here before I came;*
> *All that is here now bears my name.*

Socrates provided a philosophical way to transcend the fear of death. He may have had selfhood, but there is no evidence that he was preoccupied with self*ness*. In all the accounts of Socrates that Plato has given us, the mentor seems out of touch with himself in our sense of what *himself* means. His choice of death by poison rather than life in exile without being able to teach indicates that the freedom to think and communicate rational thought was more important to him than simply being alive. In the accounts Plato has written, Socrates, in his final days, is shown to be a man genuinely interested in seeking wisdom and not at all in making people feel sorry or afraid for him. After he has drunk the hemlock prescribed by law, surrounded by the young students who adore and are weeping for him, he shows a singular absence of self-consciousness.

When one of those students, Phaedo, observes that the master drank his poison "cheerfully," we have no reason to believe Socrates was struggling to put on a brave act in front of his young friends. And then comes a most telling statement:

> *And hitherto most of us had been able to control our sorrow; but now when we saw him drinking, and saw too that he had finished the draught, we could no longer forbear, and in spite of myself my own tears were flowing fast; so that I covered my face and wept, not for him, but at the thought of my own calamity in having to part from such a friend.*[6]

The passage reminds us that the loss of someone we love can also be tinged with self-interest. Phaedo has not learned from the selfless behavior of his teacher.

One reason loss is hard to separate from self-interest is that only very strong people do not need others to reinforce their identity. You can miss those who die, but you should be able to survive without them. Insecure lovers sometimes test each other with questions like "If I should die, would you ever get over it?" A reply such as "Surely you would want me to find someone else and be happy" would not be understood, or there would not have been a question to begin with.

Models of Life-Affirmation

14.5 *What models have been created to help humanity affirm life?*

What the arts can do for us is this: Help us grasp the profound realization that the potential for a productive, exciting life belongs to each of us. *We* control our attitudes, as Zeno the stoic would be quick to remind us. **Life-affirmation** is recognizing not only that <u>life is worth living</u>, but that real death happens only once and, in a sense, does not happen to us at all. In this final section, we will look at ways of refusing to allow the shadow of death to eclipse the sunlight of living.

The Phoenix

An ancient symbol of life-affirmation is the phoenix, a mythological bird of rare and exotic plumage and supernatural powers (Figure 14.7). The Greek historian Herodotus reported that the phoenix actually existed and was known to have visited the Egyptians every 500 years. The Roman belief was that each era bears witness to the birth of one phoenix, that it lives for a very long time, and that at the moment of its death it generates a worm that becomes the phoenix for the next age. Yet another version of the legend is that the phoenix is a bird from India that lives for 500 years and then flies to a secret temple where it is burned to ashes upon the altar, only to rise from the ashes three days later, young and resplendent.

In folklore, poetry, and song, in literature and drama, the phoenix has endured through time as a symbol of rebirth, new growth, regeneration, and redemption. The phoenix Fawkes is the pet of Hogwarts headmaster Albus Dumbledore in the Harry Potter books by J.K. Rowling; Fawkes helps Harry escape from several misadventures and, when Dumbledore dies, sings a mournful dirge for him. Religions have counterpart symbols: gods who die

Figure 14.7 The phoenix, a symbol of rebirth.
Do you agree that we can re-invent ourselves, like the bird?

Christos Georghiou/Shutterstock

or descend into the underworld, there to remain for a time and then to rise, reborn and renewed.

The phoenix model—a literary structure in which the protagonist dies either figuratively or literally and is then reborn—underlies many masterworks, including Dante's *Divine Comedy*, in which the poet, seeking a vision of God in Paradise, must travel through the very depths of hell before his wish is granted. The phoenix model has suggested to many people certain ways of thinking about events. Thus "I've been through hell" often prefaces an account of some happier turn of events—or at least invites the listener to effect a happy change for the sufferer through lavish sympathy and compassion.

GOETHE, *FAUST* The epic poem *Faust* (published in sections beginning in 1790) by the German poet Johann Wolfgang von Goethe (1749–1832) makes inspiring use of phoenix mythology. The legend dates from the Christian Middle Ages: Faust was an alchemist (someone who attempts to transform ordinary metal into gold) and trades his soul for the ability to discover *all* of earth's secrets. Goethe turns the story into his own version of the phoenix myth, one that echoes nineteenth-century German romanticism and its strong belief in the power of individuals to reinvent themselves.

There are two distinct parts to Goethe's masterpiece, but only Part One is widely read. In it, the protagonist, having wearied of his intellectual efforts to probe the secrets of life, is willing to part with his soul in exchange for a lifetime of unlimited sensory pleasures without having to think (Figure 14.8). He bargains with Mephistopheles, an agent of the devil, who promises to grant his every wish, but on one condition: *He must never be so satisfied within a given moment that he would want time to stop.* He must live from day to day at a frantic pace, never looking back, never wishing to hold onto anything or anyone.

Figure 14.8 An advertisement featuring Faust and Mephistopheles, c. 19th century.
Faust bargains with the devil for a life filled with constant pleasure. Do you think he makes a good deal?
Lebrecht Music and Arts Photo Library/Alamy

Part Two (published after the poet's death) is less dramatic, as the term is generally understood, and requires long hours of reading and analysis, but it eventually rewards the patient reader with the true meaning of the entire work: not the triumph of the devil, but the triumph of humanity. In its entirety, Goethe's *Faust* offers the perfect phoenix model, a work of ringing life-affirmation in the very confrontation of life's harshest realities.

In Part One, Faust readily agrees to the condition laid down by Mephistopheles. He has decided that life has no meaning beyond the enjoyment of each passing moment. There is no truth; there is only continual change. Why should anyone ever want to hold onto a moment?

In Part Two, older and a bit tired of a life that offers nothing but a variety of sensory experiences, the protagonist begins to long for an accomplishment, something to show for his having lived. He is also tired of serving only himself. He becomes mayor of a small seaside village built on land so low that it is constantly threatened by the encroaching waves. His project as mayor is to build a seawall—but each time the wall is extended a little further, he sees that the sea has already begun to erode what was already built. The task, he realizes, is impossible. The wall will *never* be finished.

Yet this realization only fills him with a raging passion to challenge the sea. He will continue to build, constantly repairing what was built before. He will keep on, knowing that each day he builds provides another few days of sustainable life for the people of the town. Even if the floods eventually come, the people will have raised food—perhaps a little more each year.

The need for human courage to accept continual change and to meet challenges head-on regardless of whether the effort is successful—the thought that actions are worth doing even if the work of one individual's life cannot be finished—hits Faust with the force of lightning. If he cannot ultimately win, he shall not ultimately lose.

> *He only earns both freedom and existence*
> *Who must reconquer them each day.*
> *And so, ringed about by perils, here*
> *Youth, manhood, age will spend their strenuous year.*
> *Such teeming would I see upon this land,*
> *On acres free among free people stand.*
> *I might entreat the fleeting minute:*
> *Oh linger awhile, so fair thou art!*[7]

But those words—"linger a while . . ." are precisely the ones that Mephistopheles warned Faust not to utter when the bargain was first struck. Faust has asked time to stop so that he can enjoy the beauty of his realization, and he loses the bargain. Mephistopheles comes for him, but God intervenes; angels lift Faust out of Mephistopheles's grasp and bring him to heaven.

Eventually, all of us run out of time. Life ends. Yet it is within our power to believe that we have not lost anything, *provided* we know that we reconquer our freedom and existence every day. Faust's original pact is made because he wants everything—wants to experience every sensation that life has to offer. His victory is recognizing that "everything" is present completely in every moment and that it is far more than sensory pleasure. It is realizing that we have confronted every challenge and done all that was possible and thus have not wasted one precious second. Faust knows he has given everything for the good of his people, and what one gives is what one also *has*. To give nothing to life is to gain nothing from life.

Thinking about Time: Accepting That There Is Only Now

The late actress and teacher Uta Hagen was giving a workshop to several young aspiring actors and asked a girl to prepare a scene in which she would play a 50-year-old woman. At the appointed time, the girl made her entrance in a wheelchair and spoke in a cracking voice, sounding much like the witch in *Snow White*.

"What in the world are you doing?" Hagen asked.

"Trying to physicalize the character's age," was the answer.

"Do you feel like you're 50?" Hagen asked.

Hagen told her to play 50 as she would play 16—the girl's actual age—because, barring unfortunate accidents of fate, she would feel no different inwardly when she really *was* 50 and therefore there was no reason to indulge in external and false signs of aging *now*.

Time is physical in the contemporary world of science. It forms part of Einstein's fourth dimension and can be measured. Time for us human beings is a habit, a social construct, numbers or hands on a watch that let us keep appointments. In terms of actual experience, what is it? Can we experience yesterday? In memory, to be sure, but we can also choose *not* to remember. Can we experience tomorrow? Only in imagination, and again we can decide against it. What we *cannot* control is the presence of the present moment—and regrettably, we are often so busy, either with tasks or with our own inner thoughts, that we lose the sense of that moment. The more we actually experience, the less significant is the myth of time. Someone once said, "Time is important only when you're doing it—in prison," but even prisoners can choose not to keep marking the days off their calendars.

Ways of thinking about time are well within our power. The poet William Wordsworth, to whom we return again and again for his quiet wisdom, has left us with this definitive statement about living in the eternal Now:

MY HEART LEAPS UP

My heart leaps up when I behold
A rainbow in the sky:
So was it when my life began;
So is it now I am a man;
So be it when I shall grow old,
Or let me die!
The Child is father of the Man;
And I could wish my days to be
Bound each to each by natural piety.

Did you ever think that life can run a course that is the opposite of the popular way of depicting it? Your childhood can be your tomorrow. The future has not yet even begun, and you can choose never to have it. Like the protagonist in the 2008 film *The Curious Case of Benjamin Button*, starring Brad Pitt, you can live backwards, getting younger as the years unfold. The great Picasso urged us to remain as children, filled with wide-eyed wonder.

Internal imagery can be adjusted. To break the illusion of time rushing by to an inevitable aging and death, we can replace pyramids with circles. In pyramid imagery, we visualize ourselves rising through the ranks (in school, in athletics, on the job), reaching a peak or a crest ("Ah! At last I've made it!" or, negatively, "This is as far as I'm going!") and then feeling we are "over the hill." In circle imagery, on the other hand, life is like a Ferris wheel, rising, cresting, going back down, and then starting up all over again. This is a particularly effective image because riders of Ferris wheels know that moving around is preferable to being stuck on top.

EINSTEIN AND TIME   Einstein showed that time is absolute only with respect to bodies moving at uniform speed. If A is traveling in a train side by side with B on an adjacent train and both trains have the same speed, A and B could wave to each other whenever they wished; for both, the length of the trip would be the same. The theory of relativity also demonstrates that as one travels faster and faster time slows down. If astronauts could travel at the speed of light, they would never grow old. Though it is unlikely that this particular part of the relativity theory will be tested anytime soon, it does nonetheless remind us that time—absolute time—is a variable even in the universe of science.

One way to explain relativity is to think of identical twins, one of whom takes off in a spaceship that will travel at the speed of light (186,282 miles per second), while the other remains on Earth. The mission lasts 20 years as measured on Earth by the homebound twin. When the space twin returns, he will find his brother 20 years older, while he himself looks the same as when the mission began. It is possible to live your life as if moving at the speed of light because, unless you *want* to feel old inside, you need be conscious only of where you are *now* and what you are doing.

The most famous work by the French author Marcel Proust (1871–1922), *À la recherche du temps perdu*, is titled *Remembrance of Things Past* in its customary English translation, but literally the title is *In Search of Lost Time*. Memories are pleasant diversions for a rainy afternoon, but to actually wish we could go back in time (time-travel mythology notwithstanding) is not life-affirming.

ASIAN CONCEPTS OF TIME   In Asian thought, mind, or consciousness, is infinite. Awareness is always with us. Even memories of past events are alive within us in the everlasting moment. We carry time with us. There is no such thing as the past and therefore no reason to lament that it's gone. Those who try to hold onto time are the ones suffering the most, for they come to recognize how quickly it flies by. Those who do not try to seize it are living vividly in the Now.

Asian philosophers tell us that we become dismayed by the passing of time because we create the illusion of *beginning*, which we date from the instant of our birth, and of *ending*, which is death. Books end, movies end, the party is over—always the same pattern, so that ending becomes ingrained in us. The Chinese poet and philosopher Chuang Chou, who lived over 2,000 years ago, had fun with verbal dazzle that is also profound:

> . . . *there is never beginning to have a beginning, there is never beginning to never begin to have a beginning. There is existence, there is nonexistence. There is never beginning the existence of nonexistence* . . .[8]

How can the beginning begin? Where was it before? If the beginning cannot begin, then it cannot end either. In this philosophy, all of us live between the two poles, but where that is cannot be precisely defined, can it?

Reinventing Ourselves

It's easy enough to say that memory imprisons us in time, but not so easy to erase memory. Memory is a distinguishing attribute of our species. It can brighten the darkest of days, offer consolation for loss, and link us to the past so that we don't have the sense of drifting aimlessly through life. But memory can also exert a ferocious hold over us, triggering negativity. Too many of us accumulate self-determined bad karma from the past; we refuse to let go of it and thus see no way of ever changing. What is desirable is that we learn to put memory in proper perspective, to recognize that what we have done or what has been done to us in the past may have relevance to the present but *not in the same form*. We do ourselves harm when we act and react *now* as if it were still *then*.

There are those, however, who carry the pain of yesterday into the way today is experienced and finally decide to terminate their existence. Committing even symbolic suicide is in its own way a termination of existence. Psychologists who treat suicidal patients usually try first to convince them to reaffirm life, to consider what is good in it. Sometimes their counseling fails, and in retrospect, some of them have said that self-inflicted death can be a highly rational act, a meaningful, if somber, way of reinventing oneself that is not to be recommended—only, on occasion, understood.

The Greeks and Romans generally believed self-inflicted death served four purposes: to show bereavement, to preserve honor, to avoid pain, and to benefit the state. Socrates disagreed, warning that human beings did not create themselves and therefore were not at liberty to dispose of their bodies as they willed. Most religions that oppose suicide do so on similar grounds.

Jewish law forbids self-inflicted death, but many Jews did in fact kill themselves to avoid capture by the Romans. Early Christians, also oppressed by Romans, frequently took their own lives, apparently without fear of God's retribution. Christianity now expressly forbids the act, but Christians through the centuries accepted martyrdom, essentially committing suicide. These include Thomas à Becket, Archbishop of Canterbury, who refused to say the king was greater than the pope and was slaughtered on his altar; Joan of Arc, who refused to sign a paper confessing she did not hear heavenly voices urging her into battle and was burned at the stake; and Bernadette of Lourdes, the peasant girl who, having discovered a spring that was said to have cured many hopelessly ill pilgrims, suffered from a terminal disease which she never mentioned until medical help was no longer possible, and who maintained that heaven would not allow her to use the water for herself.

THE INABILITY TO REINVENT A LIFE: ARTISTS AND SUICIDE   What seems sad, however, is that artists sometimes end their lives prematurely, overlooking the fact that, of all people, they possess the creativity to reinvent themselves. Sometimes the reason is, tragically, the very excess of their own genius. Compulsively driven to create what we now acknowledge as masterpiece after masterpiece, van Gogh was increasingly victimized by lack of recognition and the thought that his work must, after all, deserve its obscurity. Earlier in his short life he *was* able to tell himself, defiantly, that he would paint as he liked no matter what others thought. This attitude was reinvention, but van Gogh ultimately lost the power to do it.

Sylvia Plath (1932–1963) had two small children and a husband, the poet Ted Hughes, who had his own creative and emotional needs. Many such literary marriages are full of tension, and Plath had a history of emotional breakdowns. As she neared her thirtieth birthday, she began to fear that she could no longer write, and that fear became too much for her.

We can only watch sadly, wondering what beauties the world has lost, as creative people find life too difficult to face. The musician Kurt Cobain (1967–1994), leader of the Seattle grunge band Nirvana, put a shotgun to his head after a short life filled with success, but also with both mental anguish and physical pain. The acclaimed writer David Foster Wallace (1962–2008) prepared well for his death: He left a note about how he wanted his last novel edited and published before hanging himself. He too had a long history of depression and had been on and off medication for much of his life. And Amy Winehouse (1983–2011), an extravagantly talented British blues and soul singer, chose another route, dying of alcohol poisoning at only 27. Winehouse was not unusual in the annals of rock and roll. In the 1960s, when the music was first emerging, many young lives were lost: Jim Morrison of The Doors, Janis Joplin, Jimi Hendrix—all aged 27, like Winehouse. Although their deaths were not officially suicides, all were caused by reckless choices—too many drugs, too much alcohol. Choosing to live a life of excess is surely one way of choosing death—a Faustian bargain, perhaps.

Ibsen's *A Doll's House* is a play about a woman who realizes she has been denied the truth about life and is therefore unfit to be a mother and a wife. Leaving her husband and children, she slams the door behind her—a sound effect that shocked many in the original audiences. Her choice to leave her previous life behind can be seen, in retrospect, as the very model of self-reinvention.

Guilt and Forgiveness

Perhaps the most life-affirming action any of us can take is to forgive—to forgive not only others but also ourselves. Almost all of us feel guilt about something. The child of divorce feels responsible for her parents' problems. The sibling feels guilty to have bullied a younger brother or sister. The student feels guilty about having cheated on a test or borrowed a paper from the Internet; an office worker feels guilty about playing video games during work hours. A single mother feels guilty that she is unable to give her children a better life. An alcoholic or drug addict feels guilty for all the people he has hurt along the way.

The existentialist advises us that we are free to determine our own destinies—but sometimes we cannot find the key to remove the shackles of our early lives.

Those who can afford it may spend months, even years, in the psychiatrist's office, willing to confront their guilt, only to have it revived by the therapy and the whole cycle start up again. Or else they find that original guilt has been joined by a lot of new guilt. After all, *I'm a terrible person, and I know that everything bad that happens is my fault.* The result can be a decidedly neurotic individual. Those who cannot afford, or do not believe in, therapy may try to sort out their feelings on their own, or with the help of a friend, a teacher, or a priest. Our last model of life-affirmation, then, is finding a way to forgive ourselves and move on.

SURVIVOR GUILT   Testimony from those who escaped death in Nazi concentration camps during World War II indicates that their suffering did not cease just because they were still alive; instead, most felt tremendous grief, and considerable shame, that they had survived when so many others perished. William Styron's classic 1979 novel *Sophie's Choice* tells the story of a Polish concentration camp survivor, now relocated to New York, who struggles daily not simply with the fact that she is still alive, but also with the memory of a choice that was forced on her at the camp: to decide which of her two children should die. It's hard to imagine anything more horrifying, and Sophie, although offered the possibility of life with a young man who cares deeply for her, finally makes another choice: unable to grant herself forgiveness, she commits suicide.

Too frequently natural disasters—earthquakes, mudslides, wildfires, tsunamis, hurricanes, and tornadoes—cause death and devastation for thousands, sometimes hundreds of thousands. We watch anguished survivors walking amid the rubble, dazed and tearfully searching for lost wives, husbands, children. How many of these victims harbor a secret feeling that somehow the disaster is punishment for past sins? How many of us feel relief—"There but for the grace of God go I"—and then feel our own version of guilt? To hope that saying "Life goes on" will take care of the problem is unrealistic and often unkind.

FINDING FORGIVENESS   Yet somehow, we do need to get on with life, and that involves forgiving ourselves for both our real offenses and our imagined ones. The famous 12-Step Program developed by Alcoholics Anonymous suggests that we relieve ourselves of guilt only by listing all the people we have harmed and making amends—seeking their forgiveness—and then continuing throughout our lives to keep a personal inventory, to admit when we are wrong, and to make it right.

Another possibility that some find helpful is a Goodbye to Guilt party or other forgiveness ritual that involves coming together with friends and family, stating the things we regret, and casting them aside—perhaps writing down the worst thing we think we have ever done, wadding up the paper, and throwing it into a fire or into a hole dug in the ground. Forgiveness rituals can be planned or spontaneous, but they should be somehow designed to let everyone take a deep breath of satisfaction when they are done.

Hebrew tradition has for centuries encouraged a forgiveness ritual.

> *[T]he Jewish practice known as* tashlikh *(Hebrew for "throw") is derived from a verse from the prophet Micah, "And You [God] shall throw their sins into the depths of the sea" (7:19). Based on the prophet's words, a Jewish custom arose during the Middle Ages. On the first day of Rosh ha-Shana . . . Jews go to a river and symbolically cast their sins into the water. In many communities, people pull out their pockets and shake them, emptying them of the sins they contained.[9]*

Alternatively, we can create a private ritual—perhaps sitting quietly in a corner, concentrating very hard on the guilt we don't want to share, gathering up all of it into a tight ball, and then, calmly and deliberately, imagining ourselves hurling the ball straight up into the sky. See? There it goes. The ball of guilt suddenly becomes a bird winging its way over a cloud, becoming lost in an azure infinity, never to be heard from again.

Death itself—biological death, the single stroke that happens only once to each of us—will come as it may. In this chapter, we have not really been discussing that event. We have been talking about how the resources in the humanities can, even in the face of overpowering disasters or overwhelming personal guilt, help us to affirm the value of life.

The most distressing aspect of a death-denying culture is the fact that we die (or cause others to die) *symbolically*: that is, psychologically experiencing the death of self-worth and the loss of the power to reinvent ourselves. We may laugh heartily at the guilt-ridden, anxiety-filled neurotics in movies or on television, but they can also be looked upon as tragic examples of how to waste a life.

We end the chapter, however, on a positive note. The humanities are sources of life-affirming models—the myth of the phoenix bird, the possibility of reinvention—that we have the power to use as we continue to be born anew.

Looking Back

In this chapter,

- we described ways in which death is imagined and celebrated,
- we discussed how death is portrayed in popular culture and why these portrayals are so compelling for many of us,
- we talked about the various strategies people use to affirm life and deal with the fear of death, including a belief in an afterlife, avoiding talk about death, using humor, and beautifying the experience of death,

- we explored the ways in which the humanities—literature, music, philosophy—provide experiences that help us understand death and affirm life, and
- we analyzed various models of life-affirmation, including the story of the phoenix, a realization that we can to some extent control time and memory, our ability to reinvent ourselves, and the need to recognize guilt and embrace forgiveness.

Key Terms

fatalism The belief that all events, including the nature, time, and place of one's death, have been predetermined.

life-affirmation The belief that life is essentially good and worth living; the ability to free oneself from unnecessary burdens of guilt and a lack of self-esteem as well as fears of growing older and eventually having to die, and

substituting the realization that death happens only once, not every day.

program music Musical genre, an orchestral poem telling a story or following a scenario in the composer's mind, knowing which adds to the listener's enjoyment.

Chapter 15
Nature

Figure 15.1 Bushman rock art from the Kamberg Nature Reserve, South Africa.
Humanity leaves its imprint on nature, sometimes intentionally, and sometimes unintentionally. Is that imprint an improvement or a desecration? Might it be both?
Anthony Bannister/Gallo Images/Documentary Value/Corbis

Today, the word "natural" has any number of meanings. Natural foods are supposed to be free of chemicals and laboratory-injected ingredients (although it is often hard to pronounce whatever is taking their place). Those opposed to gay rights brand homosexuality and transgenderism as "unnatural." Those who put business interests ahead of environmentalism say that nature knows what it is doing—leave it alone. Environmentalists, however, hasten to say that nature has been ruthlessly tampered with and may soon reach a point of no return.

On the whole, the humanities have been friendly toward **nature**, although some artists and philosophers have been indifferent to the natural world: Key figures in the Greek cultural explosion beginning in the sixth century BCE focused on the mind and its powers; theirs was a city-oriented society. The same could be said for the Romans, who believed their mighty city was the true measure of humankind.

Long before those two civilizations, Asian philosophers were reverent toward the force that ruled the universe, the force that the West ultimately called nature and that philosophers in India called *Brahman*, in China, the *Tao*, and Buddhists, the *Dharma*. In both Asia and the West, this force had an outward appearance (trees, mountains, and so on) but also an inner soul or rationality operating in accordance with unchanging principles that either were always there or were created by a divine power. In our time, scientists in both hemispheres continue to probe the natural world for its secrets, guided by the belief that such rationality must indeed exist.

In this chapter, we'll explore the role that nature has played in the humanities throughout history—and the role that humanity is playing in nature at this moment.

Early Views of Nature

15.1 *How does the view of nature expressed through the arts change from biblical times to the Middle Ages to the age of Shakespeare?*

Despite his country's urban orientation, the Roman poet Lucretius (c. 99–55 BCE) wrote a vast poem entitled *Of the Nature of Things* in which he attributes the beginning of the natural world to a mighty collision of atoms. He predicts that eventually this primal atomic energy will reassert itself and the world will end in a violent explosion. His prediction is not early environmentalism; Lucretius does suggest that we respect nature not as a loving, kind mother who will always be there for us, but as an awesome power not to be trifled with.

The relationship between nature and humankind was a matter of concern well before the Roman Empire was founded. Some cite Genesis when placing blame for the belief that humans should rightly control earth's resources.

> So God created humankind in his image, in the image of God he created them; male and female he created them. God blessed them, and God said to them, "Be fruitful and multiply, and fill the earth and subdue it: and have dominion over the fish of the sea and over the birds of the air and over every living thing that moves upon the earth."

Genesis 1:27–28

But others—particularly those involved in **environmentalism**—hasten to add that this biblical passage does not mean that humankind has the right to *trash* the garden. Perhaps the perception that God is a disinterested creator may encourage some to think *they* are the owners, in the way a building superintendent, left in charge by an absentee landlord, might eventually grow cocky and begin believing that the building is actually his. But we should keep in mind a later line from Genesis: "The Lord God took the man and put him in the garden of Eden to till it and keep it" (Genesis 2:15), which suggests that we are, in fact, caretakers and not owners of the earth. The Islamic Qur'an echoes the same sentiments.

The Middle Ages

During the early Middle Ages—from the sixth to the eleventh centuries—much of nature must have been in a pristine, unspoiled state. Yet for the most part, people in that time probably did not venture very much outside their villages, their walled fortresses, or their monasteries. Medieval nature seems to have been perceived as something "out there," with little direct relationship to human beings. And the pressures of religion nudged individuals in another direction: Why spend time looking at clouds and flowers when nothing in this vale of tears mattered as much as preparing oneself for salvation in the next world?

During the eleventh and twelfth centuries, however, a new kind of literature appeared, written by rebellious young men studying for the priesthood who objected to the rigors of their austere training and to the otherworldly bent of their elders. Poems by the young rebels urge their fellow students to discover the natural world outside.

> Cast aside dull books and thought,
> Sweet is folly, sweet is play;
> Take the pleasure Spring hath brought
> In youth's opening holiday!
> Right it is old age should ponder
> On grave matters fraught with care,
> Tender youth is free to wander,
> Ever to frolic, light as air.[1]

Here was the earliest stirring of what would become a great poetic theme, one that still resonates today: the identification of unspoiled nature with youth and joy and all good things.

As the walled fortresses turned into walled cities, as plague and pestilence and poverty snaked along insidiously behind those walls, many looked on the city as a place of death, decay, and evil. Crime was prevalent. The countryside became a place of blessed escape. But not everyone shared this view. For the religious traditionalists, one could find God without frolicking in the spring air. Centuries later, the philosopher Baruch Spinoza (1632–1677) argued that God and nature were one and the same.

The Forest of Arden

Like other Renaissance poets, the young William Shakespeare wrote about imaginary, unspoiled countrysides, where the joys of love were abundant. By the time he came to London in the late sixteenth century, that city was already a den of filth, poverty, and crime. Aristocrats who patronized poets and bought their work could ignore the truth of the city. Why worry about the wretched poor, gasping for breath in their crowded rooms, when there isn't anything we can do about it? The patrons of art in their airy, comfortable homes enjoyed the literature of escape, subsidizing handsomely those who could please their taste.

The popularity of idealized country settings—far away from the reality—led Shakespeare to capitalize on this form of escapism. *A Midsummer Night's Dream* (1594) is set in a Disney-like woodland, with charming fairies and lovers who will stay young forever. Shakespeare's presumed final play, *The Tempest* (1611), takes us to a faraway desert island, a "brave new world" removed from urban reality, where a magician named Prospero controls everything (Figure 15.2).

SHAKESPEARE, *AS YOU LIKE IT* *As You Like It* (c. 1599), one of Shakespeare's most enduring comedies, contains a decidedly premature environmentalism. An aristocrat identified only as Duke Senior has been exiled by his evil brother. He and a small band of followers move to the Forest of Arden, the author's version of the Garden of Eden, where they enjoy a simple existence free of the corruption found in court.

Sweet are the uses of adversity;
Which like the toad, ugly and venomous,
Wears yet a precious jewel in his head;
And this our life, exempt from public haunt,
Finds tongues in trees, books in the running brooks,
Sermons in stones, and good in everything.[2]

This would not be the last time a writer would suggest that one can receive a better education in nature than in the library.

The duke's followers, however, are urbanized men, accustomed to the food of city-bred people. Instead of leaving their paradise the way they found it, they begin to kill the wild deer, which sorely grieves one of the duke's attendants, Jaques, a brooding, melancholy individual. Jaques, the duke is told, "swears you do more usurp/ Than doth your brother that hath banished you."[3] In fact, Jaques angrily denounces what they're doing to nature, insisting it is worse than the court corruption that exiled them in the first place. At one point Jaques witnesses the excruciating death throes of a wounded stag:

"Poor deer," quoth he, "thou mak'st a testament
As worldlings do, giving thy sum of more
To that which had too much."[4]

Then he cries out to the herd of still-surviving deer that they should hide themselves from the tyrants who have come to destroy the animals in their "assigned and native dwelling place."

In Shakespeare's time, nature and humanity were not considered part of each other. Humanity should therefore not try to meddle with a natural universe in which everything has its rightful place and function. The tragedy of Jaques is that he *feels* the agony of animal destruction without being able to do anything to help. All he can do is be seen "weeping and lamenting/Upon the sobbing deer." His misanthropy, fueled by the corruption of the forest, drives him almost mad. Despite his true helplessness, he develops the delusion that he can reform the world.

Invest me in my motley, give me leave
To speak my mind, and I will through and through
Cleanse the foul body of th' infected world,
If they will patiently accept my medicine.[5]

We know he will never be successful. At the play's conclusion, when the exiled and usurper brothers are reconciled and the four young lovers are to be happily married, Jaques wishes everyone peace and joy, but then declares that he cannot stay in their midst; he is "for other than dancing measures." When they beg him to return to their urban civilization, he refuses. "To see no pastime I. What you would have/I'll stay to know at your abandoned cave."

Figure 15.2 Helen Mirren as Prospero in Julie Taymor's 2010 film of Shakespeare's *The Tempest*.
The British writer Aldous Huxley titled his novel about a futuristic, mechanized society *Brave New World* (1931). What might have appealed to the 20th-century writer about this Shakespearean phrase?
Newscom

Nature and the Romantics

15.2 *What did the Romantic movement mean by the terms the* **picturesque,** *the* **beautiful,** *and the* **sublime***? How are these concepts expressed in the literature and music of the period?*

During the late eighteenth and early nineteenth centuries, on both sides of the Atlantic, the humanities were dominated by a vast movement in art, literature, music, and philosophy called *Romanticism*. The Romantics brought an intensity

Figure 15.3 J.M.W. Turner, *Rotterdam Ferry-Boat*, 1833.
Can you feel nature's power in Turner's depiction of the sea? What techniques does Turner use to convey that power?

Courtesy of National Gallery of Art/Ailsa Mellon Bruce Collection

of emotion to their work that they felt had been missing in the arts for some time—even, some felt, since before the Renaissance. They were reacting to the emphasis on reason and intellect endorsed during the eighteenth-century Age of Enlightenment, and their work emphasized feelings over intellect, heart over head. The emotions they were seeking were not necessarily comfortable ones; the Romantics also embraced horror and awe, and in particular, the awe inspired by the power of nature, like the turbulent seas (Figure 15.3) often painted by J.M.W. Turner (1775–1851).

Even though the Romantic movement began after the Revolutionary War, its basic ideas undoubtedly influenced the philosophy of those who brought the United States into being, who equated the words "natural" and "free." *Natural rights* are still the cornerstone of democracy. Before the coming of civilization, human beings living in nature were free to roam where they wanted, settle where they wanted, and create a social order that suited their needs. Implicit in the Declaration of Independence is the equation of human and natural rights.

The Vocabulary of Romanticism

Of central importance to Romanticism were the complementary concepts of beautiful, sublime, and picturesque, all terms to clarify the relationship between nature and humanity. The first two terms were established by the philosopher Edmund Burke in his 1757 work, *Philosophical Inquiry into the Origin of Our Ideas of the Sublime and the Beautiful*; the third was added to the discussion as landscape painting became a key component of nineteenth-century art. Critics and scholars typically define the *beautiful* as portrayals of nature that are balanced, serene, and pleasing to the eye, the *picturesque* as portrayals that show rougher edges and more rustic settings, and the *sublime* as portrayals that reflect the awe-inspiring (and sometimes horrible) power of nature—great mountains, cataclysmic storms, jagged and deep valleys.

Painting was not the only nineteenth-century art form that showed the general preoccupation of the time with nature. The first efforts at urban planning also emerged from that century. As cities grew darker and dirtier, governments began to realize that citizens needed access to green spaces. Visionary designers created the parks that we still value today: Frederick Law Olmsted and Calvin Vaux, in New York City and Chicago; Daniel Burnham in Chicago; John Nash in London. Many of these parks were designed to include all three of Romanticism's concepts of nature: pleasing green fields, rougher wooded paths, and, here and there, even huge boulders, trucked in from who knows where, to instill a sense of awe in the viewer.

Romanticism and Naturalism in Literature

Romanticism was also a dominant force in early nineteenth-century literature. A major voice was William Wordsworth (1770–1850), whose most famous work is "I Wandered Lonely As a Cloud" (1807). Here is a passage from the poem that can still inspire joy toward nature.

> *I wandered lonely as a cloud*
> *That floats on high o'er vales and hills,*
> *When all at once I saw a crowd,*

A host, of golden daffodils;
Beside the lake, beneath the trees,
Fluttering and dancing in the breeze.

Continuous as the stars that shine
And twinkle on the milky way,
They stretched in never-ending line
Along the margin of a bay:
Ten thousand saw I at a glance,
Tossing their heads in sprightly dance.

In 1836, the American **transcendentalist** Ralph Waldo Emerson (1803–1882) wrote a long essay entitled "Nature." What he said still has the power to move those of us who have ever stood on a mountain and gazed in awe at the surroundings.

Nature, in the common sense, refers to essences unchanged by man; space, the air, the river, the leaf . . . If the stars should appear one night in a thousand years, how would men believe and adore; and preserve for many generations the remembrance of the city of God which had been shown! But every night come out these envoys of beauty, and light the universe with their admonishing smile.

The stars awaken a certain reverence, because though always present, they are inaccessible; but all natural objects make a kindred impression, when the mind is open to their influence.[6]

Emerson taught that all of us should look for nature in ourselves (a traditional Asian philosophy), should feel that we and "it" are parts of the same whole. To love ourselves is to love the world that enfolds us. The separation of nature from humanity—the belief that humankind has the right to impose its will on nature—may in fact be a base cause of our present environmental crisis.

WALT WHITMAN AND HERMAN MELVILLE   American literature of the nineteenth century offers two extraordinary examples of writing about (but of course not *only* about) nature and humankind: Walt Whitman's "Song of Myself" from his expansive collection called *Leaves of Grass* (published multiple times in multiple versions, but first appearing in 1855); and Herman Melville's *Moby-Dick*, in which nature, in the form of a white whale and a tormenting sea, is the inevitable victor in a struggle of wills.

Canto 6 of Whitman's "Song of Myself" depicts the poet musing on a blade of grass—and concluding, finally, that humankind and nature are one:

A child said What is the grass? *Fetching it to me with full hands,*
How could I answer the child? I do not know what it is any more than he.
I guess it must be the flag of my disposition, out of hopeful green stuff woven.
Or I guess it is the handkerchief of the Lord,
A scented gift and remembrance designedly dropt,
Bearing the owner's name someway in the corners, that we may say and remark, Whose?
Or I guess the grass is itself a child, the produced babe of the vegetation.[7]

One of literature's most compelling portrayals of nature as both beautiful and sublime appears in Chapter 87, called "The Grand Armada," of Melville's *Moby-Dick* (1851). The whaling ship the *Pequod*, captained by Ahab and carrying the narrator, Ishmael, enters a narrow strait between Java and Sumatra, driven by a "fair, fresh wind." This is prime hunting ground, and soon the whales are spotted ahead—not one or a handful, but hundreds of them, "forming a great semi-circle, embracing one half of the level horizon, a continuous chain of whale-jets . . . sparkling in the noon-day air . . . This host of vapory spouts, individually curling up into the air . . . showed like a thousand cheerful chimneys of some dense metropolis, descried of a balmy autumnal evening."

The *Pequod* gives chase—but soon another massive group of whales appears behind them, and the ship is both pursuing and pursued. As the *Pequod* emerges from the straits into more open waters, the whales ahead turn back toward it "forming in close ranks and battalions, so that their spouts all looked like the flashing lines of bayonets," but then seem to lose focus, swimming round and round, while the smaller boats are launched and the harpooners begin their work. Why do these whales seem suddenly indecisive, vulnerable?

Finally, the sailors look down, beneath the surface, where

> *another and still stranger world met our eyes as we gazed over the side. For suspended in those watery vaults, floated the forms of the nursing mothers of the whales, and those that by their enormous girth seemed shortly to become mothers. The lake . . . was to a considerable depth exceedingly transparent; and as human infants while suckling will calmly and fixedly gaze away from the breast, as if leading two different lives at the same time; and while yet drawing mortal nourishment, be still spiritually feasting upon some unearthly reminiscence;—even so did the young of these whales seem looking up towards us.*[8]

The slaughter of whales that inevitably follows this scene is all the more horrific to the reader, especially as one of the harpooners, Queequeg, pulls a baby out of the water by its umbilical cord.

THE AMERICAN "NATURALIST": HENRY DAVID THOREAU Henry David Thoreau (1817–1862) called himself a **naturalist**, meaning someone who chooses to live far from society in a natural environment. (Thoreau was also a political activist, which at one point landed him in jail overnight for refusing to pay a poll tax imposed on would-be voters. Thoreau called voting a *natural* right.)

Thoreau's naturalism was supported by his lack of need for the human companionship and conversation found in urban surroundings. In his great work *Walden; or, Life in the Woods* (1854), he observes he "could easily do without the post office" because he "never received more than one or two letters . . . that were worth the postage." He did not organize marches to protest what greedy factory owners were doing to the environment, but he *did* equate urbanism with a sad way to live. He pitied those who were imprisoned in daily city labor and never saw birds feeding or hatchlings emerging. His animosity toward urban society gave rise to his most famous, often quoted observation.

> *The mass of men lead lives of quiet desperation. What is called resignation is confirmed desperation. . . . A stereotyped but unconscious despair is concealed even under what are called the games and amusements of mankind. There is no play in them, for this comes after work. But it is characteristic of wisdom not to do desperate things.*[9]

Nature, for Thoreau, is not a universal cause. It is the road to personal happiness. Let those who choose to toil in the city do so; it's their business. Instead, he migrated into the woodland surrounding Walden Pond, outside Boston and not far from Concord, Massachusetts, where he built himself a one-room cabin for $23.44. (A television spoof suggested that the hut would cost $75,000 in today's dollars. One doubts he could have gotten a mortgage!) He lived in his cabin for close to two years, and the book he wrote based on his experiences there is comprised of short chapters with titles such as "Sounds," "The Ponds," "Solitude," "The Pond in Winter," and "Spring." Thoreau's naturalism is a prescription for *noticing things*, which he believed was impossible in crowded Concord.

> *I did not read books the first summer; I hoed beans. Nay, I often did better than this. There were times when I could not afford to sacrifice the bloom of the present moment to any work, whether of the head or hands. I love a broad margin in my life. Sometimes, in a summer morning, having taken my accustomed bath, I sat in my sunny doorway from sunrise till noon, rapt in a revery, amidst the pines and hickories and sumachs, in undisturbed solitude and stillness, while the birds sang around or flitted noiseless through the house, until by the sun falling in my west window, or the noise of some traveller's wagon on the distant highway, I was reminded of the lapse of time.*[10]

Reading Thoreau makes us realize that, even if a woodland retreat with its solitude and perfect stillness is not readily available, we are still free to notice things. There are birds in the backyard or on the roof of the building across the street. There are wildflowers and trees, working hard to assert themselves even in the most depressingly rundown sections of our poorest cities.

Romanticism in Music

The Romantic preoccupation with nature and its emphasis on sensual and emotional responses, as opposed to intellectual ones, also influenced early nineteenth-century music, particular in Germany. The German composer E.T.A. Hoffman (1776–1822), better known as a writer of children's tales, including *The Nutcracker*, was also a critic. In one of the seminal essays on musical Romanticism, his 1813 essay on Beethoven's instrumental works suggests that music is

> *the most romantic of all arts, one might almost say the only one that is genuinely romantic, since its only subject-matter is infinity. Orpheus's lyre opened the gates of Orcus. Music reveals to man an unknown realm, a world quite separate from the outer sensual world surrounding him, a world in which he leaves behind all precise feelings in order to embrace an inexpressible longing. . . .*[11]

Hoffman suggested that the roots of Romanticism in music are found in Haydn and Mozart, but that it came to full flower in the work of Beethoven. Certainly Germany was the center of the Romantic movement in music. Richard Wagner's infatuation with medieval legend in works such as *Tristan and Isolde* and the *Ring* cycle aligned with Romanticism's interest in what the Romantics saw as the more natural and less intellectualized art of the Middle Ages.

Nationalism was another prominent component of Romanticism in all the arts but was perhaps most prominent in music. Romantic artists were interested in the early histories of their respective countries, particularly in the folkloric legends, and composers from a number of countries began creating music based on national themes or musical tropes: the *mazurkas* and *polonaises* of Frédéric Chopin (Poland, 1810–1849); Jean Sibelius's *Finlandia* (Finland, 1865–1957); and Richard Wagner's epic operas drawn from early Germanic legends, for example.

Romantic artists also sympathized with the revolutionary movements that were sweeping Europe, including the French Revolution (1789–1799), the Greek War of Independence (1820–1831), the Belgian Revolution (1830–1831), and the wars of unification in Germany and Italy (both of which formally ended in the establishment of independent states in 1871). The British composer Edward Elgar (1857–1934) wrote grand marches such as *Pomp and Circumstance*, while John Philip Sousa did the same in the United States. Writers were not immune to the revolutionary spirit either. The British poet Lord Byron (1788–1824) died from a fever in Greece, where he had gone to help in the Greek struggle for independence, and Italy's great poet of the *Risorgimento*, Giacomo Leopardi (1798–1837), after a youthful period of imitating the Greek classics, published a collection of various writings, *Zibaldone di pensieri*, contrasting the innocence of nature with the corruption of modern, rational man.

Asian Visions of Nature

15.3 *How do Asian visions of nature compare to those expressed by Western artists?*

Nature is, and has always been, a central element in much art created in Asia—China, Japan, the Indian subcontinent. From delicate ink drawings and watercolors to etchings on bronze household pots of the early Chinese dynasties, image after image includes creatures of nature, both real and unreal—snakes, flowers, dragons—and natural formations, in particular, mountains and caves. The natural world as conceptualized in Chinese thought is complex and regenerating, always in flux, always changing. It offers the possibility of purification (from the earliest days, Taoist holy men sojourned in the mountains to find renewal and to seek herbs that might prolong life) and calm respite (city dwellers built country homes to escape smoke and grime, not to mention political corruption). Taoist teachings—that humankind is an integral part of the natural world, not a dominant one, and that we must all struggle to follow the flow of nature's rhythms—were integrated into later Chinese belief systems, including Confucianism and Buddhism.

Art from the Han dynasty (206 BCE–220 CE) is rife with images of mountains imbued with a mystery befitting their status as the homes of magical grottoes, sometimes thought of as entries to other worlds, and medicinal herbs and plants. Gradually these images became more domesticated in elegant landscape paintings, and by the time of the late Tang dynasty (618–906 CE), nature paintings, especially those depicting gardens or parks with temples and palaces, had become a prominent genre. These depictions of nature responded to what may be a universal human longing to escape from the everyday world into a more innocent and natural setting.

Similarly, Japanese art has long celebrated the primacy of the natural world, although often the focus is on its necessary evanescence, as evidenced in the changing of the seasons. Such seasonal changes are central to the Japanese belief system of Shintoism, and seasons are often welcomed with festivals or picnics, which Japanese painters and writers have long used as inspiration. The inevitability of change is captured in the distinctive convention in Japanese landscape painting of depicting all four seasons in a single work that might include some trees in full blossom, others just beginning to bloom, and still others bare of any foliage.

Much art of the Indian sub-continent also focuses on the relationship between humankind and nature—predictably, since the major Indian belief system, Hinduism, teaches that human nature and the natural world are inextricably linked. The belief that Siddhartha reached a state of truth while seated beneath a great bodhi tree may account for the prominence of trees and other plants in many Indian designs and paintings.

The Rise of Urbanism

15.4 *What impact did the rise of urbanism have on humankind's relationship to nature, particularly in the United States?*

The Athenians of the fifth and fourth centuries BCE were partly responsible for developing the attitude that civilization meant the urban world. When asked why he never went for walks in the countryside, Socrates simply stared and replied that being by himself in lifeless nature could never take the place of stimulating conversation with his companions. The city meant for him culture, sophistication, the arts, and philosophy—life itself.

As cities (and their industries) grew in the nineteenth century, urban parks became substitutes for nature in the raw. New Yorkers in the early twentieth century took their new automobiles and drove out of the city on *parkways*, created especially for the purpose of offering pleasant Sunday drives, rather than for simply getting from here to there. Those who could afford it took special trains north to the Adirondack Mountains, where sprawling wood-frame hotels welcomed them, and they could sit on benches made from tree branches and look out over the picturesque beauty of Lake George. In the United States, huge swaths of land were designated as national parks, beginning with Yellowstone in 1872 and followed by some 58 others, preserving them for those of us who really wanted to see what "nature" looked like. For many of us, city and suburb dwellers, nature took on almost an unreality; it was the place where we vacationed, no longer an integral part of our lives.

The mythology of the United States is essentially urban. Early settlers were the "trailblazers," brave pioneers who "fought and tamed a wilderness"—so have cried the trailers for endless films about the subject. In Hollywood Westerns, the pioneers and cowboys were the "good guys," and they, with the help of the U.S. Cavalry, cleared the land of its original occupants—the Native Americans—through war, massacre, or resettlement to designated reservations. The land needed to be cleared because towns needed to be built; such towns represented civilization. The lives loved by Native Americans, often nomadic, almost always in harmony with the natural world, stood in the way.

In 1845, a journalist named John Louis O'Sullivan, defending the annexation of Texas, coined the phrase **Manifest Destiny**, the underlying implication of which was that the superior nation was *obliged* to spread the gospel of civilization to the "less developed world." Development—putting in place the systems and cities that would allow the newcomers to *use* the land rather than letting it defeat them—was inevitable.

And so the cities of the United States grew: New York, Chicago, San Francisco, Atlanta, Los Angeles. Detroit, with the rise of the automobile. Dallas and Houston, with the rise of the oil business. Just as cities across the globe had thrived for centuries—London, Rome, Mumbai, Beijing, Rio, Mexico City, Dakar—cities in the United States grew bigger, developed personalities. And we loved them, these magnificent cities, with their towering buildings (skyscrapers, they started calling them in Chicago), their dazzling lights (Figure 15.4), their powerful financial centers, their Broadways and Rodeo Drives.

Poets of the American Cities: Whitman and Sandburg

Even Walt Whitman, whose love of nature was transcendental, got caught up in the excitement of American urbanity. He lived in Brooklyn; he edited a newspaper there. He looked across the river to Manhattan, and this is what he saw:

> Rich, hemm'd thick all around with sailships and steamships, an island sixteen miles
>   long, solid-founded,
> Numberless crowded streets, high growths of iron, slender, strong, light splendidly
>   uprising, toward clear skies,
> Tides, swift and ample, well-loved by me, toward sundown,
> The flowing sea-currents, the little islands, larger adjoining islands, the heights, the
>   villas,
> The countless masts, the white shore steamers,
>   the lighters, the ferry-boats, the black sea-
>   steamers well model'd,
> The downtown streets, the jobbers' houses
>   of business, the houses of business of the
>   ship-merchants and money-brokers, the
>   river-streets,
> Immigrants arriving fifteen to twenty thousand
>   in a week,
> The carts hauling goods, the manly race of
>   drivers of horses, the brown-faced sailors.
> A million people—manners free and superb—
>   open voices—hospitality—the most
>   courageous and friendly young men,
> City of hurried and sparkling waters/city of
>   spires and masts!
> City nested in bays! My city![12]

Figure 15.4 Times Square, New York, at night.
How does this "landscape" compare to the one depicted by J.M.W. Turner in Figure 15.3? Are there any words that might apply to both images?
Gary Burke/Moment/Getty Images

The other muscular American city, Chicago, had its own poet laureate in Carl Sandburg (1878–1967), who in 1914 wrote this about *his* city.

Hog Butcher for the World,
Tool Maker, Stacker of Wheat,
Player with Railroads and the Nation's Freight Handler;
Stormy, husky, brawling,
City of the Big Shoulders:

They tell me you are wicked and I believe them, for I have seen your painted women
*   under the gas lamps luring the farm boys.*
And they tell me you are crooked and I answer: Yes, it is true I have seen the gunman
*   kill and go free to kill again.*
And they tell me you are brutal and my reply is: On the faces of women and children
*   I have seen the marks of wanton hunger.*
And having answered so I turn once more to those who sneer at this my city and
*   I give them back the sneer and say to them:*
Come and show me another city with lifted head singing so proud to be alive and
*   coarse and strong and cunning.*
Flinging magnetic curses amid the toil of piling job on job, here is a tall bold slugger
*   set vivid against the soft little cities;*
Fierce as a dog with tongue lapping for action, cunning as a savage pitted against
*   the wilderness.*[13]

Sandburg and Whitman are not museum pieces. Their respective attitudes bring millions of tourists each year into the sprawling cities, where hordes continue to gaze in awe at the skyscrapers. And interestingly, cities are proving their worth in these days of environmental worries. By most calculations, urban centers use less energy per resident than rural or, especially, suburban communities. City-dwellers rely on public transportation rather than private cars; they don't waste water on lawns. Urban residents collectively leave a smaller "carbon footprint" than any other group. But what is lost when we turn away from the serenity of nature?

Contemporary Antiurbanists

We do find the occasional Thoreau among us, of course—the individualist who retreats "off the grid" and builds, or tries to build, a self-sufficient life. Such retreats were particularly popular in the 1960s, when a cottage industry grew up around supporting these efforts, including *The Whole Earth Catalog* (1968–1998), a publication focused on ecology and self-sufficiency that listed vendors and products for digging wells, grinding flour, and the like, and *Foxfire*, a quarterly magazine published first in 1966 that gathers together interviews and oral histories in an effort to sustain the culture and crafts of the Appalachian Mountains.

More recently, some city-dwellers throughout the country have engaged in efforts to recapture the feel of a smaller, more manageable society. In New York, the borough of Brooklyn is famous (and occasionally laughed at) for its collection of bearded artisanal cheese-makers, bee-keepers, and micro-breweries. San Francisco is home to the original "locavore" food movement, which emphasizes the need to eat foods grown locally, on small farms, without chemicals or artificial conditions.

The argument can be made that, despite the rise of the great American city, there has always been a back-to-nature push in this country. John D. Rockefeller, founder of the Standard Oil Company, which for decades dominated the business of refining and selling oil throughout the world, tells us in his autobiography that God was responsible for his financial success. We might assume that, since much of that success involved the large-scale depletion of fossil fuel, Rockefeller was implying that God approved of this assault on the earth's resources. Or perhaps he was suggesting that a God-fearing man who benefitted humanity through the employment he provided and the fuel to drive cars and run factories was an instrument through whom God's plans were carried out.

But not so fast. Perhaps Rockefeller was in fact aware of the biblical admonition that humanity must "till and keep the Garden." Perhaps he saw that too much of nature was being despoiled, and he realized he was in a position to do something about it. Whatever his reasons, late in his life, Rockefeller purchased a good portion of Wyoming wilderness and willed it to the United States with the proviso that it be kept forever as a natural reserve. This land became the basis for two of the nation's first national parks, Yellowstone and Grand Teton.

The Force of Nature

15.5 *What is meant by the force of nature when we talk about works such as Melville's* **Moby-Dick** *and Mary Shelley's* **Frankenstein?**

Romantic artists invested nature with the awesomeness that Dante and Michelangelo attributed to God. The vast canvases of nineteenth-century English painter J.M.W. Turner, like the one shown in Figure 15.3, depict nature as a force that is both terrifying and majestically beautiful. The most comprehensive collection of Turner's work is in the recently added wing of London's Tate Gallery. There the viewer will find landscapes and, especially, seascapes, in which the furious energy at the heart of nature bursts forth in riotous colors and monstrous ocean waves—an elegy that seems impossible to comprehend and never to be ignored, but always worshiped by humanity that is part of but in no way superior to its grandeur.

The early work of American artist Winslow Homer (1836–1910) depicts calm seas and families enjoying themselves on a day at the beach. He studied in Paris, where his work was influenced by the soft colors of the Impressionists. Then he returned to spend the rest of his life in Maine. His work, under the influence of Turner, displays the sea as an awesome power to be respected but never tamed (Figure 15.5).

Melville, *Moby-Dick*

In the work of Turner and Homer, we find early environmentalism of a kind that cries "Love it, worship it, but keep your distance!" In the very year of Turner's death, Herman Melville (1819–1891) published his epic novel *Moby-Dick* (1851), written in a sweeping, breathtaking style that is the verbal equivalent of Turner and Homer. *Moby-Dick* follows the tragic attempt of one man to find and destroy a white whale that has taken off his leg in a previous encounter and that symbolizes all of nature's, and therefore God's, power. The narrator, the young sailor Ishmael, talks frequently about the terrors of confronting nature—not simply because of its physical powers, but because it can consume us psychologically as well. In Chapter 35, called "The Masthead," for example, he describes his experience standing guard high above the ship, "lulled into such an opium-like listlessness of vacant, unconscious reverie" by the "blending cadence of waves with thoughts, that at last he loses his identity; takes the mystic ocean at his feet for the visible image of that deep, blue bottomless soul, pervading mankind and nature."[14]

Figure 15.5 Winslow Homer, *The Gulf Stream*, 1899.
Homer advised young artists to look to nature for their inspiration. How does this painting differ from the Turner seascape in Figure 15.3? Does that difference impact the power of the image?
SuperStock

Moby-Dick has been compared to the great Greek tragedies as well as to the Book of Job and called a warning against moral pride, or *hubris.*

Earlier in the nineteenth century, another novel also warned against pride, rooted in science.

The Frankenstein Monster

Many attempts have been made by science to control or manipulate nature, but perhaps none have been so vividly portrayed in literature as the monster created by Victor Frankenstein in *Frankenstein; or, the Modern Prometheus*, by Mary Wollstonecraft Shelley (1797–1851), the wife of the famous poet. Shelley's fable has since become a classic; it has added terminology to our vocabularies and spawned innumerable films.

The tale was written when Mary Shelley was 19, in response to a bet posed while she was vacationing with her husband and Lord Byron about who could write the most frightening ghost story. She based her story on the ancient myth of Prometheus, a figure half human and half god, whose godly nature causes him to seek unlimited power. When he attempts to steal fire from the gods, he is caught in the act and sentenced to an eternity of anguish; he is chained to a rock while a vulture eats his liver—a torture that can never end because the devoured liver always grows back.

Mary Shelley's Dr. Victor Frankenstein is not the mad scientist of the well-known movie adaptations but rather a sensitive, gentle person, intrigued from childhood by science (then called "natural philosophy") and eager to learn everything that can possibly be learned in order to create a better life for all people. As he matures, he finds himself particularly concerned with the way the body functions.

> *Wealth was an inferior object, but what glory would attend the discovery if I could but banish disease from the human frame, and render man invulnerable to any but a violent death.*[15]

Yet, he asked himself, how am I to find the secret of immortality unless I first learn where life comes from?

Like her husband and other Romantic writers, Mary Shelley saw nature as a wondrous mystery full of almost divine secrets. She and Percy Bysshe Shelley, whom she married at the age of 16, especially loved the grandeur of lakes and mountains. Switzerland, the locale of the novel, was her favorite spot on earth. For her, nature should be admired, adored, worshiped—but never analyzed. Nature should be left alone.

Victor Frankenstein's tragic flaw is that he wants to be more than a *part* of nature. Not content with understanding how the spark of life enters lifeless matter—from electricity, he is convinced—he must take a further step. He will assemble parts of cadavers into an 8-foot superman who will represent the perfection of the species and live forever.

The outcome of his experiment is, as everyone knows, not what he expected.

> *I had selected his features as beautiful. Beautiful—Great God! His yellow skin scarcely covered the work of muscles; and arteries beneath; his hair was of a lustrous black, and flowing; his teeth of a pearly whiteness; but these luxuriances only formed a horrid contrast with his watery eyes, and seemed almost of the same colour as the dun white sockets in which they were set.*[16]

Nonetheless, the "daemon," as the author calls him, is at first as kind and gentle as his creator. He is a creature of nature; and the author believes nature, undisturbed, is good at heart. But society will not leave the daemon alone. Because of his frightening appearance, he is rejected, scorned, and ultimately becomes a vicious killer. Before his transformation, he has shown the noblest of feelings. He is a vegetarian, believing it immoral to eat animal flesh. Overhearing an account of how America was discovered, he weeps at the fate of the original inhabitants. Hiding out in a farmhouse, he stops stealing the food for which he desperately hungers when he observes how little food the family has for itself.

In an extraordinary finale, anticipating *Moby-Dick* by over 30 years, the doctor pursues the daemon to the ends of the earth, insanely believing, as does Captain Ahab, that once the monster is destroyed all evil will vanish from the earth. In the end it is Frankenstein, not the daemon, who dies. The daemon is reclaimed by nature, his true and only parent. Dwarfed by the frozen mountains of the polar circle, he sails on a raft of ice into a mist, there to meet who knows what destiny. We feel that he belongs in this primordial limbo outside of time, deep within which lie the ultimate secrets glimpsed and even unleashed but never grasped or fully controlled by human intelligence.

If Mary Shelley were alive today, she might advise us to hold on to—or acquire— the sense of mystery that the Romantic writers attributed to nature. A mystic reverence for the power of nature is well understood by our greatest scientists, Albert Einstein and Stephen Hawking among them. Victor Frankenstein was a scientist also, but one who lost sight of his own limitations. Who was the "daemon" in this great novel? Frankenstein, like Ahab, ultimately pursued his own glory.

The humanities have not been afraid to face the grim possibility that such pursuits are in conflict with the primal innocence of the natural world. That world can be violent and terrifying, but the terrors it produces—the storms, tsunamis, and earthquakes—are indigenous to that innocence.

Leaving an Imprint

15.6 *What role does nature play in Native-American culture and arts?*
  In site-specific and environmental art?

Since well before written history, humankind has been leaving its mark on the natural world. Cave paintings and rock art dating back as far as 40,000 BCE can be found across Europe, Asia, Africa, the Americas, and the Pacific and may have been forms of early communication or of support for religious ceremonies (see Figure 15.1). They were not, scholars think, purely decorative, since they often occur in places without other signs of habitation, or in hard-to-access places. Similar evidence of human creativity can be found in the American Southwest and in Latin America. These paintings use natural pigments and typically represent animals, but some also show human handprints, sometimes with abstract decorations, or geometric abstractions.

Nature and Native Americans

Native Americans enjoy a long tradition of a deeply spiritual relationship with nature. Their gods watch over nature's varied aspects: rivers, the hunting of animals, the cycles of birth and death, and so on. Their rituals with songs and dances celebrate and intensify this relationship, and their language is filled with the understanding of nature's deepest secrets. Nature inspires Native-American art and also provides the raw material for it: Pueblo potters in the Southwest use clay from the earth and natural glazes for their graceful black and red pots (Figure 15.6); Navajo weavers use natural dyes for the patterned rugs they still produce;

Figure 15.6 An early ceramic container from the Rio Grande Valley, near Albuquerque, NM, uses a typical bear claw design.
What makes an everyday item like a pot or a basket art?
Diane N. Ennis/Shutterstock

totem poles in the Pacific Northwest and Canada are carved from massive tree trunks and painted with colors made from natural elements.

In his collection of oral histories labeled creative nonfiction called *The Wolf at Twilight*, the American writer Kent Nerburn, whose work often explores Native-American culture, interviews a 90-year-old Lakota elder named Dan. How can he tell, Dan is asked, how deep a nearby creek is? Dan replies:

> *I'd have to sit and listen. If the creek giggled, it was shallow because it meant there were rocks close to the surface. If it whispered, it was deeper, but not so deep you couldn't walk across it. If it was silent, you had to be careful. That's how you knew where to cross in the darkness—by listening to how the creek talked.*[17]

Crowfoot (c. 1830–1890), of the Blackfoot nation, sees all existence from nature's viewpoint.

> *What is life? It is the flash of a firefly in the night. It is the breath of a buffalo in the winter time. It is the little shadow which runs across the grass and loses itself in the Sunset.*[18]

The difference between those who identify with nature and those who believe it is their privilege to bend nature to their will is expressed by a venerable Native-American holy woman.

> *The white people never cared for land or deer or bear. When we Indians kill meat, we eat it all up. When we dig roots we make little holes. When we burn grass for grasshoppers we don't ruin things. We shake down acorns and pinenuts. We don't chop down trees, kill everything. The tree says, "Don't. I am sore. Don't hurt me." But they chop it down and cut it up. The spirit of the land hates them.*[19]

Regardless of how much urban society has wrought changes in some Native-American quarters, the fact remains that they *have* a long history of oneness with nature, and much of their traditional wisdom can be seen in the proud displays of native clothing and the performances of traditional dances and songs, most of which have roots in the natural world. The imprint they leave on the natural world is light.

Site-Specific and Environmental Art

Cave paintings and totem poles were often placed specifically in locations where their creators felt they belonged for cultural or spiritual reasons. In the twentieth and twenty-first centuries, the term **site-specific art** was created to describe works, often sculptures, that are similarly designed to fit into one place and one place only. Often these use the contours or materials of the natural landscape as part of their design, and whether they are intended to be temporary or permanent, they cannot be sold, removed, and rebuilt in a museum or a living room. They belong only where they are.

Site-specific installations can refer to works created for both natural settings (like *The Gates*, pictured in Figure 5.43, by Christo and Jean-Claude) or urban ones. Sculptures by the American George Segal, for example, are primarily of human figures, and they startle viewers as they cross a street on the campus of Montclair State University in New Jersey or sit in a park near the site of the Stonewall "riots" in 1969 in New York City as a monument to the gay rights movement. But much site-specific art, also called **environmental art**, nestles in natural landscapes, sometimes calling attention to the damage that humankind has done to these landscapes over the centuries.

ROBERT SMITHSON The American Robert Smithson (1938–1973), after an early career as a figure painter, became intrigued by natural materials and settings. Also a critic and essayist, Smithson wrote widely on—and was clearly influenced by—nineteenth-century landscape painting and the park designs of Frederick Law Olmsted. He noted the fluidity both of nature itself and of those settings that had been created to mimic nature, like Olmsted's Central Park. The park was designed to be *picturesque*. By the late twentieth century, however, it had become anything but. Writing in the 1970s, Smithson noted:

> *Now the Ramble has grown up into an urban jungle, and lurking in its thickets are "hoods, hobos, hustlers, and homosexuals," and other estranged creatures of the city. . . . Walking east, I passed graffiti on boulders. . . . In the spillway that pours out of the Wollman Memorial Ice Rink, I noticed a metal grocery cart and a trash basket half-submerged in the water. Further down, the spillway becomes a brook choked with mud and tin cans.*[20]

In the 1960s, Smithson began creating monumental earthworks designed to demonstrate his theories about the changes that occur constantly in nature. His most famous work is *The Spiral Jetty* (1970), which comprises a 1,500-foot-long spiral-shaped jetty built from rocks and earth that extends into the Great Salt Lake in Utah. The jetty has periodically disappeared, submerged as the lake waters rise, reappearing in times of drought.

ANDY GOLDSWORTHY   Unlike Smithson, the British sculptor Andy Goldsworthy (born 1956) is an active environmentalist. But like Smithson, he is also interested in the natural cycles of growth and decay. He is a skilled photographer—almost necessarily, since much of his work is open to the elements and transient, even ephemeral. His entryway to San Francisco's DeYoung Museum is a courtyard of granite cracked to mimic the effects of an earthquake—a frequent occurrence in San Francisco—but more typically he creates in natural settings: tree trunks laid end to end to form a pathway; polished rocks balanced in precarious piles; small arches of natural stone; structures of red clay.

More than an Inconvenience

15.7 *What implications does humanity's disregard for nature over the past 100 years have on our future?*

In his sonnet "The World Is Too Much with Us," Wordsworth speaks of the "getting and spending" which cause us to lose touch with the natural world. Nature for him was a force capable not only of healing itself but of healing the troubled hearts of those who were willing to flee urban society. Many today may believe that they need do nothing to help in the healing process, that it will take place magically, as it did for the Romantic poets. Not everyone agrees, including a modern poet named David Kwiat.

HURRICANE SEASON, THE NATURE OF WAR

The winds like war have wreaked
their havoc once again,
Upturned, bent, crushed and crushing,
bringing along roots, grass, concrete and
God help us, coffins.
These giants, so many of them a century in the
making; sprung from this brackish earth and water,
these once towering, yawning canopies
are reconciled to their befallen state—
duly pacified in the knowledge of their role
in the greater scheme;
the one that is incomprehensible
in the here and now.
The one that says the winds are nature's
cleansing power and that these
earthly steeples have not died in vain.
The reasoning of an ecological 'sound bite'

as buzz-sawed trunks rot
and limbs still quiver
in a calmer wind.[21]

The concerns expressed by Kwiat are not new. Some writers and artists have long been dismayed by the tendency of humankind to take what it will from the earth and ignore the consequences. For centuries, we have indulged our need to "civilize"—to tame both nature and its inhabitants, sometimes even its human ones—but at what cost?

"The Horror! The Horror!"

In 1902, Joseph Conrad (1857–1924) published the novella *Heart of Darkness*, still one of the strongest indictments of human arrogance every written. Conrad, born in Poland but a naturalized British citizen who wrote in English, spent his early years working on ships that took him to remote corners of the globe, including what was then called the Belgian Congo, a relatively unexplored, largely impenetrable, but potentially resource-rich land in central Africa. The narrator of the story, a Conrad alter ego named Marlowe, is hired by a trading company that sends him into the Congo looking for the company's principal trader, an Austrian named Kurtz, who has not been heard from in months.

Early in the narrative, Marlowe describes what it felt like to enter the eerie, forbidden land, a region truly primal:

> *Going up that river was like travelling back to the earliest beginnings of the world,*
> *when vegetation rioted on the earth and the big trees were kings. An empty stream,*
> *a great silence, an impenetrable forest.*[22]

On the way up the river, Marlowe hears legend after legend about Kurtz, who is considered a wilderness tamer, even a god, in the eyes of the African natives. White men in outlying posts refer to Kurtz as "a prodigy . . . an emissary of pity and science and progress." What we gradually learn, however, is that Kurtz represents all that went wrong with civilization, beginning with the myth that humanity was the noblest achievement of evolution. Armed with a belief in the infallibility of "civilization" and in the inherent rightness of "taking over," Kurtz is convinced that his way of dealing with the natives is in their best interest. But Marlowe soon realizes that the mythical aura in which Kurtz has enveloped himself masks the real "heart of darkness."

> *But the wilderness had found him out early, and had taken on him a terrible vengeance*
> *for this fantastic invasion. I think it had whispered to him things about which he did*
> *not know.*[23]

In one of the most dramatically anticipated confrontations in all of literature, Marlowe finds Kurtz, but only after the latter has been mortally wounded in an explosive and bloody uprising. "I had immense plans," Kurtz insists. "I was on the threshold of great things." What these were to have been, we never find out—but presumably he intended to impose the order and discipline of his own brand of civilization on the people who now surrounded him.

We also do not find out all the sins Kurtz has committed, but we do learn that he presided "at certain midnight dances ending with unspeakable rites," has been party to the wanton killing of elephants for their ivory, and has committed multiple murders when others stood in his way. In Francis Ford Coppola's 1979 adaptation of the story into film, *Apocalypse Now*, the camera pans along rows of shrunken heads on poles outside Kurtz's home, a terrifying image that also occurs in the novella. As he dies in Marlowe's presence, Kurtz, perhaps realizing at last the damage he has done in the name of civilization, whispers *"The horror! The horror!"*

But when Marlowe returns to London and meets with Kurtz's fiancée, he cannot bear to tell the truth: His last words, he tells her, were about you.

One characteristic of a classic is that it continues to resonate. *Heart of Darkness* can be read today as an allegory of the damage we have done—and continue to do—to the earth's resources, our arrogance in thinking that human needs trump those of all other creatures and, indeed, of the earth itself.

Modern Environmentalism

The environmental movement that exists today began in the 1960s, following the publication of Rachel Carson's *Silent Spring* in 1962 and, only a few years later, the first major U.S. oil spill, off the coast of Santa Barbara, California, in January 1969. Its roots can be traced to much earlier times—the Romantic obsession with pure landscapes, and the rising concern in the early twentieth century about smoke and water pollution—but Carson's book was the trigger. It warned about the deadly effects of the pesticide DDT, and it was followed in the next decades by other, equally alarming works, including *The Fate of the Earth* (1982, Jonathan Schell) and *The End of Nature* (1989, Bill McKibben).

In the 1980s, scientists began issuing stern warnings that the increasing levels of carbon emissions into the atmosphere would inevitably cause chaotic change in the climate and that this change would eventually prove devastating to our civilization. They warned that big businesses who chopped down massive swaths of trees, particularly in South American rain forests, failed to realize how necessary these forests are to our own breathing cycle of oxygen and carbon dioxide. They warned people not to drive unnecessarily because the carbon emissions from automobiles alone could ruin the planet—not to mention that our levels of gas and oil consumption would eventually deplete the earth's supplies.

AN INCONVENIENT TRUTH   The 2006 Academy Award–winning documentary *An Inconvenient Truth*, written and narrated by former U.S. Vice President Al Gore, offers a strong and sobering message to all who choose to listen. The film features graphic photographs of disasters that have already taken place, including the melting ice sheets in Greenland, the Arctic Circle, and Antarctica, as well as a picture seen around the world of a polar bear clinging to a slender piece of ice in its desperate search for food.

Eminent environmental scientists in the film point out that carbon levels in the Antarctic are higher than in any of the last 650,000 years. They argue that if the ice sheet that has surrounded Greenland for millennia continues melting (and they are certain that it will), sea levels could rise as much as 20 feet, leaving all of Florida and much of the East and West coasts under water—not to mention submerging multiple island nations throughout the world. And they tell us that animals will seek new habitats, deserts will appear where fertile fields once produced food, and drinkable water will become scarce.

We are already seeing these predictions come to pass. Biologists are identifying animal species in locations where they have never before appeared; sea levels are rising and more polar bears are being stranded; much of North Africa has shifted from arable land to desert; massive storms like Hurricanes Katrina (2005) and Sandy (2013), formerly predicted to occur once or twice in a century, now come every few years; California is suffering a drought of four years and counting, and the governor is rationing water consumption. (See Figures 15.7 and 15.8.) All of

Figure 15.7 A polar bear clings to a tiny ice floe in an environment where ice used to exist as far as the eye can see.
Jan Martin Will/Shutterstock

Figure 15.8 A beach on the shore of Lake Tahoe, in Nevada, shows the results of a four-year drought.
Do you think climate change can be reversed? Or would we be better off spending our energies trying to find new ways to accommodate to these changes?

David N Braun (www.Gowestfoto.com)/Moment Open/Getty Images

this is the result of climate change. Whether or not the problem is reversible at this point is a matter of debate. Many scientists say no, no matter what changes we make, which leads many to a fatalistic attitude: If nothing I do makes a difference, then why do anything? Others feel there is still hope, but only if the nations of the world agree to work together to halt consumption and emissions.

The problem is staggering. If you ask people on the street whether they worry about the health of the planet, the answer would probably be yes, but they might add, "What can I do about it? I have to commute a long way to my job." Summit meetings on global warming have resulted in much agreement and little change. Like Conrad's Marlowe, we may all have to be content with the lie. Or we can hope that the few scientists who assure us that global warming is part of a natural cycle that has repeated itself time and again are right. We may have to cling to a tiny ice floe and hope for the best.

Looking Back

In this chapter,

- we discussed the changing view of nature expressed through the arts from biblical times to the Middle Ages to the age of Shakespeare,

- we differentiated among Romantic views of nature defined as the picturesque, the beautiful, and the sublime, and examined examples of Romanticism in literature and music,

- we explored visions of nature expressed in Chinese and Japanese art,

- we discussed the rise of urbanism, particularly in the United States, and its implications for the arts,

- we talked about the awesome force of nature—its indifference, and its horrors—and offered examples from Melville's *Moby-Dick* and Mary Shelley's *Frankenstein*,

- we compared the way nature is used in Native-American, site-specific, and environmental art, and

- we explored how our disregard for nature—its resources and its power—for the past 100 years will inevitably affect our future.

Key Terms

environmentalism A movement based on the beliefs that the proper role of humankind is stewardship of the earth's resources, that greenhouse gases are causing climate change and endangering all life on the planet, and that all humans should properly be concerned about actions that adversely affect the planet.

environmental art An umbrella term for art that incorporates nature, but more often is used specifically to refer to art that is motivated by ecological, often political, concerns.

Manifest Destiny Popular phrase coined in 1845 by John Louis O'Sullivan to support the annexation of Texas. It came to mean, for some, that the United States has an obligation to become a world leader and a role model for "less advanced" nations.

naturalist One who prefers to live apart from society, in the country, observing day-to-day events taking place in nature. Henry David Thoreau was such an observer.

nature A term with multiple meanings: a reference to the nonurban world; the system of laws governing the universe; an indwelling spirit or mind governing the universe; and the environment and the ecosystem within it.

site-specific art Artwork that is created to exist in a specific place, where the artist has taken the location into consideration when designing the art.

Transcendentalism The belief that divinity pervades all nature and that thought and spirituality are more real than material things and the ordinary actions of life.

Chapter 16
Freedom

Learning Objectives

16.1 Explain early views of freedom, including the role of religion in discussing freedom.

16.2 Describe various determinist arguments, including political, institutional, and economic determinism, character as fate, behaviorism, and genetic determinism.

16.3 Describe various arguments supporting the existence of free will, including those based on theories of Schopenhauer, William James, and Freud.

16.4 Explain the term *existentialism* and its relationship to the debate about free will and determinism.

16.5 Discuss why true freedom needs limits.

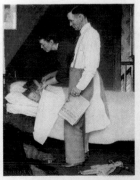

OURS...to fight for

Freedom of Speech   *Freedom of Worship*

Freedom from Want   *Freedom from Fear*

Figure 16.1 Norman Rockwell, *The Four Freedoms*, 1943.
Do you agree that these four — freedom of speech and of worship, freedom from want and from fear— define the most important freedoms for humankind? What else might you add to this list?
Pictorial Press Ltd/Alamy. Art © Norman Rockwell Trust

427

Humanists believe freedom is vital to the art of being human: the freedom to create and to enjoy what others create; the freedom to think and listen to the thoughts of others, whether in agreement or not; the freedom to examine one's options and then decide upon the wisest course of action.

This chapter focuses on the question of *whether or not the will is truly free*. If it is not, then what does it mean to be a truly free individual? We will look into the two major sides of the debate. **Determinism** holds that freedom of the will does not exist, that too many factors govern our choices. Arguments for free will hold just the opposite: that we do indeed act freely, and that there are ways to prove this.

Throughout modern history, education has been considered the best way to guarantee freedom: An education that focuses on the humanities, or the **liberal arts**, and on critical thinking will prepare individuals to be thoughtful citizens with the ability to analyze arguments critically, communicate their own positions effectively, and find paths to compromise and agreement. In the last few decades, however, increasingly powerful arguments have emerged that suggest something very different: Education should be, above all else, a path to a good job. Students should be taught the skills necessary to do the jobs that the economy offers—not the skills necessary for analysis, innovation, effective communication, and creativity. But because the world is always changing, the jobs that the economy offers today will not necessarily be there tomorrow. Analysis, innovation, communication, creativity—these are the skills that will allow humankind to survive under *any* conditions.

Early Views of Freedom

16.1 *What are some early views of freedom? What role does religion play when we discuss freedom?*

As with other important ideas, freedom has not had the same meaning in every historical context. The Greeks, for example, developed the concept of democracy and passed on as their legacy the model of the democratic state in which citizens are free to think, to question, and to speak out. At the time, however, free citizens comprised only about 5 percent of the adult Greek population; the rest were slaves and women, who were generally deemed too irrational and irresponsible to be trusted with political decisions.

The Roman state also denied freedom to much of its population and held many thousands in slavery. The early Roman Empire believed it had the right to enslave the conquered in the name of civilization, which it thought it was bringing to the barbarian world. In 212 CE, however, the emperor Caracalla granted full citizenship to all free men within the Roman Empire (where before only those living in the region around Rome could be citizens)—a move that many historians believe is at least partially responsible for the long success of Roman rule over such a wide territory. (Women held a more limited form of citizenship.) Rome also famously had its forum, where duly qualified citizens had the right to exchange ideas and debate the laws, even when emperors as tyrannical as Caligula and Nero ruled with iron hands.

And there were examples such as Epictetus, a Greek philosopher who was held in captivity and tortured by the Romans but was finally released when his brilliance was recognized. Presumably even in his early years as a slave, Epictetus enjoyed freedom to think as he pleased. His years in slavery may also have contributed to his development of the concept of stoicism.

Religion and Free Will

For most major religions, a central question is whether the actions of humankind are undertaken freely or are part of an overall plan of destiny created by God. Christianity has struggled for centuries with the complexity of freedom. Do human beings have free will or not? If God is all-powerful, he must be all-knowing; he must have advance knowledge of what people will do. If human actions have already been determined, in what sense, then, can free will exist?

The Christian writer St. Augustine (354–430) proposed one solution: God possesses foreknowledge, but this does not mean that humanity is not held responsible for its sins. On the divine level, there is no free will, but on the human level, there is. Augustine believed in predestination (the divine level), but since humanity did not have this foreknowledge, individuals were actually free to do as they pleased—free by God's grace and predestined because of God's power. Detractors, however, argue that Augustine is trying to have it both ways. Either we are free or we are not free.

The teachings of Hinduism are in some ways similar to those of Augustine: People are responsible for their own actions, but they are part of a world created and controlled by an omniscient and omnipotent figure. The key is to realize that Brahman is in control. As long as individuals believe that they have free will, they will indeed be free to make their own decisions and follow their own paths, but those paths will lead only to a cycle of births and deaths; such individuals will not advance toward a purer state. Those who surrender completely to the worship of Brahman will then be freed from the consequences of actions they have taken and will benefit from God's benevolence.

Like Buddhism, Hinduism does not endorse fatalism. Even though we live in a world controlled by God, we are expected to live good and fruitful lives and to make good and fruitful choices. Similarly, adherents of Islam are free to either follow Allah's path or choose to go astray.

Free to Do . . . What?

When we argue that we should be free to do what we really want to do, how do we know what we really want? Perhaps many forces are pushing us in one direction or another. How much of what we are, what we think, and what we do was determined long before we ever entered this world and reached an age when making choices was possible? A great many scientists, philosophers, sociologists, economists, and psychologists maintain that total freedom is an impossibility, even in a free society.

Some have equated free will with natural rights. The British poet William Blake was a strong believer in the rights of the individual. In the very proper eighteenth century, he and his wife demanded the right to go naked in their own garden. Blake loved nature and loved being out of doors in his original state. He viewed clothing as a symbol of society's oppression. He saw the right to do as one pleased as nature's bequest, and he believed nature (or heaven, which had the same meaning for him) responded ferociously when that right was denied. In "Auguries of Innocence," he put the matter succinctly:

> *A robin redbreast in a cage*
> *Puts all Heaven in a rage.*

Determinism

16.2 *What are some of the arguments supporting determinism, including political, institutional, and economic determinism, character as fate, behaviorism, and genetic determinism?*

Freedom of will can be defined as the ability to choose between alternatives, ranging from fairly straightforward ones—obeying the speed limit or driving faster than the law permits; going to class or sleeping in; spending a paycheck on video games or putting it in the bank—and more complicated ones—choosing to live together, get married, or stay single; choosing to continue to worship in your parent's faith, find a new one, or turn your back on organized religion. Listing the number of options with which we are faced each day, from deciding how many spoonfuls of sugar to put in our morning coffee to picking the time to turn off the iPad at night, might cause us to think we are indeed free.

Yet stop a moment and reflect on even one of these options. We can't decide whether to speed or obey the limit if we don't have a car. We can't buy a car without money or at least a decent credit rating. We can't have money or credit without a job (unless, of course, we inherit wealth—which offers a whole other set of decisions to make). Even if we have a job, the *kind* of job will determine what kind of car we can afford. If we aren't able to afford the right kind of education, our choice of jobs may be limited.

It gets complicated fast.

Rigid determinists believe the limitations integral to our lives are too numerous for there ever to be any question of making a *free* choice. Social class lays down the parameters of our lifestyle. Responsibilities incurred by marriage and family force some of us to continue reporting to jobs we may not like. Economic circumstances force some parents to work two or three jobs in order to earn the money to provide for children necessarily left in the care of others. Other parents feel obligated to put careers on hold in order to care for children—role switches that may result not in greater freedom but in different limitations.

Determinism emerged from the eighteenth-century revolution in philosophy triggered by science—in particular, the impact of the view that every effect must have a cause. Applying this scientific law to human behavior, some philosophers argued that all choice is limited by a prior condition—limited so severely that it cannot be considered a free choice. Each of us, they suggest, is in fact the product of a chain of *cause and effect* stretching back to the very dawn of existence. Among the causes they cite are those imposed by politics and economics, by institutions, by the makeup of our own characters, by behavioral limitations, and by genetics and sociobiology.

Political Determinism

Obstacles to freedom of choice and action are the restrictions imposed on the individual by groups in power. It is hard to imagine that when people are aggressively denied freedom of action, freedom of thought is readily available to them.

An independent film titled *Chinese Dream* (2004) deals with uneducated, poverty-stricken young men in China who are lured into signing up for work in the United States with promises of unlimited opportunities but who are smuggled into the country, brought to New York without being told where they are, forced into menial labor for long hours every day in the stifling heat of a restaurant kitchen, and made to live in dirty, crowded, airless dormitories, never seeing sunlight. The sensitive young protagonist asks only for cigarettes and a magazine showing pictures of New York, the promised land of his dreams. Finally escaping one night, he is penniless and bewildered by the roaring traffic and frenetic pace of the big city, a vast neon wasteland in which he will never be free to create his own destiny.

Millions exist in countries that deny freedom to all but a privileged few. Azar Nafisi, now a professor at Johns Hopkins University and author of *Reading Lolita in Tehran* (2003), formerly taught literature at a university considered the most liberal in her country of Iran. It did admit some women, but they were not treated as the equals of the male students.

> *I felt helpless as I listened to their endless tales of woe. Female students were being penalized for running up the stairs when they were late for classes, for laughing in the hallways, for talking to members of the opposite sex.*[1]

Thwarted in her attempts to enlarge the scope of her students' reading background and their critical-thinking skills, Nafisi decides at one point she will never be allowed to teach books that invite a free exchange of ideas and so offers her resignation, which is promptly refused on the grounds that only the university has the right to decide when employment is to be terminated. At length she does manage to leave, but not without regret that she has been unable to fulfill completely her mission as a teacher dedicated to opening the minds of her students so that they might think for themselves.

Facing up to the reality of freedom denied to a large portion of the world's population can be unpleasant to those who sigh, then shrug their shoulders, as if to say, "But what can I do about it? Let's just be glad *we're* free." Yet understanding that "free" is not a word to be tossed about lightly or to be simply *assumed* is the first, absolutely essential step we must take. Even if we are lucky enough not to be penalized for laughing in the hallway, so goes the determinist argument, too many other forces must at some point be recognized, all the more frightening because they have no human face.

Institutional Determinism

Though he is known as one of the staunchest advocates of freedom from oppression, the French philosopher Jean-Jacques Rousseau (1712–1778), whom many consider the major architect of the French Revolution, is also famous for his analysis of the forces that limit freedom. If he could be asked if he were a determinist, his answer might well be: "I wish I were not, but the conditions under which we live require me to adopt this belief."

Rousseau's thinking was as radical as that of any activist of the modern era. He was vehemently against any repressive government with the power to limit human choice, for, he reasoned, we should be free to create the ideal form of government. Total freedom was for him impossible, given the uncontrollable forces stacked against everyone. But to take what freedom remained and surrender it to one human being or group of human beings was an affront to all civilized people. He believed the ideal government did not exist for personal power or prestige but was answerable to the entire population.

ROUSSEAU, "A DISCOURSE ON THE ORIGIN OF INEQUALITY"   In fanning the revolutionary flames that were beginning to sweep through a France increasingly outraged at the decadence of the aristocracy and the injustices suffered by the common people, Rousseau constructed a mythical account of the origin of the human species to back up his claim that freedom was both a *natural condition* and a *natural right*. In "A Discourse on the Origin of Inequality," Rousseau draws a romantic picture of a lost age of innocence when early people lived in peace and harmony, sharing the fruits of the abundant earth through a common realization that nature provided equal bounty for everyone. In this age of innocence, no laws or government existed because, obviously, law and government are not necessary when everyone is happy and there is no crime.

Many artists, poets, and religions have been inspired by the idea of a pristine state of innocence. Judaism, Christianity, and Islam all share the belief that our earliest ancestors lived in the Garden of Eden before their fall (Figure 16.2).

In his "A Discourse on the Origin of Inequality," Rousseau says one day a man with a stick

Figure 16.2 Edward Hicks, *The Peaceable Kingdom,* **ca. 1820.**
Do you believe such a paradise once existed? Could it exist again?
Courtesy of National Gallery of Art/Gift of Edgar William and Bernice Chrysler Garbisch

decides to grab more than his natural share. He is the first person to abuse nature's gift of freedom by using it to his own advantage. With his stick, he carves out a private piece of territory for himself.

> *The first man, who, after enclosing a piece of ground, took it into his head to say, "This is mine," and found people simple enough to believe him, was the true founder of civil society.*[2]

The man with the stick was the founder of society as Rousseau understands it because, by creating the model of the exploiter, he and his followers became an ever-present threat to the rights of the others. The exploiters therefore had to be suppressed by the gradual development of law, government, and all other institutions dedicated to the curtailment, or the limitation, of natural rights. But these safeguards of liberty, once in place, become despotic.

Here Rousseau's position becomes revolutionary. The philosopher asserts that revolution, even if violent, is a genuine alternative to exploitation and may often be the *only* means by which to deal with it. Rousseau explains and justifies revolution in the name of natural rights belonging to all, but he does *not* in his myth account for the origin of the man with the stick. What made this one man decide to become possessive when the others were joyously bobbing for golden apples in an age of sun and fun? Or was he merely the first to manifest himself? Did the potential for exploitation lie deep within *every* member of that "innocent" society? If so, when were institutional safeguards ever *not* needed?

THE NATURAL STATE OF HUMANKIND Rousseau's anti-institutional bias is based on the assumption that in the *state of nature* (a phrase hotly debated then and since) humankind is decent, tame, moral, and benevolent. Only when held in check, only when threatened with punishment for disobedient acts, do people become hateful, aggressive, and violent—particularly when rebelling in a just cause. But what Rousseau did not know, because he died a decade before the revolution he predicted, was that Napoleon Bonaparte would rise from the ashes of France and, sword in hand, create a new age of exploitation, perhaps even more oppressive than the one it supplanted. History shows us that this cycle of oppression, liberation, and further oppression has been repeated many times over.

A tragic example of a revolutionary cause turned lethal occurred on November 18, 1978, when over 900 members of a religious sect called People's Temple were ordered to commit suicide by drinking cyanide-laced Kool-Aid. From all accounts, their leader, Jim Jones, was earnest in the beginning about establishing a communal agricultural society, which, had it come to pass, would have resembled Rousseau's free and benevolent community. But when many became disillusioned and tried to defect, the community turned into a prison.

One member was able to secretly contact outside sources and describe Jones's manic, self-absorbed leadership, forced sexual intercourse, and brutal beatings administered to those who disobeyed his rules. Four Americans, including U.S. Representative Leo Ryan and several relatives of Jones's prisoners, visited the camp but were gunned down before they could reboard their plane. With time running out, Jones ordered the mass suicide. Among the dead were 270 children. A memorial service was held, and one speaker said: "Remember the people of Jonestown, not for their horrible deaths, but for who they were—people in search of a better world."

If a strong-willed person leads a once-benevolent cause, Rousseau might have said, it sometimes turns into "forced benevolence," which then must be autocratically monitored. Is the stick inborn into certain people, who become a menace to civilized life and must in turn be controlled? Are the institutions of control inevitable? And can *they* in turn become oppressive, acting as curtailments on everyone's freedom?

Rousseau believed he had solved the problem when he advanced the theory of the *social contract*. By this he meant that the only way to guarantee the protection of human rights was not through unlimited freedom but through each citizen's willingness to hand over some rights to institutions dedicated to the maintenance of order within society. The social contract is a cornerstone of **institutional determinism**, which holds that government controls are needed to protect people from other people. Yet what happens when institutions insist they must have more and more power in order to do their job? Will the man with the stick suddenly reappear?

Economic Determinism

The two major competing economic ideologies of the twentieth century were **communism** and capitalism. By the 1990s, capitalism had essentially won the battle; the central communist power, the Soviet Union, had broken apart, and most other major communist countries (China, North Korea, Vietnam, Cuba) were moving further and further from the original communist ideal, either toward something close to capitalism or to dictatorship.

MARX AND THE THEORY OF COMMUNISM   The writings of the German economic philosopher Karl Marx (1818–1883) profoundly influenced the Bolshevik Revolution of 1917 in Russia and the subsequent spread of **socialism** throughout much of the world. Despite the failure of the communist experiment in the Soviet Union and elsewhere, the theories of Marx continue to influence economic theory.

Not nature, not humanity, but *money* calls the tune, so believed Marx. As an economist, he developed a theory explaining that our behavior, our hopes and aspirations, our career choices are all determined by the social class into which we are born: The rich want to hold onto their money and tend to favor legislation designed to keep their holdings intact; the poor desire to better themselves, and in some cases, this desire becomes an obsession, eclipsing everything else in their lives. And those in the middle class want to climb to the top—while making sure that those below are not following too closely.

Marx believed that **economic determinism**—the quest for money and property that controls thinking and dictates actions—would inevitably lead to a society divided into two classes: the affluent **bourgeoisie**, who control all means of production, and the **proletariat**, or those who work. Sooner or later, however, the proletariat, made furious by the unfair distribution of wealth, will unite, rise up, and seize the means of production for themselves. Marx believed this radical change could—but would not necessarily—take place without violence.

Marx's theory was influenced by the thinking of an earlier German philosopher, Georg Wilhelm Friedrich Hegel (1770–1831), whose theory of knowledge stated that we reach philosophical certainty through a method he called the **dialectic**—that is, by analyzing opposing views and combining them into a *synthesis*. Marx took Hegel's abstractions and applied them to the concrete realities of the class struggle. The opposition of the bourgeoisie, who want to hold onto money and power, and the proletariat, who are bent on seizing some of it, would lead to a synthesis that Marx called the *classless society*.

THE SOVIET EXPERIMENT   Communism, a social system based on the idea of the classless society, was the banner of the 1917 revolution in Russia. The revolutionists agreed with Marx that violence would sometimes prove to be the only way to bring about the workers' paradise. They had grown tired of waiting. Vladimir Lenin (1870–1924) had redefined Marxism to make violent revolution a necessity. The first dramatic, world-shaking event was in February of 1917, when Czar Nicholas II was forced to abdicate. (He and his family were executed the following year.) In October of that same year, the Bolshevik Revolution led to the establishment of the Soviet Union and a new social order, communism, whereby most private property would be state-owned and the private sector nearly abolished.

The Communists were careful to say "public," not "state-owned," but the result was the same: Workers were forced into collectives, both agricultural and industrial, and their shared labor was used to support the nation as a whole. The Soviet Union (the political entity comprising Russia and the satellite nations it had drawn into its orbit) soon realized that public ownership of all means of production was not an easy sell. Farmers, for example, really weren't interested in raising crops and livestock for society as a whole. Some rebelled; some burned crops in protest—and many were sent, in retaliation, to the prisons of the *gulag* in Siberia. The vast majority of the Soviet population under communism was given assigned jobs, and everybody was paid what was considered a decent, if modest, wage. The housing program was also administered by the state under the strictest of guidelines, providing so many square feet per person.

As time went on, the Soviet state recognized the need for more and more private ownership. The classless society never really materialized, and, because the private sector grew, a handful of people prospered while the mass of workers looked on with envy. Propaganda was strong, constantly assuring the people that their sacrifices were for the good of all; as time went by, workers began to wonder when the "paradise" was coming (Figure 16.3). It began to look as though the Marxist separation of the rich and the poor was still there. Without being able to satisfy their self-interest, most workers could not be motivated to produce more goods or provide more efficient service.

Whether or not the classless society envisioned by Marx could ever actually exist, Marxist theory is still invoked by many as a way of explaining, at least in part, what motivates human behavior. The fact is that much of Europe now adheres to socialism, a less rigid interpretation of Marxian theory, which puts the welfare of the people squarely in the hands of the state. Although individuals select their own careers and earn their own paychecks, they also pay high taxes in order to ensure that everyone will enjoy the benefits of free education, parental leave, health care, and mandated vacation time.

Figure 16.3 A Soviet propaganda poster from 1967, showing workers uniting for the good of the state.
In theory, does Marxism sound like a good idea? Why does Marxism seem to work in some places but not in others?
Sovfoto/Universal Images Group/Getty Images

ADAM SMITH AND THE THEORY OF CAPITALISM The Scottish moral philosopher Adam Smith (1723–1790) argued that capitalism is the natural driving force behind human life. Smith suggests that greed, which is natural to all of humanity, is good because it ensures a free market system. If businesses are allowed the freedom to do what they like, they will provide employment, which in turn will give everyone disposable income, which in turn will move the economy upward. When there is too much money to spend or too little product to sell, then businesses will raise prices until a point is reached at which buying slows down, and prices will begin to fall.

Marxism and capitalism share one basic, common underlying assumption: *Economic needs dominate.* Some economists believe both philosophies are flawed, because there are never enough material resources to satisfy everybody. In a communist society, workers may not be motivated to produce abundantly. In a capitalist society, the affluent can afford to buy whatever they want regardless of price, but inflated costs eventually harm those less fortunate. The case for determinism at this point becomes very strong: *Can anybody escape the desire for more money?* The more one has, the less one is likely to be satisfied. The less one has, the more obsessive one's needs become. According to economic determinists, all human behavior can be understood in terms of how much money is or is not available.

ECONOMICS AND THE ART OF BEING HUMAN   Traditional humanists find it degrading to suppose that money alone is necessarily the source of well-being. Surely we find pleasure in things other than material resources: In fact, we find pleasure in the creative endeavors that this book has discussed and that have marked human progress throughout time. The art of being human does not entail making a choice between the humanities and money. We cannot deny the importance of economics to the way we live. But the art of being human *does* require that we observe ourselves in action. If economic motives are not the *sole* reasons that we do what we do, we must admit that they are sometimes the *major* ones.

Creative artists, once romantically thought to be somehow "above" the vulgarity of economic determinism, nevertheless retain agents, negotiate hefty contracts, charge high fees for television interviews and college lectures, and go on promotional tours to boost the sales of their latest film, recording, or publication.

Whether we like it or not, the science of economics often dominates our lives. We stay in jobs we hate because we need the money; we lose homes to foreclosure; we juggle bills to stay alive. Still, to admit that our lives are at least partially determined by economics is not the same as being either a rigid Marxist or a crass materialist. The important thing is at all times to recognize—or at least try to recognize—the roots of our behavior. The more we wear blinders to allow us to ignore reality, the more chronically unfree we become. We take a step on the path to freedom when we begin to see the things that limit us—or when we impose the limitations on ourselves.

Character as Fate

Achilles may be a hero, but determinists would say he is made so by the strengths of his own character—just as Oedipus must come to a tragic end because of his flawed character. Many enduring characters in memorable works of fiction—Don Quixote, Becky Sharp, Huckleberry Finn, Frodo, Katniss Everdeen, among others—stay in our minds because they are idiosyncratic and make what sometimes feel like unpredictable choices, but also because they eventually fulfill the fates that we, from the beginning, have seen in store for them. Their authors—Cervantes, Thackeray, Twain, Tolkien, Collins—provide us as readers with the information we need to understand where they will end up. In each case, character suggests destiny.

Are the lives of these characters examples of determinism, then—of lives that finally follow a predictable path not because money drives them, or power drives them, but precisely because of who they are? Their very particular flaws (Don Quixote's inability to perceive reality, Becky Sharp's ambition) or strengths (Huck's innate moral compass, Katniss's compassion) are the engines that drive them.

The early Greek philosopher Heraclitus (535–475 BCE) famously said that "character is fate." Many modern psychologists would agree.

Behaviorism

Behaviorism is a school of thought founded on the work of B.F. Skinner (1904–1990) that says we are not what we *are* (as the character-as-fate believers might) but rather what we *do*, and that how we behave is determined by a series of rewards and punishments that begins to weave its web as soon as we are born.

If humanity has a nature, it lies, according to Skinner (Figure 16.4), in *the capacity to be conditioned*. Everything we do is the result of a reinforcement of behavior.

Figure 16.4 The psychologist B.F. Skinner.
Skinner argued that all behavior is based on conditioning—
the application of rewards and punishments. Do you agree?
AP Images

Those actions that are followed by pleasant consequences tend to be repeated; those followed by unpleasant or painful consequences tend to be avoided. Behaviorism is both a philosophy and a method used by some psychologists to alter patterns of human behavior that run counter to individual wishes or societal or institutional standards. In both theory and practice, behaviorists believe that what people do is determined by responses to the consequences of their actions: The child who repeatedly drops food on the floor is scolded or otherwise punished until, finally, she stops doing it.

According to Skinner, freedom is simply the effort to escape from the unpleasant consequences of certain actions. We slap at an attacking mosquito to prevent the itching that will follow a bite if we don't; we send a crying child to bed to avoid the sound of crying (and then sometimes relent when the crying continues in order to avoid the sound of *more* crying). Whatever the motive for escape, say behaviorists, the fact remains that the *desire* to escape is a determining force. Moreover, if freedom is defined as escape from unpleasantness, no such state as pure and absolute freedom exists, because freeing oneself from *all* unpleasantness is impossible.

Behaviorists argue that people identify absolute freedom as a state in which "aversive control" is absent—that is, when there is no apparent oppression, people imagine themselves to be free. Skinner calls such people "happy slaves," molded unknowingly by hidden controls. Their freedom is an illusion. In Skinner's view, victims of oppression are better off than deluded happy slaves; at least they know where they stand. "The literature of freedom has been designed to make men 'conscious' of aversive control, but in its choice of methods it has failed to rescue the happy slave."[3] Activists who fight against oppression typically concern themselves solely with obvious victims and rarely with enlightening those who believe they are free but in fact are not.

SKINNER, *BEYOND FREEDOM AND DIGNITY*   We cling to the notion of "freedom," Skinner suggests, because we believe that human dignity is lost if humanity is not, nor ever can be, considered free. If we are not free, then how do we account for the great imaginative creations of humankind—works of art, literature, music, philosophy? Are they simply responses to conditioning? If so, how can we define human dignity?

In one of his most influential works, *Beyond Freedom and Dignity*, Skinner redefines these two key words in strictly behavioral language. Since people are going to be conditioned anyway, the focus should be on the *good* controls that *can* exist. He writes: "The problem is to free men, not from control, but from certain kinds of control, and it can be solved only if our analysis takes all consequences into account."[4] Eventually, Skinner argues, an ideal society can be designed in which people develop their abilities to the maximum—even creative ones—through carefully preplanned reinforcements. Such a society would have no crime, no aggression, no exploitation. The question is: *Would we want such a carefully pre-planned society?*

Genetic Determinism

Does **DNA** determine our fate? The science of *genetics* explores the role played by biological factors in determining how plants, animals, and human beings develop their characteristics. In what seems like an almost miraculous outcome, geneticists are mapping the structures of the infinitesimal cells that comprise various forms of life, discovering, in effect, the very secret of life itself.

We understand now that a predisposition toward many diseases, including Type 1 and Type 2 diabetes, Alzheimer's disease, cystic fibrosis, Huntington's disease, and certain forms of cancer, can be inherited. More tentative arguments suggest that a predisposition to addiction, including alcoholism and other dependencies—once thought to be socially acquired—may also be inherited.

Genetic research moves quickly. Now that the strands of DNA have all been identified and labeled and genetic maps are being constructed for more and more organisms, gene replacement therapy has become both a major goal—and a major concern in medical science. Soon, inherited birth defects or the propensity toward a genetic disease may be stopped in their tracks by locating and replacing the responsible gene.

How far off, then, is the ability for parents to decide what color hair they would like their child to have? How smart she should be? How good an athlete? Is this kind of research, as many religious leaders suggest, a slippery slope? How much control do we want, and how much should we have, over future humankind? At what point do our demands become arrogance, with risks of unintended consequences outweighing benefits? Debates over the ethics of interfering with natural process are likely to continue.

Gene replacement has already been amazingly successful, particularly in mice and chimpanzees. Using their knowledge of genetic codes, scientists have cloned animals. This means they already have in their hands the process of bringing about prearranged genetic results. Athletes have used genetic manipulation for years, injecting growth hormones and other muscle-building genetic materials. Scientists suggest that the ease and accessibility of gene therapy technology is easy to subvert.

On the other hand, consider the advantages that successful gene therapy, performed with the intention of curing once-fatal illness or prolonging human life span, may bring. If we can live longer, healthier lives, might we be freer to realize our full creative potential as human beings?

SOCIOBIOLOGY   In the social sciences, the role of genetics becomes intertwined with the long debate about heredity versus environment (**nature versus nurture**), which asks which has more impact on our personalities and the choices we make: our genes, or the influence of family, peers, education, and the social structure around us? Replacing a faulty gene is one matter; replacing external influences at will is quite another.

The science of **sociobiology** assumes the absence of free will and studies human behavior in terms of *genetic investment*. The basic assumption is that everything we do is driven by our genetic strain. Love between two people is a matter of genes: The decision to settle down with a partner and procreate is based on the desire to make a *genetic investment* in continuing our line. How we feel about genetic propagation determines how we conduct intimate relationships.

Traditional definitions of love are thus displaced. People who share the same genetic attitudes are likely to attract each other. Even family ties result from sharing a similar gene pool. Sociobiology also redefines the term *altruism*, or self-sacrifice. A mother sacrifices for her children because they represent the continuing life of her own genes, but she would not necessarily do the same for someone else's child. Soldiers who die to save their battalion do so because the battalion has become a substitute family.

The sociobiologist contends that *all* decisions—political, religious, educational, financial—relate in one way or another to genetics. If nothing else, genes determine *who* we are, and who we are determines what we stand for, and apparently we cannot decide to walk a different path.

Free Will

16.3 *What are some arguments supporting the existence of free will, including those based on theories of Schopenhauer, William James, and Freud?*

Thus far in this chapter we have presented determinist views—arguments suggesting that human beings do not have free will to choose their own actions. Determinist arguments are too powerful to be ignored. Economics, politics, innate character, genetics and biology—these are forces that, we must admit, come into play in most lives. But does the existence of these forces necessarily mean that we have no real freedom? It may depend on how we define freedom.

A Pessimist's View of Free Will: Reading Schopenhauer

Many argue that the phrase "free will" is redundant; that if one *has* a will at all, and that will can be exercised, then it is necessarily free. The *existence* of will implies freedom. But does the will in fact exist? Or is what some philosophers have called "will" nothing but causation, working through our conscious level, making us *think* we are doing what we want, and not what we must? B.F. Skinner argues that the will cannot be detected, cannot be felt. So *where* is will located? Not everyone agrees on an answer.

Here is how the German philosopher Arthur Schopenhauer (1788–1860) objectified will:

- Stand in front of a mirror and observe yourself.
- Think you would like to raise your left arm.
- Then raise your left arm.

In the first instant, the desire to raise the arm is locked inside the mind, the consciousness. In the next instant, the will is visibly present in the action you see in the mirror.

But having made will visible, Schopenhauer went on to ask: *What is the will for?* Here is an imaginary conversation:

US:	*It's obvious. The will makes free choices among available options.*
SCHOPENHAUER:	*Indeed, but is making free choices enough to justify optimism about the human condition?*
US:	*We don't understand.*
SCHOPENHAUER:	*Is a free choice always a good choice? Suppose the choice is to kill someone. Does the fact that it was a free choice in any way soften the horror of the crime? Do we take a measure of comfort in knowing that the decision to murder was determined solely by the will of the murderer? Would it not be far better had the potential killer been conditioned by a religious upbringing that taught benevolence toward one's fellows?*

FREE WILL AS SELF-INTEREST Schopenhauer believed the will is actually the will *to live*. The will drives us to actions that we think will benefit us, actions that will ensure our survival. Often these are downright evil.

> *Unjust or wicked actions are, in regard to him who performs them, signs of the strength of his affirmation of the will to live, and thus how far he still is from true salvation, which is denial of this will.*[5]

In other words, while not denying our freedom to act, Schopenhauer is saying that each of us is constrained, is *forced*, to use the power of will to further our own ends, even if that means harm to others. The freedom of *not* acting also exists, but too often this results from a fear of being caught—or at least, of not profiting from the act—and cannot be construed as a true denial of will.

Schopenhauer seems to believe that freedom is possible in the *denial* of will. While remaining pessimistic about human nature in general, he entertains the hope that a rare few will understand and curb their own aggressive drives. He encourages us to willfully turn aside from the pleasures and successes life offers, because the free pursuit of them only makes us evil in our intentions—that is, solely self-centered. A disillusioned idealist, Schopenhauer longed for a world of peace and *good* will, but he saw little chance that it would ever come about. And in a twenty-first century filled with reality shows that encourage narcissism above all, it is hard to disagree with his conclusion.

Regret and Relief as Signs of Free Will: Reading William James

The American philosopher William James (1842–1910) reviewed the case for pure determinism as set forth by European philosophers and concluded they were wrong. In fact, James developed a theory he pointedly called **indeterminism**, which presents the world as a random collection of chance happenings. Determinism, for James, was too coldly logical: Cause A leads to effect B. Determinism made people seem like well-run, well-oiled machines. James said people, on the contrary, are typically indecisive and unpredictable—exactly the opposite of machines.

Regret, for example, is a universal phenomenon. At any given moment, people are able to think back over a hundred choices they wish they had not made. But at the same time, regret cannot be meaningfully experienced unless there exists an opposite—satisfaction—that gives regret its identity. In other words, within the random collection of happenings, people sometimes make what they consider the right move and many times make what they consider the wrong move.

If everything were predetermined—that is, if the will were not free—looking backward could not reveal missed chances. We could not see them unless they had existed, though we may have been blind to them at the moment of choice. How often do murderers think back and realize that they had options—that they did not *have* to carry a gun, for example? It's possible that at some point in the future, even Kim Kardashian will regret having issued an entire book of selfie photos and called it *Selfish*. For James, hindsight is proof that genuine alternatives always exist. For the determinist, alternatives not chosen have no real existence; something always makes us choose one—and only one.

Each of us can probably list a few things we might have done last week but chose not to, and that we are now relieved we didn't do. When we consider the wrong moves that might have been made but were not, we are aware of having chosen wisely. We were *free* to do so because we *could* have made the wrong decision. Nothing except our own intelligence determined the choice. Relief (like regret), then, is a sign of free will.

Most of us probably live more or less split down the middle, with good moves (that we are relieved to have made) on one side and bad moves (that we regret having made) on the other. That we can say we have made many mistakes is an admission that we know ourselves to be free agents. That we have sometimes chosen wisely may cause us to think, "If the good choice was predetermined, then I freely embrace determinism!"

Psychoanalysis and Free Will: The Impact of Freud

Many psychologists theorize that the choices we make, the things we do, are impelled by causes of which we are not always aware. **Psychoanalysis** examines dreams, the thought processes evidenced in conversations, and the free association of ideas in

Figure 16.5 Sigmund Freud's couch, c. 1930.
Here Freud explored the buried psyches of a long succession of patients. Do you agree that we may find keys to our character and behavior in long-forgotten events of our childhoods?
Bjanka Kadic/Alamy

an attempt to help people figure out why they do what they do (Figure 16.5). It aims to lead people to a rational state of mind in which free choice is possible because the causes of deviant, antisocial, or uncharacteristic actions are revealed. Once the cause is discovered, psychiatric theory suggests, the forces driving actions can be fully or at least partially controlled. For people who undergo treatment because they don't like who they are or what they do, therapists hold out the hope that, through understanding and proper guidance, they can change. They can, in fact, become less "determined" than they were before.

Psychoanalysis, developed by Sigmund Freud (1856–1939) to assist people toward mental health, is based on the assumption that painful past events hidden away in the unconscious mind cause some people to have bizarre dreams, make odd statements, and perform incomprehensible actions. In other words, their lives are determined by unconscious prior causes: sometimes by guilt-ridden emotions they have refused to deal with; often by desires of the *id*, that primitive, animal self human beings possessed long before they developed the rational *ego*.

In the Freudian view, the ego is the Apollonian conscious mind, and the id, the Dionysian self, which contains the sexual and aggressive drives that society has taught us to suppress. Freud called the values imposed upon us by family, education, religion, the law, and the opinions of others the *superego*: the voice inside the mind that tells us what we may or may not do. Yes, the will is free to disobey this voice, but chances are those who do so will be plagued by guilt. And, yes, we are free *not* to think about our guilt, but, for Freud, denying it only makes matters worse.

The aim of the Freudian therapist is to uncover the hidden self that is responsible for neurotic—that is, disordered—behavior and to lead the patient to a happier life dominated by the ego. Successfully psychoanalyzed, the patient is released from the determining phantoms of the past and is free to exercise will, which can reside only in the fully conscious ego.

FREUD IN CONTEMPORARY THOUGHT   In recent years, Freud's theories have been viewed with increasing skepticism. Critics suggest that human behavior is far more complex than Freud theorized. Not all behavior can be traced to childhood events or buried causes, they argue, and the ego, or conscious self, is not always capable of rational, sustained thought once buried causes are uncovered.

One reason for the changing views of Freud's theories is that the role of the superego is far less pronounced today than it was in his day. Sexual mores, in particular, are far less rigid, violations less apt to instill guilt. Women have more freedom to determine their reproductive choices; homosexuality, once considered an illness, is now accepted as a biological fact. In much **psychotherapy** of today, the therapist and client focus more on changing unwanted behaviors (anger management, stopping addictions) than on opening closets full of forgotten skeletons.

FREUD, FREE WILL, AND THE HUMANITIES   Despite recent controversies, Freud's impact on the humanities in the twentieth and twenty-first centuries is undeniable. Without Freud, there would presumably be no Hulk (who is all id) or *X-Men*'s Professor Xavier (who is all ego). The psychological traumas reflected in the characters of Batman—damaged by watching the murder of his parents as a child—or Tony Soprano—in therapy to get rid of his debilitating dreams—would be unimaginable. And certainly without Freud, some of our most beloved children's books, in particular those by the American author and artist Maurice Sendak (1928–2012), would not have been written. Sendak said on multiple occasions that his own psychoanalysis allowed him to access childhood memories that he then was able to "tame" through books such as *Where the Wild Things Are* (1963).

Countless films and books have, because of Freud and his followers, focused our attention not on *Who done it?* but on *Why was it done?* or even *What is that character afraid to face?* This last question is central to the films in the 2000s built around the character of the amnesiac special agent Jason Bourne (Matt Damon). Haunted by memories and appalled by the skills he seems to possess, Bourne, who has been trained as an elite assassin, spends the first three movies searching for the key to his ability to kill so easily. He finally uncovers the truth—as well as his real identity—and sets out to rid himself of guilt by righting the wrongs he has committed. The need to explain his nightmarish memories is the engine that drives Jason Bourne forward.

Psychoanalytic films were extremely popular during and just after World War II. Many of them focused on the relationship between a troubled character and a sympathetic therapist. The endings were usually happy (often with marriage in the offing between patient and therapist). Interestingly, the popularity of Freudian-based entertainment coincided with the recovery of the American economy from the dismal Depression of the 1930s, as well as with the recognition that the United States would have to enter World War II to help free those overrun by fascist forces. The need for the literature and drama of freedom was apparently an insatiable one.

Writers unconvinced that anybody can readily be freed from a suppressed past show little optimism, and a few have given us memorable modern tragedies. Tennessee Williams's milestone work *A Streetcar Named Desire* (1947) presents audiences with a harrowing study of mental illness culminating in madness. The heroine, Blanche DuBois, tries to give the impression that she is a genteel Southern belle, carrying on the elegant traditions of the Old South, but as the play deepens, she exhibits unmistakable signs of an unstable mental condition that causes her to denounce her sister's uncouth husband while she is at the same time driven by a fierce sexual attraction to him. Recognizing this attraction and thinking of his own sexual gratification, the husband rapes her violently. The abuse causes Blanche to retreat into a fantasy world from which she will never escape. The author himself was in therapy for a good part of his life but was apparently unable to free himself from the demons of his own past.

Of course, determinists can always argue that the liberation of the unconscious and the confrontation with reality may provide the illusion of freedom, but only for a time. Stamping a patient's chart *CURED* does not guarantee freedom from all determining influences. Just as physicists discovered that matter is composed of particles within particles within particles, so too may the self be a circular staircase leading down into an infinity of shadows. Freud understood this and was generally cynical about human existence, but his theories provided hope that many could ascend that staircase into the clear light of day.

Studying the humanities of the past century would be difficult indeed without recognition of Freud's role. Many schools of psychotherapy continue to be rooted in his thought, and millions have been restored to mental health through psychoanalytical methods. That Freud's views may not represent an all-inclusive means to human freedom from the determining past should not eclipse the importance of these views to both the arts and to modern psychology.

Existentialism

16.4 *What is* **existentialism?** *How does it relate to the debate about free will and determinism?*

At the end of World War I, many older beliefs were swept out the door. European countries sought new ways of thinking about freedom, perhaps through some kind of global cooperation. But Roman-style nationalism—the belief that one's country was superior to all others and had a right to subjugate the rest of civilization—reared its head once more in the person of an Austrian house-painter named Adolf Hitler, and the terrors of war resumed. This time they were accompanied not simply by slaughter of soldiers but also slaughter of civilians deemed "inferior"—Jews, Roma (gypsies), homosexuals.

Hitler and his allies were defeated in 1945, and once again, the world was exhausted. The definition of freedom that emerged from that exhaustion was called **existentialism**. Born in the middle of the nineteenth century, the philosophy remained obscure until post-war cynicism began to take root, especially in France, a nation that prided itself on being the cultural center of Western civilization but that had been devastated by Nazi occupation. After the war, France found itself without a guiding philosophy, and its art reflected hopelessness and despair. The rediscovery of existentialism provided a strong light of free choice at the end of a long, dark tunnel—but with a price to be paid.

Religious Existentialism

Søren Kierkegaard (1813–1855) is considered the first existentialist philosopher. He was raised in an austere religious environment in Denmark, rebelled against it for a time, then returned to it as a matter of conscious choice, without the need of mystic revelations. For Kierkegaard, religion became a psychological reality freely accepted, rather than a revealed truth that required acceptance. When one reached a point of absolute despair (as indeed he did) and felt ready to turn to God, one could, Kierkegaard argued, take a **leap of faith**.

In that leap, however, lie undeniable anxieties. The leap must be made over many counterarguments and without any scientific or tangible proof of the existence of a God or gods. On our knees in the darkness of a church, we might feel our prayers soaring heavenward and have a sense of union with God, but we can never *know* if God is listening—or is even there at all.

To dramatize the plight of the believer, Kierkegaard recounts the biblical tale of Abraham and Isaac in his book *Fear and Trembling* (published in 1843 under the pseudonym *Johannes de silentio*, or "John of the silence"). An angel appears to Abraham and tells him God demands the sacrifice of his son Isaac. Abraham is appalled, but what can he do? If God wants the sacrifice and he is God's servant, he must obey. His unquestioning willingness to do as God commands is a leap of faith. In that leap, in that raising of the knife, must not Abraham experience unutterable anguish (Figure 16.6)? Suppose the message was not really from God—what then? The anguish of Abraham represented for Kierkegaard the existential dilemma of all people. An existential dilemma is knowing that one is free to make a choice, but who knows whether it is the right, or even the best, choice?

TWENTIETH-CENTURY RELIGIOUS EXISTENTIALISM: MARTIN BUBER The philosopher Martin Buber (1878–1965), like Kierkegaard, found his way to religion through nontraditional means. He is most famous for defining two kinds of relationships a person can have:

- The "I/it"—our objective relationship with objects and events with concrete reality. Here there is no God, but only the existential moment. For Buber, an "it" must be defined; it has to be justified as concrete reality, otherwise there can be no relationship.

- The "I/Thou"—the bridge representing our relationship to God. A "Thou" is not defined, but addressed.

The difference is clear: If you can address someone (whether a person standing in front of you or God, unseen), objective definition is beside the point. The fact that you are addressing anyone means that for you, at least, they exist. When it comes to "I/it," objective proof is possible. The "it" is out there for all to see. When it comes to "I/Thou," the experience of God comes through feeling, through intuition, through an overpowering sense of God's presence, and is not out there for all to see. That sense of God's presence cannot be challenged. Buber and Kierkegaard are very close on this point.

Early in his adult life, Buber approached religion intellectually. He was a scholar of sacred Hebrew texts concerned with the interpretation of traditional religious history as being a matter of myth and legend, yet he sought the fundamental truth behind them. God was not a "Thou" until the reading of one particular text—just a few sentences, really—changed his life forever.

Figure 16.6 Michelangelo Merisi da Caravaggio, *The Sacrifice of Isaac,* **c. 1590.**
An angel stays Abraham's hand as he is about to murder his son Isaac at God's command. What emotions do you assume Abraham and Isaac are feeling? How does Caravaggio convey those emotions?
Erich Lessing / Art Resource, NY

> I opened a little book entitled the Zervaat Ribesh—that is the testament of Rabbi Israel Baal-Shem—and the words flashed toward me: "He takes unto himself the quality of fervor, for he is hallowed and become another man and is worthy to create and is become like the Holy One, blessed be He, when he created his world." It was then that, overpowered in an instant, I experienced the Hasidic soul.[6]

We might call this a Dionysian religious experience. Buber discovered that truth in religion comes from irresistible feeling, not analytical thought. From that moment on, he became a Hasid—a member of a Jewish sect that emphasizes joy in God's closeness to humanity and the warm fellowship with other members of God's family.

Buber was then led to a passionate concern for the sacredness of human relationships, for in human contact he also found God. Every person with whom one connects was for him a "Thou," and every "Thou" contained the spirit of God. This belief—that there is God in every living being—is common to a number of Eastern religions, as well as the Protestant denomination of Quakerism, or the Society of Friends.

"I/Thou" created a revolution in modern ethics. Here was a philosopher who dispensed with the rules, who challenged the moral absolutes of the Socratic tradition as well as those of many of the world's major religions. The existential philosophers argued that we are all free—that moral goodness exists in every human heart, provided we seek it. Not everyone will find it, but each of us is free to make the search.

Secular Existentialism

When existentialism re-emerged after World War II, it was of a very different kind. The secular existentialism that swept Europe fitted readily into the depressed mood of countries that had been devastated by fighting and loss. And yet, its inherent belief in freedom as a natural condition helped to stir up some optimism.

Belief in God entails obeying commandments, as well as believing that humankind is put here for the purpose of submitting to God's will and deserving God's love and mercy. Secular existentialism does not seek to address a God whose existence we cannot prove; it opposes a religious teaching that human beings have an *essence* which defines their humanness.

The basis of secular existentialism is this: All we can be sure of is *existence*. Once we recognize that fact, we can begin to shed the sense of abandonment that necessarily derives from the notion that we are alone in a bewildering universe that exists for no comprehensible reason. This acknowledgment—that the only fact we can really know for sure is that we exist—means that each of us is free. We have no obligation to a higher force or indeed to anything else. But this kind of freedom can be both confusing and terrifying.

We choose religion—or some other authority with equally rigid and intimidating guidelines for living—because that relieves us of making up those guidelines for ourselves. Even if we don't obey them, we have at least a perspective. We know what we are *supposed* to be doing. And that can be reassuring. Abandoning that reassuring belief, although ultimately freeing, is initially frightening.

THE FRENCH EXISTENTIALISTS: SARTRE, DE BEAUVOIR, AND CAMUS   Central to the secular existential movement are the writings of three twentieth-century French philosophers: Jean-Paul Sartre (1905–1980), Simone de Beauvoir (1908–1986), and Albert Camus (1913–1960). Sartre, the most influential of the three, bases his belief in the human right of self-definition on the absolute certainty that God cannot exist. He is opposed to the acceptance of God as a matter of psychological necessity. Deep down, he argues, we must know that each of us is alone in a world that makes no sense—a statement that must have seemed all too true to many war-weary survivors in Europe.

Sartre maintains there is no such thing as human nature. People *talk* about human nature, but who has ever seen it? We cannot assume people are fundamentally good *or* bad, when in fact they are *neither* at birth. No one comes into this world to serve any purpose or to fulfill some preexisting definition of what it means to be human.

> *If man, as the existentialist conceives him, is indefinable, it is because at first he is nothing. Only afterward will he be something, and he himself will have made what he will be. Thus, there is no human nature, since there is no God to conceive it.*[7]

Saying that humankind is born without any identifying nature is in direct conflict with earlier philosophies that describe everyone as having an essence. In Christianity, for example, that essence is the soul. For Aristotle, it is rationality. The religious existentialist insists that individuals create an essence that is spiritual and longs for union with God. Secular existentialists, however, say that individuals must work at developing an essence that can be defined as human, an essence that includes good will and a strong, clear sense of moral responsibility to others. Thus the ringing declaration of both religious and secular existentialism is *Existence precedes essence.*

According to Sartre, only natural phenomena and manufactured objects have essences from the beginning. A paper cutter was "born" to cut paper. If it doesn't cut paper, you have the right to demand your money back. A storm was "born" to bring wind and rain (or snow) and maybe knock down a few buildings in its path. Even animals have essences, for they too are natural phenomena. A tiger has to growl and be carnivorous. But human beings somehow escaped *having* to be anything.

The bright side to this picture is that human beings *are* capable of *reason*, a faculty we develop through experience. Some of us choose to exploit this capacity more than others do. Some decide they cannot live without an essence, without a purpose, without a way of defining themselves. But each person must find the definition all alone. To borrow an essence from the past, from the traditions and beliefs of one's ancestors, or to be influenced by peer pressure or educational or religious institutions is to forfeit the right to define oneself.

SARTRE: "DOOMED TO FREEDOM" Once we realize that we have no essence, each of us has to create one freely. As Sartre puts it, we are "doomed to freedom." Each of us, having declared our essence, must then take responsibility for it. We cannot decide we are going to be such-and-such only to deny, when our actions harm someone else, that we ever made that decision. No one is free to be *morally unaccountable*. True freedom carries a hefty price tag. Reason does not guarantee the right to behave any way you want to unless, as Immanuel Kant would say, you are willing to accord that right to everyone else. In that case, you'd have to be careful not to turn your back on anyone. Do we *really* want to live in a society in which no one is responsible for anything?

Many people, of course, find it simpler to believe that they serve a purpose and that what they do was meant to be. Sartre tells the story of a young man who, on failing examinations for various professional careers, insists that he was meant to fail because his true destiny was to become a priest. Nonsense! Sartre declares. The young man—like all of us—was always in charge of his own life. He should not have turned to the priesthood solely on the hunch that destiny was forcing him into it. Freedom is painful sometimes. If we choose to use a paper cutter (which has to fulfill its essence by cutting paper and sometimes other things) and we cut our finger, we are tempted to swear at the paper cutter. But inanimate objects have no moral responsibility. Only we have moral responsibility. If we blame something or someone else for our failures, we deny the truth of our freedom.

The true existentialist—like Abraham—has to make choices and is always confronted with anguish. An existentialist holds himself accountable for the decisions he makes, no matter how horrifying they may be. An authentic person is one who defines herself, stands behind the definition, and willingly accepts either praise or blame.

DE BEAUVOIR, *THE SECOND SEX* Sartre's companion Simone de Beauvoir, a feminist writer, focused on the ways in which women must create essences for themselves. She called for the creation of bold new ones; her route to existentialism was the feminist rejection of male rules and the essences males imposed on females.

In her most famous work, *The Second Sex* (1949), de Beauvoir explores the wide-ranging reasons that women have, historically, been devalued, from the biological "problem" of motherhood, which ties women to their bodies in ways that men are not tied to theirs and leaves women open to subjugation by men, to the economic theory of private property, which led to the legal status of women as property. Very early on, de Beauvoir argues—by the time humankind reached the stage of written mythology and law—the patriarchate was established:

> [T]he males were to write the codes. It was natural for them to give woman a subordinate position, yet one could suppose that they would look upon her with the same benevolence as upon children and cattle—but not at all. While setting up the machinery of woman's oppression, the legislators were afraid of her.[8]

Women were "duped," de Beauvoir argues, by the label that men put on them: They were priceless, too valuable to be permitted out in the world. In order to be free, women need to fight for absolute equality:

> [W]omen raised and educated exactly like men would work under the same conditions and for the same salaries; erotic freedom would be accepted by custom, but the sexual act would no longer be considered a remunerable "service"; women would be obliged to provide another livelihood for themselves; marriage would be based on a free engagement that the

spouses could break when they wanted to; motherhood would be freely chosen—that is, birth control and abortion would be allowed—and in return all mothers and their children would be given the same rights.[9]

Women made great progress toward equality in the twentieth century. For centuries confined to their roles as homemakers, with little political or economic power, women began to break free in the late nineteenth and early twentieth centuries. The right to vote was won, first in Finland in 1906, in 1920 in the United States, and in most of Europe and the Americas by the beginning of the Second World War. In 2011, the last country in the world to continue to deny women the vote, Saudi Arabia, decreed that Saudi women would be able to vote beginning in 2015.

More women began to work outside the home in the twentieth century, too, first because they were needed to keep factories running during World War II and later as they found such work fulfilling—and often economically necessary. And the development of birth control devices and the Supreme Court decision permitting abortion gave women significantly increased control over when they would choose to have children, although that control continues to be threatened by religious leaders and politicians who feel they are better suited to make such decisions. Certainly, de Beauvoir would find women freer in the twenty-first century than they were in 1949 when she wrote *The Second Sex*—but she would no doubt argue that there is still a long way to go.

CAMUS: FREE WILL AND SUICIDE If not the most influential of the French existentialists, Albert Camus was surely the most poetic—and dramatic. In his three major essays, "An Absurd Reasoning," "The Absurd Man," and "The Myth of Sisyphus," he makes the existential case that rationality is found not in the universe but in the human mind. The intellect, attempting to make sense out of reality, realizes that the task cannot be accomplished. Why then are we rational? To what end? Reason leads us to one conclusion: That living is absurd, meaningless.

Having said this, Camus begins "An Absurd Reasoning" with his most often quoted statement: "There is but one truly serious philosophical problem, and that is suicide." Where Sartre believed that abandonment in a meaningless universe opened the door to freedom, Camus goes deeper, analyzing that condition of abandonment and insisting that life is not worth living if we cannot assign a value to it. Yet if life is absurd, what value *can* it have?

Camus's answer is that it has an absurd value. What we think and do may not make any ultimate sense, but perhaps "ultimate sense" ought never to have been the goal. That there is only this existential moment, this here and now, does not imply that the moment is not worth experiencing. Unlike his colleagues, Camus talks about the colors, the sounds, the continually unfolding wonders of the universe. Absurd, yes, in that they have no meaning beyond themselves—but this fact does not make suicide the inevitable, the *only* recourse.

If we do not (as Hamlet famously does not) choose suicide, then we must have a purpose. That is, if we *had* chosen suicide would it not be said that our purpose was to do away with ourselves? If choosing suicide is purposeful, then choosing life must also be purposeful. But if the world is absurd and we choose to remain in it, it must follow that we accept the absurdity and move on from there. In that lies our freedom, and with freedom comes an infinite number of possibilities.

To dramatize his point, Camus recounts the Greek myth of Sisyphus, "the wisest and most prudent of mortals," who also questioned the meaning of life. To find the answer, he stole secrets from the gods, who retaliated by condemning him to roll a heavy rock up a steep hill. When, through exhausting labor and physical pain, he reached the top, the rock rolled back down, and Sisyphus had to start all over again. This was to continue for eternity.

I leave Sisyphus at the foot of the mountain! One always finds one's burden again. But Sisyphus teaches the higher fidelity that negates the gods and raises rocks. He too concludes that all is well. This universe henceforth without a master seems to him neither sterile nor futile. Each atom of that stone, each mineral flake of that night-filled mountain, in itself forms a world. The struggle itself toward the heights is enough to fill a man's heart. One must imagine Sisyphus happy.[10]

The view of freedom expressed in much existential philosophy and literature has been widely questioned. Is it the freedom to behave without regard for others? If we create our own values, can anything we do be morally wrong? True, the existentialists insist that we be held accountable for speech and actions. But are we free to lie? To behave toward others in a way that will draw praise and make it easy to manipulate them? And if we use our freedom for our own profit, are we *really* free—or simply victims of our own selfishness?

Freedom Within Limitations

16.5 *Why does true freedom need limits?*

By now, you may have realized that the philosophies of freedom and free will that we have been discussing were all generated by Western thinkers living in comparatively open societies in which freedom of thought and expression were and are taken for granted (see Figure 16.1). Even Augustine, within the confines of Christianity, was at liberty to express his doubts. Determinists such as Marx and Skinner were not threatened with jail for saying that our choices are not freely made.

Sometimes a philosopher of freedom does in fact live under an oppressive government: Rousseau, for example, in a rigid monarchy; Sartre, during the Nazi rule in France. Both fought against tyranny: Rousseau through his pen, and Sartre through his work in the French Underground, an organized covert attempt to help those being sought or persecuted by the Nazis. Neither philosopher abandoned his belief that freedom was the natural condition of humanity. That belief tends to be echoed throughout the humanities in different ways.

What does freedom mean to those who grow up in societies that have long, rigidly defined traditions of behavior that govern everyday life? What about those in societies that have been or are now embroiled in bitter religious or territorial disputes that severely limit choices? Is freedom a narrowly Western idea?

Buddhism and Freedom

Japanese society is nothing if not rule-driven, Western influences notwithstanding. Zen Buddhism, a dominant practice in much of Asia, requires long hours of meditation. Similarly, to excel in any of the martial arts so valued in some Asian nations demands many years of training in body coordination and muscular development. These arts are also products of civilized societies in which ethics and good manners are essential. Even in a sport as incomprehensible to Western minds as *sumo* wrestling, opponents must bow to each other as a mark of deep respect.

The love of the beautiful found in many Asian cultures dictates, for example, how tea is prepared and served in Japan, how flowers are arranged in a vase, how calligraphy is drawn on a scroll. All of these requirements might strike some in the West as cumbersome impositions—even as imprisonments of the will. Yet it is doubtful that their practitioners would agree.

One of the foremost modern spokespersons for Buddhist thought and practice was Chögyam Trungpa, who fled Chinese persecution in his native Tibet and founded a still-thriving American Buddhist community in Boulder, Colorado.

Among those who came there to absorb his teachings was poet Allen Ginsberg (1926–1997). Ginsberg was a major voice of the American Beat Generation, the label applied to a post-World War II group of writers, artists, and composers who were disillusioned with the greed they saw on all sides and with what they perceived as a growing materialism in American society. The Beats proclaimed themselves social dropouts, adrift in a land that called itself the cradle of liberty, the home to the American dream of social mobility—but that more and more offered its citizens only shoddy values and corrupt politics.

Many, like Ginsberg, saw in Buddhism the one true path to freedom from this emerging enslavement through the discipline of meditation and the renunciation of materialistic desires. In *The Myth of Freedom*, Trungpa implies that the Western definition of "freedom" includes an absence of external control and the right to disobey the rules whenever it suits—or the right to become the chief and impose one's own rules. In order to be free in the Buddhist sense of the word, Trungpa maintains, one must first wake up to the reality of pain and suffering. It is absurd to suppose that following the American Dream and striving for wealth and the pleasures it can buy will avoid pain and suffering. If anything, wealth and pleasure only add to the pain because (as Epicurus points out) there is never enough pleasure to satisfy us. Even if we have all the money we want and are "free" to spend our lives doing whatever we please, there remains the excruciating pain of recognizing that death will eventually bring an end to it all. According to Trungpa:

> [W]e must begin by seeing the experience of life as it is. We must see the truth of suffering, the reality of dissatisfaction. We cannot ignore it and attempt to examine only the glorious pleasurable aspects of life. If one searches for a promised land, a Treasure Island, then the search only leads to more pain. We cannot reach such islands, we cannot attain enlightenment in such a manner. So all sects and schools of Buddhism agree that we must begin by facing the reality of our living situations. We cannot begin by dreaming.[11]

Trungpa defines true freedom as surrendering to reality and, by accepting things as they are, liberating ourselves from pain—which is, after all, a goal of the free person. In his view, even the imprisoned can be free, because no one can put chains on our thoughts and feelings. This doctrine of freedom through personal choice despite limitations has inspired hundreds of Trungpa's followers.

Choosing Freedom

Would Trungpa's doctrine bring solace to the many who still live in slavery or under severe autocratic rule? It seems unlikely. And yet there are ample examples throughout history of free will being exercised under the most horrific of conditions. Mahatma Gandhi, Martin Luther King, Jr., Nelson Mandela, and many others have fought for freedom from inside prison walls. Enslaved Africans fought for freedom in this country and elsewhere both physically—in armed rebellions—and psychologically—by finding ways to stay alive while retaining their dignity. African Americans suffering the indignities of segregation rose up against it (Figure 16.7). The German priest Martin Luther threw off the tyranny of a corrupt religion; the founder of Quakerism, George Fox, was imprisoned and beaten for preaching that every person contains God.

Although historians tell us that fewer wars are currently being fought than at most times in the past millennia, still it

Figure 16.7 Freedom Riders in Mississippi, 1964.
What movements toward freedom have happened in your lifetime?
Paul Schutzer/The LIFE Picture Collection/Getty Images

feels—perhaps because social media now bring war onto our tablets and iPhones—as though conflict is everywhere. Everywhere we look, people are living under conditions that seem unimaginable to those of us who are not forced to endure them. Fundamentalists of many religions—Muslim, Christian, Jew—seem determined to impose their beliefs on the rest of the world.

And yet we seek freedom. We search for the possibility. The Arab Spring rises, and even if the result seems disappointing, we know it happened once—and so it may eventually happen again. Things that seemed impossible 20, even 10, years ago are now written in law: Our gay brothers and sisters and children can marry in much of the world, including the United States.

Perhaps all one can say now is that there are many paths to freedom and that some of them still have impassable barriers. This gives us all the more reason to be grateful if we have the right to choose.

Coming to a Close: Understanding the Limits of Freedom

It seems appropriate to close this book with a theory—and it is just that—by means of which we can apply the word *free* to ourselves. According to this theory, derived from a number of sources, freedom is achieved *only* when we place limits on our options.

People who jog know all about the relationship between freedom and limits. They will tell you about a consciousness of freedom in running, pushing against the wind and feeling their arms and legs equal to the demands made by the will; runners, in contrast to what Skinner has said, *do* feel their will. When there is a sharp incline, runners must draw upon reserve strength. On the downward slope, they know that power needs to be conserved. If they run flat-out, they may not have enough left for the final mile. If they are running against others and there is a need to win, they accelerate. If all they want to do is complete the course, they adopt a more leisurely pace.

But the vivid experience of will does not happen all of a sudden. In the beginning, jogging is a distinct effort accompanied by pain and soreness. There is the inevitable pulling of muscles, the labored breathing, the tendency to overheat rapidly. In the beginning, joggers often stop running for the slightest excuse. After a time they set a goal: to the end of the road and then back; one mile; two miles; down to the county line. Self-imposed limits are crucial; the goal must be met. Even wind and rain are not likely to keep the determined runner at home. The ultimate feeling of liberation—the sense of floating, the so-called runner's high—-occurs when the runner's body is equal to the task set by the will. And runners experience the will when they feel at ease within the limitations they impose on themselves.

In the sonnet form, a poet's choices are determined by the requirement of 14 lines. It would be easy for the poet to complain that the length limitation prevents the free expression of an idea—and indeed, many poets have chosen to write in free verse for which no restrictions exist. The Romantic poet William Wordsworth did not see the rigid sonnet rules as constraints upon freedom.

NUNS FRET NOT

Nuns fret not at their convent's narrow room;
And hermits are contented with their cells;
And students with their pensive citadels;
Maids at the wheel, the weaver at his loom
Sit blithe and happy; bees that soar for bloom,
High as the highest Peak of Furness-fells,
Will murmur by the hour in foxglove bells:
In truth the prison unto which we doom

Ourselves, no prison is: and hence for me,
In sundry moods, 'twas pastime to be bound
Within the Sonnet's scanty plot of ground;
Pleased if some Souls (for such there needs must be)
Who have felt the weight of too much liberty,
Should find brief solace there, as I have found.

Why, one asks, is freedom so vital? If Sartre is right in saying that most people prefer not to be free, why should we *have* to be free? Or, if freedom and liberty are not the same, what's wrong with seeking liberty for its own sake? What's wrong with going through life unfettered by rules and behaving in any way we desire? Why do we need to define ourselves at all—and then be responsible for what we do?

When you put a tight lid on a pan of boiling water, the energy inside will become intense. So too will the joy of living be intense to the degree that we face a limited number of choices. Liberty is bewildering. Liberty does not know what to choose. Defining oneself as a certain kind of person is the first limitation. Unless we can do that, we become scattered to the winds, at the mercy of every gust. Narrowing the range of possibilities and *then finding the best way to work within that range* might, after all, be the answer. And what is the question? It is: *How can I do the most with the one life I have after I take inventory of how much freedom of choice is available to me?*

Of course, determinist arguments are powerful, and one has the right to believe there is no free will and thus one cannot be held responsible for anything. If one adopts that view, one must accept the fact that no one else is responsible either. Determinism is the only logical course for some. Many artists and philosophers do not agree. If a painting is decried by those who fund the exhibit, we don't hear the artist saying, "But I came from a bad environment that forced me to paint that way." Instead, the artist defends the work and decries the funders. Without *this* kind of freedom, there can be no pride in any accomplishment.

If determinism is chosen, is the chooser forced to make that choice? Surprisingly enough, many *do* choose determinism without realizing it. How many people do we know who seem to be happy only when they find someone who will listen to their tragic tales of victimization—by other people, by the law, by the government, by their parents, and on and on? Never by themselves. As Jean-Paul Sartre continually reminds us, the only way to be an authentic person is to admit that you're free and to take responsibility for the bad choices you make. We have conceded many times that not everyone is lucky enough to have the right to choose. Those who do and who prefer to see themselves as helpless victims without responsibility would do well to recognize that they were nonetheless free to reject that responsibility.

Authentic people advertise their natures. We always know what to expect from them. Inauthentic people, backed into a corner after being blamed for something, try to plead their innocence by saying something forced them to make a wrongful choice. If free will is a fact of life it cannot be accepted here and rejected there at one's convenience.

In the final analysis, true freedom may reside in the limitations we impose upon ourselves freely. To believe that freedom means having unlimited options is to be trapped in infinity. Only by deliberately narrowing our range of options can we experience the exhilarating sense of being truly our own persons. It is freedom to say we can do this or that. It is not freedom to say we can do this, or that, or perhaps that other thing, or even its opposite, and on and on forever. When we come to this realization, we also see we need not trap ourselves by always choosing the easy way. At a sumptuous buffet we can gorge ourselves or decide to enjoy fully a limited amount of delicious food.

Those who achieve the strength of inner control are not only authentic persons; they are *good people.* They never want to harm others, for doing so would mean being at the mercy of uncontrollable passions, becoming the victims they choose not to be.

A study of the humanities looks into the minds and hearts of creative and thoughtful human beings and reveals many innovations in art and philosophy. Countless artists and philosophers have changed the course of human consciousness and given us options our ancient ancestors could not have dreamed of: options for experiencing the beautiful, the different, even sometimes the shocking, and, of course, the thought-provoking. How predetermined were *they* when the greatest of them did what nobody else had ever done? If they were predetermined, why was there not more than one Beethoven or Shakespeare or others who might have been similarly directed? The humanities would seem to be the study of the free spirit, and from this study each of us can know that more can be done with our lives. It is your birthright as a human being to reach up and mentally redo the Sistine Chapel ceiling if you don't happen to like it. Once you have investigated the past, it is your birthright to let go of it, but knowingly and with full awareness of what you want the present to be. It is your birthright to reach into the darkness and from it pull forth a new lantern, however unfamiliar the shape, however irregular the beam of light.

Reaching beyond ourselves is a natural right. Without the risk of failure, there can be no possibility of success. The American novelist and poet Stephen Crane sums it all up:

I SAW A MAN PURSUING THE HORIZON

I saw a man pursuing the horizon;
Round and round he sped.
I was disturbed at this;
I accosted the man.
"It is futile," I said,
"You can never—"
"You lie," he cried,
And ran on.[12]

Looking Back

In this chapter,

- we explained some early views of freedom, including the role religion plays in any discussion of freedom,
- we described the various arguments supporting determinism, including political, institutional, and economic determinism, character as fate, behaviorism, and genetic determinism,

- we described some arguments supporting the existence of free will, including those based on theories of Schopenhauer, William James, and Freud,
- we talked about *existentialism* and its relationship to the debate about free will and determinism, and
- we discussed why true freedom needs limits—because unlimited freedom is not really freedom at all.

Key Terms

behaviorism Both a philosophy and a school of psychology that believe people are what they do and what they do is determined by systems of rewards and punishments.

bourgeoisie In Marxism, refers to the affluent upper class.

communism A system of governing in which nearly all property is state (or publicly) owned and there is very little entrepreneurship in the private sector.

determinism Philosophy that believes everything has a prior cause and consequently free will cannot exist.

dialectic Philosophical method of Georg Hegel, involving the presentation of one idea, followed by an analysis of its opposite, and then arriving at a synthesis that combines the two; adopted by Karl Marx to describe the conflict between the proletariat and the bourgeoisie and the eventual synthesis of a classless society.

DNA Abbreviation for *deoxyribonucleic acid*, the hereditary material present in nearly all living organisms. It carries genetic information throughout the body.

economic determinism Another name for the philosophy of Karl Marx, maintaining that our behavior is controlled by the need for money.

existentialism A philosophy with either a religious or a secular foundation that maintains humanity is free to create its own essence.

indeterminism Philosophy expounded by William James that whatever happens does so randomly, without a clear-cut prior cause, and therefore we have free will to make choices.

institutional determinism Name given to Jean-Jacques Rousseau's belief that the will is governed by restrictive forces of law, education, and religion, all necessary because of the inborn depravity of a few people.

leap of faith Phrase invented by Søren Kierkegaard to indicate that religion can be freely chosen, but to do so one must bypass reason and thus can never be sure if the choice is right.

liberal arts In classical Greece, those skills that allowed individuals to participate in civic life, including rhetoric, logic, and grammar. Later, those disciplines that define humanity: literature, language, history, history and appreciation of art, history and appreciation of music, philosophy, mathematics, and science.

nature versus nurture A debate about whether an individual's character is impacted more by DNA or by life experiences and environment.

proletariat In Marxism, the working classes that will eventually rise up against the affluent bourgeoisie, leading to the classless society.

psychoanalysis A technique invented by Sigmund Freud that examines a patient's dreams and patterns of free association of ideas in an effort to diagnose the causes of neurotic behavior and mental illness.

psychotherapy Clinical treatments of mental and emotional disorders.

socialism A system of governing in which more property is owned and there is more entrepreneurship in the private sector than in communism.

sociobiology A social science that believes human behavior can be analyzed in terms of genetic investment or the lack of it—that is, the extent to which one is motivated by the need to propagate his or her genes either directly through a sexual relationship or indirectly through the need to survive physically, socially, or economically.

Endnotes

Chapter 1

1. Leonard Cohen, "Anthem." Available at http://www.azlyrics.com/lyrics/leonardcohen/anthem.html
2. Taylor Mali, *What Learning Leaves* (Newtown, CT: Hanover Press, 2002). Available at http://www.taylormali.com/poems-online/totally-like-whatever-you-know.

Chapter 2

1. William Wharton, *Dad* (New York: Avon, 1981), 419–420.
2. Daniel Mendelsohn, "But Enough about Me," *The New Yorker*, January 25, 2010, 68–74.
3. Alex Ross, *The Rest Is Noise* (New York: Farrar, Straus and Giroux, 2007), xii.
4. Alastair Macaulay, "Review of Joffrey Ballet Production of *Cinderella*," *The New York Times*, Monday, February 22, 2010.
5. William Wordsworth, "The World Is Too Much with Us," *The Major Poets, English and American* (New York: Harcourt Brace, 1954), 257.

Chapter 3

1. June Singer, *Boundaries of the Soul: The Practice of Jung's Psychology* (New York: Doubleday, 1972), 79.
2. Ibid., 79.
3. Joseph Campbell, *The Myths of God: Oriental Mythology* (New York: Viking Penguin, 1976), 243.
4. Ibid., 342.
5. Ibid., 9–10.
6. Edith Hamilton, *Mythology* (New York: New American Library, 1969), 63.
7. John Milton, *Paradise Lost*, Book VII, ll. 211–217.
8. Hamilton, *Mythology*, 89.
9. Rose Anna Mueller, "La Llorona, The Weeping Woman," *Community College Review* 20, no. 1 (1999): 28–33.
10. Alfred, Lord Tennyson, from "The Lotos-eaters," in *English Poetry III: From Tennyson to Whitman*, Vol. XLII, *The Harvard Classics* (New York: P.F. Collier & Son, 1909–14). Bartleby.com, 2001. www.bartleby.com/42/.
11. J.R.R. Tolkien, *The Return of the King* (New York: Ballantine Books, 1966), 384.
12. Paraphrased from R.H. Blythe, *Zen and Zen Classics* (Tokyo: Hokuseido Press, 1960–1970).
13. Walter de la Mare, *Memoirs of a Midget* (New York: Knopf, 1921), 379.

Chapter 4

1. John Steinbeck, *The Grapes of Wrath* (1939; reprint, New York: Penguin Books, 1992).
2. *The Iliad*, trans. Augustus Taber Murray (London: W. Heinemann, 1929). Available on Google Books.
3. Sappho, "Ode to Aphrodite," trans. J. Addington Symonds, in *Our Heritage of World Literature*, ed. Stith Thompson and John Gassner (New York: Dryden Press, 1942), 258. Available at www.gutenberg.org.
4. The source for this and all other Shakespeare quotations in this volume is *The Complete Works of Shakespeare*, 7th ed., ed. David Bevington (New York: Pearson, 2013).
5. Petrarch, "Love's Inconsistency," in *The Sonnets of Europe*, ed. Samuel Waddington (London: Walter Scott, 1888); Bartleby.com, 2012. http://www.bartleby.com/342/.
6. John Donne, "Holy Sonnet XIV," in *Metaphysical Lyrics & Poems of the 17th c.*, ed. Herbert J.C. Grierson (Oxford: The Clarendon Press, 1921); Bartleby.com, 1999. http://www.bartleby.com/105/.
7. William Blake, "The Tiger" and "The Lamb," in Quiller-Couch, Arthur Thomas, Sir. *The Oxford Book of English Verse* (Oxford: Clarendon, 1919, [c1901]); Bartleby.com, 1999. http://www.bartleby.com/101/.
8. Gerard Manley Hopkins, *Poems* (London: Humphrey Milford, 1918); Bartleby.com, 1999. http://www.bartleby.com/122/.
9. Emily Dickinson, "After great pain," *The Atlantic Monthly*, February 1929.
10. Georgia Douglas Johnson, "Black Woman," in *The Portable Harlem Renaissance*, ed. Daniel Levering Lewis (New York: Penguin Books, 1995.)
11. Audre Lorde, *The Collected Poems of Audre Lorde* (New York: W. W. Norton and Company Inc., 1997)
12. F. Scott Fitzgerald, *The Great Gatsby* (New York: Scribner Paperback Edition, 1995), 160–161.
13. John Updike, *My Father's Tears and Other Stories* (New York: Knopf, 2006), 89.
14. Ibid., 112.
15. Walt Whitman, *Leaves of Grass* (Philadelphia: David McKay, [ca. 1900]). Bartleby.com, 1999, http://www.bartleby.com/142/.
16. A. E. Housman, *A Shropshire Lad* (London: K. Paul, Trench, Treubner, 1896). Bartleby.com, 1999. http://www.bartleby.com/123/.
17. Wilfred Owen, *The Poems of Wilfred Owen*, ed. Jon Stallworthy (New York: W.W. Norton, 1986). Available at http://www.poetryfoundation.org/poem/176831

Chapter 5

1. Bruce Cole and Adelheid Gealt, *Art of the Western World* (New York: Summit, 1985), 271.
2. Somerset Maugham, *The Gentleman in the Parlour: A Record of a Journey from Rangoon to Haiphong* (London: W. Heinemann, 1930).
3. Jonathan Lipman, *Frank Lloyd Wright and the Johnson Wax Building* (New York: Rizzoli, 1986), xii.

Chapter 6

1. "I Been Workin' on the Railroad," *Carmina Princetonia: The University Song Book*, 8th Edition (Martin R. Dennis & Co., 1894), pp. 24–25.

2. "John Henry." Author anonymous. Lyrics vary from version to version. This version available at http://www.ibiblio.org/john_henry/early/.

3. Joan Baez, "Joe Hill," http://www.ilyric.net/Lyrics/J/JoanBaez/JoeHill.html/.

4. "The Moonshiner." Author anonymous. Lyrics vary from version to version. This version available at http://www.celtic-lyrics.com/lyrics/337.html/.

5. "Deep River." Author anonymous. First published in Marsh, J.B.T., *The Story of the Jubilee Singers: with Their Songs* (London: Hodder & Stoughton, 1876).

6. "His Eye Is on the Sparrow." Civilla De. Martin, 1905. First published in Alexander, Charles, *Alexander's Gospel Songs* (Philadelphia: Westminster Publishing Co., 1908).

7. Alan Bullock and R. B. Wooding, eds., *20th Century Culture* (New York: Harper & Row, 1983), 212.

8. Charlie Gillett, *The Penguin Book of Rock and Roll Writing*, ed. Clinton Haydin (London: Penguin, 1992), 11.

9. Ibid., 14.

10. Rolling Stone, *100 Greatest Rolling Stone Songs*. 15 October 2013. Accessed 25 June 2015. http://www.rollingstone.com/music/lists/100-greatest-rolling-stones-songs-20131015/gimme-shelter-1969-19691231

11. Gillett, *op cit*, 212.

Chapter 7

1. *Henry V*, IV, Prologue, 1–9, 22–28.

2. Sophocles, *Antigone*, in *The Oedipus Cycle*, trans. Dudley Fitts and Robert Fitzgerald (Orlando, FL: Harcourt, 1941).

3. *Othello*, V, ii, 338–344.

4. *King Lear*, V, iii, 306–308.

5. *Aristotle*, trans. Philip Wheelright (New York: Odyssey, 1951), 296.

6. *Othello*, V, ii, 91–97.

7. *Romeo and Juliet*, II, ii, 2–3; 5–6.

8. *Hamlet*, III, iv, 162; 164–165.

9. *Hamlet*, III, ii, 1–8.

10. *Hamlet*, V, ii, 217–222.

11. *Macbeth*, V, v, 17–28.

12. Jean Racine, *Phaedra*, trans. Robert Bruce Boswell. A volume in the Harvard Classics series, ed. Charles W. Eliot (New York: P. F. Collier & Son, 1909–1914).

13. *Henry IV, Pt. II*, V, v, 47–51.

14. Harold Bloom, *Shakespeare and the Invention of the Human* (New York: Riverhead, 1996), 271–272.

15. Ibid., 272.

16. Molière, *Tartuffe*, trans. Richard Wilbur (New York: Roundhouse, 1997).

17. Oscar Wilde, *The Importance of Being Earnest* (London: Methuen & Co., 1915).

18. Henrik Ibsen, *A Doll's House*, trans. Rolfe Fjelde, in *Literature of the Western World*, ed. Brian Wilke and James Hurt (New York: Macmillan, 1988), 1303.

19. Eugene O'Neill, *Long Day's Journey into Night* (New Haven, CT: Yale University Press, 1955), 165–166.

Chapter 8

1. John D. Drummond, *Opera in Perspective* (Minneapolis: University of Minnesota Press, 1980), 278.

2. William G. Hyland, *Richard Rodgers* (New York: Yale University Press, 1998), 127.

3. Ibid., 131–132.

Chapter 9

1. Gerald Mast, *A Short History of the Movies* (New York: Macmillan, 1986), 68.

2. Roger Ebert, "Great Movie: The Films of Buster Keaton," http://www.rogerebert.com/reviews/great-movie-the-films-of-buster-keaton, November 10, 2002. Accessed 10 April 2015.

3. Ephraim Katz, *The Film Encyclopedia*, 3rd ed. (New York: Harper Perennial, 1998), 121.

4. David Denby, "A Fine Romance: The New Comedy of the Sexes," *The New Yorker*, July 23, 2007.

5. Nick Poppy, "Frederick Wiseman," 30 January 2002. http://www.salon.com/2002/01/30/wiseman_2/. Accessed 10 April 2015.

6. Newton N. Minow, "Television and the Public Interest." Address to the National Association of Broadcasters, Washington, D.C., May 9, 1961.

7. Alison Bechdel, *Dykes to Watch Out For* (Ann Arbor: Firebrand Books, 1986).

Chapter 10

1. Wendy Doniger, *Merriam-Webster's Encyclopedia of World Religions* (Springfield, MA: Merriam-Webster, 1999), 434.

2. *Buddhist Scriptures*, trans. Edward Conze (London: Penguin Books, 1959), 51.

3. *The Republic and Other Works by Plato*, trans. B. Jowett (New York: Doubleday Anchor Books, 1989), 470.

4. Ibid.

5. *Aristotle*, ed. and trans. Philip Wheelright (New York: Odyssey Press, 1951), 4–5.

6. Rabbi Joseph Telushkin, *Jewish Literacy* (New York: William Morrow, 1991), 102.

7. *The Confessions of Saint Augustine*, Book VI (New York: Airmont Publishing Company, 1969), 213.

8. Karen Armstrong, *A History of God* (New York: Alfred A. Knopf, 1993), 142.

9. Edwin Arlington Robinson, "The Man Against the Sky," in *American Poetry and Prose*, ed. Norman Foerster (Boston: Houghton Mifflin, 1947), 1275–1276, ll. 305–314.

10. Charles S. Peirce, "How to Make Our Ideas Clear," *Popular Science Monthly* 12, January, 1878.

11. Peirce, "The Fixation of Belief," in *The Search for Meaning*, ed. Robert F. Davidson (New York: Holt Rinehart Winston, 1967), 259.

12. Peirce, "How to Make Our Ideas Clear."

13. Stephen Crane, "God fashioned the ship of the world carefully," Poem VI in *The Black Riders and Other Lines* (Boston: Copeland & Day, 1895). Available online at http://www.theotherpages.org/poems/crane02.html.

14. Walt Whitman, *Leaves of Grass* (New York: Heritage Press, 1936), 25.

Chapter 11

1. Plato, *The Republic*, trans. Benjamin Jowett (New York: Doubleday, 1973), 44ff.

2. Ibid., 44ff.

3. Henry David Thoreau, "On the Duty of Civil Disobedience." (Originally published as "Resistance to Civil Government," 1849).

4. Thomas Hobbes, *Leviathan* (London: Printed for Andrew Crooke, 1651).

5. Jonathan Swift, "A Modest Proposal for Preventing the Children of Poor People from Being a Burden to Their Parents or Country" (Dublin: Printed for S. Harding, 1729).

6. John Stuart Mill, *On Liberty* (London: John W. Parker and Son, 1859).

7. John Donne, "Meditation XVII," in *Devotions upon Emergent Occasions* (1623)

8. Huston Smith, *The World's Religions* (San Francisco: Harper, 1991), 290–291.

9. John A. Hutchinson, *Path of Faith*, 2nd ed. (New York: McGraw-Hill, 1973), 121–122.

10. Leo Tolstoy, "What Is Art?" trans. Alymer Maude. (New York: Funk & Wagnalls, 1904).

11. Nicholas D. Kristof, "In Japan Nice Guys (and Girls) Finish Together," *The New York Times*, April 15, 1998.

Chapter 12

1. Epicurus, *The Extant Remains*, trans. Cyril Bailey (London: Oxford Universirty Press, 1926), 64.

2. Ibid., 65.

3. *The Complete Short Stories of Ernest Hemingway* (New York: Scribners, 1982), 289–290.

4. Viktor Frankl, *Man's Search for Meaning: An Introduction to Logotherapy*, preface by Gordon W. Allport (New York: Washington Square, 1998), 90.

5. Anne Frank, *The Diary of a Young Girl*, ed. Otto J. Frank and Miriam Pressler, trans. Susan Massotty (New York: Doubleday, 1991), 28.

6. Ibid., 54.

7. Ibid., 190.

8. Dalai Lama, *The Path to Tranquility* (New York: Viking Arcana, 1999), 163.

9. Ibid., 303.

10. Ibid., 395.

Chapter 13

1. Petronius Gaius, "Doing, a Filthy Pleasure Is, and Short," trans. Ben Jonson, in *99 Poems in Translation*, eds. Harold Pinter et al. (London: Faber and Faber, 1994).

2. William Shakespeare, *Venus and Adonis*, in *The Annotated Shakespeare*, ed. A. L. Rowse (New York: Clarkson N. Potter, 1978), ll. 7–12.

3. Translated from the Middle English by the authors.

4. *The Rubáiyát of Omar Khayyám*, trans. Edward Fitzgerald, *The College Survey of English Literature*, rev. ed. (New York: Harcourt, Brace & World, 1951), ll. 393–396.

5. Ibid., ii. 217–220.

6. *The Essential Rumi*, trans. Coleman Barks (New York: HarperCollins, 2004).

7. Plato, *The Symposium*, trans. B. Jowett (New York: Doubleday, 1989).

8. "The Death of the Hired Man," in *The Poetry of Robert Frost*, ed. Edward Connery Lathern (New York: Holt, Rinehart and Winston, 1969).

9. Confucius, "Classical Rites," in *Anthology of World Literature*, ed. Robert E. Van Voort (Belmont, CA: Wadsworth, 1999), 152–153.

10. Dante, *La vita nuova*, trans. D. G. Rossetti (New York: Viking, 1947), 547–548.

11. Dante, *The Divine Comedy*, trans. Lawrence Binyan (New York: Viking, 1947), 30.

12. Gabriel García Márquez, *Love in the Time of Cholera* (New York: Knopf, 1988), 339.

13. Hannah Kahn, "Signature," in *Eve's Daughter* (Coconut Grove, FL: Hurricane House, 1962), 17. Reprinted by permission of the poet.

Chapter 14

1. Sherwin B. Nuland, *How We Die* (New York: Knopf, 1993), 10.

2. Christopher Hitchens, "Topic of Cancer," *Vanity Fair*, November, 2010.

3. Oscar Wilde, *The Picture of Dorian Gray* (New York: Dell, 1977), 33.

4. Matthew Gilbert, "Review of *House*," *Boston Globe*, November 16, 2004.

5. James Agee, *A Death in the Family* (New York: McDowell, Obolensky, 1957), 307–308.

6. *The Republic and Other Works*, trans. Benjamin Jowett (New York: Doubleday, 1989), 551.

7. Johann Wolfgang von Goethe, *Faust*, trans. Walter Arndt (New York: Norton, 1976), 294.

8. *The Essential Tao*, trans. Thomas Cleary (San Francisco: Harper, 1991), 75.

9. Rabbi Joseph Telushkin, *Jewish Literacy* (New York: Morrow, 1991), 566.

Chapter 15

1. "Invitation to the Dance, No. 23," in *Wine, Women, and Song: Medieval Latin Drinking Songs Now Translated into the English,* with an Essay by John Addington Symonds (London: Chatto and Windus, 1884).

2. *As You Like It*, II, i: 12–17.

3. Ibid., 20–27.

4. Ibid., 47–49.

5. Ibid., II, vii, 58–62.

6. From Ralph Waldo Emerson, "Nature," first published anonymously in 1836 and as Ch. 1 in the collection titled *Nature, Addresses and Lectures*, 1849. Available at http://www.emersoncentral.com/nature.htm.

7. Walt Whitman, "Song of Myself," Canto 6, in *Leaves of Grass*, Riverside Edition, ed. James E. Miller, Jr., (Boston: Houghton-Mifflin, 1959). 28.

8. Herman Melville, "The Grand Armada," Ch. 89 in *Moby-Dick*, eds. John Bryant and Haskell Springer (New York: Pearson Education, 2007), 340–345.

9. Henry David Thoreau, *Walden and Civil Disobedience* (New York: Barnes & Noble Classics, 2003), 11.

10. Ibid., 90.

11. Allgemeine musikalische Zeitung (Leipzig), 1810, trans. Martyn Clarke. In David Charlton, ed., *E.T.A. Hoffmann's Musical Writings* (Cambridge: Cambridge University Press, 1989), 96–97, 98.

12. Walt Whitman, "Mannahatta," No. 161 in *Leaves of Grass* (Philadelphia: David McKay, 1900). Bartleby.com, 1999. http://www.bartleby.com/142/.

13. "Chicago," in *The Complete Poems of Carl Sandburg* (New York: Harcourt, Brace, Jovanavich, 1969).

14. Herman Melville, "The Masthead," Ch. 35 in *Moby-Dick*, eds. John Bryant and Haskell Springer (New York: Pearson Education, 2007), 154–155.

15. Mary Wollestonecraft Shelley, *Frankenstein; or, The Modern Prometheus* (Berkeley: University of California Press, 1989), 24.

16. Ibid., 51.
17. Kent Nerburn, *The Wolf at Twilight* (Novato, CA: New World Library, 2009), 161.
18. T.C. McLuhan, *Touch the Earth* (New York: Promontory Press, 1971), 12.
19. Ibid., 15.
20. Robert Smithson, *Robert Smithson: The Collected Writings*, ed. Jack Flam (Berkeley: University of California Press, 1996), 169–170.
21. David Kwiat, *A Traveler in Residence* (Miami: Three Star Press, 2010), 144.
22. Joseph Conrad, *Heart of Darkness* (New York: W.W. Norton, 2005), 34.
23. Ibid., 69.

Chapter 16

1. Azar Nafisi, *Reading Lolita in Tehran* (New York: Random House, 2004), 9.
2. Jean-Jacques Rousseau, "Principal Discourses," in *Rousseau's Social Contract and Discourses*, trans. G.D.H. Cole (New York: Everyman Library, 1923). Second Discourse, Part 2, 1.
3. B.F. Skinner, *Beyond Freedom and Dignity* (New York: Bantam Books, 1972), 37.
4. Ibid., 39.
5. Arthur Schopenhauer, *Essays and Aphorisms*, ed. and trans. R. J. Hollingdale (London: Penguin Books, 1970), 65.
6. Martin Buber, *Tales of the Hasidim* (New York: Schoken Books, 1992), viii.
7. Jean-Paul Sartre, *Existentialism and Human Emotions*, trans. Bernard Frechtman (New York: Philosophical Library, 1947), 15.
8. Simone de Beauvoir, *The Second Sex*, ed. and trans. H. M. Parchley (New York: Knopf, 1969), 79.
9. Simone de Beauvoir, *The Second Sex* [1949], trans. Constance Borde and Sheila Malovany-Chevallier (New York: Knopf, 2009), 760.
10. Albert Camus, *The Myth of Sisyphus and Other Essays*, trans. Justin O'Brien (New York: Vintage Books, 1995), 123.
11. Chögyam Trungpa, *The Myth of Freedom* (Berkeley, CA: Shambala, 1976), 1–2.
12. Stephen Crane, "I saw a man pursuing the horizon," Poem XXIV in *The Black Riders and Other Lines* (Boston: Copeland & Day, 1895). Available online at http://www.theotherpages.org/poems/crane02.html.

Credits

Chapter 1

1.2 Gifts of the Humanities

p. 8: Source: Geoffrey Chaucer; Richard Pynson, *The Canterbury tales*, London, Richard Pynson, 1491; p. 9: Greek philosopher Heraclitus Quoted in *History of Philosophy Volume 1: Greece and Rome*, Frederick Copleston, A&C Black, 01-Jun-2003; p. 9: Source: Oscar Wilde, *The Importance of Being Earnest*, Leonard Smithers and Company, 1899; p. 9: Source: *The Essential Rumi*, translated by Coleman Barks with John Moyne, New York, Harper Collins, 1995, pp. 141–2; p. 9: Source: "Leonard Cohen on Leonard Cohen" edited by Jeff Burger, Chicago Review Press, 2014, page 294; p. 10: Source: Taylor Mali, "Totally like, whatever, you know?" www.TaylorMali.com; p. 10: Source: Albert Einstein quoted in *Introduction to Critical Thinking and Creativity: Think More, Think Better* by J. Y. F. Lau, John Wiley & Sons, 22-Dec-2011.

Chapter 2

2.1 The Importance of Critical Thinking

p. 16: Source: William Wharton, *Dad* (New York: Avon, 1981), 419–420; p.17: Source: Daniel Mendelsohn, "But Enough about Me," New Yorker, January 25, 2010, 68–74.

2.4 A Guide to Critical Viewing, Professional and Personal

p. 26: Source: Pauline Kael, Will Brantley, Conversations with Pauline Kael, Univ. Press of Mississippi, 1996; p. 27: Source: Alex Ross, *The Rest Is Noise* (New York: Farrar, Straus and Giroux, 2007), xii; p. 27: Source: Alistair Macauley, "Review of Joffrey Ballet Production of Cinderella," *New York Times*, Monday, February 22, 2010; pp. 27–28: Source: William Wordsworth, "The World Is Too Much with Us," *The Major Poets, English and American* (New York: Harcourt Brace, 1954), 257; p. 29: Source: Thomas R. Lounsbury, ed. (1838–1915). Yale Book of American Verse. 1912, 173. Rock Me to Sleep, Elizabeth (Akers) Allen. 1832–1911.

2.5 Literalists and Figuratists

p. 31: Source: Winston Churchill; p. 31: Source: Shakespeare, *Hamlet*.

Chapter 3

3.2 Archetypes in Mythology

p. 36: Source: June Singer, *Boundaries of the Soul: The Practice of Jung's Psychology* (New York: Doubleday, 1972), 79; pp. 36–37: Source: June Singer, *Boundaries of the Soul: The Practice of Jung's Psychology* (New York: Doubleday, 1972), 79; pp. 39: Source: *St. Joan*, Summary and Analysis Epilogue by George Bernard Shaw; p. 40: Source: Joseph Campbell, *The Myths of God: Oriental Mythology* (New York: Viking Penguin, 1976), 243.

3.3 Myth as Explanation

p. 40: Source: Joseph Campbell, *The Myths of God: Oriental Mythology* (New York: Viking Penguin, 1976), 342; p. 46: Source: Joseph Campbell, *The Myths of God: Oriental Mythology* (New York: Viking Penguin, 1976), 9–10; p. 47: Source: *Paradise Lost*, Book VII, ll. 211–217; p. 49: Source: Hamilton, *Mythology*, 89; p. 52: Source: Sophocles.; E D A Morshead, *Oedipus the king*, London : Macmillan, 1885.

3.6 How Myth Influences the Humanities

p. 58: Source: J. R. R. Tolkien, *The Return of the King* (New York: Ballantine Books, 1966), 384; p. 58: Source: Paraphrased from R. H. Blythe, *Zen and Zen Classics* (Tokyo: Hokuseido Press, 1960–1970); p. 60: Source: Walter de la Mare, *Memoirs of a Midget* (New York: Knopf, 1921), 379.

Chapter 4

4.2 Literature as History

p. 64: Source: John Steinbeck, *The Grapes of Wrath* (1940; reprint, New York: Penguin Books, 1992); p. 67: Source: *The Iliad*, translated by Augustus Taber Murray.

4.3 Poetry

p. 69: Source: translation by John Myers O'Hara, Project Guttenberg http://www.gutenberg.org/files/42166/42166-h/42166-h.htm; p. 70: Source: A Good Soldier, Edgar Albert Guest; p. 70: Source: William Shakespeare Sonnet 18, Shall I compare thee to a Summer's day?; p. 71: Source: Sir Thomas Wyatt (1503–1542); p. 72: Source: William Shakespeare, *Hamlet* Act 1, scene 5, 186–190; p. 72: Source: William Shakespeare, SONNET XXIX; p. 73: Source: John Donne (1572–1631), *Holy Sonnets: Batter my heart, three-person'd God*; p. 75: Source: William Blake, "The Lamb", *Songs of Innocence and Experience*; p. 75: Source: William Blake's, "The Tyger" and "The Lamb", *Songs of Innocence and of Experience, copy Z*; p. 76: Source: King James bible, Psalm 23; pp. 76–77: Source: Gerard Manley Hopkins, 1877; p. 77: Source: The Atlantic Monthly, Vol 143, published in 1929; p. 78–79: "Black Woman." Source: Georgia Douglas Johnson, "Black Woman," in The Portable Harlem Renaissance, ed. Daniel Levering Lewis (New York: Penguin Books, 1995.); p. 80: Source: "From the House of Yemanja", from *The Collected Poems of Audre Lorde* by Audre Lorde. Copyright © 1997 by the Audre Lorde Estate. Used by permission of W.W. Norton & Company, Inc.

4.4 The Novel

p. 81: Source: Gabriel García Márquez: *A Life*. Vintage Books, 2010; p. 83: Source: F. Scott Fitzgerald, *The Great Gatsby* (New York: Scribner Paperback Edition, 1995), 160–161.

4.5 The Short Story

p. 87: Source: John Updike, *My Father's Tears and Other Stories* (New York: Knopf), 89.

A Critical Focus

p. 88: "Come Up from the Fields, Father." Source: Walt Whitman, Come Up From the Fields Father; p. 89: Source: A. E. Housman, "To an Athlete Dying Young," 1896; p. 89: Source: *Original Text: Wilfred Owen, Poems By Wilfred Owen with an Introduction by Siegfried Sassoon* (London: Chatto and Windus, 1921): 15. PR 6029 W4P6 Robarts Library.

Chapter 5

p. 92: Source: Robert Thiele.

5.2 Creating Likeness in Different Styles

p. 104: Source: (Mark: 14:18), New Revised Standard Version (Anglicized Edition) bible.oremus.org.

5.4 Art as Alteration

p. 117: Source: Bruce Cole and Adelheid Gealt, *Art of the Western World* (New York: Summit, 1985), 271.

5.6 Architecture

pp. 129–130: Source: Somerset W Maugham, *Gentleman In The Parlour*, New York : Doubleday, ©1930; p. 132: Source: Jonathan Lipman, *Frank Lloyd Wright and the Johnson Wax Building* (New York: Rizzoli, 1986), xii.

Chapter 6

6.1 The Basic Elements of Music

p. 142: Source: Mickey Hart.

6.3 Music Beyond the Concert Hall

p.156:Source:I'veBeenWorkingontheRailroad,1894;pp.156–157:Source:JohnHenryTheSteelDrivingMan-http://www.ibiblio.org/john_henry/early; p. 157: Source: Joan Baez, "Joe Hill," http://www.ilyric.net/Lyrics/J/JoanBaez/JoeHill.html/; p. 157: Source: The Moonshiner - http://celtic-lyrics.com/lyrics/337.html; p. 159: Source: Deep River - http://www.hymnlyrics.org/hymns_spirituals/deep_river.php; p. 159: Source: lyricist Civilla D. Martin and composer Charles H. Gabriel (1905); p. 160: Source: Scott Joplin, Maple Leaf Rag. 1899; p. 161: Source: Alan Bullock and R. B. Wooding, eds., *20th Century Culture* (New York: Harper & Row, 1983), 212; p. 163: Source: Booker T. Jones, William Bell, *Born Under a Bad Sign*; p. 165: Source: Charlie Gillett, *The Penguin Book of Rock and Roll Writing*, ed. Clinton Haydin (London: Penguin, 1992), 11; p. 166: Source: Charlie Gillett, *The Penguin Book of Rock and Roll Writing*, ed. Clinton Haydin (London: Penguin, 1992), 14; p. 167: Source: http://www.rollingstone.com/music/lists/100-greatest-rolling-stones-songs-20131015/gimme-shelter-1969-19691231; p. 168: Source: © Pearson Education, Inc.

Chapter 7

7.1 Drama and Tragedy in Theater History

p. 175: Source: Henry V, IV, Prologue, 1–9, 22–28; p. 177: Source: Sophocles, *Antigone*, trans. Dudley Fitz and Robert Fitzgerald; p. 177: Source: *Othello*, V, ii, 338–344; p. 178: Source: *King Lear*, V, ii, 306–308; p. 178: Source: Aristotle, trans. Philip Wheelright (New York: Odyssey, 1951), 296; p. 181: Source: *Othello*, V, ii, 91-97; p. 181: Source: William Shakespeare, *Romeo and Juliet*, ACT II SCENE II; pp. 181–182: Source: *Hamlet*,III,iv,162;164–165;p.182:Source:*Hamlet*,V,ii,217–222; p. 182: Source: *Macbeth*, V, v, 17–28; p. 184: Source: *Phædra*, by Jean Racine; translated by Robert Bruce Boswell. The Harvard Classics series. Charles W. Eliot ed. New York: P.F. Collier & Son, 1909–14.

7.2 Comedy in Theater History

p. 187: Source: Aristotle; p. 189: Source: *Henry IV*, Pt. II, V, v, 47–50; pp. 189–190: Source: Harold Bloom, *Shakespeare and the Invention of the Human* (New York: Riverhead, 1996), 271–272; p. 192: Source: Molière, *Tartuffe*, trans. Richard

Wilbur (New York: Roundhouse, 1997); p. 192: Source: Lady Bracknell from *The Importance of Being Earnest* (1952); p. 193: Source: Lady Bracknell from *The Importance of Being Earnest* (1952).

7.3 The Nineteenth Century: The Roots of Modern Theater

p. 195: Source: Henrik Ibsen, *A Doll's House*, trans. Rolfe Fjelde, in *Literature of the Western World*, ed. Brian Wilke and James Hurt (New York: Macmillan, 1988), 1303.

7.4 A Century of Dynamic Change

p. 202: Source: Eugene O'Neill, *Long Day's Journey into Night* (New Haven, CT: Yale University Press, 1955), 165–166.

A Critical Focus

pp. 207–208: Source: from Arthur Miller's *Death of a Salesman*, Viking Press.

Chapter 8

8.1 Opera

p. 218: Source: John D Drummond, Opera in perspective, Minneapolis : University of Minnesota Press, ©1980.

8.3 The Broadway Musical

pp. 223 and 224: Source: William G. Hyland, *Richard Rodgers* (New York: Yale University Press, 1998), 127.

8.4 Dance

p. 229: Source: Alice Gomme, 1898.

Chapter 9

9.2 Early Milestones in Film

p. 244: Mast quote. Source: Gerald Mast, A Short History of the Movies (New York: Macmillan, 1986), 68.

9.3 Major Film Genres

p. 247: Source: Robert Ebert, The Films of Buster Keaton, Nov. 10, 2002 - http://www.rogerebert.com/reviews/great-movie-the-films-of-buster-keaton; p. 251: Source: David Denby, *New Yorker* (July 23, 2007); pp. 256–257: Source: Frederick Wiseman, The grandfather of cin NICK POPPY, THURSDAY, JAN 31, 2002, http://www.salon.com/2002/01/30/wiseman_2/; p. 248: Ephraim Katz, *The Film Encyclopedia*, 3rd ed. (New York: Harper Perennial, 1998), 121.

9.6 The "Small Screen": Television

p. 268: Source: Newton N. Minow, "Television and the Public Interest", address to the National Association of Broadcasters, Washington, D.C., May 9, 1961.

9.7 A Word on Critical Viewing

p. 270: Source: Bechdel, Allison. *Dykes to Watch Out For.* Firebrand Books (October 1, 1986).

Chapter 10

10.1 The Importance of Religion in the Humanities

p. 275: Source: Kings 16:30, King James Version.

10.2 The Belief in Many Gods

p. 278: Source: Wendy Doniger, Merriam-Webster's Encyclopedia of World Religions (Merriam-Webster, 1999), 434.

10.3 Belief in an Amorphous or Universal Divinity

p. 282: Source: Siddhartha, Quoted in Nick Smith, The Demon Revels, Lulu.com.2009; p. 282: Source: Buddhist

Scriptures, trans. Edward Conze (London: Penguin Books, 1959), 51; p. 286: Source: *The Republic and Other Works by Plato*, trans. B. Jowett (New York: Doubleday Anchor Books, 1989), 470; p. 286: Source: *The Journal of Education*, Volume 14; Volume 24, Published by William Rice, 1892, page 422; p. 286: Source: *Aristotle*, ed. and trans. Philip Wheelright (New York: Odyssey Press, 1951), 4–5.

10.4 The Belief in One God

p. 288: Source: Job 1:11, New Revised Standard Version (Anglicized Edition) bible.oremus.org; p. 289: Source: Job 3:23, New Revised Standard Version (Anglicized Edition) bible.oremus.org; p. 289: Source: Rabbi Joseph Telushkin, *Jewish Literacy* (New York: William Morrow, 1991), 102; p. 289: Source: Lamentations 2:17, New Revised Standard Version (Anglicized Edition) bible.oremus.org; p. 289: Source: Isaiah 7:14, New Revised Standard Version (Anglicized Edition) bible.oremus.org; p. 290: Source: Exodus 20:3, New Revised Standard Version (Anglicized Edition) bible.oremus.org; p. 290: Source: Matthew 7:12, New Revised Standard Version (Anglicized Edition) bible.oremus.org; p. 290: Source: Qur'an, Sunnah.com - http://sunnah.com/riyadussaliheen/1/183; p. 290: Source: Genesis 1:1-3, New Revised Standard Version (Anglicized Edition) bible.oremus.org; pp. 291–292: Source: *The Confessions of Saint Augustine*, Book VI (New York: Airmont Publishing Company, 1969), 213; p. 293: Source: Karen Armstrong, *A History of God* (New York: Alfred A. Knopf, 1993), 142.

10.5 Understanding Good and Evil: The Problem of Faith

p. 295: Source: Plato, *Apology* 41d, Perseus Project (www.perseus.tufts.edu) Plato. Plato in Twelve Volumes, Vol. 1 translated by Harold North Fowler; Introduction by W.R.M. Lamb. Cambridge, MA, Harvard University Press; London, William Heinemann Ltd. 1966; p. 295: Source: Genesis 3:5, New Revised Standard Version (Anglicized Edition) bible.oremus.org; p. 296: Source: Genesis 8:21, New Revised Standard Version (Anglicized Edition) bible.oremus.org; p. 296: Source: Muhammad Asad, *The Message of the Quran*, first published in Gibralter in 1980. Revised edition 2008 by the Book Foundation. http://web.archive.org/web/20100926172730/http://www.wikimir.com/message-of-quran-by-muhammad-asad-004.

10.6 Doubt

p. 299: Source: Carl Sagan (1934–1996); p. 299: Source: "The Man Against the Sky: A Book of Poems" The Macmillan Company, 1916 by Edwin Arlington Robinson; p. 300: Source: Charles S. Peirce, "How to Make Our Ideas Clear," *Popular Science Monthly*, 1878; p. 300: Source: Peirce, "The Fixation of Belief," in *The Search for Meaning*, ed. Robert F. Davidson (New York: Holt Rinehart Winston, 1967), 259; p. 301: Source: Charles S. Peirce, "How to Make Our Ideas Clear," *Popular Science Monthly*, 1878; p. 301: Mencken quote. H. L. Mencken quoted in *Making Sense of It All: Pascal and the Meaning of Life*, Thomas V. Morris, Wm. B. Eerdmans Publishing, 06-Oct-1992; p. 301: Source: Author Stephen Crane, *Black Riders came from the sea*.

10.7 Religion and the Arts

p. 302: Source: Walt Whitman, *Leaves of Grass* (New York: Heritage Press), 25; p. 303: Source: William Wordsworth, Lines Composed a Few Miles Above Tintern Abbey on the Banks of the Wye.

Chapter 11
11.1 Defining Morality

p. 307: Butler's definition of morality. Source: Samuel Butler (1835–1902), British author. First published in 1912. Samuel Butler's Notebooks, p. 55, E.P. Dutton & Company (1951).

11.2 The Morality of Self-Interest

pp. 309 and 310: Source: Plato, *The Republic*, trans. Benjamin Jowett (New York: Doubleday, 1973), 44ff; p. 312: Source: Henry David Thoreau, "Civil Disobedience," 1849, 1; p. 310: Source: Plato, *The Dialogues of Plato*, Vol. 1, translated by B. Jowett, Oxford at the Claredon Press, 1771, page 369; p. 316: Source: Thomas Hobbes, *Leviathan* (London); p. 317: Source: Jonathan Swift, "A Modest Proposal" 1729.

11.3 Moral Alternatives to Self-Interest

p. 320: Source: John Stuart Mill, *On Liberty*; p. 322: Source: John Donne, "Meditation XVII," in Devotions upon Emergent Occasions (1623).

11.4 Morality and Religion

p. 324: Source: Huston Smith, *The World's Religions* (San Francisco: Harper, 1991), 290–291; p. 324: Source: Matthew 5:38–39, New Revised Standard Version (Anglicized Edition) bible.oremus.org; p. 324: Source: John A. Hutchinson, *Path of Faith*, 2nd ed. (New York: McGraw-Hill, 1973), 121–122; p. 325: Source: Luke 23:42–43, New Revised Standard Version (Anglicized Edition) bible.oremus.org.

11.5 Morality and the Arts

p. 326: Source: Leo Tolstoy; p. 328: Source: Ludwig van Beethoven *Heiglnstadt*, [*Heiligenstadt*] October 6th, 1802; p. 328: Source: Bernard Schoenbaum, *New Yorker* cartoon (July 18, 1988).

11.6 Moral Relativism

p. 330: Source: Nicholas D. Kristof, "In Japan Nice Guys (and Girls) Finish Together," *New York Times*, April 15, 1998.

Chapter 12
12.1 Hedonism: Happiness Is Pleasure

p. 335: Excerpt from "To the Virgins." Source: Robert Herrick, To the Virgins, to Make Much of Time, 1591–1674; pp. 335–336: Source: To His Coy Mistress by Andrew Marvell (1621–1678).

12.2 Epicureanism: Happiness Is Living Moderately and Avoiding Pain

p. 337: Source: Epicurus, *The Extant Remains*, trans. Cyril Bailey (London: Oxford University Press, 1926), 64; p. 238: Source: *The Complete Short Stories of Ernest Hemingway* (New York: Scribners, 1982), 289–290.

12.3 Stoicism: Happiness Is Survival

p. 341: Source: Becket, Thomas À (c.1118-1170).

12.5 Models of the Happy Life

p. 347: Source: Viktor Frankl, *Man's Search for Meaning: An Introduction to Logotherapy*, preface by Gordon W. Allport (New York: Washington Square, 1998), 90; pp. 347–348: Source: Anne Frank, *The Diary of a Young Girl*, ed. Otto J. Frank and Miriam Pressler, trans. Susan Massotty (New York: Doubleday, 1991), 28.

12.6 Buddhist Paths to Happiness

p. 351: Source: Dalai Lama, *The Path to Tranquility* (New York: Viking Arcana, 1999), 163.

Chapter 13
13.1 Eros

p. 357: Source: Petronius Gaius, "Doing, a Filthy Pleasure Is, and Short," trans. Ben Jonson, in *99 Poems in Translation*, eds. Harold Pinter et al. (London, Faber and Faber, 1994); p. 357: Source: William Shakespeare, *Venus and Adonis*, in *The Annotated Shakespeare*, ed. A. L. Rowse (New York: Clarkson N. Potter, 1978), ll. 7–12; p. 358: Source: Trans. from the Middle English by the authors; p. 360: Source: *The Rubáiyát of Omar Khayyám*, trans. Edward Fitzgerald, The College Survey of English Literature, rev. ed. (New York: Harcourt, Brace & World, 1951), ll. 393–396; p. 360: Source: *The Essential Rumi*, trans. Coleman Barks (New York: HarperCollins, 2004).

13.2 Agape

p. 361: Source: Ben Jonson, Peter Whalley, *The Dramatic Works of Ben Jonson*: Printed from the Text, John Stockdale, 1811 - Englishdrama-721 pages; p. 362: Source: Plato, *The Symposium*, trans. B. Jowett (New York: Doubleday, 1989); p. 363: Source: John Keats, *Ode on a Grecian urn : and other poems*, Boston : Houghton, Mifflin, ©1898.

13.3 Family and Friendship

p. 363: Source: Voltaire (1694–1778); p. 363: Source: "The Death of the Hired Man," in *The Poetry of Robert Frost*, ed. Edward Connery Lathern (New York: Holt, Rinehart and Winston, 1969); p. 366: Source: Ruth: 1:16, King James Version; p. 367: Source: Confucius, "Classical Rites," in *Anthology of World Literature*, ed. Robert E. Van Voort (Belmont, CA: Wadsworth, 1999), 152–153; p. 369: Source: William Shakespeare, Hamlet Act 1 Scene 3; p. 369: Source: Henry Fielding, *Tom Jones*, New York : H.M. Caldwell.

13.4 Romantic Love

p. 374: Source: Dante, *La Vita Nuova*, trans. D. G. Rossetti (New York: Viking, 1947), 547–548; p. 375: Source: The Society of Authors as the Literary Representative of the Estate of Laurence Binyon.

13.6 Variations on a Theme

p. 379: Source: Gabriel García Márquez, *Love in the Time of Cholera* (New York: Knopf, 1988), 339; p. 381: Source: Hannah Kahn, "Signature," in *Eve's Daughter* (Coconut Grove, FL: Hurricane House, 1962), 17. Reprinted by permission of the poet.

Chapter 14
14.1 Being Mortal: How We Portray and Celebrate Death

p. 385: Excerpt from *Henry V*. Source: The Life of King Henry the Fifth, *Henry V*, Act 4, Scene 3; p. 386: Source: Peace Prayers, eds. staff (San Francisco: Harper, 1963).

14.3 Strategies for Dealing with Death

p. 389: Source: Sherman B. Nuland, *How We Die* (New York: Knopf, 1994), 10; p. 389: Source: Christopher Hitchens, "Topic of Cancer," Vanity Fair, November, 2010; pp. 391–392: Source: John Donne, A Valediction: Forbidding Mourning; p. 392: Source: After dark vapors have oppress'd our plains, John Keats; p. 395: Source: Oscar Wilde, *The Picture of Dorian Gray* (New York: Dell, 1977), 33; p. 396: Source:

Matthew Gilbert, "Review of *House*," *Boston Globe*, November 16, 2004.

14.4 Life-Affirmation in the Humanities

p. 397: Source: James Agee, *A Death in the Family* (New York: McDowell, Obolensky, 1957), 307–308; p. 400: Source: *The Republic and Other Works*, trans. Benjamin Jowett (New York: Doubleday, 1989), 551.

14.5 Models of Life-Affirmation

p. 402: Source: Johann Wolfgang von Goethe, *Faust*, trans. Walter Arndt (New York: Norton, 1976), 294; p. 403: Source: W. Wordsworth, Francis T. Palgrave, ed. (1824–1897). The Golden Treasury. 1875; p. 404: Source: *The Essential Tao*, trans. Thomas Cleary (San Francisco: Harper, 1991), 75; p. 406: Source: Rabbi Joseph Telushkin, *Jewish Literacy* (New York: Morrow, 1991), 566.

Chapter 15
15.1 Early Views of Nature

p. 409: Source: Genesis, 1:27–28, King James Version; p. 409: Source: Genesis 2:15, King James Version; p. 410: Source: "Invitation to the Dance, No. 23," in Wine, Women, and Song: Medieval Latin Drinking Songs Now Translated into the English, with an Essay by John Addington Symonds (London: Chatto and Windus, 1884); p. 411: Source: *As You Like It*, II, i: 12–17; p. 411: Source: *As You Like It*, II, i: 47-49; p. 411: Source: *As You Like It*, II, iv: 58-62

15.2 Nature and the Romantics

pp. 412–413: Source: William Wordsworth "I Wandered Lonely As a Cloud" (1807); p. 413: Source: From Ralph Waldo Emerson, "Nature," first published anonymously in 1836 and as Ch. 1 in the collection titled *Nature, Addresses and Lectures*, 1849; p. 413: Source: Walt Whitman, "Song of Myself," Canto 6, in *Leaves of Grass*. Edited by James E. Miller, Jr., Riverside Edition, (Boston: Houghton-Mifflin, 1959). 28; p. 413: Source: Herman Melville, *Moby Dick ; or The Whale*, Dixon Publisher; p. 414: Source: Herman Melville, *Moby-Dick*, Ch. 89, "The Grand Armada." Edited by John Bryant and Haskell Springer. (New York: Pearson Education, 2007), 340-345; p. 415: Source: *Allgemeine musikalische Zeitung* (Leipzig), 1810, trans. Martyn Clarke. In David Charlton, ed., E.T.A. Hoffmann's Musical Writings (Cambridge: Cambridge University Press, 1989), 96–7, 98; p. 414: Source: Henry David Thoreau; Thomas Carew, *Walden, or, Life in the woods*, Boston : Ticknor and Fields, 1854; p. 414: Source: Henry David Thoreau, *Walden and Civil Disobedience* (New York: Barnes & Noble Classics, 2003), 11; p. 414: Source: Henry David Thoreau, *Walden and Civil Disobedience* (New York: Barnes & Noble Classics, 2003), 11.

15.4 The Rise of Urbanism

p. 417: Source: Walt Whitman, *Leaves of Grass*, Rees, Welch & Co, Philadelphia 1882; p. 418: Source: "Chicago" by Carl Sandburg, *Poetry*, March 1914.

15.5 The Force of Nature

p. 419: Source: Herman Melville, *Moby-Dick*, Ch. 35, "The Masthead." Edited by John Bryant and Haskell Springer. (New York: Pearson Education, 2007), 154–55; p. 420: Source: Mary Wollestonecraft Shelley, *Frankenstein, or The Modern Prometheus* (Berkeley: University of California Press, 1989), 24, 51.

15.6 Leaving an Imprint

p. 422: Source: Kent Nerburn, *The Wolf at Twilight* (Novato, CA: New World Library, 2009), 161; p. 422: Source: T. C. McLuhan, *Touch the Earth* (New York: Promontory Press, 1971), 12, 15; p. 423: Source: Robert Smithson, *Robert Smithson: The Collected Writings*, Ed, Jack Flam (Berkeley: University of California Press, 1996), 169–70.

15.7 More than an Inconvenience

pp. 423–424: Source: David Kwiat, *A Traveler in Residence* (Miami: Three Star Press, 2010), 144; p. 424: Source: Joseph Conrad, *Heart of Darkness* (New York: Norton), 34, 69.

Chapter 16

16.1 Early Views of Freedom

p. 429: Source: William Blake, Auguries of Innocence.

16.2 Determinism

p. 430: Source: Azar Nafisi, *Reading Lolita in Tehran* (New York: Random House, 2004), 9; p. 432: Source: From Rousseau's "Principal Discourses," translated by G.D.H. Cole, *Rousseau's Social Contract and Discourses*, (Everyman Library, 1923). Second Discourse, Part 2, 1; p. 436: Source: B. F. Skinner, *Beyond Freedom and Dignity* (New York: Bantam Books, 1972), 37.

16.3 Free Will

p. 438: Source: the German philosopher Arthur Schopenhauer (1788–1860); p. 438: Source: *Arthur Schopenhauer, Essays and Aphorisms*, ed. and trans. R. J. Hollingdale (London: Penguin Books, 1970), 65.

16.4 Existentialism

pp. 443–444: Source: Martin Buber (1878–1965); p. 443: Source: Martin Buber, *Tales of the Hasidim* (New York: Schoken Books, 1992), viii; p. 444: Source: Jean-Paul Sartre, *Existentialism and Human Emotions*, trans. Bernard Frechtman (New York: Philosophical Library, 1947), 15; p. 445: Excerpt from *The Second Sex*. Source: Simone de Beauvoir, *The Second Sex*, ed. and trans. H. M. Parchley (New York: Knopf, 1969), 79; pp. 445–446: Source: Beauvoir, Simone de. *The Second Sex*. [1949] Trans. Constance Borde and Sheila Malovany-Chevallier. (New York: Alfred A. Knopf, 2009), 760; p. 447: Source: Albert Camus, *The Myth of Sisyphus and Other Essays*, trans. Justin O'Brien (New York: Vintage Books, 1995), 123.

16.5 Freedom Within Limitations

p. 448: Source: Chögyam Trungpa, *The Myth of Freedom* (Berkeley, CA: Shambala, 1976), 1–2; pp. 449–450: Source: William Wordsworth 1770–1850, Nuns Fret Not; p. 451: Source: Bonnie Szumski, ed., *Readings in Stephen Crane* (San Diego: Green Haven Press, 1998), 194.

Index

Note: Page numbers followed with f refer to Figures

BCE	HISTORY	HUMANITIES
c. 7000	Native Americans May Have Migrated from Northern Asia	
c. 3200	Egyptian Civilization Established	
c. 1500	Hinduism Develops in India	The Vedas, the Upanishads
c. 14th century	Amenhotep IV Establishes Monotheism Tutenkhamen Reestablishes Polytheism	
c. 13th century	Moses Leads Exodus from Egypt	
c. 1200	Presumed Period of Trojan War	
c. l027–256	Golden Age of Chinese Philosophy	Lao-tzu, 6th century Confucius (557–479)
c. 700	Age of Homer and Greek Mythology	*The Iliad*
6th century	Buddhism in India Festivals of Dionysus in Athens	Siddhartha Gautama (564–483) Sappho (early 6th century) Aeschylus (525–456)
5th century	Golden Age of Athens	Sophocles (496–406) Euripides (484–406) Socrates (469–399) Plato (c. 427–347)
4th century	336–323, Reign of Alexander the Great	Aristotle (c. 382–322)

CE		
1st century	Christianity in Rome	
c. 400	410, Sack of Rome by the Goths	Augustine (354–430)
6th century		Mohammed (571–632)
8th century	Moors Occupy Spain	
10th century		Lady Murasaki Shikibu (978–1031) *Tale of Genji,* Japan, earliest known novel
11th century	1066, Norman Conquest of England	Bayeux Tapestry
12th century	Japanese Feudal Period, Rise of Samurai	Angkor Wat Moses Maimonides (1135–1204)
13th century	High Middle Ages in Western Europe	Notre Dame Cathedral Thomas Aquinas (1225–1274) Dante Alighieri (1265–1321)
14th century	Emergence of the Ottoman Empire 1347–1351, Black Death Devastates Europe	Geoffrey Chaucer (1340–1400)
15th century	High Renaissance Starts in Italy 1492, Columbus Sails to the New World	Leonardo (1451–1519) Michelangelo (1475–1564) Raphael (1483–1520)
16th century	1517, Martin Luther's Reform Proposals 1519, Conquest of Mexico by Cortes 1533–1603, Reign of Elizabeth I	Sophonisba Anguissola (c. 1532–1626) Cervantes (1547–1616) William Shakespeare (1564–1616)